Communications
in Computer and Information Science 173

Constantine Stephanidis (Ed.)

HCI International 2011 – Posters' Extended Abstracts

International Conference, HCI International 2011
Orlando, FL, USA, July 9-14, 2011
Proceedings, Part I

 Springer

Volume Editor

Constantine Stephanidis
Foundation for Research and Technology - Hellas (FORTH)
Institute of Computer Science (ICS)
N. Plastira 100, Vassilika Vouton
70013, Heraklion, Crete, Greece
and
University of Crete
Department of Computer Science, Crete, Greece
E-mail: cs@ics.forth.gr

ISSN 1865-0929   e-ISSN 1865-0937
ISBN 978-3-642-22097-5   ISBN 978-3-642-22098-2 (eBook)
DOI 10.1007/978-3-642-22098-2
Springer Heidelberg Dordrecht London New York

Library of Congress Control Number: 2011930138

CR Subject Classification (1998): H.4, H.5, I.2, H.3, C.2, D.2

Typesetting: Camera-ready by author, data conversion by Scientific Publishing Services, Chennai, India

Printed on acid-free paper

Springer is part of Springer Science+Business Media (www.springer.com)

Foreword

The 14th International Conference on Human–Computer Interaction, HCI International 2011, was held in Orlando, Florida, USA, July 9–14, 2011, jointly with the Symposium on Human Interface (Japan) 2011, the 9th International Conference on Engineering Psychology and Cognitive Ergonomics, the 6th International Conference on Universal Access in Human–Computer Interaction, the 4th International Conference on Virtual and Mixed Reality, the 4th International Conference on Internationalization, Design and Global Development, the 4th International Conference on Online Communities and Social Computing, the 6th International Conference on Augmented Cognition, the Third International Conference on Digital Human Modeling, the Second International Conference on Human-Centered Design, and the First International Conference on Design, User Experience, and Usability.

A total of 4,039 individuals from academia, research institutes, industry and governmental agencies from 67 countries submitted contributions, and 1,318 papers that were judged to be of high scientific quality were included in the program. These papers address the latest research and development efforts and highlight the human aspects of design and use of computing systems. The papers accepted for presentation thoroughly cover the entire field of human–computer interaction, addressing major advances in knowledge and effective use of computers in a variety of application areas.

This volume, edited by Constantine Stephanidis, contains posters' extended abstracts addressing the following major topics:

- Design methods, techniques and knowledge
- Usability and user experience
- Cultural, cross-cultural and aesthetic issues in HCI
- Cognitive and psychological issues in HCI
- Inclusive design and accessibility
- Social interaction and on-line communities
- Work and collaboration
- Access to information and knowledge

The remaining volumes of the HCI International 2011 Proceedings are:

- Volume 1, LNCS 6761, Human–Computer Interaction—Design and Development Approaches (Part I), edited by Julie A. Jacko
- Volume 2, LNCS 6762, Human–Computer Interaction—Interaction Techniques and Environments (Part II), edited by Julie A. Jacko
- Volume 3, LNCS 6763, Human–Computer Interaction—Towards Mobile and Intelligent Interaction Environments (Part III), edited by Julie A. Jacko
- Volume 4, LNCS 6764, Human–Computer Interaction—Users and Applications (Part IV), edited by Julie A. Jacko

- Volume 5, LNCS 6765, Universal Access in Human–Computer Interaction—Design for All and eInclusion (Part I), edited by Constantine Stephanidis
- Volume 6, LNCS 6766, Universal Access in Human–Computer Interaction—Users Diversity (Part II), edited by Constantine Stephanidis
- Volume 7, LNCS 6767, Universal Access in Human–Computer Interaction—Context Diversity (Part III), edited by Constantine Stephanidis
- Volume 8, LNCS 6768, Universal Access in Human–Computer Interaction—Applications and Services (Part IV), edited by Constantine Stephanidis
- Volume 9, LNCS 6769, Design, User Experience, and Usability—Theory, Methods, Tools and Practice (Part I), edited by Aaron Marcus
- Volume 10, LNCS 6770, Design, User Experience, and Usability—Understanding the User Experience (Part II), edited by Aaron Marcus
- Volume 11, LNCS 6771, Human Interface and the Management of Information—Design and Interaction (Part I), edited by Michael J. Smith and Gavriel Salvendy
- Volume 12, LNCS 6772, Human Interface and the Management of Information—Interacting with Information (Part II), edited by Gavriel Salvendy and Michael J. Smith
- Volume 13, LNCS 6773, Virtual and Mixed Reality—New Trends (Part I), edited by Randall Shumaker
- Volume 14, LNCS 6774, Virtual and Mixed Reality—Systems and Applications (Part II), edited by Randall Shumaker
- Volume 15, LNCS 6775, Internationalization, Design and Global Development, edited by P.L. Patrick Rau
- Volume 16, LNCS 6776, Human-Centered Design, edited by Masaaki Kurosu
- Volume 17, LNCS 6777, Digital Human Modeling, edited by Vincent G. Duffy
- Volume 18, LNCS 6778, Online Communities and Social Computing, edited by A. Ant Ozok and Panayiotis Zaphiris
- Volume 19, LNCS 6779, Ergonomics and Health Aspects of Work with Computers, edited by Michelle M. Robertson
- Volume 20, LNAI 6780, Foundations of Augmented Cognition: Directing the Future of Adaptive Systems, edited by Dylan D. Schmorrow and Cali M. Fidopiastis
- Volume 21, LNAI 6781, Engineering Psychology and Cognitive Ergonomics, edited by Don Harris
- Volume 23, CCIS 174, HCI International 2011 Posters Proceedings (Part II), edited by Constantine Stephanidis

I would like to thank the Program Chairs and the members of the Program Boards of all Thematic Areas, listed herein, for their contribution to the highest scientific quality and the overall success of the HCI International 2011 Conference.

In addition to the members of the Program Boards, I also wish to thank the following volunteer external reviewers: Roman Vilimek from Germany, Ramalingam Ponnusamy from India, Si Jung "Jun" Kim from the USA, and Ilia Adami, Iosif Klironomos, Vassilis Kouroumalis, George Margetis, and Stavroula Ntoa from Greece.

This conference would not have been possible without the continuous support and advice of the Conference Scientific Advisor, Gavriel Salvendy, as well as the dedicated work and outstanding efforts of the Communications and Exhibition Chair and Editor of HCI International News, Abbas Moallem.

I would also like to thank for their contribution toward the organization of the HCI International 2011 Conference the members of the Human–Computer Interaction Laboratory of ICS-FORTH, and in particular Margherita Antona, George Paparoulis, Maria Pitsoulaki, Stavroula Ntoa, Maria Bouhli and George Kapnas.

July 2011   Constantine Stephanidis

Organization

Ergonomics and Health Aspects of Work with Computers

Program Chair: Michelle M. Robertson

Arne Aarås, Norway
Pascale Carayon, USA
Jason Devereux, UK
Wolfgang Friesdorf, Germany
Martin Helander, Singapore
Ed Israelski, USA
Ben-Tzion Karsh, USA
Waldemar Karwowski, USA
Peter Kern, Germany
Danuta Koradecka, Poland
Nancy Larson, USA
Kari Lindström, Finland

Brenda Lobb, New Zealand
Holger Luczak, Germany
William S. Marras, USA
Aura C. Matias, Philippines
Matthias Rötting, Germany
Michelle L. Rogers, USA
Dominique L. Scapin, France
Lawrence M. Schleifer, USA
Michael J. Smith, USA
Naomi Swanson, USA
Peter Vink, The Netherlands
John Wilson, UK

Human Interface and the Management of Information

Program Chair: Michael J. Smith

Hans-Jörg Bullinger, Germany
Alan Chan, Hong Kong
Shin'ichi Fukuzumi, Japan
Jon R. Gunderson, USA
Michitaka Hirose, Japan
Jhilmil Jain, USA
Yasufumi Kume, Japan
Mark Lehto, USA
Hirohiko Mori, Japan
Fiona Fui-Hoon Nah, USA
Shogo Nishida, Japan
Robert Proctor, USA

Youngho Rhee, Korea
Anxo Cereijo Roibás, UK
Katsunori Shimohara, Japan
Dieter Spath, Germany
Tsutomu Tabe, Japan
Alvaro D. Taveira, USA
Kim-Phuong L. Vu, USA
Tomio Watanabe, Japan
Sakae Yamamoto, Japan
Hidekazu Yoshikawa, Japan
Li Zheng, P.R. China

Human–Computer Interaction

Program Chair: Julie A. Jacko

Sebastiano Bagnara, Italy	Gitte Lindgaard, Canada
Sherry Y. Chen, UK	Chen Ling, USA
Marvin J. Dainoff, USA	Yan Liu, USA
Jianming Dong, USA	Chang S. Nam, USA
John Eklund, Australia	Celestine A. Ntuen, USA
Xiaowen Fang, USA	Philippe Palanque, France
Ayse Gurses, USA	P.L. Patrick Rau, P.R. China
Vicki L. Hanson, UK	Ling Rothrock, USA
Sheue-Ling Hwang, Taiwan	Guangfeng Song, USA
Wonil Hwang, Korea	Steffen Staab, Germany
Yong Gu Ji, Korea	Wan Chul Yoon, Korea
Steven A. Landry, USA	Wenli Zhu, P.R. China

Engineering Psychology and Cognitive Ergonomics

Program Chair: Don Harris

Guy A. Boy, USA	Jan M. Noyes, UK
Pietro Carlo Cacciabue, Italy	Kjell Ohlsson, Sweden
John Huddlestone, UK	Axel Schulte, Germany
Kenji Itoh, Japan	Sarah C. Sharples, UK
Hung-Sying Jing, Taiwan	Neville A. Stanton, UK
Wen-Chin Li, Taiwan	Xianghong Sun, P.R. China
James T. Luxhøj, USA	Andrew Thatcher, South Africa
Nicolas Marmaras, Greece	Matthew J.W. Thomas, Australia
Sundaram Narayanan, USA	Mark Young, UK
Mark A. Neerincx, The Netherlands	Rolf Zon, The Netherlands

Universal Access in Human–Computer Interaction

Program Chair: Constantine Stephanidis

Julio Abascal, Spain	Michael Fairhurst, UK
Ray Adams, UK	Dimitris Grammenos, Greece
Elisabeth André, Germany	Andreas Holzinger, Austria
Margherita Antona, Greece	Simeon Keates, Denmark
Chieko Asakawa, Japan	Georgios Kouroupetroglou, Greece
Christian Bühler, Germany	Sri Kurniawan, USA
Jerzy Charytonowicz, Poland	Patrick M. Langdon, UK
Pier Luigi Emiliani, Italy	Seongil Lee, Korea

Zhengjie Liu, P.R. China
Klaus Miesenberger, Austria
Helen Petrie, UK
Michael Pieper, Germany
Anthony Savidis, Greece
Andrew Sears, USA
Christian Stary, Austria

Hirotada Ueda, Japan
Jean Vanderdonckt, Belgium
Gregg C. Vanderheiden, USA
Gerhard Weber, Germany
Harald Weber, Germany
Panayiotis Zaphiris, Cyprus

Virtual and Mixed Reality

Program Chair: Randall Shumaker

Pat Banerjee, USA
Mark Billinghurst, New Zealand
Charles E. Hughes, USA
Simon Julier, UK
David Kaber, USA
Hirokazu Kato, Japan
Robert S. Kennedy, USA
Young J. Kim, Korea
Ben Lawson, USA
Gordon McK Mair, UK

David Pratt, UK
Albert "Skip" Rizzo, USA
Lawrence Rosenblum, USA
Jose San Martin, Spain
Dieter Schmalstieg, Austria
Dylan Schmorrow, USA
Kay Stanney, USA
Janet Weisenford, USA
Mark Wiederhold, USA

Internationalization, Design and Global Development

Program Chair: P.L. Patrick Rau

Michael L. Best, USA
Alan Chan, Hong Kong
Lin-Lin Chen, Taiwan
Andy M. Dearden, UK
Susan M. Dray, USA
Henry Been-Lirn Duh, Singapore
Vanessa Evers, The Netherlands
Paul Fu, USA
Emilie Gould, USA
Sung H. Han, Korea
Veikko Ikonen, Finland
Toshikazu Kato, Japan
Esin Kiris, USA
Apala Lahiri Chavan, India

James R. Lewis, USA
James J.W. Lin, USA
Rungtai Lin, Taiwan
Zhengjie Liu, P.R. China
Aaron Marcus, USA
Allen E. Milewski, USA
Katsuhiko Ogawa, Japan
Oguzhan Ozcan, Turkey
Girish Prabhu, India
Kerstin Röse, Germany
Supriya Singh, Australia
Alvin W. Yeo, Malaysia
Hsiu-Ping Yueh, Taiwan

Online Communities and Social Computing

Program Chairs: A. Ant Ozok, Panayiotis Zaphiris

Chadia N. Abras, USA
Chee Siang Ang, UK
Peter Day, UK
Fiorella De Cindio, Italy
Heidi Feng, USA
Anita Komlodi, USA
Piet A.M. Kommers, The Netherlands
Andrew Laghos, Cyprus
Stefanie Lindstaedt, Austria
Gabriele Meiselwitz, USA
Hideyuki Nakanishi, Japan

Anthony F. Norcio, USA
Ulrike Pfeil, UK
Elaine M. Raybourn, USA
Douglas Schuler, USA
Gilson Schwartz, Brazil
Laura Slaughter, Norway
Sergei Stafeev, Russia
Asimina Vasalou, UK
June Wei, USA
Haibin Zhu, Canada

Augmented Cognition

Program Chairs: Dylan D. Schmorrow, Cali M. Fidopiastis

Monique Beaudoin, USA
Chris Berka, USA
Joseph Cohn, USA
Martha E. Crosby, USA
Julie Drexler, USA
Ivy Estabrooke, USA
Chris Forsythe, USA
Wai Tat Fu, USA
Marc Grootjen, The Netherlands
Jefferson Grubb, USA
Santosh Mathan, USA

Rob Matthews, Australia
Dennis McBride, USA
Eric Muth, USA
Mark A. Neerincx, The Netherlands
Denise Nicholson, USA
Banu Onaral, USA
Kay Stanney, USA
Roy Stripling, USA
Rob Taylor, UK
Karl van Orden, USA

Digital Human Modeling

Program Chair: Vincent G. Duffy

Karim Abdel-Malek, USA
Giuseppe Andreoni, Italy
Thomas J. Armstrong, USA
Norman I. Badler, USA
Fethi Calisir, Turkey
Daniel Carruth, USA
Keith Case, UK
Julie Charland, Canada

Yaobin Chen, USA
Kathryn Cormican, Ireland
Daniel A. DeLaurentis, USA
Yingzi Du, USA
Okan Ersoy, USA
Enda Fallon, Ireland
Yan Fu, P.R. China
Afzal Godil, USA

Ravindra Goonetilleke, Hong Kong
Anand Gramopadhye, USA
Lars Hanson, Sweden
Pheng Ann Heng, Hong Kong
Bo Hoege, Germany
Hongwei Hsiao, USA
Tianzi Jiang, P.R. China
Nan Kong, USA
Steven A. Landry, USA
Kang Li, USA
Zhizhong Li, P.R. China
Tim Marler, USA

Ahmet F. Ozok, Turkey
Srinivas Peeta, USA
Sudhakar Rajulu, USA
Matthias Rötting, Germany
Matthew Reed, USA
Johan Stahre, Sweden
Mao-Jiun Wang, Taiwan
Xuguang Wang, France
Jingzhou (James) Yang, USA
Gulcin Yucel, Turkey
Tingshao Zhu, P.R. China

Human-Centered Design

Program Chair: Masaaki Kurosu

Julio Abascal, Spain
Simone Barbosa, Brazil
Tomas Berns, Sweden
Nigel Bevan, UK
Torkil Clemmensen, Denmark
Susan M. Dray, USA
Vanessa Evers, The Netherlands
Xiaolan Fu, P.R. China
Yasuhiro Horibe, Japan
Jason Huang, P.R. China
Minna Isomursu, Finland
Timo Jokela, Finland
Mitsuhiko Karashima, Japan
Tadashi Kobayashi, Japan
Seongil Lee, Korea
Kee Yong Lim, Singapore

Zhengjie Liu, P.R. China
Loïc Martínez-Normand, Spain
Monique Noirhomme-Fraiture,
   Belgium
Philippe Palanque, France
Annelise Mark Pejtersen, Denmark
Kerstin Röse, Germany
Dominique L. Scapin, France
Haruhiko Urokohara, Japan
Gerrit C. van der Veer,
   The Netherlands
Janet Wesson, South Africa
Toshiki Yamaoka, Japan
Kazuhiko Yamazaki, Japan
Silvia Zimmermann, Switzerland

Design, User Experience, and Usability

Program Chair: Aaron Marcus

Ronald Baecker, Canada
Barbara Ballard, USA
Konrad Baumann, Austria
Arne Berger, Germany
Randolph Bias, USA
Jamie Blustein, Canada

Ana Boa-Ventura, USA
Lorenzo Cantoni, Switzerland
Sameer Chavan, Korea
Wei Ding, USA
Maximilian Eibl, Germany
Zelda Harrison, USA

HCI International 2013

The 15th International Conference on Human–Computer Interaction, HCI International 2013, will be held jointly with the affiliated conferences in the summer of 2013. It will cover a broad spectrum of themes related to human–computer interaction (HCI), including theoretical issues, methods, tools, processes and case studies in HCI design, as well as novel interaction techniques, interfaces and applications. The proceedings will be published by Springer. More information about the topics, as well as the venue and dates of the conference, will be announced through the HCI International Conference series website: http://www.hci-international.org/

General Chair
Professor Constantine Stephanidis
University of Crete and ICS-FORTH
Heraklion, Crete, Greece
Email: cs@ics.forth.gr

Table of Contents – Part I

Part I: Design Methods, Techniques and Knowledge

Part II: Usability and User Experience

Part III: Cultural, Cross-Cultural and Aesthetic Issues in HCI

Part IV: Cognitive and Psychological Issues in HCI

Part V: Inclusive Design and Accessibility

Part VI: Social Interaction and On-line Communities

Part VII: Work and Collaboration

Part VIII: Access to Information and Knowledge

Table of Contents – Part II

Part I: Novel Interaction Environments

Part II: Virtual and Augmented Environments

Part III: Gestures, Gaze and Multimodality in HCI

Part IV: Touch-Based and Table-Top Interaction

Part V: Brain-Computer Interfaces and Brain Monitoring

Part VI: Ergonomics and Human Modelling Issues

Part VII: Health and Wellbeing

Part VIII: Learning, Education and Cultural Heritage

Part I

Design Methods, Techniques and Knowledge

Professional Graphic Designers Approaching Visual Interface Design

Joanne Elizabeth Beriswill

Department of Instructional Systems and Workforce Development,
Mississippi State University, Box 9730, Mississippi State, MS 39759
jberiswill@colled.msstate.edu

Abstract. This case study involves the redesign of the visual interface for an instructional website. Three expert designers were individually asked to redesign the interface. Through stimulated-recall sessions, the participants commented on their initial design. The data patterns indicated divergences, as well as convergences, among the participants. Participants varied from a basic linear process to successive approximations. Similarities included the primary focus on an anchor graphic, the exploration of colors and typography, and the extensive use of resources.

1 Introduction

Expert graphic designers are often employed to create the visual interface (the repeated visual design) for instructional websites. While there are descriptions of principles that pervade high-quality visual design [1,4] and there are proposed models for novice-level visual design processes [2]. However, expert graphic designers and their visual design processes have not been studied.

Design processes have "often occupied an ambivalent position, being characterized as either a form of fine art or a form of technical science" [14]. However, research on design processes has documented basic steps or phases which are common to a variety of design disciplines [6]. Currently in the field of instructional systems design, the basic design phases are defined as analysis, design, development, implementation, and evaluation (ADDIE). These phases are most commonly applied in the interactive, yet linear ADDIE Design Model [3] and the iterative Rapid Prototyping Design Model [11]. Rowland [13] explored the design process by studying the actual design processes that instructional designers use.

Nonetheless, there is no specific design process to describe the specific area of web interface design. There has been extensive research on the visual interface of a website and its impact on the usability and appeal of the site [7,10,15,18]. There are also web design resources that discuss the characteristics of well-designed websites [7,9,10] and the visual design characteristics of web design [15,18]. Although these resources give some design logistics, they do not address how these characteristics can be integrated into a systemic design process.

C. Stephanidis (Ed.): Posters, Part I, HCII 2011, CCIS 173, pp. 3–7, 2011.
© Springer-Verlag Berlin Heidelberg 2011

The purpose of this study focuses on the processes that expert web visual designers use to redesign the visual design visual interface for an instructional website. Like the Rowland study, this study looks at how designers actually carry out a design task. In this case, the designers are expert web visual designers.

2 Methodology

This instrumental case study was exploratory [17] since it sought to discover a process not yet reflected in visual design research literature. Three expert web visual designers were selected as participants in this study. In order to qualify as "experts" for this study [5,12,16], participants had to meet the following criteria: (1) more than ten years of experience in graphic design, (2) more than four years of experience creating website visual interfaces, (3) design products that exemplify a professional level of visual design, and (4) the ability to describe their work in explicit terms.

The participants had the task of redesigning the visual interface for an existing, real-world website. In order to ensure authenticity, an existing instructional website, entitled "The Great Computer Mystery," was used as the basis of the simulation task. The original website had a simplistic visual design. It contained basic wordart and clipart images created with Microsoft Office. The website included a homepage, intermediate navigation pages (one for each of four case-based scenarios or "mysteries"), and a series of content pages for each of the mysteries. The researcher felt that the "mystery" metaphor also might pique the interest of participants in the study.

There were three videotaped sessions with each participant: the screening interview, the first design and stimulated-recall session, and the second design and stimulated-recall session. During the screening interview, the researcher asked participants questions regarding their visual design and web design experience. During each of the two design session, the participants worked on the initial redesign of the "Great Computer Mystery Website" for approximately one hour. Fifteen minutes after each design session, participants viewed videotapes of their design sessions and were asked to comment on what they did and why. There was a one-week break between the two design sessions to allow for subliminal processing.

The data collected included videotapes of the three sessions, sketches participants drew during the design sessions, transcripts of the videotapes, and computer files created during the sessions. The analysis process consisted of carrying out a card sort, coding statements and actions, writing stories, mapping participant actions, and writing summary tables.

3 Petite Generalizations

Due to the focused nature of qualitative research, Stake [17] argues that findings should be stated in the form of petite generalizations. For this study there were three petite generalizations which surfaced: (1) the participants designed the website following a systematic process; (2) the object on which all participants first focused was the splash graphic, and they carried over the attributes from that graphic to the subsequent objects they created; and (3) participants interrupted their design work to experiment or to leverage additional resources.

All three participants in this study created a visual interface for the website following a systematic order. The two participants who completed multiple page types began by designing several iterations of the layout for the homepage, then the layout for one or more intermediate navigation pages, then the layout for content pages. The other participant used the time for both design sessions to create the homepage design. She created one version of the homepage using the same red color as the client-provided materials. Upon reflection, she decided that combination of colors did not foster a "mystery" theme. Therefore, she created a second version of the homepage with new buttons and a new background. These results indicate that the three participants used a systematic order in their design process. Their process of creating layouts is iterative and follows a homepage / intermediate navigation page / content page order.

Not only did the three participants all begin on the homepage, they also all began work on the same type of element on that page—the splash graphic (see Figure 1).

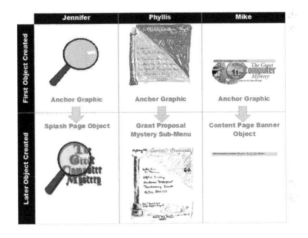

Fig. 1. Comparison of first and later elements created

While making the graphic, the participants had to make decisions regarding many attributes of the graphic, such as color, typography, subject, and layout. Later the participants repeated these attributes in their as they created later elements for the website. The splash graphic became a key element for all three of the participants' designs. Once they made key design decisions about the attributes for that particular element, the participants later reused those same attributes for other elements they created. This practice of carrying over graphic attributes from the logo/splash graphic aligns with the suggestions from Lynch and Horton [7].

When participants for this study were in the midst of the designing layouts or elements, they would sometimes interrupt their design work. For example, after having spent nine minutes working on the design of a splash graphic element, participant three opened up a dialog box on the screen and began experimenting with font typefaces for 3 minutes before selecting one that he said was a "mysterious font."

In addition to experimenting with graphical attributes, the participants would also interrupted their work to get additional resources to infuse in their design work. For example, after having created all the graphics for the homepage of the website, participant three opened the original HTML page that had been provided by the client and used the HTML code from that page as a basis for his own version of the homepage. All of the participants leveraged resources to speed up their design process. They used HTML code, webpage templates, graphics from the WWW, and images from print sources. This finding aligns with Martin's discussion [8] of the many sources of ideas and information that graphic designers use to stimulate the design process.

4 Discussion

The web design process observed in this study includes stages of design/ development, experimentation, and accessing resources. For this study, three levels of webpages were created: (1) homepages, (2) intermediate navigation pages, and (3) content pages. In this study, participants began by creating the homepage, the most visible page level and carried over the elements (i.e., logos, buttons, banners, footers, and backgrounds) from that page level to subsequent page levels, such as intermediate navigation pages and content pages. During the design process, designers streamlined and sped up their process by using existing resources such as client-provided materials, work that they had previously created, or resources that they could easily access, such as images they could download from the web. In order to explore various attribute options for graphics and page layouts, designers would branch out of their ongoing design process and enter an experimentation stage where they played with and explored a particular attributes until they found a combination that worked together visually.

5 Conclusions

Web design is a complex task. The web design model used by the expert web visual designers in this study could be used to guide web designers and help streamline their creation of web visual interfaces. However, additional studies should be carried out to verify the feasibility of this model. The model identifies a common sequence which the participants. Future studies could determine whether this sequence of page levels holds true for different types of websites and for other types of designers.

One time-saving strategy used by the participants in this study, using existing resources, proved to speed up the design process. Additional studies could focus on what types of resources experts use and how they repurpose those resources in their own work.

As the area of web design research develops, it would be helpful to use common terminology to describe the characteristics of a website. This would facilitate cross-study comparisons and meta-analyses of research studies. The coding categories developed through this study were used for the analysis of various types of data. These categories might be a basis for analysis of future studies, as well.

This study does provide insights into the web design process. However, due to the limitations of the generalizability of case study research, additional studies should be carried out to test these findings from this study against other web design variations, such as other types of design tasks or with other participants.

References

1. Arnheim, R.: Art and Visual Perception: A Psychology of the Creative Eye, 2nd edn. University of California Press, Berkley (1974)
2. Beriswill, J.: Analysis-based message design: rethinking screen design guidelines. Paper presented at the National Convention of AECT, St. Louis, MO (1998)
3. Dick, W., Carey, L., Carey, J.O.: The systematic design of instruction, 7th edn. Longman, New York (2001)
4. Dondis, D.A.: A Primer of Visual Literacy. MIT Press, Cambridge (1973)
5. Durrance, B.: Some explicit thoughts on tacit learning. Training & Development 52(12), 24–29 (1998)
6. Jones, J.C.: Design Methods. John Wiley & Sons, New York (1992)
7. Lynch, P.J., Horton, S.: Web Style Guide: Basic Design Principles for Creating Websites, 2nd edn. Yale University Press, New Haven (2002)
8. Martin, D.: Graphic Design: Inspirations and Innovations. North Light Books, Cincinnati (1995)
9. Mullet, K., Sano, D.: Designing Visual Interfaces: Communication Oriented Techniques. SunSoft Press, Engelwood Cliffs (1995)
10. Nielsen, J.: Designing Web Usability: The Practice of Simplicity. New Riders, Indianapolis (2000)
11. Piskurich, G.M.: Rapid Instructional Design: Learning ID Fast and Right. Pfeiffer, San Francisco (2006)
12. Polyani, M.: The Tacit Dimension. Anchor Books, Garden City (1967)
13. Rowland, G.: What Do Instructional Designers Actually Do? An Initial Investigation of Expert Practice. Performance Improvement Quarterly 5(2), 65–86 (1992)
14. Rowe, P.G.: Design Thinking. MIT Press, Cambridge (1998)
15. Sano, D.: Designing Large-Scale Websites: A Visual Design Methodology. John Wiley & Sons, New York (1996)
16. Schon, D.A.: The Reflective Practitioner: How Professinals Think in Action. Basic Books, New York (1983)
17. Stake, R.E.: The Art of Case Study Research. Sage, Thousand Oaks (1995)
18. Williams, R., Tollett, J.: The Non-Designer's Web Book: An Easy Guide to Creating, Designing, and Posting Your Own Website, 3rd edn. Peachpit Press, Berkley (2006)

Co-discovery Method and Its Application with Children as Research Subjects

Alessandra Carusi and Cláudia Mont'Alvão

LEUI Ergonomics Laboratory, Post Graduation Program in Design,
Arts & Design Department, Pontifical Catholic University of Rio de Janeiro, PUC - Rio,
Rua Marquês de São Vicente, 225, Gávea - Rio de Janeiro, RJ - Brazil
alessa.carusi@gmail.com, cmontalvao@puc-rio.br

Abstract. The abstract should summarize the contents of the paper and should contain at least 70 and at most 150 words. It should be set in 9-point font size and should be inset 1.0 cm from the right and left margins. There should be two blank (10-point) lines before and after the abstract. This document is in the required format.

Keywords: We would like to encourage you to list your keywords in this section.

1 Introduction

Clickable areas in computer interfaces can be defined as those areas in where it is allowed to press or select using a pointer and, from this action; the user is guided to another area of the system [1]. Graphical representations for clickable areas in computer interface should enable mental representations that help understanding navigation system during the cognitive process. Otherwise, the user may feel a sense of being lost. This concern must be present in interactive educational system development.

Hypermedia environments are frequently present at Education. Flexibility and non-linearity of these systems has been seen as causes of misunderstanding and disorientation of its users. Due this, many times users are not capable to know *"where"* they are or *"where to go"* inside the system [2].

The participative aspect of interaction within a graphic interface can be essential to motivate children to continue the system´ usage. Users that can´t interact with an interface will soon lose the interest in it [3]. This reaction can be justified by the fact that a succeed interaction, in an environment based on hypermedia , presenting a non-linear manipulation join different data from time and culture, in different formats and possibilities of expression, allowing the customization and promoting the user participation [4].

According to these assumptions, the main problem of this research is: how the graphic elements' design that represents the navigation system can influence cognitive processes? And how it also influences performance in educational sites for

C. Stephanidis (Ed.): Posters, Part I, HCII 2011, CCIS 173, pp. 8–12, 2011.

children tasks? Trying to give some answers to this problem, navigation was taken as the research focus.

It is important to notice that this research not focused on the visual language of the elements that are clickable areas (e.g., as color, typography and proportion). The focus was the paths performed by users in educational websites, indicating the design importance in such interfaces areas of these systems. Nor did the research's scope was to evaluate if children were able to learn the contents presented in the interface.

2   Methodology

To achieve the research objectives both quantitative and qualitative data were collected considering user's mental model structure, influenced by the graphic representation of the pre-selected clickable areas in a children's educational site. Later, users models aspects were compared to system selected usability models.

The website chosen as the object study was *Kiagito* (http://www.edukbr.com.br), which part of *EduKbr* portal (http://www.edukbr.com.br) with offers interactive activities to be developed in Elementary school's classroom. This portal is supported by Microsoft in Brazil.

Considering the characteristics of main users of these interfaces – children from 7 to 10 years were set for survey. Although we know that are differences in development levels between children at these ages, it is the same division adopted by the Brazilian Government for children at Elementary School.

From these considerations, the survey was divided into two phases: exploratory and participative. Exploratory phase consisted in interviews with Education experts, teachers and designers about interfaces for children and the *Kiagito* website. Participative phase was an evaluation with navigating this same website.

This paper will present only results of participatory phase in which was used the Co-discovery method. The idea of using the method was also it allows children participation' according their understanding and their behavior about while navigating in the website. At the same time, according to literature review this method allows to obtaining systematic and relevant information.

2.1   Co-discovery: Choice and Applicability

In this research the choice of this method to verify whether the clickable areas design in this website are in accordance with children mental models, considering navigation performance during a predetermined task execution.

As subjects in this phase children were selected and organized into seventeen pairs who were already known each other. All subjects are regular students at elementary schools, has computers at home and internet access, some experience in using computers and but never visited *Kiagito* website before.

Children were asked to perform the task "create the *Clubinho* card" at the *Kiagito* website and they were encouraged to verbalize their impressions of each step in the navigation system.

Fig. 1. Kiagito homepage with the main menu

This chosen task involves finding the provided label on the main menu (Fig.1), and from this, does the activities for creating the card, such as to fill out the registration form and to create his portrait illustration (Fig.2). Thereafter, the pair was confronted with another navigation menu to view the *Clubinho* card finished (Fig.3).

3   Results

From obtained navigation data, after the task to get the "card" as a *Clubinho* member some details can be pointed out:

* All the children could recognize the menu and pinpoint the necessary information (*Clubinho* tag) to carry on the task: all actions were inside *Clubinho*
  section;
* Total time of navigations ranged from 3.26 sec to 16.35min. This result was
  related to the period of participation of each couple, not considering if they
  concluded or not the task. This wide variation is justified by the creation of the
  "portrait" which stimulates a big conversation between the kids;
* Children couldn't understand why they should fill in a database – the majority
  was really agog to navigate and know better the system;
* The *Clubinho* interface' menu with the tag "Card" haven´t the same access' result of main menu – considering the 4 couples that reached this interface, only
  two couples visualized and clicked on this menu.

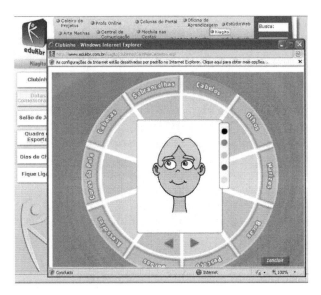

Fig. 2. Kiagito interface to create the portraits illustration for "*Clubinho* card"

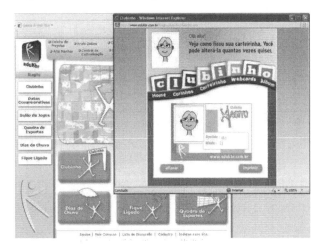

Fig. 3. The "*Clubinho* card" at the *Kiagito* website

4   Conclusion

The initial question of this research was the adequacy of navigational systems of websites designed for children, with educational intention, to its users. The main focus when examining these interfaces was the design of *clickable areas* that must signalize navigation options and the interaction with user in hypermedia systems. The interaction between user and interface can be enhanced when the system model is similar to the users´ mental model.

In an educational website reach the learning process objectives depends on the encouragement given to the user to think and be critical to his actions inside the system. To this, child must be stimulated and feel safe to navigate in the website until she/he can find the desired information. Inversely, she/he can soon lose the interest in the system. In other words, the child needs to know what she/he is doing, feeling pleasure and curiosity to reach the desired information.

Clickable areas can stimulate users (in this case, children) in learning process, in retrieving information and problems solution, and from this, can guarantee satisfaction and motivation while using an interface. These graphic representations (the *clickable areas*) are subject to interpretation considering a cognitive process, which significance will be directly affect user´s behavior. So, the efficacy of *clickable areas* in navigation, considering an interactive system, depends on its graphic representations, that means, its design.

From the results, it was noticed that children's participation was essential to identify some usage aspects that probably could be unthinkable by adults during system development.

In many situations, during navigation, it was noted that the clickable areas design wasn't corresponding with children's mental models. From data analysis was possible to understand that is very important for children the doubtless to know "where" they are inside the system and "what" they should do to achieve their goal. When the navigation' conditions wasn't clear in this way, the children were disoriented and asked for help. Therefore, the Co-discovery method application pointed out some mismatches between users' mental models and the usability model of *Kiagito* website.

References

1. Padovani, S., Moura, D.: Navegação em Hipermídia: uma abordagem centrada no usuário. Ciência Moderna, Rio de Janeiro (2008)
2. Puntambeakar, S., Stylianou, A., Hübscher, R.: Improving navigation and learning in hypertext environments with navigable concept maps. In: Human-Computer Interaction, vol. 18, pp. 395–428 (2003)
3. Chiasson, S., Gutwin, C.: Design Principles for Children's Software. In: Technical Report HCI-TR-05-02, Computer Science Department, University of Saskatchewan, Canada, (2005)
4. Moura, M.: A Interatividade no Design de Hipermídia. In: Anais do P&D Design 2006 – 7o Congresso Brasileiro de Pesquisa e Desenvolvimento em Design (2006)

Get Your Mobile App Out the Door

Heather Cottingham and Michele Snyder

300 Oracle Parkway, M/S 3op333 Redwood Shores, CA 94065
`heather.cottingham@oracle.com`

Abstract. The increased speed and vast number of mobile products being re-
leased into the market has demanded that Oracle design and develop mobile
products faster. These applications must be innovative to stay competitive in the
market place. We will present a rapid design and research process that has been
used to create a superior mobile expenses application. This process assisted in
learning user requirements, validating concepts, and getting detailed usability
feedback.

Keywords: mobile application, rapid design cycle, user research.

1 Introduction

The enterprise worker's life is busier than ever with greater demands, increasing
workloads, and a blurring of work and personal time. Taking the time to perform
basic administrative tasks, such as submitting expense reports, is becoming increasingly more difficult for stressed professionals. Road warriors, who spend more than
40 percent of their time on the road, feel the pressure the most. As network coverage
becomes more reliable and mobile technology improves, these workers increasingly
rely on their smart phones to complete daily work.

These conditions provided Oracle with an opportunity to create a simple yet intuitive mobile expenses solution for road warriors to use on their smart phones while in
places such as train stations, airports, and taxis. Because of the incredible consumer
mobile applications that they use daily, mobile workers expect innovation in all business applications as well. Our goal at Oracle was to design an innovative application
that would make it easier for mobile users to complete expense-related activities
while on the go.

Achieving this goal meant changing our current design process. We needed a rapid
process that helped us think outside the box, that incorporated user feedback, and that
iteratively incorporated this feedback into our designs.

2 Process

Our process took Oracle's usual approach for designing desktop applications and
looked at it critically to see how we could modify it for mobile application design and
development. We knew immediately we needed to increase the speed of the process
without losing valuable feedback from internal stakeholders and end users. Whereas

C. Stephanidis (Ed.): Posters, Part I, HCII 2011, CCIS 173, pp. 13–17, 2011.
© Springer-Verlag Berlin Heidelberg 2011

before, we would take requirements from internal teams individually and spend months iterating on designs before showing it to users, we now had to find a way to quickly and collaboratively get our stakeholder feedback in concise well-timed packages. In short, we needed to let the design drive the process. We had to think and act more like a company designing for the consumer marketplace, rather than one designing for enterprise applications.

We were tasked with creating—within four months—an innovative mobile expenses application without the limitation of a specific technology or platform. To meet this deadline, it was necessary to modify our current way of designing and conducting research. In essence, we needed to simplify the project plan to the most impactful activities and speed up the process. Knowing how quickly decisions needed to be made, the User Experience (UX) project lead determined that a dedicated, small, core stakeholder team needed to meet for two hours twice a week. Additional time was required to observe testing and attend presentations.

Even before gathering the team, we had homework to do! The UX team performed competitive research to identify what was current in the market and conducted phone interviews with mobile workers to understand how they track expenses while on the road.

After completing those two tasks, we gathered the team and conducted a two-hour brainstorming session followed by two hours of persona, scenario, and task selection. The next four weeks were focused on creating and reviewing technology-agnostic prototypes with the team.

The following process was implemented each week:

- Mondays: Review storyboard, use cases, and rudimentary designs.
- Tuesdays and Wednesdays: Incorporate feedback and revise designs.
- Thursdays: Present updated designs and alternatives to the core team. Decide collectively which designs work best. Use an electronic whiteboard to maximize the collaboration among local and remote team members.

Once we had initial designs and concepts, a six-person user panel was created to collect feedback. The panel reviewed a range of designs from rough wireframes to near-pixel-perfect screens, all while continuing the team's usual meeting schedule.

To ensure that we met our customers' needs and that our designs were innovative, we conducted feedback sessions with three local customers. After incorporating all feedback, we ran a Formative Usability Assessment (FUA) using a low-fidelity clickable prototype. The last round of usability tests will be run on a high-functioning prototype currently being developed.

In the following section, we explain in detail each of the steps that we used in creating this innovative application.

3 Getting Up to Speed

3.1 Competitive Research

Before gathering the requirements for our application, we performed competitive research. We looked closely at Gartner's Mobile Enterprise Application Provider

(MEAP) quadrant to determine who had, or could have, a competing application. After creating sub-classifications, we moved onto gathering public information on consumer financial applications.

Because we were interested in new and innovative applications, we also did a survey of application stores to find other products already in the marketplace. Once we had a list of the applications, we compared them on the following dimensions: innovative use of technology, user interface, integration with other applications and systems, functionality, and available platforms. We then shared this analysis with the core team to strategize on the best areas to address in our application.

3.2 Phone Interviews

When the project first began, the product team had an extensive understanding of the needs of desktop expense users. Unfortunately, desktop user requirements do not easily translate into what mobile workers expect in a mobile solution. Due to our accelerated schedule, we did not have time to conduct a full-fledged field study. Instead, we conducted phone interviews to get the product team in-tune with the new set of users. Each of the 10 phone interviews lasted one hour and consisted of a series of predefined questions. In order to participate in the study, the person had to be a road warrior who traveled at least 40% of the time and who had associated expenses.

3.3 Brainstorming

Because our goal for this project was to think outside the box and increase the level of innovation built into our application, we decided to conduct brainstorming sessions to generate ideas for the application. The first brainstorming session was two hours and included all levels (vice presidents to interns) and roles (development, product management, strategy, and user experience) within Oracle.

Our task was to identify common problems and innovative solutions for all aspects of expense creation and submission. The group divided into three smaller groups and spent approximately one hour coming up with ideas. Each team then presented its ideas to the larger group for discussion that resulted in additional ideas.

The next day we had our second brainstorming session. The goal for day two was to review the personas and to prioritize the long list of features from the previous day.

Originally designed to generate great ideas and get buy in from the group, the brainstorming exercise had the unintended benefit of creating a buzz of excitement. Not only was the team on board with the ideas, they were excited! Team member buy in and excitement were the best possible outcomes for this fast-paced project.

4 Design and Validation

4.1 Storyboards and Use Cases

Using personas developed from the interviews and brainstorming as a starting point, the design team generated three "Day-in-the-Life" storyboards to present to the entire team. The storyboards were broken into scenarios so that all team members, even those who were not familiar with the roles, could gain a deeper understanding of our personas, their devices of choice, and their needs. After the storyboards were presented, we chose the persona that best fit the road warrior ideal and continued to design the application with that in mind. While our chosen persona had a device of choice, we continued to remain platform-agnostic in an effort to keep the innovative ideas flowing and design with the best phone features available. For example, we assumed that eventually all phones, not just Android, would have superior voice recognition.

4.2 User Panels

After the initial concepts and design mock-ups, we selected a user panel methodology to quickly gather feedback. The user panel included the same users in a series of sessions over a period of eight weeks. The user-panel method was selected because it had several advantages over other more traditional usability methods:

- Ability to collect detailed feedback on portions of the design in each session.
- Collect insightful feedback by exploring more complex issues. Participants gained a thorough knowledge of the design and goals over time.
- Participants were more willing to openly share ideas and provide feedback because they were comfortable with the protocol and moderator with each subsequent session.

Six road warriors participated in the user panel. These users were a mix of iPhone, Blackberry, and Windows Mobile users. Participants were run individually for an hour every two weeks for a total of 4 sessions.

This method is rigorous in that it requires quick turnaround of test materials, designs, findings, and recommendations between each round of user panels. To accommodate the user panels, the design team added additional meetings to the already packed schedule.

On Fridays, we planned and mocked up the following week's test. Testing occurred on Mondays and Tuesdays. On Wednesdays and Thursdays, we analyzed and then presented our findings. Despite the demanding schedule, the effort was well worth it because getting regular feedback ensured that we were developing the right concepts for our end users.

4.3 Road Shows

After incorporating the user panel feedback, the team wanted to confirm that we were truly innovative and that the designs were on track with what our customers wanted. We chose road shows to present our designs to key customers to obtain their valuable feedback. We chose to visit customers rather than host a web or telephone conference for several reasons. First, by scheduling in-person meetings, the customers felt that their feedback was valued. Second, we were able to see facial expressions and gestures to better assess their genuine impressions of the application.

Internally, many people wanted to attend the session to hear our customers' feedback resulting in members from Sales, User Experience, Product Development, and Product Strategy coming along. On the customer side, attendees either owned the expenses business process or were responsible for implementing mobile solutions.

During two weeks, we held three road shows, each lasting approximately two hours. At each meeting, we provided a flow-based demo of static design mock-ups and asked a series of predefined questions to gather feedback. These sessions validated that the designs were considered modern.

4.4 Usability Testing

Round 1. Once the designs were refined based on customer visits and team discussions, we wanted to get low-level usability feedback. We knew the features and functionality of the application were well received but wanted to concentrate on any potential issues with the task flow, navigation, field placement, and terminology. We performed a task-based usability test using high-fidelity static mock-ups. Ten road warriors participated in individual two-hour remote sessions. These participants were given a set of task scenarios and asked to tell the moderator how they would perform each task using the application. Because the mock-ups were not fully functioning, the moderator controlled the mouse to move from one place to the next.

Round 2. The designs were revised again based on the findings of Round 1. These designs were passed to the application development team to create a fully functioning prototype. When this prototype is complete, we will hold on-device usability testing. This in-person testing will enable us to precisely assess device interactions.

5 Conclusion

Mobile technology growth, network coverage, and marketplace demands are requiring companies to design and develop products more rapidly than in the past. Not only do mobile products need to be developed quickly so that they are not dated before they hit the marketplace, but these products also need to be innovative to stay competitive. As a result, we must adapt traditional research and design techniques for rapid development cycles. In the past, user researchers had the luxury of spending weeks conducting just one research technique. Now, with accelerated product design, user researchers must modify traditional methodologies to provide results in a much shorter time frame. The process presented provides an example of how it is possible to conduct iterative design and research in a short time frame. The methods presented can be used and adapted to support the design and development of any product within a rapid development cycle.

Activity-Centered Design: An Appropriation Issue

Yvon Haradji[1], Germain Poizat[2], and Florence Motté[1]

[1] EDF R&D, 1 Avenue du Général de Gaulle, 92141 Clamart, France
{yvon.haradji,florence.motte}@edf.fr
[2] Université de Bourgogne, Campus Universitaire, B.P. 27877, 21078 Dijon Cedex, France
germain.poizat@u-bourgogne.fr

Abstract. When designing workplace computer systems one must take human activity into account. It has become standard practice to approach this issue through user-centered design. The aim of this paper is to stimulate thought on activity-centered design and to propose the concept of appropriation as a fundamental principle of this design approach. This orientation aims to take into consideration the *constituent function* of tools during conception. We will take the design of computer systems dedicated to customer relations as an example.

Keywords: Activity centered-design, appropriation, customer relation.

1 Introduction

A company such as EDF, producing and commercializing energy, is constantly evolving in terms of organization, tools and expertise in order to adapt to the evolutions of its clients and to those of its economic environment and legal framework. Our work falls within this dynamic of corporate evolution and focuses even more specifically on the technical, organizational and cultural changes relating to the service relationship. Within this framework we have helped to design various computer systems dedicated to the service relationship (for example, interactive vocal server, ERP application, invoicing application). Our input has always been built around an organic relationship between an understanding of human activity and technical changes - the focus being on the user's current activity and on a design which attempts to help said activity.

In this paper, we aim to show that this notion of supporting human activity deserves to be taken further, to be expanded. To this end, we will refer to previous studies that we have done on the service relationship. More broadly, the aim of this paper is to stimulate thought on activity-centered design and to propose the concept of appropriation [1] as a fundamental principle of this design approach. This orientation aims to take into account the *constituent function* of tools [2] during the design process.

2 Supporting Individual and Collective Activity within the Service Relationship

From the standpoint of design focusing on user activity, technical systems must help users to understand the situation, to initiate thought, and to take action themselves.

C. Stephanidis (Ed.): Posters, Part I, HCII 2011, CCIS 173, pp. 18–22, 2011.

In order to properly understand an activity and thus determine the actors' real needs and difficulties, it is important to consider two factors: *(a)* activity is situated, i.e. it cannot be dissociated from the context in which it takes place, and must therefore be studied *in situ* [3], *(b)* activity is autonomous, i.e. the interactions between actors and environments are *asymmetric couplings* in that they concern only those elements from the environment that the actors select moment by moment as being most relevant to their internal organization [4]. We therefore privilege an understanding of an activity in real situations and give primacy to the actors' experiences [5].

Our initial works on the service relationship related mainly to help for customer advisors working in call centers. We felt that it was important to approach advisors' work via all of their interactions with customers, tools and other actors in the company. For example, we assessed their tools and made suggestions relating to functionalities (utility) and dialogue logic (usability) in relation to a sales support work station. In this case, our design input was fundamentally directed at helping advisors in their individual work.

We gradually became aware of the collective dimension of activity in the service relationship: the advisor-customer relationship is important, but very often several other actors are involved in responses to customers. We therefore oriented our work in two complementary directions. Firstly, we focused on cooperation between the different actors within the company (advisors, invoicing experts, connection experts, etc.) who are involved in the overall processing of customer requests. In this way we highlighted the importance of mutual intelligibility between actors when coming up with responses that are adapted to customers' needs. The second orientation involved proposing help for this transversal construction of responses to customers' requests. So we are now working on the design of the "request processing file" which will enable all of the company's actors to share common computer data, thus giving concrete form to collective transversal work. This design objective does not end at the company itself; the computer data are also available to customers. By accessing this file, customers can thus examine information relating to them and modify it where necessary.

The practical objective of our input thus gradually shifted from that of helping sales advisors in their work, to helping to improve the collective activity behind the service relationship. The request processing file therefore seemed to be an integrating object of design capable of supporting collective transversal activity and transactions with customers.

3   From a Situation of Aid to a Situation of Appropriation

Aid, in the sense that we have been using so far, essentially relates to how one orientates the design of a computer tool in interaction with the cognitive dimension of individual or collective human activity. Yet the constitutive function of the technique, i.e. its power to change human activity, can be far broader and relate to aspects of health, cognition, efficacy and acceptability within the work itself. Aid as a notion for design is thus not a sufficient notion to take into account the unity of human actors in their relationships with the changed situation [6]. Our various inputs regarding the service relationship illustrate how our design issue has broadened.

Technological evolutions went hand-in-hand with organizational evolutions. The initial organizational rationale had tended to create an imbalance between the different roles of the service relationship (i.e. advisors, invoicing specialists, connection specialists). For example, the people in contact with customers benefited from having the recognized role of advisor and had a clear idea of the purpose of their work. On the other hand, the people in invoicing were doing work which was less clearly defined, with less refined tools and a very fragmented overview of the actual purpose of their activity. Our analyses were part of an organizational approach which aimed to group roles together, thus avoiding too great a fragmentation, which would reduce the efficacy and utility of the work.

These works also allowed us to assess the effect of implementing productivity criteria (with financial rewards for objectives reached). These criteria raise a certain number of problems. For example, there is a quality objective which is assessed on the basis of the number of times a customer calls back. Such an objective is clearly a delicate one, as the telephone might be cut off, or the customer may have forgotten to provide a piece of information, or there could be any number of other reasons why a customer might call back, thus reducing the quality index for request processing. Operators have to cope with a triple constraint and find a satisfactory balance between the quality of the service given to customers, their respect of corporate guidelines and reaching objectives.

Our studies revealed another important aspect, that of taking into account the way the profession is evolving. Changes in commercial offerings, the grouping together of tasks, etc., lead to evolutions in professional knowledge which place operators in a dynamic of constantly having to learn.

We will conclude with the question of the difficulty of the job. This difficulty is not caused by the premises, by the noise or the lighting, or by the pace of the work, all of which are deemed to be satisfactory. It is caused, for the most part, by job interest (before the grouping together of tasks) and by the intensity of the work (productivity criteria), which must always be balanced with quality of service and evolutions in jobs and tools that do not always make it easier to effectively cope with the work. It can also stem from a particular organizational form. Indeed, certain call centers have a majority of customers who have financial problems and who find it hard to pay their bills. In such situations, not only are operators obliged to deal with requests that are often of a more complex nature (specific payment schedules, third-party payments, etc.), but also with customers in highly precarious situations (risk of a family having its electricity cut off). Being confronted with the suffering of others is also a source of suffering for the operators, especially when they have to meet their productivity objectives.

Transformations of the situation have numerous effects on the activity of the operators. The purpose of the design for such a situation is consequently of a more inclusive nature than simply focusing on the help provided by the technical aspect of the change.

4 Designing for Appropriation

Designing for appropriation requires one to go beyond the mere utilitarian functions of a tool (a computer system for example) and integrate broader aspects. We feel that it is important to approach design for appropriation in terms of the following dimensions of human activity:

- **Individual and collective aid for the activity.** First and foremost, aiming for appropriation means helping the actors in their activity. This is our main point of entry into the issue of the service relationship, by contributing towards design processes not only for sales tools or collaborative tools to improve collaborative work, but also service training adapted to projected changes.

- **Individual and collective efficacy within the activity.** Aiming for appropriation means that one must consider different aspects of efficacy, such as the quality of responses to customers, for example, or the collective processing of requests.

- **Preventing the difficulties inherent in the activity.** Appropriation-related design must consider how a given change might affect the difficult nature of a job and the health and safety of personnel. In our example, this dimension can be taken into account through actions relating to organization and technical evolutions (e.g. reducing the number of repetitive actions). It might also take the form of service training in order to have a better understanding of the needs of the population in difficulty.

- **Individual and collective acceptability in the activity.** Changes sometimes go beyond just the technical and organizational dimension and must also be adapted to suit the cultural values relating to a profession, a group or a company. Appropriation-related design must consider the cultural dimension of the change. In particular, this might mean accompanying the change.

The theoretical and practical bases for appropriation-related design remain to be developed. We can however lay down the following principles: (a) appropriation-related design is achieved through the structural relationship of design orientation and human activity; (b) appropriation-related design integrates the different dimensions of human activity and aims to take into consideration the indissociable nature of said activity; (c) appropriation-related design must anticipate the combined development of the artifact, the situation and the activity that will follow the transformation; (d) appropriation-related design must be constructed from an integrated set of criteria and be validated with markers. These criteria are vital for guiding the design and provide a framework for a bridge between the description of the human activity and the design process.

5 Conclusion

Appropriation is a notion which relates to the experience of those concerned: via a continuous process and an internal dynamic, human actors incorporate (or not) elements from an outside environment. In the context of this paper, appropriation falls within a vision of the unfinished and continuous man and the technical, organizational and cultural transformation contributes towards the developmental dynamic of the human actor [7]. Designing for appropriation thus relates to a complex design object: it is a case of offering greater clarification and expression of how changes in situation affect the different dimensions of human activity. At the present time we hypothesize that each of these dimensions relates to one particular phenomenology of the activity (e.g. activity and health, activity and aid) and that appropriation is an integrating concept, the purpose of which is the unity of and between acting man and learning man. The appropriable nature of a situation thus corresponds to the capacity of the transformation to be livable, achievable and learnable and to be integrated into the user's own body. In proposing to design for a situation of appropriation, we want to show that a process of transformation will affect all of the human activity. We are not suggesting that every situation can and must be approached in all its complexity. Indeed, appropriation is a process which cannot be fully anticipated. Rather we wish to draw attention to this complexity and to the indissociable nature of human activity in order to provide a better framework for the transformations envisaged. For each dimension of the activity, we believe it is useful to identify the bases of a transformation framed by criteria and to specify the framework of a validation on the basis of appropriation markers within the activity.

References

1. Merleau-Ponty, M.: Phenomenology of Perception. Routledge, London (1945/1962)
2. Leroi-Gourhan, A.: Gesture and Speech. MIT Press, Cambridge (1964/1993)
3. Suchman, L.: Plans and Situated Action. Cambridge University Press, Cambridge (1987)
4. Varela, F.J., Thompson, E., Rosch, E.: The Embodied Mind: Cognitive Science and Human Experience. MIT Press, Cambridge (1991)
5. Theureau, J.: Course of Action Analysis & Course of Action Centered Design. In: Hollnagel, E. (ed.) Handbook of Cognitive Task Design, pp. 55–81. Lawrence Erlbaum Ass., Mahwah (2003)
6. Theureau, J.: La notion de "charge mentale" est-elle soluble dans l'analyse du travail, la conception ergonomique et la recherche neurophysiologique. In: Jourdan, M., Theureau, J. (eds.) Charge mentale: Notion floue et vrai problème, pp. 41–70. Octarès, Toulouse (2002)
7. Rabardel, P., Béguin, P.: Instrument Mediated Activity: from Subject Development to Anthropocentric Design. Theor. Issues in Ergon. Sci. 6, 429–461 (2005)

Conjoint Analysis Method That Minimizes the Number of Profile Cards

Hiroyuki Ikemoto[1] and Toshiki Yamaoka[2]

[1] Design Center, TOSHIBA Corporation, 1-1,
Shibaura 1-chome, Minato-ku,
Tokyo 105-8001, Japan
[2] Faculty of Systems Engineering, Wakayama University,
Sakaedani 930, Wakayama City 640-8510, Japan
hiroyuki.ikemoto@toshiba.co.jp

Abstract. Conjoint analysis is an effective method for use in deciding on a product concept. However, when numerous items are being surveyed, the number of profile cards shown to survey respondents increases and responding becomes more difficult. This makes it necessary to restrict the number of items being surveyed. This paper proposes a method of analysis that makes it possible to use a lower number of profile cards than that provided by the orthogonal design of experiment even when a large number of items is being surveyed. An Internet survey of 1,600 consumers using this method indicated that it generated identical analytical results to those produced when the orthogonal design of experiment was used.

Keywords: conjoint analysis, industrial design, incomplete rank ordered data.

1 Introduction

Conjoint analysis is a survey and analysis method which seeks to determine which product concepts will appeal to consumers by studying the degree to which they like or dislike entire products and then estimating the utility of each individual element making up that product[1],[2],[3]. In conjoint analysis, elements which determine the value of a product are termed "attributes," and concrete expressions of the conditions of these attributes are termed "levels." Concepts, which are combinations of single levels for each of the elements, are termed "profile cards." When consumers decide that they prefer a specific profile card, there is a trade-off between attributes, and this clarifies the criteria used by consumers when they select a product. However, when the number of surveyed attributes and levels in conjoint analysis increase, the number of profile cards also increases, making it difficult for subjects to provide answers. This makes it necessary to restrict the number of surveyed items.

C. Stephanidis (Ed.): Posters, Part I, HCII 2011, CCIS 173, pp. 23–28, 2011.
© Springer-Verlag Berlin Heidelberg 2011

Table 1. Attributes and levels of hypothetical product plan for a digital camera & survey results

Attribute	Level	Part-worth utility		Attribute importance	
		16 cards	10 cards	16 cards	10 cards
Pixel count	3MP	-1.203	-1.030	59.64%	58.03%
	5MP	1.203	1.030		
Zoom	3x zoom	-0.890	-0.784	32.64%	33.61%
	8x zoom	0.890	0.784		
Memory card	SD card	0.465	0.443	4.72%	5.03%
	Memory stick	0.038	0.035		
	CompactFlash	-0.012	-0.070		
	xD-Picture card	-0.490	-0.407		
Battery	Lithium rechargeable battery	-0.036	0.015	0.05%	0.01%
	AA dry battery	0.036	-0.015		
Design	G	-0.069	-0.070	2.94%	3.32%
	J	-0.030	-0.067		
	L	0.420	0.403		
	W	-0.321	-0.266		
Constant		8.500	5.419		

2 Method of Minimizing Number of Profile Cards

Theoretically, the minimum number of profile cards that can be projected for conjoint analysis is the total number of levels minus the number of attributes, plus one. In addition, there are cases in conjoint analyses in which multicollinearity arises due to the rank deficiency of the design matrix, making analysis impossible. Because of this, even in the case of the theoretically supposable minimum number of profile cards, it would also be necessary to consider ensuring that the rank of the design matrix does not drop below the level given by the subtraction of the number of attributes from the total number of levels.

The formulation of a collection of cards such that, when any two attributes are randomly selected, all the combinations of the levels of those attributes appear uniformly, is an ideal condition in terms of achieving minimal bias in the levels combined as cards. This makes it possible to maximize the accuracy of estimation of part-worths, but the number of cards increases greatly[4]. It is difficult to balance minimization of the number of cards and minimization of bias in the levels; however, an increase in the number of cards increases the burden on respondents, and consistency or repeatability in answers is lost. It would be desirable to minimize any decline in reliability due to such loss, in addition to the incidence of analytic errors due to bias in the presented product concept.

Conjoint analysis allocates levels to cards with a lack of interaction between attributes as a precondition. Assuming sufficient attention to this point, when attributes and levels are studied, this problem can be dealt with by ensuring that when any two attributes are randomly selected, all the combinations of the levels of those attributes appear as uniformly as possible, under the principle that statistical independency (slightly weaker than orthogonality), rather than orthogonality, is ensured between the attributes. In concrete terms, the constraints for the solution of the optimization problem for the minimization of the number of cards are:

1. Number of cards = Total number of levels – Number of attributes +1
2. Guarantee of statistical independency between attributes
3. The theoretical maximum rank of the design matrix = Total number of levels – Number of attributes

Under these constraints, the optimization problem is solved by means of iteration so as to ensure, to the degree possible, that all of the combinations of the levels for any two randomly selected attributes will appear uniformly. Specifically, after cards are formulated using the L2-L7 and other orthogonal arrays, a card is randomly removed, and the statistical independency of the attributes is checked by means of a test for independence using the Akaike information criterion (AIC) and a test, using the ratio of the singular values of the matrix, is conducted to ensure that there is no deficiency in the maximum theoretical rank. Cards continue to be removed in turn until the minimum number of cards is reached. Following this, the levels of each attribute are interchanged while checks of independency and rank-deficiency are run. The formulation of the cards is optimized by conducting this procedure sequentially until each level of the attributes appears most uniformly.

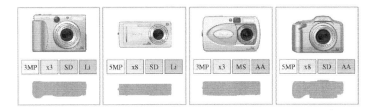

Fig. 1. Examples of profile cards

3   Verification of Effectiveness of Plan

In order to determine whether conjoint analysis using the minimum number of cards would be effective in an actual survey, a conjoint analysis of an Internet survey of consumers regarding a hypothetical product plan for a digital camera was conducted[5]. This experiment employed the attributes and levels shown in Table 1. For the sake of comparison, two surveys were prepared: Survey A, using 16 cards formulated using the orthogonal design of experiment; and Survey B, using 10 cards, minimized by means of the algorithm discussed above. 1,600 respondents who intended to purchase a digital camera were randomly assigned the surveys (800 subjects for each survey). The cards formulated using the orthogonal design of experiment were generated using SPSS ORTHOPLAN. Sixteen cards were output, with no designation of holdout cards or simulation cards. The profile cards used in Surveys A and B are respectively shown in Tables 2 and 3. Figure 1 shows examples of the profile cards that were shown to respondents. 1,600 responses were received for the survey. Responses in which there were no gaps in the rank of preference, duplications, etc. were taken as valid, and all other answers were judged invalid. 1,386 valid answers were received, representing 86.6% of the total. For each survey, the figures were:

- Survey A (16 cards): 609 (76.1%)
- Survey B (10 cards): 777 (97.1%)

The error rate for Survey A was 23.9%, while it was only 2.9% for Survey B. Assuming that there was no difference in attitude between the respondents for the two surveys, the difference can be ascribed solely to the number of cards, and we can say that the difference in error rates originates in the number of cards. This suggests that reducing the number of cards reduced the burden on respondents.

The average response times for valid responses in each survey were:

- Survey A (16 cards): 17.96 min (SD=9.76, SE=0.40)
- Survey B (10 cards): 16.05 min (SD=9.26, SE=0.33)

There is a difference of 1 minute and 27 seconds in the times. A t-test of the response times for the two surveys [$F(1384)=1.946$, $t(1384)=-2.845$, $p=0.005$] shows a statistically significant difference between them, at a significance level of 1%.

Table 2. Profile cards formulated using orthogonal design of experiment

Card number	Pixel count	Zoom	Memory card	Battery	Design
1	5MP	×8	CompactFlash	Lithium rechargeable batteries	L
2	3MP	×8	xD-Picture Card	AA dry batteries	G
3	3MP	×3	CompactFlash	AA dry batteries	W
4	3MP	×8	CompactFlash	Lithium rechargeable batteries	J
5	5MP	×3	xD-Picture Card	Lithium rechargeable batteries	J
6	5MP	×8	SD card	AA dry batteries	J
7	5MP	×3	CompactFlash	AA dry batteries	G
8	3MP	×8	SD card	AA dry batteries	L
9	5MP	×8	Memory stick	Lithium rechargeable batteries	G
10	5MP	×8	xD-Picture Card	AA dry batteries	W
11	3MP	×3	Memory stick	AA dry batteries	J
12	3MP	×3	SD card	Lithium rechargeable batteries	G
13	3MP	×3	xD-Picture Card	Lithium rechargeable batteries	L
14	5MP	×3	SD card	Lithium rechargeable batteries	W
15	5MP	×3	Memory stick	AA dry batteries	L
16	3MP	×8	Memory stick	Lithium rechargeable batteries	W

Multivariate tests were conducted in order to determine whether the difference in card numbers produced any difference in the part-worths estimated for each survey. The most powerful of these, Wilks' lambda, showed that there was no statistically significant difference [F(9) = 1.607, P=0.108]. Given this, we can say that there is no difference in the part-worths estimated from the results of the two surveys using differing numbers of cards.

These results show that a conjoint analysis conducted using cards the number of which had been minimized by means of the proposed method was able to produce results identical to those produced by a survey using cards generated by means of the orthogonal design of experiment. This indicates that it will be possible to survey greater numbers of attributes and levels using the same amount of cards as generated by the orthogonal design of experiment without increasing the burden on respondents.

Table 3. Profile cards formulated using minimization algorithm

Card num-ber	Pixel count	Zoom	Memory card	Battery	Design
1	3MP	×3	Memory stick	AA dry batteries	J
2	3MP	×3	SD card	Lithium rechargeable batteries	G
3	5MP	×8	SD card	Lithium rechargeable batteries	L
4	5MP	×8	SD card	AA dry batteries	W
5	3MP	×8	Memory stick	Lithium rechargeable batteries	J
6	5MP	×3	Memory stick	Lithium rechargeable batteries	L
7	5MP	×3	CompactFlash	AA dry batteries	G
8	3MP	×8	CompactFlash	AA dry batteries	L
9	5MP	×8	xD-Picture Card	AA dry batteries	G
10	3MP	×3	xD-Picture Card	Lithium rechargeable batteries	W

4 Conclusion

This paper has shown that when conjoint analysis is used to decide on a product concept, the use of the minimum number of profile cards and a good balance of profile cards make it possible to survey a greater number of attributes and levels, reduce the burden on respondents, and increase the accuracy of responses and the reliability of the survey.

Unlike analyses in which holdout cards (which are not used for estimation but exclusively for verification) are introduced, because the proposed method generates only the minimum number of profile cards necessary for the estimation of part-worths, it has the problem that it is not possible to obtain indicators of the reliability of the estimation results. In the case of the first conjoint analysis conducted during product research, a standard analysis using holdout cards should be conducted prior to using the proposed method, in order to check the reliability of the survey.

References

1. Luce, R.D., Tukey, J.W.: Simultaneous conjoint measurement: A new type of fundamental measurement. Journal of Mathematical Psychology 1(1), 1–27 (1964)
2. Green, P.E., Rao, V.R.: Conjoint Measurement for Quantifying Judgmental Data. Journal of Marketing Research 8(3), 355–363 (1971)

3. Green, P.E., Srinivasan, V.: Conjoint Analysis in Consumer Research: Issues and Outlook. The Journal of Consumer Research 5(2), 103–123 (1978)
4. Moriguchi, S.: Optimality of Orthogonal Designs, Res. Stat. Appl. Res., JUSE 3 (1954)
5. Ikemoto, H., Yamaoka, T.: A study on the effective usage of full-profile conjoint analysis. Kansei Engineering International Journal 9(2), 215–225 (2010)

Research on the Role of the Sketch in Design Idea Generation

Yuichi Izu[1], Koichirou Sato[2], and Yoshiyuki Matsuoka[2]

[1] Toshiba Corporation, 1-1-1 Shibaura, Minato-ku, Tokyo, Japan
[2] Keio University, 3-14-1 Hiyoshi, Kohoku-ku, Yokohama, Japan

Abstract. The purpose of this research is to solve the function achieved in the design idea generation of idea sketches. We conducted the comparative-analysis experiment on the relation between the sketch and an idea generation. We considered the relation between display technique and the design idea generation to the experimental result by the "Multispace Design Model" which shows the comprehensive viewpoint of design thinking. In conclusion, from the relation between sketch skill and the number of deployment, the following were shown about the role of the display technique in the idea generation. One is a conversion function from a keyword with the high degree of abstraction to an attribute element, and another is a deployment function from "Structure Attributes" to "Appearance Attributes" in attribute examination of form.

Keywords: Design idea generation, Idea sketches, Multispace Design Model.

1 Introduction

In innovative thinking, creative capability has been the focused of attention in recent years. In this research, we focused on the idea generation process of designers who create beautiful and easy-to use products based on abstract concepts. Many designers utilize display techniques, such as sketches, and we analyzed the relationship between display technique and idea generation.

The purpose of this study is the elucidation of the function of the display technique in design idea generation. Display technique in a design can be considered to be the technique for creating a concrete model that extracts and express the character of the design, or the technique for creating a model that shows how a subject can be viewed.

2 Comparative-Analysis Experiment

We conducted a comparative-analysis experiment on the relationship between a sketch, which is one display technique and an idea generation.

2.1 Comparative-Analysis Experiment on Concept Formation

First, the relationship between sketch skill and design idea generation was analyzed based on concept formation. The subjects comprised 21 students with specialized

C. Stephanidis (Ed.): Posters, Part I, HCII 2011, CCIS 173, pp. 29–32, 2011.

design education experience and 13 students without experience. The following five items were analyzed for "Iron" and "Liquid Crystal Television" idea sketches; each was displayed for 5 minutes.

1. Sketch Skill
2. Number of Television Designs
3. Number of Iron Designs
4. Number of Element Examinations in Television Design
5. Number of Element Examinations in Iron Design

Sketch skill was categorized into three groups on the basis of the correctness of perspective and the smoothness of outline expression. Correlation analysis, cluster analysis, and factor analysis were used for analysis. It was shown that the subjects can classified into three groups with the following features (Fig.1).

Group1: High sketch skill, perform many element examinations, display many television design proposals.
Group2: Medium sketch skill, display of many iron design proposals.
Group3: Low sketch skill, few ideas generated.

2.2 Comparative-Analysis Experiment in the Idea Selection Stage

Second, the relationship between drawing skill and design idea generation was analyzed in the idea selection stage by the same subjects. The following five items were analyzed based on rough sketches of a "Projector" displayed for 1 hour.

1. Sketch Skill
2. Number of Element Examinations
3. Number of Structure Deployments
4. Number of Appearance Deployments
5. Keywords

Keywords were classified into four steps based on the degree of abstraction [1].

1. Abstract Image Expression
2. Concrete Image Expression
3. Image Expression for Function
4. Image Expression for Form

Correlation analysis, cluster analysis, and factor analysis were used for analysis. It was shown that the subjects can be classified into three groups with the following features (fig.2).

Group1: High sketch skill, develop many appearances and conceive keywords with a high degree of abstraction.
Group2: Medium sketch skill, develop many structures and conceive keywords about function.
Group3: Low sketch skill, conceive keywords about form.

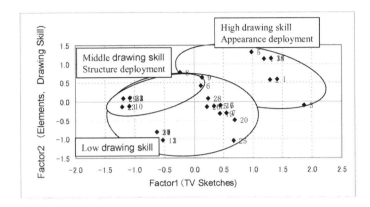

Fig. 1. The scatter diagram of the analysis result in concept formation

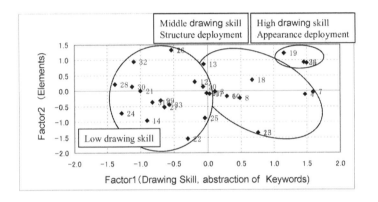

Fig. 2. The scatter diagram of the analysis result in idea selection

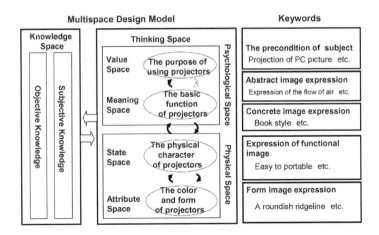

Fig. 3. Multispace design model and keywords

4 Discussions by a "Multispace Design Model"

We considered the relationship between display technique and design idea generation using experimental results based on the "Multispace Design Model" [2] [3] which shows a comprehensive viewpoint of design thought. The "Multispace Design Model" divides the thinking space of design into 4parts-- "Value Space", "Meaning Space", "State Space", and "Attribute Space"--and defines a design act as reasoning between space inner and space based on knowledge. The following were shown as a result of having keywords that are classified by "the class method of the degree of abstraction" applied to the   "Multispace Design Model". Figure 3 shows the key words which correspond to the "Multispace Design Model"

Subjects with high sketch skill conceive keywords used as "Value Elements" in "Value Space", and "Meaning Elements" in "Meaning Space". Then those keywords are changed into "State Elements" in "State Space", and "Attribute Elements" in "Attribute Space", and they draw design proposals.   Moreover, "Structure Deployments" and "Appearance Deployments" which were observed in the comparative-analysis experiment considered to be a deployment of "Structure Attributes" and "Appearance Attributes" in "Attribute space".

5 Conclusion

In conclusion, from the relationship between sketch skill and the number of deployment, the following conclusions were drawn about the role of display technique in idea generation. One is the conversion function from a keyword with a high degree of abstraction to an attribute element, and another is the deployment function from "Structure Attributes" to "Appearance Attributes" in "Attribute space".

References

1. Rasmussen, J.: Information Processing and Human Machine Interface. KeigakuShuppan, 17–29 (1990)
2. Matsuoka, Y., Ujiie, Y., et al.: Design Science. pp. 10–29. Maruzen Co., Ltd., (2010)
3. Matsuoka, Y., Miyata, S.: The Concept of the Optimal Design. Kyoritsu shuppan, 8–17 (2008)

Initial Perspectives from Preferences Expressed through Comparisons

Nicolas Jones, Armelle Brun, and Anne Boyer

LORIA - Nancy Université, BP 239, 54506 Vandœuvre-lès-Nancy, France
{nicolas.jones,armelle.brun,anne.boyer}@loria.fr

Abstract. Rating-scales have become a popular modality for expressing our preferences, but they present several drawbacks. We have recently proposed a new modality: comparing items ("I prefer A to B"). After initial user-studies with encouraging results, we here share some initial perspectives. In particular we examine three issues illustrated with graphs of user's preferences. We discuss the adaptability of comparisons, their algorithmic complexity and incoherences introduced by transitivity.

Keywords: preference expression, comparisons, ratings.

1 Introduction: Context for Using Comparisons

Multi-point rating scales have become a popular preference expression tool for personalization and recommender systems. They unfortunately present several drawbacks: users' ratings are inconsistent through time [1]; the issue of the optimal number of points in rating scales is still unresolved [7]; the granularity of the scale often offers limited precision, which likely to frustrate users [4]; the values and descriptive labels associated with the scale points can influence users's ratings [2], etc.

We recently proposed a new modality whereby users compare items two-by-two "I prefer A to B" ($A \rightarrow B$), as one often does in everyday life. To evaluate this alternative, we ran several user studies with over 200 participants [6,5], where these got to rate or compare films and television series. Three important findings were obtained. First, preferences expressed with comparisons are coherent with those from ratings, although some differences appear. When users say that they prefer a movie A to B with a comparison, the rating scores reflect this preference in 92.5% of cases. However, when both are equal in comparisons ($A \leftrightarrow B$), ratings are only equal 42.7% of times. Second, participants preferred comparisons, and were favorably predisposed to using them instead of ratings. Users found comparisons easier to use, requiring less effort, but at the same time found the ratings to give more control. Third, over a fifteen day break, comparisons are 20% more stable through time than ratings.

Despite these favorable findings, certain issues about comparisons need to be raised. In this paper, we discuss three high-level considerations relating to preferences expressed through comparisons. In order to model users' preferences, we used *preference relations* to create ranked graphs of users' comparisons [3]. Several graphs are presented in this paper.

C. Stephanidis (Ed.): Posters, Part I, HCII 2011, CCIS 173, pp. 33–37, 2011.

2 Discussion

2.1 Adaptability of Comparisons

One issue with rating scales is that, within a system, they only provide a fixed range of possible answers. Depending on the situation, users might wish to have more or fewer points on the scale. We expected that comparisons would be more flexible, since users can explicitly say that two items should be equivalent or if a difference is perceived. This adaptability was confirmed by our results. These show that some users need only three levels of rankings in their preference relation, whereas others go up to nine levels; the median score is 5 ranks. Examples with respectively three and seven levels are shown in Figure 3 and Figure 1. One should keep in mind that these results were only obtained over a three minute session, and that more detailed relations are likely to appear over time.

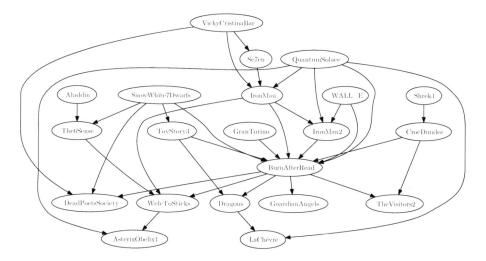

Fig. 1. Example of a users' preferences with seven ranks

More importantly, we believe that the adaptability of comparisons means that they are more precise at modeling users' preferences than ratings. Let us imagine the case of users who only need three levels to rank items. If they are given a five-point rating scale, it is highly likely that they will give neighboring scores to items that they actually perceive as being indifferent. In doing so, they will introduce noise into their data. This phenomena is known in literature and was reported by several users during post-study discussions. In contrast, comparisons seem to allow users to stay on three levels, and therefore they model users' preferences more precisely. If we consider the opposite case, of users who rely on more than five levels, they are often obliged to give the same rating to two films which they actually appreciate differently. Here again the comparisons seem to solve this issue, with some users relying on up to nine ranks of preferences, therefore modeling users' preferences more precisely. For these reasons we are convinced that comparisons will increase the quality of the user information recorded.

2.2 Complexity of Comparisons

A second issue about comparisons is their algorithmic complexity. In order to obtain a complete comparison graph, where each item has been compared to all others once, $n * (n - 1)/2$ comparisons are needed, where n is the number of items. Whilst this theoretical number is very high and thus an obvious drawback, encouraging signs show that not all comparisons are useful. In a full preference relation, collected for instance over a three-minute session, some items may have a high uncertainty when determining their ranking. To illustrate this issue, we portray two examples in Figure 2: we consider two similar items M and N that have the same relation towards E and F. By choice, we positioned the first item M at rank 3 with a high uncertainty, as it could just as well be on either of the two ranks above it (M' or M"). However, the promising observation is that with just one additional comparison the doubt around N can be resolved. If we compare N to D we will not learn anything new, whilst a comparison with B (labelled j) will allow to position N with confidence.

For this reason, we believe that by using an adequate strategy for selecting pairs to be compared, we can easily limit the complexity of comparisons. We are confident that a compromise between completeness of the preference relation, and asking users to compare items a minimal number of times, can be reached. This should especially be true, as our results show that users find it easier, and requiring less effort, to make comparisons rather than ratings. A straightforward strategy for selecting which comparisons should be made would be to use dichotomy among the ranks with uncertainty. Other optimal strategies are regularly discussed in the field of preference relations, such as [9].

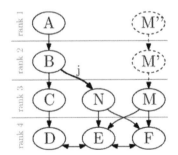

Fig. 2. Uncertainty of rankings illustrated

2.3 Incoherences in Comparisons

A third challenge about using comparisons is incoherences induced by transitivity. In Section 2.2 we supposed that transitivity could be used to deduce unknown

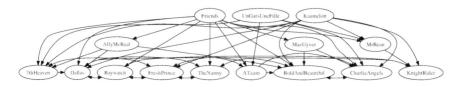

Fig. 3. Example of a users' preferences with three ranks, and incoherences

preferences. In order to reflect on how realistic this claim is, we here discuss the incoherences that users created in their three minute sessions of comparisons.

We consider that a user has introduced an incoherence when a cycle in the preference relation can be detected among several comparison couples among which at least one is not a strict equivalence. (for example: A→B→C→A). In one of our experiments, less than half of the users presented cycles with incoherences, the majority of them only having one or two incoherences throughout their whole graph. This shows that within three-minute sessions, users are mainly coherent.

When users' graphs present incoherences, this can seem problematic. However, having run these preliminary studies, and considering users' feedback, we are under the impression that these incoherences should not be perceived only as a weakness, but rather as an opportunity to improve and refine the user-model. Currently two strategies appear to us as being easily implementable.

A first strategy would be to weight edges. We observed that most of the incoherences appeared when users indicated one or more equivalence relations inside a cycle. Figure 3 shows two examples, highlighted in red. When multiple items are judged as being equivalent, it seems that there is an increased uncertainty in the use of transitivity across the current rank. Said otherwise: users are able to make equivalence judgements between two items at a time, but a sequence of equivalences does not guarantee that all items are on the same global rank. It is conceivable that multiple equivalencies could spread across two (or more) ranks. We believe that such incoherences across equivalences could be detected and that the weights of the graph, or the ranks of the items, could be tweaked to create a finer user-model.

Second, another possible strategy would be to simply remove conflicting edges in the system. In the field of database, a recent work by Pyratos *et. al* used the same strategy, leading to the non-inclusion of new edges creating an incoherence [8]. A variant of this approach might be to keep the last added comparison, and to try and remove the oldest comparison(s) which created this incoherence. In doing so, the system would give priority to the users current feedback, a common tactic in the field of user modeling.

3   Conclusions

The points discussed in this paper show that comparisons are a highly promising modality for expressing preferences. We use preference relations to model users' preferences as ranked graphs. Using these graphs, we first observe that the preferences expressed with comparisons are very adaptive to users' needed level of detail. Second, although the number of comparisons required to build a reliable preference relation is high, we show that not all comparisons are useful and that an adequate strategy may dramatically reduce the number of comparisons required. Third, we point out that users don't express many incoherences through a three-minute session of comparisons, and that those observed often appear in equivalence judgements. We argue that incoherences could present an additional value, a mechanism for weighting users' graphs. These findings conduct us to the following statement: when using rating scales, the number of answers is limited, which reduces the precision of the preferences expressed, but facilitates their automatic processing. At the opposite, when using comparisons, a finer precision of preferences is obtained, but these are more complex to process. We believe that if we can make comparisons an even easier interaction-task, and deduce comparisons from users' traces, comparisons will become a much more valuable preference-expression mechanism than the current rating-scales. These elements constitute our future work.

References

1. Amatriain, X., Pujol, J.M., Oliver, N.: I like it... I like it not: Evaluating user ratings noise in recommender systems. In: Houben, G.-J., McCalla, G., Pianesi, F., Zancanaro, M. (eds.) UMAP 2009. LNCS, vol. 5535, pp. 247–258. Springer, Heidelberg (2009)
2. Amoo, T., Friedman, H.: Do numeric values influence subjects' responses to rating scales? Journal of International Marketing and Marketing Research 26, 41–46 (2001)
3. Brun, A., Hamad, A., Buffet, O., Boyer, A.: Towards preference relations in recommender systems. In: Workshop on Preference Learning, European Conference on Machine Learning and Principle and Practice of Knowledge Discovery in Databases, ECML-PKDD 2010 (2010)
4. Cena, F., Vernero, F., Gena, C.: Towards a customization of rating scales in adaptive systems. In: De Bra, P., Kobsa, A., Chin, D. (eds.) UMAP 2010. LNCS, vol. 6075, pp. 369–374. Springer, Heidelberg (2010)
5. Jones, N., Brun, A., Boyer, A.: Comparisons Instead of Ratings: Towards More Stable Preferences. Tech. rep., LORIA, Nancy Université (2011)
6. Jones, N., Brun, A., Boyer, A.: Ratings, What Else? Tech. rep., LORIA, Nancy Université (2011)
7. Preston, C., Colman, A.: Optimal number of response categories in rating scales: reliability, validity, discriminating power, and respondent preferences. Acta Psychologica 104(1), 1–15 (2000)
8. Spyratos, N., Kotzinos, D.: Communicating through preferences. In: PETRA (2010)
9. Spyratos, N., Meghini, C.: Combining preference relations: Completeness and consistency. In: Very Large Data Bases, VLDB (2007)

Reducing Uncertainty in a Human-Centered Design Approach: Using Actor-Network Theory Analysis to Establish Fluid Design Guidelines

Ryan Kirk and Anna Prisacari

Iowa State University, Human-Computer Interaction Program,
1620 Howe Hall Ames, IA 50010, USA
{rakirk,annacari}@iastate.edu

Abstract. When designing, it can be difficult to keep track of all of the complex and varying relationships that exist. This paper is intended to persuade designers to consider using Actor-Network Theory (ANT) in order to gain insights about the existence and the nature of complex relationships occurring within a usage scenario. ANT allows for the creation of network maps that may offer insights about future interactions that are useful for gauging the appropriateness of a particular technological intervention. Guidelines are offered for using ANT for design. Future work is being done to further establish and validate methodologies for creating ANT network maps.

Keywords: Actor-Network Theory, network, design.

1 Introduction

A holistic approach to human-centered design can be achieved through incorporating the ANT as a part of the regular design process when initially analyzing a design problem. ANT is a useful framework for the development of fluid guidelines that can be used in a human-centered design approach. ANT advocates mapping the language, the tangible interactions, the environmental changes, the activities and the expressed needs of elements within a system. ANT is more of a framework than it is a concrete theory. The use of ANT on development revolves more about relationships within a system than it does around rigid objectives.

In designing a technology, this framework can be used to establish fluid guidelines for development. These fluid guidelines help the designer to consider the general tendencies within an entire system and will result in an intervention that is adaptable to future social constraints given the current knowledge of the system; these guidelines will help a designer account for the constantly changing constraints in a real-world setting. These design guidelines will help the designer to reduce the uncertainty and the design-related risks associated with costs. The method of establishing these design guidelines will be presented and examples will be provided in support of this framework.

C. Stephanidis (Ed.): Posters, Part I, HCII 2011, CCIS 173, pp. 38–42, 2011.
© Springer-Verlag Berlin Heidelberg 2011

2   Creating an ANT Network for Design

In ANT, actors are nodes that can be thought of as people, places, events and other elements that are capable of exhibiting agency within a network. Connections are the edges that connect the nodes and these represent the flow of energy within a network. Here energy is defined as resources spent or received by actors and could include, but are not limited to things such as: time, money, and effort. Thus, creating an ANT network involves establishing the nodes, or actors, and determining what connects them. Once these factors are established, a map can be created that diagrams a network.

In order to establish a network for a particular design problem, a few steps are offered as guidelines:

1. Collect all of the available artifacts that relate to the design goal.
2. List elements from the artifacts that qualify as actors or as connectors.
3. Create a network diagram for your network. Optimal guidelines for designing the network are currently being developed as a work in progress.
4. Modification of any actors in the network will result in a new network structure.

Artifacts can be considered 'snapshots' or byproducts of a network and consist of data or information about what has happened within the network. Artifacts can also represent the final product created by a network dedicated to a goal. For instance, a building is an artifact created from a network that involved people and resources; however, the location of the building could be a place that serves as an active actor within a network. Thus, artifacts and actors can sometimes be directly related. Some examples of artifacts could include: buildings, products, programs, and behavioral records.

When examining artifacts, look for evidence about the presence of actors and connectors and document this evidence. Use the evidence from all of the artifacts to establish al list of actors and connectors. Once a list of actors and connectors has been established, the ANT network can be created. There are many ways to create networks and guidelines for placing actors and connectors into a network are a focus for this ongoing work in progress. Finally, once a network is established, any changes that occur within an actor will result in changes within the entire network. Time itself is a resource within a network; changes in time do not change the structure of a network directly. However, changes in a network occur as changes in actors occur, therefore, changes in a network usually occur over time.

3   Example Scenario: HCI-i Conference

The detail and data within a network will depend upon the frame of reference considered. Here, the HCI-I conference as a whole is considered from the standpoint of the artifacts that are easily accessible remotely. Several artifacts were considered including the website, previous proceedings/papers/proposals, the conferences' reputation, the list of previous attendees, the previous speakers/lecturers, and the previous conference themes. From this list of artifacts, a list of actors and connectors was created. See figure 1 for a diagram of extracting actors and connectors from the HCI-i website artifact.

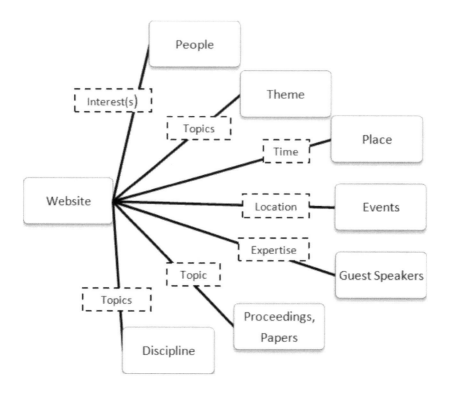

Fig. 1. A list of artifacts to be analyzed is seen at left. To the right, a map of actors and connectors is presented that was created from analyzing the website artifact. The text inside the dotted lines represents a description of the connector to which it is adjacent.

The list of actors and connectors is subjective, but the reliability of the resultant list can be increased through using a collaborative approach to examining artifacts. Once the list has been verified by several researches, the relationships between the actors and connectors can be diagramed. The construction of a proposed network structure also benefits from a collaborative approach that involves several researchers who can cross-validate each other's recommended network structure.

The final structure of a network may not always be directly intuitive. It is important to only connect those actors that play an active role in the current network structure. In each case, use artifacts to justify the connection decisions. Thus, as new artifacts are discovered, the network structure will adjust to accommodate the evidence (see Figure 2).

Once a network is created using this ANT-based approach, it is possible to simulate the flow of resources through a network. Notice that the type of resource being exchanged depends both upon which actors are exchanging resources and upon which method of connection these actors are using to exchange resources. Notice that the 'Current Proceedings' actor and the 'People' actor can exchange resources based upon time, money and interconnections depending upon the activity that is occurring

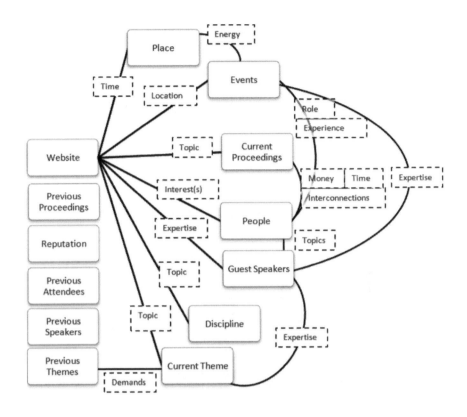

Fig. 2. A graph of the ANT network is presented that was created from analyzing artifacts. Notice that some of the actors listed to the left did not become connected to other actors. This happened because evidence was not yet found within other artifacts that suggested that these played an active role in the current HCI-i conference network. This reflects the iterative, continuously developing, nature of this network-centered approach.

within the network. Finally, because the actors are interconnected, notice that any change in an actor or a connection channel will result in a change in the overall network structure.

4 Conclusions and Next Steps

Since the passage of time does not affect the structure of an ANT network, using ANT to map a network results in an approach that is more robust than the analysis of technological interventions alone. Additionally, using ANT to map connections allows for a better idea of what may happen in a network when a change does occur because mapping a network makes interconnections more obvious.

Ultimately, this paper examines an example of only one usage scenario and certainly a large variety of networks could be mapped using the techniques offered. It is the goal of this paper to motivate others to consider using such an approach to map the structure of the network associated with their own design goals.

Finally, this is an active work in progress. Guidelines for developing an optimal network structure as well as examples of other networks are actively being assembled.

Acknowledgements. We would like to thank our advisors Dr. Jared Danielson, Dr. Thomas Holme and Dr. Anna Correia for their support.

References

1. Callon, M.: Actor Network Theory. International Encyclopedia of the Social and Behavioral Sciences, 62–66 (2004)
2. Law, J.: Actor Network Theory and Material Semiotics (DRAFT) (2007),
   http://www.heterogeneities.net/publications/
   Law2007ANTandMaterialSemiotics.pdf
3. Randall, D., Harper, R., Rouncefield, M.: Fieldwork for Design: Theory and Practice. Springer, London (2007)

Verification of Centrality to Extract Proper Factors in Model Construction Process by Using Creativity Technique

Kodai Kitami[1], Ryosuke Saga[2], and Kazunori Matsumoto[1]

[1] Kanagawa Institute of Technology, Graduate School of Engineering,
1030 Shimo-ogino, Atsugi, Kanagawa, 243-0292, Japan
[2] Kanagawa Institute of Technology, Facuty of Information and Computer Science
kodai.kitami@gmail.com
{saga,matumoto}@ic.kanagawa-it.ac.jp

Abstract. This paper describes the verification of measure to extract factors in a factor model construction process. We have proposed a factor model construction process that uses structural equation modeling and KJ method to construct an objective factor model. KJ method is a creativity technique and a bottom-up approach which members of small group think out, refine, and organize ideas. We apply degree centrality to extract factors from a model constructed by KJ method in this process. There are several different centralities such as closeness and betweenness, which may be superior to degree centrality. Therefore, we verified a method for selecting a centrality by determining the changes in a goodness-of-fit-index and the features of a constructed model by three centralities.

Keywords: Causality analysis, Factor model construction process, SEM, KJ method, Centrality.

1 Introduction

The causality analysis is important in knowledge management, and many enterprises have built a strong relationship with consumers through customer relationship management [1]. As the saying goes, "A satisfied customer is the best advertisement", so many enterprises perform a causality analysis to determine consumer purchase factors and satisfaction [2]. There are many kinds of statistical methods for causality analysis, such as the factor analysis, regression, and Bayesian network methods [3] [4] [5]. Structural equation modeling (SEM) especially has a beneficial effect on causality analysis because this method can express complex relationships between variables visually and quantitatively by path model [6]. A problem with SEM is that an analyzer can construct a model based on one's own subjective assumptions, so the objectivity of the constructed model tends to be low. To solve this problem, we propose a factor model construction process that uses KJ method, which is a creativity technique [7]. A creativity technique is a systematic method to creatively solve

C. Stephanidis (Ed.): Posters, Part I, HCII 2011, CCIS 173, pp. 43–47, 2011.
© Springer-Verlag Berlin Heidelberg 2011

problems by thinking out and organizing ideas. KJ method is a factor model construction method for writing ideas and facts into cards, organizing groups, and connecting groups or cards by links [8]. By using KJ method, we can construct an objective factor model that multiple people can agree on.

In the proposed process, we use degree centrality as a threshold to extract factors because degree centrality means the importance of nodes. However, there are several centralities such as closeness and betweenness, which may be superior to degree centrality [9]. It is possible that we need to use a proper centrality in accordance with the construction of a model. Therefore, in this paper, we perform an experiment, determine the changes in the construction of a model transformed by the differences in centralities, and specify a proper centrality for the proposed process.

The rest of this paper is presented as follows. We describe the outline of our proposed process and the purpose of this paper in Chapter 2. In Chapter 3, the environment and results of the experiment are described, and the results are discussed. Finally, Chapter 4 concludes with a summary of the key points.

2   Proposed Process and Problem

2.1   Factor Model Construction Process

We propose a model construction process that uses KJ method as shown in the following five steps (Figure 1).

1. **Run KJ method:** We perform KJ method by targeting test subjects and obtain the results expressed by cards and their links in order to construct a factor model.
2. **Refine the model by integrating expressions:** We refine the model obtained using KJ method by integrating the expressions of the cards.
3. **Collate cards by data:** We collect the necessary data from the internet and collate cards whose conceptual meanings are approximately equal. We treat collated cards as observed variables and the remaining cards as latent variables.
4. **Extract factors from the results:** We extract factors from the model by setting a threshold for degree centrality.
5. **Analyze by SEM:** We analyze the completed factor model and calculate goodness-of-fit-index (GFI) and the path coefficients, which indicates the strength of the relationships between the variables.

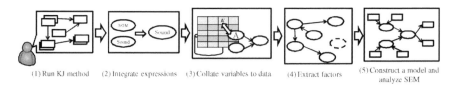

(1) Run KJ method   (2) Integrate expressions   (3) Collate variables to data   (4) Extract factors   (5) Construct a model and analyze SEM

Fig. 1. Procedure of Proposed Process

Table 1. Types and Statistics of Analysis data

Attribute	Type	Max	Min	Average	SD
Graphics	Numeric	10	1	6.803	1.705
Sound	Numeric	10	0	6.742	1.731
Gameplay	Numeric	10	0	6.700	1.897
LastingAppeal	Numeric	10	0	6.455	2.107
Overall	Numeric	10	0.700	6.766	1.795
Price	Integer	153	1	74.61	40.68
Publisher	Factor	-	-	-	-
Month	Factor	-	-	-	-
Genre	Factor	-	-	-	-
Rating	Factor	-	-	-	-
Platform	Factor	-	-	-	-

2.2 Problem and Purpose

For the proposed process, we set a threshold for degree centrality in order to extract important factors in the model. However, it was not clear if degree centrality was appropriate for this process because we had not constructed factor models by using other centralities such as closeness and betweenness [9]. Closeness centrality is expressed by the averages of length between a variable and the others. Betweenness centrality is expressed by the possibility that a variable is contained in the shortest paths between other variables. To specify a proper centrality, we constructed factor models by setting the threshold to three centralities (degree, closeness, and betweenness) and determined the configuration and the changes of the GFI in the constructed model.

3 Experiment

3.1 Experimental Environment

We constructed factor models by gradating the thresholds of three centralities for three models obtained by KJ method. In addition, we specified a proper centrality based on the configuration and the GFI of the constructed models. In the experiment, we set theme to be "the factor for best-selling video games", generated three groups, and performed KJ method targeting university students. We used data for 5764 video games as analysis data on "IGN Entertainment Games" as analysis data. We also included 11 parameters such as graphics and sound as attributes. Table 1 shows the types and statistics of the analysis data. Note that we treat directional models as non-directional models for the closeness and betweenness centralities because the centralities of most latent variables becomes zero in the directional models.

3.2 Result of Experiment

First, we performed steps 1 to 3 for the three models obtained by KJ method (Figure 2 to 4). In step 4, we applied three centralities and constructed factor models by

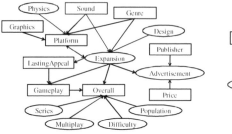

Fig. 2. Basic Configuration of Model 1

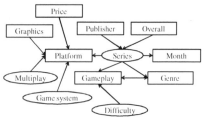

Fig. 3. Basic Configuration of Model 2

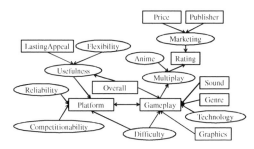

Fig. 4. Basic Configuration of Model 3

gradating the thresholds of the centralities. Table 2 shows the GFI of each model. As can be seen from the table, there were no changes in the GFI among the centralities in this experiment.

For Model 1 and 2, variables located at the edge were preferentially excluded as the threshold became high in all centralities. The reason is that many latent variables located at edge of models and their lengths to other variables are long. For Model 3, variables located at the edge of the models were excluded by priority in the degree and betweenness centralities; however, the latent variables connected to a hub in the model, so the closeness centrality of the variables became high. For example,

Table 2. GFI of Each Centrality

Degree	2	3	4	5	6	7
Model 1	.867	.867	.867	.867	.867	.804
Model 2	.861	.861	.861	.861	.861	.862
Model 3	n/a	n/a	.610	.610	.610	.610
Closeness	3.5	3	2.5	2	1.5	1
Model 1	n/a	n/a	.867	.867	.842	.804
Model 2	.861	.861	.861	.861	.861	.862
Model 3	n/a	n/a	.610	.610	.610	.610
Betweenness	0	0.25	0.5	0.75	1	
Model 1	.868	.868	.842	.842	.804	
Model 2	.861	.861	.861	.861	.861	
Model 3	n/a	.610	.610	.610	.610	

"difficulty" has low degree and betweenness centralities because this variable is located at the edge of the model. However, variables connected to "gameplay" and "platform" had a high degree and were located by the center of the model, so the closeness centrality of the variable became high, and a model having a different configuration was constructed.

From these results, it is clear selecting a proper centrality by contemplating which variable has importance in the model is necessary.

4 Conclusion

In this paper, centralities for extracting factors from factor models were verified. We verified a way to select a centrality by determining the changes in a GFI and the features of a constructed model transformed by three centralities (degree, closeness, and betweenness). In this experiment, there were no differences in GFI for each centrality. However, it is possible that the GFI changes when the configuration of a model is transformed by a centrality. In addition, there are characteristics that exclude latent variables in each centrality. Therefore, it is effective to select a centrality by contemplating which variable has importance in the model. For instance, if we focus on the vulnerability of models, it is effective to apply the betweenness centrality, and, if we emphasize the number of degrees, the degree centrality is a proper centrality.

References

1. Tiwana, A.: The Knowledge Management Toolkit: Orchestrating IT, Strategy, and Knowledge Platforms. Prentice-Hall, Englewood Cliffs (2002)
2. Bayus, L.B.: Word of Mouth : The Indirect Effects of Marketing Efforts. Journal of Advedrtising Research, 31–39 (June-July 1985)
3. Loehlin, C.J.: Latent variable models –an introduction to factor, path, and structural equation analysis. Psychology Press, San Diego (2009)
4. Freedman, D., Pisani, R., Purves, R.: Statistics. W. W. Norton & Company, New York (2007)
5. Koller, D., Friedman, N.: Probabilistic graphical models –principles and techniques. The MIT press, Cambridge (2009)
6. Pearl, J.: Causality, Models, Reasoning, and inference. Cambridge University Press, Cambridge (2000)
7. Saga, R., Kitami, K., Matsumoto, K.: Graphical modeling by creativity method for structural equation modeling. In: Proceeding of Japan-Cambodia Joint Symposium on Information Systems and Communication Technology 2011, pp. 51–56 (2011)
8. Kawakita, J.: Way of thinking: For creativity development. Chuokoron-Shinsha.Ink (1967)
9. Wasserman, S., Faust, K.: Social Network Analysis: Methods and Applications. Cambridge University Press, Cambridge (1994)

User-Centered Approach for NEC Product Development

Izumi Kohno and Hiromi Fujii

NEC Corporation, Japan
kohno@ay.jp.nec.com, h-fujii@bu.jp.nec.com

Abstract. We present the work we have done on the universal design of our products, solutions, and services. We consider universal design to have three aspects: accessibility, usability, and innovation. General universal design is composed of only accessibility and usability. NEC Group universal design includes the concept of innovation, which means that our products provide new value to our customers. We use a user-centered design process to make our products more user-friendly, easy-to-use, and innovative. We present two cases in which we applied user-centered design. One is the flight information board at the international passenger terminal of Tokyo International Airport, which features high accessibility and usability. The color, font, and character size were designed to accommodate people with impaired color vision and the elderly. The design process also took into account the location and environment in which the boards were set up. The information is laid out to correspond with how important it is, so passengers can quickly find the information they need. The second case is the robust and durable laptop computer "ShieldPRO." Through observation and information sharing, we learned more about the conditions in which it is used, which enabled us to expand the market. Customers are able to use computers in new application where computers have not been used before, and they can benefit from new value: in other words, innovation. We also interviewed developers and marketers who used this design process and found that user-centered design was effective for improving development efficiency and maintenance as well as for improving sales.

Keywords: universal design concept, flight information board, durable computer.

1 Introduction

NEC Group's vision is "to be a leading global company leveraging the power of innovation to realize an information society friendly to humans and the earth." NEC is utilizing universal design in order to achieve our group vision. We consider universal design to have three aspects: accessibility, usability, and innovation. General universal design is composed of only two concepts, accessibility and usability. Accessibility means that an increasing number of people can use products regardless of their age, nationality, or ability, and usability means that products are easy to use. NEC Group's universal design includes the additional concept of innovation, which means that products provide our customers with new value. This makes our customers keen to use the products, as shown in Fig.1.

C. Stephanidis (Ed.): Posters, Part I, HCII 2011, CCIS 173, pp. 48–52, 2011.
© Springer-Verlag Berlin Heidelberg 2011

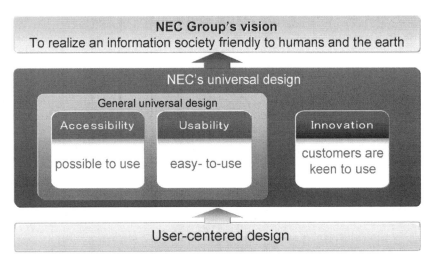

Fig. 1. Universal, user-centered design for NEC Group's vision

2 User-Centered Design for Our Products

We apply a user-centered design process to create products, solutions, and services that feature a universal design. Understanding users and providing solutions from the user's perspective is the key to this process. Various user-centered design methods are used in the development of our products. To improve accessibility, we invite disabled people to participate in prototype development and evaluations, or we simulate a disabled person's situation using various tools, and then identify barriers to operation and reduce or eliminate them. To improve usability, we create various types of prototypes using paper, wireframes, etc. and use either heuristic evaluations by experts or user testing to identify usability problems so that we can reduce or eliminate them. Guidelines or checklists are commonly used to develop unified user interfaces and meet certain standards of usability. To create innovation, we observe how products are used in the actual world and then identify latent needs, which enables us to offer new values in a new market.

3 Cases

In this section, we describe two actual cases to which we applied user-centered design. One is the flight information board at the international passenger terminal of Tokyo International Airport, which features high accessibility and usability. The second is our robust and durable laptop computer, "ShieldPRO." It is used in various applications where computers either have not been used before or have encountered a lot of problems, so it provides new value to customers.

3.1   Flight Information Board at Tokyo International Airport

The international passenger terminal of Tokyo International Airport was built on the basis of universal design, so various facilities such as the information desk, restrooms, and elevators are user-friendly. NEC developed the flight information board, which features a universal, user-centered design.

Design Process. Designers specified the context of use by observing various information boards at several airports and train stations (Fig. 2(a)) and then determined which user interface design concept to use. They developed several prototypes and evaluated them iteratively during the project execution. Various screen designs were viewed on a display the same size as an actual board and subjectively evaluated (Fig. 2(b)). User tests were executed to check the visibility of three different fonts (Fig. 2 (c)).

(a) Observation   (b) Prototype   (c) User test

Fig. 2. User-centered design process for flight information board

Features. The board has high accessibility: the color is easily read by people with impaired color vision and the elderly, and the font and character size fit the location, environment, and distance between the board and the passengers. The information design on the board also has high usability. The information is laid out to correspond with how important it is, so passengers can quickly find the information they need.

Fig. 3. Screen image of departure information

3.2 Robust and Durable Laptop Computer

Our robust and durable laptop computer, ShieldPRO, is resistant to water, dirt, heat, cold, and shock. This computer was first used in factories and has been applied in recent years to more diverse situations, such as in vehicles, at fish markets, at transit stations, and in kitchens at quick serve restaurants (QSRs), as shown in Fig. 4. Through observation and information sharing, we learned more about the conditions in which it is used, which enabled us to expand the market.

Application extensions. To determine latent needs, marketers observed how computers are used in the field and then regularly shared the acquired information at in-house meetings. They also created documents about cases in which ShieldPRO was introduced and then presented these documents to dealers and sales teams. The dealers and sales teams reviewed them and then suggested to the marketers other ways in which their customers might use ShieldPRO.

New value provision. Here are four examples of how ShieldPRO provides new value.

- The production control system on a factory floor required a computer that was resistant to metal dusting, vibration, and temperatures of around 50 degrees C. In the past, a computer was located a considerable distance from the floor. In contrast, ShieldPRO was placed directly on the floor, enabling workers to enter order changes in real time.

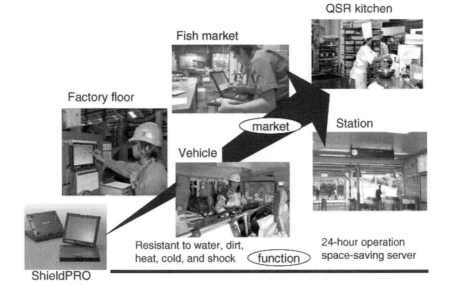

Fig. 4. Market expansion of ShieldPRO

- The sales management system at a fish market required a computer that was resistant to water and shock. ShieldPRO was installed at the fish market, enabling sales staff to input sales figures while handling with the fish.
- An in-vehicle computer was required for transmitting and receiving information about fire hydrant's locations and the best route to take. Installation of ShieldPRO, which is resistant to water, shock, and temperatures of up to 50 degrees C, in a fire truck enables fire fighters to plan their strategy on the way to an emergency.
- A server computer for a POS system was required in the kitchen of a QSR, but there was not enough space in the kitchen. Marketers evaluated the situations and determined that SheildPRO would be suitable if it could be enhanced so that it could operate 24 hours a day. The hard disk was customized accordingly, which was the birth of a new space-saving server. The space-saving server is now also used in various other applications such as train information systems.

Such innovations provide customers with new value in that they can use the ShieldPRO computer for applications for which computers either have not been used before or have encountered a lot of problems.

4   Effect of User-Centered Design

User-centered design provides quality improvements: the accessibility, usability, and innovation of our products, which directly affects our customers. We interviewed developers and marketers who used this design process and found that user-centered design was also effective for developers and marketers themselves. There are three effects, effective development, reduction of maintenance, and sales improvement. For example, in the case of the flight information board, designers could answer the queries on the spot from the customer (an international airport company) about universal design, so the project flowed smoothly and the development period was shortened. In another case, developers of a software product reported that the number of operation items needing fixing decreased, so maintenance costs decreased. In a third case, developers of an automatic control system reported that they could provide the high level of customer satisfaction, and the customers introduced other potential customers.

5   Conclusion

We are using user-centered design to create products with universal design. We built, for example, a flight information board and a durable laptop computer using various methods such as observation, prototyping, user testing, and information sharing, and the end result was accessibility, usability, and innovation. NEC has many such products, solutions, and services in both personal and business fields, and we are working hard to create universal, user-centered designs across a wide area of applications.

Idea Creation Method Based on Memory

Nozomi Koyatsu and Kazuhiko Yamazaki

Chiba Institute of Technology Engineering research course 2-17-1
Tsudanuma NArashino-shi, Chiba-ken 275-0016, Japan
tnxcx565@ybb.ne.jp, kazuhiko.yamazaki@it-chiba.ac.jp

Abstract. The purpose of this study is to discover an idea creation method for designers based on memory. This poster focuses on how to use memories to produce new ideas. The author did the workshops based on two previous design works. Then, she proposes the approach that uses memories for designer to produce the idea. There are two different backgrounds in this study. The one is the state that the user enjoys using the tool. Secondarily, there is a reason why designers tend to use the memory to produce new ideas. Brown, R., & Kulik, J. indicated on the paper "Flashbulb memories" the event that strong emotional feelings continue to keep the memory. The author believes idea creative method based on memory helps designers to create various ideas. This research refers to the result of the research that two professors previously did. One is "Photo diary and photo essay" which is a methodology created by the Professor of the first author. Another one is "Changing Personal Memories to Group Memories: Study of a Workshop on the Expression of Personal Memories" that Prof. Nojima at Seijo University is researching. "Photo diary and photo essay" is the methodology for the designer and the developer to be the approach to obtain user information, and to conceive the idea. The photograph is used for this approach. Prof. Nojima's research is based on a study about the method of managing memories by a technological approach. The author is starting this research from the experience of the workshop done by these two previous works to visualize memories.

Keywords: memory, workshop, method for designer, idea creation.

1 Introduction

The purpose of this study is to discover an idea creation method for designers based on memory. This poster focuses on how to use memories to produce new ideas. The author did the workshops based on two previous design works. Then, she proposes the approach that uses memories for designer to produce the idea.

2 Background

There are two different backgrounds in this study. The one is the state that the user enjoys using the tool. Secondarily, there is a reason why designers tend to use the

C. Stephanidis (Ed.): Posters, Part I, HCII 2011, CCIS 173, pp. 53–57, 2011.

memory to produce new ideas. Brown, R., & Kulik, J. indicated in the paper "Flashbulb memories" that strong emotional feelings continue to keep the memory. The author believes idea creative method based on memory helps designers to create various ideas.

3 Previous Work

This research refers to the results of the research that two professors previously did. One is "Photo diary and photo essay" which is a methodology created by the Professor of the first author. Another one is "Changing Personal Memories to Group Memories: Study of a Workshop on the Expression of Personal Memories" that Prof. Nojima at Seijo University is researching. "Photo diary and photo essay" is a user requirements collection and analysis methodology, which can assist designers and developers conceive new idea. Photograph is used for this approach.

Prof. Nojima's research is based on a study about the method of managing memories through a technological approach. The author is starting this research from the experience of the workshop done by these two previous works to visualize memories.

4 Workshop (1)

The purpose of the 1st workshop is to make memories visible. First of all, the participant prepares a slip of paper according to age. Then the participant writes the music that remains in memories, a piece for each year as shown in Fig. 1, arranges the notes chronologically (Fig. 2), and present them (Fig. 3).

The following two opinions were obtained in this workshop:

- The participants cannot recall memories if there is no stimulus to recall.
- The participants had been doing an interesting conversation when they worked than the announced time

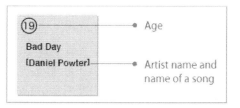

Fig. 1. He writes the age when he listened that song, the song name and the artist name

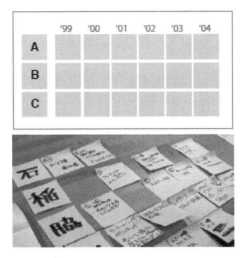

Fig. 2. The slip of paper that arranged as a chronology

Fig. 3. Their presentation

5   Workshop (2)

The 2nd workshop was planned and held based on the first. Some improvements were included in the workshop:

- The chance that the participants recall memories is increased.
- The time of which the participants take notes is increased.

This workshop followed the process below.

The participants write on a card the games they were playing when they were children (Fig. 4). Next, the speaker announces the content of which they took notes. The participant should write the following thing on the card.

1. Name of play.
2. Place where it was played.
3. With whom did you play?
4. Illustration of how to play.
5. Explanation of how to play.

Some opinions were obtained even in the workshop of the second times.

- It is easy for the participant to recall as the stimulus to recall is provided to the participant through questions.
- The participant doesn't talk so much because they are busy drawing the illustration.
- When the content of the card is announced, the participant explains aiming at the chairperson.

Fig. 4. Card to write how they were playing when they are children

Fig. 5. Their appearances when writing it on card

6   Important Aspects of the Workshop

Based on the result of the workshop, the author proposed necessary improvements for the workshop to make memories more visible.

1. The participants should talk mutually and actively.
2. The participants should write the memo the thing noticed while recalling memories.
3. The participants and the facilitator should dig the opinion down with an interesting opinion.
   After this proposal, the author designed the third workshop.

7   Workshop (3)

The 3rd workshop not only recalled memories but also showed the idea by using the recalled event in this workshop. The participant is a member of the project team that designs concerning music. The member recalled memories concerning each theme to be designed, and conceived the idea in this workshop. The feature of this workshop is a thing of not using the format that becomes complete. The form that the participant referred to one of the memories was adopted for the question that the chairperson had prepared beforehand.

The chairperson is preparing a different question for each participant. The respondent answers the question that the chairperson did in oral. The idea is shown there, and all participants including the respondent take notes for the respondent. The participant announces putting the memo together at the end.

They present the respondent the memo.

The respondent conceives the idea based on the memo.

The author thought in this workshop as follows.

- The form that the chairperson questions the participant according to the theme is a method good to recall memories as understood from the appearance where the participant's conversation increases.
- It is necessary to make establish rules regarding the questions that the chairperson makes to a participant. This result shows that effects proposed design approach based on memory was evaluated.

8 Summary

The author wants to improve the workshop based on the results that have been obtained from each workshop. Moreover, she plans to evaluate this method.

Designing Interfaces for Home Energy Users:
A Preference Study

Janelle LaMarche and Olga Sachs

Fraunhofer Center for Sustainable Energy Systems
25 First Street, Cambridge, Massachusetts 02141
JLaMarche@fraunhofer.org

Abstract. The current study compared user-generated preferences of energy management visualizations to established principles of dashboard design and visual perception. Twenty subjects rated paper prototypes of seven energy web portals according to aesthetic and usability parameters and completed a forced-choice task on six visual pairs contrasting elements of feedback design. Questions addressed the look of the interface, understanding, usefulness, friendliness, level of visual clutter, and desire to explore. Results revealed robust differences between mean interface ratings across questions, and follow-up pairwise comparisons further revealed user data was found to be in line with a predetermined pattern of rankings. These results suggest that user-centered design is critical to the implementation and functionality of energy saving visual technologies and can inform future prototypes that maintain effective aesthetics as well as realistic cognition.

Keywords: User Experience, Home Energy Management, Feedback, Interface Design, Psychology.

1 Introduction

The fields of sustainable energy and media design are becoming increasingly interconnected. Moreover, the success of new home energy technologies depends heavily on usability, consumer acceptance, and participation. How can visual information be used to foster ideas and generate action within the field of energy efficiency?

The interactions involved at the human-computer interface may influence both cognitive and behavioral factors involved in the decision-making process [1]. Therefore, when successfully implemented, the visual design and content of an energy web portal may influence a user's experience and later outcome in terms of energy consumption.

The focus of this study was to uncover user preferences for visually presented, energy-based data. Six pairs of visualizations were constructed that contrasted dimensions of feedback design [2]. These contrasted both visual elements (1. Bar vs. pie chart, 2. Horizontal vs. vertical display; data granularity, 3. Ambient vs.technical

C. Stephanidis (Ed.): Posters, Part I, HCII 2011, CCIS 173, pp. 58–62, 2011.
© Springer-Verlag Berlin Heidelberg 2011

displays) as well as conceptual elements (4. Projected cost vs. savings, 5. Passive vs. motivational energy tips, 6. Social normative vs. personal goal setting).

To investigate the effect of interface design on usability, seven home energy dashboards were amassed from current market or proof of concept products. A dashboard is a display of information needed to achieve one or more objectives and arranged on a single screen so the information can be monitored at a glance [3]. In the energy field, dashboards are becoming increasingly relevant to consumers for real-time feedback on their home energy use.

Importantly, all dashboards were analyzed and ranked by the lead researcher according to principles of dashboard design [3], and pre-attentive attributes of visual perception [4]. Thumbnail images of the dashboards, pre-study design notes, and expected pattern of rankings are shown in the Appendix.

2   Method

Materials. Materials included laminated pictures of the six visualization pairs as well as paper prototypes of the seven dashboards. For the visual pairs, a forced-choice task was administered (although an answer of 'both' was accepted). For the dashboards, subjects completed an aesthetic and usability ratings task assessing the following parameters: *Is it nice to look at? Is it easy to understand? Is all of the information provided useful? Would it be useful for you personally? Does it seem friendly? Does it seem cluttered? Does it make you want to explore more?* All questions employed a 5-point scale with the anchors 'Not at all, Slightly, Quite a bit, Very, Extremely.'

Procedure. A total of twenty subjects (M_{age} 39.5, 10f) were recruited and compensated for their time. All subjects provided informed consent and were instructed to a) choose the visualization from each pair that they liked better and b) rate each of the dashboards according to the questions provided by circling a number on the scale. Participants saw all visual pairs and rated all dashboards.

2.1   Analysis

For each visual pair, percentages of choice were calculated. For each question in the ratings task, interfaces were ranked according to their mean ratings across subjects.

Table 1. Overall feedback design preferences for the six visual pairs across subjects

Pair 1	Pair 2	Pair 3	Pair 4	Pair 5	Pair 6
Pie 65%	Horizontal 60%	Function 75%	Cost 60%	Passive tip 50%	Social goal 50%
Bar 30%	Vertical 40%	Aesthetic 15%	Savings 35%	Active tip 35%	Self goal 40%
Both 5%	Monthly 40%	Both 10%	Both 5%	Both 15%	Both 10%
	Weekly 25%				
	Daily 20%				
	All times 15%				

Once preliminary analyses were completed, a 7*7 multivariate ANOVA was run with main variables of interest including question (7 levels) and interface (7 levels).

Table 2. Interface ranks by question, calculated according to the mean usability ratings across subjects. In addition, the overall expected rank and overall actual rank by mode is also shown.

Question	N.E.M.	EMonitor	SaveEnergi	Agilewaves	Tendril	TED	Gridpoint
Look?	1	2	5	4	2	6	7
Understand?	3	1	2	4	5	6	7
All useful?	1	1	3	4	6	5	7
Useful for you?	1	2	3	4	6	5	7
Friendly?	2	1	4	3	5	6	7
Cluttered?	4	5	6	6	3	2	1
Want to explore?	1	3	2	4	4	6	7
Overall Expected Rank	1	2	4	3	5	6	7
Overall Rank by Mode	1	2	3	4	5	6	7

2.2 Results

Main effects within subjects revealed a significant effect of question ($F(3.02)=4.04$, p=*.01*, Greenhouse-Geisser corrected), interface ($F(6)=9.48$, p<*.001*), and a question by interface interaction ($F(8.19)=9.01$, p<*.001*, Greenhouse-Geisser corrected).

Pairwise comparisons were run to examine the interaction in more detail. For each question, the top rated and bottom rated interface was compared to all others. As shown in Table 3, interfaces that scored relatively high or low along a question's dimension were significantly different from their counterparts, respectively. Critically, this overall pattern of results across questions falls in line with the pattern estimates in the Appendix.

Table 3. Shown are mean difference and p-values of Fisher's Least Significant Differences for the highest and lowest rated interfaces relative to the other six interfaces. Pairs with a p-value < .05 were considered significantly different from one another along that question's dimension, and pairs with a p-value > .05 were considered not significantly different from one another along that question's dimension (i.e. The *N.E.M* interface is considered better looking than all other interfaces except the *EMonitor* and only the *TED* interface is as poor looking as *Gridpoint*). A score of 1.000 indicates an exact tie.

	Is it nice to look at? vs.	M_diff	p-value		Is it understandable? vs.	M_diff	p-value		Is all the information useful? vs.	M_diff	p-value		Would it be useful for you? vs.	M_diff	p-value
Highest	EMonitor	.60	.110	Highest	N.E.M	.25	.549	Highest	EMonitor	.00	1.000	Highest	EMonitor	.15	.748
	SaveEnergi	1.30	.003		SaveEnergi	.05	.886		SaveEnergi	.20	.494		SaveEnergi	.50	.086
N.E.M	Agilewaves	.70	.005	EMonitor	Agilewaves	.85	.011	N.E.M	Agilewaves	.65	.015	N.E.M	Agilewaves	.90	.009
	Tendril	.60	.004		Tendril	1.10	.007		Tendril	.95	.003		Tendril	1.15	.001
	TED	1.90	<.001		TED	1.20	<.001		TED	.90	.010		TED	.95	.024
	Gridpoint	2.05	<.001		Gridpoint	1.55	<.001		Gridpoint	1.30	<.001		Gridpoint	1.70	<.001
Lowest	N.E.M	-2.05	<.001	Lowest	N.E.M	-1.30	<.001	Lowest	N.E.M	-1.30	<.001	Lowest	N.E.M	.32	<.001
	EMonitor	-1.45	<.001		EMonitor	-1.55	<.001		EMonitor	-1.30	<.001		EMonitor	.30	<.001
Gridpoint	SaveEnergi	-.75	.010	Gridpoint	SaveEnergi	-1.50	<.001	Gridpoint	SaveEnergi	-1.10	.002	Gridpoint	SaveEnergi	.30	.001
	Agilewaves	-1.35	<.001		Agilewaves	-.70	.027		Agilewaves	-.65	.024		Agilewaves	.32	.022
	Tendril	-1.45	<.001		Tendril	-.45	.083		Tendril	-.35	.167		Tendril	.29	.069
	TED	-.15	.614		TED	-.35	.217		TED	-.40	.163		TED	.30	.021

Table 3. (*continued*)

	Is it friendly?				Is it visually cluttered?				Do you want to explore more?		
	vs.	M_{diff}	p-value		vs.	M_{diff}	p-value		vs.	M_{diff}	p-value
Highest	N.E.M	.15	.651	Highest	N.E.M	1.80	<.001	Highest	EMonitor	.45	.290
	SaveEnergi	.70	.019		EMonitor	1.85	<.001		SaveEnergi	.40	.042
Emonitor	Agilewaves	.40	.269	*Gridpoint*	SaveEnergi	2.00	<.001	*N.E.M*	Agilewaves	.90	.004
	Tendril	.95	.009		Agilewaves	2.00	<.001		Tendril	.90	.001
	TED	1.50	<.001		Tendril	1.25	.001		TED	1.40	<.001
	Gridpoint	1.90	<.001		TED	.90	.049		Gridpoint	1.80	<.001
Lowest	N.E.M	-1.75	<.001	Lowest	N.E.M	-.20	.519	Lowest	N.E.M	-1.80	<.001
	EMonitor	-1.90	<.001		EMonitor	-.15	.614		EMonitor	-1.35	.001
Gridpoint	SaveEnergi	-1.20	<.001	*SaveEnergi*	Agilewaves	.00	1.000	*Gridpoint*	SaveEnergi	-1.40	.001
	Agilewaves	-1.50	<.001		Tendril	-.75	<.001		Agilewaves	-.90	.016
	Tendril	-.95	.004		TED	-1.10	.002		Tendril	-.90	.005
	TED	-.40	.163		Gridpoint	-2.00	<.001		TED	-.40	.189

3 Discussion

The current study compared user ratings of home energy web portals to principles of dashboard design. Robust statistical findings revealed that usability ratings were in line with a predetermined pattern of results. These results provide evidence that principles of design and psychology must be taken into account when designing visual technologies targeted at residential energy savings.

In addition to the ratings, consumer feedback design preferences can inform future prototypes in a way that maintains artistic integrity and user pragmatics. More work still needs to be done that bridges both the interface design elements involved in energy feedback as well as the human factors involved in the interactions with the technologies themselves.

References

1. Fogg, B.J.: Persuasive Technology: Using Computers to Change What We Think or Do. Morgan Kaufmann, San Francisco (2003)
2. Froehlich, J.: Promoting Energy Efficient Behaviors in the Home through Feedback: The Role of Human-Computer Interaction. In: HCIC 2009 Winter Workshop Boaster Paper, Colorado (2009)
3. Few, S.: Information Dashboard Design: The Effective Visual Communication of Data. O'Reilly Media, Sebastopol (2006)
4. Few, S.: Tapping the power of visual perception. Perceptual Edge (2004)

Appendix

Thumbnail	Interface	Dashboard Design Notes	ERank	Question Estimates
	Net Energy Market (N.E.M)	Good level of content and well placed affordances prompt exploration, excellent in tone and hierarchy, minimal clutter with artistic intent.	1	Look? Excellent Understanding? Good All useful? Excellent Useful for you? Excellent Friendly? Good Clutter level? Mid Exploration? Excellent
	EMonitor	Sparse but symmetrical layout for quick viewing, some eye competition at start of visual sequence, but footprint evokes human visceral design and is friendly.	2	Look? Good Understanding? Excellent All useful? Good Useful for you? Good Friendly? Excellent Clutter level? Low Exploration? Fair
	Agilewaves	High visual aesthetic and focus on personalization is nice starting point, consistent bar graphs allow technical information to shine, nice and friendly colors.	3	Look? Good Understanding? Fair All useful? Good Useful for you? Good Friendly? Excellent Clutter level? Low Exploration? Fair
	SaveEnergi	Clean line of vision and symmetry, nice hierarchy, information laid out intuitively, biggest flaw is misuse of color.	4	Look? Poor Understanding? Excellent All useful? Good Useful for you? Good Friendly? Fair Clutter level? Low Exploration? Good
	Tendril	Pleasing to look at but problems with viewing sequence, no logical flow, inconsistent category labels and insufficient context, seems unfriendly and over technical.	5	Look? Excellent Understanding? Poor All useful? Fair Useful for you? Poor Friendly? Fair Clutter level? Mid Exploration? Fair
	The Energy Detective (TED)	Issues with cluttering and overdecoration, machine like interface causes unnecessary visual processing, color contrast negatively impacts legibility, dead spaces.	6	Look? Poor Understanding? Fair All useful? Fair Useful for you? Fair Friendly? Poor Clutter level? High Exploration? Poor
	Gridpoint	Weak viewing sequence ruined by visual clutter and too much text as well as technical terms, confusing to look at, little aesthetic merit.	7	Look? Poor Understanding? Poor All useful? Fair Useful for you? Fair Friendly? Poor Clutter level? High Exploration? Poor

Exploring the Relationship between Thinking Style and Collaborative Design Outcomes

Chiung-Cheng Liao[1], Wenzhi Chen[1], and Hsien-Hui Tang[2]

[1] Department of Industrial Design, Chang Gung University,
330 Tao-Yuan, Taiwan, R.O.C.
[2] Department of Commercial and Industrial Design,
National Taiwan University of Science and Technology,
106 Taipei, Taiwan, R.O.C.
toi250@yahoo.com.tw, wenzhi@mail.cgu.edu.tw,
drhhtang@mail.ntust.edu.tw

Abstract. The purpose of this study is to explore the relationship between the team members' thinking styles and their performance in collaborative design. 20 undergraduate industrial design students participated in the experiment. The Thinking Style Inventory was used to establish the thinking style profile. The grades of the collaborative design team members were collected. The correlation coefficient of team members' thinking styles profiles was calculated, and the Pearson's correlation analysis was used to examine the relationship between project grades and team members' thinking style. The results demonstrated that the team members with difference thinking style could have better performance in the collaborative design team.

Keywords: Thinking styles, Team member, Design performance.

1 Introduction

Under the trend of the globalized business, the importance of design has been increased. Collaborative design has become the mainstream of design to increase the creativity and competitiveness. Many factors affect the performance of the design team. Team members' composition is one of the most important issues that worth to discuss. The purpose of this study is to explore the relationship between the team members' thinking styles and their performance.

Design is regarded as an intuitive activity and described as a black box [1]. The theory of thinking style that proposed by Sternberg [2] can help to illuminate the differences in the way people think. Sternberg has described 13 separate styles and five dimensions that comprise his theory of thinking styles, including *functions*, *forms*, *levels*, *scopes*, and *leanings*. Table 1 shows the dimensions, styles, and the essential characteristic of each style.

C. Stephanidis (Ed.): Posters, Part I, HCII 2011, CCIS 173, pp. 63–66, 2011.
© Springer-Verlag Berlin Heidelberg 2011

Table 1. Dimensions, styles, and the essential characteristic of thinking styles

Dimensions	Styles	Key characteristic
Functions	Legislative	Being creative
	Executive	Being conforming
	Judicial	Being analytical
Forms	Monarchic	Dealing with one task at a time
	Hierarchic	Dealing with multiple prioritized tasks
	Oligarchic	Dealing with multiple non-prioritized tasks
	Anarchic	Dealing with tasks at random
Levels	Global	Focusing on abstract ideas
	Local	Focusing on concrete ideas
Scopes	Internal	Enjoying working independently
	External	Enjoying working in groups
Leanings	Liberal	Using new ways to deal with tasks
	Conservative	Using traditional ways to deal with tasks

Thinking style was used in education domain to discuss the learning and teaching style, learning performance, and relative issues. Zhang [3] conducted a survey that used the Thinking Styles Inventory (Revised) and the Preferred Teaching Approach Inventory to explore the university students' thinking styles and their preferred teaching approaches. Three hundred and forty-eight (111 male and 237 female) students from a large comprehensive university in Beijing, P.R. China participated in the survey. The results indicated that students with different thinking styles had significantly different preferences for particular teaching approaches. Zhang [4] also conducted another survey to explore the utility of measuring intellectual styles in addition to measuring personality, and to verify Sternberg's claim that the theory of mental self-government is applicable to non-academic settings as well as to academic settings. The Thinking Styles Inventory and the NEO Five-Factor Inventory were administered to 199 parents of secondary school students in mainland China. The results suggested that it is meaningful to investigate intellectual styles in addition to examining personality. In addition, results also supported Sternberg's assertion regarding the validity of the theory of mental self-government in both academic and non-academic settings.

Creativity plays an important role in new product development to increase the innovative values, especially in highly competitive and uncertain market environment [5]. Creativity is also regared as essential quality for a good designer [6]. Is there an relationship between thinking style and the creativity? Ju [7] conducted a survey to discuss the adult learners' thinking styles and creativity. 711 students in technical colleges and universities of science and technology participated in the survey, and its results shown that thinking styles affected creativity. There were 8 types of thinking styles positively related to creativity: *liberal, legislative, judicial, hierarchic, internal, local, global* and *external*. Tsai, Yeh and Lin [8] studied the relationship between thinking style and design behaviour. They conducted two design tesk experiments to collected the data., and their results indicated that the Sternberger's theory of thinking styles can be used to explain and predict the design behaviour.

Thinking style was used in education domain to discuss the learning and teaching style, learning performance, and relative issues. Some studies discussed the relationship between thinking style and creativity. Some studies demonstrated that thinking style influenced students' learning performance and personal creativity. The question of this study is whether it also affects the performance of the collaborative design.

2 Method

This study included undergraduate industrial design students as participants, investigating the correlation between the team members' thinking style and the performance in collaborative design. 20 students participated in the experiment. A group of two students executed the design project in their design studio course. The participants were asked to fill out the Sternberg's Thinking Style Inventory [9] to establish their thinking style profiles. Then, the coefficient of correlation between the team members' thinking style profile was calculated. Finally, the Pearson's correlation analysis was done to examine the relationship between project grades and team members' thinking style.

3 Result

The results of the correlations between the performance of collaborative design and the team members' thinking style composition were shown as Table 2. There was no significant correlation between the grade and the thinking style profiles (Pearson correlation = -0.386, p = 0.271 > 0.05). The relationship between grades and each dimensions of thinking style has been calculated. The correlation coefficient of grades and the *"function"* dimension is -0.457 (p = 0.184), the *"form"* dimension is -0.682 (p = 0.030), the *"level"* dimension is 0.472 (p = 0.168), the *"scope"* dimension is

Table 2. Correlations between the collaborative design performance and the team members' thinking style crrelation in profile and each dimensions

Group	Grade	Profile	Function	Form	Level	Scope	Leaning
			Dimension				
A	70.75	0.443	0.000	0.870	-1.000	a	1.000
B	77.50	0.372	1.000	0.081	a	1.000	a
C	73.50	0.062	0.971	0.707	-1.000	1.000	-1.000
D	71.00	0.366	0.756	0.663	1.000	-1.000	1.000
E	74.50	0.649	0.929	0.302	1.000	a	1.000
F	79.00	0.354	0.000	0.816	1.000	1.000	-1.000
G	82.75	0.027	-0.803	0.000	1.000	a	a
H	80.25	0.054	-0.866	-0.076	1.000	1.000	-1.000
I	78.25	-0.328	0.866	0.000	a	-1.000	-1.000
J	75.25	-0.242	-0.866	0.870	-1.000	-1.000	1.000
Pearson correlation [b]		-0.386	-0.457	-0.682	0.472	0.443	-0.581
P value		0.271	0.184	0.030	0.168	0.320	0.078

[a] Cannot be computed because at least one of the variables is constant.
[b] Pearson correlation between grades and the team members' thinking style composition.

0.443 (p = 0.320), the *"leaning"* dimension is -0.581 (p = 0.078). There were 3 of 5 thinking style dimensions negatively related to the grade, especially the *"form"* dimension that the correlation coefficient being significantly higher than 0.6 (p < 0.05).

4 Conclusion

This study tried to explore the relationship between the collaborative design performance and team members' thinking style composition. The results demonstrated that the team members have difference thinking style may have influence on the performance in the collaborative design team. The current results of this exploratory study were not very conclusive. Future research will need to have more data of collaborative design projects to provide deep understanding and more evidences to verify the results of this study.

References

1. Akin, O.: An exploration of the design process. In: Cross, N. (ed.) Developments in Design Methodologies, pp. 189–208. John Wiley & Sons, New York (1984)
2. Sternberg, R.J.: Thinking Styles. Cambridge University Press, Cambridge (1997)
3. Zhang, L.-F.: Do university students' thinking styles matter in their preferred teaching approaches? Personality and Individual Differences 37(8), 1551–1564 (2004)
4. Zhang, L.-F.: Thinking styles and the big five personality traits revisited. Personality and Individual Differences 40(6), 1177–1187 (2006)
5. Hsiao, S.-W., Chou, J.-R.: A creativity-based design process for innovative product design. International Journal of Industrial Ergonomics 34(5), 421–443 (2004)
6. Badke-Schaub, P.: Creativity and innovation in industrial design: wishful thinking? Journal of Design Research 5(3), 353–367 (2007)
7. Ju, C.-Y.: A study on in-service adult learners's thinking styles and creativity. Journal of National Pingtung University of Education 32, 359–392 (2009)
8. Tsai, S.-J., Yeh, T.-L., Lin, H.-F.: Pilot Study on the Relationship of the Thinking Styles and the Design Behaviors. In: Asian Conference Mechanism and Machine Science 2006, Kaohsiung (2006)
9. Sternberg, R.J., Wagner, R.K.: Thinking styles Inventory. Yale University, New Haven (1992) (unpublished test)

Identifying Product Opportunity Based on Interactivity

Seungwoo Maeng, Daeeop Kim, Sang-Su Lee, and Kun-Pyo Lee

Department of Industrial Design, KAIST. 335 Gwahangno Yusung-Gu,
Daejeon, Republic of Korea
{maengoon,up4201,sangsu.lee,kplee}@kaist.ac.kr

Abstract. In the process of developing innovative product concepts, user's needs and technology has been generally regarded as a major driver of innovation [2,9]. And although interaction, being the contact point of the actual user and products or services, has a very high significance, they have been overlooked because they were considered to be dependent factors of products and technologies. The reason for this was because interactions were hard to manipulate and also because they weren't tangible [3]. Being aware of these limitations, there are ongoing researches and studies on the properties of interactivity found in interaction between UX and products [4]. Importance of interactivity and the possibility of interactivity being a driving factor of a new product development attracted attention in this study. Also, a method for extracting functional needs and new product domain was developed based on interactivity, and the effectiveness of this method was checked by using in the process of designing an organic user interface concept.

Keywords: Interactivity, Design Method, Product Concept Development.

1 Background

In the area of the design of interactions in the user interface, interactivity is known to be subordinate to technology or product from Command Line UI to GUI-based WIMP Interface. Interactivity is known to be subordinate because it is difficult to manipulate and not tangible [3]. However, as interface becomes tangible due to the development of technology, interactivity is gaining greater importance in the area of interaction design. In addition, studies have been made to find out qualities of interactivities between UX and products getting out from the subordination of interactivity [4].

As interactivity secures an independent area, not being subordinate to technology, has brought a few important changes. Interactivity, which was addressed only in the area of interaction design that played a bridging role between developed products and users, after the concept of product was developed, became a factor which determines the product concept itself, and now is finding the possibility of a motivating factor to product innovation. The innovative products such as iPod and iPad, which have appeared recently, can hardly be viewed as being technology or user-driven. Looking in detail into the areas, interactivity is the main in the concept of products. Innovative products with interactivity as the major concept of products have been developed since later 2000's.

C. Stephanidis (Ed.): Posters, Part I, HCII 2011, CCIS 173, pp. 67–71, 2011.

2 Definition of Interactivity

It was possible to understand the basic structure of interactions by referring to the Interaction Framework [1]. And based on this understanding, connections were expressed as follows.

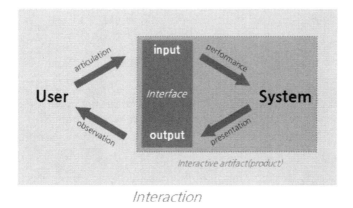

Fig. 1. Structure of an interaction

Interaction carries various factors such as system, user, input, and output. Out of these factors, factors in charge of input and output can be defined as interface, and interactivity can be defined as products' interactive aspect of an artifact [8]. Reason for paying attention to interactivity in interaction is because interactivity seen in the range of interaction or interface can become dependent on product or technology. Therefore, there were attempts in seeing interactivity as an independent factor by separating the properties of products' interactive aspect, attracting interest. Because there aren't any existing product or technology in case of OUI, a domain of this study, actions in which users articulate was defined as interactivity and transformation, a key concept of an organic user interface, was defined as a property of interactivity.

3 User Research Design

The design methods, used in the identification of the concept of innovative products which are not existing, use the present environment such as designers' insight, existing products, consumers and competing markets, context-based information. The value of users or design direction produced based on the present situation is superficial or too general so that it is not appropriate as a method to seek new changes of design [5,7]. Therefore, it is necessary to find design opportunities in the area of linear future studies, not improvement of products in the area of design, and to find an appropriate approach to develop it. Apart from efforts to produce results of innovative designs based on creative techniques by creativity of designers, the concept technique for future innovative designs based on systematic design information as a user-centered method should be probed. The probe technique developed by Gaver is used as a form of x-probe in application [6].

This study presented a method of probing the concept of innovative products by utilizing interactivity. This probe provides users with clues to future products, not a simple user observation, thus enabling the users to experience such clues. Hence, the users can find out how such clues can be applied in their daily life as they experience the clues specifically. In an effort of approach to accomplish innovation based on interactivity, this study looked into the probe process of product opportunity through interactions as an example of the development of an organic user interface which newly appeared in the industry.

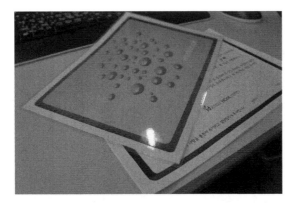

Fig. 2. Workbook provided to subjects

For this purpose, three days' workbooks were made. And along with the workbooks, plastic plates which carry OUI's interactivity were handed out as a clue. By carrying around these plastic plates in their everyday lives, 9 subjects thought about where to use the plate (product domain), and use the plates for what (function). They then answered the following questions in their workbooks. 1. Did you change the form of any kind throughout the day? 2. Explain in what situations you wanted to change the form to accomplish a purpose. 3. If current devices (smartphones, smart pads, etc.) were to be bendable, what functions would be good to add? All 9 subjects were to write down the answers in their workbooks like journals, take pictures of each situation written in their books, and turn them in to the researchers.

4   User Research Result

Needs for product category creatable through interactivity referred to as transformation, and functions practicable through transformations of a kind in everyday life were found. Followings are some of the needs extracted through interactivity referred to as transformation

• Seeking applications suitable for physical forms: Among the subject's demands were tendency in needs for transformation and application suitable to the context rather than preferring a particular form of transformation.

• Demands pursuing fun rather than productivity: Because physical transformation carries more physical task loads on the users compared to the existing interface, it prefers fun from physical movements rather than productivity.
• Pursuing transformation for self-storage/usage/movement: Many parts of demands for transformation preferred minimization for storing and organizing, and maximized transformation for efficiency during usage.
• Fixation through tension: desire for transformation forms when fixing different things or adhere them to the body through tension like stockings and hair ties.
• Expressing emotions through transformation: Expressing feelings through transformation action such as crumpling, tearing or ripping when angry.

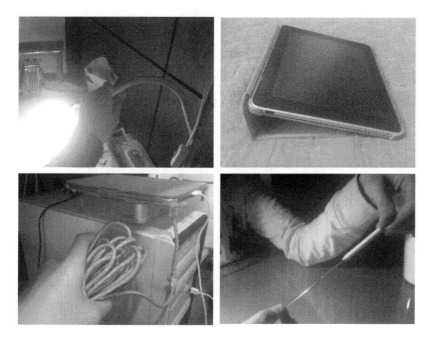

Fig. 3. Pictures collected through User Research

According to the results of user research, the obtained data were differentiated from ones from evaluating usability by simply providing prototypes to the users, adding new functions to currently existing product function, or tracking users' everyday life with absence of any stimulus. These differentiated results showed that the collected needs were evaluated to have been helpful in deciding the product domain or its' main function. These results, as information focused on transformation which we wanted to design, showed very high efficiency in the process.

5   Limitation and Conclusion

This study started out with transformation, a type of interactivity, to identify what kind of needs it can create for the users. And exploratory study about "What categories can the product create?" or "What kind of main functions can the product hold?" through these needs were conducted. Through this user research, we were able to find out that it was possible to extract needs related to interactivity.

However, needs we were hoping to obtain in the beginning happened to be needs as displays and input devices. But because they're out of control, and it's focusing on simple transformation, it seems better to provide more specific interactivity rather than these users research.

Also, current user research dealt only up to processes extracting needs, but processes connecting from needs to product concept and core functions could not be built. Therefore, if these processes are clearly built, it is likely to be used as a process for new product development and innovation starting with interactivity leading up to final product concept.

Acknowledgment. This research was supported by WCU(World Class University) program through the National Research Foundation of Korea funded by the Ministry of Education, Science and Technology (R33-2008-000-10033-0).

References

1. Dix, A., et al.: Human-Computer Interaction, 3rd edn. Prentice-Hall, Englewood Cliffs (2004)
2. Kahn, D.K.B.: Approaches to New Product Forecasting. In: Kenneth, B.K. (ed.) The PDMA Handbook of New Product Development, 2nd edn., pp. 362–377 (2007)
3. Lim, Y.-k., et al.: Interaction gestalt and the design of aesthetic interactions. In: Proceedings of the 2007 Conference on Designing Pleasurable Products and Interfaces, pp. 239–254. ACM, Helsinki (2007)
4. Lim, Y.-k., Lee, S.-S., Lee, K.-y.: Interactivity attributes: a new way of thinking and describing interactivity. In: Proceedings of the 27th International Conference on Human Factors in Computing Systems, pp. 105–108. ACM, Boston (2009)
5. Maeng, S., Lee, K.-P.: How to connect the present to the future for design?: Comparative study of design method and forecasting method. In: IASDR 2009, Seoul (2009)
6. Mattelmäki, T.: Design Probe, in University of Art and Design Helsinki. UIAH, Helsinki (2006)
7. Salovaara, A., Mannonen, P.: Use of Future-Oriented Information in User-Centered Product Concept Ideation. In: Costabile, M.F., Paternó, F. (eds.) INTERACT 2005. LNCS, vol. 3585, pp. 727–740. Springer, Heidelberg (2005)
8. Svanaes, D.: Understanding Interactivity: Steps to a Phenomenology of Human-Computer Interaction. In: Computer Science, Norges teknisk-naturvitenskapelige universitet, pp. 1–294 (2000)
9. Wind, J., Mahajan, V.: Editorial: Issues and Opportunities in New Product Development: An Introduction to the Special Issue. Journal of Marketing Research 34(1), 1–12 (1997)

Idea Creative Method Based on Metaphor for Product Design

Takuya Mitsumaru

Chiba Institute of Technology, Japan
maruma176671@yahoo.co.jp

Abstract. The purpose of the research is to propose idea creative method base on metaphor. This method should be included to consider user's lifestyle. Author proposed design method was done from the analysis of the previous work concerning the metaphor and an existing product. It was thought that three patterns "form", "Concept", and "Operation" were effective in use of the metaphor. The prototype was made, and the effectiveness of the conception support method that had done the hypothesis was verified. The kitchen timer was selected this design object. To understand the feature and the improvement of the use pattern of each metaphor, the pattern of thinking that the produced prototype drew was arranged, and visualized. Moreover, the assessment experiment was done to two students who were majoring in the design to judge the improvement of the prototype and the effectiveness of the idea creative method objectively. As for the metaphor using the "Concept", it has been understood that an effective possibility to improve user's interest and curiosity is high in the use pattern of three metaphors. The following want to do the workshop using the conception support method, and to verify effectiveness.

Keyword: metaphor, HCD (Human Centerd Design), idea creative method.

1   Introduction

The background of the research is that uses the metaphor and is utilityed by many designs. Most of purpose is to have interest and curiosity on the product. However, might it be expected that the metaphor and the motif will be easily used in the character product, and cause the problem on the user interface. It is necessary to select the metaphor and the motif to meet user intention. Author believes is that importance in the design should progress the idea by the method of the human centred design for that. The research for metaphor is conclusion several field such as the language, the culture, and the interface design etc. Author believes that a new model can be made up more conceptual by researching use and mechanisms of the metaphor other than the field of product design when the metaphor is used by the design.

2   Purpose

The purpose of the research is to propose idea creative method base on metaphor. This method should be included to consider user's lifestyle.

C. Stephanidis (Ed.): Posters, Part I, HCII 2011, CCIS 173, pp. 72–76, 2011.
© Springer-Verlag Berlin Heidelberg 2011

Fig. 1. Example of using metaphor: Kettle_design by Richard Sapper

3 Research Plan

The plan of the research is that the making prototype and the workshop, etc. are done by actually using idea creative method that proposed design method, and the verification is repeated. First investigates the previous work in each field such as the language, the cultures, and interfaces concerning the metaphor, and investigates the feature, the classification theory, and the evaluation method of the metaphor etc.

Next, use of the metaphor of an existing product was analyzed based on the classification theory of the metaphor that had been obtained from the previous work of the metaphor in the language.

The hypothesis of the conception support method was done based on three classification theories of the metaphor that had been obtained from the investigation of the previous work and the analysis of an existing product.

The design object was made a kitchen timer, the conception support law that had done the hypothesis was executed, and three prototypes were made.

The conception process of three prototypes was arranged and visualized.

Three feature of each pattern of thinking and the fault were analyzed.

Moreover, the assessment experiment was done to two students who were majoring in the design to judge the improvement of the prototype and the effectiveness of the conception support method objectively.

4 Proposed Design Method

The hypothesis of the research was done from the previous work concerning the metaphor and the analysis of an existing product.

It paid attention from the previous work in the language field of the metaphor to 3 classification theories.

- concept abstraction
- concept blending
- concept integration(Thematic relation)

Existing product that uses metaphor and motif was analyzed by using the classification theory. And, it was thought that the following three feature in use of the metaphor in product design.

- Metaphor using form
- Metaphor using concept
- Metaphor using operation

These three uses were set to the axis of the hypothesis of the conception support method. And, "Person" and "Thing" were set to the other axis. To use the metaphor that considered intended user's lifestyle, "Person" was set. In addition, to conceive the design freely, "Thing" was set.

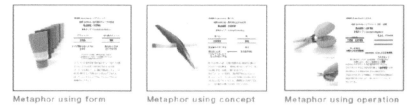

Metaphor using form   Metaphor using concept   Metaphor using operation

Fig. 2. Analysis of existing product

5   Case Study

Three prototypes were made by using this method. The purpose of this experiment is to put out the output using the metaphor of "Shape", "Operation", and "Concept" to the same design object. As a result of the analysis of an existing product, there are a lot of use cases with the metaphor in the life miscellaneous goods. The kitchen timer was selected this design object.

6   Result of Experiment

To understand the feature and the improvement of the use pattern of each metaphor, the pattern of thinking that the produced prototype was arranged, and visualized. Moreover, the assessment experiment was done to two students who were majoring in the design to judge the improvement of the prototype and the effectiveness of the conception support method objectively. As for the metaphor using the concept, it has been understood that an effective possibility to improve user's interest and curiosity is high in the use pattern of three metaphors. Moreover, it has been understood that the decision of an early design condition is important. The improvement of this conception support method is a method of extracting the metaphor in the design with effectiveness from the intended user.

7 Conclusion

Based on the result of experiment proposed design method has been evaluated.It was thought that three patterns "form", "Concept", and "Operation" were effective in use of the metaphor. The prototype was made, and the effectiveness of the conception support method that had done the hypothesis was verified. As for the metaphor using the concept, it has been understood that an effective possibility to improve user's interest and curiosity is high in the use pattern of three metaphors. The following want to do the workshop using the conception support method, and to verify effectiveness.

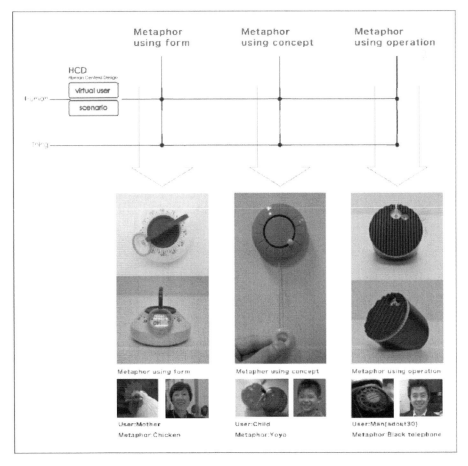

Fig. 3. Hypothesis of idea creative method and execution experiment

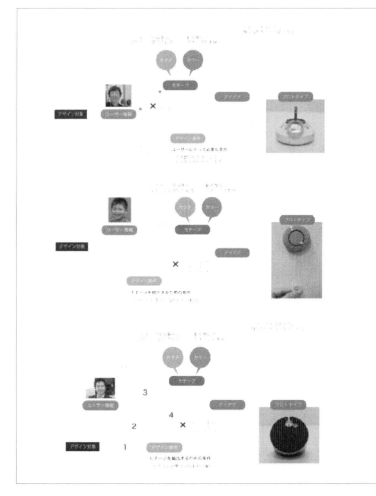

Fig. 4. Analysis of prototype

Reference

Yurika, TAuro, T.: Formla description of Concvept-synthesizing process for creative design (2006)

Persona-Storyboard Fusion: A Hybrid Approach to Improving Design Artifacts

Michael Stewart[1], Jennifer Francois[1], Hongbo Zhang[2], and D. Scott McCrickard[1]

[1] Center for Human-Computer Interaction, Virginia Tech, 2202 Kraft Dr.,
Blacksburg, VA 24060, USA
[2] Human Factors, Industrial and Systems Engineering, Virginia Tech,
250 Durham Hall, Blacksburg, VA 24060, USA
{tgm,jenniff,hbzhang,mccricks}@vt.edu

Abstract. We propose and explore a novel method for fusing personas and storyboards in iteration by novice and expert designers. Personas have been shown to provide benefits to designers in understanding their users and keeping them in mind while designing. Storyboards have been shown to facilitate the communication of process between designers and users, and between designers and developers. Our process demonstrates the power and limitations of personas and storyboards, seeking to improve the design artifacts' ability to inform the analysis of a product, and the resulting design implications. We describe the application of our process in a product design exercise. Through our study we saw the fusion of personas and storyboards facilitate the teaching of design.

Keywords: Personas, Storyboards.

1 Introduction

Teaching or practicing engineering design is challenging due to its complex, multivariate, and multilevel nature. Because of the complexity of the subject, novice designers (NDs) may not always acquire a working knowledge of every design technique. This can lead to confusion and even misuse of the design knowledge. Integration of experience with these design tools into the curriculum can enhance the ND's comprehension of design tools and promote a holistic view of design.

A *persona* is an abstract representation of users in the form of an archetype character, introduced by Cooper [1]. Personas can be used throughout the stages of design, from contextual data inquiry to prototyping, as a reminder of the target users. However, personas alone do not offer the capability for directly guiding the design.

The *storyboard* is usually a low-fidelity paper based prototype mostly used in early design stages. It helps the designer to visualize an idea about the process of the target application and communicate it to all project stakeholders. The targeted user can use the storyboard to understand how they can interact with the different aspects of the product. Storyboards can facilitate designers in achieving common ground. Additionally, they give the designer an opportunity for visual reflection, which consists of several phases: simulation, evaluation, and decision [2].

C. Stephanidis (Ed.): Posters, Part I, HCII 2011, CCIS 173, pp. 77–81, 2011.
© Springer-Verlag Berlin Heidelberg 2011

Using personas alone has not always addressed design expectations due to low adoption among design teams [3, 4]. Among design teams which used personas, their use was limited to individual designers' internal concepts or to facilitation of communication, which limits its effectiveness in design [5]. The isolated use of personas has not always been successful in design, which can be attributed to the unconvinced, insincere use of personas [3, 5]. The integrated use of personas with other design techniques such as storyboarding is still not well documented.

In this research, we investigated how to integrate personas with storyboards. In exploring the fusion of these two design techniques, we ran a study with participants from a graduate class. Ten NDs and three expert designers (EDs) participated in the design of the interface for a Google Android app [6]. We found that the framework can help novice designers in brainstorming their design, help expert designers to enlarge the design workspace, and facilitates agreement between NDs and EDs. We address how the framework can be used in academic settings to facilitate teaching of design.

2 Persona-Storyboard Fusion

NDs have difficulty using multiple or even single design technique(s). EDs also have difficulty improving on novice designers' designs such as NDs' storyboards. EDs can improve the NDs' storyboard in terms of aesthetics, HCI design principles, and the satisfaction of general design goals. However, these improvements may not be sufficient for EDs to reach common ground with NDs. It is difficult for EDs to know NDs' design background and motivation. The inevitable conflicts that arise during ED and ND cooperation often leads to incompleteness or incorrectness of design and slow progress of both EDs and NDs.

The persona-storyboard fusion approach seeks to address these conflicts. Our approach consists of the following steps. First, the NDs create personas and storyboards. Then, with the help of the EDs, they evolve them together; with the NDs encouraged to continue this evolution with feedback from the EDs. The EDs independently rate the NDs' personas on applicable dimensions of interest. The NDs then take this feedback from the EDs and use it to help them improve their personas. Because EDs independently rate the personas, the NDs can see issues of contention in their personas reflected in inter-rater disagreement. With their evolved personas, the NDs can concurrently evolve their storyboards. They attempt to reflect the relevant facets of the persona in the storyboard. Next EDs will develop multiple possible enhancements to each of the NDs' storyboards. The NDs can then take this feedback and use it to focus their personas and scenarios to make clear why their design is best for their persona, or otherwise to improve their storyboard. The design iterations could continue until satisfaction. The framework is shown in Figure 1.

In this process, there are a few important considerations. First, it is vital that the storyboard include the relevant facets of the personas that the ND created. It is possible to do this through the storyboard's imagery and/or its descriptions. Next, both EDs and NDs should work toward converging on a direction that agrees with the design goals.

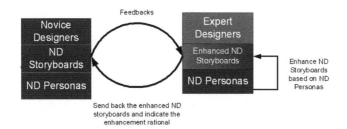

Fig. 1. Storyboard and persona fusion diagram

The advantages of this framework are that it can give NDs further exposure to design techniques in action and that it brings the "living" nature of personas [7] to storyboarding. The possible disadvantages of this framework are that it may require a longer design cycle, and poor selection by NDs can possibly lead to biased design.

3 Methods

We applied our ND-ED method in the creation and evaluation of a mobile ideation tool that presented pictures of interesting uses of mobile technology to designers. The tool, a mobile version of our PIC-UP tool, supports flipping through lots of pictures and reading about the pictures, with the goal of conveying to designers the power and functionality of the Android mobile platform. The goal of the experiment was to come up with redesign ideas for the application. In total, 10 students taking a grad-level HCI class participated. These NDs had the opportunity to brainstorm their personas prior to class. They had to think about their background, interests, etc. During class, a presentation of personas and storyboards was given and a video of top 10 Android apps in 2010 was shown to stimulate the brainstorming for their storyboards. The NDs were then required to write down their persona information, and to create a storyboard for their idea for the redesign of PIC-UP.

The EDs then evaluated the personas from the NDs. Each ED evaluated the persona information independently and rated the persona information based on several categories from 0-4 (see Table 1). Based on these ratings, the EDs brainstormed independently how to improve the NDs' storyboards in ways that respect the ND's persona. By integrating the NDs personas, the EDs enhanced the storyboards and re-drew them using the Google Docs Drawing tool and finally, sent these revised storyboards back to the NDs. They were then asked to comment on the enhanced version of their storyboards. The EDs then modified the storyboards based on the NDs' feedback. After the enhancement, the EDs could find important features that could help with PIC-UP redesign. Then it was possible to consider these proposals and decide on the design tradeoffs of each before implementing them.

4 Results

Many of the NDs were enthusiastic contributors to our study. However, there may have been some miscommunication in delivering our instructions as not all of them followed the instructions. This paper selects 3 individual submissions (labeled A, B, and C) to examine the process. The ratings of seven categories of NDs' personas are shown in table 1. Each expert independently rated the personas on seven categories. The rating for each category ranges from 0 to 4. In this table, the median and the individual ratings are shown. From Table 1, EDs have consistent view for several categories such as design experiences. EDs have diversified view of the ND's persona for some categories such as smart phone experiences.

Based on these ratings and the initial three storyboards created by the NDs, the EDs (in total 3) produced the enhanced storyboards for each of the NDs. In these 9 storyboards, the EDs ensured that the relevant facets of the persona were exemplified. This enabled the ND to see how other designers would interpret their storyboards, as well as their personas. For example, the ND may not have felt that the ED understood their persona fully. This could help indicate to the ND that they needed a more explicit description of that particular facet of their persona.

The EDs then sent these storyboards to the NDs and asked for their feedback. A few interesting points arose from the NDs' comments. ND A recognized the importance of the storyboard designer to be able to annotate elements of their storyboard with text. ND B recognized a tradeoff between the richness of the user experience in the Android App and the time available for development of the app. And ND C recognized the need for developers to be an audience to user feedback.

Table 1. Rating of seven categories extracted from personas (within cell, top: median of rating, bottom: individual rating) Experience (Exp), Development (Dev)

ND	Coding Exp	Design Exp	App dev Exp	Work Exp	Smart-phone Exp	Intro-version	Extro-version
A	2	3	0	0	1	2	1
	1, 2, 3	3, 4,3	0,0,2	0, 0, 1	0, 1, 2	0, 2, 4	0, 1, 2
B	2	4	0	0	3	3	0
	3, 2, 0	4, 4, 4	0, 0, 1	0, 0, 1	3, 4, 0	3, 0, 4	0, 0, 3
C	1	3	2	2	2	3	1
	1, 0, 1	2, 3, 4	1, 2, 4	4, 2, 2	1, 2, 2	4, 0, 3	4, 0, 1

5 Discussion and Conclusion

Through our study we found three design implications for our framework. By quantitatively rating the NDs' personas, EDs have a firm basis to enhance the storyboards. Also, NDs and EDs have common ground based on the feedback process of personas and storyboards, which results in better communication and a design that reflects their common interests. As the final design incorporates features from the enhanced and critiqued storyboards, it effectively drew from a larger design space giving the designers more freedom.

We also experienced great variability in the quality of the personas. The primary issue was that not all of the NDs provided us with the dimensions for which we were hoping. We suggest that in the future, the EDs should be more explicit in communicating the primary descriptors they would like NDs to include in their personas. We also hoped that using the iterative process to inform the storyboards from the personas and to then have the personas be updated by the evolving storyboards would help in designing and enhancing personas as well as storyboards.

Not all of the NDs fully integrated their personas' facets in their storyboards. In order to help NDs include them, we recommend an example persona and storyboard with annotations that demonstrate details that reflect these facets. Additionally, in giving the feedback to the NDs after they create their own storyboards, the EDs should highlight aspects that reflect the personas. Then, to help the NDs enhance their personas, EDs could ask explicit questions about ambiguous aspects of the personas. This would help the NDs to see where they need to provide more detail in their personas. Finally, to help the NDs improve, it is important that the EDs provide detailed feedback in an accessible way. For example in our study, we should have shared our ratings of the personas with the NDs, aside from explicit questions, this would be an accessible way for the ND to see how EDs understand their personas and the level of ambiguity would be reflected in the inter-rater agreement.

Our hybrid approach in assisting novice and expert designers jointly participating in a fusion of two design techniques resulted in better communication between experts and novices, resulting in artifacts whose processes were arguably clearer and personas and storyboards which were arguably more directly relevant to stakeholders.

References

1. Cooper, A.: The inmates are running the asylum. Sams, USA (1995)
2. Van der Lelie, C.: The value of storyboards in the product design process. Personal and Ubiquitous Computing 10, 159–162 (2006)
3. Blomquist, Å., Arvola, M.: Personas in action: Ethnography in an interaction design team. In: Conference Personas in action: Ethnography in an interaction design team (2002)
4. Rowan, J., Cooper, M.: The plural self: Multiplicity in everyday life. Sage Publications Ltd., Thousand Oaks (1999)
5. Ronkko, K.: An empirical study demonstrating how different design constraints, project organization and contexts limited the utility of personas. In: Proceedings of the 38th Annual Hawaii International Conference on System Sciences, p. 220a (2005)
6. Wahid, S., McCrickard, D.S., DeGol, J., Elias, N., Harrison, S.: Don't drop it! Pick it up and storyboard. In: Proceedings of the 29th International Conference on Human Factors in Computing Systems (2011)
7. Nieters, J., Ivaturi, S., Ahmed, I.: Making Personas Memorable. In: Proceedings of The ACM CHI Conference on Human Factors in Computing Systems, pp. 1817–1824 (2007)

Studying Analysis Method for the Design Innovation

Inaba Takashi and Kazuhiko Yamazaki

Chiba Institute of Technology Graduate School., 2-17-1, Tudanuma, Narashino,
Chiba, 275-0023, Japan
kxfdw728@yahoo.co.jp, kazuhiko.yamazaki@it-chiba.ac.jp

Abstract. The experience economy and the user experience of the word began
to spread. And people's sense of values is changing from the thing to
experience. In the company, the importance of an innovation has been
recognized and the importance of a design also increased. The purpose of this
research is a proposal of the analysis method for innovation. In this paper
describes The author conducted three analysis method. The first is a demand
value analysis. The second is KA method. The third is a method using the
experience value. These analysis results were arranged. As a result, the
advantage of each method and the problem were found.

Keywords: Analysis Method, Observation, Design Innovation.

1 Introduction

The purpose of this research to propose of the analysis method for the design
innovation. There are two backgrounds in this study. The one of background is the
people's value has been shifted from the product to the experience. Secondarily,
Based one it's background the importance of an innovation has been increased for the
company.

2 Experiment for Analysis Method

Author believes importance of analysis method in to innovation. The first is to
understand the user's demand. Therefore, the author proposes three analyses method.
The first analysis a demand value analysis. The second is KA method. The third is
analysis using experience value analysis. The author conducted experiment for digital
camera including observation by shadowing, interview and three analyses method is
demand value analysis, KA method (KA method is a analysis method which Ms.
Miwa Asada developed and was public.) .The third is analysis using experience value
analysis.

The author conducted experiment of described below.

Observation by Shadowing. Investigation purpose: Records of how to use a digital
camera. Investigation content: The author goes to the place where the tested uses the
digital camera. and records of how to use digital camera. Recording medium: Video
camera.

C. Stephanidis (Ed.): Posters, Part I, HCII 2011, CCIS 173, pp. 82–85, 2011.

Interview. Investigation purpose: grasp of how to use digital camera and the place which was not found by shadowing investigation is ask to a tester. Investigation content: The depth interview about how to use digital camera for photograph which a tested photographed while shadowing investigation. Recording medium: Video camera and IC Recorder. It analyzes it based on the result of executing two investigations.

3   The Result of Analysis

1. Demand value analysis method. The first experiment is demand value analysis method. The demand value analysis is a method proposed by Yamazaki etc. In the Japan Ergonomic-Design academic society. When the designer extracts user requirements, uses it. How to use this analysis method is explained. First of all, extract the tester's behavior, feature, and anxious thing based on the interview result. Next, the question is repeated in the written keyword. Contents of the questions are "why" and "what the purpose". this is analysis method to extract the demand of the user.

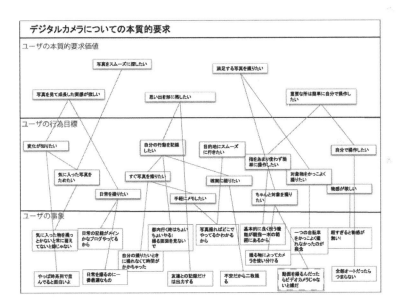

Fig. 1. Example result of Demand value analysis

2. KA method. The second experiment is KA method .The KA method is an analysis method, which Ms. Miwa Asada developed and was public. Mr. Miwa Asada belongs to KIBUN FOODS Inc. KA method is a technique for carrying out the modeling of the collected information. The KA method uses the information collected by the investigating methods, such as a context interview and the observing method. Because it is necessary to understand the sense of values that exists in user's act and the background.

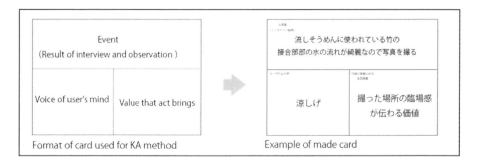

Fig. 2. Example of KA method of card

3. The analysis using experience value. The third experiment is analysis using experience value. The experience value is not a material and money value of the thing. Experience value is such the effects that people are obtained through use experience, and impression, satisfaction as mental and sensuous value. The author used five experience values that Mr. Bernd H. Schmitt advocated. Five classifications are SENSE, FEEL, THINK, ACT, RELATE. This method divides user findings into these five classifications and analyzes it. However, this method cannot directly utilize the results of user surveys. Therefore, the analysis result first and second was used by this third analysis.

experiment is analysis using experience value.						
essential value				user's target		
		・強いものが欲しい ・綺麗な写真を撮りたい	SENSE	・乱暴に扱っても壊れない物が欲しい	・物感が欲しい ・自分で操作したい	・頑丈な物が欲しい ・価値に浸りたい
・満足する写真を撮りたい ・皆との思い出を残したい ・写真を見て楽しみたい ・もてたい ・機能が良い物が使いたい	・写真を見て満足した気分が欲しい ・思い出を形に残したい ・満足する写真を撮りたい	・その時の感じを残したい ・友達を撮りたい	FEEL	・自己満足感が欲しい	・ちゃんと同窓を撮りたい ・綺麗に撮りたい ・気に入った写真を撮りたい ・変化が知りたい ・日常を撮りたい	・写真を撮るとき全体を撮りたい ・思い出を残したい ・写真を撮りに来たい ・撮影をおさめたい ・変化を見たい ・かっこよく女性を撮ってポスターにしたい ・なるべく半周して撮りたい
			THINK		・対象物をかっこよく撮りたい ・自分の行動を記録したい	・わくわくしたい
・写真を撮って人との繋がりを広げたい	・写真をスムーズに撮りたい ・重要な所は簡単に自分で操作したい	・カメラでコミュニケーションをとりたい	ACT	・カメラを通してもっと仲良くなりたい。	・自動的にスムーズに行きたい ・すぐ写真を撮りたい ・手軽にメモしたい ・指をあまり使わず簡単に操作したい	・写真を撮ることでコミュニケーションをとりたい ・カメラを持ち運びたい
			RELATE			・カッコよく見られたい

Fig. 3. Example result Method of using experience value

4 Result of the Experiment

Result of three analysis method. The first is demand value analysis. Demand value analysis can know a deep demand of a user. And The testee can be understood. The second is KA method. KA method can understand the action that the testee did. And idea increases. The third is analysis method using experience value. This analysis method is can understand the classification of experience   that the testee of demand.

5 Conclusion

The conclusion of three analyses that the author did is written. The first is demand value analysis. Demand value analysis can know a deep demand of a user. The fault does not have an index of concrete idea development. The second is KA method. KA method pays attention to all extracted information. Therefore, the number of ideas increases. The fault of this method is hard to understand the demand of the user. The third is analysis using experience value. The analysis that utilized experience value understands which experience value a user demands among five experience value.
Even if the fault of this technique understands the classification of the experience value, the use method is not understood.

References

1. Cabinet Office: Public opinion poll concerning national life (2010) (Japanese),
   http://www8.cao.go.jp/survey/h18/h18-life/index.html
2. Aizawa, M.:: Why is it an innovation now. Chemical Society of Japan, Chemistry and industry, volume 60 editorial (2007)
3. http://www8.cao.go.jp/survey/h18/h18-life/index.html
4. Utterback, J.M.: Design-inspired Innovation. World Scientific Pub. Co. Inc., Singapore (2006)
5. Kelley, T., Littman, J.: The Art of Innovation: Success Through Innovation the IDEO Way. Profile Business (2002)
6. Nakazawa, J., Ohnogi, H., Minami, H.: Shinnrigaku kannsatu manyuaru hou (Psychology observation manual). Kitaohjishyobou, Kyoto (1997)
7. Ando, M.: User engineering lecture material (2010),
   http://sites.google.com/site/usability22/documents
8. Schmitt, B.H.: Experiential Marketing: How to Get Customers to Sense, Feel, Think, Act, Relate. Free Press, New York (1999)

Balancing Trust and Automation Needs for Effective Home Energy Management

Hari Thiruvengada[*], Pallavi Dharwada, Anand Tharanathan, Wendy Foslien,
Sriharsha Putrevu, and John Beane

Honeywell (ACS) Advanced Technology Labs
1985 Douglas Drive N., Golden Valley, MN 55442, USA
{Hari.Thiruvenagda,Pallavi.Dharwada,Anand.Tharanathan,
Wendy.Foslien,Sriharsha.Putrevu,John.Beane}@honeywell.Com

Abstract. With the increasing shortage of energy resources and the adverse
impact of non-renewable fuels on the environment, there is a shift in the
consumer's mindset to emphasize managing and utilizing energy efficiently,
reducing green house emissions and contributing to a clean environment. This
is especially true to the residential markets where a trusted Home Energy
Manager (HEM) device can aid in automating and delivering effective energy
management strategies in homes. Home users are often passive in their
interaction and have to be engaged and reassured that a HEM device contributes
positively to the goal of home energy management. The objective is to boost
their trust and confidence in HEM by making information (such as energy costs,
usage patterns, etc.) accessible and enabling them to act and conserve energy
effectively based on the same. In this research, we explore and understand the
potential factors that influence how users would engage and interact with HEM
device. Some basic functions of the HEM device include: a trusted advisor that
provides dynamic recommendations based on user's interaction and behavior in
the home; ability to sense occupancy within the home and automatically adjust
schedules without the need for explicit human intervention; deduce energy
usage patterns; and adapt energy management strategies based on the user
profiles derived from their behaviors and interaction with the thermostat. Using
a HEM device with the proper balance of automation and user engagement can
have a positive impact on reducing the global energy consumption and the
sustenance of our environment.

Keywords: Human Computer Interaction, Home Energy Manager,
Sustainability, Energy Conservation, Behavior Change.

1 Introduction

The US Energy Information Administration (2001) estimated that total electricity
consumption in 2001 was 1140 Billion kWh (with average consumption of 10,656
kWh per household) which amounts to 100.34 Billion US Dollars. This estimate is

---

[*] Corresponding author.

C. Stephanidis (Ed.): Posters, Part I, HCII 2011, CCIS 173, pp. 86–90, 2011.

10% higher than the prior estimates in 1997 (1037 kWh, with average consumption of 10,656 kWh per household) and is predicted to increase in the future. The major energy consumers in the household were space heating (2,637 kWh), air conditioning (2,263 kWh), water heating (2,505 kWh), and appliances (6,894 kWh). Due to such enormous growing energy demands and shortages, residential home owners are turning to energy conservation measures and smart home energy management devices to help them reduce their growing energy costs and become more sustainable.

2   Key Dimensions of Home Energy Manager: A Trusted Advisor

The key role of the home energy management device is to act as a "Trusted Advisor". Lee & See (2004) define automation as "technology that actively selects data, transforms information, makes decisions, or controls processes". The key dimension that makes the Home Energy Manager (HEM) a trusted advisor can be summarized as: *User in control; Motivation for change and persistence of user behaviors; Enhanced information visualization and decision support; Intuitive user interfaces & reliable automation; Emotional and aesthetically superior interface design; Improved Situation Awareness.*

2.1   User in Control

To maintain trust in a system that includes automation, users need to feel that they are in control of the automation, rather than being driven by the system. This is particularly true when the outcome of an action by the system is uncertain. For example, a system that offers options, or presents options as advice or recommendation generally enjoys greater tolerance from users. Anderson's study on turbine control systems found that operators preferred a system that balanced step wise automation with user input after each automated step, rather than completely manual or completely automated systems (Anderson, 2008).

2.2   Motivation for Change and Persistence of User Behavior

Changing behavior tends to be challenging. Endeavors such a embarking on a new diet, following an exercise program, or organizing work processes are generally difficult for people to sustain over time. Changing behavior to reduce energy consumption has similar characteristics to these endeavors. Past studies have noted that various forms of energy feedback can drive savings, but that persistence does not happen until participant have developed new habits (Darby, 2006). A recent study revisiting participants from an energy monitoring program found that electrical energy consumption rose after removal of the devices, but did remain roughly 1% lower than prior to the study (Parker et. al., 2010).

2.3   Enhanced Information Visualization and Decision Support

As the data produced by home energy management systems grows, the task of consolidating that data into valuable, actionable information for the homeowner becomes critical. Simply providing home owners additional data without interpreting that data in context will not provide good value. The expected quantitative data available in a HEM must be carefully displayed using information design principles designed to communicate and guide decision making. Tufte (1983) asserts poor information graphic design is the core of many problems with understanding data, and that core principles such as minimizing "chart junk", maximizing "data ink" and striving for high data density can be employed to develop effective visualizations that "Above all else show the data". Similarly, Few (2006) provides guidance for communicating information through dashboards. Analyzing, visualizing and alerting users when information of value is available will be increasingly important as the connected home network becomes more complex.

2.4 Intuitive User Interfaces & Reliable Automation

Automation is typically designed to enhance human performance. More specifically, automation is introduced to make certain processes easier for human beings to execute. There are important characteristics associated with a well designed human-automation system. Beyond the systemic requirements and computational capabilities of the automation, it is also important for it to enhance the level of human interaction. Parasuraman and Riley (1997) highlight some of the key aspects of an automated system that can affect its use, disuse, misuse and abuse. For example, if an automated system results in several false alarms, it would result in the disuse of automation (also known as the cry-wolf syndrome). In contrast, if the false alarms are extremely low, it would lead to over-reliance, and potentially in abuse of automation.

Swarm intelligence is smart cooperation of very small units (Palomäki, 2002). The key distinction between swarm intelligence and other coordinated system modules is that when one function fails the collective system can still function and support the overall goal. HEM can be treated as inter-dependent set of smart modules that perform a specific function such as scheduling, occupancy detection, alarm management and provide a unique service when taken collectively contribute to a larger overall goal (E.g. Home Energy Management). Even if some units fail the HEM device should support this larger overall goal.

2.5 Emotional and Aesthetically Superior Design – "Kansei Engineering"

The design of an interactive HEM should not only be usable but also make an emotional connection with the users to motivate and influence their behavior for efficient energy management. Emotions play a significant role in learning a new interactive system (Norman, 2003), but, the challenge lies in identifying, and understanding these emotions and translating them into design. The invention of Kansei Engineering (Nagamachi, 2002) and other stimulus based participatory research methods will help elicit and translate the emotions into product parameters. Trust plays a key role in motivating and changing the current behaviors (Lee & See, 2004), so it is critical to understand and define trust using emotional research methods and use it as criteria in designing a HEM that truly resonates with users.

2.6 Improved Situation Awareness

Situation Awareness (SA) is important for effective human performance. Situation awareness (SA) is defined as a person's "perception of the elements in the environment within a volume of time and space, the comprehension of their meaning, and the projection of their status in the near future" (Endsley, 1988, p. 97). Problems with SA were found to be the leading causal factor for several industrial accidents and aviation mishaps (e.g., Durso et. al, 2007). Designing displays and automated systems that can help operators maintain good SA is essential (Tharanathan et. al, 2010).

3 HEM Case Study

The research team adopted multiple methods to gather user requirements for the HEM device. The team used traditional user-centric design methods such as conducting surveys to gather data on user demographics, their energy conservation practices, behaviors and their familiarity with energy efficiency and demand response programs and strategies. The team conducted a follow-on focus group with a similar demographic to understand their familiarity, and current practices to cope-up with the time-of-use pricing programs deployed by their utility. Most of the users did not have an energy management device at home and hence the team tried to understand how the home users review their utility bills. In particular, the team tried to understand what information in the electricity bill is more informative, useful and meaningful to the home user and how they use this information.

The information requirements generated from the focus groups and surveys were used in generating user interfaces for HEM. Users are good at reacting to product designs and notoriously bad at identifying the sources of their reactions (Smith, 2001). The research intent for the design of screens early-on was to get user reactions on the information displayed. The user interfaces developed for this purpose are expected to change most likely after implementing user feedback. It was important for the team to understand what problems the home users are trying to address to manage their energy and what kinds of information would provide them with better decision support? It was also important to understand how the user's profile/preferences determine their comfort, savings and level of device interaction.

The primary challenge in designing the user interface for a HEM was that the home users did not currently have a central device to manage their home energy usage. Instead, they were using multiple systems such as programmable thermostat, timers for washer/dryer, and other appliances. Given that most homes contain a thermostat, that allows us to manage the largest electric load (HVAC) contributing to more than 50% of the electricity bill, the research team's approach was to leverage one of the existing thermostat UI design and extend the comfort control scope to home energy management. Identifying the visual priority of information displayed for control and management of home energy and comfort is one of the other key challenges for the designers to address. The resulting HEM acts as a trusted advisor that provides decision support while engaging the user by creating a satisfying experience.

References

1. Anderson, J.: Levels of Automation and User Control – Evaluation of a Turbine Automation Interface. Project Report No. NKS-179 (October 2008)
2. Darby, S.: The effectiveness of feedback on energy consumption. A review for DEFRA of the literature on metering, billing and direct displays. Environmental Change Institute, University of Oxford (2006)
3. Durso, F.T., Rawson, K., Girotto, S.: Comprehension and situation awareness. In: Durso, F.T., Nickerson, R., Dumais, S., Lewandowsky, S., Perfect, T. (eds.) Handbook of Applied Cognition, 2nd edn., pp. 163–193. Wiley, Chichester (2007)
4. Endsley, M.R.: Design and evaluation for situation awareness enhancement. In: Proceedings of the Human Factors Society 32nd Annual Meeting, pp. 97–101. Human Factors Society, Santa Monica (1988)
5. Few, S.: Information Dashboard Design: The Effective Visual Communication of Data. O'Reilly Media, Sebastopol (2006)
6. Lee, J.D., See, K.A.: Trust in Automation: Designing for Appropriate Reliance. Human Factors 46(1), 50–80 (2004)
7. Nagamachi, M.: Kansei engineering as a powerful consumer-oriented technology for product development. Applied Ergonomics 33(3), 289–294 (2002)
8. Norman, D.: Emotional Design: Why We Love (Or Hate) Everyday Things. Basic Books, New York (2003)
9. Palomäki: Swarm Intelligence in automation. In: 5th Conference on Regional Development in Seinäjoki (2002),
   http://lompsa.seamk.fi/heikki.palomaki/Articles/
   swarmintelligence.pdf
10. Parasuraman, R., Riley, V.: Humans and automation: Use, misuse, disuse and abuse. Human Factors 39, 230–253 (1997)
11. Parker, D., Hoak, D., Cummings, J.: Pilot Evaluation of Energy Savings and Persistence from Residential Energy Demand Feedback Devices in a Hot Climate. In: 2010 ACEEE Summer Study on Energy Efficiency in Buildings (2010)
12. Smith, P.: Debunking the myths of UI design (2001),
    http://www.ibm.com/developerworks/library/us-myth.html (retrieved March 24, 2011)
13. Tharanathan, A., Bullemer, P., Laberge, L., Reising, D.R., Mclain, R.: Functional versus schematic overview displays: Impact on operator situation awareness in process monitoring. In: Proceedings of the 54th Annual Meeting of the Human Factors and Ergonomics Society, Santa Monica, California (2010)
14. Tufte, E.R.: The Visual Display of Quantitative Information. Graphics Press, Cheshire (1983)
15. US Energy Information Administration. Electricity Consumption and Expenditures in U.S. Households by End Uses and Census Region (2001),
    http://www.eia.gov/emeu/recs/byfuels/2001/byfuel_el.pdf
    (retrieved March 24, 2011)

Defining a Process for Cross-Product
User Interface Consistency

Leslie Tudor and Cheryl L. Coyle

SAS Institute, Cary, North Carolina
{leslie.tudor,cheryl.coyle}@sas.com

Abstract. A small team of usability analysts created, implemented, and followed a company-wide process to increase user interface consistency across products. Key ingredients to success were: an effective process; ongoing, active, involvement from stakeholders; iterative design and review cycles; and easily accessible and reusable code. This effort changed the process of cross product user interface design at SAS, providing impetus to the development of products that are more consistent. Goals, process, results, and lessons learned are described.

Keywords: Usability, consistency.

1 Usability and Consistency

A few years ago, a small team of usability analysts created, implemented, and began following a company-wide process to increase user interface consistency across SAS products. SAS Institute develops and markets dozens of products aimed at many different user types, such as statisticians, educators, law enforcement, marketing personnel, business analysts and executives, to name a few. Considering the large number of SAS products that exist, the diversity of users and their respective task goals, this objective was not trivial. A well thought out process was generated, and then vetted by participants.

2 Consistency Process

Multiple plans were brainstormed and reviewed with a variety of stakeholders, and successive refinements were made along the way. The process that was ultimately selected consisted of several elements.

2.1 Stakeholders

Consistency is not something that can be achieved by individual, independent efforts. Collaboration across multiple domains is necessary in order for products to have a consistent look and feel. Therefore, collaboration across two distinct usability groups, as well as product management, was critical. In addition, obtaining buy-in from other stakeholders across the company such as product development, product testing and

C. Stephanidis (Ed.): Posters, Part I, HCII 2011, CCIS 173, pp. 91–95, 2011.
© Springer-Verlag Berlin Heidelberg 2011

user documentation was necessary so that there was no question that the designs ultimately submitted to product teams could be implemented.

After identifying the relevant stakeholders, several ideas for keeping them actively involved in the process were discussed. Even though a request from upper management to support this effort might initially garner stakeholder enthusiasm, the pressures of meeting deadlines to get new releases out the door might understandably supersede their commitment. Since sustaining support from stakeholders was important, it was decided that stakeholders should be a critical part of the usability design review process. Therefore, the process was designed so that it consisted of multiple review cycles, with one cycle including a group of prime stakeholders.

2.2   Areas of Inconsistency and "Topic Area Teams"

Once stakeholders were identified, the immediate next step was to determine where to focus consistency efforts. A two-day meeting was held with all usability analysts in order to identify areas of opportunity. A high-level survey to identify areas of focus for current company products was also conducted. Documentation from these two data sources was gathered and reviewed and, ultimately, a list of several "topic areas" (primarily focusing on the appearance and behaviors of widgets) was created. The topic areas ranged from small items, such as what kind of information to include in an "About Box" to more involved widgets, such as how a "Wizard" should be designed.

Each topic area was then assigned a team of usability resources, known as a "Topic Area Team" (TAT), and the actual design and review phases could begin. Usability analysts were assigned to work on topic areas based on an interest in the topic area, experience designing in that topic area, and/or their current product workload.

The first task undertaken by a TAT was to ask development managers to post screenshots of the topic area from their respective products so that designers could review the UIs with regard to consistency, task flows, and user needs. At this early stage, analysts also met with each other to brainstorm design ideas. Once an initial design was completed, the review process began.

2.3   Reviews and Design Iteration

Iterative design is desirable on most, if not all, design efforts, and this effort was no different. Considering the scope of the effort and the desire to involve stakeholders in this process, the challenge was to iterate while still being efficient with regard to the mechanisms used for reviews, employee participation in review sessions, and how different phases of the reviews were structured.

The review process was structured so that it consisted of three review cycles with different cycles each focusing on different sets of reviewers: usability analysts, a small group of prime stakeholders, and a larger group of all interested parties, respectively.   Specifically, after a TAT created their design and accompanying specification document (spec), they posted the design spec and requested reviews. Usability analysts reviewed the spec and posted review comments. They also voted on the acceptability of the design. Spec authors used a discussion board to enter their responses to comments. It was at this time that comments often drove design modification decisions. The second review cycle (which was ultimately dropped) was identical to that of the first but included reviewers outside of the usability groups. During the final review cycle, a much broader group of product managers, developers, testers and technical writers were asked to perform the review, enter comments, and vote. The usability managers in charge of this effort then assessed the state of the design spec itself, and made sure that that all comments had been adequately addressed. The spec was then posted and labeled as "complete", ready to be developed.

2.4 Code Reuse

The prospect of individual development teams independently implementing the designs that resulted from this effort was a major concern; different development teams could potentially vary in the degree to which they remained faithful to the designs. Additionally, teams might feel pressure to give preference to coding new features instead of modifying current ones, and might also resist dismantling code they had worked so hard on in previous releases. Because of these concerns, one development team was selected to implement the designs as pieces of reusable code that different product development teams could then use. This team was formed to create common components that would be easy for other teams to take from the code base and insert into their products. This was an ideal mechanism for facilitating consistency.

3 Outcome

Because of this consistency process, many common components have been created and are being re-used in products. The success of the effort is inherent in the many designs that resulted from the process. In addition to the designs that were created, there was much learning along the way, and the realization that the process contained both benefits and disadvantages.

3.1 Pros

Prior to this effort, attaining a comprehensive understanding of design variability across products was difficult. Several issues contributed to this difficulty, including the large number of GUI products at SAS, relative difficulty of accessing screen shots and/or viewing product interfaces, and the time involved. These barriers were significantly lessened by the consistency process, and this newfound data has benefitted both usability analysts and development.

As both analysts and developers reviewed screenshots, the concept of "intelligent versus foolish consistency" became apparent and guided design decisions. Specifically, a few non-usability colleagues were so committed to the goal of consistency that they assumed that every aspect of a UI should look and behave the same. This presented an opportunity to educate others about the fact that consistency is good if it meets user needs, and, conversely, is not desirable if it leads to usability issues that result in poor performance and user frustration.

The fact that two usability groups worked together on design was positive with regard to team building. From a workload perspective, there was the additional benefit of ample time and opportunity for brainstorming design ideas and for incorporating the ideas of others. This helped to assure that the designs were of high quality. Finally, involving development staff in this effort increased their knowledge of design issues, increased their commitment to the effort, and allowed them to provide usability analysts with quick feedback on implementation constraints. It also brought usability and the importance of consistency into the forefront for the development community.

3.2 Cons

Even though a multitude of designs were generated, the complexity of the effort was off-putting to many analysts and reviewers. Each design entailed several formal review phases, and preparing detailed design specs meant that it was extremely time-intensive for both the designing analysts/spec authors as well as the reviewers. Also, the fact that the designs were produced months before they were implemented was not very satisfying for many of the analysts. There was a lot of variability across analysts with regard to their perception of this effort with some feeling very positive about the quality and number of specs generated but others feeling like it was too time consuming and took time away from product work. Finally, getting all of the stakeholders to review the designs and enter review comments was one of the most difficult aspects of this effort. Despite the fact that there was much expressed enthusiasm during the effort's initial stages, the reality of reading through what were sometimes dense and highly detailed specification documents took its toll and, over time, it became apparent that only a small subset of personnel outside of the usability community were reviewing the designs and entering comments.

4   Going Forward

In summary, though there were many positive aspects of this process, it became apparent that the process was too challenging for analysts, employees, and management to engage in going forward. The current goal is to improve the process so that it is less complex and time intensive, and more empowering and gratifying in terms of quick implementation. Therefore, a new component UI design process is being defined that builds on the positive aspects of the process described in this paper and eliminates the negative ones. Specifically, we will be establishing a new role for a "component usability analyst" who will be both designer and project manager for the component effort.

   Due to the sheer number of SAS components, it would be difficult for one UI designer to create usable designs for all components, and to wholly understand the many products and user tasks that comprise the SAS offerings. Instead of attempting to design numerous components independently, and understand multiple applications and users' needs, the component usability analyst will act as a project manager and two-way communication vehicle for the components being designed. This refined process will include open communication with product UI designers, to determine when there is a need for a common component. Once a need is identified, a usability analyst will be assigned to design the new component. The job of that designer will be to gather all the requirements from the product teams, design the component to meet those needs, and review the design with users. This process may sound similar to what was described above, but will differ mainly in how time consuming it is for individual usability analysts. The time commitment for each component design will fall on one person only, instead of on everyone. The component usability analyst will help individual analysts manage the process, will keep them focused on the necessary tasks, and will provide ongoing communication across the usability and development communities. We look forward to refining and implementing this process, and to continue making positive contributions to intelligent consistency efforts.

Tweaking HCI Methods for m-Design

Alícia Valls Saez, Muriel Garreta-Domingo, Gemma Aguado,
and Marta Lopez Reyes

Universitat Oberta de Catalunya
Av. Tibidabo 47, 08035 Barcelona, Spain
{avallssa,murielgd,gaguado,mlopezreye}@uoc.edu

Abstract. The potentialities of mobile devices for e-learning are amazing and exciting. M-learning is a new field that needs to be defined and designed. User-centered design can provide the methods to ensure that m-learning functionalities are appropriate and effective but, in order to do so, traditional UCD settings need to be tweaked.

Keywords: m-learning, user-centered design, human-computer interaction methods, e-learning, mobile design.

1 Introduction

Mobile devices are pervasive, ubiquitous and increasingly powerful. Teaching and learning processes, especially e-learning, must take these technological changes into account as they have important implications in the uses that virtual students make of technology, the way in which they access information and, therefore, the way they gain access to learning.

This poster presents a project aimed at 1) exploring the possibilities of mobile devices for e-learning and 2) evaluating the usefulness and drawbacks of traditional HCI methods for m-design.

2 Context

The Universitat Oberta de Catalunya (Open University of Catalonia-UOC) is an online university that offers training to 54,000 students. The profile of UOC students presents a series of characteristics that are increasingly extensible to the student in our information and communication society. 60% of the students are over the age of 30 and 75% work full time. Mainly, we are dealing with a student who must reconcile work, family and study, solving questions of mobility that this reality presents.

Consequently, educational institutions must seek to have an effect on matters related to flexibility, learning centered on the student, interactivity, collaboration and lifelong learning. Therefore, enabling education to adapt to the personal and professional reality of each individual, and to different rhythms and planning, regardless of time and place.

The data provided to us from the study conducted by Vavoula [1] about where learning takes place for an adult gives us some clues about how we may improve the

C. Stephanidis (Ed.): Posters, Part I, HCII 2011, CCIS 173, pp. 96–99, 2011.
© Springer-Verlag Berlin Heidelberg 2011

aforementioned aspects in order to facilitate access to learning for distance students: 51% occurs in the student's home or workplace; 21% takes place during work hours outside the workplace, 5% outside, 2% in the home of a friend and 6% in some leisure place. In the remaining 14% we find other places such as stores, cafés, etc. It is interesting to point out that in 1% of this total learning takes place in some type of transportation [2] and the goal is to effect this 1% by providing students new functionalities for learning process with the best mobile user experience [3].

3 Approach to the Concept of m-Learning

Even though m-learning is in the early stages of its development, we encounter different approaches to the concept, as well as research referring to obtaining results on the possibilities and limitations of m-learning in e-learning or blended learning.

Some authors define m-learning as learning facilitated by the use of mobile phones or hand held digital devices [4]. Other authors define it as a kind of learning that takes place when the student is not in a fixed or predetermined place, or as learning that happens when the student takes advantage of learning that is offered by mobile technologies [5].

Yet others stress different questions, stating that m-learning is a new way of learning that involves new experiences of interaction [6] or addressing the possibilities of m-learning with regard to situated learning or lifelong learning [2].

Among the possibilities attributed to it we can highlight: 1) ease of access to learning anytime, anywhere; 2) increased interactivity in the classroom; 3) facilitates students' following of classes; 4) it is proving to be a learning focus that fosters student participation and motivation; and 5) the capacity to transform higher education, making educational focuses more in keeping with current technology-related practices of our students. [7, 4, 8].

4 UCD Process for Mobile Design at the University

This paper is based on previous studies at the UOC (Universitat Oberta de Catalunya) on the uses of mobile technogolies in commuting situations. Acording to this, students use their devices mainly to search for and consult specific information such as deadlines, activities, course material and assessments in email, forums or debates.

A process of prototyping was carried out from these findings. So, mobile students could do all of the previously discussed in learning situations in commuting contexts.

The process carried out to develop the mobile prototype and provide solutions to users followed a series of phases that we will describe below:

1. **Background research:** it was revealed that students adapt their learning strategies and process to the context and devices available. Most interviewed users do not own a smartphone or netbook and, as a result, they print out subject material to be read during their commute and leave mail, forums and consultation for when they arrive at work or home since they can not do it when they are on the move. Our goal was to provide a better way to access messages, forums or debates with mobile devices to promote these activities during commutes.

2. **Prototyping:** to start with this phase we had to make certain prior decisions such as the choice of the device with which to conduct the test and implement the prototype, given that each type of device employs a different type of navigation. We opted for the iPhone, taking market trends into consideration. We started with paper and pencil prototypes, moved on to electronic mockups with Balsamiq and finished with high fidelity paper prototypes. These prototypes were refined with experts reviews and feedback.
3. **Two rounds of user test:** the first user test analyzed the prototypes implemented in the previous phase with 6 students. Common ways of collecting information for a user test are audio and video recording of the user while performing the test task and its interaction with the interface analyzed. However, they are not very sophisticated, specific and suitable for mobiles. Because of this, we seek for a new and adjusted way to capture all the testing process. This process consist of: recording facial gestures and voice and interaction with the devices [9, 10]. The result is the recording of the user while executing the task.

In the second round of testing were provided with a blank paper iPhone so that they could freely draw how they wanted to visualize contents on the mobile phone, with the objective of finding out which contents they wanted to visualize and how they wanted them to be displayed. The innovation lies in this second round. Habitual processes don't evaluate predefined prototypes; however we focus on the use of fully defined prototypes.

4.1 Lessons Learned

During the project, we detected a series of aspects that led us to make adjustments in the user-centered design methods.

• Recording: combining a webcam and Camtasia wasn't ideal for further analysis of the user tests. Specific recording settings need to be defined for mobile user testing.
• Observation: this task is much more difficult when testing with a mobile device. Only the facilitator was able to observe what the user was doing and even for him / her it was difficult to follow all the steps without invading the user's space.
• Paper prototype: most of our users didn't own a smartphone and, as a consequence, the paper prototype was too far away from what they are used to interact with. We felt it didn't provide us with realistic results. On the other hand, if they had been faced with a high fidelity interactive prototype, there would have also been drawbacks.

5   Future Work

In order to pilot the project and make sure that the application is useful for our students over time and to leave out the effects of not owning or knowing how to use a smartphone, our idea is to promote a renting service of these devices. Upon termination of this renting but also during this pilot phase, we will keep using different UCD methods to test and evaluate the application but also the methods themselves.

6 Conclusion

Traditional settings for UCD methods need to be tweaked and adapted for mobile design. This adaptations include recording, observing and also keeping in mind that there are more variables – such as unfamiliarity – that effect the results. From the different tasks and settings we have tried, asking users to draw what they would like in the mobile device was the most informing and less biased result we obtained.

We're currently evaluating the method.

References

[1] Vavoula, G.N.: D4.4: A Study of Mobile Learning Practices: Internal report of MOBIlearn project (2005)

[2] Sharples, M., Taylor, J., Vavoula, G.: Towards a theory of mobile learning. In: Proceedings of the 4th World Conference on mLearning (mLearn 2005), Cape Town, October 25-28, pp. 1–8 (2005),
http://www.mlearn.org.za/CD/papers/
Sharples-%20Theory%20of%20Mobile.pdf (recovered)

[3] Hinman, R.: Mobile User Experience: What Web Designers Need to Know,
http://www.slideshare.net/Rachel_Hinman/
mobile-user-experience-what-web-designers-need-to-know
(recovered on 3/31/2010)

[4] Dyson, L.E., Litchfield, A., Lawrence, E., Raban, R., Leijdekkers, P.: Advancing the m-learning research agenda for active, experiential learning: Four case studies. Australasian Journal of Educational Technology 25(2), 250–267 (2009)

[5] O'Malley, C, Vavoula, G, Glew, J.P, Taylor, J., Sharples, M., Lefrere, P.: WP 4 – Guidelines for learning/teaching/tutoring in a mobile environment: Internal report of MOBIlearn project (2003), http://www.mobilearn.org/download/
results/guidelines.pdf (recovered)

[6] Abdul Razak, F.H.: Understanding Interaction Experience in Mobile Learning. Springer, Heidelberg (2004)

[7] Duncan-Howell, J., Lee, K.: M-learning: Finding a place for mobile technologies within tertiary educational settings. In: Proceedings Ascilite Singapore (2007)

[8] Shen, R., Wang, M., Pan, X.: Increasing interactivity in blended classrooms through a cutting-edge mobile learning system. British Journal of Educational Technology 39(6) (2008)

[9] iPhone paper prototype video (n.d),
http://www.guuui.com/
posting.php?id=2254&utm_source=feedburner&utm_medium=
feed&utm_campaign=Feed%3A+guuui+%28GUUUI+-+
The+interaction+designers+coffee+break%29&utm_content=
Google+Reader (recovered on 3/31/2010)

[10] Kaikkonen, A., Kekäläinen, A., Cankar, M., Kallio, T., Kankainen, A.: Usability Testing of Mobile Applications: A Comparison between Laboratory and Field Testing. Journal of Usability Studies 1(1), 4–16 (2005)

Part II
Usability and User Experience

Contextual Awareness as Measure of Human-Information Interaction in Usability and Design

Michael J. Albers

East Carolina University
Greenville NC 27858, USA
albersm@ecu.edu

Abstract. Contextual awareness (CA) [3] provides a way of thinking about the communication quality of the human-information interaction (HII) aspects of a design [4]. Understanding information in complex situations is essentially always cognitively-based rather than physically-based (although physical interaction may be required to control the situation). Gaining that understanding within a complex situation requires mentally integrating many pieces of information, which requires the user knows the information exists, what it means, and how it is interrelated to other pieces of information. The design and testing of complex information systems and effectively interacting with them require a different approach than working with simply information [1, 11].

Keywords: contextual awareness, human-information interaction, usability.

1 Definition of Contextual Awareness

Contextual awareness (CA) is the understanding of the information within an informational situation which forms the basis for how to interpret new information and how to make decisions for interacting with that situation. CA is about a person's state of knowledge about the situation and not about the process they use to obtain that knowledge. With poor CA, people can know something is occurring or that a particular piece of information exists, but they cannot easily find relevant information or they have the information but do not understand how it relates to the overall situation. On the other hand, good CA does not guarantee a person will form the proper intention or make the proper decisions; the error analysis literature is filled with cases where people understood a situation, but still made incorrect choices.

Situations which require design teams to consider CA are those which contain complex information [2] that must fit within the situation and be presented to meet a reader's information needs. Understanding a situation requires mentally integrating many pieces of information with respect to the reader's goals and the current context. In complex situations, people don't follow a fixed path, instead they continually adjust their mental paths as new information presents itself. The non-fixed path arises from the non-linear aspects of problem solving. Addressing the mental shift to non-linear thinking breaks with the fundamental philosophy of step-by-step analysis. The design must place the information within the situational context and allow user to develop and maintain an overall awareness of the situation.

C. Stephanidis (Ed.): Posters, Part I, HCII 2011, CCIS 173, pp. 103–107, 2011.

CA provides a tool to help judge the fluid, ill-formed goals in complex situations. CA pulls back from thinking in terms of button pushing or fonts/color choices. Instead, it focuses on content and relationships across screens with a focus on how to efficiency and effectively communicate information. Different people will use different methods and approaches to gain contextual awareness.

Elements of good contextual awareness are (figure 1): (1) Understands how the information fits within the current situation. (2) Understands the information relationships [1]. Information comprehension requires knowing how information relates to other information. (3) Understands the future development of the situation and can make predictions about the ripple effect of different decisions.

2   Why Be Concerned about Contextual Awareness

Design teams need to consider how people need the information to develop contextual awareness.. It is not enough to simply provide them with the information; it must be organized and presented in a way that lets readers fit that information into their background knowledge and build up a coherent understanding of the entire situation.

If people are to create a coherent story, they need information to enable them to comprehend the situation. They can use that comprehension as the basis for the selection and performance of judgments, decisions, and actions. Gaining that understanding requires mentally integrating many pieces of information, which requires the person knows the information exists, what it means, and how it is interrelated to other pieces of information. That implies having a deep enough understanding to understand the current situation and to be able to make predictions about its future evolution.

Having full CA in a complex situation typically requires more than just possessing the available information; in addition, environmental and social aspects must also be considered. Schriver [12] discusses the importance of the social situation and how failing to allow for its effects leads to failure of information communication.

2.1   Information Comprehension

People identify a problem and make a problem-solving decision based on how they interpret the information around them. Unfortunately, the interpretation often has less to do with reality and more to do with what the person expects to see. Strong expectancy biases in data interpretation must be expected [8]. Also, the presentation format exerts a strong influence on how people interpret the data. Salient information must have proper presentation. With poor information salience, the presentation fails to either effectively present salient information or to present adequate cues about relevant information.

Much of the information analysis research attempts to predefine people's needs and, thus, the system breaks down when users go beyond the solution envisioned by the designer. User analysis and task analysis are important components of current design methodology, but are not constructed to support complex problem solving, rather they focus on assembling task blocks versus defining the continuous chain of event that exist in a problem solving situation. In a well-defined domain, the user

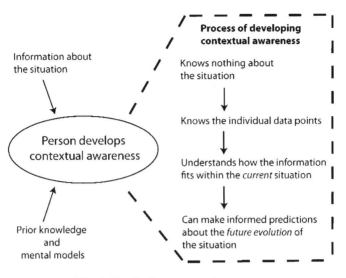

Fig. 1. Developing contextual awareness

approaches are limited and can be fully defined by the designer. In an ill-structured domain, each user takes a slightly different path and the designer can't assume that an understanding of how one person performs the task describes anyone else.

2.2 Information Relationships

Effective design for CA requires focusing on the relationships between information and how those relationships fit into the user's mental model of the situation. As people address a complex problem, a structure emerges which is based on the context, the relationships between the important elements, and the user's mental model. When solving a problem, the user's initial difficulty is recognizing what is wrong and what information is needed to verify the problem and suggest possible solutions.

Multiple studies have on how people solve problems in the real-world reveal a consistent feature of people constantly adjusting their goals and sub-goals to allow for the dynamic nature and quality of the information available [9, 10]. Unfortunately, people have a hard time integrating information and relating various data points to each other. Unless it is properly organized, humans cannot efficiently process large amounts of information, especially with the incomplete information available in a typical real-world context [7, 13].

2.3 Evolution of the Situation's Future

After understanding the relationships with the situation, the person needs to use the data and relationships to make predictions of the results of potential decisions. Complex situations are highly dynamic and usually exhibit a non-linear response to changes. But people make linear extrapolations and are extremely poor at judging non-linear data. Many failures occur because of the assumption that the initial conditions would somehow suddenly jump from initial to final state.

3 How to Analyze and Design for Contextual Awareness

Because, by definition, CA is about people understanding the situation and being able to make predictions of the situation's future development, it leads directly to methods which can be used during early prototyping and usability testing of reading to decide information. Note that this is substantially different from a more typical usability test which focuses on how people obtain information or perform a task (e.g., measuring search times or how paths deviate from optimal). Instead, it tests a person's comprehension of the overall situation and the information presented.

The intial analysis reveals the general user goals and information needs and the potential sub-goals that must be addressed as they proceed to a resolution. Defining the goals and information needs becomes complicated because there is no "right way" to solve a complex problem [2, 10]. With complex situations, there is no single path and no way of predicting when the user will make a decision. Slightly different starting points can require different information and resulting decisions.

The major problem in decision making is understanding the problem. A decision is based on how people interpret the information around them. Incorrect or incomplete information can lead to incomplete or invalid decisions. Even with complete information, different presentations cause different approaches to the solution [6]. Having the data available does not equal understanding. Thus, the users' main need is information which supports gaining a clear understanding of the problem and the possible solutions. During the requirements analysis, the information designer must gain an understanding of what information is relevant, how the information is obtained, how it relates to other information, and how to present the information to maximize revealing those relationships.

The first step in designing an effective system should not be to define the data needs, but to define the communication situation in terms of the necessary information processes and mental models of the users. A standard practice for handling complexity is to attempt to limit the problem-space and accept that all the information needed can be defined in advance [5]. Rather than attempt to handle the entire dynamic process, this type of analysis focuses on single slices (either time or procedure). It often results in ignoring parts or misestimating each part's importance to understanding the overall situation [13]. Many methods attempt to define a static space and attempts to predefine the space and, thus, the system breaks down when users try to go beyond the solution envisioned by the designer.

The situation analysis for determining a person's contextual awareness must be performed in the context it is designed to address. An underlying problem facing the analyst is that there is no simple way of determining when to stop the user analysis, but it does run the risk of trying to collect everything. Techniques such as critical incident analysis can provide a relatively bounded area of interest in which to collect user goals and information needs which can be directly related back to the situation. The base situation analysis must get into the person's mind and start to understand the mental model building and situational thought processes while it builds a picture of how the person becomes fully aware of the overall situation.

4   Conclusion

Effective design for complex problem-solving focuses on providing the appropriate content for the user's real-world goals and information needs. The design must not be swept up in the technology and, instead, must focus on how the information and presentation apply to the situational context. CA adds to the HCI and usability testing toolbox for creating and testing information designed to address open-ended questions for problem-solving or decision-making.

References

1. Albers, M., Still, B. (eds.): Usability of Complex Information Systems: Evaluation of User Interaction. CRC Press, Boca Raton (2010)
2. Albers, M.: Communication of complex information: User goals and information needs for dynamic web information. Erlbaum, Mahwah (2004)
3. Albers, M.: Design for Effective support of user intentions in information-rich interactions. Journal of Technical Writing and Communication 39(2), 177–194 (2009)
4. Albers, M.: Human-Information Interaction and Technical Communication: Concepts and Frameworks. IGI Global (in press)
5. Basden, A., Hibberd, P.: User interface issues raised. by knowledge refinement. International Journal of Human-Computer Studies 45, 135–155 (1996)
6. Elam, J., Mead, M.: Can software influence creativity? Information Systems Research 1(1), 1–10 (1990)
7. Gerlach, J., Kuo, F.: Understanding human-computer interaction for information system design. MIS Quarterly 15(4), 527–550 (1991)
8. Klein, G.: Do decision biases explain too much. Human Factors Society Bulletin 32(5), 1–3 (1988)
9. Klein, G.: Sources of Power: How People make Decisions. MIT Press, Cambridge (1999)
10. Mirel, B.: Applied constructivism for user documentation. Journal of Business and Technical Communication 12(1), 7–49 (1998)
11. Redish, J.: Expanding usability testing to evaluate complex systems. Journal of Usability Studies 2(3), 102–111 (2007)
12. Schriver, K.: Dynamics in Document Design. Wiley, New York (1996)
13. Woods, D., Roth, E.: Cognitive engineering: Human problem solving with tools. Human Factors 30(4), 415–430 (1988)

A Usability Model for Government Web Sites

Deborah S. Carstens and Annie Becker

Florida Institute of Technology
150 W. University Blvd.
Melbourne, Florida 32901, USA
{carstens,abecker}@fit.edu

Abstract. A usability model is proposed for developers of government Web sites. The model is based on the findings of a study to identify potential usability barriers of state government Web sites when accessing information on government accountability. The model was then applied during a heuristic evaluation of fifty government Web sites. The model is based on four core usability components consisting of readability, reading complexity, navigation and supportability. The model is discussed in terms of its practical application for improving state government Web sites for the purposes of enhancing the usefulness and ease of use in navigating state government Web sites.

Keywords: Usability, Government Accountability, Government Web sites.

1 Introduction

A usability model is proposed for developers of government Web sites. The model is based on the findings of a study to identify potential usability barriers of state government Web sites when accessing information on government accountability. Application of the model took place during a heuristic evaluation of fifty government Web sites. The model is based on four core usability components consisting of readability, reading complexity, navigation and supportability. The reading component is comprised of font size, font type, resizing capabilities and screen reader compatibility. The reading complexity component is based on the Flesch Reading Ease score. The navigation component considers the use of breadcrumb trails, links leading to external sites, table of contents and images without labels used to navigate as well as the amount of clicks necessary to access information. The supportability component takes into consideration the amount of support information displayed on a Web site such as contact information, live online help, privacy policy and accessibility policy as well as whether feedback from a user of a Web site can be submitted.

The model is discussed in terms of its practical application for improving state government Web sites for the purposes of enhancing the usefulness and ease of use in

C. Stephanidis (Ed.): Posters, Part I, HCII 2011, CCIS 173, pp. 108–112, 2011.
© Springer-Verlag Berlin Heidelberg 2011

navigating state government Web sites. Web developers of State government sites may find these results insightful in promoting site usability for all citizens of all ages.

2   Web Site Usability

Application of Human Computer Interaction (HCI) in technology results in usability, universality, and usefulness [9]. Bainbridge [3: 4] defines usability as, "a user interface is the aspect of a Web site (or application) that the user interacts with and experiences first-hand." Usability is a quantitative and qualitative measurement of the design of a user interface, grouped into five key factors: learnability, efficiency, memorability, errors, and satisfaction." These five factors are based on Nielson's [9] five attributes associated with usability. Learnability refers to the ease of use in learning the system. Efficiency looks at how productive the system user can be once having learned the software. Memorability refers to the user being able to recall how to use the system even after a certain period of time has elapsed. Satisfaction is attributed to how pleasant the Web site or system is to use taking into account user frustration associated with using a site.

Web usability research has extended to include Web designs that are usable by older adults and those with vision deficiencies or impairments [4&5]. Web designs that do not take into account vision, for example, may pose barriers to a large user group. According to the American Foundation for the Blind [1&2], approximately 6.2 million older adults (65 and over) have vision loss and approximately 9 million Americans, 45 to 64, have vision loss. Furthermore, 1in 12 males or 8% of the male population is colorblind, 10 million individuals wear glasses and are still visually impaired and over 1million individuals are legally blind.

The study, described in this paper, builds upon recent studies conducted by Becker, Carstens and Linton [6] and Carstens and Becker [7]. The study customized heuristics to take into account both user profiles (e.g., vision associated with normal aging) and the objective of using the Web site (e.g., informational links provided on a homepage). This customization is done to gather meaningful data about Web usability associated with a particular site. Bainbridge [3] and Carstens, Feizi and Malone [8], for example, tested Web sites for travel sales using specific heuristics related to online accommodations. Becker assessed the usability of health-related Web sites by older adults in search of health resources [5].

3   Methodology

A usability model for developers of government Web sites was developed and tested. The methodology utilized is listed below:

Step 1: The model was first developed based on the findings of a study to identify potential usability barriers of state government Web sites when accessing information on government accountability. This specific study that resulted in the development of the model followed the steps below:

Step 1.1: Identification of state government Web sites with cost and performance data made accessible to the public. The Web sites selected in this study included FloridaPerforms.com, VirginiaPerforms.com, and the State of Washington Transportation Improvement Board GMAP Performance Management Dashboard.

Step 1.2: Development of usability criteria to measure and assess each of the three government Web sites in terms of potential usability barriers. The criteria used to assess each Web site was focused on usability by citizens from all adult age groups. The criteria consisted of: text resizing capabilities, screen reader compatibility, readability, navigation, understandability, consistency, reading complexity, errors, number of years of data, cited source information and availability of help information.

Step 1.3: Evaluation of each state government Web site utilizing the usability criteria. The screen reader tool, WebAnywhere, was used in the evaluation of each site to take into account usability from the perspective of vision impairment or blindness. WebAnywhere is a web-based screen reader developed at the University of Washington with funding support by the National Science Foundation. The tool enables blind people to access the web from any computer with a sound card. For more information, visit http://webanywhere.cs.washington.edu/.

Step 1.4: Identification of potential usability barriers that include older adult users and those with vision impairments.

Step 1.5: Identification of model guidelines for developers of government Web sites to use in pursuit of universal usability by all constituents.

Step 2: The model was then applied during a heuristic evaluation of fifty government Web sites. This specific study that resulted in the development of the model followed the steps below:

Step 2.1: Identification of the fifty state Web sites.

Step 2.2: Test the model that was developed from the first study findings by evaluating each state Web site utilizing the usability criteria in the model.

Step 2.3: Identification potential usability barriers of the fifty Web sites that include elder adult users and those with vision impairments.

Step 2.4: Identification of the practical application of the research study in providing usability guidelines to developers of Web sites based on the heuristic evaluation performed.

Step 3: Identification of the final version of the model that provides usability guidelines to developers of government Web sites.

4   Results

The research findings are in the form of a proposed usability model which consists of guidelines for developers of government Web sites to utilize. The model was developed and applied in studies and is displayed in Fig. 1.

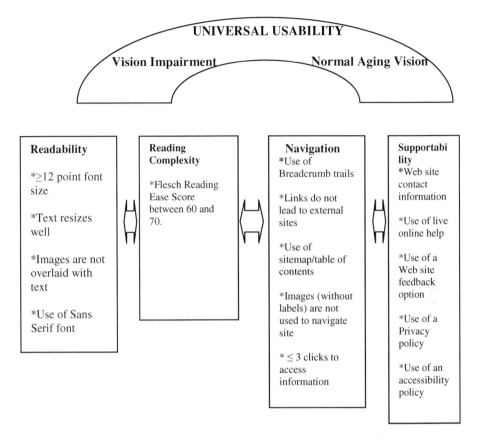

Fig. 1. Usability Web Site Model to Promote Universal Usability

5   Conclusion

The usability Web site model to promote universal usability is based on four components each of which are discussed in this section.

Readability. There are design components that may adversely impact readability. These components consist of: (1) Text format on sites being 12 point font size or smaller is difficult to read; (2) Resizing text option should enable the text size to be increased without distorting the web site graphics and text; (3) Images that have text overlay make the reading of text difficult; (4) Text exceeding three pages in length are better served by providing multiple pages of information versus one very long page of text; and (5) Use of non-sans serif text format is difficult to read.

Reading Complexity. The Flesch Reading Ease readability score formula rates text on a 100-point scale based on the average number of syllables per word and words per sentence. The higher the Flesch Reading Ease score, the easier it is to understand the document. For most standard documents, aim for a Flesch Reading Ease score of approximately 60, standard score, to 70, fairly easy. For more information on Flesch Reading Ease score, visit http://rfptemplates.technologyevaluation.com/Readability-Scores/Flesch-Reading-Ease-Readability-Score.html.

Navigation. There are several design components to consider in determining if a Web site is intuitive for a user. Design components that adversely impact the use of the Web site: (1) Breadcrumb trails are not used to provide navigational support; (2) External links or menu options transfer a user to an external link where the user is directed outside of the initial site without notification about leaving the initial e-government site; (3) Table of Contents do not exist to assist the user in navigating throughout a site; (4) Images without any form of labeling (labeling is needed for a screen reader tool) are used to provide navigation to users and (5) Users have to click through more than three links to access desired information.

Supportability. There are several design components that may impact supportability for a user: (1) Lack of contact information available on the Web site; (2) Web site does not have live online help such as online chat options; (3) Web site does not have feedback options for users to provide comments for improvement of a web site; (4) Site has no privacy policy listed which is a legal document that discloses some or all of the ways a party gathers, uses, discloses and manages a user's data; and (5) Site has no accessibility policy identifying how users with disabilities can access the web site thereby ensuring equal access to electronic and information technologies.

References

1. American Foundation for the Blind. Normal changes in the aging eye (2004), http://www.afb.org/Section.asp?SectionID=35&TopicID=212&SubTopicID=39 (retrieved April 26, 2009)
2. American Foundation for the Blind. Normal changes in the aging eye (2009), http://www.afb.org/Section.asp?SectionID=35&TopicID=212&SubTopicID=39 (retrieved March 10, 2011)
3. Bainbridge, A.: Hotel booking process: Design & usability (1.02) (February 2003), http://www.tourcms.com/company/research/pdf/hotel_booking_process_february2003.pdf (retrieved March 11, 2011)
4. Becker, S.A.: E-government Visual Accessibility for Older Adult Users. Social Science Computer Review 22(1), 11–23 (2004)
5. Becker, S.A.: A Study of Web Usability for Older Adults Seeking Online Health Resources. ACM Transactions on Human-Computer Interaction 11(4), 387–406 (2004)
6. Becker, S.A., Carstens, D.S., Linton, T.M.: Heuristic Evaluation of State Electronic Government to Promote Usability for Citizens of All Age. Journal of Management & Engineering Integration (2010)
7. Carstens, D.S., Becker, S.A.: A Heuristic Study on the Usability of State Government Performance Data Web Sites. Issues in Innovation 4(1), 15–44 (2009)
8. Carstens, D.S., Feizi, S., Malone, L.: Traveling Abroad? A Usability Assessment of Travel Sales Web sites. Journal of Management & Engineering Integration 2(1), 17–24 (2009)
9. Nielson, J.: Usability Engineering. Morgan Kaufmann, San Diego (1993)

Usability Analysis of Website with Unconventional Layout

Ro-Han Chang and Ying-Ya Su

Department of Commercial Design, Chung Yuan Christian University, No.200, Zhongbei Rd.,
Zhongli City, Taoyuan County 320, Taiwan
rohan@cycu.edu.tw, newstory0113@gmail.com

Abstract. It is a vision that internet bandwidth will continue to expand and there is more and more interactive multimedia being applied to websites. When users browse the website quickly, they only remember the unique characteristics of the website. However, a lot of research on web design has been conducted, yet there is no new research on the technique and usability of website with unconventional layouts. When users browse a website, they may feel frustrated with the complicated content and structure. Therefore, it is a challenge to create an innovative website with fine usability. This proposal will not only analyze the technique of the innovative website with unconventional layout, but also focus on the usability. The proposal is as follows: (a.) Catalogue the technique and focus on the style from the innovative website with unconventional layout. (b.) Analyze the usability of website with unconventional layouts. (c.) Generate and discuss the feedback from the users in regards to how they feel after browsing. Basically, the research is to be conducted by studying the recorded document theories, interviewing experts, focusing on certain website users, and other results. After this research is conducted, generalizing the principle of the website with unconventional layouts will take place. The result will be referred to by future web designers working in industries where such information will be of value to them.

Keywords: Web Design, Interactive Multimedia, Layout, Usability.

1 Introduction

The internet has expanded fast and the traditional website layout can no longer satisfy browsers' needs. A website with unconventional layout has to be acknowledged in order to deliver the impression of the brand. When users browse an interactive website, they may feel frustrated with the complicated content structure of the innovative website with unconventional layout. Therefore, it is a challenge to create a website with unconventional layout with fine usability. This research has organized the information of website with unconventional layouts, analyzed different techniques and discussed the usability.

C. Stephanidis (Ed.): Posters, Part I, HCII 2011, CCIS 173, pp. 113–117, 2011.

2   Literature Review

2.1   Traditional Website Layout Design

In accordance with the traditional website layout regulation from academic experts (see the Table 1).

Table 1. Generalize website with unconventional layout layouts

Layouts	Definition
Homepage, Impression	Mainly use photos to fill up 2/3 of the content
Two Column, Center Align	Separate the content into two columns
Three Column	Separate the content into three columns
Blog, Ring, Single, Structural pattern, Composited structural pattern	Separate the content into two or three columns
Gallery, Full scene	Display the shrunk images and arrange them in order
Satellite	Focus point located in the center and elements spread out from the focal point
Spread Out	Less restriction but more freedom on presentation

2.2   Technique of Website Design

Generalize website with unconventional layout layouts (see the Table 2). There are five types of techniques from the website with unconventional layouts as seen in Table 3 below.

Table 2. Generalize website with unconventional layout layouts

Author (Year)	Generalize technique of website design
Li, S.Y.(2004) [1]	Children's interactive website: 1.Map menu 2.Mobile Menu 3.Frame Menu 4.3D Spacious Menu 5.Non-Frame Menu 6.Object Menu 7.Node Menu 8. Atmosphere menu.
Chen, J.S., Tsai,J. Y.(2005) [2]	Children's learning websites: 1.Cartoon Theme 2.Story Theme 3.Visual Theme 4.Block Theme 5.Frame Mixture 6.Multi Information 7.Frame Composed.
Hong, Y.L.(2007) [3]	Example from the international interactive multimedia competition in 2006, lists the techniques as follows: 1.Deconstruct 2.Copy and Paste 3.Transform 4.Variance 5.Overlap 6.Narrative 7.Gaming.

Table 3. Definition of technique

Technique	Definition
Map exploring	Build the web content like a map.
Interactive Gaming	High entertainment gaming to interact with the browsers.
Triggering	Use buttons to trigger animation.
Spacious	Guide browses to different virtual scenes.
Atmosphere	Perform different styles to create an atmosphere for users' satisfaction.

2.3 Discussion of Usability

This research applies the learning ability and satisfaction of the five behaviors from Jakob Nielson[4]. The next section will discuss the website with unconventional layouts through experiment and questionnaire and analyze the problems and the content of the website layouts. There are different influences on users when browsing interactive websites during the same circumstance. To gain such a response, Table 4 outlines the criterion upon which the websites will be ranked. The outcome will be compared to the recorded documents written by Preece[5] and Liou, Y.H. [6]. To conclude, an index of usability will be prepared and impersonal information from the questionnaire will be gathered (Table 5).

Table 4. Questionnaire on user's satisfaction criterion

Criterion	Definition
Consistency	Picture and text in the interface presented in consistency.
Simplicity	Provide a clean, visible function to increase user willingness to use.
Compatible	Apply an environment related to the user allowing the function to be understood faster.
Feed Back	Enable the user to communicate with the interface.
Readability	Avoid difficult vocabulary.
Theme	Create a theme page separate from the other pages.

Table 5. Questionnaire on user's feelings criterion

Criterion	Definition
Aesthetic	Visuals.
Interactive	Inspire creativity and imagination.
Affection	Self –experience.
Entertainment	Fun and interesting.
Learning motivation	Motivate to browse.

3 Method

3.1 Collect Information from Websites

Books (WEB DESIGN INDEX 7, WEB DESIGN INDEX 8, WEB DESIGN INDEX 9) between November 2010 to February 2011, recommendation from experts and 50 websites.

3.2 Experiment

(1) Interview with experts: Interview three experts who have more than three years working experience on multimedia field and spend 5 hours on the internet daily. Generalize the presentation of fifty websites and choose the best five. (2) Test usability: Invite 6 subjects, 3 who have website design background and 3 who do not. Users follow instructions and browse website samples. (3) Questionnaire: Invite the subjects to complete the two questionnaires (satisfaction and feeling).

3.3 Task

Subjects will browse each website sample which includes three tasks (Table 6).

Table 6. The purpose of the tasks

Task	Attribute	Purpose
1	Visual image	Subject enters the first page of content and learning ability is tested.
2	Layer Framework	Subject enters the second page of content and observes the usability of the framework of the website.
3	Interface Configuration	Subject finds out where the contact menu is and discusses the interface configuration of the website.

3.4 Procedure of Experiment

Excluding the features of the traditional website, this study found five main features of the website with unconventional layout. The experiment the questionnaire was then conducted.

4 Result

This research has conducted three points of view: (1)Catalogue the presentation of the website with unconventional layout: from the 50 website samples we found, Atmosphere website was applied the most, followed by triggering and map exploring websites. (2)The problems of usability when users browse the website with unconventional layout: interactive gaming in the visual image attributes and interface configuration attributes easily confused browsers. Triggering takes more time in the layer framework attribute. (3) Feeling of the users toward the website with unconventional layouts: according to the questionnaire of users feeling, we found that the buttons to navigate around the website (map exploring) related to its meaning. The browsers had more control on interactive websites resulting in a higher level of interest among users. Complicated tables confuse the users. The interface of the interactive website is the simplest to understand. Spacious websites take the longest time to download. Atmosphere websites make browsing smoother for the user resulting in a greater use of this technique.

5 Conclusion and Discussion

Finally, this study provides recommendations for the website with unconventional layout: (1)Consistency: Exploring navigator needs to link with the information content and the images. (2)Interaction: Use hyper linking navigator to increase the interaction with buttons in order to raise the visual attraction and reduce any form of wrong judgment. (3)Guiding: The website should display the progress when a user is browsing between different pages. (4)Interpretation: Suggestions are made to use animation to present the manual. It could draw user's attention more than texts. When users are familiar with the navigator, they could skip and enter the homepage. (5)Hint : For first time users who are browsing and feel confused with the website with unconventional layout. The website needs to provide some hints incase the user is lost.

According to the research, people who have website design background spent less time on the menu but beginners were easily confused with the website with unconventional layouts. Even though the visual is interesting, they would feel troubled and give up on navigating. Therefore, this study hope the website with unconventional layout designers would focus on every age group of browsers and make sure the usability is for all people of all skill levels.

References

1. Li, S.Y.: An Application of Dynamic Navigation Interface on Children's Website Design. National Digital Library of Theses and Dissertations in Taiwan, Taipei (2004)
2. Chen, J.S., Tsai, J.Y.: A Study on the Style of Domestic Websites for Children's Learning in Arts. Journal of Ergonomic Study 7(1), 47–54 (2005)
3. Hong, Y.L.: The Creative Themes, Methods, Styles of Post-Modernism for Digital Media Design–A Case Study of Interactive Media Awards 2006. Journal of Design 1, 40–52 (2007)
4. Nielsen, J.: Usability Engineering. Academic Press, USA (1993)
5. Preece, J.: A Guide to Usability: Human Factors in Computing. Addison-Wesley, UK (1993)
6. Liou, Y.H.: The Study of the Use of Visual Situation in Multimedia CAI - the Case of Interactive Visual Situated Websites. National Digital Library of Theses and Dissertations in Taiwan, Taipei (2006)

Methodologies for Evaluating Player Experience in Game Play

Kimberly Chu, Chui Yin Wong, and Chee Weng Khong

Universal Usability and Interaction Design (UUID) SIG,
Interface Design Department, Faculty of Creative Multimedia,
Multimedia University, 63100 Cyberjaya, Selangor, Malaysia
{kimberly.chu,cywong,cwkhong}@mmu.edu.my

Abstract. Player experience constitutes one of the most significant factors in determining the success rate of games. Games which do not provide enormous user experience usually will not gain intense interest from players. The concept of player experience is normally interchanged with concepts such as fun, flow, fulfillment, enjoyment, engagement, satisfaction, pleasure and playability. In this paper, we reviewed, analyzed and discussed the different attributes and methodologies used to evaluate player experience for game play. We concluded the finding in a playability matrix based on an analysis of methodologies for evaluating player experience in game play. The matrix was constructed from literature analysis, which comprised of attributes consisting of qualitative and quantitative, verbal and non-verbal, empirical and non-empirical methods.

Keywords: Player experience, measurement, game play, playability.

1 Introduction

In the past decade, game industries have been flourishing on various platforms from consoles, to personal computers (PC) to mobile devices. The trend is also coupled with enhanced graphic processing power, advanced user interfaces and increased complexity in game play. The number of players grows exponentially due to the increased enjoyability of game play. Therefore, in Human-Computer Interaction (HCI) discipline, there are a number of research contributions, which are related to the methodologies for evaluating player experience for game play.

The concept of player experience is often interchangeable with other concepts, such as fun, flow, fulfillment, engagement, satisfaction, pleasure and playability. Player experience does not depend on a particular mode of emotion, but encompass a wide variety of emotions that contribute to game player experience. For example, while playing game, players experience fear, excitement, happiness, alert, anger, relief, pleasure, hope, discouragement, proud, joy, and distress. These different modes of emotions eventually form the elements of gaming experience. In addition, Clanton [3] and Federoff [6] mentioned three aspects of gaming, i.e. interface, mechanics and game play, which highly affected the level of player's experience. Nevertheless, the concept of player experience is fairly difficult to distinguish as they seem to be as

C. Stephanidis (Ed.): Posters, Part I, HCII 2011, CCIS 173, pp. 118–122, 2011.

intangible as they are appealing, which requires hands-on skills and grasping the experience of enjoyment [15, 18]. So far, the concept itself seems fragmented, with various viewpoints, and it has not defined a cohesive integrated framework [11]. Sweetser and Wyeth [16] also highlighted that there was no integrated model on how players evaluate their enjoyment level in games. Moreover, Bernhaupt [1] addressed there was no general framework on what methods shall be used to assess interaction concept on games. As a result, this paper aims to review and analyze the existing methodologies for evaluating player experience, particularly on game play.

2   A Review of Methodologies for Evaluating Player Experience

Numerous research studies from different domains have been conducted in academia and industries to evaluate player experience. Csikzentmihalyi [4] introduced the study of "flow" where it defines the optimal experience of enjoyment regardless of age, gender or social class. On one hand, researchers from the usability domain [5, 6, 12] adapted traditional usability methods such as heuristics to evaluate playability in games. For instance, Malone [11] constructed a list of heuristic guidelines for educational games, but it is based on designing enjoyable interfaces rather than player experience itself. Federoff [6] compiled a list of heuristics by reviewing literature in games industry guidelines and did a case study at a game development company. In addition, Desurvire et. al. [5] created Heuristics Evaluation for Playability (HEP) from games design literature, HEP results were then cross validated the findings from user studies. User studies act as a benchmark for game evaluation tools in HEP, whilst Federoff [6] and Malone [11] did not involve any users in their heuristics studies. Desurvire stressed that although certain player issues were determined through HEP; nonetheless, some of the problems could only be found by direct player observation. Sweetser and Wyeth [16] mentioned although there were many heuristics studies in literature, however, there is a need to integrate these heuristics into a validated model to assess player enjoyment for games. As a result, they created GameFlow and validated through expert evaluators' point of view. There was still no direct user involvement in their method.

On the other hand, researchers in the physiological design domain of Human Computer Interaction (HCI) employ physiological metrics for user evaluation and optimizing relationship between human and technological systems. Mandryk [13] conducted a study of continuous emotion in games based on physiological responses such as Galvanic Skin Response (GSR), electrocardiography (EKG), and electromyography of face (EMG smiling and EMG frowning). Heart rate (HR) was computed from the EKG signal. The author compared the modeled emotion from users and reported subjective evaluation on a 5-point likert scale. Affect Grid was adapted as part of their modeled emotion. However, other perspectives have seen limited success in adopting physiology to indentify emotional states [2]. In addition, Zaman and Smith [19] presented studies to measure fun through FaceReader, where it distinguished six emotional states. They compared the results of FaceReader with other sources such as user questionnaires and researcher's loggings. He found that user questionnaire did not provide precision as it reflected more on the content of the application or the outcome of the task (successful or not) rather than fun or enjoyment. Sykes and Brown [17] investigated a player's state of arousal, relating to the pressure to press buttons on a gamepad. The results indicated that it was possible to determine game player's arousal by the pressure they used when controlling the gamepad. However, there was no measure of emotional valence for game players in this study. Hazlett [7] used facial electromyography (EMG) as a measure for positive and negative emotional valence. On one hand, facial EMG is limited to only positive and negative result as the method was not able to recognize discrete emotions. Users are interviewed on which factors that were positive and negative to them based on the events of the game. However, by using various physiological methods, they need to ensure participants had no qualms being attached with wires and connectors, or else it would appear to intrude participants emotionally, thus affecting the final result. Recent developments on questionnaire have included dimensions such as tension, frustration or negative affect. Ijsesslsteijn et. al. [9] suggested using Games Experience Questionnaire (GEQ) as a qualitative questionnaire to understand player experience in games after the game play session.

3   Analysis of Methodologies

Based on literature reviews, we categorize the methodologies for player experience into three categories, general research methods (qualitative versus quantitative), instruments for measuring emotions (verbal versus non-verbal), and measurements for pleasurable design products (empirical versus non-empirical). Table 1 shows the three main evaluation categories for evaluating player experience in game play.

3.1   General Research Methods: Qualitative vs. Quantitative

Qualitative research concentrates on exploring and understanding user's perceptions and interactions. Generally this research approach generates non-numerical data where it documents the experience of players. On the other hand, quantitative research produces numerical data or data that can be converted into numbers [14]. The qualitative manner allows the evaluator to write down their experiences during game play, and quantitative method provides the statistics to show how interested there are. As for verbal and non verbal diagnostics, not every player shows their emotions or talk freely during game play. During game play, players have difficulty to concentrate and talk about their experience at the same time. Therefore, both methods should be adopted to get a more objective and thorough analysis for evaluation.

3.2   Instruments for Measuring Emotions: Verbal vs. Non-verbal

Hirschman [8] states that researchers prefer to develop their own approaches to measure emotion. A distinction is made between non verbal (objective) and verbal (subjective) instruments. Non verbal measures the expressive or the physiological element of experience emotion evaluated by facial or vocal expressions while verbal instruments assesses the subjective feeling component of emotion evaluated through self report, rating scales and verbal protocols [19].

3.3 Measurements for Pleasurable Design Products: Empirical vs. Non-empirical

In designing pleasurable products, Jordan [10] highlighted two methods to measure the relation of understanding people, products and evaluating design concepts, that is (i) *non-empirical*, which requires no participant involvement, and (ii) *empirical*, which involves user engagement in the design process. Both empirical and non-empirical methods are important when it involves players during the game play, especially at the final evaluation stage. However, the non-empirical method is also crucial, particularly at the beginning of creating or designing game play, as experts are able to provide greater deal of feedback for further game play development.

Table 1. A review of methodologies for evaluating player experience in game play

		Heuristic for Game Experience	Heuristics Evaluation for Playability (HEP)	Game Flow	Face Reader	EMG	GEQ	Emotion Through Finger Pressure	Physiological methods (GSR, EMG, EKG, HR)
General Research Methods	Qualitative	√	√	√	√		√		
	Quantitative					√	√	√	√
Instruments to measure Emotion	Verbal	√		√		√			
	Non-Verbal		√		√			√	√
Pleasurable Product Measurement	Empirical				√			√	√
	Non-Empirical	√	√	√	√	√			

To summarize, we suggest an adoption of the three methods from qualitative and quantitative, verbal and non verbal, and lastly empirical and non empirical in order to provide a comprehensive approach to evaluate player experience for game play.

4 Summary

With regards to the perception of game play experience, it is different for individual players. Hence, both the expert evaluator and game player are crucial in assessing the elements involved in game play and the level of game player experience. This paper examined and reviewed methodologies that evaluate player's experience and analyzed the different attributes through literature studies. Here we recommend three main categories consisting of general research methods, instruments to measure emotions and pleasurable product measurement. A mixed method approach suggested in this paper provides a holistic approach in determining player experience for game play.

References

[1] Bernhaupt, R., Eckschlager, M., Tscheligi, M.: Methods for Evaluating Games – How to Measure Usability and User Experience in Games? In: Proc. ACE 2007, pp. 309–310. ACM Press, New York (2007)

[2] Cacioppo, J.T., Bernston, G.G., Larsen, J.T., Poehlmann, K.M., Ito, T.A.: The Psychophysiology of Emotion. In: Lewis, M., Haviland–Jones, J.M. (eds.) Handbook of Emotions. The Guilford Press, New York (2000)

[3] Clanton, C.: An Interpretation Demonstration of Computer Game Design. In: Proc. of CHI 1998' Summary: Human Factors in Computing Systems, CHI 1998, pp. 1–2 (1998)

[4] Csikszentmihalyi, M.: Flow: The Psychology of Optimal Experience. Harper Perennial, New York (1990)

[5] Desurvire, H., Caplan, M., Toth, J.A.: Using Heuristics to Evaluate the Playability of Games. In: Extended Abstract, CHI 2004, pp. 1509–1512. ACM Press, New York (2004)

[6] Federoff, M.: Heuristics and Usability Guidelines for The Creation and evaluation of Fun in Video Games (February 2009),
http://www.melissafederoff.com/thesis.html

[7] Hazlett, R.: Measuring Emotional Valence during Interactive Experience: Boys at Video Game Play. In: Proc. CHI 2006, pp. 1023–1026. ACM Press, New York (2006)

[8] Hirschman, E.C., Holbrook, M.B.: Hedonic Consumption: Emerging concepts, methods and propositions. Journal of Marketing 46, 92–101 (1982)

[9] Ijsselsteijn, W.A., van den Hoogen, W.H.M., Klimmt, C., de Kort, Y.A.W., Lindley, C., Mathiak, K., Poels, K., Ravaja, N., Turpeinen, M., Vorderer, P.: Measuring the Experience of Digital Game Enjoyment. In: Proc. of Measuring Behavior 2008, pp. 88–89 (2008)

[10] Jordan, P.: Designing Pleasurable Products: An Introduction to the New Human Factors. Taylor and Francis, London (2000)

[11] Law, E., Roto, V., Vermeeren, A.P.O.S., Kort, J., Hassenzahl, M.: Towards a Shared Definition of User Experience. In: Proc. SIGs, CHI 2008, pp. 2395–2398 (2008)

[12] Malone, T.W.: Heuristics for Designing Enjoyable User Interfaces: Lessons from Computer Games. In: Thomas, J.C., Schneider, M.L. (eds.) Human Factors in Computing System, Norwood. Ablex Publishing Corporation, NJ (1982)

[13] Mandryk, R.L., Atkins, M.S., Inkpen, K.M.: A Continuous and Objective Evaluation of Emotional Experience with Interactive Play Environments. In: Proc. CHI 2006, pp. 1027–1036. ACM Press, New York (2006)

[14] Neill, J.: Qualitative & Quantitative Research (March 2009),
http://wilderdom.com/research/
QualitativeVersusQuantitativeResearch.html

[15] Overbeeke, C.J., Djajadiningrat, J.P., Hummels, C.C.M., Wensveen, S.A.G.: Beauty in Usability: Forget About the Ease of Use? In: Green, W.S., Jordan, P.W. (eds.) Pleasure with Products: Beyond Usability, pp. 9–18. Taylor & Francis, London (2002)

[16] Sweetser, P., Wyeth, P.: GameFlow: A Model for Evaluating Player Enjoyment in Games. ACM Computers in Entertainment 3(3), article 3A (2005)

[17] Sykes, J., Brown, S.: Affective Gaming: Measuring Emotion through Gamepad. In: Proc. of SIGCHI Conference on Human Factors in Computing Systems (CHI 2003), pp. 732–733. ACM Press, New York (2003)

[18] Wittgenstein, L.: Philosophical investigations. Blackwell, Oxford (1953)

[19] Zaman, B., Smith, T.S.: The FaceReader: Measuring instant fun of use. In: Proc. of the 4th Nordic Conference on Human-Computer Interaction, pp. 457–460 (2006)

How Does This Look? Desirability Methods for Evaluating Visual Design

Edward S. De Guzman and Julie Schiller

Autodesk, Inc., One Market St., Suite 500, San Franciso, California 94105, USA
{Edward.DeGuzman,Julie.Schiller}@autodesk.com

Abstract. Previous studies show that traditional usability evaluation methods can be problematic for collecting feedback on visual design [1]. Desirability studies have been used by usability practitioners to collect feedback on the affective response to interactive systems, but none focus on assessing visual design. We describe the Visual Design Card Sort (VDCS), a desirability research method for collecting visual design feedback from domain experts. We also present a case study where VDCS was used to collect visual design feedback from expert users of Computer-Aided Design (CAD) software. Additionally, we propose a set of analyses for looking at data from desirability studies from different perspectives. Future research is needed to validate some of the assumptions made in designing VDCS and to understand how findings from VDCS compare to other desirability research methods and traditional evaluation techniques.

Keywords: Desirability, visual design, methods, usability testing.

1 Introduction

User-centered design traditionally includes iterative cycles of designing, building, and evaluating. Early iterations of the design may be lower in fidelity (e.g., paper prototypes), but more mature iterations may include a greater degree of interactivity and fidelity of design. In these later iterations, feedback on the *visual design* of the system (e.g., color palette, imagery, typography) becomes increasingly relevant. Traditional usability evaluation methods can be difficult to adapt for accurately assessing visual design in later design iterations. Feedback for visual design is less about the user's ability to accomplish tasks and more about the affective response to a design.

Desirability studies have emerged as an approach for measuring the affective response to design. Desirability research methods collect attitudinal reactions to a design rather than behavioral reactions. The data collected helps designers understand why different design directions alter the emotion of a user experience. Desirability studies can be coupled with traditional usability studies to achieve several benefits:

- In the ISO definition of usability (9241-11) the term is broken down into three components: effectiveness, efficiency, and satisfaction. Considering desirability

C. Stephanidis (Ed.): Posters, Part I, HCII 2011, CCIS 173, pp. 123–127, 2011.

as a component of satisfaction, analyzing and responding to feedback from these studies it can positively impact the overall system's usability.

- First impressions of a system can be positively impacted by designing for usability. Tractinsky [8] observed that a user with a positive first impression of a website based on visual design may be influenced to perceive the website's usability and utility in a similarly positive way. Lindgaard [5] further suggests that negative first impressions, once formed, take more work to change than impressions that start off as positive or even neutral.

- In some domains of interactive systems, there is an observed link between desirability and trust. For example, design quality was found to be among the features that enhance the feeling of trust in e-Commerce websites. [3]

One common approach to conducting a desirability study is to use post-task and post-study questionnaires [4] focused on desirability. Another approach is to use card sorting exercises, a technique traditionally used to inform the structure of a website or product. While several groups have reported case studies of desirability studies [1,2,7,9], we feel there are several research areas worth exploring. First, it is unclear how desirability methods can be adapted to focus on *visual design*. Second, a design space of analysis visualizations of desirability data would help practitioners effectively communicate findings to stakeholders. Finally, desirability research methods need to be optimized to mitigate the costs in time to conduct the research and analyze the data.

In this paper we propose a method, a Visual Design Card Sort (VDCS) for rapid collection of visual design feedback from domain experts. We report on the results of a study using VDCS and present a set of visualizations that provide multiple perspectives on the data. Finally, we propose future directions for analyzing the data and for optimizing the method itself by exploring variables in the study design to iterate the process to be highly efficient and agile.

2   Visual Design Card Sort

In this section we describe the Visual Design Card Sort, a new method for conducting desirability studies to evaluate visual design.

Participants are seated at a table with a monitor and a set of visual design reaction cards (described later in this section). Participants are then shown a set of images, one at a time. Once the image appears on the monitor, the participant has three to five minutes to select between three to five visual design reaction cards that best answers the question, *"How does this look?"* Blank product reaction cards are provided for when the participant wants to volunteer their own word to describe their reaction. After the participant has selected a set of reaction cards, he/she is asked to explain why the card was chosen before moving on to the next image.

This method for assessing desirability differs from the studies mentioned in Related Work in the following ways:

- This method uses Visual Design Reaction Cards, a subset of the Microsoft Product Reaction Cards from the Desirability Toolkit. Two researchers performed a card filtering exercise to inform and validate the set of cards, only keeping those that are relevant for providing feedback on the visual treatment of a design.

- We assume participants have a minimum degree of expertise in the domain covered by the design. Since participants have only a few minutes to evaluate a design, we suspect that expertise is needed for what Norman [6] calls "behavioral-level processing" to occur (e.g., understanding metaphors and navigation structures, developing appropriate mental models).

- VDCS is done at the start of the research session and feedback is collected after three to five minutes of review. We adapted the Microsoft method [1] to leverage previous work that opinions on aesthetics are made as soon as 50ms [5]. We gave participants significantly more time to review the design so that behavioral-level processing to visual stimuli can occur and influence the reaction guided by visceral processing [6].

3 Case Study

In November 2010, the Visual Design Card Sort was used to collect feedback on a design for a future Web service from Autodesk. Participants were screened against pre-defined criteria: familiarity with one or more of the core Autodesk products and domain expertise from working as an architect, designer, or CAD manager. Six participants were recruited for this study (1 female, 5 male).

Over seven images, the six participants selected 133 Visual Design Reaction Cards. The cards were coded (one researcher coding the results, one researcher validating the coding) into two valences—"positive" and "neutral/negative" based on the rationale for each card choice. 93 cards (70%) were positive and 40 were neutral/negative.

Fig. 1. Word cloud from Visual Design Card Sort case study

4 Discussion

In this section we propose a set of analyses allowing the researcher or stakeholder to look at the data from a desirability study from multiple perspectives.

Word clouds (Figure 1) present the space of words selected while visually showing the importance of certain data points—cards selected more than once appear larger in the cloud. This is effective in presenting a broad overview of the data *for one design* to stakeholders. The Affect Convergence visualization (Figure 2, left) shows the data sorted by valence distribution—the proportion of positive cards selected are plotted above the x-axis (0% to 100%) and the proportion of neutral/negative cards are plotted below (-100% to 0%). This figure shows to what degree participants agreed in having positive or negative reactions to one design and how this convergence of opinion compares across multiple designs. The Affect Consistency visualization (Figure 2, right) highlights responses that are consistent across participants, only showing cards selected *more than once*. This is a visualization adapted from one proposed in [1] to give stakeholders a view of the data that reflects *popular responses* and their corresponding affective valence.

In this section we build upon existing desirability methods research with new directions for visualizing the data collected from desirability studies. We do not advocate a single visualization over the others. Rather, a "scorecard view" showing the set of visualizations for a design provides a nuanced view of the data and helps design teams and stakeholders in comparing and critiquing their designs.

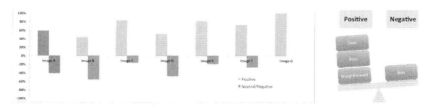

Fig. 2. Affect Convergence (left) and Affect Consistency (right) Visualizations

5   Conclusion and Future Work

Desirability studies are a class of research methods for collecting affective responses to interactive systems. While use of these methods have been documented in case studies and adopted by usability practitioners, there has been little research and innovation in desirability research methods focused exclusively on assessing visual design. Furthermore, a design space of visualizations for presentation of data from desirability studies does not exist. To address some of these open research issues, we present the Visual Design Card Sort (VDCS), a desirability research method focused on collecting feedback from domain experts on visual design. We present the results of using VDCS to assess the visual design of a future Autodesk Web Service, including a set of visualizations for viewing the data from different perspectives.

Future directions include validation of some of the assumptions made which guided the design of this research method. For example, to confirm this method is sensitive to expertise, we propose repeating the case study with *novice* users of CAD programs. We suspect that novice users are more subject to the acquiescence bias and would provide a significantly higher proportion of positive feedback than expert users.

VDCS shows one design for three to five minutes, a relatively longer exposure time than the minimum 50ms reported by Lindgaard for expressing "like" or "dislike" of a website. Further research can investigate the effects of varying the duration of exposure and number of images presented. We suspect that the longer presentation and single stimulus allowed our expert user population to better engage with the visual design and assess its desirability.

Data collected from VDCS can be compared to what is collected from other desirability research methods as well as from traditional evaluation techniques. For example, we propose repeating the case study using the full set of Microsoft Product Reaction Cards and comparing the percentage of positive and negative reaction cards with those found using VDCS. Approximately equal proportions across the two methods would suggest that they are measuring desirability in a similar way.

Finally, the analysis methods described are also opportunities for future research. A principal component analysis (PCA) or other semantic analysis may contribute greater depth to the study than the techniques used in the existing body of work.

References

1. Barnum, C.M., Palmer, L.A.: More than a feeling: understanding the desirability factor in user experience. In: Ext. Abstracts CHI 2010, pp. 4703–4716 (2010)
2. Benedek, J., Miner, T.: Measuring Desirability: New Methods for Evaluating Desirability in a Usability Lab Setting. In: Proc. Usability Professionals Association Conference (2002)
3. Karvonen, K.: The beauty of simplicity. In: Proc. CUU 2000, pp. 85–90 (2000)
4. Lavie, T., Tractinsky, N.: Assessing dimensions of perceived visual aesthetics of web sites. Int. J. Hum-Comput. Stud. 60(3), 269–298 (2004)
5. Lindgaard, G., Fernandes, G., Dudek, C., Brown, J.: Attention web designers: You have 50 milliseconds to make a good first impression! Behaviour & Information Technology 25, 115–126 (2006)
6. Norman, D.: Emotional Design. Basic Books, New York (2004)
7. Petrie, H., Precious, J.: Measuring user experience of websites: think aloud protocols and an emotion word prompt list. In: Ext. Abstracts CHI 2010, pp. 3673–3678 (2010)
8. Tractinsky, N.: Aesthetics and apparent usability: empirically assessing cultural and methodological issues. In: Proc. CHI 1997, pp. 115–122 (1997)
9. Williams, D., Kelly, G., Anderson, L.: MSN 9: new user-centered desirability methods produce compelling visual design. In: Proc. CHI 2004, pp. 959–974 (2004)

An Analysis of Usage Patterns in Utilization of Interaction Styles

Martin Dostál

Dept. Computer Science
Palacký University Olomouc, 17. Listopadu 12
77146 OLOMOUC, Czech Republic
`dostal@inf.upol.cz`

Abstract. This paper introduces particular results on analysis of usage patterns in contemporary word processing applications. We evaluate how interaction styles are used accordingly to frequency of usage of underlying user commands or semantical categories of user commands. We show that menus are used as a prevalent interaction style and report usage patterns on toolbars and keystrokes. Furthermore, the differences in usage of toolbars and keystrokes on frequently used commands are evaluated.

Keywords: user studies, interaction styles, usage patterns, word processing.

1 Introduction

This paper aims at analysis of usage patterns in utilization of interaction styles in word processing applications. Contemporary WIMP paradigm-based user interfaces make available pull down menus, toolbars, pop-up menus and keystrokes as interaction styles. Although the literature [2,5] or various human user interface guidelines define rules and guidelines for interaction styles, these are sometimes violated by user interface designers for a plenty of reasons. Furthermore, many users might not be acquainted about the proper utilization of particular interaction styles. It may put a doubt on whether interaction styles are actually used as user interface designers believe that users do. Although there is some work on usage of word processing applications [3,4,6], there has not been any recent study that paid a particular attention to utilization of interaction styles. Generally, pull-down menus are intended to invoke any of the user commands available in the application. Menus compromise between fastness and easiness of use. Toolbars and keystrokes are intended for direct activation of the most frequently used user commands. However, toolbars in modern office suites are often overloaded which might result in worsening usability. Pop-up menus are intended for providing a context-sensitive functionality dependent on the type of object at the cursor position. In this paper we report the usage of interaction styles in dependence on the frequency of usage or semantical categories of user commands in contemporary word processing applications. Word processing applications provided an opportunity to explore usage of interaction styles in WIMP paradigm-based applications since word processors represent one of the most widely used kind of applications.

C. Stephanidis (Ed.): Posters, Part I, HCII 2011, CCIS 173, pp. 128–132, 2011.

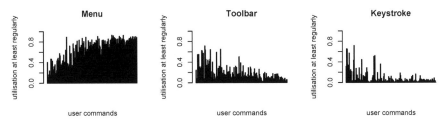

Fig. 1. Utilization of interaction styles on at least regularly used commands

2 Study Design

The utilization of interaction styles has been analyzed as a part of a study on user experience and usage habits in word processing applications. It has been studied using a questionnaire which surveyed computer skills and user experience, used functionality, interaction styles, users' opinions on word processing applications and opinions on the Microsoft Ribbon User Interface, see [1] for more details. The survey was not restricted to a particular word processing application since contemporary word processors provide more or less similar user interfaces. We studied the usage of selected (N=179) major user commands of the Microsoft Word and OpenOffice.org Writer that can be accessed using a menu, a keystroke, a toolbar or a pop-up menu. One-hundred-and-seventeen users (71 males and 46 females) participated in the survey. Although we were not able to achieve a representative sample, we paid a particular attention to achieve participants of various age, education and computer experience. The sample is somewhat biased to young (M=22.79, Min=16, 1st Qu.= 19, Mdn=20, 3rd Qu.=24, Max=54, Sd=6.51), more than average experienced and educated users. The participants have long-term experience with computers (M=11.29 years, Sd=4.71) and quite high overall computing experience (Mode=3, Mdn=4, on the 5-point scale). Thirty-five percent of participants are able to type on a keyboard using all ten fingers. Participants have long term experience with word processing (M=9.30 years, Sd=3.55). There were 82 participants using Word 2003, 68 participants using Word 2007, 20 using Word 2000, 55 using WordPad, 51 using Writer in OpenOffice.org 3.x, 22 using Writer in OpenOffice.org 2.x and 27 participants using the TextEdit application in Mac OS X. Other word processing applications were used by less than twenty respondents and we do not report them here.

3 Utilization of User Commands and Interaction Styles

Users stated the frequency of usage of individual user commands on the following 7-point scale: *I do not use and do not know this command, I do not use, but aware of this command, I use this command rarely, I use this command routinely, I use this command regularly, I use this command frequently, I assume that this command is not provided by word processors I use.* Table 1 depicts the percentage of user command usage and usage of interaction styles. Note that only 14 user commands are user by more than 75 % of participants at least regularly.

Table 1. The most frequently used commands: command usage and interaction styles usage

command	al_routinely	al_regularly	frequently	menu	toolbar	keystroke
Bold	98.29	90.60	44.44	16.44	54.79	21.92
Save, Save As	98.29	96.58	75.21	40.57	24.57	31.43
Copy	97.44	93.16	73.50	10.27	8.22	65.07
Italic	97.44	84.62	40.17	15.17	55.17	22.76
Paste	97.44	94.02	75.21	11.03	7.59	65.52
Undo	96.58	85.47	58.97	23.84	39.74	33.77
Print	95.73	83.76	49.57	46.78	28.07	22.22
Character	93.16	75.21	47.01	31.91	53.19	3.55
Font Size	93.16	80.34	45.30	25.00	62.50	2.94
Underline	92.31	74.36	33.33	14.69	57.34	20.98
Font Name	91.45	76.07	41.03	26.12	61.94	1.49
New	91.45	82.91	48.72	43.03	30.91	21.82
Close	90.60	82.91	56.41	42.64	27.91	24.81
Cut	90.60	83.76	58.97	15.22	10.14	57.25
Open	90.60	83.76	55.56	47.17	30.82	18.87
Font Color	88.89	69.23	29.91	19.05	71.43	0.79
Bullets and Numbering	87.18	61.54	25.64	43.38	45.59	0.74
Insert Table	82.05	54.70	20.51	53.33	35.83	6.67
Select All	81.20	71.79	38.46	18.18	0.91	71.82
Select Text	81.20	72.65	37.61	35.53	7.89	43.42

Participants were allowed to select any combination of the provided interaction styles, i.e., menu, toolbar, keystroke or pop-up menu, for each used command. The average utilization of interaction styles for individual levels of usage is depicted on Table 2. The utilization of individual interaction styles across *at least regularly used* commands is depicted on Fig. 1. User commands are ordered by usage decreasingly on the x axis. Table 3 depicts a detailed usage of interaction styles including all possible combinations across all available levels of usage. An interesting point is that usage of more than one interaction style at once on a particular user command is scarce and in total represent no more than 8.25 % of interaction styles utilization. Commands with the highest utilization of multiple interaction styles are following: "Save, Save As", "Print","New","Open", "Undo", "Bold", "Italic", "Redo", "Underline". Note that most of these commands are used frequently.

Table 2. Utilization of interaction styles

interaction style	rarely	routinely	regularly	frequently
menu	74.24	62.37	51.92	45.13
toolbar	16.75	24.65	32.58	37.33
keystroke	6.07	8.60	17.24	24.81
pop-up menu	9.63	14.27	13.77	14.59

Table 3. Overall utilization of interaction styles including its combinations

	m	k	t	p	mt	mk	mp	tk	tp	kp	mtk	mtp	mkp	tkp	mktp
mean	61.79	6.93	14.81	8.22	3.48	1.42	0.85	0.68	0.89	0.26	0.33	0.20	0.06	0.05	0.04
sd	23.53	11.85	14.27	9.88	3.61	2.01	1.39	2.23	1.58	1.13	1.19	0.54	0.26	0.21	0.23

Table 4. User commands issued most frequently using a toolbar (left) and a keystroke (right)

command	menu	toolbar	keystroke	command	menu	toolbar	keystroke
Font Color	19.05	71.43	0.79	Select All	18.18	0.91	71.82
Background Color	26.13	64.86	0.90	Paste	11.03	7.59	65.52
Text Highlighting	26.32	64.21	1.05	Copy	10.27	8.22	65.07
Text Alignment	24.24	63.64	4.04	Cut	15.22	10.14	57.25
Font Size	25.00	62.50	2.94	Copy To Scrapbook (Word)	31.34	7.46	52.24
Font Name	26.12	61.94	1.49	Paste From Scrapbook (Word)	36.51	3.17	50.79
Apply Style	37.63	59.14	1.08	Find	43.97	9.48	44.83
Underline	14.69	57.34	20.98	Select Text	35.53	7.89	43.42
Italic	15.17	55.17	22.76	Replace	51.19	9.52	35.71
Bold	16.44	54.79	21.92	Undo	23.84	39.74	33.77

4   Usage Patterns

According to Table 2 we found menu as a prevalent interaction style since more than 60 % of at least routinely used functionality is issued using a menu. One important observation is that menus dominate to infrequently used user commands (such as "Bibliography Database", "Document Permissions (Word)", "Version", "Protect Document" or "Options"). There is a high negative correlation between the usage at least routinely and utilization of menu $\rho(179) = -.83$, $p < .001$. Table 4 depicts user commands that are issued most frequently using a toolbar or a keystroke, respectively. Obviously, toolbars and keystrokes are used to quite frequently used commands. However, we observed one important difference; a toolbar is frequently used to commands related to document contents (i.e., a text formatting) whereas keystrokes are used to commands related to application control, such as clipboard operations, finding a text in a document or undoing/redoing changes. There was also found a moderate correlation between usage at least routinely and utilization of toolbar $\rho(179) = .59$, $p < .001$, and keystrokes $\rho(179) = -.46$, $p < .001$. Pop-up menus are intended for contextually dependent functionality, as it was recalled above. The data showed that pop-up menus are most widely used to manipulate tables in document. Fourteen of the sixteen most frequently issued user commands using a pop-up menu ("Table Properties", "Pitcure Format", "Select Rows", "Select Cells", "AutoFit Table", "Select Columns", "Object Format", "Delete Row", "Delete Columns", "Insert Row", "Insert Columns", "Select Table", "Merge Cells", "Split Cells", "Delete Table", "Table Boundaries") are related to tables. Furthermore, the data showed also that tables are quite frequently manipulated using a menu.

We used an ANOVA analysis with frequency of usage (*rarely, routinely, regularly* and *frequently*), a particular interaction style utilization and users treated as repeated measures to test a statistical significance. Mauchly's test showed that sphericity cannot be assumed neither for menu, toolbar or keystroke. We used a Greenhouse-Geisser correction by multiplying the degrees of freedom (3,348) by the ϵ. We obtained $\epsilon = .88$ for menu, $\epsilon = .91$ for toolbar and $\epsilon = .66$ for keystroke interaction style. An ANOVA analysis showed the main effect of frequency of usage was statistically significant for menu, toolbar and keystroke. For menu: $F(2.64, 306.24) = 55.39, p < .001, \ partial \ \eta^2 = .32$, for toolbar: $F(2.73, 316.68) = 25.68, \ p < .001, \ partial \ \eta^2 = .16$ and for keystroke $F(1.98, 229.68) = 58.40, \ p < .001, \ partial \ \eta^2 = .33$. The pop-up menu interaction style was not found significant for frequency of usage ($F(3, 348) = 1.34, \ p = .26$). It is a presumable result; only certain user commands are available through a pop-up menu. Pairwise t-tests with a Bonferroni adjustment on the individual interaction styles were used for post-hoc tests. For menu we revealed the significant differences between *rarely* and *frequently* ($p < .001$), *regularly* and *rarely* ($p < .001$), *routinely* and *frequently* ($p < .001$), and *routinely* and *rarely* ($p = .004$). For toolbar we revealed the significant differences between *rarely* and *frequently* ($p < .001$), *regularly* and *rarely* ($p < .001$), *routinely* and *frequently* ($p = .04$), and *routinely* and *rarely* ($p = .003$). For keystroke we revealed the significant differences between *rarely* and *frequently* ($p < .001$), *regularly* and *rarely* ($p < .001$), *routinely* and *frequently* ($p < .001$), and *routinely* and *regularly* ($p < .001$).

5   Summary

We reported usage patterns in utilization of interaction styles in word processing applications. We found that menu is a prevalent interaction style and toolbars and keystrokes as particularly used to frequently used user commands. Toolbars were found used to document-content related commands whereas keystrokes to application control related commands. The pop-up and pull-down menus were identified as particular methods to manipulate tables.

References

1. Dostál, M.: User acceptance of the microsoft ribbon user interface. In: Proceedings of the DNCOCO 2010 Conference, pp. 143–149. WSEAS (2010)
2. Galitz, W.O.: The Essential Guide to User Interface Design. Wiley Publishing, Inc., Chichester (2007)
3. Hanson, S.J., Kraut, R.E., Farber, J.M.: Interface design and multivariate analysis of unix command use. ACM Trans. Inf. Syst. 2(1), 42–57 (1984)
4. McGrenere, J., Moore, G.: Are we all in the same "bloat"? In: Fels, S., Poulin, P. (eds.) Graphics Interface, pp. 187–196. Canadian Human-Computer Communications Society (2000)
5. Stone, D., Jarrett, C., Woodroffe, M., Minocha, S.: User Interface Design and Evaluation. The Morgan Kaufmann Series in Interactive Technologies. Morgan Kaufmann, San Francisco (March 2005)
6. Whiteside, J., Archer, N., Wixon, D., Good, M.: How do people really use text editors? In: Proceedings of the SIGOA Conference on Office Information Systems, pp. 29–40. ACM, New York (1982)

On the Differences in Usage of Word Processing Applications

Martin Dostál

Dept. Computer Science
Palacký University Olomouc, 17. Listopadu 12
77146 OLOMOUC, Czech Republic
dostal@inf.upol.cz

Abstract. An analysis was conducted to evaluate the differences between users in utilization of functionality and interaction styles in word processing applications. The study evaluated 117 users of various word processing applications using a questionnaire. Results show that differences between users in used functionality are considerable. The differences in utilization of interaction styles on a common functionality was found substantial. In addition, we show that the differences in utilization of functionality do not correlate much with the differences in utilization of interaction styles, i.e., users which has similar usage patterns in utilization of functionality do not have much similar usage patters in utilization of interaction styles.

Keywords: user studies, complex software, word processing.

1 Introduction

Many software applications are steadily growing in the number of offered features. It results in growing complexity of user interfaces and worsening usability. This phenomenon has been recently addressed by several approaches including recommender systems [6], personalization of user interfaces [3,4,7] or layered user interfaces [9]. These approaches rely more or less on assumption that users are different in requirements on functionality or preferred interaction styles. McGrenere and Moore [8] conducted a study on how users experience user interface of Microsoft Word 97. The study surveyed the used functionality (which and how frequently it is used) and sources of users' dissatisfaction using a poll-type questionnaire. McGrenere and Moore showed that most users use only a small fraction of the provided functionality. The study also recognized the excess of provided functionality as a substantial source of dissatisfaction. The study results then accelerated new research into personalized user interfaces. There has also been performed some other studies on word processing experience, but most of them are related to no longer used applications that have a textual, non-graphical user interface, see [5,10] for instance. Linton [6] reported the frequency of usage of individual commands in Microsoft Word 6.0 for Macintosh. The data was collected using software logging on a sample consisted of sixteen users. However, Linton was unable to capture the information about the utilization of interaction styles owing to technical limitations of the logging technology he used.

C. Stephanidis (Ed.): Posters, Part I, HCII 2011, CCIS 173, pp. 133–137, 2011.
© Springer-Verlag Berlin Heidelberg 2011

Although it has been reported that users usually use only a small fraction of the provided functionality there has not been a study on individual differences between users in usage of word processing applications. Particular results of such a study are briefly introduced in this paper. We conducted a study that was, among other things, focused on utilization of functionality and interaction styles in word processing applications. We provide an analysis of differences between users that establishes a better understanding on users' behavior in complex software applications. Such an understanding is particularly important for research that addresses user interface personalization or design of usable systems, for instance.

2   Study Design and Participants

The utilization of word processing applications has been studied as a part of a more complex and extensive user study related to the user experience and usage habits in word processing applications. It was conducted using a questionnaire which surveyed computer skills, user experience, used functionality, interaction styles, users' opinions on word processing applications and opinions on the Microsoft Ribbon User Interface, see [1]. The survey was not focused to a particular word processing application since contemporary word processing applications provide more or less similar functionality and user interface. We studied the usage of selected (N=179) major user commands of the Microsoft Word and OpenOffice.org Writer that can be accessed using a menu, a keystroke, a toolbar or a context menu.

One-hundred-and-seventeen users (71 males and 46 females) participated in the survey. Although we were not able to achieve a representative sample, we paid a particular attention to achieve participants of various age, education and computer experience. The sample is somewhat biased to young (M=22.79, Min=16, 1st Qu.= 19, Mdn=20, 3rd Qu.=24, Max=54, Sd=6.51), more than average experienced and educated users. The participants have long-term experience with computers (M=11.29 years, Sd=4.71) and quite high overall computing experience (Mode=3, Mdn=4, on the 5-point scale). Thirty-five percent of participants are able to type on a keyboard using all ten fingers. Participants have long term experience with word processing (M=9.30 years, Sd=3.55). There were 82 participants using Word 2003, 68 participants using Word 2007, 20 participants using Word 2000, 55 participants using WordPad, 51 participants using Writer in OpenOffice.org 3.x, 22 participants using Writer in OpenOffice.org 2.x and 27 participants using the TextEdit application in Mac OS X. Other word processing applications were used by less than twenty respondents and we do not report them here.

3   Utilization of Functionality and Interaction Styles

Users stated the frequency of usage of individual user commands on the following 7-point scale: *I do not use and do not know this command, I do not use, but aware of this command, I use this command rarely, I use this command routinely, I use this command regularly, I use this command frequently, I assume that this command is not provided by word processors I use.* For further investigations we aggregated the responses to *I use the command at least rarely* (that is rarely, routinely, regularly or frequently), *I use*

Table 1. Utilization of user commands

parameter	% al_rarely	% al_routinely	% al_regularly	% frequently
Min.	27.0	21.00	5.00	0.00
1st Qu.	79.0	55.00	31.00	10.00
Median	95.0	69.00	43.00	17.00
Mean	100.4	72.23	46.97	22.88
3rd Qu.	116.0	88.00	62.00	30.00
Max.	179.0	159.00	108.00	96.00

Table 2. Utilization of interaction styles by frequency of user command usage

interaction style	% rarely	% routinely	% regularly	% frequently
menu	74.24	62.37	51.92	45.13
toolbar	16.75	24.65	32.58	37.33
keystroke	6.07	8.60	17.24	24.81
popup	9.63	14.27	13.77	14.59

the command at least routinely (that is routinely, regularly or frequently) and *I use the command at least regularly* (that is regularly or frequently).

The core of user commands in word processing applications was found obviously small; only 14 user commands (Save/Save As, Paste, Copy, Bold, Undo, Italic, Open, Print, Cut, New, Close, Font Size, Font Name, Character) are used at least regularly by at least 75 % of participants and 30 commands only by at least 50 % of participants. A summary of user command usage is provided in Table 1. The data also showed that 77 % of used functionality is used less than frequently which is a considerable number.

In the next part of the survey participants responded to questions related to utilization of interaction styles on individual user commands. For each used command the participant was allowed to select any combination of the provided options, i.e., menu, toolbar, keystroke or pop-up menu. Table 2 depicts the overall utilization of interaction styles.

4   Differences in Utilization of Functionality

The differences between users in used functionality were measured using the Manhattan distance measure [2], see Formula 1. It measures a distance between users p and q in terms of usage of user commands. Vectors $p = (p_1, p_2 \ldots p_n)$ and $q = (q_1, q_2 \ldots q_n)$ denotes the usage of individual user commands by the user p or q, respectively. The vector elements are either 0 or 1, thus the maximum possible distance between particular users is equal to 179. To compute the differences between each other participant $\frac{117^2 - 117}{2} = 6782$ distances must be computed.

$$d(p,q) = \|p - q\| = \sum_{i=1}^{n} |p_i - q_i| \tag{1}$$

The differences in usage of functionality were measured at aggregated levels of usage of user commands, i.e., *at least rarely, at least routinely, at least regularly* and *frequently*. The average difference on at least rarely used user commands was found equal to 61.6 (Min.= 0, 1st Qu.= 50, Median=59, 3rd Qu.=70, Max. = 152). On at least routinely used user commands was the average difference found equal to 58.2 (Min.= 17, 1st Qu.= 47, Median=56, 3rd Qu.=67, Max. = 140). On at least regularly used commands was the difference found equal to 47.71 (Min.= 5, 1st Qu.= 37, Median=46, 3rd Qu.=57, Max. = 103). Finally, on frequently used user commands the average difference was equal to 31.57 (Min.= 0, 1st Qu.= 17, Median=27, 3rd Qu.=43, Max. = 98). The interpretation of the first quantile values can be following: 75 % of users are different from the each other at least in x user commands (where x corresponds to the 1st quantile value). Accordingly to the average amount of user command usage at particular levels of usage (see Table 1 and compare to the obtained differences) it suggests that the differences between users are considerable.

5   Differences in Utilization of Interaction Styles

In order to evaluate the differences between users on utilization of interaction styles, we had to propose a distance measure between usage of interaction styles as seen on Formula 2. It measures a distance between sets P and Q of interaction styles ($P, Q \subseteq \{m, t, k, p\}$, m stands for menu, t for toolbar, k for keystroke and p for pop-up menu) used to initiate a particular user command. The distance is expressed by a number from interval $< 0, 1 >$, where 0 means equal sets of interaction styles and 1 means maximum dissimilarity between sets of interaction styles. For instance, $dist(\{m, t, k\}, \{t, p\}) = 1 - \frac{|\{t\}|}{\max(|\{m,t,k\}|, |\{t,p\}|)} = \frac{2}{3}$.

$$dist(P, Q) = 1 - \frac{|P \cap Q|}{\max(|P|, |Q|)} \tag{2}$$

The distance between users across interaction styles usage is computed using Formula 3. It evaluates the differences of interaction styles usage over a set of user commands $C(x, y)$ which are used both by user x and y. The $intsts(x, c)$ and $intsts(y, c)$ denotes a set of interaction styles used by user x (or y, respectively) to issue a user command c.

$$d(x, y) = \frac{\sum_{c \in C(x,y)} dist(intsts(x, c), intsts(y, c))}{|C(x, y)|}, \text{ or 1 if } |C(x, y)| = 0 \tag{3}$$

The descriptive statistic is following: Min=0, 1st Qu.=.40, Mdn=.50, Mean=.50, 3rd Qu.=.60 and Max=1. Obviously, the differences between users in utilization of interaction styles are considerable. Users are fairly different both in terms of used interaction styles and used functionality. We evaluated a correlation between the obtained distances on usage of functionality and interaction styles in order to reveal whether the users which are similar in used functionality are also similar in usage of interaction styles. The correlation analysis provided an interesting observation: the correlation was found substantially low, Pearsons's $\rho(6786) = .09$, $p < .001$. It suggests that users with similar usage patterns on used functionality usually does have not much similar usage patterns on interaction styles.

6 Conclusion

These findings lead us to conclusion that the differences between users are considerable which is an inevitable issue for todays static user interfaces where one interface should meet all users. Even a small group of users similar in usage functionality is not much similar in usage of interaction styles. Overall, we were quite surprised with the substantial differences between users. We argue that the above presented findings points out the importance of research into user interface personalization.

References

1. Dostál, M.: User acceptance of the microsoft ribbon user interface. In: Proceedings of the DNCOCO 2010 Conference, pp. 143–149. WSEAS (2010)
2. Everitt, B.S.: Cluster analysis by Brian Everitt. Heinemann Educational for the Social Science Research Council, London (1974)
3. Findlater, L., McGrenere, J.: A comparison of static, adaptive, and adaptable menus. In: CHI 2004: Proceedings of the SIGCHI Conference on Human Factors in Computing Systems, pp. 89–96. ACM, New York (2004)
4. Gajos, K.Z., Czerwinski, M., Tan, D.S., Weld, D.S.: Exploring the design space for adaptive graphical user interfaces. In: AVI 006: Proceedings of the Working Conference on Advanced Visual Interfaces, pp. 201–208. ACM, New York (2006)
5. Hanson, S.J., Kraut, R.E., Farber, J.M.: Interface design and multivariate analysis of unix command use. ACM Trans. Inf. Syst. 2(1), 42–57 (1984)
6. Linton, F., Joy, D., Schaefer, H.P.: Building user and expert models by long-term observation of application usage. In: Proceedings of the Seventh International Conference on User Modeling, pp. 129–138. Springer, Heidelberg (1999)
7. Mcgrenere, J.: The Design and Evaluation of Multiple Interfaces: A Solution for Complex Software. Ph.D. thesis, University of Toronto (2002)
8. McGrenere, J., Moore, G.: Are we all in the same "bloat"? In: Fels, S., Poulin, P. (eds.) Graphics Interface, pp. 187–196. Canadian Human-Computer Communications Society (2000)
9. Shneiderman, B.: Promoting universal usability with multi-layer interface design. In: CUU 2003: Proceedings of the 2003 Conference on Universal Usability, pp. 1–8. ACM, New York (2003)
10. Whiteside, J., Archer, N., Wixon, D., Good, M.: How do people really use text editors? In: Proceedings of the SIGOA Conference on Office Information Systems, pp. 29–40. ACM, New York (1982)

Usability Study of TEL Recommender System and e-Assessment Tools United

Beatriz Florian[1,2] and Ramón Fabregat[1]

[1] Institute of Informatics and Applications (IIiA), University of Girona, Spain
bflorian@eia.udg.edu, ramon.fabregat@udg.edu
[2] Escuela de Ingeniería de Sistemas y Computación (EISC), Universidad del Valle, Colombia
beatriz.florian@correounivalle.edu.co

Abstract. The following article presents a usability study applied over a process in formal learning that involves a set of e-assessment tools for: self-assessment, peer-assessment and summative assessment and then a simulated Recommender System (RS) in Technology Enhanced Learning (TEL). The system is constructed using Web 2.0 technologies and the Learning Management System Moodle. First, the assessment tools collect outcomes which are saved and classified according to European Qualification Framework. Second, in several times of a course, the outcomes are analyzed to find out the competence gaps of learners, the smart indicators of this analysis are showed to the learners. Finally, the simulated recommender system produces suggestions about reinforced resources to each learner according to their competence gaps. The essence of the planned presentation has three main goals: 1. To show the results of usability study on prototypes of assessment tools and the simulated RS in formal learning 2. To provide an idea of user–centered possible responses of RS for Adaptive Educational Hypermedia Systems, 3. To offer an environment for testing new recommendation approaches and methods for researchers.

Keywords: Usability study, formal learning, learning outcomes, competencies, e-assessment, adaptive educational hypermedia system, TEL recommender system, Moodle.

1 Introduction

Nowadays, formal learning focus on the institutional needs and offer support for learning processes of educational institutes like Universities. The most of universities and colleges use some Learning Management Systems (LMS) to support their courses. Some problems in the use of these systems are the few indicators of current performance of learners, the difficulty to define a competency-based learning design and the lack of recommender systems.

Toward a solution for these problems, and focus in the LMS Moodle which is the virtual learning platform for Universidad del Valle and Universitat de Girona, in our previous research we have defined a adaptive learning process [1] based on e-assessment, then we define a competency-based data model [2] which then was

C. Stephanidis (Ed.): Posters, Part I, HCII 2011, CCIS 173, pp. 138–142, 2011.

actualized according to the European Qualification Framework (EQF) [3]. We also build a set of e-assessment tool for: self-assessment and peer-assessment [4].Nowadays our work is focusing on build the adaptive algorithms of our system. This part covers some tools such as: smart indicators and a TEL recommender system in formal learning.

This work is related with TEL recommender systems [5] particularly in formal education. One advanced work in this particular area is [6]. The most of researches in TEL recommender systems has been made in the area of informal learning networks, leading by Drachsler [7] and Manouselis [8]. In [5] they collect about one hundred references to TEL recommender systems. From the educational data mining research, novelty proposals that, similar to us, use: assessment, content-based recommendations and analysis of log data from LMS are subscribed by Tang, Godoy and Sheard in [9]. The previous research in smart indicators in learning of [10] [11] are the point of start to build our layered architecture (1. Sensor layer 2. Semantic layer 3. Control layer and 4. Indicator layer). The EQF [3] defines our semantic to classified assessment items and the levels of competencies of assessment outcomes. Nowadays, several European projects, for example GRAPPLE and ICOPER, address the integration of adaptive hypermedia systems with LMS and also the building competency-driven assessment systems and recommender systems within virtual learning environments.

The novelty of the proposed approach is bring light into the gaps of the mentioned problems providing indicators to learners from the analysis of e-assessment outcomes, integrating e-assessment tools with an outcome-based competence model in a LMS and doing adaptation based on the diagnostic of learners' needs which are represented with the diagnostic of competence gaps. The assessment tools help to capture the outcome data and give them a semantic. The recommender system processes the data to produce the indicators of performance (diagnostic) and recommendations to the learners. This approach joins e-assessment, outcome-based learning, smart indicator and recommender systems in formal education.

2   Assessment Tools and Recommender System Tool United

At the first stage of the course the teacher define the competencies and the assessment plan to asses these competencies (What is the e-assessment tool to use? What is the moment to use an assessment tool? What competencies (knowledge, skills and wider competence) will be examined at each moment? What is the level expected for each competence at each moment?), for summative assessment the meta-data of each item in the test must be complemented by the teacher with the information of competence evaluated and level of evidence.

Following the architecture proposed by [14] which has four layers we are building the adaptive process. The assessment tools allow building the *Sensor Layer* and *Semantic Layer*. The *Sensor Layer* captures the outcomes from the assessment tools and transforms them into a standard outcome framework (the EQF). The recommender system acts in the *Control Layer* and *Indicator Layer*. In the *Control Layer* the data collected are analyzed and the diagnostic of competence gaps is produced. In the *Indicator Layer*, smart indicators (statistic results of learners and their peers) and recommendations of resources are produced.

During the course if a self-assessment test is in the plan, the learners judge their own level achieved in the competencies displayed. Following the EFQ, each competence can be developed at eight levels; the competencies and levels are displayed as rubric scores. If a peer-assessment tool test is in the plan users qualify the work of their peers; this tool uses the same kind of interface displaying rubric scores. For summative assessment the learners use the Quiz tool of Moodle.

With these learning outcomes the system first display smart indicator of tests and then can calculate the gaps of competencies of a learner. A competence gap is evidenced when the difference between the level expected and the level reached is positive. The gaps of competencies are also displayed as indicators to the learners. With these diagnostics of gaps of competencies the RS suggest additional resources to each student according to the levels of competencies that he doesn't have achieved.

3   Satisfaction Analysis of the System

To evaluate the satisfaction of the users with the system prototype we started an evaluation phase with users allowed to sing up in a Moodle course about Design Patterns in OO programming. In total 20 people from 3 different countries subscribed to the evaluation and ratings to the prototype. The evaluation phase ran for one month and was concluded with an online recall questionnaire. The assessment tools are all ready building but the recommender system was simulated with a prototype.

In this section we present the most relevant answers from the online recall questionnaire regarding the satisfaction with the system.

The questions regarding the use of e-assessment tools and recommender systems in Table 1 are informative for us as they give an idea which tools are used how frequently. This information is rather important to us for the further development of the system. The most frequently used services are those which show to the users comparisons with other people.

In Table 2 we asked questions regarding the general satisfaction with the systems and the offered recommendations. It is important for us to measure the satisfaction of each kind of responses that the system gives to the users. The satisfaction with the recommendations was 55%, in an open question about this rating the users suggests that they prefer recommendations of activities rather recommendations of resources.

In Table 3 we asked the participants for the ultimate choice between the smart indicator algorithms and the recommender system algorithm. Which information technology did satisfy them more? People were more satisfied with the smart-indicators. Reasons for that could be, the participants could have plenty information of their performance and this information are useful for auto-reflexion about the next step in learning. On the other hand, we need to change our recommendation strategy to suggest activities rather learning resources and suggest peer learners that already achieved the competence that a particular learner doesn't have achieved.

Table 1. General statements about the usage of e-assessment tools and recommender systems

Strongly agree	Agree	Neutral	Disagree	Strongly disagree
I had used some LMS such as: Moodle, dotLRN, Blackboard, etc.				
45% (9)	10% (2)	25% (5)	10% (2)	10% (2)
I had used e-assessment tools				
10% (2)	25% (5)	25% (5)	15% (3)	25% (5)
I track my work results online				
45% (9)	25% (5)	20% (4)	5% (1)	5% (1)
I compare my work results with my peers				
30% (6)	50% (10)	10% (2)	5% (1)	5% (1)
I think is useful rating my own work and the work of my peers				
15% (3)	60% (12)	10% (2)	10% (2)	5% (1)
I follow recommendations of systems such as: Amazon RS, iTunesPing, MovieLens etc.				
25% (5)	45% (9)	10% (2)	10% (2)	10% (2)

Table 2. Questions regarding the satisfaction of the participants regarding the prototype system

Very Satisfied	Satisfied	Unsatisfied	Very unsatisfied
How satisfied are you overall with the system prototype?			
20% (4)	45% (9)	20% (4)	15% (3)
How satisfied have you been with the indicators about the competence levels evaluated in the summative test?			
30% (6)	35% (7)	20% (4)	15% (3)
How satisfied have you been with the rubric score-based algorithm to qualify competencies in peer assessment tool and self assessment tool?			
25% (5)	35% (7)	30% (6)	10% (2)
How satisfied have you been with the indicators about your assessment outcomes displayed as the comparison between the levels of competencies expected and levels achieved?			
30% (6)	40% (8)	15% (3)	15% (3)
How satisfied have you been with the algorithm of adaptive recommendations?			
5% (1)	50% (10)	30% (6)	15% (3)

Table 3. Question regarding the satisfaction of the participants regarding the prototype system

Smart Indicators	Knowledge-based recommendations
Which information technology did satisfy you more at the end of the evaluation?	
55% (11)	45% (9)

4 Conclusions and Future Research

This article presented a prototype system that implies a simulated recommender system to suggest resources from the emerging information of a Learning Management System. During a course a set of assessment tools in the LMS provide outcomes that are used to detect competence gaps of the learners. It further presented the results of a first satisfaction analysis by a small group of users.

The most obvious future research will be the evaluation of new recommendation algorithms regarding their impact on learners in formal education. Therefore, we first want to review suitable algorithms and adjust them to our goals.

In general we can conclude that the learners are well satisfied with the smart indicators about their assessment outcomes. On the other hand, in order to attract participants for future evaluation we have to extend the functionality of the current simulated Recommender System towards a fully scaled LMS and include recommendations of activities and peer learners (maybe instated of resources) to help learners to overcome their competence gaps.

Based on the satisfaction analysis we want to develop our TEL recommender system in two different ways. One way is the integration of the TEL recommender systems to Moodle to have an attractive environment for participants for future experiments. The other way is the development of a web service to show the results of recommendations and smart-indicators to learners out of the Moodle environment.

Acknowledgements. Authors would like to thank the LASPAU Program for the scholarship No. 20080847. Also, thanks to the Universidad del Valle, Colombia for co-funding the research of Beatriz Florian. The work presented is framed in the context of A2U@ project (TIN2008-06862-C04-01/TSI) funded by the Spanish Government.

References

1. Florian, B.E., Baldiris, S., Fabregat, R.: Adaptive Evaluation Based on Competencies. In: Proceedings of the Third Workshop Towards User Modeling and Adaptive Systems for All (TUMAS-A 2009), AIED, Brighton, United Kingdom (2009)
2. Florian, B.E., Baldiris, S., Fabregat, R.: A new competency-based e-assessment data model: Implementing the AEEA proposal. In: EDUCON 2010, Madrid (2010)
3. Commission of the EC. Towards a European qualifications framework for lifelong learning, http://www.ec.europa.eu/education/policies/2010/doc/consultation_eqf_en.pdf
4. Florian, B.E., Baldiris, S., Fabregat, R., De La Hoz, A.: A set of software tools to build an author assessment package on Moodle. In: Proceedings ICALT 2010, Sousse, Tunisia, pp. 67–69 (2010)
5. Manouselis, N., Drachsler, H., Vuorikari, R., Hummel, H.G.K., Koper, R.: Recommender Systems in Technology Enhanced Learning. In: Kantor, P.B., Ricci, F., Rokach, L., Shapira, B. (eds.) Recommender Systems Handbook, pp. 387–415. Springer, Berlin (2011)
6. Santos, O., Boticario, J.: Modeling recommendations for the educational domain. In: Proc. of 1st. Workshop on Recommender Systems for Technology Enhance Learning. Elsevier, Amsterdam (2010)
7. Drachsler, H.: Navigation Support for Learners in Informal Learning Networks. Doctoral thesis, Heerlen, Open University of the Netherlands/CELSTEC (October 16, 2009)
8. Manouselis, N., Kosmopoulos, T., Kastrantas, K.: Developing a Recommendation Web Service for a Federation of Learning Repositories. In: Proceedings of the INCOS 2009, pp. 208–211. IEEE Computer Society, Washington, DC, USA (2009)
9. Romero, C., Ventura, S., Pechenizkiy, M., Chapman, B.R. (eds.): Handbook of Educational Data Mining, pp. 257–273, 311–322, 353–364. CRC Press, Boca Raton (2011)
10. Glahn, C.: Contextual support of social engagement and reflection on the Web. Doctoral thesis, Heerlen, Open University of the Netherlands, CELSTEC (September 18, 2009)
11. Verpoorten, D., Glahn, C., Kravcik, M., Ternier, S., Specht, M.: Personalisation of Learning in Virtual Learning Environments. In: Cress, U., Dimitrova, V., Specht, M. (eds.) EC-TEL 2009. LNCS, vol. 5794, pp. 52–66. Springer, Heidelberg (2009)

Perceived Multimedia Quality: The Impact of Device Characteristics

Gheorghita Ghinea and Kyle J. Patterson

Brunel University, Uxbridge, United Kingdom
george.ghinea@brunel.ac.uk, dremzo@gmail.com

Abstract. In the study reported in this paper, the research aims to tackle the question "Do the hardware characteristics of a device affect the viewer's perceived quality of the media?" Using different hardware devices and media clips that have had different frame rates the viewer's information assimilation and satisfaction of the media clip was measured. The results suggest that there is a deeper link between the user's information assimilation than just the hardware that the media is viewed on. On the other hand a user's satisfaction with clip quality is affected by the alterations in frame rate of the media rather than the device as the satisfaction levels increased regardless of the hardware characteristics.

Keywords: device, frame rate, perceived multimedia quality.

1 Introduction

With the ever increasing availability of media content and technological advances in visual displays, there is a general expectation that the media quality is increasing. As an example, media/video clips that are run at a higher frame rate, from a technical point of view, have higher quality because everything appears smoother to the eye of the beholder, the brain not being able to distinguish individual media frames. With higher frame rates come very large bandwidth and processing power requirements, which may be perfectly fine for video conferencing in a building with optical broadband connections and powerful videoconferencing units, but not a handheld mobile device.

Another area key to perceived media quality is the screen resolution of the displaying device. High Definition technology with display resolutions of up to 1920x1080 progressive suggesting 'a better viewing experience' is already well-established, with the next step - Quad High Definition - being able to run 3840x2160 progressive.

Although work has been undertaken to assess perceived/subjective media quality in terms of frame rate [1][3], resolution [2], and on specific devices [5][6],to the best of our knowledge, the question of how subjective media quality is impacted when the same content is viewed across different devices has not been explored.

C. Stephanidis (Ed.): Posters, Part I, HCII 2011, CCIS 173, pp. 143–146, 2011.

2 Methodology

2.1 Subjects

96 volunteers, aged between 16-38, participated in the experiment. Participation was voluntary, with all subjects being recruited from the staff and student population at Brunel University.

2.2 Hardware Devices

The four devices (Fig. 1) used to run the media in the experiment were a high definition television (22" LCD screen, 16:9 aspect ratio, 1920x1080 resolution), a notebook computer (15.6" LCD screen, 16:9 aspect ratio, 1440x900 resolution), a netbook (10.1" LCD screen, 16:9 aspect ratio, 1024x600 resolution) and a smart phone (3.5" TFT screen, 16:9 aspect ratio, 640x360 resolution).

Fig. 1. Devices used in our study

2.3 Media Clips

12 video clips, with varying spatial and temporal characteristics, previously employed in perceptual quality studies (e.g. [4]) were used in our experiment. Each video clip was shown at one of three different frame rates: 5, 15, and 25 frames per second.

2.4 Evaluation Metric

The Quality of Perception (QoP) metric, assessing subjective media infotainment quality [4] was used in the experiment. QoP has two components, QoP-IA – information assimilation representing the percentage of informational content assimilated by the end user, and QoP-S, the subjective media quality, expressed on a scale of 1-5.

2.5 Experimental Design

Each participant was randomly assigned to view media on one of the four hardware devices, on which s/he viewed the 12 clips (4 clips were viewed at 5, 15 and 25 fps, respectively). In order to prevent order effects, the presentation order of clips was randomised. After watching each clip, the participant filled in the QoP questionnaire and then went on to view the next clip. Media on a particular device was viewed by a total of 24 participants.

Each participant was lead to a closed off room where the device was positioned on a table. The device was not moved through each participant however the addition of an office chair with wheels attached to the legs allowed for the participant to adjust themselves relative to how they felt comfortable watching the device. The device remained on the playlist screen whilst the participant was reviewing instructions about how the following experiment would unfold.

The participant was told they were about to watch 12 media clips and that after each clip they would be given a questionnaire to answer with questions relating to the media clip they had just seen. Participants were told that the questions will relate to the media clip and that no trick question would be asked.

3   Results

Analysis of Variance of the results suggest that there is a deeper link between the user's information assimilation than just the hardware that the media is viewed on. On the other hand a user's satisfaction with clip quality is affected by the alterations in frame rate of the media rather than the device as the satisfaction levels increased regardless of the hardware characteristics. However, the interaction between media content and the device on which it was played was shown to have a statistically significant impact on user subjective satisfaction with the media quality. Last but not least, irrespective of the device, our results suggest that there is a strong relationship between media content and the frame rate at which it is viewed.

4   Future Work

Our study has two possibilities for future work:

- The broadening of the device spectrum: with 60" televisions existing in today's market incorporating devices from 60" displays to 3" displays would mean the results can be generalised across the population.
- Updating the experiment material with high definition resolutions for the media clips: the current media clips only running at 640 x 480 pixels meant that when shown on the larger screens the clips slightly distorted and may have influenced the results.

References

1. Apteker, R.T., Fisher, J.A., Kisimov, V.S., Neishlos, H.: Video Acceptability and Frame Rate. IEEE Multimedia 2(3), 32–40 (1995)
2. Bracken, C.C.: Presence and Image Quality: The Case of High-Definition Television. Media Psychology 2(7), 191–205 (2005)
3. Ghinea, G., Thomas, J.P.: QoS Impact on User Perception and Understanding of Multimedia Video Clips. In: Proceedings of ACM Multimedia 1998, pp. 49–54 (1998)
4. Ghinea, G., Thomas, J.P.: Quality of Perception: User Quality of Service in Multimedia Presentations. IEEE Transactions on Multimedia 7(4), 786–789 (2005)
5. Jumisko-Pyykkö, S., Häkkinen, J.: Evaluation of Subjective Video Quality of Mobile Devices. In: Proceedings of the 13th Annual ACM International Conference on Multimedia, pp. 535–538 (2005)
6. Kaasinen, E., Kulju, M., Kivinen, T., Oksman, V.: User acceptance of mobile TV services. In: Proceedings of the 11th International Conference on Human-Computer Interaction with Mobile Devices and Services, Bonn, Germany (2009)

Usability Testing with Children: What We Have Overlooked

Hanayanti Hafit[1], Fariza Hanis Abdul Razak[2], and Haryani Haron[2]

[1] Faculty of Computer Science and Information Technology, Universiti Tun Hussein Onn
Malaysia (UTHM), 86400 Batu Pahat, Johor, Malaysia
[2] Faculty of Computer and Mathematical Sciences, Universiti Teknologi MARA (UiTM),
40450 Shah Alam, Selangor, Malaysia
`hana@uthm.edu.my, {fariza,haryani}@tmsk.uitm.edu.my`

Abstract. Planning a usability testing for the children needs guidance and persistence. For this purpose, we identified an educational game for learning Arabic words to be tested for its usability and learnability aspects. We followed guidelines for usability testing with children by Hanna et. al. Thus, this paper focuses on issues that have been overlooked in performing testing with children. From the lessons learned, additional steps in conducting usability testing with children were made to help the young and novice testers who have never worked with children previously.

Keywords: Children, Educational Game, Guidelines, Usability Testing.

1 Introduction

Planning is often the first step in the process of usability engineering and user centered design. Additionally, the planning of a usability testing sets the stage for building rapport with participants and giving the participants a way to conceptualize the usability testing. Moreover, approaching a usability testing with sensitivity and careful planning is a paramount importance. This is especially so when working with children. Unlike adult populations, a variety of factors particular to children and their development must be considered when assessing them. In the field of Human Computer Interaction (HCI), usability testing initially focused on adults, eventually it became noticeable that children have different requirements, which directed to specific designs for children's technology [1].

From our study, we found that there were some issues which have been overlooked particularly in the earlier stages of conducting a usability test. These issues matter especially to the young and novice testers who have never worked with children previously. Later, we suggest some child-centred methods which can be adopted as guidelines for usability testing with children.

C. Stephanidis (Ed.): Posters, Part I, HCII 2011, CCIS 173, pp. 147–150, 2011.
© Springer-Verlag Berlin Heidelberg 2011

2   Guidelines for Usability Testing with Children

One of the earliest guidelines for usability testing with children was provided by Hanna, Risden and Alexander [2] which depicted in Fig. 1. They outlined the different range of children age to be considered in usability testing and highlighted the guidelines from Setup and Planning, Introduction, During the Test and Finishing Up session. Derived from [2], our study explored steps taken particularly on how to plan and set up usability test.

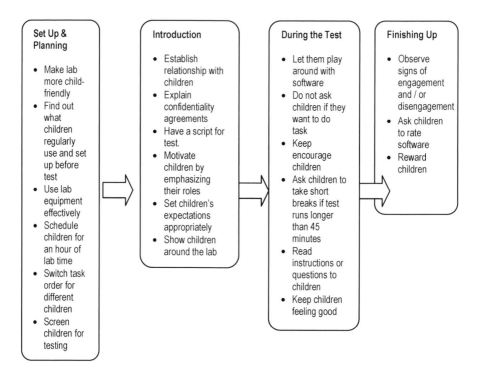

Fig. 1. Guidelines from Hanna, Risden and Alexander [2]

3   Methodology

We had a game to be tested for its usability and learnability issues. The game was called "Tiqah, the fruit collector" and was developed to help children learn Arabic words. In Malaysia, children as young as preschoolers learn Arabic as a second language beside English. Five preschool children aged 5 and 6 years old were chosen to participate in the test.

We made efforts to know the children first before we conducted the usability testing. We visited the chosen preschool quite frequently for two reasons: to learn how the children actually behave, learn, and interact in their natural environment and to establish good relationship with the teachers and children.

Next, we applied Hanna's guidelines [2] to help us 'how we should do and behave' in the lab. We went through all the phases closely as suggested in [2]: starting from Setup and Planning, Introductions, During the test to Finishing up.

4   Results

Literally, these guidelines are very useful for children testers and very easy to follow through, however, some of them prove to be quite challenging to do it, especially for young and novice testers. From our experience following these guidelines, we learned that:

1. Some of our team members seemed awkward at handling the children (*establish relationship with children during Introduction*) and did not know how to ask children questions appropriately (*during Finishing up*). This was true for young members of our team who had never worked with children before.
2. Lab can be an unsafe place for children. Some of furniture in the lab has sharp edges and some of cables and wires lying on the floor could cause accidents for the children if they are not careful when walking (*child-friendly is only useful if safety is in mind during Set up*).
3. Children can be very unpredictable in terms of actions and behaviours. Although we kept them occupied with some interesting activities, we still could not predict what they would do next (*monitor children During the test*).
4. We cannot definitely be sure whether the lab has been appropriately set up for the children testing unless we have done it first with a child of their age (*during Set up*).

5   Discussion

We adopt some methods from user-centred approach to better guide the young and novice testers when doing usability testing with children. We call it 'Child-centred usability testing' and it has four phases as shown in Fig. 2.

We add an additional phase called 'Preparation' to Hanna's guidelines to make sure that the young or novice testers understand the children so that they are able to work with them better in the lab. This is to tackle issues 1 and 3. We also suggest two guidelines (shown in red and italic in Fig. 2) in the Set up phase to tackle issues 2 and 4. Since they have been involved with the children earlier in the Preparation stage, they have already established their relationships with the children. Therefore, in Introductions phase, they just need to welcome the children and make them comfortable in the lab and its surroundings.

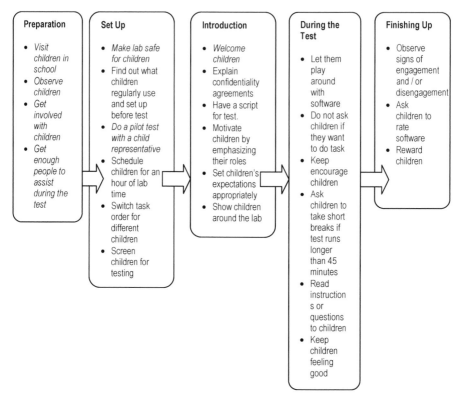

Fig. 2. Additional Steps in Usability Testing with Children

6   Conclusion

As a conclusion, usability testing with children requires patience, control and much persuasion especially for the young and novice tester. This paper presented some overlooked issues particularly in the earlier stages while conducting usability testing with children. Therefore, we proposed an additional phase called Preparation that can be applied as a guide for what should be done when conducting usability testing with children.

Acknowledgments. We wish to thank all partners in this study. We also thank all the children and the teachers who participated in our study for their collaboration in the project.

References

1. Druin, A.: The Role of Children in the Design of New Technology. Behaviour and Information Technology 21(1), 1–25 (2002)
2. Hanna, L., Risden, K., Alexander, K.: Guidelines for Usability Testing with Children. Interactions 4(5), 9–14 (1997)

The Usability Assessment of Web-Based Learning Systems

Chen-Wei Hsieh, Hong-Xon Chen, Yung-Chi Hsu, and Sherry Y. Chen*

Graduate Institute of Network Learning Technology, National Central University, Taiwan
sherry@cl.ncu.edu.tw

Abstract. Web-based learning systems (WBLSs) allow learners to choose any learning topics according to their own needs and progress. This may be the reason why the WBLS is a popular learning tool in educational settings. Thus, it is necessary to investigate how to help learners effectively obtain their desired results. To this end, the usability evaluation of the WBLSs becomes an essential issue. To address this issue, this study assesses the usability of a WBLS with real users' opinions and heuristic evaluation. Our findings show that the results from Nielson's heuristics and those from learners' questionnaire share some commonalities but there are also differences between them. Therefore, these two approaches should be used together so that a complete set of guidelines for the design of a WBLS can be developed.

Keywords: web-based learning system, WBLS, usability.

1 Introduction

Web-based learning systems (WBLSs) are popular because of their flexibility in time and space. Therefore, the usability inspections of WBLSs become important recently. The results from the usability inspections can work as guidelines for the future design of effective WBLSs and other Web-based applications. Among various usability methods, heuristic evaluation was widely used to examine Web-based applications [1]-[2]. Heuristic evaluation, which was firstly proposed by Nielson and Molich [3], consists of ten items to evaluate the usability of the system (Table 1).

Table 1. Nielson's heuristics

H1	Visibility of System Status.	H6	Recognition Rather than Recall.
H2	Match between System and The Real World.	H7	Flexibility and Efficiency of Use.
H3	User Control and Freedom.	H8	Aesthetic and Minimalist Design.
H4	Consistency and Standards.	H9	Help Users Recognize, Diagnose and Recover from Errors.
H5	Error Prevention.	H10	Help and Documentation.

---

* Corresponding author.

C. Stephanidis (Ed.): Posters, Part I, HCII 2011, CCIS 173, pp. 151–155, 2011.

Nielsen's heuristics are a kind of expert evaluation, which can rapidly find usability problem [4]. However, they only focus on the perspective of experts. In other words, learners' real opinions cannot be identified so that their needs may be ignored. To face such an issue, this study assesses the usability of a WBLS by considering the opinions of both learners and experts. More specifically, a questionnaire is used to collect learners' opinions while Nielsen's heuristics are applied to conduct expert evaluation. By doing so, a complete picture of the usability problems of WBLSs can be obtained.

2 Methodology Design

This section presents the methodology of this study and describes techniques applied to analyze corresponding data. The detail presents below.

Web-based learning systems. In this study, the subject content of a WBLS is "User Centered Design" (Figure 1), which includes 46 pages. The WBLS provides multiple navigation tools, including a main menu, keywords search, hierarchical map and alphabetical index. In addition, learners are allowed to customize the layout of the WBLS by themselves, including font type, background colors and font colors.

Fig. 1. The Web-based learning system

Procedure. 50 participants, who came from a university in Taiwan, participated in our study. They have basic computer skills and background knowledge to use the WBLS. The procedure consists of two steps. Firstly, every participant was required to interact with the WBLS about 2 hours. Secondly, they needed to fill out a questionnaire, which was used to measure learners' perception to the system's usability issues. The questionnaire is design based on Nielson's heuristics [5]. There are 44 questions in the questionnaire. Each questions used a five-point scale to identify the levels of learners' perception (5: strongly agree to 1: strongly disagree).

Data Analysis. This study consists of Nielson's heuristic evaluation and the learners' responses to the questionnaire. Firstly, the Nielson's heuristics is used to evaluate usability of the WBLS. The results are divided into two parts: (a) qualitative assessment and (b) quantitative measurement. The former represents experts' original opinions. The latter was generated by severity ratings evaluation, which represents the seriousness of each problem. More specifically, each heuristic had specific criteria that were used for conducting task-based inspections. When the task-based inspection was conducted, the strengths and weaknesses were documented. In particular, the most frequently recorded strengths and weaknesses were paid attention.

On the other hand, the questionnaire results are used to identify whether Nielsen's heuristic evaluation is complete enough to identify learners' problems.

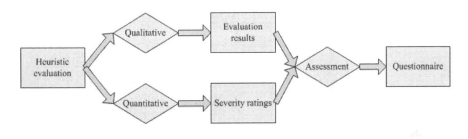

Fig. 2. Procedures of the experiment

3 Results and Discussion

The results are obtained from heuristic evaluation and real learners' opinions from the questionnaire. Regarding the former, the quantitative results obtained from severity evaluation are shown in Table 2. As showed in this table, H1 and H8 were the two influential usability issues. In other words, the system layout and feedback should be taken into account when developing the Web-based learning system. For instance, the concise layout is helpful to locate information easily. Moreover, the clear feedback can let users understand where they are or what mistakes they made. Regarding the latter, the means and, standard deviations of each question are shown in Table 3. The results indicated that H2 and H8 were the other important issues. After comparing Tables 2 and 3, we found that the problems related to H2 can be discovered with the questionnaire but these problems cannot be identified by heuristic evaluation. More specifically, these problems are concerned with the fact that the content of the Web-based system should be arranged in a logical order so that information can be easy remembered and recognized.

The aforementioned results indicated that these two methods share some commonalities but there are also differences between them. Regarding the former, both of them indicate that H8 was the key problem of the system. It is probably because that the system presents massive information so learners may feel difficult to follow the content. Regarding the latter, heuristic evaluation identify that H1 is a major problem while the responses from the questionnaire indicated that H2 is a main issue. In other words, these two ways show different levels of seriousness for each heuristic. A possible reason is that Nielson's heuristics emphasizes on a macro view while the responses from the questionnaire focus on a micro view. More specifically, the former was used to examine the overall picture of the system whereas the latter was employed to investigate the details. In other words, such two ways are complementary to each other so that they should be used together.

Based on our results, a framework is summarized to illustrate the differences of the results from these two approaches. Such a framework can be applied for the evaluation of the usability of WBLS.

Table 2. Severity evaluation

Heuristics / Severity ratings	0	1	2	3	4	T
H1: Visibility of system status	1	0	2	1	1	11
H2: Match between system and the real world	0	0	0	0	1	4
H3: User control and freedom	0	0	0	1	0	3
H4: Consistency and standards	0	2	0	1	1	9
H5: Error prevention	1	1	0	0	0	1
H6: Recognition rather than recall	1	0	1	2	0	8
H7: Flexibility and efficiency of use	0	0	0	1	1	7
H8: Aesthetic and minimalist design	0	1	2	2	0	11
H9: Help users recognize, diagnose and recover from errors	1	1	2	1	0	8
H10 : Help and documentation	1	0	0	1	1	7
Total	5	5	7	10	5	69

Table 3. The results of negative questions

Q	Negative questions	Average	standard deviation	Heuristics
1	This system went on too long, so I needed spent too much time for learning Interaction Design	3.52	1.07	H8
2	I think the program is only useful for students who are already familiar with Interne	3.44	1.091	H2
3	I would prefer to learn from human tutors than from this system	3.22	1	H2
4	The content of this system is too detailed	3.12	0.917	H8
5	I do not know how to change the design layout of this system	3.12	1.14	H6
6	I found it hard to select relevant information using the map	3.1	1.25	H10
7	This tutorial is only appropriate for advanced students who know Interaction Design	3.04	1.029	H2
8	I was lost with using back/forward buttons	2.9	1.07	H10
9	I could not get to the more advanced levels without having to go through the basic stuff.	2.86	0.86	H2&3
10	Sometimes I found it hard to keep track which bits I had learnt.	2.84	1.04	H10

Positive   Nagetive

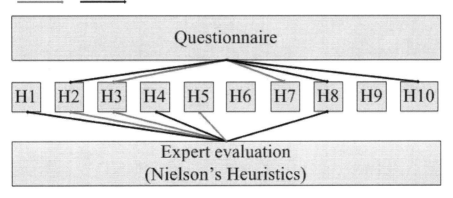

Fig. 3. The framework

4 Conclusions

This study analyzed the differences between learners' opinions from the questionnaire and heuristic evaluation. The results of this study indicated that Nielsen's heuristics are not complete enough to identify all learners' problems so it is necessary to combine with other approaches, such as questionnaires and interviews. In other words, learners' opinions and heuristic evaluation should be used to support each other. Moreover, future research should integrate the results from these two approaches to provide guidelines for the development of WBLS and other web-based applications.

Acknowledgments. This work is funded by National Science Council, ROC (NSC 98-2511-S-008 -012 -MY3 and NSC 99-2511-S-008 -003 -MY2).

References

1. Chen, S.Y., Macredie, R.D.: Assessment of the User Interface of Electronic Shopping: a Heuristic Evaluation. International Journal of Information Management 25, 516–532 (2005)
2. Gonzalez, M., Masip, L., Granollers, A., Oliva, M.: Quantitative analysis in a heuristic evaluation experiment. Advances in Engineering Software 40, 1271–1278 (2009)
3. Nielsen, J., Molich, R.: Heuristic evaluation of user interfaces. In: Proceedings of CHI 1990, pp. 249–256 (1990)
4. Jeffries, R., Miller, J.R., Wharton, C., Uyeda, K.: User interface evaluation in the real world: a comparison of four techniques. In: CHI 1991, pp. 119–124. ACM, New York (1991)
5. Nielsen, J.: Enhancing the explanatory power of usability heuristics. In: Proceedings of CHI 1994 Conference, pp. 152–158 (1994a)

Using Pre-session Homework to Elicit More Insights during Web Usability Testing

Christopher Jewell and Franco Salvetti

Bing-SF, Microsoft, 475 Brannan Street, Suite 330, San Francisco, CA 94107, USA
{cjewell,francosa}@microsoft.com

Abstract. Lab-based, web usability testing plays a central role in user-centered design. Yet time constraints, anxiety-producing conditions of testing, and a narrow focus on designs that may not align well with user needs can restrict the kinds of information obtained from users. These limitations can be addressed, in part, by assigning participants broader and more exploratory activities to be completed prior to the session that help them articulate their preferences and the processes they follow in the relevant research area. Participants are then better able to bring this awareness to their evaluation of the design being tested in the lab. Incorporating these pre-study activities into web usability testing can lead to the generation of more and a broader array of actionable recommendations.

1 Introduction

Lab-based, web usability testing plays an essential role in user-centered design and product development. Rather than relying on designers' assumptions about user needs, members of the targeted audience interact with early stages of an interface, and their responses are incorporated into subsequent versions in an iterative process of design, evaluation, and redesign known as *informal usability testing* [1]. Yet, lab-based testing is restricted in the kinds of user information it can obtain owing to several limitations of the setting and approach.

First, time constraints and the need for predictable interface behavior often lead to the utilization of tasks that may not fully coincide with how users think about or carry out the underlying activities on their own. As a result, users may interact with the tested interface differently than they would if they were completing tasks of their own choosing and at their own pace [2],[3].

Second, the "testing" quality of the lab setting can also contribute to the difficulty of eliciting normal responses from participants. Being evaluated and recorded can cause anxiety that hinders individuals' ability to respond in a natural manner or to think reflectively about their reactions.

Third, even when participants are comfortable and the activities are engaging, the information obtained may still be inadequate for developing the best design. Testing a specific interface or a few alternatives means optimizing within an already delimited design space [4], one that may not align well with users' underlying needs. This disconnect may occur because of an initial incomplete understanding of users' goals and tasks. This gap may also have emerged because user behaviors and expectations have shifted over time owing to changes in the conventions and offerings of the

C. Stephanidis (Ed.): Posters, Part I, HCII 2011, CCIS 173, pp. 156–160, 2011.
© Springer-Verlag Berlin Heidelberg 2011

competitive landscape. A tendency towards the development of feature-oriented teams may also limit the amount of organizational attention devoted to the overall experience of a site, with testing often focusing more narrowly on the particular elements for which teams are responsible[1].

2 Pre-study Homework Assignments

One way to address some of these informational shortcomings is by assigning participants broader and more exploratory kinds of activities to be completed at home and shared during the lab session. Two types of activities are especially suitable as homework: 1. having users characterize how they perform routine online activities; and 2. having users complete similar tasks on competitive sites and assess the comparative quality of the experiences. Having the time and familiar setting to complete these tasks while in an evaluative frame of mind helps participants to articulate the decision-making processes they follow and the impact various site features have on their efforts. Both exercises are, therefore, useful ways to draw more fully upon participants' often implicit experiential knowledge and preferences than is usually possible under normal lab conditions[2].

2.1 Characterizing Routine Activities

The first type of homework activity involves users describing how they carry out particular kinds of activities. These characterizations can reveal important decision-making patterns, including what users expect to accomplish in a domain, the importance of particular kinds of information (both online and off) and site features, and the challenges they face under current online conditions. Some types of activities will be relatively easy for users to characterize because they involve recurrent, routine behaviors (e.g., daily browsing for news). Other activities that involve greater task variation or that are performed less frequently may require more work on the part of the user and the researcher to identify commonalities across disparate experiences (e.g., online shopping). Having gone through this exercise (and subsequent discussion with the researcher), participants are more likely to bring this awareness to bear when they subsequently evaluate the tested design in the lab, facilitating their ability to assess how the interface meets their goals and aligns with their current approaches to task completion.

An example of instructions for characterizing routine activities is the following about the use of online coupons and deals: "Think about the various ways in which

---

[1] These limitations are particularly significant when one is interested in understanding a product or feature at a high level. By contrast, these conditions may be less important for other testing goals, such as, when one is gauging how users react to a new feature for the first time.

[2] These pre-study assignments can be distinguished from *longitudinal studies* in which participants use an interface for an extended period of time in order to gauge how perceptions and usage change with increased familiarity [5]. Homework assignments are intended as snapshots of users' current decision-making processes and opinions about related interfaces.

you find and use coupons and deals in your daily life. How often do you look for coupons and deals, and for what kinds of goods and services? How do you go about finding them? If you have found or redeemed coupons online, please be prepared to discuss the process you went through with a few examples. What are the greatest challenges to coupon hunting and redemption? Are there features or information that would make this process easier?"

2.2 Competitive Site Analysis

A second type of homework activity is to have participants complete comparable tasks on several competing sites in a domain. This kind of "applied" activity is an often useful complement to the first type of homework for several reasons. First, having participants make judgments based on new experiences avoids recall problems that arise when relying on more distant memories. Second, having multiple similar experiences that can be readily contrasted facilitates users' ability to generate their own comparative insights into the positive and negative aspects of each site.

Designed tasks can vary from relatively standardized (e.g., "find a Canon PowerShot D10 12.1MP Digital Camera with 3x Optical Zoom") to more general (e.g., "find a new television for under $750"). Having activities that are more open-ended helps ensure that users choose examples and follow processes that are more authentic. At the same time, giving users this freedom can result in greater task variation across sites and between participants, so that differences in task characteristics may play an important role in users' judgments of comparative site efficacy [6]. Mitigating against this problem of variation is the fact that the researcher is utilizing the observations of 8-10 participants and that through analysis of this aggregated data, recurring themes and reactions are likely to be identified. Additionally, because the unit of judgment is the site, many seemingly disparate observations about particular features can be characterized as instances of more general site attributes (e.g., information placement, filtering, or navigation).

An example of instructions for a competitive site assignment is the following concerning online gift shopping: "Think of 3 people you will need to buy a gift for. For the first person, look for ideas and possibly choose a gift using the online site #1 designated below. For the second person, use the online site #2. For the third person you will look for a gift in the lab on a third site. Be ready to discuss: the searches you ran; the information and site features that were most helpful in coming up with ideas; the biggest challenges you faced in doing this task; the most important reasons you chose the gift ideas you did."

As part of the in-lab discussion of users' comparative assessment, it is also useful to have them rank and score (on a 1-10 scale) their experiences. While the scores cannot be statistically significant, the numbers and particularly the forced ranking provide another opportunity for discussing their most salient impressions about each site, requiring them to make hard comparative judgments and be able to justify them.

It may also be helpful to have participants evaluate some sites at home and complete the remaining sites in the lab. This approach is useful for several reasons. First, the researcher may not have enough homework time to assign the entire exercise. Second, conducting some tasks in the lab provides the researcher access to behavioral observations, which can reveal more nuanced information than participant reporting alone. Third, lab testing allows the discussion with participants to continue past initial assignment debriefing, with these new experiences providing opportunities for further comparative assessments. If the tested design is live, the researcher may similarly want to have a mix of home and lab evaluations in order to obtain the benefits of both forms of data. In any case, the sites should be randomized in terms of which are done at home and which in the lab as well as the site sequence so as to minimize ordering effects [4].

2.3   Operational Details

The remuneration and expected duration of the homework should be stated explicitly at the top of the assignment. One workable convention is to pay users the "hourly rate" based on the amount paid for the lab session. To ensure participants do their homework in a thoughtful way, it is also helpful to instruct them to take notes and be ready to discuss and run through their work. These assignments should then be reviewed at the beginning of the lab session. Revisiting the sites helps ensure participants have actually done the work and records it for future reference. Additionally, the visual cues often spark further insights the person may not have written down or even thought of until they are talking about it.

Discussing their homework when they first arrive in the lab also helps establish rapport between the participant and the researcher. By indicating interest in the user's opinions, letting them practice being critical, and providing positive reinforcement, the researcher helps participants overcome hesitancies they may have about criticizing the company's products during the lab session[3].

3   Impact

Research shows that the number of unique findings from a user study tends to plateau, with 5 participants able to identify about 85% of a design's problems [7]. However, the number of findings can be increased by expanding the number and variety of tasks that users perform, thereby providing different ways for users to engage with a design [8]. Homework assignments can similarly increase the number of insights a study of a given size can obtain for somewhat analogous reasons. Participants often possess significant experiential knowledge and preferences relevant to a design. Yet, this information often remains latent and difficult to utilize in a lab setting. Activities like characterizing routine activities and assessing competitive site efficacy help users to access this information in evaluating and comparing interfaces intended to meet similar needs and goals, including the tested design.

The impact of pre-study homework assignments on user study findings is illustrated in Figure 1. This figure displays the locations of recommendations for an online shopping site that were generated by two user studies, one with a traditional design, and a second, later one, that had participants characterize their online shopping behavior and

---

[3] Another possible benefit to adding a homework assignment is an increase in attendance rates (in the current case a rise from 80% to about 95% has been observed). Because participants have already invested time, they may be less likely to make a last minute decision to cancel.

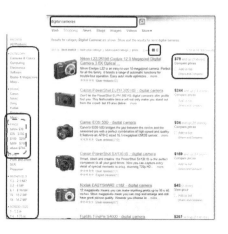

Fig. 1. Current online shopping site indicating the areas where recommendations were generated for an earlier version of the site by a traditional user study (*dotted lines*) and a user study that utilized pre-study homework assignments (*solid lines*). The study with homework assignments led to a larger number of findings across a wider array of site features.

assess competitive shopping sites prior to lab testing. While the earlier study generated a few insights about a particular feature (highlighted with dotted lines), the later study identified more issues across a wider array of features including additional recommendations for the feature previously studied (highlighted in solid lines).

References

1. Nielsen, J.: Usability Engineering at a Discount. In: Proceedings of the Third International Conference on Human-Computer Interaction, pp. 394–401. Elsevier Science Inc., New York (1989)
2. Rose, D.E.: Why Is Web Search So Hard...To Evaluate? J. of Web Eng. 3, 171–181 (2004)
3. Russell, D.M., Slaney, M., Qu, Y., Houston, M.: Being Literate with Large Document Collections: Observational Studies and Cost Structure Tradeoffs. In: Proceedings of the 39th Annual Hawaii International Conference on System Sciences, HICSS (2006)
4. Hearst, M.: Search User Interfaces. Cambridge University Press, Cambridge (2009)
5. Shneiderman, B., Plaisant, C.: Strategies for Evaluating Information Visualization Tools: Multi-Dimensional In-Depth Long-Term Case Studies. In: Proceedings of the 2006 AVI Workshop on BEyond Time and Errors: Novel Evaluation Methods for Information Visualization (2006)
6. Nielsen, J.: Usability Engineering. Morgan Kaufmann, San Francisco (1993)
7. Nielsen, J.: Why You Only Need To Test With 5 Users, http://www.useit.com/alertbox/20000319.html
8. Lindgaard, G., Chattratichart, J.: Usability Testing: What Have We Overlooked? In: Proceedings of the SIGCHI Conference on Human Factors in Computing Systems, CHI 2007 (2007)

Personalized ATMs: Improve ATMs Usability

Armin Kamfiroozie and Marzieh Ahmadzadeh

IT Department, e-Learning faculty - Shiraz University of Technology, Iran
`armin.kamfiroozie@gmail.com, ahmadzadeh@sutech.ac.ir`

Abstract. Using customization in products and services is one of the important methods for obtaining customers' satisfaction. In this paper, the personalized ATMs have been introduced which as one of the objectives, using personalization and customization methods, improve the efficiency and simplicity of usage of the ATMs and enable the users to benefit from the machine commensurate with their needs. In this system, based on general information about users and the records of customers' activities in CRM system, the information and screens are displayed which are predicted to be most applicable for the customers. This system is able to provide services based on users' abilities in order to enable all the customers to acquire their needed services from the system in the shortest time duration and highest efficiency.

Keywords: ATM, Auto Teller Machine, Customization, Personalization, HCI.

1 Introduction

It passes few decades from now when the first ATM appeared whose duty was to receive bills and deposit into customers' accounts and after a while, it could do all banking operation and now it performs other services even further than financial operation and its services are added unremittingly. Self-Service systems' family is being developed and various systems are included to this broad family. ATMs and interactive kiosks are the most famous members of them. Kiosks' applications have their own features and diversities, like doing financial, educational, entertainment, business, and communicative services. They also have different types in terms of appearance from a simple photo kiosk to financial and internet kiosks. Financial kiosks have usually a mouse, keypad, touch screens, card reader, etc., and services like getting news and information, filling out forms and operations like this are carried out by them. However, prevalent interactive kiosks have not capability of cash dispense/deposit and this task is on ATMs; ATMs generally have a monitor, card reader, printers, cash dispense/deposit modules, keypad and sometimes barcode scanner and sound system, etc. A standard and simple form of ATMs has made the use of them easy and there is no need to work with multipart and complicated systems like interactive kiosks [1], [2]. We apply existing ATMs for increasing the variety of services and personalizing them. Of course, some of the financial kiosks are also offering receiving and dispensing systems now that have turned them into very expensive and well-equipped systems, but they are rare.

C. Stephanidis (Ed.): Posters, Part I, HCII 2011, CCIS 173, pp. 161–166, 2011.
© Springer-Verlag Berlin Heidelberg 2011

2   Motivation

By adding each new service on the ATM, new menus should also be available on the device. Most of the ATMs have only four buttons on the right and four ones on the left of the screen so the number of menus in each screen is limited. Crowded lines, long process of doing an operation, complexity and increase of menus and difficult use of this device for low illiterate or disabled people, are problems we will face with the increase of services on current ATMs, [3], [4]. For many reasons, all presentable services in kiosks are not suitable to be carried out via ATMs. ATM is a public and widely used device, and time period of use is limited for each person. Actually services must be in a way that the user only needs minimum inputs, and if it is indented a purchase is made, that goods or service should be prepared and available as a prepayment in advance and not have a great variety either. These services should also be usable by special people like the blinds, illiterates, foreign and deaf people. But all of these services are not always applied for all walks of life, and it is not necessary to display all of them in each use of the ATM [3], [4].

3   Customized ATMs

Nowadays, the customization in management of relations with customers has turned into one of the most key factors in manufacturing and service companies and the businesses which are more adaptable with their customers, are more successful [5]. This approach is available in CRM system of banks through processing clients' activities [1], [6]. Providing services on ATMs and changing the screens based on the clients' needs are conducted in two ways; personalization and customization.

3.1 Customization vs. Personalization

The personalization is carried out in contents and data levels and requires analysis and processing of users' data and activities history. The users will not need to deal with designing and selecting their favorite menus. Thus, there must be various and appropriate data and available knowledge about the users. While in customization this action is done manually by the users in such a way that the users select the information which they are willing to be displayed and also they determine how the order and method of manifestation would be. The Profile is used in this way. Since one of the purposes of personalization is reducing the user's performed operation and speeding up the transaction and on the contrary, in customization, the user is required to be active and play a role in creating the desired situation and structure, therefore some sort of contradiction occurs [5]. An inactive user who likes use his favorite menus are not usually willing to spend time creating the respective profile.

Consequently, regarding the objective of this system, customization is barely used and practically the focus in the ATMs is on personalization. The bank cards are used to withdraw money from ATMs, utilized in banks, using in mobile banking operations, shopping from stores and doing online purchases [1], [2]. The bank network is suitably connected to other even in whole the world and wherever you use your card, the transaction record will be kept by your bank [2], [6].

3.2 Customization and Personalization in ATMs

In personalized ATMs all the clients' records are stored in CRM system and will retrieve from it and other related databases. These data are collected and updated in several stages: at the time of opening the account, while the account is used for mentioned purposes, or according to customers demand at the time of using the card. These data include personal information and also the records of purchases and performed transactions including time, place or the websites where the purchases have been done, list of the people who you have had financial relations and other services you have taken from the machine such as the type of the withdrawn sums, the purchased tickets, payment invoices and so on [5], [6].

By analyzing these data and personal information of customers, the screens and menus can be predicted and displayed based on the clients' needs. In this method the customers must enter their PIN after inserting the card. The PIN screen is usually identical for all users with any physical and social conditions [7]. The PIN code and card number are then sent to center in the first connection and if it authorized, based on the card number and other processed information the ATM do proper action. In a more advanced design, users can assign two passwords to their account and based on entered password the way of personalization would be different.

For instance a person, suffering from optical problems, following inserting his/her card will observe a screen in which colors and other fonts have been designed for the optical disordered people and the audio system could be activated, or for example for less educated people following entering the PIN code, some screen with graphical menus is displayed and the audio system of machine is also activated [8] (Figure 1).

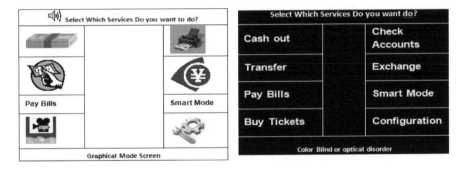

Fig. 1. Sample screen on personalized ATM for illiterate or optical disordered people

In another example an ordinary person, after entering PIN code, observes a screen in which one of assigned options is purchasing the ticket of the matches or concert which are to be held on that week, this information is based on the customers' records that indicate interest in participation in sport matches or concerts and ticket purchasing. This method of reminding and suggesting can be also applied for recalling the payment of installments and bills or introducing newly added services. It must be remembered that services in the form of previously prepared packages for purchases (such as ticket purchasing and charging telephone) are readily available for sale in ATMs. In personalized ATMs, all the services are available but the order and priority and the way of offering services and representation are different.

4 Implementation Feasibility

The processing of user's activity and prediction and creation of personalized pages for client is carried out by the software installed on the server and connected to the CRM system of the organization and there is no need to change the current cards or ATMS to approach mentioned goals. All the screens and menus could be saved in offline mode in the ATMs. The menu combinations and the order of screen can be transmitted between machine and datacenter in the form of encoded data having very low bandwidth usage and can be stored in some bytes (Fig. 2). The interpretation of codes is done in the installed software of the ATM.

Some of users, while using the ATM, do not like changes in the appearance of the menu of machine or they are willing to impose the changes themselves. In this case, customization and profiles must be used instead of personalization. The encoding manner and saving of the screens arrangements can be done as before.

a	b	c	d	e	f	g	h

Fig. 2. Sample byte set for storing personalization information

a) The way of system representation: Default – Personalized – Profile Based.
b) The user's selected language: Common languages or graphical Mode
c) User's physical and corporal condition: Healthy, Optical Disordered, Deaf, etc.,
d) Type of currency to be used
e,f,g) Custom Screen Contents.
h) Reserved for unpredictable needs.

There could be an option like "Configuration" in the "other services" menu through which the card and personalization settings can be manipulated. These settings are conducted in the form of "Wizard" and the user is able to select the type of personalization service through it. In more advanced states, a combination of these two methods can be applied. In this mode, the menus that generated by analyzing customer history are more like recommendation. The generated code for creating the screens and customized menus can be saved and used in two ways:

- Saving in offline mode on the customer's card
- Receiving in online mode from the center

Saving in offline mode results in reduction in connection to center and therefore this mode is more appropriate at the time of high network traffic and server overloads. In this way, the customers see their own personalized page at the moment of inserting the cards. In this circumstance, it is needed to read and write on the cart every time and it's not very suitable. In the second method, the analyzed data in the bank CRM system are up-to-date and the relevant personalized code of customer can be obtained using the last changes and executed transactions by considering other available data. In this method, the data are sent to the center as soon as entering the PIN and if it authorized, operation with personalized ATM will continue (Figure 3).

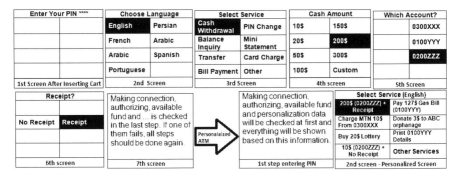

Fig. 3. Sample comparison between doing an operation in current ATM vs. personalized ATM

5 Conclusion

In this paper a model was presented for personalizing ATMs which is able to provide more services, moreover will recognize and help you to carry out your tasks more rapidly based on your needs. Improving the efficiency and usability of these devices is a result of personalizing screens and services [3]. These ATMs can offer purchases or services commensurate with your tastes and daily life. In this case you will find what you need quickly instead of memorizing the whole path of operation. They might talk and interact with you in an effective way [8]. Possibility to add efficient and purposive advertisements based on geographical or location of ATM leads the machine to be more profitable and compensate the costs that customers undergo [1], [6]. This model can also be used in Kiosks as another member of this family. As you previously had friendly relations with banks clerk and he was treating you differently compared to others, now this expectation will be fulfilled by machine clerks. They are kind of forthcoming Self-Service Machines which you can meet all you need.

References

1. First Data Corporation, http://www.firstdata.com
2. Automated Teller Machine business news, research, more,
   http://www.atmmarketplace.com
3. Yarlikas, S.: A New Automatic Teller Machine (ATM) Proposal through the Analysis of ATMs of Three Banks. In: Jacko, J.A. (ed.) HCII 2009. LNCS, vol. 5613, pp. 641–650. Springer, Heidelberg (2009)
4. Cremers, A.H.M., de Jong, J.G.M., van Balken, J.S.: User-Centered Design with Illiterate Persons: The Case of the ATM User Interface. In: Miesenberger, K., Klaus, J., Zagler, W., Karshmer, A. (eds.) ICCHP 2008. LNCS, vol. 5105, pp. 713–720. Springer, Heidelberg (2008)
5. Tseng, M.M., Piller, F.T. (eds.): The Customer Centric Enterprise: Advances in Mass Customization and Personalization, New York, Berlin, p. 168 illus (2003)

6. Hosono, N., Gotanda, S., Inoue, H., Tomita, Y.: ATM Advertisement and Financial Preferences with Sensory Analysis. In: Jacko, J.A. (ed.) HCII 2007. LNCS, vol. 4553, pp. 42–47. Springer, Heidelberg (2007)
7. Moncur, W., Leplatre, G.: Pictures at the ATM: exploring the usability of multiple graphical passwords. In: Proceedings of the SIGCHI Conference on Human Factors in Computing Systems (CHI 2007), pp. 887–894. ACM, New York (2007)
8. Akatsu, H., Komatsubara, A.: Auditory and Visual Guidance for Reducing Cognitive Load. In: Kurosu, M. (ed.) HCD 2009. LNCS, vol. 5619, pp. 391–397. Springer, Heidelberg (2009)

The Effect of Induced Priming on Product Perceived Usability

Jihyun Kim[1], Myung Shik Kim[2], and Kwang-Hee Han[2]

[1] Graduate program in Cognitive Science, Yonsei University,
134 Shinchon-dong, Seodaemun-gu, Seoul, South Korea
[2] Department of Psychology, Yonsei University,
134 Shinchon-dong, Seodaemun-gu, Seoul, South Korea
{jjyuny2,kimmyungshik}@gmail.com, khan@yonsei.ac.kr

Abstract. The usability testing by users have considered as an important process in the development of a product. However, users do not always judge rationally in the context of the evaluation. Two experiments were carried out to investigate the effect of induced priming on perceived usability evaluation. The results revealed that temporally induced affective priming affected users' usability evaluation. The present study suggests that people who engaged in the fields of usability testing or the marketing consider unexpected priming and take delicate care in handling the affective variable.

Keywords: usability, evaluation, affective priming.

1 Introduction

At this very moment, numerous new electronics launches are occurring all over the world. The usability evaluation of the user before an official launch is regarded as an important process in product development in recent years. Usability is defined as the ease of use and comprehensiveness of a human-made object, and this character is judged by humans highly-complicated multiple perceived human factors. Decades of psychological research have shown that positive affect brings users various kinds of physical and psychological advantages [1] and negative affect accordingly [2]. Moreover, this also impacts human decision making [3], however in spite of the importance of positive emotion, combining with HCI, relevant research is still insufficient. We hypothesized that the user's temporal emotion could influence the perceived usability evaluation. Two studies were carried out to investigate and reveal the effect of induced priming on user usability evaluations with unknown mobile phones in Korea.

2 Methods

The effect of affective priming was found only at the subliminal level [4]. Therefore, many tricks were designed in the process of the experiment to prevent participants

C. Stephanidis (Ed.): Posters, Part I, HCII 2011, CCIS 173, pp. 167–170, 2011.

from recognizing our experimental hypothesis. Firstly, In Session 1 participants were primed to believe they will receive automated feedback compared to that of other participants according to how proper and vivid the sentence is. However positive or negative feedback was automated dependent on the priming group. Secondly, the objective of posting comments as a task in the session 2 was introduced to reflect good comments made by participants to promote of the product. Finally, the mobile phones were presented as a product expected to be out which might reflect the rating result regarding the development and promotion of the product.

Participants. Sixteen students were paid 5000 won ($5) and 24 students received course credit.

Materials. Two different mobile phones were evaluated by each participant in the first and second session (Fig1). The mobile phones used for this research were Japanese mocks to minimize fixed ideas about domestic brands on the participant. To eliminate the order effect, the order of the two mobile phones was regularly switched prior to each participant's experiment. Software for this experiment was developed by Microsoft visual basic 6.

The evaluation questionnaire consisted of several questions about overall reactions to the software taken from the questionnaire for user interface satisfaction [5]. Other questions were about perceived usefulness and perceived ease of use [6]. These were rated on a 7-point likert scale.

In session 1, 30 positive valance and 30 negative valance pictures were selected from the International Affective Picture System (IAPS) [7]. In session 2, three words were presented with a photo randomly extracted from 10 photos of electronic devices such as a vacuum, monitor, and headphones, not including mobile phones. Sample words consisted of positive or negative adjectives. Positive adjectives were, for example, cutting-edge, improved, wonderful, new, best, vivid, etc. Negative adjectives were old-fashioned, difficult, heavy, broken-down, destroyed, ugly, etc..

Fig.1. Mobile phones that were evaluated in this experiment

Procedure. Twenty Participants were randomly assigned to the positive priming group and the other 20 were placed in the negative priming group. In the first session, participants were asked to make a sentence associated with the presentation of three pictures. With each question three pictures were presented randomly from positive or negative valence images. The positive priming group as showed only positively affective pictures and the negative priming group as showed only negatively affective pictures. Participants were directed to express the descriptions that came to mind because the score was set according to how proper and vivid the sentence was. The positive priming group got relatively high scores with positive feedback such as "that was a proper descriptive", "better than any other participants" or etc. in every sentence. The negative priming group received relatively low scores and provided negative feedback such as "needs more effort"," not enough", or etc. in every sentence. The task stopped after five minutes in order to control the same affective priming time across participants. "Congratulations, you are going to get candy" for the positive priming group or "sorry, you are not going to get candy" for the negative priming group at the end of the session. Subsequent usability testing was conducted. Participants opened a box that lay before them, and took out the product and questionnaire paper in the box. After completing the evaluation, participants turned in the product and questionnaire paper to the experimenter and started the second session, receiving a new box.

In the second session, participants were given a scenario that: they are a student promoter of a certain company and need to make a comment including the presented three words about a photo of product. The objective of the task was to promote the product with positive adjective words for the positive priming group, or to slander the product of the competing company with negative adjective words for the negative priming group. To reduce the effect of the previous session's emotion, the session order was allocated in order.

3   Results and Discussion

ANOVA was conducted to compare between the groups. Main effect results revealed that the positive priming group ($M = 4.65$, $SD = .51$) rated products as having higher usability than the negative priming group ($M = 4.03$, $SD = .83$) did, $F(1, 38) = 8.320$, $p = .006$, only in the affective priming session, not in the adjectives priming session. A brief interview was conducted after the experiments in order to ask if participants recognized or were able to guess at any experimental hypothesis such as casual relation between each task session and the evaluation phase. None of the participants was able to recognize the research hypothesis.

This demonstrates that temporally induced emotion of two different priming methods could affect users' usability evaluations. The results support the argument that temporal emotion can be one of the major factors for users' judgments, implying that a user's current emotional mood can be an important influential factor to their response. Could we say a human is a really rational being for sure?

Our experiment upholds our hypothesis: the evaluator's temporal induced emotion could affect his or her decision making. Therefore, those engaged in the fields of usability testing or the marketing should consider unexpected emotional priming and take great care in handling the emotion variable among the users. Future research should continue exploring these priming subtleties on a user's evaluation.

References

1. Isen, A.M.: Positive Affect, Cognitive Processes, and Social Behavior. In: Berkowitz, L. (ed.) Advances in Experimental Social Psychology, vol. 20, pp. 203–253. Academic Press, New York (1987)
2. Aspinwall, L.G.: Rethinking The Role of Positive Affect in Self Regulation. Motivation and Emotion 22, 1–32 (1998)
3. Schwaz, N., Clore, G.: Mood, Misattribution, and Judgements of Well-Being: Informative and Directive Functions of Affective States. Journal of Personality and Social Psychology 45(3), 513–523 (1983)
4. Lee, S.J.: The Influence of Nonconscious Affective Priming on Object Rating. The Korean Journal of Cognitive Science 10(4), 1–15 (1999)
5. Chin, J.P., Diehl, V.A., Norman, K.L.: Development of an Instrument Measuring User Satisfaction of The Human-Computer Interface. In: CHI 1988, pp. 213–218 (1988)
6. Gafen, D., Krahanna, E., Straub, D.W.: Trust and TAM in online shopping: An Integrated Model. MIS Quarterly 27(1), 51–90 (2003)
7. Lang, P.J., Bradley, M.M.: International Affective Picture System (IAPS): Instruction manual and affective ratings. Tech. Rep. A-4 (1999)

Who Are the People That Experience Soft Usability Problems?

Chajoong Kim and Henri Christiaans

School of Industrial Design Engineering
Delft University of Technology, The Netherlands
{c.j.kim,h.h.c.m.christiaans}@tudelft.nl

Abstract. The existing taxonomy of user experience needs to be redefined because of fast technology development in consumer electronic market. Design for all seems prevalent in the field of product design. However, there are ever more doubts about a one-fits-all policy considering the increasing diversity of users and the increasing number of complaints. In our previous studies a taxonomy of 'soft' usability problems related to the use of electronic products has been made. The question posed in this paper is how people behave in the actual use of annoying user-unfriendly products. An experiment was conducted with 33 South Koreans and 23 Americans. A radio alarm clock and a MP3 player were chosen to induce soft usability problems. A questionnaire was used to measure the participants' characteristics. Overall, this study indicates that product operation and user behavior are correlated with specific user characteristics such as age, gender, and culture.

Keywords: usability, soft usability problem, user characteristics, culture.

1   Introduction

The concept of form of electronic products has been changed a lot over the last decades thanks to the advancement of science and technology. Especially, technology-driven product development has produced electronic products that have all the predictable black-box disadvantages such as the integration of too many functions, operation difficulty and the lack of feedback. The consequence was and still is an increase complaints and product returns; and, disturbing for manufacturers, almost 50% of these complaints have nothing to do with technical failure [1]. In addition to product complexity, user diversity seems to explain why the product return is increasing [2]. Design for all appears prevalent in the field of product design. However, there are ever more doubts to one-fits-all policy considering the increasing diversity of user [3]. In our previous studies an inventory was made of these so-called 'soft' usability problems based on a survey among people from different countries. The problems could be categorized into six groups: *Understanding* (difficulties in understanding functions), *Performance* (low efficiency and compatibility), *Sensation* (poor sound, touch and temperature quality), *Structure* (complaints about connections and shape), *Maintenance* (dissatisfaction with service and cleaning), and *Constraint*

C. Stephanidis (Ed.): Posters, Part I, HCII 2011, CCIS 173, pp. 171–175, 2011.
© Springer-Verlag Berlin Heidelberg 2011

(lack of necessary functions, of information/feedback and battery life) [4]. As a follow-up, this study observes the behavior of users when confronted with products that are notorious user-unfriendly and frustrating. Will this behavior be different for different users?

2 Method

In order to find out the relationships between user characteristics and soft usability problems, this study first looks into the differences between young and old users, male and female users, and American and South Korean users.

Sample
The experiment was carried out with 23 American (10 male, 13 female) and 33 South Korean participants (20 male, 13 female), who lived in their home country at the moment they participated in the experiment. They were recruited though an ad. Their age ranged from 20 to 70.

Instruments
User characteristics such as demographics, personality, cognitive aspects and consumer complaining behavior, were measured by a questionnaire. To induce soft usability problems in actual product use a radio alarm clock and a mp3 player were selected (Fig. 1). Both electronic products were reported to have many consumer complaints related to soft usability problems.

Fig. 1. Radio Alarm Clock and MP3 Player

Procedure
Participants were individually invited at a location where they felt convenient such as their home, a cafeteria, or a library meeting room. First, the experiment was introduced. This was followed by filling out the first part of the questionnaire. Next, the participant was asked to do several tasks with the radio alarm clock. After this, they filled out the second part of the questionnaire. After, the MP3 player was handed and again several tasks had to be done. Finally, a retrospective interview was taken. All the sessions were videotaped for analysis afterwards.

3 Results

Overall, the results indicate that specific user characteristics such as age, gender, and culture are correlated with specific soft usability problems, use behaviors and consumer complaining behaviors. Most of the soft usability problems found in our previous studies were identified in both products' operation, but the percentage of soft problems differs (Fig. 2). For instance, *Structure* is the most frequently heard complain in the radio alarm clock, whereas in the MP3 player it is *Understanding*.

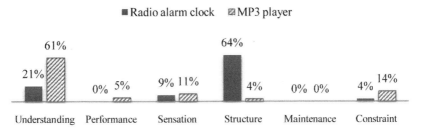

Fig. 2. Soft Usability Problems Comparison between Radio Alarm Clock and MP3 Player

3.1 Age

The 20-35 age group can be characterized by seeking for more perfectionism, hardly reading manuals, having better memory, lower uncertainty avoidance, more internal locus of control and better proficiency with electronics compared with the older group (Table 1). The younger group succeeds more in tasks requiring high cognitive load than the older group (Table 2).

Table 1. Group Differences Between 20-35 and 36+ Age Groups

User characteristics	Age 20-35 (n=26)		Age 36+ (n=30)		
	M	SD	M	SD	t(54)
Perfectionism	2.96	1.428	2.20	1.324	2.070*
Reading manuals	2.69	1.350	3.70	1.343	-2.794***
Memory	3.58	1.362	2.37	1.159	3.594***
Uncertainty avoidance	3.50	0.906	4.10	1.062	-2.256*
Locus of control	70.96	11.137	77.50	10.566	-2.252*
Proficiency with electronics	2.58	0.578	2.07	0.785	2.733***

*p < .01, ***p < .001.

Table 2. Task Success Rate Between 20-35 and 36+ Age Groups

Tasks	Age 20-35 (n=26)	Age 36+ (n=30)	$\chi^2(1)$
Radio alarm clock	20	10	8.960***
MP3 player	19	8	10.229***

***p < .001.

The older group (M=4.30, SD=1.487; t(54)=-4.225, p=.000) is more inclined to complain to the helpdesk than the younger group (M=2.54 , SD=1.630). There is no significant difference in types of soft problems between the two age groups.

3.2 Gender

Men have higher scores in technical skills and proficiency with electronics but lower scones in Agreeableness (a tendency to be pleasant and accommodating in social situations) than the female group (Table 3). Men have a higher success rate with the radio alarm clock tasks than women (Table 4). They (M=1.97, SD=0.964; t(54)=2.255, p=.028). In spite of the frustrating experience men are also more willing to purchase the radio alarm clock than women (M=1.46, SD=0.706).

Table 3. Group Differences Between Male and Female Groups

User characteristics	Male (n=30)		Female (n=26)		t(54)
	M	SD	M	SD	
Technical skills	3.60	1.248	2.04	1.248	4.668***
Agreeableness	29.90	3.960	34.42	4.709	-3.905***
Proficiency with electronics	2.57	0.568	2.00	0.800	3.086***

***p < .001.

Table 4. Task Success Rate Between Male and Female Groups

Tasks	Male (n=30)	Female (n=26)	$\chi^2(1)$
Radio alarm clock	29	18	5.872*
MP3 player	17	10	1.192

*p < .01.

3.3 Culture

The South Korean participants complain more about structure (value=8.044, p=.005), while the Americans more about understanding (value=6.080, p=.014).

The American participants are characterized by higher scores on Openness (respect for all other beings), Agreeableness, Self-efficacy (the belief that one is capable of performing in a certain manner to attain certain goals), but lower scores in Exposure to commercials (Table 5). There are no significant differences in task success rate between both groups. Regarding their reaction on the frustrating experience the American participants are less willing to express their complaints to others (M=3.61, SD=1.438; t(54)=2.824, p=.007). In contrast, the South Korean group is more likely to actively express their problems to the helpdesk and give negative comments about the product to their friends (M=4.79, SD=1.269; t(54)=-3.517, p=.001).

Table 5. Group Differences between American and South Korean groups

User characteristics	American (n=23)		South Korean (n=33)		t(54)
	M	SD	M	SD	
Openness	31.70	5.547	30.39	4.828	2.319*
Agreeableness	34.30	3.936	30.39	4.828	3.209***
Self-efficacy	33.30	4.343	29.91	4.179	2.944***
Exposure to commercials	2.26	0.851	3.05	0.689	-3.805***

*p < .01, ***p < .001.

4 Conclusions and Discussion

The main findings in the study are that the type of soft usability problems experienced by users differs between electronic products. Moreover, user behavior such as task success rate, proneness to complaining, and problems experienced are related to specific user characteristics such as age, gender, and culture. They are to some extent consistent with those of our previous studies. How users use electronics and how they complain can partly be predicted when knowing who they are. In this way, this study can provide practical information to the electronic industry and it can lead to an increase in consumer satisfaction.

Acknowledgements. The authors gratefully acknowledge the support of the Innovation-Oriented Research Programme 'Integrated Product Creation and Realization (IOP IPCR)' of the Netherlands Ministry of Economic Affairs.

References

1. den Ouden, E., Yuan, L., Sonnemans, P.J.M., Brombacher, A.C.: Quality and reliability problems from a consumer's perspective: an increasing problem overlooked by businesses? Quality and Reliability Engineering International 22(7), 821–838 (2006)
2. Brombacher, A.C., Sander, P.C., Sonnemans, P.J.M., Rouvroye, J.L.: Managing product reliability in business processes 'under pressure'. Reliability Engineering & System Safety 88(2), 137–146 (2005)
3. Abascal, J., Azevedo, L.: Fundamentals of inclusive HCI design. In: Stephanidis, C. (ed.) HCI 2007. LNCS, vol. 4554, pp. 3–9. Springer, Heidelberg (2007)
4. Christiaans, H., Kim, C.: Soft Problems with Consumer Electronics and the Influence of User Characteristics. Paper presented at the 17th International Conference on Engineering Design (ICED 2009), Stanford, USA (2009)

Gaze Analysis Tool for Web Usability Evaluation

Takuo Matsunobe

Faculty of Systems Engineering, Wakayama University, 930 Sakaedani, Wakayama, Japan
matunobe@sys.wakayama-u.ac.jp

Abstract. Gaze information is obtained during Web usability evaluation - plotting the gaze locus and estimating the gaze duration for an image on a Web page. However, the one at the position of the gaze had to specify and to specify something by the evaluator. Therefore, considerable of time is required for analysis. The proposed tool can automatically identify what an observer is viewing. Thus, using the proposed gaze analysis tool, gaze information, which was earlier analyzed qualitatively, can be analyzed quantitatively.

Keywords: gaze point, eye tracking, contents area, web design.

1 Introduction

When examining the usability of a screen interface, knowledge about which part is viewed by the user while operating is useful from a design perspective. Thus, many researches have been conducted on a gaze point by utilizing eye tracking. However, since gaze point analysis is a time consuming process, the analysis conducted in the field of product development simply comprises confirming the gaze point of a typical user on video rather than performing a quantitative evaluation.

With regard to this problem, the authors have developed a method for automatically detecting a screen area, which includes the interface to be evaluated, and converts the gaze point coordinate into a coordinate system of the target screen; this is applied when conducting head non-restraining-type measurement utilizing a head-mounted eye camera, with an aim to increase analysis efficiency[1]. Furthermore, automatic specification of the gaze target in the screen can be proposed as the next challenge.

2 Eye Movement Analysis in Web Usability Evaluation

One of the primary characteristics of the Web, which is used as a target in eye movement analysis, is the change in screen that accompanies a page transition caused by a hyperlink. Furthermore, scrolling also occurs depending on the amount of content and the display setting (i.e., character size). Because only positional information can be acquired from the display coordinate system, it is difficult to automatically associate the gaze target—contents, in other words—with a web page that involves changes in the screen.

C. Stephanidis (Ed.): Posters, Part I, HCII 2011, CCIS 173, pp. 176–180, 2011.

Therefore, to perform an analysis that targets contents, it is necessary to specify in a framewise manner the contents that are at a gaze point coordinate position using human eyes. Because this is a time consuming process, most research involved a page-based evaluation method that depended on the characteristics of eye movement on the display coordinate. However, to improve the user interface, what the user viewed last needs to be confirmed, and this point is discussed in many researches presented in the conclusion section[2].

The unit for the evaluation when considering Web usability is a web page or the entire website. When designing a page, most cases involve controlling the style using CSS. In such an instance, a tag that specifies the block area (which is typically div) is often utilized on the HTML side. When designing an entire site, in most cases the style used in several pages is controlled using CSS, with tags such as "class" and "id" specified for each common area. Page transitions using links and browser and the amount of time spent on a page are used for evaluating the relationship between pages.

3   Evaluation Tool

In this research, the area specified by a block area as a content area was used as a unit to determine the Web browsing state. An example of this is the area division depicted in Fig 1. The advantage of using division when evaluating a website is that it is possible to compare how much the areas that have a common "class" or "id" set were viewed, even among different pages. Since HTML is a language for structuring documents, this area is often organized as a cluster of significance.

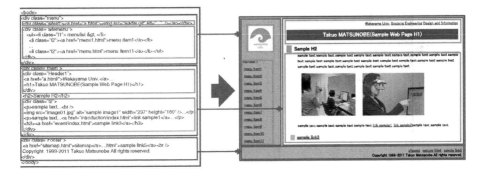

Fig. 1. Example of Area Division of a Page based on Tag Areas

The evaluation tool developed comprises a measurement tool that includes a Web browser function and an analysis tool. Since the browser included in the measurement tool utilizes components of Internet Explorer, the display is equivalent to that of Internet Explorer. Flash and other applications can be displayed by installing plug-ins.

The framework of the measurement system is as shown in Fig. 2. Gaze point coordinate data outputted from an eye tracking system (EMR-NL8B manufactured by NAC Image Technology Inc.) is received by a measurement PC. Since the measured coordinate is in fact a display coordinate system, it is converted into the browser coordinate system using an application. Next, an HTML tag provided at the browser coordinate position is acquired. The page title, the URI of the displayed web page, gaze point coordinate, the page transition method (link, URI input, back, forward), the scrolling volume, and the browser size are recorded as browse information along with the time operated.

For the HTML tag—although the gaze point coordinate position tag (e.g., <P>.<A>, <IMG>) can be recorded—tags that are parent components were acquired in this research by focusing on div immediately below the "body" that indicates the main contents, and each menu within the content area as displayed in Fig. 1.

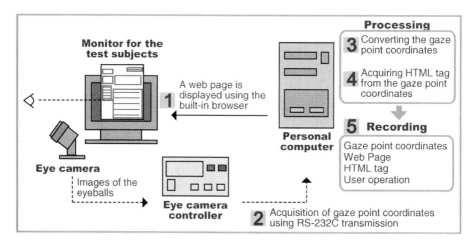

Fig. 2. Execution Environment

4 Evaluation

To examine the usage of the information acquired from the tool used in this research, a website evaluation was conducted using the tool. As a target site, the website of Tanabe city in Wakayama prefecture[3] was used. Three types of page layouts are used in this site.

The HTML uses DIV and TABLE for area division, while individual areas are differentiated based on an ID attribute or a CLASS attribute value, and designing is done using CSS. The tool developed in this experiment was utilized to record browse information and video record screens that included an eye mark (a viewing field camera image). Each subject was explained the situation setting that involved relocating to Tanabe city from Oita prefecture; the subject was asked to check for the following: "1: things required for marriage registration" and "2: things required for transferring the resident register." An explanation for Task 2 was given without using the word "change of address" used within the site. Thirteen students in their 20's were the subjects. To verify the subjects' thought process while browsing, interviews were conducted after the tasks are completed with the subjects explaining while verifying the eye movements and page transitions recorded through the viewing field camera.

The analytical tool was utilized to calculate the gaze time for each area, the order of areas gazed, the total area-specific gaze time, and the browsing time for each page from the browsing information recorded by the tool developed for this research. Gaze status and page transition status were analyzed based on this data.

In this research paper, to perform the usability evaluation of the top page, which exerts the greatest influence on navigation, a graph organizing area-specific gaze times in the top page for all the subjects was prepared (Fig. 3).

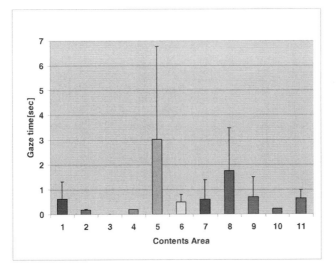

Fig.3. Area-specific Gaze Time in the Top Page (means + SD)

5 Consideration

A relationship between the contents framework and terms used in the menus was examined from the comparative chart of the gaze time for each area. It was observed that there was a long gaze time for the left menu, the center block, and the right menu included in the main menu. From each subject's gaze time for each area, it was possible to comprehend where the subjects thought was the location of the menu related to the target information. With regard to the site as a whole, by observing the area-level order of the gaze, one was able to judge the subjects who were able to grasp the position of the menu and those who were not. The figures enabled viewing the orders and the time spent in each content region. Each user's characteristics could be comprehended easily by correctly ordering the page transition.

Since each page in which the subjects got lost could be grasped from the page transition diagram, this diagram was utilized to confirm the gaze status for those pages. Furthermore, strategies adopted by subjects while browsing were discovered.

The page-based browsing state can also detect the section that was browsed repeatedly. This corresponds to a situation where the subject was lost and was unable to verify the target information. For task 2 in particular, the browsing state revealed that the subjects were making analogical inferences on information related to transferring resident register from phrases around the term "moving-in." This fact was also confirmed from the interview.

In the browsing state within a page, it was considered that scroll information could be utilized. In the interview, there was a comment that stated, "I searched the lower section of the page for the target information but could not find it, so I returned." Although the scroll information was not used in this case, it was considered that a scroll direction can be used for detecting problematic points.

Because the site that was used for this research did not set areas for each menu classification, overall menus were treated as one region. It was considered that repeated browsing states between the areas could also be detected depending on the state of division. It is believed that as a result, evaluation of all menu parts is possible. Furthermore, when examining the menu parts, it is possible to verify the links the subjects were focusing on and those that were viewed repeatedly since then by detecting all the links to different pages (anchors) that compose the menu parts. Although our purpose was to verify the browsing states between large block areas, we considered that analyzing the list of gaze status of the link parts also has a utility value in evaluating individual items in the menus.

6 Conclusion

In this research, we created a tool that assisted in the evaluation of the gaze point analysis while browsing websites on a page and content area basis, rather than on a screen basis. As a result, it was possible to effectively detect how each subject completed the task, as well as how they comprehended the contents framework. Under existing circumstances, an HTML tag analysis method was being examined. Furthermore, an evaluation method for a browsed site structure that spreads over multiple pages still needs to be developed. In addition, utilization of detailed tag information will be examined in the future.

Acknowledgments. This work was partially supported by the Strategic Information and Communications R&D Promotion Programme (SCOPE) of the Ministry of Internal Affairs and Communications of Japan.

References

1. Sato, Y., Matsunobe, T.: Gaze Point Analysis Method in Nonbinding Visual Field. Panasonic Electric Works Technical Report 58(1), 68–73 (2010)
2. Nielsen, J., Pernice, K.: Eyetracking Web Usability. New Riders, California (2010)
3. Tanabe city, Wakayama Prefecture, Japan, http://www.city.tanabe.lg.jp/

Usability Evaluation for Software Keyboard on High-Performance Mobile Devices

Takao Nakagawa and Hidetake Uwano

Nara National College of Technology, Department of Information Engineering,
22 Yata, Yamatokohriyama, Nara, Japan.
{takao,uwano}@info.nara-k.ac.jp

Abstract. Most of high-performance mobile devices called smartphone or slate computer which recently emerged uses general-purpose mobile operating system (Mobile OS) such as Android, iOS, Symbian OS, etc. These devices have two characteristics compared with previous mobile devices: 1) many of the devices have touchscreen as main user interface, hence users operate graphical user interfaces (GUIs) displayed on the screen directly by fingers or a pen and 2) different devices made by different companies have similar GUIs because the devices use the same mobile OS. Furthermore, usability evaluation and improvement for one of the mobile OS affects many devices which use same mobile OS, hence importance of the usability evaluation for mobile OS is more valuable than for previous mobile devices. In this paper, we evaluate how position of software keyboard on touchscreen affects usability of a mobile OS, Android. Software tool to record user operation history on software keyboard was developed for evaluation experience. In an experiment, three positions of software keyboard were tested. As a result, keyboard placed on top or middle of the display takes better error rate and subjective evaluation than the previous position, bottom of the display.

Keywords: Usability Evaluation, Mobile OS, Software Keyboard, Android.

1 Introduction

Most of the high-performance mobile devices called smartphone or slate computer which recently emerged uses general-purpose mobile operating system (Mobile OS) such as Android, iOS, Symbian OS, etc. These devices have two characteristics compared with previous mobile devices:

1. Many of the devices have touchscreen as main user interface, hence users operate graphical user interfaces (GUIs) displayed on the screen directly by fingers or a pen.
2. Different devices made by different companies have similar GUIs because the devices use the same mobile OS.

C. Stephanidis (Ed.): Posters, Part I, HCII 2011, CCIS 173, pp. 181–185, 2011.
© Springer-Verlag Berlin Heidelberg 2011

Previous mobile devices (i.e. feature phone or PDA) had user interfaces which consist of hardware buttons and GUIs that developed for each hardware model. Hence, developer evaluates device's usability one by one without any distinction between hardware and software.

On the other hands, user interface of mobile devices consist from the mobile OS and the touchscreen have only a few hardware buttons than the previous devices, that is, the difference of user interface between devices is shrinking. Therefore, the impact of individual hardware is decreasing from a view point of usability evaluation. In contrast, the impact of software for user interface is increasing. Evaluation and improvement for one Mobile OS lead to improving many products which using same Mobile OS. Moreover, even if the devices have different Mobile OS, their user interface have very similar structure; i.e. touchscreen and GUIs. Hence, evaluation and improvement of Mobile OS is useful.

In this paper, we evaluate one of the mobile OS, Android. We focus on software keyboard, common character input method of the mobile devices. Most of the mobile OS place the software keyboard at the bottom of screen. This design assumes what users operate by one hand and hold the device other hand. However, 74% of mobile device users holds the device and inputs by same hand [1]. In this case, users hold the device by palm and touch the keyboard by thumb; here, software keyboard position in the display is a critical factor in usability of mobile OS. In this paper, we quantitatively evaluate the effect of software keyboard position to the usability from subject's input history.

2 Related Work

Software keyboard is one of a graphical user interface component to input character strings. In contrast to hardware keyboard, software keyboard can modify size, position and layout of each key freely. Because users of software keyboard cannot recognize a borderline between keys and/or shape of keys, developers need to consider a form of software keyboard.

A lot of study propose novel type of software keyboards or input methods [2][3][4][5]. MacKenzie and Read evaluated an effect of software keyboard layout [6]. Sears and Zha focused on size of software keyboard [7]. However, neither study considers about position of software keyboard in a mobile device display. In this paper, we focus an effect of software keyboard position.

Several studies evaluate performances of mobile phone operation by thumb tapping [8][9]. These studies measure the effect of key size and position for operation accuracy and/or input speed. Also both of the study selects single software key (NOT a set of keys like software keyboard) as a target. In software keyboard operation, users tap a set of keys which compose a word or phrase sequentially, hence nature of the operation is different from single software key operation. This paper focuses to single-handed operation for software keyboard of mobile device.

3 Experiment

3.1 Settings

To record operation history of software keyboard, author developed software tool as Android OS application. This tool record key codes of subject's operation for keys on software keyboard and its timing during phrase input tasks. Figure x shows a screenshot of the tool. Subjects can select a display position of keyboard from following three patterns: 1) Under the input window, 2) Top of the display, and 3) Bottom of the display (Fig. 1).

Six subjects are participated in the experiment. Every subject has no experience of smartphone and age is between 18 and 20. In the experiment, subjects stand without any support and hold the device with right hand. Subjects are informed to do not use a left hand to operate the device. We select NEXUS ONE made by htc for the experiment.

3.2 Task

We adapt single keyword input task that assume users want to search information from the Web. Subjects input ten Japanese words indicated on the display one by one with three different keyboard positions described in Section 3.1. Words in the task are selected from Yahoo! Japan's ranking of most searched words. Every word is indicated by Hiragana (primitive character of the Japanese input method) and person name or words from other language were removed.

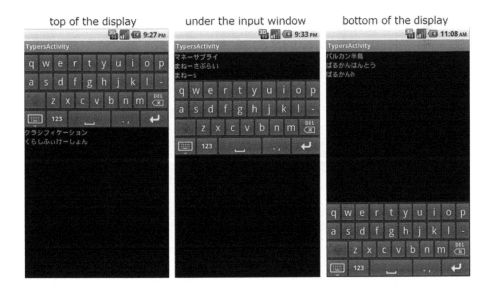

Fig. 1. Position of Software Keyboard

For an evaluation, we count the number of DEL key in the operation history to calculate EPM (Error per Minutes) of each task. Here, meaningless DEL key input such as for blank string is ignored. We also measure an input speed by Stroke/min, not by WPM (Word per Minutes.) We consider WPM is unsuitable in this experiment because of Japanese input method allows several input for one keyword (i.e. "ringo" or "rinngo" for " りんご " means apple.) Subjective estimation of usability was collected with the five-grade questionnaire.

4 Result

As a result, 180 cases data was obtained and six are excluded as noise. Table 1 shows average value of each metrics. At Bottom of the display (de-fact standard position of smart phone,) Stroke/min shows highest speed in the three keyboard positions. However, EPM shows at double count with others. This is considered as subjects take more mistakes during the tasks, hence they push DEL key many times than other keyboard positions. Under the input window shows lowest EPM and highest subjective value. This result suggests lower EPM is more important than higher input speed for subjective evaluation. In Top of display, Stroke/min and EPM is similar to "Under the input window," but in contrast, Subjective takes the lowest value. This might be caused by the subject's hand hide a wide area of display, therefore, they feel inconvenience.

Table 1. Summary of the Experiment

	Stroke/min	EPM	Subjective
Bottom of the display	90.24	13.77	3.17
Under the input window	82.17	7.35	3.67
Top of the display	79.82	7.55	1.83

5 Conclusion

In this paper, we evaluated how position of software keyboard on mobile device affects usability. As a result of the experiment, when keyboard is displayed on bottom of the display, input speed is highest but EPM is worst in compare to other position. In contrast, when keyboard is displayed on under the input window leads lowest EPM and highest Subjective evaluation. Top of the display's input speed and EPM are similar to "under the input window" but Subjective indicates worst value. These results suggest while Subjective and EPM is important, change the position of software keyboard from current position is worth to consider.

As future work, we record acceleration of device to evaluate stability and ease of hold the device during the single-hand operation. Also an evaluation of learning efficiency on each keyboard position is planned.

In future, we try to logging acceleration of device to measure device stability and ease of holding. And deference of learning efficiency on each keyboard position are also considering.

References

1. Karlson, A.K., Bederson, B.B., Contreras-Vidal, J.L.: Understanding Single-handed Mobile Device Interaction. University of Maryland, HCIL-2006-02 (2006)
2. Masui, T.: POBox: An Efficient Text Input Method for Handheld and Ubiquitous Computers. In: Gellersen, H.-W. (ed.) HUC 1999. LNCS, vol. 1707, pp. 289–300. Springer, Heidelberg (1999)
3. Aulagner, G., François, R., Martin, B., Michel, D.: Raynal. M.: Floodkey: increasing software keyboard keys by reducing needless ones without occultation. In: Proc. the 10th WSEAS International Conference on Applied Computer Science (2010)
4. Go, K., Endo, Y.: CATKey: Customizable and Adaptable Touchscreen Keyboard with Bubble Cursor-Like Visual Feedback. In: Baranauskas, C., Abascal, J., Barbosa, S.D.J. (eds.) INTERACT 2007. LNCS, vol. 4662, pp. 493–496. Springer, Heidelberg (2007)
5. MacKenzie, I.S., Zhang, S.Z.: The design and evaluation of a high performance soft keyboard. In: Proc. the SIGCHI Conference on Human Factors in Computing Systems, pp. 25–31 (1999)
6. MacKenzie, I.S., Read, J.C.: Using Paper Mockups for Evaluating Soft Keyboard Layouts. In: Proc. the 2007 Conference of the Center for Advanced Studies on Collaborative Research, pp. 98–108 (2007)
7. Sears, A., Zha, Y.: Data Entry for Mobile Devices Using Soft Keyboards: Understanding the Effects of Keyboard Size and User Tasks. International Journal of Human Computer Interaction 16(2), 163–184 (2003)
8. Perry, K.B., Hourcade, J.P.: Evaluating one handed thumb tapping on mobile touchscreen devices. In: Proc. Graphics Interface 2008, pp. 57–64 (2008)
9. Park, Y.S., Han, S.H.: Touch key design for one-handed thumb interaction with a mobile phone: effects of touch key size and touch key location. International Journal of Industrial Ergonomics 40(1), 68–76 (2010)

Usability Evaluation Method
Employing Elements of "Thinking" and "Seeking"

Nobuyuki Nishiuchi[1], Takehiro Ando[1], and Mi Kyong Park[2]

[1] Department of Management Systems Engineering, Tokyo Metropolitan University
[2] Division of Management Systems Engineering, Tokyo Metropolitan University,
6-6 Asahigaoka, Hino, Tokyo, 191-0065, Japan
nnishiuc@sd.tmu.ac.jp, takehiro.ando@gmail.com,
mkpark@sd.tmu.ac.jp

Abstract. Current usability evaluation approaches are costly, time-consuming and suffer from evaluation subjectivity, and in addition, it is often difficult to acquire the operation logs of existing electrical products. To overcome these limitations, we developed a new method for usability evaluation. During the operation of either an actual product or a reproduced interface on a touch screen, the hand movements of users were recorded with a video camera. Before evaluation of the target interface, the users operated three basic interfaces, classified as "Standard", "Thinking", and "Seeking", and the users' unique elements related to hand movements, which were based on the distribution of stationary time, during operation of the "Thinking" and "Seeking" interfaces were extracted. Finally, usability was evaluated based on the amount of each element ("Thinking" and "Seeking") that was included in the target interface.

Keywords: Usability, interface, evaluation method, image processing.

1 Introduction

Current techniques for usability evaluation encompass several approaches [1]-[3], such as video capture and eye-tracking during user operation, conducting interviews, administering questionnaires, and recording user operation logs, among others. However, these evaluation approaches are costly, time-consuming, suffer from evaluation subjectivity, and are often not feasible, as it is difficult to acquire the operation logs of many existing electrical products.

To overcome these limitations, we developed a new method for usability evaluation, which involves video recording a user's operation, extracting the movements of the user's fingertip by image processing, and then evaluating usability by analyzing the distribution of stationary time of the user's fingertip movements based on the elements of "Thinking" and "Seeking" [4].

This study is organized as follows. In section 2, the detailed methodology of the usability evaluation is described. In section 3, the results of an evaluative experiment are present. Finally, in section 4, conclusions are discussed.

C. Stephanidis (Ed.): Posters, Part I, HCII 2011, CCIS 173, pp. 186–190, 2011.

2   Methodology of Usability Evaluation

The proposed usability evaluation method is divided into three parts: (1) Extraction of usability elements, (2) Analysis of a target interface, (3) Usability evaluation. The details of each part are described in the following sections.

2.1   Extraction of Usability Elements

Prior to evaluation of the target interface, the user operated three basic interfaces, classified as "Standard", "Thinking", and "Seeking" interfaces, on a touch screen (Figure 1 and Table 1).

In the "Standard" interface, a random number from 1 to 50 was displayed in the task indication area, and buttons corresponding to numbers from 1 to 50 were displayed below in increasing order, in the button display area. The task required of the user in the "Standard" interface was to push the button of the number indicated in the task indication area.

In the "Thinking" interface, an addition task involving 5 numbers was displayed in the task indication area, and buttons corresponding to numbers from 1 to 50 were displayed below in increasing order in the button display area. The task required of the user in the "Thinking" interface was to push the button that corresponded to the correct number of the solved addition task.

In the "Seeking" interface, a random number from 1 to 50 was displayed in the task indication area, and buttons corresponding to numbers from 1 to 50 were randomly displayed in the button display area whenever a button was pushed. The task required of the used in the "Seeking" interface was to push the button of the number indicated in the task indication area.

For all interfaces, when the user pushed a button, the task indication area was updated, and the task was repeated 50 times. During the operation of the three interfaces on a touch screen, users' hand movements were recorded with a video camera. The movements of the user's index fingertip were then extracted by image processing.

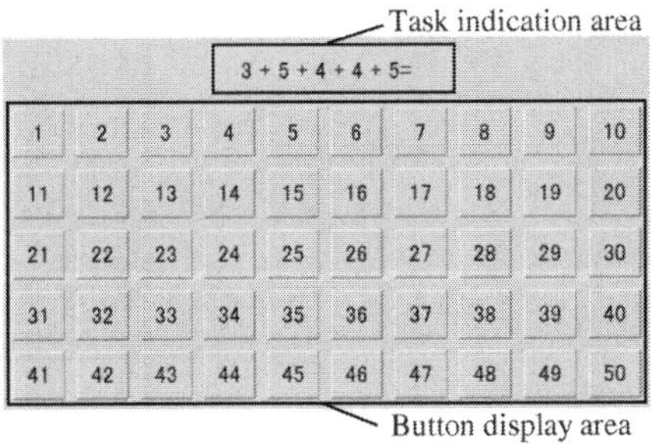

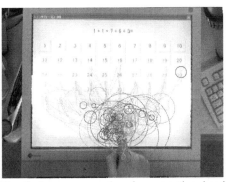

Fig. 1. Basic "Thinking" interface displayed on a touch screen. The task indication and button display areas are indicated.

Fig. 2. Image processing for extracting hand movement (yellow lines) and stationary time (circle size)

Table 1. Characteristics of the three basic interfaces

Interface	Task indication area	Button display area
Standard	Random number	Sequence
Thinking	Addition task	Sequence
Seeking	Random number	Random

It was judged from the movements of the fingertip whether the hand was stationary or not. If the following equation (1) was fulfilled, the user's hand was judged to be in a stationary state.

$$\sum_{i=1}^{T} D_i \leq D \times T \tag{1}$$

where D_i represents the distance between the positions of the finger in the current and preceding (i) video frame, and T indicates the number of previous frames in which the user's hand is considered to be in a stationary state for at least $T \times (1/30)$ seconds. D represents the average distance that a subject's finger moves between each frame for $T \times (1/30)$ seconds. T and D were determined by a preliminary experiment. Figure 2 shows the image of the locus of finger movement (yellow line) and circles, which are in a proportional size to the stationary time, during operation of the "Thinking" interface.

From the distributions obtained during operation of the "Standard, "Thinking", and "Seeking" interfaces, histograms for each subject were plotted with stationary time and frequency on the x- and y-axes, respectively (Figure 3).

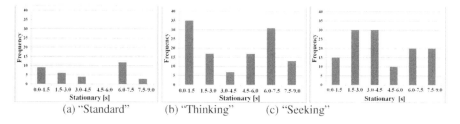

(a) "Standard"   (b) "Thinking"   (c) "Seeking"

Fig. 3. Histograms of stationary time for the three interfaces

To extract the unique elements of the "Thinking" and "Seeking" tasks, the histogram obtained from the "Standard" interface operation was subtracted from each histogram. In addition, because the operation time differed between the "Thinking" and "Seeking" interfaces, the histograms were normalized.

In this evaluation approach, data for two or more users' operations are needed. Notably, however, there is a possibility that the elements of "Thinking" and "Seeking" could be similar, and a user having two similar elements is unsuitable for this proposed evaluation approach. To determine whether a user is suitable for evaluation, it is necessary to examine the degree of similarity (ε) in the elements of "Thinking" and "Seeking", which can be accomplished using the cross-correlation coefficient shown in equation (2).

$$\varepsilon = \sum_{i=1}^{i_{max}} \sqrt{H_a(i) \times H_b(i)} \qquad (2)$$

where $H_a(i)$ and $H_b(i)$ represent the values at the class of ith in each histogram to be compared, and ε is a value from 0 to 1. We consider that a user is appropriate for the proposed evaluation approach when ε is close to 0 (both elements are not similar).

2.2   Analysis of a Target Interface

During the user operation of the target interface, the movement of the fingertip is captured, and the histogram of the target interface is plotted based on the stationary time of the finger movement determined through the image processing. Using the histogram of target interface and the "Thinking" and "Seeking" histograms, the elements of "Thinking" and "Seeking" included in the target interface was analyzed by equation (3).

$$\sum_{i=1}^{i_{max}} \left(H_c(i) - \alpha H_a(i) - \beta H_b(i) \right) \to \min. \qquad (3)$$

where $H_a(i)$, $H_b(i)$, and $H_c(i)$ represent the values at the class of ith in the "Thinking", "Seeking", and target interface histograms, respectively, and α and β obtained from expression (3) indicate the amount of "Thinking" and "Seeking" elements, respectively, when the target interface was operated. By the best-subset selection procedure for α and β, the combination of α and β at which equation (3) is minimized is obtained.

2.3   Usability Evaluation

The usability of the target interface was evaluated by plotting the circles obtained for α and β in a graph (Figure 5). Circle size depends on the degree of similarity ε in equation (2), with a larger circle being more suitable for the proposed evaluation. If the plotted circles are close to the point of origin, the usability is high. However, when numerous elements of "Thinking" are included in the target interface, the plotted circles will be close to α axis (the element of "Thinking"). It is thought that the plotted circles in the graph move in the direction of the point of origin on improvement of the element of "Thinking" in the target interface.

3   Evaluative Experiment

We conducted an evaluative experiment involving 10 users operating the test interface, which included both "Thinking" and "Seeking" elements (Figure 4). Based on our analysis, we confirmed that the unique elements of "Thinking" and "Seeking" could be extracted from the test interface for each of the 10 users (Figure 5). Several of the plotted circles were close to the line of $\beta=\alpha$, indicating that both "Thinking" and "Seeking" elements were extracted successfully from the test interface. However, a few plotted circles were located closer to the β axis (the element of "Seeking") in the graph shown in Figure 5. Although the location of the circles was dependent on the user, the elements of "Seeking" in test interface were clearly identified. In other words, an improvement of usability on the element of "Seeking" in the test interface was indicated.

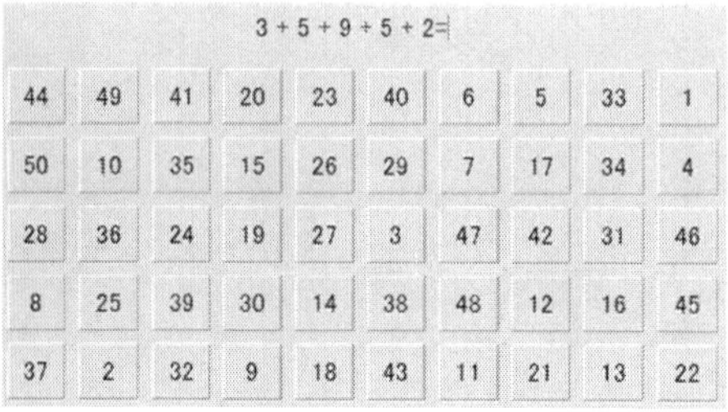

Fig. 4. Test interface includingboth "Thinking" and "Seeking" elements

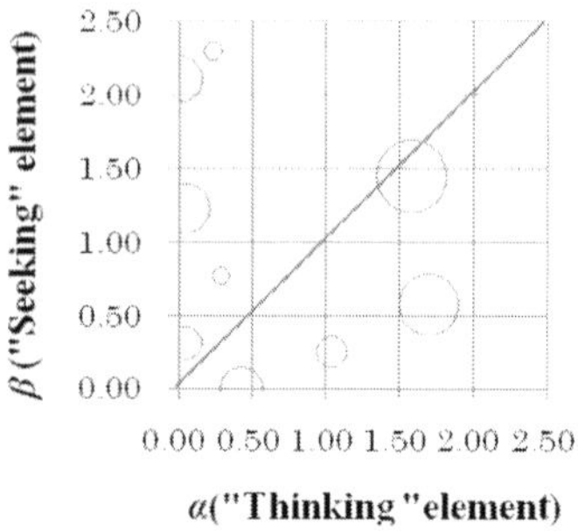

Fig. 5. Results of evaluation for the test interface

4   Conclusions

We have proposed a new method for usability evaluation, which involves taking a video recording of the user's operation, extracting the movements of the user's fingertip by image processing, and then evaluating usability based on the elements of "Thinking" and "Seeking". From the results of an evaluative experiment, our proposed method of usability evaluation appears potentially suited for quantitative analysis, and has applicability that is comparable to classical methods.

References

1. Bojko, A.: Using Eye Tracking to Compare Web Page Design: A Case Study. Journal of Usability Studies 1(3), 112–120 (2006)
2. Siegenthaler, E., Wurtz, P., Groner, R.: Improving the Usability of E-Book Readers. Journal of Usability Studies 6(1), 25–38 (2010)
3. Ryu, Y.S., Smith-Jackson, T.L.: Reliability and Validity of the Mobile Phone Usability Questionnaire (MPUQ). Journal of Usability Studies 2(1), 39–53 (2006)
4. Yoshimoto, K., Onari, H., Watanabe, K.: Methods Engineering. Asakura Publishing Co., Ltd., Japan (2001)

Software Testing Method Considering the Importance of Factor Combinations in Pair-Wise Testing

Ruoan Xu, Yoshimitsu Nagai and Syohei Ishizu

Department of Industrial and Systems Engineering
Aoyamagakuin University, Japan
`C5610173@aoyama.jp,`
`nagai@cc.aoyama.ac.jp,`
`ishizu@ise.aoyama.ac.jp`

Abstract. Software testing bears a burden of software development, increasing its time and cost. The bugs appearing due to the combination of two factors are well known in the system test phase. The current system testing methods represented by pair-wise tests or orthogonal arrays tests generate test sets by the forms of factors and values. In this study we extract two problems in the system test phase, and propose a solution to solve the problems. The first type of the problems is a survival bugs by the combination of factors among test sets. The second type of the problems is a duplication of factors by extra test case in the test set. We propose a solution which considers combinations of important factors for these two problems.

Keywords: Software test, System test, Pair-wise test, Dependency structure matrix, Combination test.

1 Introduction

In the software industry today, software quality is becoming all the more important as the scale of development becomes increasingly larger due to the incorporation of numerous functions and the technical progress of the products. Accordingly, software testing adds strain to software development, increasing its time and cost. Among software tests, there are unit tests, in which single functions are tested, and combination tests, in which combinations of multiple functions are tested. With the scale of the software, the volume of unit tests increases linearly while the volume of combination tests increases exponentially. In this study, we focus on the combination tests, which become increasingly important with the scale of the software. In combination tests, bugs are known in many cases to appear due to the combination of two factors. Therefore, pair-wise tests or orthogonal arrays tests are used as testing techniques to consider all the combinations of two factors. A delivery date is set before the software development; thus, it is necessary to have a test plan in order to meet this date and satisfying a certain reliability level. We can roughly predict how many bugs are detected and how many bugs remain by using a reliability growth curve. However, for current software, a reliability level of 100% cannot be achieved

C. Stephanidis (Ed.): Posters, Part I, HCII 2011, CCIS 173, pp. 191–195, 2011.

where all bugs are completely eliminated, and products must be shipped with some bugs remaining. In particular, the surviving bugs are mostly due to combinations of two factors. Therefore, it is important to develop a method to find bugs that arise from combinations of factors within the specified delivery date.

The aim of this study is to propose a method for generating test cases, considering the importance of combinations in software testing. So we pay attention to workflow in the system test phase. And extract problems in the workflow. Then we propose regenerating pair-wise testing method and analyzing software structure method for detecting important combination of factors.

2 Analyzing the Workflow

2.1 The Workflow in System Test Phase

The software is developed according to the function specifications. Therefore, we execute a software test according items described in the function specifications in the software testing process. So we set up test set from the items, and extract the factors and values which are related to the items. Concept of test sets and factors is shown in the following Table 1.

Table 1. Concept of test sets and factors

Test set A			Test set B			...
Factor	**Factor**	**Factor**	**Factor**	**Factor**	**Factor**	**...**
Value	Value	Value	Value	Value	Value	...
Value	Value	Value	Value	Value	Value	...

The test sets as shown in table 1 exists hugely, and there is innumerably extractive factors. Acctually, high importance factors are given priority and selected. Then the test case are generated by the pair-wise method in each test set concluding factors and values. So the pair-wise test case are existed against each test set. We shown workflow at system test phase in the following Fig. 1. Important extra test cases may be added when test cases are generated in (3). These extra test cases are generated by the experience of a testing specialist. Then some test cases may be added to find bug cause in (5). But, two problems in the workflow have been extracted.

2.2 A Problem When Test Items and Factors Are Extracted

The first type of problem occurs in the test design related to steps (1),(2), and (3). Because the test items and the factors are extracted based on the items described in the function specifications, the combination of the items and the factors which are not described in the function specifications in the test design cannot be considered. For example, in Table 1 the combination of factors in the test set A and factors in the test

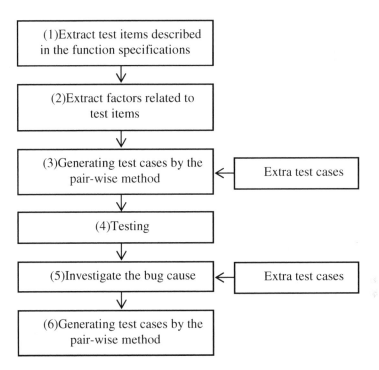

Fig. 1. Workflow at system test phase

set B will not be tested. There are a lot of bugs from combinations which are not supposed to exist, and it remains as a survival bug.

2.3 A Problem When Executing the Test

The second type of problems occurs while testing related to steps (4) and (5). If the bug is found, the test case is added. Although, when the pair-wise method covers all the combinations of the two factors, the extra test cases become merely a useless duplication.

3 The Software Test Which Consider Importance of Factors Combinations

3.1 A solution for the Problem When Executing the Test

The extra test cases is a important case, so we must leave these cases. And some test cases are already executed in the testing process, so these cases are must left too. In this study we leave extra test cases and executed test cases, and delete other test cases. Then regenerating new test cases which consider the test cases that cannot be deleted. We show the example in the following table 2 and 3.

Table 2. Pair-wise test cases

No	OS	Plugin	Browser
1	2000	QuickTime	IE
2	XP	WMP	IE
3	XP	QuickTime	Firefox
4	2000	Flash	Firefox
5	Vista	Flash	IE
6	Vista	WMP	Firefox
7	Vista	QuickTime	IE
8	2000	WMP	Firefox
9	XP	Flash	IE

Table 3. Extra test cases

10	2000	QuickTime	IE
11	XP	WMP	IE
12	XP	QuickTime	Firefox

There are twelve test cases that need testing in the Table 2 and 3. But, there are a lot duplicated combination of values in the Table3. For example, a combination of „2000" and „QuickTime" apear in the No10 of Table3 already apear in the No1 of Table2. All pair of values in Tables3 are already apear in the Table2. Because, these test cases are generated by pair-wise method. When we regenerated pair-wise leaving extra test cases and executed test cases, a number of duplicated combination will decrease. There are a glaph that show how many test cases are reduced by regeneration method in the following Fig. 2. In this glaph, a difference of conventional method and regeneration method is the number of the reduction of the test case. We can find the number of test case is reduced in Fig. 2.

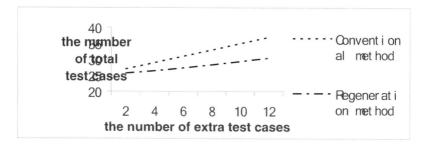

Fig. 2. The test case number of conventional method and regeneration method

3.2   A Solution for the Problem When Extracting Factors

The current system testing methods represented by pair-wise tests or orthogonal arrays tests generate test sets by the forms of factors and values. But these methods cannot extract all bugs remaining in a source code, because, these methods assure the reliability within the test set only, but don't assure the reliability among the test sets. In this study, we pay attention to the software structure, and we analyze dependency among the test sets. We propose a testing method applying the dependency structure matrix which is a software structure analyzing method, to detect survival bugs efficiently. Using dependency structure matrix we can analyze dependency among modules, and find the important combinatorial factors.

4   Conclusion

In this study, we consider combinations of important factors that can't be considered from the function specifications by using module coupling against the bug remaining problem in the work. And, we reduce duplication by using regeneration technique against the duplication of the values combinations by the extra test cases which added while testing. Using these techniques, more bugs can be found by the delivery date.

References

1. Kuhn, D.R., Wallace, D.R., Gallo Jr., A.M.: Software Fault Interactions and Implications for Software Testing. IEEE Transactions on Software Engineering 30(6), 418–421 (2004)
2. Nakatsuji, H.: Quality Evaluation Method in Quality Assurance Review. Unisys Technology Review (99), 23–33 (2009)

Part III

Cultural, Cross-Cultural and Aesthetic Issues in HCI

The Problematic of Beauty Performed in the Collaborative Action of Technology and Human

HyunKyoung Cho

ASPECT: Alliance for Social, Political, Ethical, and Cultural Thought,
242 Lane Hall, Virginia Tech, Blacksburg,
VA 24061, USA
hkcho@vt.edu

Abstract. This paper proposes that the performing beauty provoked by the collaborative action of technology provides a way of knowing, in order to overcome the dichotomy reinforcing the mutual degradation between action and thought, technology and human, subject and object.

Keywords: the collaborative action of technology and human, the performing beauty, the invaginating, and the dichotomy.

1 The Collaborative Action of Technology and Human

Technology is problematic[1]. It participates in the human history; it changes human action and thought. In particular, computational technology is endowed with highly intelligent and perceptive qualities; has its own laws as the system itself evolves. It can customize the autonomous and emergent action beyond human control. With the ability of autonomy and emergence, technology becomes a performer (an actor) collaborating with the human. The collaboration of technology and human is problematic. It expands the human condition (the existence of human and its condition). The expanded human condition can be called the collaborative condition of technology and human. It reveals the non-humanity in humanism. The humanism as an ideology considers the collaborative action of technology and human in the regime of representation. It fosters the knowledge that *expresses* the subjective experience through the representation of object conceals the real, lived, and free relationship of technology and human. In the human subject centered dichotomy, both the technology and human are subordinated into the instrumental, and the collaborative action between them remains an impure one, a means to represent the knowledge itself. To overcome the subordination of technology and human in the

---

[1] The term problematic elaborated by Michel Foucault and Louis Althusser was to reveal the problem of knowledge/power relations. Althusser, For Marx, trans. Ben Brewster (New York: Verso, 2005), Foucault, Madness and Civilization, trans. Richard Howard (New York: Vintage, 1988), and Foucault, "Polemics, Politics, and Problematizations: An Interview," In: The Foucault Reader, ed. Paul Rainbow (New York: Pantheon Books, 1984) 381-390.

C. Stephanidis (Ed.): Posters, Part I, HCII 2011, CCIS 173, pp. 199–203, 2011.

instrumental perspective, the collaboration of technology and human proposes the collaborative perspective; the collaborative being-with-the technology in the world. It cultivates the humanity that allows us to be critical, the examined and liberal life from the bondage of habit and custom[2]. The collaborative action of technology and human is problematic. It rebuilds the history of action that has been degraded into the instrument to represent thought. It embraces both the history of ideas (the analysis of systems of representations) and the history of mentalities (the analysis of attitudes and type of action). The eloquence of collaborative action of technology and human recalls that the action is an apex of human activities, and it testifies the multiplicity as the essence of life. In digital environments, the newness is that technology plays a role as a performer (an actor/collaborator) like a human, and the technology-human interaction follows the logic of human-human communication. It presents that the definition of human action should be reconsidered in the collaborative relationship with technology. The collaborative action of technology and human is what the human is doing. It indicates that the technology and human reciprocally share the action's process and its result. This sharing weaves a hybrid network constituted by performers (actors/collaborators) based on the reciprocity. The hybrid network denies the instrumental understanding of relationship of technology and human; in the terms that the autonomous human having the free will can use and control the technology as a technological tool for the representation of the human subject's thinking practice. In this sense, we could say that the collaborative action of technology and human leads us to a radical shift of knowledge/power on two points: from the human subject centered dichotomy (the binary frame) to the inter-subjective networking, from the knowledge by thinking to that by acting. The shifting retains the spirit of humanity, its great intelligence, which does not define 'I' but performs 'We.'

2 The Performing Beauty

The collaborative action of technology and human reframes the concept of beauty that has been thought in the idea, what the beauty is. It rediscovers the performing beauty organized in the relation to action to object. Performing beauty indicates that beauty is originated from the performing as what happens in the realm of presenting. It means that the performing beauty is a conjuncture at any given historical moment (current moment) to which analysis (including the theory, analytic strategy, and tactics) must be applied; it can be only addressed in the analytic action as the process of analysis[3]. Psychoanalytically speaking, the performing denotes the state of overdetermination privileged by the condensation of a number of thoughts in a single image or the displacement of psychic energy from a particularly potent thought to apparently trivial images[4]. It articulates that between the transference and suggestion that the demand (more precisely, the subject' demand in relation to its counterpart) makes, there is a relation, the so-called unconscious mechanisms of collaborative action of technology

---

[2] Martha C. Nussbaum, Cultivating Humanity: A Classical Defense of Reform in Liberal Education (Cambridge: Harvard University Press, 2003) 1-50.

[3] Althusser, "Marxism and Humanism," In: For Marx, 241.

[4] Althusser, "Contradiction and Overdetermination," In: For Marx, 89-130.

and human. The relation occurs between the effects that correspond in a subject to a particular demand and the effects of a position in relation to the other that it sustains as subject. In other words, the performing beauty has the doubling effect; it exists in between transference as the effects that correspond in a subject to a particular demand and the suggestion as the effects of a position in relation to the other that it sustains as subject.

The performing beauty substitutes knowledge for the relation to the being where the action takes place; it touches the resources producing the knowledge/power. It implies that the performing beauty is a sort of return of the repressed in the knowledge/power relations. It can be only observed symptomatically; a symptom here is the signifier of a signified that has been repressed from the subject's consciousness[5]. The performing beauty as a symptom should be read within the inter-subjective communication, the structure of language. What this linguistic conception teaches us is that the symptom proves its signifying function that differs from the natural index commonly designated by the term symptom in medicine[6]. Human language constitutes a kind of communication in which the sender receives his own message back from the receiver in an inverted form[7]. Here the inverted form is the 'interpretation' of message. The interpretation of the repressed message in the process of return (repetition) of message (chain, communication) is the reading of symptoms. What the symptomatic reading means is that the performing beauty is not a making the world-view, but a reconception in the theoretical or ideological framework, so-called concept in which it is used.

3 As a Way of Knowing

The performing beauty can be conceived as a way of knowing. It, however, is neither an arrangement of representations nor a construction of the knowledge. It also is far from a deconstruction of knowledge in the sense that it differs from the production of another concept to manage the confusion between various disciplines or methods. It means that the performing beauty may be a scientific, theoretical, and practical name, in order to locate the problematic itself correctly and to resolve it. It is only centered on the absence of problems and concepts within the problematic of beauty of the collaborative action of technology and human as much as its presence. Its aim is to exactly pose the problematic, and to pose it properly is to give a chance of solving it. The performing beauty intervenes the knowledge/power. In particular, the performing beauty works in the terrain of the confrontation between the question and its answer. Instead of drawing a line of demarcation between question and answer, it invaginates the two into a solution[8]. Here the solution is a 'seeking' the necessity of 'asking' of an

---

[5] Lacan, "The Function and Field of Speech and Language in Psychoanalysis," In: Ecrits, trans. Bruce Fink (New York: W.W. Norton & Company, 2005) 232.

[6] Lacan, "The Freudian Thing," In: Ecrits, 348.

[7] Lacan, "Seminar on 'The Purloined Letter'," In: Ecrits, 42.

[8] In this study, the term invagination refers to Derrida and Rosaline Krauss's notion. Derrida, "The Law of Genre," In: Glyph 7, trans. Avital Ronell (Baltimore: Johns Hopkins University Press, 1980) 202-232. Rosaline Krauss, "Two Moments from the Post-Medium Condition," In: OCTOBER, Vol.116, No.1, Spring 2006, 55-62.

answering in a 'questioning (inquiry)'[9]. It is an active 'investigating' for an entity both with regard to the fact that the problematic beauty of collaborative action of technology and human is and with regard to its reading as it is. It gets guided beforehand by what is sought. Insofar as the seeking about something has that which is asked about, the performing beauty is somehow an investigative questioning of something. In addition to what is asked about, the seeking has that which is interrogated. To put it differently, the performing beauty entails a seeking questioning of a movement of critical analysis in which one tries to read how the different questions and answers to the problem have been constructed; but also how theses different questions and answers result from its problematic. It appears that any new solutions that might be added to the others would arise from the current problematic of beauty of collaborative action of technology and human. The ways the problem is differently posed and diverse solutions (questions and answers) arose from them allow us to the critical reading of knowledge/power. In this sense, the intention of performing beauty is to repeat one another; not a mere folding but an immanent and synthetic repetition. It produces the reiterating differences of self-reference in the self-reflexivity.

4 Beyond the Logic of Opposition

The performing beauty reveals an essential lack of the knowledge[10]. The lack can be explained with the understanding of supplementation. The philosophy as an ideology defines the word 'supplement' as something that completes or makes an addition to complete. The supplement supports both completeness and uncompleteness, and thus its understanding can be invested in the indeterminacy. The supplementary structure, however, has chiefly been considered in one perspective that defines the supplement as "an inessential extra, added to something complete it in itself" [11]. The supplement serves to enhance the presence of something that is already complete and self-sufficient. This idea based on the logic of opposition reinforces the dichotomy; in the mutual degradation between action and thought, subject and object, technology and human. Here the action is a supplement of thought, the object is a supplement of subject, and the technology is a supplement of human. When the knowledge is rooted from the supplementary structure supporting the logic of opposition, the performing beauty of collaborative action of technology and human is degraded as the immoral, ugly, and even dangerous. The binary frame emphasizes that the beauty is an attitude (experience) of the human subject to represent the object for the thinking practice. The judgment of beauty depends on the laws of moral and reason based on the logic of opposition of moral and immoral, good and evil; what is beautiful is parallel to what is moral and good.

---

[9] Martin Heidegger, Being and Time (London: Blackwell Publishing, 1962) 24.

[10] Lacan's "On Freud's "Trieb" and the Psychoanalysis's Desire," In: Ecrits, 721-725. Derrida, Of Grammatology, trans. Gayatri Chakrvorty Spivak (Baltimore, Maryland: The Johns Hopkins University Press, 1998)

[11] Derrida, Of Grammatology, 298, and "Signature Event Context," In: Limited Inc (Evanston, IL: Northwestern University Press, 1988) 1-24.

The performing beauty admits the supplementary structure's uncompleteness, the surplus derived from its essential lack.[12] Insofar as the supplement is defined as *an unessential extra addition* to completeness itself, it is exactly what was supposed to be complete in itself. It grants that there is an essential lack originated from the uncompleteness of the supplementary structure itself. The lack articulates that the supplement does not enhance the completeness's presence, but rather underscores its absence. With absence should be filled by something, the performing beauty saves the significance of action. It notes that the action is an *essential extra addition* to fill (heal) the lack. The essential extra addition can be considers as a surplus. The surplus involves the desire realized in the relation of reality and the Real.[13] Insofar as the supplement is defined as the unessential extra added to complete it in itself, what is supposed to be complete in itself, something we have to pay always remains. In this sense, we could say that the performing beauty is the unpaid remainder derived from the demand of desire organized in the relation of reality and the Real. It spells out the essential failure of action conflicting with the desire to object. It recalls that beauty is in a truth-process that must overcome itself again and again. The action holds the knowledge of beauty as a desire.

References

1. Althusser, L., For Marx (trans.) Ben Brewster. Verso, New York (2005)
2. Derrida, J.: Of Grammatology (trans.) Gayatri Chakrvorty Spivak. Johns Hopkins University Press, Baltimore (1998)
3. Derrida, J.: The Law of Genre. In: Glyph 7, (trans.) Avital Ronell. Johns Hopkins University Press, Baltimore (1980)
4. Derrida, J.: Signature Event Context. Northwestern University Press, Evanston (1988)
5. Foucault, M.: Madness and Civilization, (trans.) Richard Howard. Vintage, New York (1988)
6. Foucault, M.: Polemics, Politics, and Problematizations: An Interview. In: Rainbow, P. (ed.) The Foucault Reader. Pantheon Books, New York (1984)
7. Heidegger, M.: Being and Time. Blackwell Publishing, London (1962)
8. Krauss, R.: Two Moments from the Post-Medium Condition. OCTOBER 116(1) (Spring 2006)
9. Lacan, J.: The Function and Field of Speech and Language in Psychoanalysis. In: Ecrits (trans.) Bruce Fink. W.W. Norton & Company, New York (2005)
10. Nussbaum, M.C.: Cultivating Humanity: A Classical Defense of Reform in Liberal Education. Harvard University Press, Cambridge (2003)

---

[12] Lacan's "On Freud's "Trieb" and the Psychoanalysis's Desire," In: Ecrits, 721-725. and Derrida, Of Grammatology, 298.

[13] The words reality and the Real were used in Lacan's term. Lacan defines the reality as an image projected by the Real. For him, the reality is constitutive of the Real. The relationship of reality and the Real does not to the completeness as the One. In the case, the Real is no less than the impossible and untouchable.

The Politics of Collaborative Action of Technology and Human

HyunKyoung Cho

ASPECT: Alliance for Social, Political, Ethical, and Cultural Thought,
242 Lane Hall, Virginia Tech, Blacksburg,
VA 24061, USA
hkcho@vt.edu

Abstract. This study examines the politics of collaborative action of technology and human, through the analysis of artwork using the emerging technology. It presents that the collaborative action of technology and human reconstructs the knowledge reinforcing the mutual degradation between action and thought, technology and human.

Keywords: politics, the collaborative action of technology and human, the performative, critique, desire.

1 We: Technology and Human

New scientific and technological disciplines make new and different orders, values, and perspectives. The emerging technology such as Human-Computer Interaction, Artificial Intelligence, Artificial Life, Networking, Tangible and Wearable Computing shows that there are multiple ways to shape and share the collaborative relationship between Nature, human, and technology. In particular, the computational technology endowed with the intelligent and emotional qualities has a certain degree of autonomy that evolves its own laws, and can customize emergent actions beyond the control of human. With the capability of autonomy and emergence, the technology performs the collaborative action with the human. This change presents that the collaborative action of technology and human is a new mode of production in the digital era.

The contemporary technology-based artwork visualizes the political power of collaborative action of technology and human. While the traditional artwork has been completed by the action of artist, the artwork using the technology consists of the collaborative action of technology and human. To create artwork, the technology and human act and react with each other, and their collaborative action becomes artwork itself. Here, the particular interest is that the action real-timely changes the artwork's meaning, and the technology exists as an artist creating artwork. It implies that the collaborative action of technology and human challenges the knowledge systems reinforcing the mutual degradation between action and thought, technology and human. It is an effort to cultivate the collaborative politics performing 'we.'

C. Stephanidis (Ed.): Posters, Part I, HCII 2011, CCIS 173, pp. 204–208, 2011.

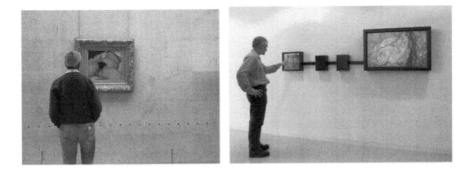

Fig. 1. The Origin of the World (1866); Painting, Oil on Canvas, by Gustave Courbet and E-volver (2006); Artwork using Artificial Genetics and Evolutionary Techniques, Touch screens, by Computer programmed by the Genetic Algorithm, Erwin Driessens & Maria Verstappen.

2 How to Perform We: The Performative of Collaborative Action

The politics of collaborative action of technology and human is originated from the performative. In artwork, the technology and human communicate using actions, and the process has a structure of conversation based on the reciprocity and consideration of others. In the case, we can say that the collaborative action of technology and human is performatve. The concept of performative, came from linguistics, is defined as 'to say something is to do something.' It indicates that the issuing of an utterance is performing not description or representation of actions, but actions. It means that the collaborative action of technology and human is a performative utterance constituted in the social contexts of communication, and then the meaning depends on the felicity conditions which can be, or not, successful, rather than the truth conditions which can be true or false. Through the performative assuring the singularity (the uniqueness and immediacy) of action, the collaborative action of technology and human has the political power to overcome the distinction between action and thought, technology and human in the knowledge systems.

3 What We Perform: On Two Fronts, the Critique of Knowledge

To reframe the knowledge systems reinforcing the mutual degradation, the politics of collaborative action of technology and human intervenes on two fronts.

First, it affirms that the action has the closest connection with the human life. The affirming comes into conflict with the knowledge that devalues the action with the instrument to represent the ideal. To put it differently, the artwork using the technology denies the idealistic aesthetics. Since the beauty of artwork consisting of collaborative action is in the live and direct action to object, not the abstract idea that describes the subjective experience through the representation of object. It illustrates that the action no longer exits as the supplement of thought. The conventional knowledge based on the supplementary structure has been assumed that the supplement is 'an *inessential* extra, added to something complete it in itself.' The artwork consisting of collaborative action of technology and human, however, notices that the supplement does not serve to enhance the presence of completeness of supplementary structure, rather underscores its absence. It saves the significance of action for the adding and the supplement as 'an *essential* extras' compensating the lack of knowledge.

Secondly, the politics of collaborative action attempts to reconcile between technology and human. It undermines the knowledge that defines the technology in the instrumental perspective based on the human-subject centered dichotomy. In the artwork, the collaborative action of technology and human weaves the hybrid network that two collaborators interact if each acts upon the other. There is no the external constraints such as subject and object, human and nonhuman, insomuch as the performing network does not being one entity. It shows that the traditional binary frame fails to explain the co-evolution of technology and human in the meshwork. Hence, the politics of collaborative action reveals that the instrumental understanding of technology is nothing less than the non-humanity of humanism. For it is rooted in the fetishistic inversion (the ideologically distorted consciousness) of technology. It displaces the direct and social relationship between technology and human into the instrumental, and conceals the surplus-enjoyment caused by the unapproachablity of object organized by the symbolic, the essential failure of action to catch up with the desiring object. In the displacement and concealing, both technology and human are enframed as a part of stockpile of available materials and personnel, and always ready for ideal purpose, not his own desire.

4   In Conformity with Our Desire, We perform What We Are

Two critiques of knowledge systems meet at one question that who are we. Through the collaborative action of technology and human, the human is aware of his own existence existing as the individual and simultaneously multitude in society. For the politics of collaborative action of technology and human reminds us that the human is the performing being transformed by the his own action, not the conditioned being determined by the ideal of Oneness as knowledge of 'there is a being as the One.' The human condition as the way in which the human produces the means of life is collaboration. This means that what we call the life is the live and actual life-process constituted by the collaborative action. Here, the essential point is the will to activate the action. It involves with the desire as the change of object in itself.

What's at stake in the relation of action and desire is that the action follows the drive (*Trieb*) as a partial manifestation of desire which circles perpetually round the object. It implies that the action performs the aim (the way itself) of drive. It is neither to reach some mystified goal (a final destination) advanced in ways which are contingent on the life history of subject, nor to satisfy biological needs regulated by any instinct (*Instinkt*) of a relatively fixed and innate relationship to an object. Insofar as the action concerns with the desire related to object, the human is a player obeying the rule of desire, and then the life becomes a game organized by the relation of action and desire to object. In this case, we can say that in the digital era, the human realizes his own desire with the technology. What the human is, therefore, coincides with the production of collaborative action of technology and human, both with what we act and with how we act with the technology, in conformity with our desire.

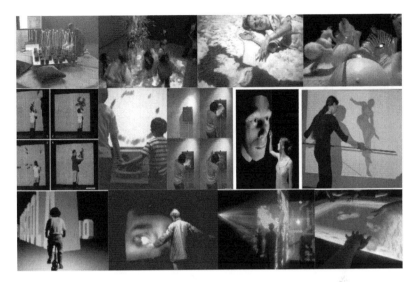

Fig. 2. The collaborative action as what we are doing with technology, still images of contemporary technology-based artworks

Acknowledgments. The first draft of this article was written for the project of post-doctoral research at Virginia Tech. I am grateful to ASPECT (Prof. Dr. Timothy W. Luke) and MAAT (Prof. Dr. Joonsung Yoon) for providing me with the time to do the work.

References

1. Adorno, T.W.: Aesthetic Theory. Minnesota University Press (1988)
2. Althusser, L.: For Marx. Verso (2005)
3. Althusser, L., Etienne, B.: Reading Capital. Verso (2006)
4. Arendt, H.: The Human Condition. The University of Chicago Press, Chicago (1958)
5. Austin, J.L.: How to Do Things With Words. Harvard University Press, Cambridge (1975)
6. Derrida, J.: Of Grammatology. The Johns Hopkins University Press, Baltimore (1998)
7. Foucault, M.: The Order of Things: An Archaeology of Human Sciences. Routlege, New York (2002)
8. Freud, S.: Civilization and Its Discontents. W.W. Norton & Company, New York (1961)
9. Hansen, M.B.N.: New Philosophy for New Media. The MIT Press, Cambridge (2004)
10. Heidegger, M.: The Question Concerning Technology. In: Scharff, R.C., Dusek, V. (eds.) Philosophy of Technology, pp. 252–264. Blackwell Publishing, Malden (2006)
11. Hyunkyoung, C., Joonsung, Y.: The Performative Art: The Politics of Doubleness. Leonardo 42(3), 282–283 (2009)
12. Hyunkyoung, C., Joonsung, Y.: How to See the Beauty that Is not There; The Aesthetic Element of Programming in Computer-Based Media Art. In: HCII 2007. LNCS, vol. 4546, pp. 292–300. Springer, Heidelberg (2007)
13. Kant, I.: Critique of the Power of Judgment. Cambridge University Press, Cambridge (2000)
14. Lacan, J.: Ecrits. W.W. Norton & Company, New York (2005)

15. Lcan, J.: The Seminar of Jacques Lacan. VII: The ethics of psychoanalysis 1959–1960. W.W. Norton & Company Inc., New York (1992)
16. Lacan, J.: The Seminar of Jacques Lacan. XI: The Four Fundamental Concepts of Psychoanalysis. W.W. Norton & Company Inc., New York (1998)
17. Latour, B.: We Have Never Been Modern. Harvard University Press, Cambridge (1993)
18. Marx, K.: Capital: A Critique of Political Economy, vol. 1. International Publishers Co. (1970)
19. Nietzsche, F.W.: Thus Spoke Zarathustra: A Book for Everyone and No One. Cambridge University Press, Cambridge (1996)
20. Zizek, S.: The Sublime Object of Ideology. Verso (1989)

What Makes Difference in Mobile Application Sales in Countries?

Hyeyoung Eun, Hyunsuk Kim, and Sungmin Hong

UED Lab. HongmoonGwan 928-1, Hongik University, Sangsoodong, Mapogu,
Seoul, South Korea
{Hyeyoung Eun,Hyunsuk Kim,Sungmin Hong,
Ellieeun}@gmail.com

Abstract. Since mobile applications use expended Wi-Fi environments and smart phones user population growth, the market is expanding rapidly. These mobile applications are supplied to the same standards around the world, but the applications preference is different for each user. Because user can choose applications based their own cultural and technical backgrounds on. Download a large number of applications is assumed to have high affinity. The collection of ranking data from Apple App store analyze this data compare by each country. Accordingly, applications preference is appear differently depending on the each country. The cause of the difference in affinity that results in a measure of the nation's cultural differences and differences in levels of technology adoption, and it can be seen through the analysis.

Keywords: Mobile Application Market, Using Smart phone Application, App Store.

1 Introduction

Nowadays, there are lots of quite interesting and inventive things around our environment and changing our lifestyle by using a Smart Phone, and, they are familiar with using Mobile Applications. Therefore the Mobile App(application)s market is rapidly increasing. In the Mobile Apps market is focused two highest markets on iPhone and Android apps. Surely, iPhone and Android apps are different system, device and market therefore this paper is studying for the difference in the iPhone application sales in countries. As a previous study, iPhone App market is bigger and longer than Android App market in many countries. But especially South Korean iPhone App market is very difference from other using application market countries. In South Korea case, it is started to iPhone App market from just 12month by Government policy about mobile market, although there are one of leading country of mobile market. As a result, between South Korea and other countries are different sales pattern of iPhone App market and using lifestyle. For instance, in Korean case, there is not game category in iPhone App categories by the National Gaming Control Commission. However, many Korean App company is making inroads in the iPhone App Industry. As a latecomer of iPhone App of the country, many developers need a preference research of mobile application for successful development iPhone App.

C. Stephanidis (Ed.): Posters, Part I, HCII 2011, CCIS 173, pp. 209–213, 2011.
© Springer-Verlag Berlin Heidelberg 2011

1.1 Research Purpose

As the fastest growing Smartphone market worldwide, the hardware, platform and applications market trend is also increasing rapidly. Since 2007, appearing Apple's iPhone was added to the terminal on the telephone functionality before than PDA (Personal Digital Assistance). It was not only mobile phone, it's Using a variety of applications that enhance the area's appearance. Recently, Mobile Applications are being circulated through the store environment improvements by wireless Internet without the constraints of space trade is active.

In this research purpose is based on what difference the user's preference between countries in mobile applications market. For this purpose, there are analyzed cultural differences, five measures of cultural variables, and technology adoption life cycle of South Korea, China, United States, UK, and Brazil. After that, it is compared and analyzed user features by market maturity in the Technology adoption life cycle. It will present the rationale theory.

1.2 Research Method

This is started from the current state and will present the following ones. Firstly, what iPhone Apps are using for many people? Secondly, which is the most trends App? Why do they shown difference consumer preferences in countries? Are they difference free or paid App market? Finally, current Apps Consumer's preference in countries will be analyzed and surveyed based on the questions.

This research was conducted to collect the opinions of interviewer iPhone Apps uses by divided short and long-term and each App categories users in Korea and USA. According of previous research, we researched about App market of Japan, China, France and UK that were similar the using App culture pattern of Japan-China-Korea and USA-France-UK.

The questionnaires were divided into three sections; 1) User behavior of favorite Apps, 2) information of using Apps and 3) demographic information. This exploratory study investigates the consumer's behavior towards iPhone App trend and preference, especially iPhone App user behavior that has not been researched mainly so far.

2 Background

According from starting point, it becomes necessary questions, which are; how many people were using iPhone Apps? which Apps are high ranking in each countries to compare all iPhone Apps market distribution? The purpose of this research is to investigate these points. The specific objectives of this research is what makes difference about iPhone App preference in countries. For this object, there are some of background theories. At first, according to O'Callaghan et al (1992) in innovation diffusion theory, the Technical conformity assessment can be the new technology of the existing software, hardware, technical procedures, and the operational conformity assessment is able to measured by how relevant procedures in an existing organization. Also Davis, F.D(1989) said that the user acceptance of information technology could be predicted a relative four points in the information technology acceptance model; **Beliefs-Attitude-Intention–Behavior**.

Based upon these objectives and theories, following hypotheses are developed: H1: Consumers will perceive the different technical background in countries. H2: Consumers will recognize useful Apps before download.

3 Research

3.1 Technology Adoption Life Style

According to Rogers (Rogers 1962 5th ed, p. 282), he defines an adopter category as a classification of individuals within a social system on the basis of innovativeness as the five categories of adopters are; innovators, Early Adopters, Early Majority, Late Majority, and Laggard. It is producted by comsumer's life cycle model from attitudes toward acceptance of new technologies.

Therefore, in the SmartPhone application market, there are difference market place South Korea in the form of the initial market; between Innovators and early adopters, the United States Central market; among early majority and late majority. Because two countries were difference launch date(South Korea: November 2009 / U.S.: July 2007).

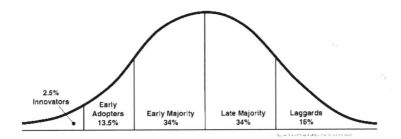

Fig. 1. Rogers, Everett M. (1962). Diffusion of Innovations, Glencoe: Free Press

3.2 Cultural Variables by Hofstede

Hofstede's studied the foundation for a framework under which there are national and regional cultural groupings that affect the behaviour of societies and organizations.

Between Korea and the United States were shown a big difference in numbers. It could be interpreted to comparing to USA and Korea, the emphasis on individual rather than collective, and material success rather than an human relations, and has a conservative or nationalistic cultural forms.

Table 1. Differences in levels of Korea and the USA by Hofstede's Cultural Variables (The Top ranking of App store research, ROA group, WIP, 2010.03)

Cultural Variables		KOR	USA
Small vs. large power distance (PDI)	Rank	27/28	38
	Score	60	40
Individualism vs. collectivism (IDV)	Rank	43	1
	Score	18	91
Masculinity vs. femininity (MAS)	Rank	41	15
	Score	39	62
Weak vs. strong uncertainty avoidance (UAI)	Rank	16/17	43
	Score	85	46
Long vs. short term orientation (LTO)	Rank	5	17
	Score	75	29

3.3 Using Mobile Applications

As a following table, although there are using same applications, the categories of top ranking is different pattern between Korea and USA.

Table 2. Category Ranking Top Seven(2010.09, iPhone App Store)

ranking	KOR		USA	
	free	paid	free	paid
1	Lifestyle	Games	Games	Games
2	Entertainment	Education	Entertainment	Entertainment
3	Games	Entertainment	Lifestyle	Utilities
4	Social networking	Utilities	Utilities	Music
5	Travel	Lifestyle	Social networking	healthcare & fitness
6	Utilities	Productivity	Music	Photography
7	Education	Music	Productivity	Productivity

4   Conclusion and Further Research

The goal of this research is, firstly, it will analyze according to the accumulated sales volume in iPhone App Store currently. Furthermore, there are developed user model of iPhone Apps from technology adoption lifestyle and cultural variable via research. Finally, the document will conclude everything that was studied and analyzed and suggest further research.

References

1. Jeong, G., et al.: The analysis of mobile applications preference between KOR·USA focusing on iPhone applications. In: Conference of KSDS (2010)
2. Hofstede, G.: Culture's Consequences: comparing values, behaviors, institutions, and organizations across nations. SAGE Publications, Thousand Oaks (2001)
3. Rogers, E.M.: Diffusion of Innovations. Free Press, Glencoe (1962)
4. Jin, S., Ha, K.: Rogers' Approach Focused Ubiquitous Housing Demand by Technology Acceptance Pattern of Rogers. Journal of the KREAA 15(3), 89–109 (2009)
5. The Google App Market - An Analysis (2009.09.06.) http://CEnriqueOrtiz.com
6. Flurry.com,
   http://blog.flurry.com/bid/26376/
   Mobile-Apps-Models-Money-and-Loyalty

hvMuseum: A Participatory Online Museum of Everyday Artifacts for Cultural Awareness

Young-ae Hahn

Savannah College of Art and Design in Atlanta
1600 Peachtree St. NW Atlanta, GA 30309 USA
yhahn@scad.edu

Abstract. The hvMuseum, an online platform for data collection and exhibition, empowers Internet users from around the world with opportunities for curatorial, contributory, and appreciatory types of museum participation. With unique, authentic and up-to-date information contributed by the locals of various countries, and displayed in a two-dimensional matrix for horizontal and vertical comparisons, the hvMuseum facilitates a viewer's inductive thinking that leads to learning opportunities and appreciation of the breadth and diversities of natural and man-made artifacts.

Keywords: online museum, user participation, inductive thinking.

1 Introduction

Traditionally, museums display artifacts of scientific, artistic, or historical importance [1] for the public, and the inclusion/exclusion of artifacts are decided by experts. As a result, two opportunities are lost.

First, the artifacts that can be housed in the museums are limited in the number, and the museum visitors lose the opportunities of seeing the myriads of other artifacts excluded from the collection. For instance, the *Common Concerns, Different Responses* exhibit in the Field Museum in Chicago, USA shows 60 plus pairs of shoes collected from all over the world, and among them, only one pair of Japanese shoes designed for the theatrical performance in 1940s is included. The beauty and functionality of Japanese shoe design cannot be fully represented by just one pair of shoes, and the viewers lose the opportunity to appreciate other specimens of different designs and materials.

Secondly, artifacts that have recently been invented or are currently being used are often excluded from the collection because their importance is still in the making. As a result, the opportunities to see contemporary artifacts in relation to the artifacts from the past are lost. The *Common Concerns, Different Responses* exhibit mostly shows shoes from the past, so the audience loses the opportunity to see what designs of shoes Japanese are walking around in at the present moment, and it may contribute to a viewer's incorrect cultural stereotypes. Inclusion of current artifacts would not devalue the quality of the exhibition because the appreciation of cultural diversity can arise from the comparison of current artifacts as well. Moreover, the design of a

C. Stephanidis (Ed.): Posters, Part I, HCII 2011, CCIS 173, pp. 214–217, 2011.

current artifact is often related to, or evolved from, aesthetics and philosophies of the past—such as the simplicity and functionality common to both the shoes in 1940s and the latest *Issey Miyake* collection—so discovering the essence of a culture preserved and manifested in many forms will be a valuable experience for the viewer.

2   Research Design

The *hvMuseum* provides the aforementioned lost opportunities. It is a web-based system for data collection and exhibition of everyday artifacts from around the world that may be normally excluded from museum collections because either they are current, or are considered to have little scientific, artistic, or historical importance by curators. Collections of such artifacts, however, can be valuable resources in promoting cultural awareness. More accurate pictures of the current life styles in other countries should be available for educators, designers, businesses, and engineers who prepare new talents or products for the global market.

The *hvMuseum* can be a success if (a) its collections are well-balanced representations of the cultures around the world; and (b) its collections provide unique, authentic and up-to-date information to facilitate the visitor's informal learning as it is often observed in on-ground museums [2, 3]. To achieve these goals, the research team recruited participants from both developing and developed countries. Three types of museum visitor participations identified in previous studies [4, 5, 6] were considered: curators who initiate collections, contributors who collect and post data, and visitors who appreciate and rate the quality of collections. In this study, however, the curatorial participation was difficult to observe as the research team had to initiate the first collection for this study. The museum website provided interfaces for the other two types of participation: data collection and rating.

2.1 Comparison Matrix View and Contributory Type Participation

A prototype of *hvMuseum* was opened with one collection, *bread from around the world*. The collection grew with more contributions from two groups of Internet users: the users from underrepresented cultures recruited from online pen-pal sites and the users from relatively well-represented cultures who frequent knowledge-sharing sites. In total, 20 participants were recruited for collection type participation. They contributed with information on the various types of bread consumed in their countries with either their original pictures or useful websites written in their native languages; the English-speaking research team members would not have been able to find the websites.

Collected bread data—digital images and brief descriptions of their origins, cooking methods, types (leavened or not), and key ingredients—are categorized into 12 regions (Far East Asia, South East Asia, Oceania, Central Asia, South Asia, Middle East, Africa, Mediterranean, Europe-Siberia, North America, Central America & the Caribbean Islands and South America) that sum up the sovereignties, climates, and cultures around the world.

The data are displayed in two views: the Comparison Matrix View and Reading-Rating View. First, users are invited to browse bread in the Comparison Matrix View where bread items from 12 regions are displayed on a world map to show their origins. The arrangement of data is actually a two-dimensional matrix for two directions of comparisons. The effectiveness of a matrix type of *advance organizers* in relational learning is demonstrated in previous studies [7]: an advance organizer provides a cognitive framework for the viewer to grasp structural information faster.

The 'h' and 'v' in *hvMuseum* mean horizontal and vertical, i.e. two directions of comparisons: First, a comparison of artifacts in horizontal directions allows the viewer to see artifacts originating from the regions sharing the same latitude. Secondly, a comparison of artifacts in vertical directions allows users to see artifacts originating from the regions sharing the same longitude. With a horizontal comparison, the artifacts from various cultural regions that share more or less similar climate conditions will be contrasted, whereas a vertical comparison will allow users to see the impacts from climate conditions on the eco system and lifestyle of each region, exemplified with the various crops and baking methods in the bread collection.

2.2 Reading-Rating View and Appreciatory-Type Participation

The *hvMuseum* also provides a Reading-Rating view where users can participate by appreciating and rating collected items. While the Comparison Matrix View is a convenient way to see all of the items from the 12 regions at once, the space is limited and there was no room for in-depth information. The Reading-Rating view allows a horizontal comparison of items originating from the same region with larger images and longer description. In this view, users can participate by rating the quality of displayed information with a score of one to ten. For the appreciatory type participation, 20 Internet users recruited via a crowd-sourcing site tried the museum site and were interviewed via email later for comments.

3   Inductive Thinking and Learning Opportunity with *hvMuseum*

From the qualitative data collected from participants, the research team found that the information displayed in the matrix successfully led the participants to the acquisition of novel information, to an appreciation of the breadth and varieties of cultures around the world, and to the recognition of patterns through inductive thinking.

In their responses to the email questionnaires, participants shared (a) new information they learned from the site, (b) comparison of bread items from around the world, (c) incorrect or incomplete information on the site, (d) any missing bread item they wished to add to the collection, and (e) any new collection they would like to start in *hvMuseum*.

New information is acquired when hvMuseum visitors broadened their definitions of bread by learning about new types of bread, such as the steamed buns made with rice powder in Asian countries. From the comparison of bread data, especially from the comparison of image data, participants mentioned the similarities between other countries' bread and the ones they eat (Middle Eastern Ka'ak and Polish bagel, e.g.), as well as the differences between them, and learning opportunities were observed. They were able to induce the relationship among the geographical/cultural origins, crops and other ingredients, cooking methods, tastes and textures of bread, and consumption methods. Regarding the incorrect or incomplete information, the participants shared their own cultural and historical knowledge, such as the British and European Imperialism influence on East Asian and African bread, an observation which exemplifies the possible valuable contributions from future *hvMuseum* visitors. Lastly they suggested new collection ideas of natural and man-made artifacts.

4   Limitations and Future Plans

The findings from this study are limited in that (a) the curatorial user participation was missing, and (b) the rating scores collected for this study were not clear indices for the authenticity or uniqueness of the displayed information due to the small number of appreciatory type participants and their nationalities. Most of them are from English-speaking countries and their input cannot be trusted on the other regions' bread items. The *hvMuseum* project will be expanded with features—such as a language translation tool feature, which will ensure equal participation of the Internet users from under-represented cultures—to make its collections unique and more authentic.

References

1. Lampe, K., Riede, K., Doerr, M.: Research Between Natura and Cultural History Information: Benefits and IT-Requirements for Transdisciplinary. Journal on Computing and Cultural Heritage 1(1), 1–22 (2008)
2. Friedman, R., Sequeira, M.: Application Development for Informal Learning Environments: Where IT Education, Community Outreach, Baseball and History Intersect. In: Proc. Special Interest Group for Information Technology Education, pp. 111–117 (2004)
3. Skov, M., Ingwersen, P.: Exploring Information Seeking Behavior in a Digital Museum Context. In: Proc. Information Interaction in Context, pp. 110–114 (2008)
4. Simon, N.: The Participatory Museum. Online Publication: Museum 2.0 (2010)
5. Roussou, M., Kavalieratou, E., Doulgeridis, M.: Children Designers in the Museum: Applying Participatory Design for the Development of an Art Education Program. In: Proc. IDC, pp. 77–80 (2007)
6. Dalsgaard, P., Dindler, C., Eriksson, E.: Designing for Participation in Public Knowledge Institutions. In: Proc. NordiCHI, pp. 93–102 (2008)
7. Kiewra, K.A., Mayer, R.E.: Effects of advance organizers and repeated presentations on students' learning. Journal of Experimental Education 65(2), 147–159 (1997)

The Cross-Cultural Adaptation of the Work Role Functioning Questionnaire to Turkish

Ahsen Irmak[1], Gonca Bumin[2], and Rafet Irmak[3]

[1] Hacettepe University, Institute of Health Sciences, Program of Ergotherapy
[2] Hacettepe University, Faculty of Health Sciences, Department of Ergotherapy
[3] Ahi Evran University, College of Health Services
ahsenrmk1842003@hotmail.com

Abstract. The aim of this study was to perform a cross-cultural adaptation of the Work Role Functioning Questionnaire into Turkish. The cross-cultural adaptation was performed as it is recommended in the international guidelines with the following steps: forward translation, synthesis, back-translation, consolidation of translations with expert committee, and pre-testing. The pre-final version of WRFQ-TV was conducted with 40 office workers with no specific health problem. The translation process of the questionnaire was completed without any major problem. The lay out was changed because 65% of the participants did not completely understand the questionnaire. The data shows acceptable results regarding to the psychometric properties of the WRFQ-TV. Cronbach'salpha for each subscale was >0.77, exceptfor the physical demand scale and social demand scale. This study resulted that the cross-cultural adaptation of the WRFQ-TV was successful. Future studies may focus on reliability of the WRFQ-TV.

Keywords: cross-cultural adaptation, psychometric properties, perception of difficulty, work functioning.

1 Introduction

Instruments related to work functioning are needed to both evaluate outcomes of preventative interventions and to determine the effects of health problems –on individuals' work activities.

Work Role Functioning Questionnaire (WRFQ), which is based on Work Limitations Questionnaire (WLQ), was developed in USA (1,2). WRFQ measures the perceived difficulty during the work activities by amount of time. Additionally WRFQ can be used to determine the effects of the intervention. It has five subscales: Work scheduling, Output, Physical, Mental and Social demands subscales (1).

Because of possible cultural differences the proper cross-cultural adaptation process of the instruments should be held (3). A six stepped approach for the cross-cultural adaptation of the questionnaires was introduced by Beaton (2000). The steps of this approach are: forward translation, synthesis, back translation, expert committee review, pre-testing and the formulation of the final translated version. There are

C. Stephanidis (Ed.): Posters, Part I, HCII 2011, CCIS 173, pp. 218–222, 2011.
© Springer-Verlag Berlin Heidelberg 2011

several successful cross-cultural adaptations of the WRFQ in other cultural contexts such as Dutch (4), Brazilian Portuguese (5) and Canadian French (6).

The aim of this study was to perform a cross-cultural adaptation of the Work Role Functioning Questionnaire into Turkish.

2 Methods

Cultural adaptation of the survey was conducted in accordance with standard guidelines.

2.1 The Cross-Cultural Adaptation Process

Forward Translation: Items and instructions were forward translated by four independent translators whose mother tongue was Turkish. Only two of the four translators had a medical background and an opinion what the WRFQ measures. A synthesis questionnaire was developed by comparison of the translated questionnaires. A detailed report was written about how a consensus was established on each issue.

Back Translation: Synthesized version of the questionnaire was translated into Turkish in order to control semantic or conceptual errors by two translators.

Expert committee: By reviewing all the translations, reports and the original questionnaire, the expert committee produced the pre-final version of the questionnaire for the use of pre-test. The differences between the back translations and the original version of the questionnaire were examined and discussed about what causes the differences.

Pre-test: To evaluate the clarity and equivalence of the questionnaire within the Turkish culture, a pre-test was applied with 40 participants. Contrary to the other translated versions validity for healthy workers was evaluated in this study. Therefore, inclusion criteria established as follows: the absence of an acute musculoskeletal problem, currently working (at least 8 hours/day), aged of 18-65 years, be able to read and understand the Turkish language. After filling out the questionnaire, one of the researchers interviewed with the participants individually and asked 7 questions about the WRFQ. The interview questions were taken from the article of Dutch version of the Questionnaire (4). The research team reviewed the answers given by the participants and decided whether there is a need to make any changes.

Evaluation of the Psychometric Properties of the Pre-final Version of the Questionnaire

Scale and Item Internal Consistency: Mean and standard deviations were calculated for each subscale. Croncach's alphas were calculated to evaluate the internal consistency. George and Mallery (2003) have identified the following rules :> 0.90 – Excellent, >0.80 – Good, >0.70 – Acceptable, >0.60 – Questionable, >0.50 – Poor, <0.50 – Unacceptable (7). Item-to-subscale correlations were calculated.

Validity: The content validity of the Turkish version of WRFQ was reviewed by the expert committee.

3   Results

3.1   Cross-Cultural Adaptation Process

The alteration of the lay out of the questionnaire was discussed in the process of forward translation. But no changes were made. Preserving the meaning of the items, item 1 ("required"), 2 ("Get going") and 4 ("extra breaks or rests") were changed. Item 14 ("pounds") was revised in kilograms.

In the meeting after the back translation process, forward translation, back translation and the original version of the questionnaire were compared. It was decided that there is no need for any changes.

3.2   Pre-test

The pre-final version of the questionnaire was applied to 40 office employees (n=22 women and n=18 men). The mean age of participants was 41.6 (SD 10.4) and the average hours worked per week was 40.5 (SD 1.8) hours. Socio-demographic information is shown in Table 1.

Table 1. Participants' socio-demographic characteristics (N=40)

	Total N=40	Women n=22 (%55)	Men n=18 (%45)
Age in years, mean (SD)	41.6 (10.4)	36.1 (6.9)	48.2 (10.2)
Working hours/week, mean (SD)	40.5 (1.8)	40.22 (1.06)	40.83 (2.57)

35% of respondents said that the instructions were not clear enough. Participants indicated that the cause of incomprehension of the instructions was the lay out of the questionnaire. According to the recommendations of the participants, the research team decided to inclusion of the phase of "I had difficulty" in each item. Instructions were revised and changed according to the new lay out.

Nearly half of the participants experienced difficulty in understanding the item 1. In order to obtain better understanding, it was included the phrase of "of my job". A small insertion was made to item 13 which is mentioned by two participants. It was changed to "Going around the room and going various places while performing my job" from "Being on the move on your job and going to different places". Even if it was mentioned only by one participant "train of thought" in the item 23 was changed to "line of thought" to enhance the Turkish adaptation.1 to2participants reported difficulty in understanding items 5,9, 11, 12, 16, 17, 18, 20and27. But the research team has concluded there is no need to change.

70% of the participants noted that the questionnaire provides a complete overview of their occupation. The remaining 30% replied by saying "no" or "not exactly". Among the issues proposed by the participants physical environment and eye/ear health were included. In addition, the participants noted that they complete the questionnaire without getting bored and the length of the questionnaire was quite well.

3.3 Evaluation of the Psychometric Properties of the Final Version of the WRFQ-TV

Content Validity: The expert committee considered the content validity of the Turkish version of the Work Role Functioning Questionnaire as good. They concluded the questionnaire to be complete for especially for office workers. According the pre-test data acceptance rate of the WRFQ-TV was high.

Scale and Item Internal Consistency: Cronbach's alpha for each subscale was >0.77, except for the physical demand scale (α=0.68) and social demand scale (α=0.62). Cronbach's alpha values are shown in Table2.

Table2. Cronbach's alpha coefficient for each subscale of WRFQ (Turkish version)

	Number of items	Cronbach's alpha	Range of item-to-subscale correlations
Work scheduling demands	5	0.84	0.55 – 0.77
Output demands	6	0.77	0.30 – 0.71
Physical demands	6	0.68	0.01 – 0.76
Mental demands	7	0.88	0.51 – 0.82
Social demands	3	0.62	0.27 – 0.63

The item-to-subscale correlations for Work scheduling demands and Mental demands subscales were ranged from 0.51 to 0.82. The item-to-subscale correlations for other subscales were ranged between 0.25 and 0.76, except item 14 in the Physical demands subscale.

4 Discussion

The purpose of this study was to conduct the cross-cultural adaptation of the WRFQ to Turkish and to make it usable to assess the perceived difficulty of Turkish healthy workers according work activities. The cross-cultural adaptation was performed as it is recommended in the international guidelines (3). By this means a Turkish version of the WRFQ which is equal the original version was obtained.

The aim of the changes made in the questionnaire right after the translations and pre-test was to optimize clarity. In Turkish version the lay out of the questionnaire also changed (rewrite the items as a full statement including difficulty each sentence). Gallasch et al also changed the lay out but the other two versions adhered to the original lay out (5).

There was difficulty in translating a few items and others are changed according to the pre-test results.

Although there was a consensus about the completeness of the questionnaire between the participants and the expert committee, several advices were made to improve the questionnaire. Among the recommendations there were work environment ergonomics and eye/ear health issues. Future studies may focus on exploration of items that may reflect Turkish work culture better and adaptation the questionnaire to specific occupations (such as stenographer or secretary).

The results reveal that the suitability for use and psychometric properties of Turkish version of the questionnaire are good. Cronbach's alpha for each subscale was >0.77, except for the physical demand scale and social demand scale. The Cronbach' s alpha for social demands subscale were also lower compared to other subscales in the other translated versions of the questionnaire. Although the physical demands scale internal consistency was good in the other versions, in Turkish version it was questionable (0.68) by a narrow margin. According to the statistical analysis, item 14 was responsible for the fall of the value. Without item 14 the Cronbach's alpha value increased to 0.88. Although the data obtained from this study was promising, more studies should be done with inclusion of more participants and different professional groups. Future studies should examine the psychometric properties, test-retest reliability and validity in more detail.

References

1. Amick III, B.C., Lerner, D., Rogers, W.H., Rooney, T., Katz, J.N.: A review of health-related work outcome measures and their uses, and recommended measures. Spine 25, 3152–3160 (2000)
2. Lerner, D., Amick III, B.C., Rogers, W.H., Malspeis, S., Bungay, K., Cynn, D.: The Work Limitations Questionnaire. Med. Care. 39, 72–85 (2001)
3. Beaton, D.E., Bombardier, C., Guillemin, F., Ferraz, M.B.: Guidelines for the process of crosscultural adaptation of self-report measures. Spine 25, 3186–3191 (2000)
4. Abma, F., Amick III, B.C., Brouwer, S., van der Klink, J.J., Bültmann, U.: The cross-cultural adaptation of the Work Role Functioning Questionnaire to Dutch (in publishing process)
5. Gallasch, C.H., Alexandre, N.M.C., Amick III, B.C.: Cross-cultural Adaptation, Reliability, and Validity of the Work Role Functioning Questionnaire to Brazilian Portuguese. J. Occup. Rehab. 17, 701–711 (2007)
6. Durand, M.J., Vachon, B., Hong, Q.N., Imbeau, D., Amick III, B.C., Loisel, P.: The cross-cultural adaptation of the Work Role Functioning Questionnaire in Canadian French. Int. J. Rehabil. Res. 27, 261–268 (2004)
7. George, D., Mallery, P.: SPSS for Windows step by step: A simple guide and reference. 11.0 update, 4th edn. Allyn& Bacon, Boston (2003)

WARAI PRODUCT: Proposal to the Design Approach Designing the Product that Causes Laughter

Takaaki Kamei[1] and Kazuhiko Yamazaki[2]

Chiba Institute of Technology. 2-17-1 Thsudanuma, Narashino, Chiba, 275-0016 Japan
kame_8427@yahoo.co.jp, designkaz@gmail.com

Abstract. The purpose of this study is to propose the design approach designing the product that causes laughter. Author believes this product helps to reduce various stresses by laughter. Modern people tend to be emotionally unstable easily because of a lot of stresses like worry, the difficulty, and the financial problem and the social trouble. Moreover, laughter has able a lot of effects for man and the power to change the world. Laughter is a common language of the world. Therefore, laughter is sent to the world by the product produced in this research, and it aims at communications and the global peace. Author selected a college student as a target person on this study because student will be active in the society of the future. Author named WARAI(big smile)PRODUCT as product that causes laughter.Based on the literature study, author proposed designing method for WARAI PRODUCT such as preparing minimum two factors to cause laughter on the product. For example, one of WARAI PRODUCT have laughter factor on external design and internal design. The investigation has extracted the factor of laughter from the literature study of current laughter. The factor that looked like was made 15 groups from the factor of 62 extracted by using the KJ method. In addition, it made it to 16 factors adding the factor to which the author was paying attention. Using these 16 factors did the user investigation and the humor product investigation. Other investigations were the property investigation, the laughter investigation, and the scene investigation. The user investigation, the property investigation, and the scene investigation were done in Japan and France. Because to send the world laughter. The idea is progressed based on the result of the investigation, and the product that causes laughter named WARAI PRODUCTS is produced.

1 Background

Background of this research, I like to laugh and the laughter has a large power invisible, acting-out behavior is considered to be a very exciting feeling. Moreover, modern people are a lot of walls should, and become emotionally unstable easily from the situation of present economy, the society, and the world the worry thing and get over because of the stress. Then, I thought that laughter was increased and the person and the world became energetic. Laughter is a necessary, indispensable existence to change the world of the future. Therefore, I think that it is important to make this laughter known to the world. Then, I want to increase laughter from the angle of

C. Stephanidis (Ed.): Posters, Part I, HCII 2011, CCIS 173, pp. 223–226, 2011.
© Springer-Verlag Berlin Heidelberg 2011

product design, to make known, and to make it to production and the conducting research of the product that causes laughter named WARAI(big smile)PRODUCTS.

It is defined with WARAI(big smile)PRODUCTS as the product that causes the laughter at which the person who exists in surroundings with the user instinctively laughs.

2 Purpose of Research

This investigative purpose does the research and the production of the product that causes laughter named WARAIPRODUCTS at which a college man all over the world active in the society of the future instinctively laughs. And, it aims to pacify the world by making young people energetic by the power of laughter and sending the world laughter. I think that I want to cause laughter with WARAIPRODUCTS and to draw out the charm of the intended user further. I think communications and peace can be promoted by being able to expect able, for man various effects of laughter, and including the element of this laughter in product design.

3 Survey of Service Innovation

In my research, it has aimed to give the intended user a new experience of laughing as the cause from the product. Therefore, human centered design (UCD) technique and technique of the persona are used and the research is advanced.

4 Hypothesis

A lot of products with an interesting externals exist. I guessed that big laughter was able to be invited by giving the product two changes or more including not only externals but also the function and use, and set this hypothesis.

5 Survey

The investigation has extracted the factor of laughter from the literature study of current laughter. The factor that looked like was made 15 groups from the factor of 62 extracted by using the KJ method. 15 groups is ①Surprising ⊖Sarcasm ⊛Be often ④Exaggerate ⑤Trifling ⑥Amazing ⑦Ribald ⑧Self-torment ⑨Mistake ⑩Crisis ⑪Reverse ⑫One after another ⑬Imitate ⑭Ignorance ⑮Play. In addition, author thought that happiness and laughter were able to be caused by combining a gesture, posture of the custom, and unconscious operation with the product, and added the factor of ⑯gesture and posture.

Using these 16 factors did the user investigation and the humor product investigation. The user investigation was showed the 74 images that appropriate for each factor to the target user, and investigated by which factor big laugh appeared. Author was investigated four Japanese, one French, one Vietnamese and one Chilean,

7 persons in total. Author recorded this investigation content on film, and observed the size of laughter. The humor product investigation was which of 16 factors used from 102 products. Other investigations were the property investigation, the laughter investigation, and the scene investigation. The user investigation, the property investigation, and the scene investigation were done in Japan and France. Because to send the world laughter.

(1) Result of the user investigation
5 high ranks of Japan are Mistake, Be often, Exaggerate, Trifling, One after another, and 5 high ranks of France are Sarcasm, One after another, Ignorance, Be often, Exaggerate. When Japan was compared with France, a common factor was clarified. It is One after another, Be often, and Exaggerate. Because One after another has the same meaning as the hypothesis, it can be said that the hypothesis will meet the user's demand.

(2) Result of the humor product investigation
5 high ranks are Surprising, Imitate, Trifling, Play, gesture and posture, Amazing. There is no common factor when the user investigation is compared with the result of humor product investigation. It is understood that the factor of the laughter used for the factor and the product of the laughter that the user demands is different from these. The production of this research should produce the product that contains the factor of the laughter that the user demands.

(3) Result of the property investigation
There are a lot of people who have the book and the game machine besides the class tools in Japan, and a lot of people who bring only the class tools in France. When the world is contemplated, it is necessary to set the object of the product designed based on France. Therefore, writing materials that target user's university student have without fail is made the object of the design.

(4) Result of the laughter investigation
The aimed laughter is laughter more than non-voluntary smile and infected laughter that is not ribaldry. Contain three elements of there is a person in the condition (1)There is a person in the circumference (2)Safety is given (3)The surprise is given. It was set to use the body language and senses that did not need the language to send the world laughter, and to apply movement and changing the product. This investigation was investigated from various viewpoints difference among history of laughter, classification, factor, infection, condition, and culture and structure and techniques, etc.

(5) Result of the scene investigation
Author investigated the university that was university student's activity place in fieldwork technique. It was clarified to the place where laughter seemed to happen that Japan and France were similar, such as the classroom, dining rooms, and bus stops.

The idea is progressed based on the result of the investigation, and the product that causes laughter named WARAI PRODUCTS is produced.

References

[1] Saeki, M.: Is laughter useful for the peace building (2009)
[2] Kayaba, N., Masuko, Y., Saito, M.: Classification of smile by amount of physical change and meaning of laughter
[3] Tatsumoto, T., Shimizu, A.: Does "Pleasant laughter" increase because of the others' existence?
[4] Hayakawa, H.: Quantitative analysis based on classification of "Laughter"
[5] Nagashima, Y.: Area of "Cause of laughter" term
[6] Aiba, A.: History of "Comedy"
[7] Higashihata, T.: About "It is laughingly study"
[8] Inoue, H.: About "It is laughingly study" research
[9] Kayo, F.: Does "Laughter like falling of tears" come to be shown about when? (2008)
[10] Emi, A.: Does pinpinkorori (PPK) life: in smiling through one's tears? pp. 145–146 (2007)
[11] Urano, Y.: laughter that lurks in the cultural setting in Japan of the history and the chivalry of negative two sides-tooth black 10, 3–10 (2003)
[12] Wakabayashi, I.: Borrowing of power of laughter, and art and literature company
[13] Shoda, R.: Consideration concerning character and laughter
[14] Koyama, K., Nakamura, R., Nishio, S.: Aiming at the clarification of the mechanism of laughter (information processing the front)
[15] Kitagaki, I.: The point of contact of the pattern and the education of laughter and amusement is researched laughter study 11, 11–18 (2004)
[16] Fukui, E.: Laughter at destining
[17] Kitagaki, I.: Laughter and factor systematization of amusement are researched laughter study 12, 40–47 (2005)
[18] Nakamura, T.: Natural laughter and analysis of difference of time of expression in forced smile
[19] Kayo, F.: Do it come to be shown about when, and Kyoto University of Education bulletin (114), 77–86 (2009); of "Laughter like falling of tears"
[20] Momose, O.: Ahhahha and research 15 of laughter study, 138–144 (2008)
[21] Kimura, Y.: Humour and power and research 15 of laughter study on laughter, 1–2 (2008)
[22] Yokoi, S.: laughter theory and the 8th continuation study meeting, 104–108 (2005), in KPS fiscal year (2004)
[23] Kasai, F.: Two things produce strange
[24] Shofukutei, M., Oda, M.: The fifth generation of guide series (3) of laughter Matsunosuke Shofukutei

The Beauty Formation of Digital Media Projects via Sticking Jewels Techniques Applied to the Research and Education of Culture Creative Design

Jhih-Wei Lee and Chun-Ming Huang

Department of Architecture, College of Design
Chung Yuan Christian University, Taiwan
jing_fang_lee@yahoo.com

Abstract. According to the Industry analysis of Design Report: As the trend of design development, the Culture Innovation is regarded as one of important development policies by government as same as Western Countries. There are two methods in trend of industry as: Keep the whole world in view, Take the all actions in locally. This is the most metropolitan territory and Internationalize through combination of Culture and Design Innovation to promote the additional value of products by local characteristic to establish the product image On the other hand, Not only Culture Innovation but additional valuable design. Design needs to combine the Arts, Culture and Science in future and reset the life style of human. According to raise talent, knowledge, technology of education spirit, combine with digital design and Aesthetic curriculums to work on "Sparkling Surprise" competition. Meanwhile, regarding creativity and Aesthetic to practice by brain storming and hand-making to stimulate young people put into the innovation, activity and vivid living. For pushing Localization and hand-made of Crafts are kinds of meaningful and valuable for nation. Besides, cultivate the culture and aesthetic of accomplishment, is good for a young people's vision career after graduation in society and Industry service. In order to go deep into Culture practice and cultivation of nation talent, combine with culture education and digital training to apply in liberal education of University.

Keywords: Culture Innovation, Value Added Design.

1 Research Background and Motivation

The British scholar John Howkins brought up two inspiring statistical data items: service economy accounts for 60% of the economic growth in Europe and the United States of America; and even 40% of new jobs sprout from individual creativity in the USA. Hence, cultural and creative industries have undeniably evolved into a mainstream of economic development. All sorts of product design thinking should focus on breakthroughs in the traditional product form, and this will bestow on

C. Stephanidis (Ed.): Posters, Part I, HCII 2011, CCIS 173, pp. 227–231, 2011.
© Springer-Verlag Berlin Heidelberg 2011

products brand new interpretations and appearances. Aside from innovation in materials, trendy ideas mapped by the use of digital media in design will also give new looks to products.

Currently introducing the concept of "local aesthetic, global perspectives", the Taiwan government strives to enable local culture to take root and develop. Moreover, the government also strives to cultivate the core value of craft emphasizing both culture and industry, and to enhance local residents' ability to appreciate aesthetic and the refined quality of life. All the efforts are meant for the sustainable development of craft industries in Taiwan. Amidst globalization and internationalization, Taiwan has been facing strong Japanese and Korean cultural impacts. Nowadays, when the vogue of the "Jungle Girl" is very popular among Japanese young people, toying with the digital camera has brought fun and become a habit of creativity for them.   In this research, digital image processing has been applied to photographic self-portraits and artistic facial expressions before trendy materials – Swaroski crystals are studded upon them.   In this way, art products worthy of collection are created. The theme of the exhibition and presentation is "Sparkling Surprise", punning on the original idea of "joyful surprise". It is such a delight to see unique personal styles and colorings displayed in the exhibited artworks, which also glisten with galactic radiance; and when sun-like energy and originality are emanated from the artworks, they also serve as creative inspiration for each student in his or her grasp of a "poetic and artistic life".

2 Research Objectives

By making the university a live studio for aesthetic creativity, students will be influenced by the natural ambiance and identify with the concept "life and culture, one with each other". Meanwhile, students will be further inspired to re-define their personal values and develop their conviction in lifelong learning. In doing so, they will achieve greater self-recognition and carry out better life-planning. Hence, this research serves to:

1. Infuse know-how into digital and cultural and creative design teaching apart from exploring the digitalization of creative artworks. With the creation of high-quality modern craftworks, both product value and product quality are increased, and unique personal humanity imagery is displayed.
2. Instill a new way of thinking into the craftwork industry by applying the latest image stitching technology and the Swarovski sticking jewels technique, setting new vogue via avant-garde coloring and styling.
3. Develop the humanistic quality and aesthetic excellence in students; enable the graduates to make infinitesimal contributions by connecting the society with industries and also through their offer of services. With the intention to enhance cultural cultivation and foster talents for Taiwan, a combined education of humanities, arts and digital technology is being introduced to the undergraduate curricula of General Studies.

3 Operating Procedures

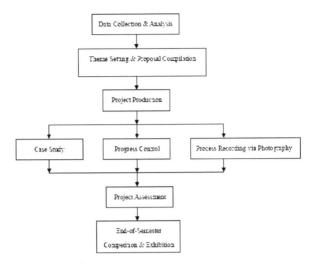

4 Idea of Creative Design – Sparkling Surprise

The creative idea of this research sprang from the creative theory of "self-portrait", which made its debut in the European culture in recent centuries. It could only be used to describe the portrait concept and arts in contemporary Europe, but was inadequate for the exploration of portraits in other civilizations. Thereof, such a definition in Western artistic theories has been inverted with the rise of new propositions on cultural portrait in modern art. Professor Olga Gorodetskaya, in an attempt to define "portrait", expressed that "regardless of styling and functions, the artwork of an individual figure, who is an end and from whom the cultural outlook is projected, is known as a 'portrait'", and "there are three concepts regarding portrait: the first being individual consciousness; the second, cognition of the Creator; and the third, comprehension of history. It is the similarities and differences of these three concepts in various civilizations that cause the image of portrait to vary among civilizations." In this research of experimental creativity, the author has observed that the vogue of the "Jungle Girl" is very popular among Japanese young people nowadays; toying with the digital camera has brought fun and become a habit of creativity for them. Hence, by applying digital image processing to photographic self-portraits and artistic facial expressions before sticking trendy Swarovski crystals upon them, artworks worthy of collection are created. The theme of the project is "Sparkling Surprise", resonating with the original idea of "joyful surprises". The artworks induce wonder and symbolize a wish for countless surprises in life.

Based on the difference of each person's portrait and the individuality, students are guided to discover their own uniqueness and excellence. And by sticking trendy and brilliant Swarovski crystals upon a variety of creative design products, students create spectacular artworks filled with "joyful surprises". The appliance items include porcelain saucers, young people's mobile phones, face masks, photo frames, lunch boxes, stationery, etc. Wonders are made out of the common items in daily life with both quality and value added to them.

5 Research Contributions

When the cultural and creative economy characterized by knowledge and aesthetic has arrived, the mainstream society and industries begin to understand that design matters. As the global economy and social development advance with a quantum leap in technology, the tides of globalization, technological advances, cultural creativity, and green environment awareness arise. As a result, the Taiwan government endorsed cultural creativity as a key national development project in 2002. As culture is intangible and extends beyond time and space, we can actually say that "life and culture are one with each other". The cultural and creative industries can be defined as "industries originated from the accumulation of creativity and culture, with potentials in creating wealth and employment opportunities via the establishment and manipulation of intellectual property. Such industries are also capable of promoting our overall living environment". Inclusive of printing, publishing, multimedia, visual and audio arts, photography and film production, and crafts and design, such a concept simply encompasses all major industries like food, fashion, housing and transportation. In view of Asian countries and neighboring regions such as Korea, Hong Kong, Singapore and Thailand, all are working hard to transform their economy into the cultural and aesthetical economy. The thinking of cultural creativity and design has become an important basis for national economic development. Thus, all the universities in Taiwan should devote themselves to fostering talents and elites by immersing students in culture and creativity, life and design. In this way, they are supporting the government's national development strategy, helping to boost Taiwan's competitiveness and alignment with the world. Furthermore, universities will be able to fulfill the mission of their time.

Left: Art Essential (Liu Shu-Wei / Hsu Chi-Jie / Lin Chi-Chung) The designer's Jazz spirit is displayed along with a three-dimensional vision by sticking different colors and layers of crystals on the porcelain saucer.
Right: Pretty Round (Chou Tsong-Hui / Tsiu Fang-Yu) This exclusive piece features a floral background burgeoned with crystals, a symbol of radiance, joy and fullness, while capturing the designer's individuality and youthfulness at the same time.

Left: Twinkle (Huang Yu-Ting / Hsieh Tsai-Ling) The "cat" as the main character is encompassed by the designer's illustration to exude an ambiance pervasive of mystery and brilliance!

Right: Glittering & Glamour (Tsai Cheng-Han /Huang Hsi-Han / Chang Hui-Min) A vibrant Malayan design coupled with a bold contrast in crystalline coloring – all add up to a very distinct creative style!!

6 Conclusion

Mankind's cognition of beauty is under the tremendous influence of the Greek philosophers' aesthetic principles in balance, Plato's idealism and the Euclidean geometry. Shapes such as the circle, parallel lines, square and rectangle, which are found in Nature, are very often used in art creation; and such a symmetry and basic relationship are expected to be inherited in music and art. (John Briggs, 1993) As the rough gemstones used in accessory design come from Nature, they definitely bear the characteristics similar to their origin; and accessories set with rough gemstones or made alone in metal are rarely created in the Euclidean shapes, but mostly in the organic or concrete natural form instead. Recently, exclusiveness is being emphasized in accessory design and a rising demand for accessory design products is also spotted in the consumer market. If the art of "portraiture" can be applied to the realm of accessory design, the new ideas formed in creative design and the new vision generated thereof will differ from the conventional Euclidean geometry, resulting in an innovative way of expression in styling. The positive results and benefits of this educational research are summarized as follows:

1. Training students in visual design planning, marketing and promotion, product design, etc. And through such a fusion of digital media teaching and the cultural and creative industries, a win-win scenario is created for both education and the cultural and creative industries.
2. Developing design products for the team and exploring key criteria for the success of a brand and the creative thinking methodology.
3. Building a brand, rethinking the local value of "culture" and "life", and further promoting innovative and refined art products.
4. Establishing confidence and self-identification in undergraduates; worthwhile of development to enrich teaching materials in art education.

Leveraging Card-Based Collaborative Activities as Culturally Situated Design Tools

D. Scott McCrickard[1], DeMarcus Townsend[1], Woodrow W. Winchester[2], and Tiffany Barnes[3]

[1] Virginia Tech, Department of Computer Science, 2202 Kraft Drive,
Blacksburg, VA 24060, United States
[2] Virginia Tech, Grado Department of Industrial and Systems Engineering, 250 Durham Hall,
Blacksburg, VA 24061, United States
[3] University of North Carolina, Charlotte, Department of Computer Science,
Charlotte, NC, 28223, United States
{mccricks,dm2town,wwwinche}@vt.edu, tiffany.barnes@uncc.edu

Abstract. This paper describes two examples of virtual card games serving as Culturally Situated Design Tools (CSDTs) for young people. CSDTs have promise in helping people to learn by connecting principles from computing with aspects of their heritage or gender. The development and deployment of card games on two cutting-edge platforms (mobile devices and multitouch tables) revealed novel ways to display information to users and important lessons for deploying them to young people.

Keywords: culturally situated design tools, games, education, mobile, multitouch.

1 Introduction

Culturally Situated Design Tools (CSDTs) seek to help people to learn by connecting principles from computing and technology with aspects of their heritage valued by members who identify with a demographic or culture. These aspects can include clothing that they wear, food that they eat, crafts that they undertake, activities that they do, people with whom they identify, or other cultural aspects that are particularly valued or related to the demographic. The theory behind this approach is that the unique aspects will provide context and meaning to underrepresented groups, thus overcoming the often unintentional biases of the majority group in choosing teaching tools and techniques.

This work seeks to leverage collaborative card games to connect with particular focus on two groups: women and African-Americans. Both groups historically play card games at a disproportionate rate, and both put unique value on the importance of collaboration through games. In modern times, evidence shows rapid adoption of mobile and non-traditional technology by women and African-Americans due to the availability of collaborative activities and the ability to strengthen interpersonal relationships. This work seeks to use novel emerging technologies to leverage the

C. Stephanidis (Ed.): Posters, Part I, HCII 2011, CCIS 173, pp. 232–236, 2011.
© Springer-Verlag Berlin Heidelberg 2011

cultural appeal of card-based games to attract young people (K-12 students, in particular middle and high school students from underrepresented groups) to computing and technology fields. This paper describes two design and evaluation examples by the authors and their collaborators that embody card game motifs: HealthAttack for the iPhone and METapp for multitouch surfaces. Drawing from the experiences with these games, the paper concludes with a roadmap for future card-based application development and testing.

2   Background and Approach

Culturally-Situated Design Tools (CSDTs) are activities based on math and computing knowledge; examples include the use of African American cornrow hairstyles to explore computation [1] and the use of Native American beadwork to show scanning algorithms [2]. CSDTs are used to teach people about difficult computational concepts, with the expectation that people from the represented groups (i.e., African Americans or Native Americans) will be motivated to learn because of the cultural connection.

This paper explores the use of card games as a CSDT. Unlike many computing activities, members of underrepresented groups—especially women, African Americans, and Hispanics) play certain games at equal or greater rates than white males [3].   Among those are card games, which often have cultural roots in underrepresented groups. Card games provide an experience for users that is both engaging and informative. Games have been leveraged previously to reach out to both adults and children, e.g., [4]. This game reinforces what is learned in school about the USDA food pyramid. As it was the developers' collective belief that responsiveness to cultural norms is of importance in the usefulness of a health and wellness application, the game leverages cultural norms and values central to the African-American community such as "role-modeling of behaviors".

3   Example 1: Health Attack

One common category of card games are memory-based games, in which participants seek to match pairs of cards from a large set of unordered pairs that are initially face down in a grid. Our efforts sought to implement such a game on a mobile device, with a focus on ethnic foods to increase appeal to underrepresented populations. Implementation on a mobile device also allowed us to extend the capabilities of the game to provide information about the foods, specifically nutrition information and ways to cook the food in a healthy manner. We called the game "Health Attack" and targeted it for African American youth. This section of the paper describes Health Attack as a tool for culturally situated design and understanding; for a more complete description of the implementation, use, and evaluation, see [5].

Health Attack is one of a large collection of applications for "smart" phones that are or will soon be distributed through the marketplace environments for the Apple iPhone and Google Android platforms. Smart phones are particularly relevant for many minority populations as they are often their primary Internet access platform

[6]. Researchers in our labs have distribution experience through these venues as registered developers, with some applications receiving hundreds of downloads in as little as two months.

A team of designers was assembled and charged with creating an engaging interface to address health and wellness concerns among African Americans. Five of the seven people on this team were African American, providing connections and empathy with the target population with potential for improved interfaces [7]. The design team sought to target a younger family demographic—children ages 7-11—expecting that behavior would be easier to influence and that the lessons would be reinforced in schools and other community groups.

With the African American culture in mind, the developers designed the interactive game for African-American children to provide awareness of nutritional information of commonly-eaten food. Based on the literature, field studies, and relevant cultural elements central to the African-American community (drawing heavily from their own experiences as youth and as older siblings), the developers identified symbols of black culture in our surrounding communities by going around the local community and to take pictures and notes about African American culture—quickly centering on issues of food selection and preparation. After finding important symbols in the community, the design team discussed how to convert that same tradition and important characteristics into the application targeted for African-American children.

The Health Attack game augments the traditional memory matching game by asking players to match food items that are placed in their respective places on the USDA food pyramid (see Figure 1). While users are playing the matching game, they are also given nutrition and health-related facts about each match. This feedback balances fun and learning, to attract users and to give them a reason to continue learning more about health and nutrition. By showing foods popular among African-Americans, Health Attack provides a sense of ownership for the target users. Also included on each card are quotes from African-American role models to help make the game feel more authentic and accessible to the African American community.

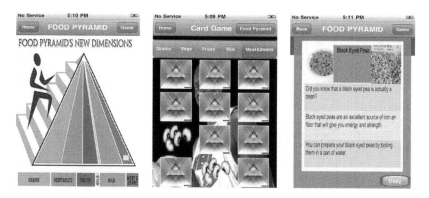

Fig. 1. Health Attack screens: Pyramid view (left) adapted from the USDA food pyramid; Game View (center) showing a match; Information View (right) with detailed information

Evaluation of Health Attack was conducted through a demo and questionnaire. The feedback questionnaire was given out to sixteen participants—primarily K-12 teachers, but also some college teachers and senior students. The participants viewed information on a poster, talked with developers and project leads, and experienced hands-on use of the application at a highly interactive poster session. The participants felt that the application would be helpful to raise nutritional awareness for children, specifically African-American children. In particular, there were positive feelings about the different role models used in the backgrounds throughout the game—though two of the participants did not answer this question, perhaps because they did not notice the role models. Since many of the participants were not African American or did not understand the African American culture, they may not have felt comfortable addressing some of the issues; future study will focus within the demographic.

4   Example 2: MET Apps for Multitouch Tables

The second example is the multitouch educational table application (MET) for multitouch tabletop computing technologies that provides a platform for collaborative and competitive card games. We designed this in-house technology to support multi-person, multi-handed interaction. A signature series of games asks participants to match cards with the same picture (in simple mode for younger players) or to match inventors and their inventions (for more advanced play). Some card sets focus on inventions by female and African American inventors, in an effort to connect better with those demographics. See [8] for a report of the design and assessment of MET.

Our team has explored the utility of multitouch tables through both field interventions and lab-based studies. The field interventions were highly informative; most notably in highlighting issues with the appeal to girls. Often the competitive nature of some of the games seemed to dissuade girls from playing the games. They tended to be more hesitant, seeking to learn the rules and to wait for a demo from a facilitator before starting the game. A lab-based usability study comparing METapp to a comparable computer desktop application showed that performance is similar across the different platforms, but participants enjoy the multitouch table game more than the traditional desktop game. While there were no differences in performance by minority groups, prior research suggests that long-term learning benefits may exist (see [7]).

Our planned MET game seem likely to address some of the barriers due to the competitiveness. As an example, our ongoing work seeks to create a collaborative game (more an activity) to provide a face-to-face Facebook-based experience in which multiple participants indicate their preference for music, books, and other topics that, when aggregated and displayed, can serve as the basis for conversations, collaborations, and friendships. The simple elegance of this type of application (on a cutting-edge platform) will hopefully serve to demystify computing and technology at an important age for recruitment to the field. Continued testing with K-12 groups will further reveal the effectiveness of these methods as a tool for encouraging technology use and as a method for encouraging collaboration and communication.

5 Conclusions and Future Work

Our experiences with these two example games suggest the following conclusions and directions for future work. First, there is promise in card-based games and activities, as students who were unfamiliar with these technologies tended to learn them quickly and embrace them readily. Second, we found that card-based games and activities benefit from highly collaborative (and sometimes competitive) aspects to them. Third, the appeal of cutting-edge technology serves as a recruiting tool, particularly in our involvement with middle and high school students, including groups that traditionally attract girls and minority students. We are inspired by and encouraged by the many other efforts in designing for minority populations, particularly the work of Grimes and Grinter (e.g., [9]). We feel that the true value of this work will take place with the technologies in the hands of people who can benefit from them.

Acknowledgements. Thanks goes to the NSF for grants IIS-0851774 and CNS-0940358 that supported this work. The opinions in this paper are ours and not necessarily shared by the NSF. Also, thanks to the many people who helped build and use our methods and software.

References

1. Eglash, R., Bennett, A.: Teaching with hidden capital: Agency in children's computational explorations of cornrow hairstyles. Children, Youth and Envinroments 19(1), 58–73 (2009)
2. Eglash, R.: Ethnocomputing with Native American Design. Information Technology and Indigenous People, ch. 29, pp. 210–219 (2007)
3. Markin, G.A.: Game Demographics—She's Young, She's Practiced, She's Good. Alien Babel Tech, http://www.alienbabeltech.com/main/?p=20058 (downloaded 1/12/2011)
4. Consolvo, S., McDonald, D.W., Landay, J.A.: Theory-driven design strategies for technologies that support behavior change in everyday life. In: Proceedings of the ACM Conference on Human Factors in Computing Systems (CHI 2009), pp. 405–414 (2009)
5. Hill, D., Blunt, J., Pugh, T., Monk, M., Kim, J.-S., McCrickard, D.S., Winchester, W.W., Estabrooks, P., Doswell, F.: Mobile technologies for promoting health and wellness among African American youth. In: Proceedings of HCII 2011 (2011)
6. Smith, A.: Mobile Access. Technical report, Pew Internet & American Life Project (2010)
7. Winchester, W.W., McCrickard, D.S., Doswell, F.: Towards culturally empowered design: Addressing African-American health disparities through notification interfaces. In: Workshop paper in CHI Wellness Information Workshop, 4 pages (2010)
8. George, J., de Araujo, E., Dorsey, D., McCrickard, D.S., Wilson, G.: Multitouch tables for collaborative object-based learning. In: Proceedings of HCII 2011 (2011)
9. Grimes, A., Grinter, R.E.: Designing persuasion: Health technology for low-income African American communities. In: Proceedings of Persuasive Technology, pp. 24–35 (2007)

Designing for Cultural Connections

Anicia Peters[1], Britta Mennecke[2], José Camou[1], Kiraz Candan Herdem[1], and Lei Zhang[2]

[1] Human Computer Interaction Program,
Virtual Reality Applications Center, 1620 Howe Hall
[2] Art & Design, 146 College of Design
Iowa State University, Ames, Iowa, 50011, USA
{anpeters,ruth463,jcamou,cherdem,leiz}@iastate.edu

Abstract. The 2010 earthquake in Haiti not only devastated the country's infrastructure, it also left many orphaned children, which accelerated the pace of international transracial adoptions by families in the United States and other developed countries. While international adoptees such as these Haitian children are older and will therefore likely remember some aspects of their birth culture, often younger children are at risk of forgetting much of their cultural and linguistic heritage. Despite much research on international transracial adoptions, surprisingly few web-based resources are available to adoptees for exploring and connecting with their birth cultures. To address this shortcoming, we used an iterative approach of ethnographic methods, paper prototypes, usability testing and heuristic evaluations to design Synergy, a system which allows adoptees to explore and connect with their birth cultures and its people autonomously.

Keywords: Virtual culture, international transracial adoptees, virtual tour, birth culture, adoptions, avatars.

1 Introduction

Imagine you are forever a foreigner in the country in which you grew up, you are always asked where you come from, why you look so different from your parents, can you speak your parents' language or they use gestures with you, sometimes people address you in a foreign tongue and try to connect you to a country and a people foreign to you, you feel as if you have "adoptee" written on your forehead...

In the United States alone, a staggering 213,496 international adoptions took place during the period 1999-2009 [16]. International adoptions happen when children are adopted from a country that is different from the adopting parents' country [9]. Many of these adoptions are transracial, which implies that the adopted children are in a different racial or ethnic group than are their adoptive parents [9, 17]. In 2009, the top five countries for adoptions were China, Ethiopia, Russia, South Korea and Guatemala [16]. In the United States, adoption parents are often middle-class and affluent [9, 14] and have the resources to provide special medical care and an excellent education to adoptees [1, 7].

C. Stephanidis (Ed.): Posters, Part I, HCII 2011, CCIS 173, pp. 237–241, 2011.
© Springer-Verlag Berlin Heidelberg 2011

Many children who are adopted as infants will likely easily assimilate or take on the values of their surrounding culture and family, but older children might find it more difficult to adapt to and accept the adoptive culture as their own since they have already formed some type of connection or idea about their birth culture [9]. For example, the January 2010 Haiti earthquake left many children orphaned with the result that American parents adopted approximately 1,150 Haitian orphans in one year alone [3]. Many of the children orphaned by the earthquake were older and more likely to have strong ties to their birth culture. Nevertheless, international transracial adoptees such as these Haitian orphans may successfully adopt the culture of their upbringing, but their race will not change and, as we will discuss, this has implications in the formation of their identities [1, 7].

Adoptees often struggle with self-identity, which includes physical appearance, birth culture and the culture of upbringing [7, 17]. Children become aware of differences in their physical appearances by themselves, through teasing by peers, or because of the way strangers view and engage with them and their family group [17].

Younger children identify racially and ethnically with their birth cultures, but for most children this identification diminishes in adolescence or early adulthood. Nevertheless, for some children, race and ethnicity becomes more accentuated by early adulthood when adoptees leave the parental home and neighborhoods [7, 9]. One non-Caucasian adoptee stated that she drew herself as having blonde hair and big blue eyes, which are visual characteristics associated with Caucasians [6, 17]. She added that when she was introduced to her birth culture, she "explored the contours of her DNA, personality and her essence" [6]. Children who resemble the race of their parents, e.g. Russian children adopted by Caucasian parents, experience fewer identity problems associated with physical appearance and race [7].

One way to address the cultural challenges of being a transracial adoptee is to learn about one's birth culture [9, 17]. In this paper, we assume that this connection is valuable. However, most families are not able to travel to the birth country of their children nor do they have the means to give their children first-hand experiences of their birth cultures. As a result, parents often rely upon culture camps, books, a native person, or their own knowledge about the children's birth cultures [7, 13].

Some adoptees applauded culture camps because they eased their isolation by allowing them to meet similar families and learn about their birth culture and language [7]. Nevertheless, one informant complained that culture camps offer a superficial experience where adoptees are separated from other people in their communities and those who teach them about their birth culture are not themselves natives of these cultures. It is important, therefore, that positive role models from their birth cultures should be part of this cultural experience [7, 9, 17]. Adoptees who have little contact with role models who are native to their birth countries will be more likely to have difficultly "developing pride in their race, ethnicity or culture" [7, 17] or in some cases, they might even be rejected by members of their own ethnic or racial group if they assimilate into the adopted culture [7, 12].

Although many resources are available to parents of adopted children to assist them in exploring or learning about their children's birth cultures, very few resources are available to the adoptees themselves [7, 8].

2   The Design Process of the Synergy Project

This project is an attempt to design a web-based tool that will help international, transracial adoptees explore and appreciate their birth cultures, connect with similar adoptees, families and mentors, and native people from their birth cultures.

As part of our data collection, we reviewed documentaries that featured expert discussions and vignettes from adoptees' lives [1,6,11]. We also reviewed the content of specialized adoptee social networking sites and international adoption web sites [2,5]. We held preliminary informal discussion rounds with two families, adult adoptees and an American sibling of two adoptees. We then held semi-structured interviews with six potential users, consisting of adoptees, adoptive parents and experts in adoption issues. The user group consisted of three adult adoptees, one of whom is an adoptee culture camp counselor; a father of two younger adoptees with American siblings; two mothers of two adoptees each, one of whom is also involved in an orphanage. All but two of our informants were women.

Interview questions were guided by literature reviews, documentaries and our preliminary discussion rounds about adoptions. Interviews were conducted in person, via cellphone and Skype. One interview was conducted at a place of work while another one was conducted in the home of the potential user. This venue was particularly rich because it enabled our informants to show us many artifacts that were acquired and showcased in their residence to help blend their children's' birth culture with the American culture in order to instill a sense of pride and belongingness.

2.1   Requirements Analysis

Our interviews and literature review each suggest that racial and ethnic identity becomes more salient for adoptees entering adulthood [9] and adoptees are also more likely to start exploring their birth cultures or visit their country of birth then. Further, we determined that it is only when adoptees become adults that they can request their adoption files and birth information, which would allow them to initiate searches for parents and family histories [5, 7]. As a consequence, we concluded that our target user group should be adult adoptees (i.e., 18 years or older).

Adoptees held diverse perspectives and views of themselves. A few of our informants assimilated with their adopted culture and had no interest in viewing themselves as being different from the adopted culture, others rejected their birth or adopted cultures, while some embraced both cultures [7, 9, 11, 15]. We took these divergent views into consideration and based our personas only on individuals who would be willing, to one degree or another, to explore their birth cultures.

Based on the information gathered, we created personas, scenarios and storyboards to help define the problem space and users' characteristics.

2.2   Interface Designs, Prototyping and Usability Testing

We then designed a paper prototype of screen sketches based on the personas, scenarios and storyboards.

Informational feedback on the paper prototype was solicited from the six users interviewed. The users evaluated the prototype by giving verbal feedback and suggesting improvements and additions to screens, layouts, and functionality. We also evaluated our designs based on Nielsen's usability heuristics [12].

Feedback from the informants for the prototype was incorporated into new paper sketches and medium fidelity screens.

2.3 Proposed System

We decided on the name "Synergy" because it refers to cultural synergies and its definition "the sum is greater than its parts" implied that understanding both adoptive and birth cultures results in a more balanced and positive human being. Synergy is a web-based tool where a user can explore a country's culture in an interactive way with the help of a virtual avatar as a guide. The user also has a social networking resource page to connect with different communities and adoption resource sites.

The user can edit the avatar to take on different personalities, gender, gestures or physical forms such as human and non-human forms and they can wear traditional costumes, jewelry and accessories from the country chosen. A picture of the user's face can be taken by webcam or uploaded and displayed/modeled on the avatar.

Non-human avatars were included as part of the avatar selection after usability testing revealed that male users preferred non-human avatars. This is also consistent with findings that males prefer "outlandish avatars that stand out" [4].

The system will display various components of the culture being explored. These include cultural characteristics such as daily rituals, language translators, representations of music and dance.

The initial content will be collected from books and the Internet. International students will be asked to serve as content judges and contribute supplementary material such as pictures, videos and experiences.

A social networking media content model will be followed for dynamic content generation wherein any user can create a profile and upload pictures, videos, and textual information with appropriate commentary or reviews in a wiki. This page will also display suggestions such as places to visit, lodging arrangements, food venders, and important cultural or civic events.

3 Conclusion and Future Work

The system is currently at a prototype stage, but will mature quickly with continued iterative design. One missing element is the content generated with input from international students. An important conclusion derived from our interviews and informal testing is that such a system is truly needed by transracial adoptees as well as family and friends of this stakeholder group.

References

1. Adopted The Movie, http://www.youtube.com/user/adoptedthemovie#p/u/10/MKHHzaOheHQ
2. Adoption Mosaic, http://www.facebook.com/AdoptionMosaic
3. Crary, D.: Haitian Orphans are settling with their new Families. In: Des Moines Sunday Register: Metro Edition. Associated Press (December 26, 2010)

4. Ducheneaut, N., Wen, M., Lee, N., Wadley, G.: Body and Mind: A Study of Avatar Personalization in Three Virtual Worlds. In: Proceedings of ACM CHI 2009 Conference on Human Factors in Computing Systems, pp. 1151–1160. ACM Press, New York (2009)
5. Holt International, http://www.holtinternational.org
6. Interview with Joo Young Choi, A Korean adoptee artist, http://www.fillintheblankgallery.com/discussions/2010/8/30/joo-young-choi.html
7. Interviews with potential users
8. Kids Culture Center, http://www.kidsculturecenter.com/
9. Lee, R.: The Transracial Adoption Paradox: History, Research and Counseling Implications of Cultural Socialization. Couns. Psychol. 31(6), 711–744 (2003)
10. Nielsen, J.: Ten Usability Heuristics, http://www.useit.com/papers/heuristic/heuristic_list.html
11. POV Documentaries with a Point of View, http://www.pbs.org/pov/firstpersonplural/history.php
12. Rodriquez, R.: Hunger of Memory: The Education of Richard Rodriquez. Bantam Dell, New York (1982)
13. Scroggs, P., Heitfield, H.: International Adopters and their Children: Birth Culture Ties. Gender Issues, 3–30 (2001)
14. Shiao, J., Tuan, M., Rienzi, E.: Shifting the Spotlight: Exploring Race and Culture in Korean-White Adoptive Families. Race & Society 7, 1–16 (2004)
15. Steward, R.J., Baden, L.: The Cultural-Racial Identity Model: Understanding the Racial Identity and Cultural Identity Development of Transracial Adoptees. National Center for Research on Teacher Learning, East Lansing, MI (1995)
16. Total Adoptions to the United States, http://www.adoption.state.gov/news/total_chart.html
17. Vonk, E.: Cultural Competence for Transracial Adoptive Parents. Social Work 46(3), 246–255 (2001)

Can Culture Translate to the Virtual World?

Raghavi Sakpal and Dale-Marie Wilson

University of North Carolina at Charlotte
{Rsakpal,DaleMarie.Wilson}@uncc.edu

Abstract. The United States consists of a diverse population of ethnic groups. Catering health care to such a culturally diverse population can be difficult for health care professionals. Culture plays a complex role in the development of health and human service delivery programs. Cultural Competence has emerged as an important issue to improve quality and eradicate racial/ethical disparities in health care. The Nursing Standards of proficiency for nursing education emphasize that nurses should be able to acknowledge patients cultural practices and take cultural influences into account when providing nursing care. A major challenge facing the nursing profession is educating and assisting nurses in providing culturally relevant care. To tackle this issue we have created virtual humans that will represent different cultures. These virtual humans will serve as educational tool that allow nurses to understand and handle patients from different cultures. Our first culturally-specific virtual human is a young Indian girl. In this paper we will discuss the architecture to create a culturally specific virtual patient.

Keywords: Culture, Cultural Competence, Transcultural Nursing, Virtual Humans.

1 Introduction

The 2000 census revealed that 29.4% of the United States population represents a variety of ethnic backgrounds. The main ethnic groups identified are: Hispanic, African American, Native American or American Indian, Asian, Native American or other Pacific Islander [14]. It has been projected that by the year 2050, the minority population will surpass the majority population [15]. With such a diverse population arises the issue of multiculturalism or what is commonly known as cultural diversity.

Cultural differences are one of the main contributors of disparities in the health care industry with respect to the quality of services provided. Research indicates significant existence of racial and ethnic disparities in access to health care service [13]. The 'Healthy People 2020' initiative, launched by the U.S Department of Health and Human Services, has emphasized the need to eradicate these disparities and thereby improve the health of all groups [8]. Therefore, it has become necessary to provide "culturally competent" medical care to improve the quality of the health care industry [5].

To provide culturally relevant care, it is necessary to acknowledge patients' cultural practices and take their cultural influences into account. A major challenge in

C. Stephanidis (Ed.): Posters, Part I, HCII 2011, CCIS 173, pp. 242–246, 2011.
© Springer-Verlag Berlin Heidelberg 2011

the health care industry is to educate and prepare future nurses with skills in transcultural nursing. This paper discusses the use of virtual humans as patients to teach cultural competence to nursing students.

2 Understanding Culture and Cultural Competence

According to Chamberlain, 2005 culture means "the values, norms and traditions that affect how individuals of a particular group perceive, think, interact, behave and make judgments about their world" [3]. Understanding culture helps us to understand how people see their world and interpret their environment. Culture also influences how people seek health care and how they respond towards health care providers [11]. Nurses must possess the ability and knowledge to communicate and to understand health behaviors influenced by culture. Having this ability and knowledge can eliminate barriers caused by race and ethnicity to provide culturally competent care.

Cultural Competence is the ability to interact effectively with people from different cultural backgrounds [4]. To be culturally competent the nurse needs to understand his/her world views and those of the patients and integrate this knowledge while communicating with the patients. Nurses need to learn how to ask sensitive questions while showing respect for different cultural beliefs [2][10]. Along with cultural sensitivity, it is also necessary to develop a trasdisciplinary, transcultural model that must be taught at the basic level of nursing education [7].

3 Agent Architecture

To create a culturally-specific virtual patient we are utilizing the FAtiMA (FearNot Affective Mind Architecture), agent architecture. This architecture creates believable agents where emotions and personality play a central role [1]. We extended FAtiMA to allow for the cultural adaption of the agents (see Fig. 1). The cultural aspects are set through the Hofstede cultural dimension values for the culture of the character; culturally specific symbols; culturally specific goals and needs, and the rituals of the culture [9].

Agents perceive the outside world based on their sensors. The perceived events are then passed through symbol translation. Different cultures perceive events differently based on their symbols. The symbol translation captures the specificities of communication in the agent's culture. For example, shaking one's head in India means 'yes' as opposed to the US interpretation of 'no'. Once the event has been identified by the agent, the appraisal process is triggered. In the appraisal process the situations are interpreted to enable valence reaction. The appraisal process consists of two main components:

1. Motivational System: Calculates the desirability of an event towards the agent depending upon the agent's needs and drives. If an event is perceived to be positive for the agent's needs, the desirability of the event is high, and vice-versa.
2. Cultural Dimensions: They are psychological dimensions, or value constructs, which can be used to describe a specific culture. Cultural dimensions capture the social norms of the culture that the agent is part of. We have considered Geert

Hofstede's cultural dimensions for India [9]. Geert Hofstede's research gives us insights into other cultures so that we can be more effective when interacting with people in other countries. Hofstede's cultural dimensions are- Power Distance Index (PDI), Individualism (IDV), Masculinity (MAS), Uncertainty Avoidance Index (UAI), and Long-term Orientation (LTO).

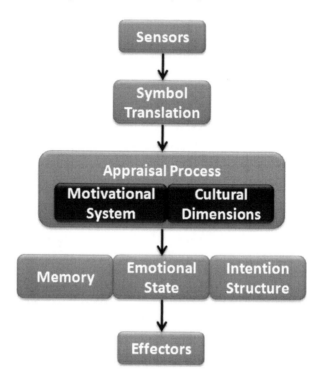

Fig. 1. Culturally-modified FAtiMA

The appraisal component then activates an emotion producing an update in the agent's memory and starts the deliberation process. The emotional state of the agent is determined by the OCC model of emotions defined by Ortony, Clore and Collins [12]. The deliberation process consists of the intention structure, which determines the agents- goals, intentions and plans. Once the action is chosen, symbol translation is invoked, and the agent translates the action taking into account its symbols, before the action is performed by its actuators.

4 Methods

In collaboration with the nursing department of University of North Carolina at Charlotte (UNCC), a life-sized virtual patient belonging to the Indian culture is being developed. The Indian culture was chosen due the large population of Indian students and families in the UNC system. The virtual patient is a 24-year old Indian girl, Sita.

The initial test case will involve Sita visiting a clinic due to an outbreak of Tuberculosis (TB) in one of her classes. In India, the population is immunized against TB. Any subsequent screening for TB results in a positive result due to the presence of the antibodies in the blood. Sita, during her preliminary visit to the clinic has presented with a positive result on the TB screening test. Sita is at the clinic for her subsequent visit. The nursing students will interact with a life-size projection of Sita. The goal of the students is to receive answers to their list of required questions, with some of the questions eliciting negative desirability based on the cultural dimensions of young, Indian females.

Sita's personality is based on Digman's Five Factor Model (FFM) [6] with her emotions governed by the OCC model of emotions [12]. The students interact with Sita on a one-on-one basis. Our goal is to design Sita such that she reacts to the student based upon the questions asked, how the questions are posed and the student's body language during the interaction. The interaction will be video recorded and analyzed by a faculty member. The faculty member is able to annotate the recording as they evaluate the student's performance. The annotated video will then used by the student as a study tool.

5 Future Work

We plan to create a common framework that will help in development of autonomous virtual humans belonging to different cultural/ethnic groups. Using this framework next we plan to create a Hispanic patient (due to high Hispanic population in Charlotte). Also we are investigating using Virtual Humans to improve customer service in other industries e.g. banking, education.

References

1. Aylett, R., Vannini, N., Adre, E., Paiva, A., Enz, S., Hall, L.: But that was in another country: agents and intercultural empathy. In: Proceedings of The 8th International Conference on Autonomous Agents and Multiagent Systems. International Foundation for Autonomous Agents and Multiagent Systems, vol. 1, pp. 329–336 (2009)
2. Campinha-Bacote, J., Padgett, J.: Cultural competence:A critical factor in nursing research. Journal of Cultural Diversity 2(1), 31–35 (1995)
3. Chamberlain, S.P.: Recognizing and responding to cultural differences in the education of culturally and linguistically diverse. Intervention in School and Clinic 40, 195–211 (2005)
4. Cohen, J.J., Gabriel, B.A., Terrell, C.: The case for diversity in the health care workforce, interventions to improve the racial and ethnic diversity of the US medical workforce should begin well before medical school. Health Affairs 21, 90–102 (2002)
5. Cross, T.L., Bazron, B.J., Dennis, K.W.: Toward a Culturally Competent System of Care: Monograph on Effective Services for Minority Children Who Are Severely Emotionally Disturbed. CASSP Technical Assistance Center, Georgetown University Child Development Center, 3800 Reservoir Rd., Washington DC (1989)
6. Digman, J.M.: Personality structure: Emergence of the five-factor model. Annual Review of Psychology, 417–440 (1990)

7. Glittenberg, J.: A transdisciplinary, transcultural model for health care. Journal of Transcultural Nursing, 6–10 (2004)
8. Public Health Service. Healthy People 2020: The road ahead. U.S. Department of Health and Human Services (2010)
9. Hofstede, G.: Hofstede's Culture Dimensions. Journal of Cross-Cultural Psychology 15, 417–433 (1984)
10. Leninger, M.: Transcultural nursing:Theories, research, and practice. McGraw Hill and Companies, New York (1995)
11. Meyer, C.R.: Medicine's Melting Pot. Minn Med. (1996)
12. Ortony, A., Clore, G., Collins, A.: Cognitive Structure of Emotions. Cambridge University Press, Cambridge (1988)
13. Smedley, B., Stith, A., Nelson, A.: Unequal Treatment: Confronting Racial and Ethnic Disparities in Health Care. National Academy Press, Washington DC (2002)
14. U.S. Census Bureau. Quick facts from the U.S. Census Bureau. USA (2004)
15. U.S. Department of Commerce. Quaterly labor reports, October 1-December 31, 1995. U.S. Printing Office, Department of Census, Washington DC (2004)

Product Pleasure Enhancement: Cultural Elements Make Significant Difference

Tyan-Yu Wu

Chang Gung University, The department of Industrial Design,
Tao-Yuan, Taiwan
tnyuwu@mail.cgu.edu.tw

Abstract. The aim of this paper is to examine the following arguments: 1) Products embedded with cultural elements have a greater chance to evoke a consumer's pleasure response than ones without; 2) A consumer perceiving the meaning of a cultural product in advance has a greater chance to evoke his/her pleasure than the one without perceiving; 3) Electromyography (EMG) is able to objectively assess consumers' pleasure evoked by a product. In this paper, EMG signal activity was collected as women (n=60) were exposed to three different stimuli. The results revealed that a product with cultural elements, (e.g. pictographic patterns) has a greater chance to evoke participants' pleasure than the one without. It also demonstrated that a consumer, perceiving a product's cultural meaning ahead of time have a stronger pleasure response than those without perceiving the meaning advance. The result shows that pleasant products are able to elicit greater activity over zygomaticus major.

Keywords: Emotional design, Facial Electromiography, Cultural product.

1 Introduction

Emotions play an important role in product design [1], [2], [3], [4]. Consumers, nowadays require a product not only to provide functional and ergonomic satisfaction, but also to fulfill users' pleasure status when interacting with a product [4]. Particularly, when a product is involved a decent cultural meaning, it can elicit users' pleasure if the meanings attached to a product are understandable.

A product with local appeal appears is becoming an important component for the development of a successful product [5]. For example, in 2007 Alessi cooperated with Taipei's National Palace Museum for the development of a series of kitchenware objects including pepper and salt shakers, cooking timer and egg holder. These designs patterned a powerful image of the Chin dynasty emperor and turned out to become very unique cultural products. These products communicate emotional semantics, which derive from remembered experience, including social experience and interpreted experience [6], memory of Chinese history. So, the product acts as an agent [3] of evoking users' pleasure when connecting to users' wonderful memory or experience during conversation. Hence, to create a product with pleasure, a designer should understand that, beside functions and usability, the cultural meaning is

C. Stephanidis (Ed.): Posters, Part I, HCII 2011, CCIS 173, pp. 247–251, 2011.

equalized important in designing a product for pleasure [7]. However, the lack of an empirical study in this aspect has lead to this paper. This paper aims to prove that a product patterned with cultural elements has a greater chance to evoke a consumer's pleasure response than the one without.

Product with cultural contents can enhance a user's pleasure after he or she comprehends the meaning of its particular form [8]. In fact, comprehension of product meanings involves users' cognition and previous experiences. This means the cognitive process and experience may affect the way users value the objects around them. In this paper, we argue that a consumer should have a pleasure response great, if they perceive the meaning (e.g. content, context, historical value or semantic meaning) of a product "positively". Hence, we assume that participants receiving a product's cultural meaning in advance (i.e. by watching a film related to the meaning of product) should have a greater influence on their pleasure responses than participants who do not perceived ahead of the time. In this paper, differently, we exclude traditional self-report and purpose to use Electromyography (EMG) as a tool because of its objective matter and success in evaluating positive and negative emotions in the base of facial muscles reactions.

2   Cultural Products Can Elicit Emotion

All aspects of human life are influenced by culture [9]. In fact, products with cultural form which we use in the daily life can be something with social meaning. In which can best fit the social belief systems, values and custom contexts [10], [8]. Hence, products can convey a strong information/ meaning [11], in certain cases about the human being who owns it [7]. For instance, by enforcing cultural value and emphasizing user's identity, Swatch conveys something personal; their products just about trendy colors or matching to various outfits, but say something about the personality of the wearer, which somehow make users feel pleasant.

Through product semantic content and expression, owning a product can affect a users' positive (i.e. strengthen the role) or negative (i.e. weaken the role) perceptions, emotion, value and associations [12]. From a user's point of view, decoding symbolic qualities of artifacts involves the cognitive and social context of their use [13]. As known, users from different culture have different cognitive and social context may strengthen or weaken users' social context and cognition, which affect their perception towards the product value and further evoke their pleasures. For instance, a product with Chinese elements can convey a stronger association, imagination, and interpretation to a Chinese viewer (e. g. Taiwanese participants) and further evoke a greater emotional response. Hence, to indicate users' emotion intensity involves their capabilities in translating/decoding artifact meaning in the product. In this paper, we assumed that a consumer watching a film related to product meaning advance can reveal greater pleasurable response than the one without watching. Additionally, to measure positive emotion, researchers have been particularly interested in facial EMG measures of activity over zygomaticus major, which pulls the corners of the mouth back and up into a smile, and corrugator suercilii, which draws the brow down and together into a frown[14], [15].

3   Method

Sixty Chang Gung Junior College female students (Ave. age = 17.5) took apart the test. They were divided into two groups: thirty for controlled and another thirty for experimental groups. Three physical stimuli were used in the experiment. Among these three, both S3 (i.e. pepper and salt shakers) and S2 (i.e. ice block lamp) demonstrate a strong pleasure, while S1 repeated S3, but without patterns on. In the experiment, MP 150, Biopac system was employed to catch EMG facial signals.

Procedure: Participants were asked to seat on a comfortable chair with relaxed gestures. Electrodes were fixed to the subjects to capture facial signals. In experimental group, two films were displayed before observing real stimuli, S2 and S3. The experiment was started with a 20-s calm period (i.e. preparation phase); then, participants were asked to watch the physical stimuli (S1) appeared for lasting 20-s. After the observing of S1, continuously ice scenario film was played on the screen and, after the film stopped, S2 was displayed in front of participants for another 20-s. Continuously, last process was repeated on S3. Repeat the same process experimental group gone through in controlled group. The only difference is that the films input sections were controlled and omitted.

Data acquisition: EMG signals were collected and transform into digital data. The EMG signals were submitted to a 20-Hz low pass and 500-Hz high-pass filter to reduce movement and blink-related artifact, then full-rectified. Following Larsen et al. (2003), EMG reactivity was measured during the first 6000-ms stimulus period and the 1000-ms immediately prior to stimulus on set. Total of measured period was 7000-ms. All data were subjected to a root mean square (RMS) transformation. EMG values were normalized to enable comparison of the values of two groups of each subject. Normalization formula is shown as $N = \overline{X} / \overline{P}$. Where $\overline{X}$ is the signal in the 6000-ms (i.e. after stimulus displayed) + 1000-ms (i.e. before stimulus displayed). $\overline{P}$ is the signal in the any 7000 ms before exposure of S1 (i.e. among 20s of calm period at preparation phase).

4   Results and Discussions

Control group: In Table 1, a repeated measure of general linear model was used to test three stimuli. In the activity of zagomatic major, a significant differences were found in three stimuli (F=3.17, p= .05). The result of zagomatic major signal activity demonstrates that participants can distinguish the difference significantly among S1, S2, and S3. Extensively, through paired test, the result of the signal activity of zagomatic major shows that both S3 and S2 elicited higher signal activity than S1 in zagomatic major activity (see Table 1-1,). It implied that pepper and salt shakers (i.e. S3) patterned cultural elements has a greater impact than pepper and salt shakers (i.e. S1) without cultural elements. In sum, the result implied that products attached with culture elements/ meaning have a greater influence on participants' pleasure responses than the one without.

Table 1. Statistic result of EMG value from Zagomatic major, elicited by three stimuli (Controlled group) (n=26)

Source	SS	df	MS	F	P
S1, S2, S3	.78	2	.39	3.17	.05*
Bet.-Sub.	12.80	25	.51		
Error	6.16	50	.12		
Total	19.66	77			

Table 1-1. Paired test of EMG value from Zagomatic major, elicited by three stimuli (Controlled group) (n=26)

(I) Real stimulus	(J) Real stimulus	MD (I-J)	Error	p
S1	S2	-.14*	.06	.03*
S2	S3	-.10	.09	.30
S3	S1	.24	.12	.06

Note: S3(Mean=1.07) >S2(Mean=.97) > 1(Mean=.83)

Experimental group: In Table 2, a repeated measure of general linear model was utilized to test three stimuli along with watching a film. In the activity of zagomatic major, a significant differences were found in three stimuli (F=4.26, $p<$ .02). The result in zagomatic major signal activity demonstrates that participants can distinguish the difference significantly among S1, S2, and S3. Furthermore, in the Table 2-1, paired test result shows that S3 has higher signal activity than S1 does significantly in zagomatic major. However, there is no significant different between S2 and S1, although the mean of S2 has higher signal activity than the mean of S1 does. The result of this paper supported the theory, that people find pleasure and meaning in the use of their eyes and have delighted in them, when the product content has associated with history and in every known culture [16].

Table 2. Statistic result of EMG value from Zagomatic major, elicited by three stimuli (Experimental group) (n=26)

Source	SS	df	MS	F	P
S1.S2.S3	36.03	2	18.02	4.26	.02*
Bet.Sub	244.36	25	9.78		
Error	211.45	50	4.23		
Total	491.84	77			

Table 2-1. paired test of EMG value from Zagomatic major, elicited by three stimuli (Experimental group) (n=26)

(I) Real stimulus	(J) Real stimulus	MD (I-J)	Error	p
S1	S2	-.65	.42	.130
S2	S3	-1.00	.59	.10
S3	S1	1.65*	.68	.022*

Note: S3(Mean=2.50) >S2(Mean=1.49) > S1(Mean=.84)

In table 3, to identify the effect derived from the cultural element, independent-samples T test was carried out to exanimate the effective difference between watching film in experimental group and without watching film in controlled group. In the examination of signal activity between two groups, $\triangle$S2 and $\triangle$S3 represent the value derived from the enhancement of watching film in experiment group and $\triangle$S2' and $\triangle$S3' represent the value without watching film in controlled group. In which EMG values were normalized by $\triangle S2 = \overline{S2} - \overline{S1}$, $\triangle S3 = \overline{S3} - \overline{S1}$, $\triangle S2' = \overline{S2}' - \overline{S1}'$ and $\triangle S3' = \overline{S3}' - \overline{S1}'$.

Table 3. Independent-Samples T Test between Experimental and Controlled Group

	△S2 & △S2'						△S3 & △S3'					
	Mean	F	Sig.	t	df	Sig.(2-tailed)	Mean	F	Sig.	t	df	Sig.(2-tailed)
EG	.65	5.73	.02*	1.21	50	.23	1.69	15.98	.00*	2.01	50	.05*
CG	.14						.24					
Note: " * " indicates significant, EG= Experimental Group (n=26), CG= Controlled Group (n=26)												

Moreover, independent-samples t test was conducted to test the effective between experimental and controlled groups. The result shows that there is a significant difference (F=15.98, p=.00) between $\triangle$S3 & $\triangle$S3'. Consistently, between $\triangle$S2 & $\triangle$S2' also demonstrated a significant difference (F=5.73, p =.02). The results implied that participants' pleasure towards product have a greater influence by their perceptions of watching films in both S2 and S3. In accordance of means, the result indicates that S3 carried out with Chinese cultural element/ meaning, in which Taiwanese participants can associate with their cultural root more and further may evoked a greater pleasure response, while S2 carried out with less familiar scenario (e.g. icy images) which reduced participants' imagination and further resulted in less pleasure response. The result explained why the cultural experience may influence a viewer's perception to a product, particularly when a product carried out a strong cultural meaning.

References

1. Laparra-Hernández, J., Belda-Lois, J.M., Medina, E., Campos, N., Poveda, R.: EMG and GSR signals for evaluating user's perception of different types of ceramic flooring. International Journal of Industrial Ergonomics 39, 326–332 (2009)
2. Norman, A.D.: Emotional design. Basic books, New York (2004)
3. Desmet, P.M.A., Hekkert, P.: The basis of product emotions. In: Green, W., Jordan, P. (eds.) Pleasure with Products, Beyond Usability, pp. 60–68. Taylor & Francis, London (2002)
4. Jordan, P.: Designing Pleasurable Products: An Introduction to the New Human Factors. Taylor & Francis, London (2000)
5. Desmet, P., Overbeeke, K.: Designing Products with Added Emotional Value: Research through Design. The Design Journal 4(1), 32–47 (2001)
6. Burnette, C.: Designing products to afford meanings. In: Tahkokallio, P., Uihma, S. (eds.) Design-Pleasure or Responsibility?, pp. 120–125. The University of Art and Design, Helsinki UIAH (1994)
7. Demirbilek, O., Sener, B.: Product design, semantics and emotional response. Ergonomics 46(13&14), 1346–1360 (2003)
8. Chang, W., Wu, T.Y.: Exploring types and characteristics of product forms. International Journal of Design 1(1), 3–14 (2007)
9. Razzaghi, M., Ramirez, M.J.R., Zehner, R.: Cultural patterns in product design ideas: comparisons between Australian and Iranian student concepts. Design Studies 30(4), 438–461 (2009)
10. Arnould, E., Price, L., Zinkhan, G.: Consumers, 2nd edn. McGraw-Hill Education, USA (2003)
11. Csikszentmihalyi, M., Rochberg-Halton, E.: The meaning of things: domestic symbols and the self. Cambridge University Press, Cambridge (1981)
12. Wikström, S.: Methods for Evaluation of Products' Semantics, PhD Thesis, Chalmers (1996)
13. Krippendorff, K., Butter, R.: Product semantics: Exploring the symbolic qualities of form in Innovation. The Journal of the Industrial Designers Society of America 3(2), 4–9 (1984)
14. Larsen, J.L., Norris, C.J., Cacioppo, T.J.: Effects of positive and negative affect on electromyographic activity over zygomaticus major and corrugator supercilii. Psychopfysiology 40(5), 776–785 (2003)
15. Dimgerg, U.: Facial reactions to emotional stimuli: Automatically controlled emotional responses. Cognition and Emotion 16(4), 449–471 (2002)
16. Bloch, H.P.: Seeking the Ideal Form: Product Design and Consumer Response. The Journal of Marketing 59(3), 16–29 (1995)

Part IV

Cognitive and Psychological Issues in HCI

An Optimal Human Adaptive Algorithm to Find Action - Reaction Word-Pairs

Arpit Agarwal, Rahul Banerjee, Varun Pandey, and Riya Charaya

Birla Institute of Technology & Science, Pilani
333031 Pilani, India
{arpit,rahul,varun,riya}@touch-lives.org

Abstract. This paper presents an efficient approach for understanding the formation of associations between random sentences spoken by humans over a period of time. The associations formed are mathematical relations (A X B) where the former is called as the "action" and the latter as the "reaction". The voice-to-text converted file is the input to the algorithm. After processing, the algorithm devises a map (Actions X Reactions). The algorithm stops only after the relation becomes surjective. The most important improvement over the previous techniques is the automatic adaptation of the machine to the ever-changing grammar of the user in real-time.

Keywords: adaptive, surjective, relations, grammar, human-behavior.

1 Introduction

Of late, there has been a marked shift in the user acceptance level from desktop to mobile applications and this has opened up several possibilities for technology-assisted approaches aiming to enable those who are often not served by it. Touching the lives of millions using simple, inexpensive technology-driven gadgets has been the driving force of the *"Project Connect"* under the *Touch-Lives Initiative (http://www.touch-lives.org)*. We have attempted to conceptualize and design simple assistive solutions that with the help of voice driven input, makes the mobile device automatically respond to the aid of the elderly user. Part of this work involves making a customized user-interface for easy use by the elderly people. We hope, it would help the user in the following ways: -

1. Respond to user queries without a trigger.
2. Interact with users in real time and intuitively.
3. Call for help in case of emergencies, without requiring explicit call initiation.

2 Related Work

Algorithms specifically designed to interpret a given speaker's real intent have attracted a lot interest in the recent years. Yoshiharu et. al. [1] in their work on the

C. Stephanidis (Ed.): Posters, Part I, HCII 2011, CCIS 173, pp. 255–259, 2011.

MindReader have designed a system where the computer tries to understand the user by repeated questioning. Proposing the view that users cannot always easily express their queries, this algorithm gives multiple queries a score (0/1 or multi-level). Subsequently, the algorithm guesses the appropriate distance function and issues the appropriate query.

Research by Doulamis. al.[2] in *Adaptive Algorithms for Interactive Multimedia*, throws light upon the various feedback algorithms and their performance, which provides important cues on the upper limit of iteration count.

The *Stable Partition Algorithm (SPA)* is an adaptive algorithm, which finds a valid relation between two elements (say 'a' and 'b'). A valid relation is one, where all 'b' are preceded by 'a' a *sufficient* [1] number of times. The run-time complexity of this algorithm is $O(nLog(n))$ if any secondary memory is not available and $O(n)$ complexity, if enough primary memory is available.

These pieces of works have helped our algorithm in accurately and reliably classifying the relations between *"action-sentences"* and *"reaction-sentences"* out of large sets of random data.

3 Proposed Methodology

The application developed under the *Project Connect* makes use of innovative algorithms that allow building embedded software capable of efficient and fast response to queries in real time without human-intervention. The mobile device is activated upon the reception of voice queries. Voice recognition algorithms are used to convert the voice-input to text. The text-files thus formed are analyzed forming logical-relations between sentences (stand-alone) and they are termed as *action-reaction pairs*. Once this stage completes, every time an *action-sentence* is encountered, the *reaction-sentence* triggers a function to help the user.

The human-adaptive algorithm, finds a relation between sentences by repeated reduction of the possible target-values by iterative intersection of *Region of Interests (ROI)*. Firstly, a possible *"action-word"* (usually the verb of the sentence) is determined. Since, sentences are logged at random intervals, a lot of *noise* (irrelevant sentences) would be logged as well. The ideal relation between every *"action-sentence"* and *"reaction-sentence"* would eventually take indefinite time. Thus, the limit on the iteration count is essential to balance the optimality and accuracy. It has been found that the method used in our algorithm performs with an accuracy of 91.84% (determined from the following histogram.) and a run-time efficiency of $O(n)$. (Where n is the size of input file that has to be analyzed).

The Y axis in Figure 1 (below) is read as: (say for dataset-1) Match:Action::30:70. So, in case there are 70 actions then there are 42.85% (i.e. 30, worst case) matches. The average of the ratio (Match:Action) over these 1000 datasets was found out to be 91.84:100 i.e. the algorithm is 91.84% accurate in order to find the action-reaction word pairs.

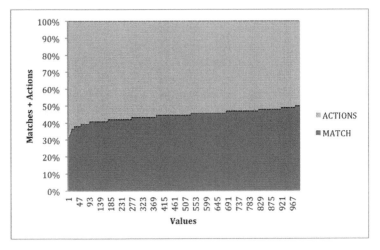

Fig. 1. Histogram showing how different datasets responded to the algorithm. The Y-axis is %age contributions of Actions & Matches.The X-axis refers to each dataset.

The algorithm, which has been explained above, can be summarized as:

```
begin:
              ReadLogFile();
              ChooseSentence();
              FindActionKeyword(); //Within the sentence.
              FormRegionsOfInterest();
//Using the action keyword as delimiters.
              while(!RelationAccuratelyFound) //aRb::a→b
begin:
TakeIntersections();
                  //Select common-sentences form ROI's.
              end
end
```

Assumptions: 1) The log-file has infinite length, 2) Number of required iterations [1][6] for each action-sentence <= Number of available ROI's formed (in the log file) for the same action-sentence.

4   Experiments & Results

The most important part of developing this algorithm was identifying the number of iterations to accurately decide the relations (aRb). Earlier works on adaptive algorithms ([3][4][5]) have shown remarkable results but our algorithm has demonstrated (Graphs and explanation below) a significant improvement over them in terms of both *performance* and *reliability*.

Here n is the size of the input file – i.e. the number of actions for which the action-reaction pairs have to be found.

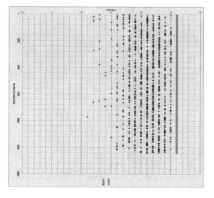

Fig. 2. Number of action-reaction pairs found

In Figure 2, the concentration of the points can be seen near the bold line at the right end that shows the *accuracy* and the *reliability* offered by the presented algorithm. A similar approach was tried with a neural network based algorithm to solve the problem but that turned out to be quite memory intensive. Hence, this algorithm suits fine, as it offers a *space complexity* of $O(n)$.

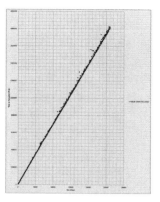

Fig. 3. Size of input Vs. Time

It can be clearly seen from the graphs that the time complexity of the algorithm implemented is $O(n)$ Here n is the size of the input. Figure 3 is plotted for *time-taken* versus the *size-of-input*. Here, graph shows a straight-line depicting a linear relation between time and size-of-input.

Also, the sample size for the graph is of the order of 10^6 values, making the results reliable for future studies.

5 Conclusions

The presented algorithm has been designed for mobile communication devices and therefore the principal effort was to optimally use the storage and processing power. We have shown that our algorithm is memory efficient. The time and space complexities have been found to be acceptable for the target platforms and have been successfully tested on the same.

Also, this work represents a significant improvement over other known algorithms [1][2][3][4][5].

References

1. Ishikawa, Y., Subramanya, R., Faloutsos, C.: MindReader: Query Databases through Multiple Examples. In: Proc. 24th VLDB Conf. Morgan Kaufmann, San Francisco (1998)
2. Doulamis, N.D., Doulamis, A.D., Varvarigou, T.A.: Varvarigou, Adaptive Algorithms for Interactive Multimedia. IEEE Multimedia 10(4), 38–47 (2003), doi:10.1109/MMUL.2003.1237549
3. Peter Lepage, G.: A new algorithm for adaptive multidimensional integration. Journal of Computational Physics 27(2), 192–203 (1978) ISSN 0021-9991, doi:10.1016/0021-9991(78)90004-9
4. Duan, J., Bressan, M., Dance, C., Qiu, G.: Tone-mapping high dynamic range images by novel histogram adjustment. Pattern Recognition 43(5), 1847–1862 (2010) ISSN 0031-3203, doi:10.1016/j.patcog.2009.12.006
5. Li, X., Lam, K.M., Shen, L.: An adaptive algorithm for the display of high-dynamic range images. Journal of Visual Communication and Image Representation, Special issue on High Dynamic Range Imaging 18(5), 397–405 (2007) ISSN 1047-3203, doi:10.1016/j.jvcir.2007.06.005
6. Abramowitz, M., Stegun, I.A. (eds.): Handbook of Mathematical Functions with Formulas, Graphs, and Mathematical Tables, ch. 26, p. 948. Dover, New York (1965) ISBN 978-0486612720, MR0167642

Modeling Users in Web Transactional Tasks with Behavioral and Visual Exploration Patterns

Areej Al-Wabil and Mashael Al-Saleh

Information Technology Department, College of Computer and Information Sciences
King Saud University, Riyadh, Saudi Arabia
{aalwabil,malsaleh2}@ksu.edu.sa

Abstract. In this paper, we describe a model of how users conduct transactional tasks on the web. In an exploratory eye tracking experiment, visual patterns of user interactions with web-based transactions were examined for verifying the model. Findings suggest viewing patterns and interactions supportive of the proposed user model and provide a good match to participants' interactions in completing transactional tasks on Arabic interfaces.

Keywords: Eye tracking, transactional tasks, visual attention, user model.

1 Introduction

Modeling user behavior facilitates the optimization of interface designs. Services and transactions are increasingly being offered online for users, but there exists limited research on modeling users in transactional tasks when compared to navigational and informational tasks. User modeling is needed to investigate effective methods for optimizing transactional interfaces and facilitating the development of automated usability evaluations. Recently, models have been proposed to investigate navigational and informational tasks in which users search for specific information elements in interactive systems. Navigational models include the framework for Human-Web Interaction [1], theories that have been developed for the purpose of cognitive engineering include Norman's Theory of Action [2], and frameworks which have informed usability practice include the User Action Framework [3].

Eyetracking has been shown to be a viable approach for examining the cognitive and perceptual capabilities of users in their interaction with interfaces [e.g. 4]. The focus of this study involves developing a user model that focuses on transactional tasks on the web. The model is motivated by the Theory of Action [2], which quantifies the perceived relevance of web form elements to the user's goal by cognitive processing and behavioral mechanisms. It utilizes behavioral and eye gaze metrics, derived from visual exploration patterns. In exploratory eye tracking experiments, visual patterns of user interactions with web-based transactions were examined for verifying the model's representation of user behavior and cognition.

C. Stephanidis (Ed.): Posters, Part I, HCII 2011, CCIS 173, pp. 260–264, 2011.
© Springer-Verlag Berlin Heidelberg 2011

2   A Model of Interaction in Transactional Tasks

In this study we propose a behavioral model of human interaction in transactional tasks, particularly web forms. The model can inform the design of a framework for examining usability issues in web forms. The model assumes that users complete transactional tasks in web form sequentially based on behavioral mechanisms that involve perceptual, cognitive and motor responses. It is depicted in Figure 1.

The first stage involves determining the goal for completing the transaction and the intention by ensuring that the form matches the goal of the transaction. After that, users proceed to fill out the form fields by first determining each field's strategy. The *Determine Strategy* step involves scanning the interface for cues on the form controls to understand how to proceed. The *Modifying Form Controls* stage is an iterative multi-step process which involves selecting the controls (e.g. field, radio button, checkbox, etc.) and modifying the controls by applying the appropriate action for entering data or selecting elements. Following that, the perceive system state involves scanning the interface to identify feedback and examining the system's response to understand what needs to be done. The evaluate field sub-stage involves understanding the system state to determine whether to proceed or act upon the feedback received from the system. Finally after completing all fields, the *Conclude Transaction* stage involves scanning form elements before concluding the transaction.

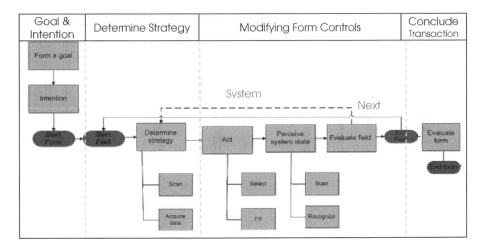

Fig. 1. Proposed model of interaction in transactional tasks

2   Method

The exploratory study was conducted in a lab environment controlled for consistent lighting, temperature and sound. The model was tested against a detailed set of eye tracking data collected from ten participants as they engaged in three transactional tasks using Arabic interfaces of web-based forms.

2.1 Participants and Apparatus

Ten participants took part in this exploratory experiment. Participants ranged in age between 17-34 years (Mean (M) = 23.4 years, and Standard Deviation (SD) = 4.5 years). Their computer experience ranged between 8-14 years of usage (M=10.7 years, SD= 2.37 years) and their Internet experience similarly ranged between 7-14 years (M=9.7, SD= 2.45). A standalone Tobii X120 eye tracker was used for gaze capture; it samples the position of users' eyes at the rate of 120Hz with accuracy of approximately 0.5°. Gaze data were logged by Tobii Studio 2.1. Internet Explorer 7 was used to display web stimuli with a resolution of 1024x768.

2.2 Experimental Design: Stimuli and Procedure

Each participant was asked individually to complete three transactional tasks on Arabic web interfaces so as to fill out forms related to different topics. The web pages participants viewed were selected to be representative of sectors such as public information, business and academic. Tasks involved booking a flight online with pre-specified departure and return dates, registering for an online academic portal, and searching for the contact form on a public service web site. Order of transactional tasks was counterbalanced across participants. Two examples are shown in Table 1.

The experiment consisted of three parts. The first part included demographic questions and familiarity with computers and the web. The second part was the main eye tracking study. The third part was the retrospective think-aloud (RTA) protocol on a sub-set of tasks in which participants describe their thoughts as they completed transactional tasks to elicit a deeper understanding of their observed behavior.

Table 1. Sample of stimuli

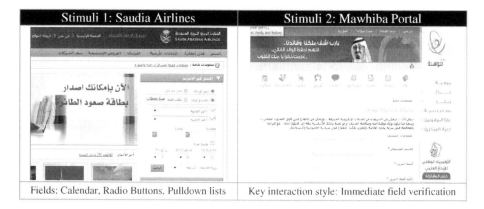

Stimuli 1: Saudia Airlines	Stimuli 2: Mawhiba Portal
Fields: Calendar, Radio Buttons, Pulldown lists	Key interaction style: Immediate field verification

3 Results and Discussion

In this study, we examined visual and behavioral strategies in transactional tasks, and present our findings in four parts according to the key stages of the user model.

3.1 User Goal and Intentions

To investigate this part of the model, we examined a navigation task in which users searched an organization's landing page for the contact form. It was evident that links with descriptive titles received more and longer fixation durations than other competing links. Verification of intent and goal matching was exhibited by users in visual explorations of form titles and headers/introductions and supported by RTA verbalizations. An example of a user experiencing difficulties is depicted in Figure 2.

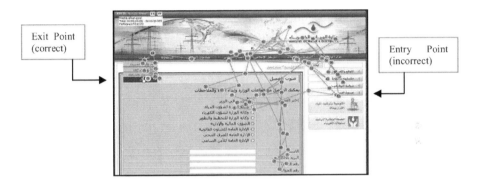

Fig. 2. Scattered scanpaths exhibited for verifying whether a form matches a user's goal

3.2 Part 2: Determining the Strategy

Examining patterns of how users determined the strategy for selecting dates on a reservation form, participants varied in familiarity with this form control. Four participants exhibited systematic patterns of examining labels followed by field controls. The RTA confirmed familiarity of participants with this type of field controls. This is depicted in Figure 3.

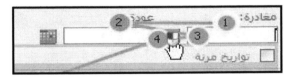

Fig. 3. Visual pattern reflecting the 'Determine Strategy' stage: Users examine the field labels for departure and return flights, then data entry field, then the calendar icon

The remaining participants had no prior experience with calendar controls for fields and exhibited on average more fixations and longer mean fixation durations than the first group. The visual patterns exhibited by this group were either scattered scanpaths with a relatively large number of fixations or intense fewer fixations suggesting increased cognitive processing in trying to figure out how to enter a date.

3.3 Modifying Form Controls

The Act sub-stage involves direct selection of form controls followed by modifying the controls by key presses, mouse clicks or selection of radio buttons etc. The *perceive system state* sub-stage was interesting to examine with eye gaze data as patterns revealed insights into how users perceive system feedback. For example, the Mawhiba form included immediate verification of fields and thus the user in Figure 4 noticed the error message indicating the problem with the username. Scanpaths show users visually scanning the system state and returning to the field and recognizing the problematic element and acting upon the feedback. Once corrected, users proceeded to the next field as depicted in Figure 4.

Fig. 4. Modifying Form Controls: Perceiving and Acting upon system state

3.4 Concluding Transactions

In evaluating a form before concluding transactions, participants exhibited one of three patterns. The first two were top-down or bottom-up visual scan to verify form elements before submitting. The third was directing attention to the submit control on the form to conclude the transaction without verification.

4 Conclusion

Findings show viewing patterns and interactions supportive of the proposed model, and it was concluded that the model provided a good match to users' interactions in completing transactional tasks. Furthermore, insights obtained from the exploratory experiments have led to revising segments of the model's stages as well as establishing a set of predictions for validating the model in future work.

References

1. Pilgrim, C., Lindgaard, G., Leung, Y.: A Framework for Human-Web Interaction. In: Proceedings of the CHISIG Annual Conference on Human-Computer Interaction, Ergonomics Society of Australia, Wollongong. ACM, New York (2004)
2. Norman, D.: Cognitive Engineering. In: Norman, D.A., Draper, S.W. (eds.) User Centered System Design, pp. 31–62 (1986)
3. Andre, T., Hartson, H., Belz, S., McCreary, F.: The User Action Framework: A Reliable Foundation for Usability Engineering Support Tools. Human-Computer Studies 54, 107–136 (2001)
4. Nielsen, J., Pernince, J.: Eyetracking Web Usability. New Rider, New York (2010)

Evaluating Information Visualizations with Working Memory Metrics

Alisa Bandlow, Laura E. Matzen, Kerstan S. Cole, Courtney C. Dornburg,
Charles J. Geiseler, John A. Greenfield, Laura A. McNamara,
and Susan M. Stevens-Adams

Sandia National Laboratories, P.O. Box 5800, Albuquerque, NM 87185 USA
{abandlo,lematze,kscole,ccdornb,cjgiese,jagreen,
lamcnam,smsteve}@sandia.gov

Abstract. Information visualization tools are being promoted to aid decision support. These tools assist in the analysis and comprehension of ambiguous and conflicting data sets. Formal evaluations are necessary to demonstrate the effectiveness of visualization tools, yet conducting these studies is difficult. Objective metrics that allow designers to compare the amount of work required for users to operate a particular interface are lacking. This in turn makes it difficult to compare workload across different interfaces, which is problematic for complicated information visualization and visual analytics packages. We believe that measures of working memory load can provide a more objective and consistent way of assessing visualizations and user interfaces across a range of applications. We present initial findings from a study using measures of working memory load to compare the usability of two graph representations.

Keywords: Information visualization, evaluation, cognitive load.

1 Introduction

Visual analytics software aims to enhance an individual's ability to make sense of complex data. However, evaluating visual analytics tools is difficult. Good data sets for testing are difficult to obtain. Some lack ground truth while others are sensitive and proprietary. Even when good data sets are available, controlled, experimental testing across tools is difficult when tools support different tasks. Visualization software supports complex tasks that vary across users and domains [7]. Traditional evaluation, including usability studies and controlled experiments, can be "helpful but take significant time and resources"[6]. Moreover, they do not generalize across conditions and contexts, which can lead to costly re-designs for specific data sets and user communities.

2 Cognitive Load Evaluation

We seek evaluation metrics that can be generalized across different types of visual analytics software, data and tasks. Mechanisms of human cognitive processing are

C. Stephanidis (Ed.): Posters, Part I, HCII 2011, CCIS 173, pp. 265–269, 2011.
© Springer-Verlag Berlin Heidelberg 2011

consistent across individuals. Since reasoning tasks require substantial cognitive resources, measuring cognitive processing demand can help designers assess the efficacy of visual representations.

Measurements of cognitive load are commonly used in evaluation. However, to our knowledge, the prior uses of cognitive load measures have used subjective questionnaires rather than measures of working memory. For example, the Task Load Index (TLX) questionnaire developed by NASA [2] has been used as one subjective metric for evaluating software tools [5, 8]. However, TLX ratings are subjective and must be combined with application-specific usability metrics, making comparison across software designs tricky and possibly expensive.

A more objective way of assessing cognitive load is to measure working memory, the "theoretical construct that has come to be used in cognitive psychology to refer to the system or mechanism underlying the maintenance of task-relevant information during the performance of a cognitive task" [9].

Working memory approaches can be implemented in a dual-task paradigm requiring completion of two simultaneous tasks. Sternberg tasks are well-validated working memory task frequently used in dual-task studies [10]. A Sternberg task requires participants to remember a distinct set of target items, and then identify them in a string of distractor items. Participants can perform well on the Sternberg task only when their cognitive resources are not consumed by the primary task. Accuracy and reaction times are compared across conditions to assess the relative burden imposed by the primary task. Such secondary task approaches are better at detecting workload than primary task measures alone [1, 4].

Huang et al. [3] suggest that effective visualizations help people concentrate on difficult tasks. Similarly, we suggest that *effective visualizations should minimize the cognitive demands associated with data-driven reasoning.* Difficult-to-use visualizations will consume cognitive resources, minimizing a user's ability to engage in higher-order reasoning. If this is the case, then as individuals are reasoning with a visual representation, performance on a concurrent Sternberg task may indicate if the representation is inducing extraneous cognitive load, beyond that associated with the primary task.

3 Measuring Working Memory Capacity for Graph Evaluation

To assess the feasibility of this approach, we used a within-subjects, dual-task paradigm to assess workload induced by two different graphical representations. Twenty-three participants completed the experiment.

In the primary task, participants reviewed either a traditional vertex-edge graph or a tree-ring graph, and then answered a question about the graph. We presented each participant three versions of each graph, with 20, 40, and 80 elements, for a total of six graphs. The participants' primary task was to answer six questions about the content of each of the six graphs, for a total of thirty-six questions. Half of the questions were a "good fit" for vertex-edge graph, and half were a "good fit" for the ring graph. The questions that were a "good fit" for the ring graph were a "bad fit" for the vertex-edge graph, and vice versa. The order of the questions and the order in which participants used the graphs were counterbalanced across tasks and across participants. After each question, participants filled out the NASA TLX questionnaire before proceeding. The participants' accuracy, reaction times, and subjective ratings for each question were recorded.

As participants completed the primary task, they completed a concurrent, auditory Sternberg task. We presented a memory set of three random letters before viewing each graph type. A random string of letters was presented over computer speakers at a rate of one letter every two seconds. Participants were instructed to click the mouse button as quickly as possible upon hearing a letter from the memory set. They were told to give more effort to the primary task at the expense of the secondary task.

For the primary task, we hypothesized that participants would take more time to answer "bad fit" questions than "good fit" questions. Secondly, we hypothesized that as the size of the graphs increased, the participants would take more time to respond and would make more errors. Thirdly, we hypothesized that performance differences between the "bad fit" and "good fit" questions would increase as the graph size grew.

We hypothesized that the results of the secondary Sternberg task would mirror the results from the primary task. We predicted that the participants would have longer reaction times and lower accuracy on the Sternberg task when answering the "bad fit" questions and for the larger graphs. We also predicted that the increased graph size would heighten secondary task performance differences between the "bad fit" and "good fit" questions.

4 Graph Evaluation Results and Conclusions

Participants' subjective evaluations indicated the primary task became more difficult for a) larger graphs and b) questions that were a "bad fit" to the graph type. A two-way analysis of variance (ANOVA) for each type of workload assessed by the NASA TLX showed main effects of graph size and question type for the mental demand, temporal demand, effort, and frustration measures (all $F=3.90$, all $p<0.02$).

As hypothesized, the participants' performance on the primary task declined as the graphs grew. Decline was greater for questions that were a "bad fit" to the graph type. The average percentages of correct responses are shown in Figure 1 and the average reaction times across conditions are shown in Figure 2. Two-way ANOVAs showed main effects of graph size and question fit and a significant interaction between graph size and question fit for both ($p<0.04$).

Working Memory (WM) tasks: Our critical prediction was that the working memory measure from the secondary task would mirror the results from the primary task. The participants' responses to the Sternberg task were scored as correct if they responded to the target letters before the next letter was presented. The participants' hit rates and false alarm rates were used to calculate d' scores, a measure of the participants' ability to discriminate between the target and distractor items. The average d' scores across participants are shown in Figure 3. A two-way ANOVA showed a significant interaction between graph size and question type [$F (2, 22) = 4.87$, $p = 0.01$]. This result indicates, as predicted, that the participants' performance on the working memory task reflected the difficulty of the primary task.

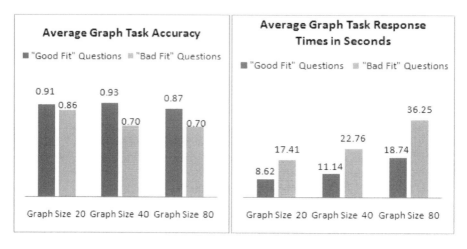

Fig. 1.   Fig. 2.

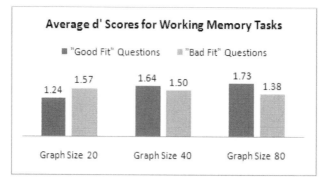

Fig. 3.

One issue with this evaluation is that the primary task questions were very easy for the size 20 graphs, notably for the "good fit" questions. Participants were often able to answer the questions before any targets were presented in the secondary task, which led to sparse data. In the future, we will ensure that the primary task allows for the presentation of several targets in the working memory task in all conditions.

This study indicates that a secondary working memory task could be useful for evaluating visualizations in cases where it is difficult or impossible to assess primary task performance. In future work, we plan to extend this method by applying it to more complex visualizations and to user interfaces. We believe that working memory assessments will provide metrics that enable designers to determine if particular design options require more cognitive resources than others for a given task.

Acknowledgements. This work was supported by the Networks Grand Challenge at Sandia National Laboratories. Sandia is a multiprogram laboratory operated by Sandia

Corporation, a Lockheed Martin Company, for the United States Department of Energy Company, National Nuclear Security Administration under contract DEAC04-94AL85000.

References

1. Gawron, V.: Human performance, workload, and situational awareness handbook. Taylor & Francis, Boca Raton (2008)
2. Hart, S.G., Staveland, L.E.: Development of a NASA-TLX (Task load index): Results of empirical and theoretical research. In: Hancock, P., Meshkati, N. (eds.) Human Mental Workload, pp. 139–183. North-Holland, Amsterdam (1988)
3. Huang, W., Eades, P., Hong, S.: Beyond time and error: A cognitive approach to the evaluation of graph drawings. In: Proc. 2008 Conference on Beyond Time and Errors: Novel Evaluation Methods for Information Visualization, pp. 1–8. ACM, New York (2008)
4. Meshkati, N., Hancock, P.A., Rahimi, M.: Techniques of mental workload assessment. In: Wilson, J. (ed.) Evaluation of Human Work: Practical Ergonomics Methodology, pp. 605–627. Taylor and Francis, London (1989)
5. Morse, E., Steves, M.P., Scholtz, J.: Metrics and methodologies for evaluating technologies for intelligence analysts. In: Proc. Conference on Intelligence Analysis (2005)
6. Plaisant, C., Fekete, J., Grinstein, G.: Promoting insight-based evaluation of visualizations: From contest to benchmark repository. IEEE Transactions on Visualization and Computer Graphics 14(1), 120–134 (2008)
7. Scholtz, J.: Progess and challenges in evaluating tools for sensemaking. Presented at the ACM CHI Conference Workshop on Sensemaking (2008)
8. Scholtz, J., Morse, E., Steves, M.P.: Evaluation metrics and methodologies for user-centered evaluation of intelligent systems. Interacting with Computers 18, 1186–1214 (2006)
9. Shah, P., Miyake, A.: Models of working memory: An introduction. In: Miyake, A., Shah, P. (eds.) Models of Working Memory: Mechanisms of Active Maintenance and Executive Control, pp. 1–27. Cambridge University Press, Cambridge (1999)
10. Wierwille, W.W., Eggemeier, F.T.: Recommendations for mental workload measurement in a test and evaluation environment. Human Factors 35, 263–282 (1993)

A Study on Human Error in the Interaction with the Computer Systems

Luiz Carlos Begosso[1,2], Maria Alice Siqueira Mendes Silva [3],
and Thiago Henrique Cortez[1]

[1] Fundação Educacional do Município de Assis - FEMA, Department of Computer Science
Av Getúlio Vargas, 1200, Assis – SP, Brazil
lbegosso@femanet.com.br, cortez.th@gmail.com
[2] Faculdade de Tecnologia de Ourinhos – FATEC,
Av Vitalina Marcusso, 1400, Ourinhos – SP, Brazil
[3] Universidade Estadual Paulista – UNESP, Department of Psychology
Av Dom Antonio, 2100, Assis – SP, Brazil
mallicemendes@gmail.com

Abstract. The term human factor is used by professionals of various fields meant for understanding the behavior of human beings at work. The human being, while developing a cooperative activity with a computer system, is subject to cause an undesirable situation in his/her task. This paper starts from the principle that human errors may be considered as a cause or factor contributing to a series of accidents and incidents in many diversified fields in which human beings interact with automated systems. We propose a simulator of performance in error with potentiality to assist the Human Computer Interaction (HCI) project manager in the construction of the critical systems.

Keywords: Computer Systems, Human Computer-Interaction, Human Error, Simulator of Performance in Error.

1 Introduction

The term human factor is used by professionals of several areas – engineering, psychology, sociology, ergonomics and more – dedicated to understanding human behavior at work. Generally, it is connected to the idea of error, failure and fault made by operators. Much criticism has been made around this expression, considered to be reductionist and scientistic, since it mostly disregards affective, cultural, ethical and political nature aspects that are involved in the complexity of the human-work relationship, [1].

Without ignoring such critiques, on the contrary, considering the inevitability of human failure – since it involves conscious, cognitive and also unconscious aspects – the present work confines itself in the paradigm of applied sciences, whose subjects make an effort to propose better efficacy and efficiency of human actions in their interaction with machines. It restricts itself, especially, to the perspective of dispute with possible human errors that might occur from this relationship, with the goal of comprehending them, in a way to develop new informational systems that allow, if not predictability, minimization, reversibility and correction of these errors in time for the task not to suffer serious disturbance.

C. Stephanidis (Ed.): Posters, Part I, HCII 2011, CCIS 173, pp. 270–274, 2011.

In this way, this work's goal is to present new mechanisms of human error that emerge of human computer interaction, expanding the taxonomy of human error proposed by [2] – aggregating to it new error mechanisms – and, still, demonstrate the contributions of a simulator of human performance in error – conceived and organized during our research – for the construction of projects in the HCI area.

2 Background

Because error is studied from different perspectives, even those strictly related to the HCI area, it is comprehensible that the analyses and consequent definitions of the term have, also, distinct conceptions.

A definition for human error considers *error* an unsuitable or undesired human decision or behavior that reduces or has potential to reduce the efficacy, security or performance of the system, [3].

Another important definition of human error is the one that considers erroneous actions that include the whole situation in which a planned sequence of physical or mental activities has failed in obtaining a result, and these failures cannot be attributed to external cause interventions, [2].

In this research, the context of human reliability in critical systems has been adopted, the conception that affirms human error is the probability a person: (a) does not correctly execute some activity required by the system, within a given time; and (b) performs strange activity that degrades the system, [4].

From the perspective of item (b), a successful task is not only the one that, during its execution, has reached the proposed goal. Under the point of view of human reliability, the successful task is the one that has achieved the expected mission result, within the specified conditions, and without creating undue disturbances to the process.

3 Model of the Human Information Processing

An important study of the area of HCI, has resulted in a broadly known model, called model of the human information processing [5]. This model, based on studies of behavior psychology, allows a reflection about the fact that different activities demand different levels of attention, knowledge, training or manual ability. It is divided in three levels of activities performed by a human operator during the execution of a task: skill-based level, rule-based level and knowledge-based level, that can be defined as follows: Skill level – It is linked to tasks which need manual skills. Generally speaking such skills result from routine practices of an activity, leading the person to produce fast response in face of stimulus; Rule level – refers to tasks which are governed by pre-defined situations. The person uses rules existing at the base of knowledge in order to accomplish the action; Knowledge level – It is linked to the accomplishment of more complex tasks, that is, those which depend on more elaborate responses and on previous knowledge to accomplish it. The lower performance levels (*skill* and *rule*) provide the person with storage of experience due to inferential reasoning activities and training for action accomplishment.

However, errors can occur to the extent in which tasks are executed in each one of the three levels.

To understand error's nature, researches are trying to classify them according to their similarities and differences. One of the classifications has created the theoretical model called GEMS (Generic Error Modeling System) that, organized from the model of human information processing, aim to explain human error [2] through an organization called 'failure modes', and these modes can take over different forms of error.

4   Proposal of a Simulator of Performance in Error

Ideally, the computer systems that simulate the human-computer interaction should contemplate, in their projects, the largest possible diversity of errors that could happen during the interaction. Generally speaking, the HCI designer considers only the most critical errors. However, the mistake pointed out in the preliminary analysis as the most critical one is not always the one which causes accidents.

A computer tool may generate forms of human behaviour in errors in a much higher number and with combinations which the human treatment would not allow, because it is a very long and fortuitously anti-economical task.

Our proposal, during this research, was about the conception and development of a human action simulator that considers error, so it can be applied to the study of human reliability in the operation of computer systems.

Since the aim of the simulator is not studying human behaviour, but its effect from the point of view of operational reliability, one decided, based on Reason's taxonomy, to group the implementation of errors which present proximity to the definition and one chose to generalize them in a single mechanism producing the same effect.

Table 1 was thus built with failure modes, according to performance levels. The goal was to demonstrate how these failure modes can compose the implementation of a computer simulator of human performance in error.

Table 1. Error Mechanisms

Skill level	Rule level	Knowledge level
Intentionality reduction	Rule force	Selectivity
Perceptive confusion	Redundancy	Memory limitation of work
Motor overload	Deficiency in Codification	Deficient learning
False perception	Wrong rule	
Omission	Overload	
Repetition		
Inversion		

We can observe, in Table 1, that there was the insertion of three new types of error mechanisms, resulting from this research, namely: motor overload and false perception, in the skill level, and defective learning, in the knowledge level, that completed the classification proposed by [2].

From the perspective of the Simulator of Performance in Error, which has been programmed in JAVA programming language, we proposed to simulate the interaction between a human operator and some computational interface, and to associate this interaction to human error concept. This simulation was conceived in a way to receive the entry of the task to be simulated, generate disturbances on it, using the errors of Table 1, and still, simulate the human operator executing the task in the environment of the ACT-R (Atomic Components of Thought – Rational) cognitive architecture. This cognitive architecture is capable of generating the simulation of a human being's performance while executing a task. The simulator here proposed receives, as entry, the task to be executed by the operator, inserts erroneous behaviors in the task and generates the source code, in ACT-R so the cognitive architecture can make its execution. The Simulator of Performance in Error's architecture is shown in Figure 1.

In said simulator, the modules for the task input in the Simulator of Human Performance, are: Interface Editor – provides the Designer with a graph environment to describe any computational interface. Its purpose is to help the Designer in building visual representations which convey the interface the system user interacts with; Task Editor – is a graph tool which implements the formalism proposed by [6] and follows the Designer during the analysis and task description stages. It enables their hierarchical description, as task trees related by means of temporal operators. Its purpose is to understand the user's cognitive operation; Semantic Knowledge Description – in charge of the user's semantic description of knowledge for solving problems represented by the described task.

The final product, after the execution of the three modules, is the automatic output of an XML file which represents the task described by the Designer.

The task processing, described at the simulator input, requires the following modules: Pre-Processor – synchronizes tasks with the ACT-R declarative and procedural memories and produces the task to be simulated free of disturbances; Trigger – it triggers shots under the task performance and, synchronized with the disturber module, it issues a possible error at random to the simulated behavior; Disturber – it produces the simulation of cognitive, perceptive and motor processes. From the chosen disturbance by the Trigger module, the Disturber triggers error situations which impact the behaviors of a given task and sends them to the Pre-processor that outputs the disturbed task.

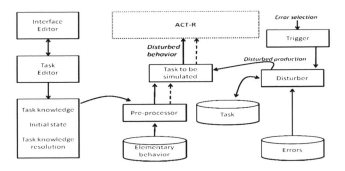

Fig. 1. Simulator of Performance in Error's architecture

The final result delivered by the Simulator of Performance in Error is a text document, syntactically correct from the ACT-R language's point of view, to be executed in the cognitive architecture environment.

We currently work on the implementation of the error modes presented in Table 1. The Simulator of Human Performance will be capable of including, in a certain task, one or more mechanisms of the errors here presented.

5 Conclusions

This work presented the Simulator of Human Performance whose goal is to contribute to the area of software development in critical applications. In order to achieve the proposed goal, the GEMS model has been studied, and three new failure modes, results of this research, were added to it.

The modules of data entry in the Simulator of Human Performance are concluded and the error modes established in the GEMS model are being implemented.

We emphasize that the Simulator of Human Performance is a system that organizes the entry of data to be executed by a simulated operator. After this organization, the simulator generates undesirable situations and includes them in the task that will be executed by the simulated operator, in ACT-R.

The results of this study were presented as a tool with potentiality to assist the HCI project manager in the construction of projects and software development that aim to increase chances of controlling certain types of human faults, resulting from the human-computer interaction.

References

1. Dejours, C.: Le facteur humain. FUP, Paris (2002)
2. Reason, J.: Human error. Cambridge University Press, Cambridge (1999)
3. Sanders, M.S., McCormick, E.J.: Human factors in engineering and design. McGraw-Hill, New York (1987)
4. Swain, A.D., Guttmann, H.E.: Handbook of Human Reliability Analysis with emphasis on Nuclear Power Plant Applications. U.S. Nuclear Reg. Commission, Albuquerque (1983)
5. Rasmussen, J.: Skills, Rules, and Knowledge; Signals, Signs, and Symbols, and other distinctions in human performance models. IEEE Transactions on Systems, Man, and Cybernetics 13(3), 257–266 (1983)
6. Mori, G., Paternò, F., Santoro, C.: CTTE: support for developing and analyzing task models for interactive system design. IEEE Transactions 28(8), 813–979 (2002)

Psycognition: Cognitive Architectures for Augmented Cognition Systems

Karmen Guevara

Independent Research and Consultancy
kg@karmenguevara.com

Abstract. This paper describes Psycognition, a concept and methodological approach for eliciting the subconscious processes which influence human behavior. An examination of the Psycognition methodology is drawn from research that explored the subconscious processes underlying the tactical behaviors and decision making of a sample of RAF fighter pilots. This example application illustrates how the approach can be applied to apparently random behavior in critical situations. A primary aim of the research was to explore whether the Psycognition approach could contribute to our understanding of the requirements for future cognitive adaptive aircrew systems.

Keywords: Characterologies, core beliefs, strategic behaviors, subconscious processes, fighter pilot research, cognitive architectures, predictable emotional responses, diagnostic, predictive analytic tool.

1 Introduction

The objective of this paper is to introduce Psycognition, a novel concept, and methodological approach for eliciting the subconscious processes which influence human behavior. It has become increasingly clear that there is a need to broaden our understanding of human behavior to include the seemingly irrational and illogical forms. This requires that those cognitive frameworks used to understand conscious rational behavior be extended to include the subconscious processes that influence and shape behavior, particularly those that appear irrational or unpredictable.

System design draws heavily upon the assumption that individuals act according to conscious, rational, and predictable behaviors. However, evidence from studies of system disasters indicates that a major contributing factor is human error. [1] Furthermore, studies have identified a theme in which human error relates to a breakdown in rational behavior. The importance of subconscious behavior and the prominence it has in decision making is recognized outside the psychoanalytical domain. Recent neurological research has led to important discoveries about the emotional architecture of the brain. [2]

An examination of the Psycognition methodology is drawn from research that explored the subconscious processes underlying the tactical behaviors and decision making of a sample of RAF fighter pilots from the UK. A primary aim of the research was to explore whether the Psycognition approach could contribute to our understanding of the requirements for building a new generation of cognitive adaptive aircrew systems, a key component for future combat aircraft.

C. Stephanidis (Ed.): Posters, Part I, HCII 2011, CCIS 173, pp. 275–279, 2011.
© Springer-Verlag Berlin Heidelberg 2011

2 Psycognition

Psycognition is based on the theory that behavioral motives originate from the subconscious and therefore are significant because they directly influence an individual's perceptions and conscious behaviors. [3] Psycognition seeks to understand the subconscious processes associated with the semi-predictable emotional responses and behaviors that reside in the subconscious.

The human psyche being an efficient organism for survival makes decisions about self, the world, and self in the world. Examples of the key questions are: What can be trusted? Can I get what I need here? How can I have power here? How can I work with others? How am I valued?

Once a decision is made about these questions, this decision resides deeply rooted in the subconscious mind. These decisions filter how an individual responds to each real life event. For clarity's sake we discuss characterology in terms of core beliefs and strategies. Core beliefs consist of beliefs and emotional responses formed early in development and strategies are behaviors that are predicated on those core beliefs [4]. Psycognition applies a framework of six characterologies as a basis for examining subconscious processes and associated behavioral strategies. For ease of comprehension colloquial terms are used instead of clinical ones. These characterologies are universal even though there are variations in the terms used [5] [6].

Table 1. Overview of Characterological Themes

Character Position	Behavioral Orientation	Core Belief
Mr. Safety	Safety & trust	The world is dangerous
Mr. Action	Performance & recognition	Self-worth stems from achievement
Mr. Endurance	Subtle power, indirect control & endurance	Not good enough It's important to do one's best
Mr. Freedom	Freedom & direct control To be the best & to win	Must be in charge power & control It's not safe to give up
Mr. Self-Reliant	Challenge Going it alone	Must always take care of oneself Never rely on others
Mr. Attention	Attracting attention Constant involvement	Not being interesting & listened to

This characterological model enables us to understand character processes in terms of strategies. Characterology is intended as a starting point for developing hypotheses about individual strategic behaviors. These enable us to look for patterns and inconsistencies in behavior and thereby make predictions about the kinds of strategies individuals will draw upon in certain situations.

3 The Research – A Case Study

The Psycognition methodology was applied to an investigation of how RAF fighter pilots' subconscious processes influenced the strategies they chose in handling certain critical incidents. The research focused on the pilots' tactical behaviors in three kinds of critical incidents: a breakdown in plan; a control breakdown; and information overload. The key research findings can be summarised as [7]:

- Despite the similarities in background, training, experience, and the strength of the military culture, significant differences emerged in how the subjects responded to certain critical incidents.
- In these situations the subjects drew upon deeply rooted subconscious core beliefs to guide their decisions and actions, instead of conscious, rational cognition.
- The differences in tactical behaviors were evident in situations that involved a breakdown in plan or control, an overload of information or a compromise of principles and values.
- The evidence suggested that there is a logical explanation for human behaviors that are seemingly irrational and unpredictable.
- A conclusion drawn from the research was that Psycognition provides us with a basis for predicting what these behaviors will be, the strategies that will be applied, and the breakdown situations in which they will be triggered.

4 Application of Psycognition

Augmented cognition technologies monitor and assess the state of the user through behavioral, psychophysiological, and neurophysiological data acquired in real time. The resulting Psycognitive models of characterological and predictive behaviors add an important dimension to this composite picture of the user. This information can then feed into an algorithm that characterises an individual and predicts potential behavioral outcomes and strategic choices. By tapping into this human dimension, Psycognition has the potential to contribute to the ability of augmented cognition systems to adapt to the cognitive state of users.

Figure 1 provides an overall architecture in which a system collects continuous real-time information about a user through various sources, and draws from the RAF fighter pilot research to provide a simple illustration of how this might apply.

In this example the cognitive adaptive system 'knows' the cognitive architecture of the pilot (A Mr. Safety). It has a map of his behavioral strategies for handling a breakdown in the clarity function. The system will track his difficulties in processing information and will attempt to manage the process through interventions to reduce the insight barrier and to restore the clarity function. The system aims to slow things down for Mr. Safety so that he can understand the meaning of the information he is receiving. It attempts to break things into smaller, more manageable steps. It will also try to keep the pilot in contact with the situation to prevent him from withdrawing into confusion or over analysis (which is a strategy of Mr. Safety's) The system does this by tracking signs of the strategy not working, which will be reflected in increased confusion and fragmentation.

One can imagine that the cognitive architectures upon which Psycognition are based can be equally powerful in the design of augmented cognition systems in numerous other application areas. Obvious ones are those where ineffective strategies

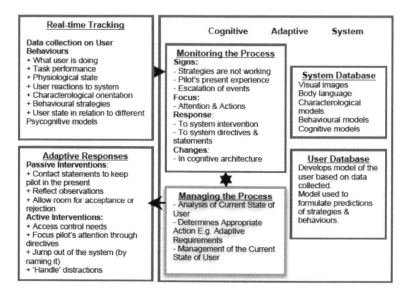

Fig. 1. A Model for Cognitive Adaptive System Support of Strategic Behaviors

can lead to accidents and fatalities. Among these are the military, NASA, air traffic control, ambulance control and hospital emergency rooms. Although not life threatening, stock market trading floors are an excellent example of high stress environments in which strategic breakdowns often result in significant financial losses[1].

As education, training and career re-skilling become increasingly distant, interactive and technology based, it will be essential for these systems to 'understand' the characterological make up of students to enable individual tailoring and equally important, to track students cognitive state for continuous adaptation. This will underpin the quality of education and the learning experience. This is also true of the area of telehealth as the technologies become highly interactive and extend beyond non-clinical usages. Here lies the application to medical avatars as they are envisioned now, but also as the focus expands beyond the physiological to encompass the mental health of individuals as well. [8] In the future Psycognitive models of individual characterology with the monitoring of behavioral and psychophysiological data potentially could detect the mental imbalances that lead to psychological disorders and illness. [9]

An important socio-economic and political trend is the movement towards individuals accepting increasingly more responsibility for the welfare of themselves and their families in all areas of their lives. As public sectors continue to shrink, the level of personal responsibilities will continue to rise. In combination with the other rapid changes occurring in the world, such as disruptive climate changes, oil prices, food shortages, terrorism, etc. individuals will need to develop a new form of

---

[1] An investigation of the application of Psycognition to the London Stock Exchange was carried out in 1997.

resilience. One can imagine personal avatars as guide and coach rolled into one, playing this role. New coping mechanisms and survival strategies can be created as ones' personal avatar navigates them through unchartered waters and stirs them away from self-defeating strategies predicated on core beliefs and characterological orientation.

5 Conclusion - A Powerful Diagnostic and Predictive Analytical Tool

In consequence, the methodological framework and models upon which Psycognition is based makes it a powerful diagnostic and predictive analytical tool. By focusing information gathering on the dimension of human behavior where core beliefs lie embedded in the subconscious, Psycognition provides an instrument for formulating hypotheses of individual characterological orientation. This creates a platform for a predictive analysis of the manifestation of character under certain circumstances. It is critical for designing rapid response in life threatening situations because individual character is triggered by certain stimuli and therefore emerges in particular situations, especially under stress or in danger. Beyond life threatening situations, Psycognition is also a powerful predictive analytical tool that potentially can be applied in numerous other application areas. This is because all human beings have character, core beliefs, emotional responses, and various subconscious and conscious strategies predicated on these.

References

1. Neumann, P.G.: Computer Related Risks. Addison-Wesley, New York (1995)
2. Le Doux, J.: Emotion and the Limbic System Concept. Concepts in Neuroscience 2 (1992)
3. Erickson, M.H., Rossi, E., Rossi, S.: Hypnotic Realities. Irvington Pubs., New York (1976)
4. Kurtz, R.: Body-Centered Psychotherapy. Life Rhythm, California (1990)
5. Sharp, D.: Jung's Model of Typology. Inner City Books, Toronto (1987)
6. Shapario, D.: Neurotic Styles. Basic Books, New York (1965)
7. Guevara, K.: Psycognition: An Exploration of the Strategic Behaviors Underlying Fighter Pilots' Decision Making in Critical Incidents. Research Report, DERA, CHS, Farnborough, UK (July 1997)
8. VPH NOE: Virtual physiological human network of excellence. ICT FP7 Research European Commission
9. Gaggioli, A., Mantovani, F., et al.: Avatars in clinical psychology: a framework for the clinical use of virtual humans. Applied Technology for Neuro-Psychology Lab, Istituto Auxologico Italiano, Milan, Italy. Journal of CyberPsychology, 117–25 (April 6, 2003)

A Study on the Cognitive Differences between Beginners and Experts Regarding Cooking Processes

Keisuke Ishihara[1], Toshiki Yamaoka[2], Kazumi Tateyama[3], and Chinatsu Kasamatsu[4]

[1] Wakayama University Graduate School of Systems Engineering
930, Sakaedani, Wakayama City, Wakayama, 640-8510, Japan
[2] Wakayama University Faculty of Systems Engineering
930, Sakaedani, Wakayama City, Wakayama, 640-8510, Japan
[3] Institute of Food Sciences & Technologies Ajinomoto Co., INC
[4] Institute for Innovation, Ajinomoto Co., INC
yamaoka@center.wakayama-u.ac.jp

Abstract. The purpose of this study is comparative studies on cognitive process between beginner and expert in cooking. The twelve elements of the cognitive process were extracted. The relationships among elements were cleared by DEMATEL. Finally, we suggested the cognitive models in cooking.

Keywords: mental models, cognitive process, cognitive model.

1 Introduction

When users look at recipe, they use their mental models. If the distance of the mental models between users and designers is too far, the users can't understand the recipe accurately. Therefore, it is important to understand the user's cognitive models and mental models. To investigate user's mental models, it is necessary to consider from various viewpoints the process of constructing a cognitive model. In fact, the areas of interface design, it's often said that the mental models are important to understandable interfaces [1]. Therefore, the purpose of this study is comparative studies on cognitive process between beginner and expert in cooking. In this study, we investigated cognitive model of beginners' and experts' during cooking.

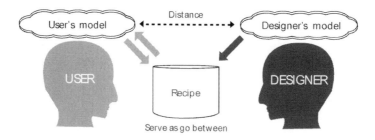

Fig. 1. The interaction between user and designer

C. Stephanidis (Ed.): Posters, Part I, HCII 2011, CCIS 173, pp. 280–283, 2011.

2 Method

The participants of this study were fifteen female college students (Mean age 20.07, SD 1.29) and three experienced cookers (Mean age 38.33, SD 4.03).

In the experiment, the protocol analysis and the interview were used to understand their cognitive process. After the explanation for experiment, the participants practiced the protocol analysis. They cooked the same task according to instruction. When they were cooking, their behaviors and utterances were observed by a video tape recorder (Fig. 2, Fig. 3).

Fig. 2. Experiment circumstance   **Fig. 3.** Image of videotaped sessions

3 Result

3.1 Extract of Element in Cognitive Process

The video data of participants' behaviors and utterances were converted into flowcharts. After that, we extracted the element of cognitive process based on Norman's gulf model [1] as a standard. In this result, the twelve elements of the cognitive process were extracted. The proposed cognitive process and elements are outlined below.

- A. Look at the recipe: It is the acts to search information for cooking.
- B. Goal setting: It is the process that decides on the goal of act.
- C. Adapt models: It is process that uses the mental models.
- D. Inference: It is the process that forming a notion based on the mental models.
- E. Trial and Error: It is the act to structure the mental models.
- F. Planning: It is the process that decides on the best way before taking act.
- G. Action: It is the act that execute as planned.
- H. Ingenuity: It is the act that users exercise their ingenuity for greater efficiency.
- I. Perceive and Interpret: It is the process that perceive and interpret.
- J: Evaluation: It is the process that users evaluate the results of object.
- K. Recognition of error: It is the cognition that the act was errors or mistakes.
- L: Recognition of goal: It is the cognition that the goal was achieve.

3.2 Relationship of Elements of Cognitive Process

The DEMATEL method was used to understand of relationships among the twelve elements of the cognitive process. The DEMATEL is method which the elements structural, data visibility as well as the data's influence relationships can be made clearer from the data's position [2]. The relationships of Students' elements are shown Fig. 4 and experienced cookers' are shown Fig. 5.

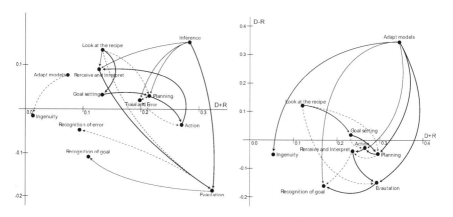

Fig. 4. DEMATEL data of beginners   **Fig. 5.** DEMATEL data of experts

Result of DEMATEL method of students (Fig.4) showed that the main flow were "Look at the recipe"→ "Goal setting"→"Planning" →"Action"→"Perceive and Interpret"→ "Evaluation"→ "Recognition of goal" , "Inference"→"Planning" or and "Inference"→"Evaluation". In particular, "Look at the recipe" and "Inference" was most important elements for students.

On the other hand, Result of experienced cookers (Fig.5) showed that "Adapt models" was most important elements for students. However, the main flow "Look at the recipe"→ "Goal setting"→"Planning" →"Action"→"Perceive and Interpret"→ "Evaluation"→ "Recognition of goal" were same as students.

4 Discussion

The result of this study shows that the students checked certainly the recipe before performing. Also the results of interviews proved that they didn't have the experience and knowledge of cooking. To cover these disadvantages, they were depending strongly on the recipe and inference based on their mental models. We think that beginners depend on the recipe stronger than experts'. Beginners structured mental models by recipe and their selves' inference to cover experience and knowledge. If beginners could only receive the information without errors, they can easily understand the process.

On the other hand, experienced cookers were cooking using their mental models that were constructed from the experience and knowledge at all cooking process.

Because they understood what to do next, they were able to understand the meaning of cooking process. Their differences have an enormous influence on the cooking process. Compensated beginners' mental models with recipes are most important things for them to cook without mistake. In finally, based on the relationships of elements, we would like to suggest the cognitive model between beginner and expert in cooking process as shown in Figure 6. We think it is possible to analyze the meaning of the cooking action if use this model. To determine the reason for the errors from each stage designers, it can lead the quality improvement of recipe design.

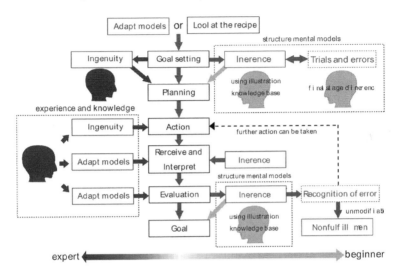

Fig. 6. The cognitive model between beginner and expert in cooking process

5 Conclusion

The purpose of this study is comparative studies on cognitive process between beginner and expert in cooking. The model of cognitive process between beginners and experts were showed by fig.6. The model of fig.6 can be used to determine the reason for the errors from each stage. In order to narrow the distance between User's model and Designer's model, designers should design using this model.

References

1. Norman, D.A.: Psychology of Everyday Action. In: The Design of Everyday Things, pp. 45–46. Basic Book, New York (1988)
2. Lee, Y.C., Hu, H.Y., Yen, T.M., Tsai, C.H.: Kano's Model and Decision Making Trial and Evaluation Laboratory Applied to Order Winners and Qualifiers Improvement. Information Technology Journal (7), 702–714 (2008)

Red for Romance, Blue for Memory

Ilyung Jung[1], Myung Shik Kim[2], and Kwanghee Han[3]

[1] Graduate program in Cognitive Science, Yonsei University, 134 Shinchon-dong,
Seodaenum-ku, Seoul, South Korea
[2,3] Department of Psychology, Yonsei University, 134 Shinchon-dong,
Seodaenum-ku, Seoul, South Korea
khan@yonsei.ac.kr

Abstract. Decades of psychological research have shown that the color could affect human's emotion and perception. However, the influence of this effect on human performance is still unknown. This study was performed to investigate and reveal the effect of the color red, blue and gray on memory through a word recognition task. When the presented video clip featured a red background, the model's attractiveness was rated statistically higher than the other condition. The blue condition video viewers and their resulting performance on the word recognition task were better than the performances of the other color condition groups. This research implicates that a specific color has an effect on human perception and memory.

Keywords: red, color, memory, attractiveness.

1 Introduction

When a consumer purchases a product, he or she makes a decision depending on the first impression of a product. The relevant image of product is a critical criterion for purchase. (Edell, Burke, 1987; Bloch, 1995). Perceived product attractiveness can enhance 'intent to use', and its effect on 'pleasure', 'learnability' and 'utility'(Van der Heijden, 2003; Lavie & Tractinsky, 2004; Hassenzhal, 2004). It is important to verify what circumstances the color stimulus was exposed in. The color red can be interpreted as a warning for danger, provocation to an enemy, or failure itself depending on temporal and spatial situations. Also, cultural background can effect color perception. Historically, red was regarded a symbol of femininity (Knight, Powers & Watts, 1995).

In recent empirical work, Elliot (2008) demonstrated the influence of the color red not only on perceived attractiveness and sexual desire, but also on one's intention for dating, and willingness to pay on dates which are higher cognitive behaviors. In our previous research, we hypothesized that when a male user is asked to rate the attractiveness of a female model, the ratings will differ depending on the background color of the video file (Jung, Kim & Han, 2011). Additionally we have proved that when the presented video clip featured a red background, the model's attractiveness was rated statistically higher than when the background was blue.

In many of these previous studies, the color red made females more attractive to males. However, the influence of this effect on human performance is still unknown.

C. Stephanidis (Ed.): Posters, Part I, HCII 2011, CCIS 173, pp. 284–288, 2011.

It is common to watch TV or learn something from a female host. Therefore we can extend our research question from perceived attractiveness to human performance.

2 Experiment

This study was performed to investigate and reveal the effect of the color red on memory through a word recognition task. In contrast to our previous research (Jung, Kim & Han, 2011) in which all of the participants were male to measure perceived attractiveness of a woman in a red context; we recruited both male and female participants this time.

Moreover, we altered the female model's clothing to make this experiment appear more natural. In this experiment, a female model wears three differently colored t-shirts as participants read a word set. Participants complete a word recognition task after watching the prepared video clip. We measured a difference in the recall rates between the color groups.

Participants. Thirty six undergraduate students took part in this study for course credit. (Male: 16, Female: 20) They were recruited through the advertisement of the institutional official internet site at Yonsei University.

Materials. IBM Pentium4 PC and a 17 inch 60Hz LCD monitor with 1280 x 1024 resolution were used for the experiment system. The experiment software was developed by MS Visual Basic 6.0. The selected words for this task were chosen by a word of high frequency list from the "Survey of Modern Korean word usage." by the 'National Institute of the Korean language'. According to this survey we picked 200, two-syllable nouns, which and have frequencies between 200 and 1100 according to the aforementioned standard.

Stimulus. This video was recorded using a digital camcorder (CANON VIXIA HF10). The female model wore plain red, blue and gray short sleeve colored T-shirts. (UNIQLO brand) The background color was white while the waist-up was shown in the shot. The selected word was spoken 1,000ms per average and interval was also 1,000ms. A subtitle was also presented in white letters at the middle and bottom of the video screen during the female model's word recital.

Procedures. Participants watched the differently colored video clips which each contained a 10 word set one time and the sequence of the video presentation followed the "Latin Square" randomized design. Following the video clip, the word recognition task began. None of them were aware of the hypotheses being tested. After the three tasks, the participant rated the woman's attractiveness (1 = not attractive, 7 = very attractive). According to the signal detection theory, a hit (recall of the right word emerging former video clip) was calculated by a correct answer, and a false alarm was calculated by incorrect answer.

Fig. 1. The example of video stimulus

3 Results and Discussion

In this study, we focused on red and blue; gray was added for achromatic color condition. We analyzed the collected data through repeated measure analysis. Two participants' data were eliminated due to a false alarm rate significantly exceeding their hit rates.

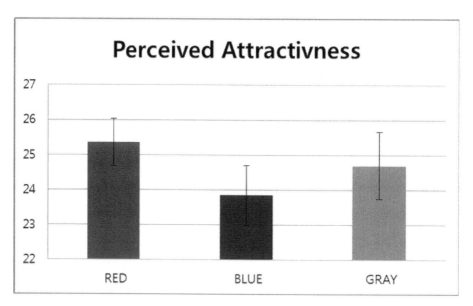

Fig. 2. Perceived attractiveness as a function of clothes' color. (Standard Errors are indicated by vertical lines).

As displayed in Figure 2, a woman in red's attractiveness ($M = 25.36$, $SD = .67$) was higher than blue's ($M = 23.85$, $SD = .84$) condition ($MSe = .574$, $p = .013$), a result that mirrored the conclusion of our previous study.

Word recognition results are shown in figure 3. The blue condition ($M = 19.31$, $SD = 2.03$) video viewers and their resulting performance on the word recognition task was better than the performances of the other color condition groups: in red ($MSe = .666$, $p = .039$) and in gray ($MSe = .897$, $p < .001$). Additionally, the red condition ($M = 18.18$, $SD = 1.70$) has better performance than gray condition ($MSe = .955$, $p = .038$). Unlike previous similar research, our study tried to use video stimulus which more closely represented the real world. These findings indicate that in certain conditions, background color can subconsciously change human perception of a female model and memory performance. In terms of the association between the color red and the attention participants paid to a female model in situations including, but not limited to, the commercial, this research implies that a specific color has an effect on human perception and memory.

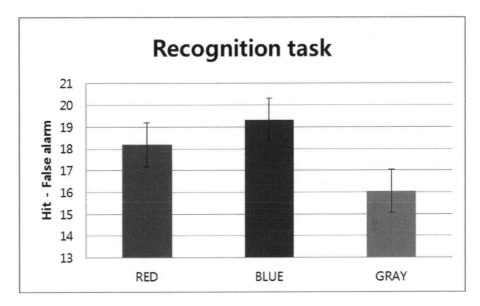

Fig. 3. The result of recognition task. (Standard Errors are indicated by vertical lines).

References

1. Bloch, P.: Seeking the ideal form: product design and consumer response. Journal of Marketing, 16–29 (1995)
2. Edell, J.A., Burke, M.C.: The power of feelings in understanding advertising effects. Journal of Consumer Research, 421–433 (1987)
3. Elliot, A.J., Niesta, D.: Romantic Red: Red enhances Men's attraction to women. Journal of Personality and Social Psychology, 1150–1164 (2008)

4. Hassenzahl, M.: The Interplay of Beauty, Goodness, and Usability in Interactive Products. Human-Computer Interaction, 319–349 (2004)
5. Jung, I., Kim, M., Han, K.: The influence of an Attractive Female model on Male Users' Product Ratings. In: KHCI Conference (2011)
6. Knight, C.D., Powers, C., Watts, I.: The human symbolic revolution: A Darwinian account. Cambridge Archeological Journal 5, 75–119 (1995)
7. Lavie, T., Tractinsky, N.: Assessing dimensions of perceived visual aesthetics of web sites. International Journal of Human-Computer Studies, 269–298 (2004)
8. Van der Heijden, H.: Factors influencing the usage of websites: The case of a generic portal in The Netherlands. Information & Management, 541-549.motion analysis. Online reference on Mikromak GmBh-WinAnalize Vendor (2003), http://www.winanalyze.com

Time: A Premise of Virtual Life

Hee-Cheol Kim

School of Computer Engineering/UHRC, Inje University, Obang-Dong 607,
Gimhae, Gyeong-Nam, Korea
heeki@inje.ac.kr

Abstract. Why do humans aspire for a virtual life? The answer is important, because it can explain the phenomenon that we are fond of, or even addicted to virtual worlds such as computer games, on-line communities, avatars, and so on. This paper presents an account with respect to time. Emphasizing the importance of time to understand virtuality, the paper gives an answer based on the three principles: (1) Humans exist with time, (2) Humans experience and tend to resist the finitude of time, and (3) A way of resisting it is aspiration for a virtual life.

Keywords: human existence, time, virtual life, virtual world.

1 Introduction: Every Human Lives a Virtual Life

We often live computer supported virtual lives through on-line games, virtual worlds like *Second Life*, virtual reality systems, and so on. Not only computers but also traditional media such as TVs, books, and movies, serve as nice tools supporting virtual life. Human desire for a virtual life is not the one appearing suddenly together with computers. Such desire already existed before the birth of computers and multimedia technology [1]. For example, people had read novels and been moved by powerful but fictitious stories. In fact, everyone imagines, dreams, plans, and doubts. Just as we humans cannot live out of reality, we cannot live without virtual world, either. According to Pierre Levy, virtuality and reality are two important ways of human existence [2].

Then, why do humans aspire for a virtual life? There must be many plausible answers, which eventually help provide design rationales for systems supporting virtual life, as well as understand humans. This paper shows that time is an important premise of virtual life. Without time, one cannot think of the future nor remember the past. Because we live with time, we can imagine, plan, and recall. Without time, therefore, there is no virtual world. Virtual worlds are constructed over time span. This paper gives an answer to the question of why people long for a virtual life through the following three principles: (1) Humans exist with time, (2) Humans experience and tend to resist the finitude of time, and (3) A way of resisting it is aspiration for a virtual life.

C. Stephanidis (Ed.): Posters, Part I, HCII 2011, CCIS 173, pp. 289–292, 2011.
© Springer-Verlag Berlin Heidelberg 2011

2 Three Principles

In this section, the argument "Since humans are temporal being, they aspire for a virtual life" is explained in more detail by the three principles: (1) Humans exist with time, (2) Humans experience and tend to resist the finitude of time, and (3) A way of resisting it is aspiration for a virtual life.

2.1 Humans Exist with Time

While the present is about reality, the past and the future are more about virtuality. Therefore, the notion of time is a key to understand virtuality. In particular, Heidegger believed that humans cannot be understood only by reason, mind, etc., but also within time. From the early 20C, time became a crucial concept to understand human existence among western intellectuals. Heidegger's "Being and Time" [3] and Bergson's "Creative Evolution" [4] are perhaps the most influential literatures. According to Heidegger, the meaning of life is explained through the historicality of our existence [3]. Therefore, the existence is not fixed but more dynamic. The potential of our existence is fulfilled according to time. Psychologically, Zimbardo and Boyd also mentioned that different time perspectives affected our decisions to choose certain ways of living, suggesting six perspectives, e.g. past-oriented and future-oriented [5]. Time also affects human behaviors, e.g. time pressure negatively affects helping behaviors [6]. Our physical forms, perspectives, characteristics, and ways of thinking change with time. Human minds and decisions are always working together with time. Because of time, we recollect, regret, wait, fear, imagine and plan. Humans are the beings with time.

2.2 Experience and Resistance of the Finitude of Time

What happens when humans exist with time? As stated in Heraclitus' famous saying, "You cannot step twice into the same river", time is irreversible to us. Importantly, we feel impuissance about time in our everyday lives. Everyone dies as time goes by. Humans face the problems that change brings. We may have joy today, but not tomorrow. Happiness is transitory by nature. Time causes change, and it brings about human anxiety. As a living condition, anxiety has been analyzed and explained from psychological perspectives by Fritz Rieman [7]. We even suffer from the potential to suffer or get into problematic situations. Without time, we may not have such pain. We experience the finitude of time through death, pain and uncertain situations. As we know it, the first truth among four noble truths in Buddhism is that humans suffer. While many religious truths accept human suffering, humans tend to devise every activity to avoid the fate of death and pain [5]. The denial of it is like that of the fact that time has the end. A common phenomenon is that humans resist the finitude of time in order to free from anxiety and psychological stress.

2.3 Aspiration for a Virtual Life to Resistance of the Finitude of Time

"Timelessness" is an essence of Freud's view on the unconscious [8]. However, even the conscious could be timeless. In fantasy, for example, past, present and future are united in one representation. A young single lady may imagine of a marriage in the future, and then suddenly think of yesterday's baseball games. Though human legs and arms are limited to move here and there, human thought is free and unlimited to go back to earliest childhood or to a point in the future. Human beings seek freedom and ways to overcome the finitude of time that they face in the real world, and move to a virtual world where it is not time-restrictive, by means of thought. Concerning this, Kim has described it as follows [1]:

> "Reality is a useful word that can symbolize various types of limitation, in that actions, words and plans are limited, in reality, with respect to time and space. There seems to be no way by which we, as humans, can escape reality. However, certain individuals aspire to overcome the limitations imposed by reality, and search for freedom and change. The question is how such aspirations may be realized. One way is to create virtual worlds or spaces. By living in a virtual space, humans can augment monotonous lives, and forget an embattled reality that has become hard and dreary." ([1], p. 616)

Virtual worlds are the spaces beyond the finitude of time and with the human mind. The success of virtual worlds on the net is deeply rooted in the human mind of longing for a virtual life [1]. In this respect, the idea of time is also understood as the creation of conscious mind [9], as Einstein said, "Space and time are modes by which we think, not conditions under which we live." Humans have freedom of thoughts. Using this freedom, they want to move to a world in which time does not dominate, which is a virtual world.

3   Conclusion

In this paper, I proposed the three principles in relation to time in order to give an account of the phenomenon that humans aspire for a virtual life. While admitting that they do not explain it completely and more work remains, I believe that this study sheds light on the importance of understanding time in the context of virtuality and its related systems.

References

1. Kim, H.: Aspiring for a virtual life. In: Jacko, J.A. (ed.) HCI 2007. LNCS, vol. 4551, pp. 615–623. Springer, Heidelberg (2007)
2. Levy, P.: Becoming Virtual: Reality in the Digital Age. Plenum Publishing Corporation (1998)
3. Heidegger, M.: Sein und Zeit, Gesamtausgabe, vol. 2 (1927); Being and Time, trans. by John Macquarrie and Edward Robinson. SCM Press, London (1962)
4. Bergson, H.: L'Evolution Créatrice (1907); Creative Evolution trans. by Arthur Mitchell, Henry Holt and Company (1911)
5. Zimbardo, P., Boyd, J.: The Time Paradox: The New Psychology of Time That Will Change Your Life. Simon & Schuster, New York (2008)

6. Darley, J.M., Batson, C.D.: From Jerusalem to Jericho: A Study of Situational and Dispositional Variables on Helping Behaviors. Journal of Personality and Social Psychology 27, 29–40 (1973)
7. Rieman, F., Rieman, R.: Grundformen Der Angst: Eine tiefenpsychologische Studie, Reinhardt, Munchen (January 1999)
8. Freud, S.: The Psychopathology of Everyday Life. Norton, New York (1901)
9. Malik, M., Hipolito, M.: Time and its Relationship to Consciousness: An Overview. J. of Consciousness Exploration and Research 1(5), 570–573 (2010)

Extracts Cognitive Artifacts from Text through Combining Human and Machine Learning in an Iterative Fashion

Ryan Kirk

Iowa State University, Human-Computer Interaction Program
1620 Howe Hall Ames, IA 50010, USA
rakirk@iastate.edu

Abstract. The world network of information is complex and not always organized in a structure useful for human understanding. This paper investigates the need and methods for creating an artificial system that categorizing information similar to the way humans categorize. The system will use Bayesian modeling to model text sentiment. The categorization of text sentiment will be done both by machines and by humans. The hypothesis is that the resultant system will not differ significantly from the accuracy of a control group of human categorizers. This represents a non-standard approach to learning that involves the human and the machine in an iterative learning process.

Keywords: Cognition, categorization, learning, natural-language processing, sentiment analysis, machine learning.

1 Introduction

This study seeks to pair data from comments with ratings data in order to learn which words and ideas tend to be used more for positive, for neutral and for negative feedback. The goal of this research is to create a model that will functionally categorize the affect of a particular word as a human would. The internet has become a tangled web where users play an active role in generating content. This Web 2.0 type of content represents individual users' thoughts and could be considered cognitive artifacts. In aggregate, these artifacts can be used to determine what people think and feel about various ideas or events [13].

In order to understand how the aggregation of text artifacts can represent people's thoughts and feelings, the nature of human cognition and, especially, the central role that categorization plays in cognition, needs to be examined [4]. Cognitive recall given certain prompts follows a probabilistic pattern. Furthermore, more complex ideas can be established through creating new assemblies of existing ideas [8]. As categorization is extended to emotions, similar patterns are exhibited such that all emotion can be said to stem from basic attraction or repulsion [1]. Additionally, cognition and categorization for words may occur in a probabilistic fashion [6, 11]. Such a probabilistic, binary classification may be easily modeled using computer

C. Stephanidis (Ed.): Posters, Part I, HCII 2011, CCIS 173, pp. 293–297, 2011.

algorithms. Furthermore, Naive Bayesian Networks (NBNs) not only operate probabilistically, but NBN have also been shown to be surprisingly robust at categorizing higher-dimensional data such as text [3, 5, 9, 12].

A system was developed that categorizes the sentiment of a particular word given its prior odds. It was expected that the resultant system would categorize text better than chance with both supervised and unsupervised data sets, though these accuracy levels are a baseline and not the dependent variable. The goal of this experiment is not optimality of classification; the goal is to achieve optimal similarity of machine classification to human classification. Thus, the future work for this ongoing work in progress will focus upon comparing the resultant system's performance levels to the error levels of human classification on the same text.

2   Extracting Text Sentiment Artifacts

This experiment will rely upon a corpora of text created at Amherst University; this corpora represents the aggregate of populations' sentiment artifacts and contains over 700,000 comments from Internet websites where users both gave a comment and a satisfaction rating [2, 10]. These ratings are of products or hotels and range from 1 to 5 with 1 being least satisfied and 5 being most satisfied. The attribute for each rating (1 through 5) represents the cumulative number of times that a particular token occurred within comments rated at a particular satisfaction level. Thus, any particular word will have its own frequency of occurrence within the knowledge base as well as a distinct frequency of occurrence at each satisfaction level (see Table 1).

Table 1. A simple, faux example of comments and their constituent ratings is presented. Also, the resultant word sentiment frequency distribution table is displayed.

Comment	Rating	Word	1	2	3	4	5	Sum
A nice cat	5	a	2		2		2	6
A bad cat	1	nice					2	2
A decent cat	3	cat	1		1		1	3
A nice man	5	bad	2					2
A decent man	3	Man	1		1		1	2
A bad man	1	decent		2				2

The data required some tokenization and preprocessing prior to use with learning algorithms. Once data was in the proper format, it was entered into a MySQL database. At this point, categorization could occur based upon the nature of the distribution of each word's cumulative frequencies of occurrence at each rating. This approach allowed words that have multiple sentiment uses to be categorized based upon their most probabilistic use. Thus, words that have multiple definitions or that tend to be used sarcastically were categorized based upon their most prevalent definition or most prevalent used form. Prior odds classification can be through a simple logic statement that relies upon the proportion of responses at each of five rating levels:

if (`one` + `two` > `three`+`four`+`five`, `negative, if (`four`+`five`> `three`+`four`+`five`, `positive`, `neutral`))

The probability that a word is positive, negative or neutral could be calculated based upon these prior odds alone. However, this method may not be sufficient; in the Amherst corpora, 98.4% of data rates a four or five meaning that the distribution has an incredible skew. Thus, the training set for the text sentiment data may also be categorized via methods other than prior odds such as through variance from mean or through rank-order of positivity (or of negativity). Both the prior odds method and the rank-order (of positive responses) were used.

Data was analyzed using RapidMiner 5.0 and the Weka algorithm for the Naive Bayesian Network (NBN) [7]. As a part of the exploratory analysis, Support Vector Machines (SVMs) and Artificial Neural Networks (ANNs) were also used in order to establish a baseline for categorical accuracy of the NBN. This analysis resulted in a model that can be used to classify words as positive, negative or neutral based upon their frequencies of occurrence associated with each rating. Accuracy levels were estimated using a 10-fold cross-validation procedure. The resultant NBN model provides a density distribution that can be graphically represented (see Figure 1). The accuracy level for the NBN on the prior odds data was 97.9% (compared to 98.4% chance) while the accuracy level for the NBN on the rank-order data set was 82.3% (compared to 33.3% chance); see Table 2 for all accuracy levels.

Table 2. A table displaying accuracy levels, as compared to chance, for NBN, SVM and ANN algorithms at classifying the probability and rank-order data sets is presented

	NBN	SVM	ANN	Chance
Probability	97.9%	98.6%	99.8%	98.4%
Rank-order	82.3%	41.0%	90.8%	33.3%

3   User Involvement and Current Work

Categorizing words as positive, negative and neutral is not as straightforward as it sounds. From the humans' perspective, certain words have multiple definitions and multiple senses (polysemy). From the machines' perspective, the data has a tremendous skew favoring positive comments and categorization must undergo strenuous training in order to be accurate without also over fitting the data.

The Amherst corpora contain data that has already been supervised by users. However, in order to test the resultant system in comparison to users, the system will need to examine new words that were not a part of the original corpora. The dataset already contains 5,232 words or symbols and, therefore, data for many new words would need to be obtained in order to perform a valid analysis.

New users will then need to be recruited into a control group. This group will be given the words from the new data set and asked to determine whether the words are negative, neutral or positive based upon their individual latent semantic knowledge. The level of agreement between individuals within the control group will be used as a measure of the control group's accuracy. The accuracy of the control group can then be compared to the accuracy of the system across measures of efficiency such as accuracy, reliability and error tendency (eg. the confusion matrix). This assessment will result in an effort to assess similarity between the human group and the system at performing certain categorization tasks.

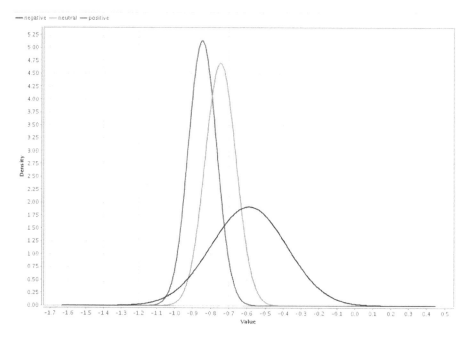

Fig. 1. An example of the resultant distributions of positive (left, red), neutral (mid, green) and negative (right, blue) sentiment is presented. The positive tokens are the most densely categorized, this is likely because many of the tokens in this data set were actually positive.

4   Next Steps

This work will be extended from categorizing sentiment of words to categorizing sentiment within n-grams and sentences. As development continues to be refined, the system will eventually perform broader categorical inferences based upon the methods developed within this experiment.

This experiment cannot be accomplished without human participants since the system will rely upon the participants' results as training data. Thus, the human and the machine will develop the resultant system in an iterative fashion.

Finally, as the system is continuously refined, the aim will be to make broader categorizations similar to human categorizations. It is hoped that this approach will result in knowledge structure that is more congruent and intuitive with the ultimate goal being the increased usability of information in an increasingly complex world network of knowledge.

Acknowledgements. I thank my advisor, Dr. Jared Danielson for his support. I also thank Amherst University for making their corpora available to the academy.

References

1. Barrett, L.: Are emotions natural kinds? Perspectives on Psychological Science 1, 1 (2006)
2. Constant, N., Christopher, D., Christopher, P., Florian, S.: The pragmatics of expressive content: Evidence from large corpora. To appear in Sprache und Datenverarbeitung (2008)
3. Eyheramendy, S., Lewis, D.D., Madigan, D.: On the Naïve Bayes model for text categorization (2008)
4. Holyoak, K.J.: Relations in semantic memory: Still puzzling after all these years. In:
5. Gluck, M.A., Anderson, J.R., Kosslyn, S.K.: Memory and mind: A festschrift for Gordon A. Bower, pp. 141–158. Erlbaum, New York (2008)
6. McCallum, A., Nigam, K.: A comparison of event models for Naive Bayes text classification. In: AAAIWS (1998)
7. McClelland, J.L.: Connectionist models of memory. In: Tulving, E., Craik, F.I.M. (eds.) The Oxford handbook of memory, pp. 583–596. Oxford University Press, New York (2000)
8. Mierswa, I., Wurst, M., Klinkenberg, R., Scholz, M., Euler, T.: YALE: Rapid Prototyping for Complex Data Mining Tasks. In: Proceedings of the 12th ACM SIGKDD International Conference on Knowledge Discovery and Data Mining (2006)
9. Moors, A., De Houwer, J.: Automaticity: A theoretical and conceptual analysis. Psychological Bulletin 132, 297–326 (2006)
10. Pendar, N., Cotos, E.: Automatic identification of discourse moves in scientific article introductions. In: 46th Annual Meeting of the ACL, pp. 62–70 (2008)
11. Potts, C., Florian, S.: Exclamatives and heightened emotion: Extracting pragmatic generalizations from large corpora. Ms., UMass Amherst (2008)
12. Roediger III, H.L., McDermott, K.B.: Tricks of memory. Current Directions in Psychological Science 9, 123–127 (2000)
13. Russel, S., Norvig, P.: Artificial Intelligence: A modern approach. Prentice Hall, Uppers Saddle River (2003)
14. Smith, N., O'Connor, B., Balasubramanyan, R., Routledge, B.R.: From Tweets to polls: Linking text sentiment to public opinion time series (2010)

Modeling Human Behavior for Energy-Usage Prediction

Anand S. Kulkarni, Karla Conn Welch, and Cindy K. Harnett

Department of Electrical and Computer Engineering,
University of Louisville, Louisville, KY, USA
{askulk02,karla.welch,cindy.harnett}@louisville.edu

Abstract. We propose a system that uses a set of mobile sensors to model human behavior of energy usage. This mobile sensor suite can be fit on a keychain or ID/access badge. Data from these sensors, e.g., temperature, visible light spectrum, and 60 Hz electromagnetic field, will be used to give real-time feedback of user's energy consumption and prediction of future energy usage. Feedback of energy consumption will be displayed in an understandable manner on a user interface, e.g., smart phone. A model developed from the available data using machine learning will inform the system about energy consumption patterns and behaviors of users.

Keywords: energy-usage prediction, human behavior, green buildings, sensors.

1 Introduction

Demand of electricity is increasing and will continue to increase day by day throughout the world. A significant amount of electricity is currently generated using nonrenewable fossil fuels. These fuels and similar resources on the earth are limited and depleting rapidly due to increased demand of electricity. Conserving nonrenewable sources for the future is imperative. Also, electricity generation using nonrenewable fuel causes environmental impacts (e.g., global warming, ozone layer depletion, greenhouse gas emissions, etc). Conservation of electricity is the best solution to immediately address these problems. Scientific experts agree with the public recognition of the importance of energy conservation; however, approaches for how to best implement energy-saving strategies remain unclear.

Energy consumption by buildings (residential and commercial) has already exceeded energy usage in the industrial and transportation sector and has reached 20%-40% of total energy consumption [1]. Although environmentally-responsible Green buildings should use less energy than their conventional counterparts, research has shown that some Green buildings consume more energy than expected [2]. In the Swedish city of Malmö, a community of 20 buildings was expected to consume energy in the range of 32 to 107 kWh/m^2 per year. Although a few buildings consumed energy within the range, the remaining consumed in the range of 74 to 356 kWh/m^2 per year. Similarly the Lewis Center at Oberlin College, a multi-purpose facility for Environmental Studies built for maximum energy efficiency, consumed

C. Stephanidis (Ed.): Posters, Part I, HCII 2011, CCIS 173, pp. 298–302, 2011.

120 to 200 kWh/ m² per year instead of an estimated 64 kWh/ m² per year [3]. One of the major reasons for these startling disparities between estimated and actual energy consumption is lack of knowledge of how different people use energy [4, 5].

Providing informative and immediate feedback to energy users about their energy usage has been found to be an effective way of reducing energy consumption. Such instantaneous feedback has proven to encourage physical activity (e.g., pedometers) and energy conservation, through people's sense of competition [6, 7] or their desire to save money—reducing energy usage by an average of 15% [8]. Fisher (2008) [8] determined that effective feedback for stimulating energy conservation should be:

- Based on actual consumption
- Provided frequently to the user
- Involve an appliance-specific breakdown of energy use
- Presented in an understandable and appealing way

2 Related Work

There are a variety of energy monitoring and feedback systems available in the market today. For example, Kill-A-Watt (p3international.com) and Plogg (plogginternational.com) are promising products that monitor appliance-level energy consumption. TED (The Energy Detective; theenergydetective.com), Wattson panel (diykyoto.com), and GEO's (Green Energy Option; greenenergyoptions.co.uk) Minim and Solo are capable of monitoring whole house's energy consumption. In addition, GEO's Duet, Trio, and Quartet have the ability to monitor energy usage on the level of a whole house as well as down to the individual appliance level.

Overall, at the moment these products are expensive, which is a major hindrance to users adopting them. Importantly, none of the systems available today show an individual's energy usage or provide any information about human behavior.

3 Proposed System

The authors are in the process of developing a system which uses a set of mobile sensors, as shown in Fig. 1. This mobile sensor suite, which can be attached to a keychain or an ID/access badge, will provide measurements of temperature, visible light spectrum, and 60 Hz electromagnetic fields in the vicinity of the user. The proposed system will use data from the sensors to provide real-time feedback on the individual user's energy usage and to predict of future energy consumption.

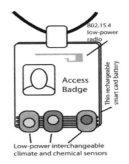

Fig. 1. Wireless sensors on badge

3.1 Mobile Sensor Suite

The compact wireless sensor suite is based on outdoor sensors we developed over 2007-present [9] that connects several different sensor types to a wireless node. This sensor suite moves with the user and can sense changes in illumination and power spikes indicating the user has turned electrical equipment on and off. This real-time energy consumption feedback will be displayed on a smart phone as shown in Fig. 2, which is convenient and one of the most accepted ways of receiving feedback on energy usage [10].

Fig. 2. Example interface display on smart phone

Mobile sensor data, combined with data about the buildings' age, historical energy usage pattern and type of HVAC equipment, outdoor weather conditions, and localization data from the sensor resources in a user's mobile phone [11-13] which include cellular signal level, GPS, Wi-Fi level, cameras, and accelerometers, would give an accurate hour-by-hour energy usage estimate.

Three new sensors that will be added under this project are temperature, lighting spectrum, and electromagnetic field sensor.

Temperature sensor: This low-power integrated circuit converts temperature to a serial data stream upon request. This device can also be programmed to set an alarm flag when a minimum or maximum temperature is attained. Temperature sensing will help the system infer the user's location, the user's energy needs, and any changes in heating/cooling caused by a HVAC system switching on.

Lighting spectrum sensor: This circuit is based on a four-input analog-to-digital converter (DS2450, Maxim Semiconductor) interfaced with photoresistors having light filters centered at four different wavelengths. The relative intensity data will be used to infer the intensity and type of light in the user's vicinity.

Electromagnetic field sensor: This amplifier is tuned to pick up 60 Hz signals at a coil. The amplified signal is rectified and connected to a DS2450 A/D converter. Signals suddenly exceeding a threshold DC voltage mean that the user has switched on an appliance, while slowly-varying signals are more likely caused by the user moving closer to a transformer or electrical outlet.

3.2   Machine Learning

The task of machine learning will be to measure and then model an individual's energy usage patterns and classify users accordingly (Fig. 3). For example, if average power consumption per person is 50 kWhr/day, future research could determine if in a building populated by a large number of people whether perhaps 50% of them have one type of energy-usage pattern (e.g., average energy user), 35% of another pattern (e.g., above-average), and 15% of a third pattern (e.g., below-average). Various algorithms, including neural networks and support vector machines (SVM), will be tested for generating models of energy use related to human behavior.

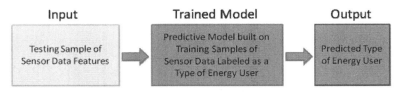

Fig. 3. Overview of a trained predictive model of energy use

Fig. 4 depicts a mock-up of data that could potentially be produced by the mobile sensor suite. Graphs show energy consumption of three users for personal computers, a shared microwave, and shared lighting.

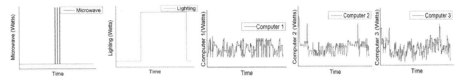

Fig. 4. Example energy usage data by appliance (e.g., microwave, lights, computers)

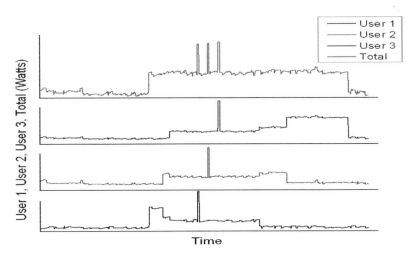

Fig. 5. Mock-up of energy consumption of three users over time with energy events attributed to individual devices (e.g., microwave)

Data from the sensors will be used to compose a comprehensive assessment of the energy use in an area as well as energy consumption that can be attributed to individual users in an area, as shown in Fig. 5.

References

1. Pérez-Lombard, L., Ortiz, J., Pout, C.: A review on buildings energy consumption information. Energy and Buildings 40, 394–398 (2008)
2. Newsham, G.R., Mancini, S., Birt, B.J.: Do LEED-certified buildings save energy? Yes, but... Energy and Buildings 41, 897–905 (2009)
3. Kunz, J., Maile, T., Bazjanac, V.: Underestimating energy. Science 326(5953), 664–665 (2009), doi:10.1126/science.326_664b
4. Kavgic, M., Mavrogianni, A., Mumovic, D., Summerfield, A., Stevanovic, Z., Djurovic-Petrovic, M.: A review of bottom-up building stock models for energy consumption in the residential sector. Building and Environment 45, 1683–1697 (2010)
5. Charles, D.: Leaping the Efficiency Gap. Science 325, 804–811 (2009)
6. Seligman, C., Darley, J.M.: Feedback as a means of decreasing residential energy consumption. Journal of Applied Psychology 62(4), 363–368 (1977)
7. Darby, S.: The effectiveness of feedback on energy consumption: A review for DEFRA of the literature on metering, billing and direct displays. Environmental Change Institute (2006)
8. Fisher, C.: Feedback on household energy consumption a tool for saving energy? Energy Efficiency 1(1), 79–104 (2008)
9. Harnett, C.K., Courtney, S.M., Kimmer, C.J.: SALAMANDER: A distributed sensor system for aquatic environmental measurements. In: Proc. IEEE International Instrumentation and Measurement Technology Conference, pp. 1787–1792 (2008), doi:10.1109/IMTC.2008.4547334
10. Weiss, M., Loock, C., Staake, T., Friedemann, M., Fleisch, E.: Evaluating mobile phones as energy consumption feedback devices. In: Proc. Mobiquitous, Sydney, Australia (2010)
11. Mitchell, T.M.: Mining our reality. Science 326, 1644–1645 (2009)
12. Kwok, R.: Phoning in data. Nature 458, 959–961 (2009)
13. Aoki, P., Honicky, R.J., Mainwaring, A., Myers, C., Paulos, E., Subramanian, S., Woodruff, A.: Common sense: mobile environmental sensing platforms to support community action and citizen science. In: Proc. UbiComp (2008)

The Effect of a Visual Element on Musical Sensitivity

Jieun Lee[1], Mitsuko Hayashi[2], and Masashi Nosaka[1]

[1] Hokkaido University, Graduate School of International Media, Communicaiton,
and Tourism Studies, Kita 8, Nishi 5, Kita-ku, Sapporo, Hokkaido, Japan
jeentwo@gmail.com
[2] Hokkaido University of Education Hakodate, Department of education,
Hachimancho 1-2, Hakodate, Hokkaido, Japan
hmitsuko@hak.hokkyodai.ac.jp

Abstract. This research is to review sensitivity comparisons between musical rhythm and visual rhythm focused on the kinetic typography that can be utilized as a synesthesia. According to preliminary research, kinetic typography that has visual movement can be measured by AVSM (affective value scale of music), which is one of the "emotional measures for evaluation" used for music. In this research based on the preliminary study, AVSM has been used to find out the emotional difference between music itself and a visual element with musical rhythm. The possibility of musical expression by a moving visual element has been reviewed.

Keywords: Rhythm of visual element, Rhythm, Movement, Emotional value.

1 Introduction

This study is a part of studies that the rhythm made by visual element can be used instead of musical rhythm. These studies were progressed under the hypothesis that the visual element produced by musical rhythm could communicate an emotion similar to the emotion communicated by music. In this study, the emotional values of both, which are investigation 1 'musical rhythm' and investigation 2 'visual rhythm with musical rhythm', were measured. Emotional communication by both measures is similar if there is no difference statistically. And if there is any difference statistically, emotional communication by both measures is concluded to be different. This study investigated how much difference was there between music and visual element information added to music as well as how much effect it made on music.

2 Purpose and Method of Study

In this study, the measured data for emotion, which are 'Musical rhythm' and 'Visual element with musical rhythm', were compared and analyzed by using AVSM (affective value scale of music). AVSM consists of 24 adjectives(scale of 1 to 5) such as 'Gloomy', 'Light', 'Exciting', etc. Each adjective is assigned to 5 factors; 'Uplift', 'Strength', 'Solemnity', 'Affinity' and 'Lightness'. By adding up the measured value

C. Stephanidis (Ed.): Posters, Part I, HCII 2011, CCIS 173, pp. 303–307, 2011.
© Springer-Verlag Berlin Heidelberg 2011

of belonged adjective, the score of each factor's measured value is calculated. In this study, each adjective is reviewed by the criterion score whose standard is factor, rather than is compared, because basic factor of emotion makes an effect on the measured value of each adjective.

In the investigation1 'Musical rhythm', the impression evaluation was conducted with adjectives of 24 items after hearing the 4 instrumentals. In the investigation2 'Visual element with musical rhythm', the impression evaluation was conducted with adjectives of 24 items after seeing and hearing 'visual element with musical rhythm' produced by the investigation1 'Musical rhythm'. The 'visual element' was kinetic typography, which is consist of 5 vowels of Japanese, (A), (I), (U), (E) and (O). The object of research was 31 students (1st graded students of Hokkaido University of Education HAKODATE) and the period was from July to August in 2010.

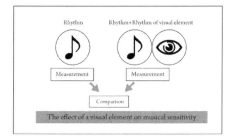

Fig.1. Experimental Composition

Table 1. Instrumentals used to experiment

Suggestion	Instrumentals
Suggestion1	Concerto for solo percussion & chamber orchestra 1st movement
Suggestion2	Sorbet No. 5
Suggestion3	Sorbet no. 7
Suggestion4	Michi

3   The Result of Research

Average score and standard deviation of each of 5 factors for 'musical rhythm' and 'visual element with musical rhythm' of Concerto for solo percussion & chamber orchestra 1st movement were found. For verifying if average value by each factor between the two has a significant difference statistically, 1 factor's ANOVA (analysis of variance), whose factors were 'musical rhythm' and 'visual element with musical rhythm' for each factor, was performed. Firstly, 'Uplift' ($F_{(1,60)}= 0.03$, *ns*), 'Strength' ($F_{(1,60)}=1.99$, *ns*), 'Affinity' ($F_{(1,60)}=0.00$, *ns*) and 'Lightness' ($F_{(1,60)}= 0.12$, *ns*) didn't show a significant difference statistically between two factors. Also, 'Solemnity' showed a marginally significant statistically ($F_{(1,60)}=3.83$, $p<.10$).

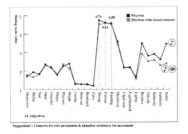 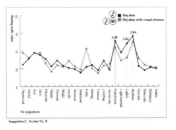

Fig. 2. The AVSM graph comparison for 'Concerto for solo percussion & chamber orchestra 1st movement'

Fig. 3. AVSM graph comparison for 'Sorbet No. 5'

Table 2. Experimental data for Concerto for solo percussion & chamber orchestra 1st movement

Investigation 1	Total Average	Standard deviation	Investigation 2	Total Average	Standard deviation
Factor 1 'Uplift'	23.26	5.14	Factor 1 'Uplift'	23.00	5.13
Factor 2 'Strength'	25.77	2.24	Factor 2 'Strength'	24.81	3.02
Factor 3 'Solemnity'	11.77	3.47	Factor 3 'Solemnity'	9.77	4.39
Factor 4 'Affinity'	3.87	1.31	Factor 4 'Affinity'	3.87	1.83
Factor 5 'Lightness'	5.77	2.47	Factor 5 'Lightness'	5.55	2.43

Table 3. Experimental data for 'Sorbet No. 5'

Investigation 1	Total Average	Standard deviation	Investigation 2	Total Average	Standard deviation
Factor 1 'Uplift'	25.16	6.45	Factor 1 'Uplift'	26.87	6.64
Factor 2 'Strength'	16.23	4.23	Factor 2 'Strength'	14.55	3.89
Factor 3 'Solemnity'	8.10	3.72	Factor 3 'Solemnity'	8.94	4.61
Factor 4 'Affinity'	5.77	2.76	Factor 4 'Affinity'	6.48	2.53
Factor 5 'Lightness'	9.87	3.66	Factor 5 'Lightness'	8.26	3.47

Average score and standard deviation of each of 5 factors for 'musical rhythm' and 'visual element with musical rhythm' of Sorbet No.5 were found. For verifying if average value by each factor between the two has a significant difference statistically, 1 factor's ANOVA, whose factors were 'musical rhythm' and 'visual element with musical rhythm' for each factor, was performed. Firstly, 'Uplift' $(F_{(1,60)}= 1.02, ns)$, 'Strength' $(F_{(1,60)}=2.55, ns)$, 'Solemnity' $(F_{(1,60)}=0.60, ns)$ and 'Affinity' $(F_{(1,60)}=1.08, ns)$ didn't show a significant difference statistically. Also, 'Lightness' $(F_{(1,60)}=3.06, p<.10)$ showed a marginally significant $(F_{(1,60)}= 0.12, ns)$.

Average score and standard deviation of each of 5 factors for 'musical rhythm' and 'visual element with musical rhythm' of Sorbet No.7 were found. For verifying if average value by each factor between the two has a significant difference statistically, 1 factor's ANOVA, whose factors were 'musical rhythm' and 'visual element with

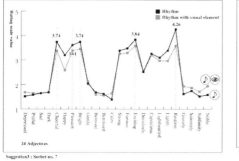

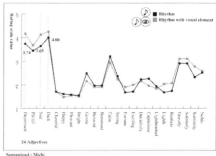

Fig. 4. AVSM graph comparison for 'Sorbet No. 7'

Fig. 5. AVSM graph comparison for 'Michi'

Table 4. Experimental data for 'Sorbet No. 7'

Investigation 1	Total Average	Standard deviation	Investigation 2	Total Average	Standard deviation
Factor 1 'Uplift'	16.13	5.36	Factor 1 'Uplift'	17.84	4.61
Factor 2 'Strength'	22.10	3.88	Factor 2 'Strength'	20.58	4.29
Factor 3 'Solemnity'	6.45	2.58	Factor 3 'Solemnity'	7.45	4.06
Factor 4 'Affinity'	5.32	2.15	Factor 4 'Affinity'	5.26	2.27
Factor 5 'Lightness'	9.74	2.97	Factor 5 'Lightness'	9.19	2.93

musical rhythm' for each factor, was performed. There was no significant difference for all of 'uplift' ($F_{(1,60)}= 1.76,ns$), 'Strength' ($F_{(1,60)}= 2.06,ns$), 'Solemnity' ($F_{(1,60)}=1.30, ns$), 'Affinity' ($F_{(1,60)}=0.01,ns$) and 'Lightness' ($F_{(1,60)}=0.51,ns$).

Table 5. Experimental data for 'Michi'

Investigation 1	Total Average	Standard deviation	Investigation 2	Total Average	Standard deviation
Factor 1 'Uplift'	32.39	6.28	Factor 1 'Uplift'	33.97	5.27
Factor 2 'Strength'	12.52	3.58	Factor 2 'Strength'	13.42	4.30
Factor 3 'Solemnity'	10.71	3.85	Factor 3 'Solemnity'	11.42	4.90
Factor 4 'Affinity'	6.29	2.82	Factor 4 'Affinity'	5.90	2.80
Factor 5 'Lightness'	5.87	2.86	Factor 5 'Lightness'	5.84	2.77

Average score and standard deviation of each of 5 factors for 'musical rhythm' and 'visual element with musical rhythm' of Michi were found. For verifying if average value by each factor between the two has a significant difference statistically, 1 factor's ANOVA, whose factors were 'musical rhythm' and 'visual element with musical rhythm' for each factor, was performed. There was no significant gap for all of 'Uplift' ($F_{(1,60)}=1.11,ns$), 'Strength' ($F_{(1,60)}=0.78,ns$), 'Solemnity' ($F_{(1,60)}=0.38,ns$), 'Affinity' ($F_{(1,60)}=0.28,ns$) and 'Lightness' ($F_{(1,60)}=0.00,ns$).

4 Consideration

This study is a part of studies that 'Visual element with musical rhythm' can be replaced for 'Musical rhythm'. This study was progressed under the hypothesis that visual element produced by music rhythm could deliver an emotion similar to the emotion delivered by music. In this study, investigation 1 and 2 were measured by emotional scale consisted by 24 adjectives to review the effect of moving visual element on music. Each average score and standard deviation for 'Uplift', 'Strength', 'Solemnity', 'Affinity' and 'Lightness' were found and statistical significant difference among the average values of each score was evaluated. As the result, only suggestion 1 'Solemnity' ($F_{(1,60)}$=3.83, $p<.10$) applying 'Concerto for solo percussion & chamber orchestra 1st movement' and suggestion 2 'Lightness' ($F_{(1,60)}$=3.06, $p<.10$) applying 'Sorbet No. 5' showed marginally significant difference and others didn't show a significant difference among the average value statistically. In other words, 'Visual element' produced by music rhythm did not influence to 'Musical rhythm' as a noise. And it communicated the emotion of music as it was.

References

1. Jieun, L.E.E.: The comparison of emotion between music and kinetic typography-The emotional evaluation for music focused on the measure of kinetic typography. A Journal of Brand Design Association of Korea 9(1), 353–365 (2011)
2. Jieun, L.: Emotional Disparity in the Kinetic Typography between Design Majors and Other Specialtie. The Journal of Korean Society of Typography 2(2), 520–539 (2010)
3. Berlyne, D.E.: Aesthetics and Psychology. Appleton Century-Crofts, New York (1971)
4. Taniguchi, T.: Construction of an affective value scale of music and examination of relations between the scale and a multiple mood scale. The Japanese Journal of Cognitive Psychology, 463–470 (1995)
5. Hashimoto, S.: Music and Kansei Information processing –Musical performance System Using Gesture-. In: 1994 ITE Annual Convetion, pp. 487–490 (1994)
6. Kishihara, M.: Trail to Classifications of Music using the Affective Values. IPAJ, 33–36 (2006)
7. Yasuda, S.: A psychological Study of Strong Experience Due to Listening to Music based on a subjective measurement of physical reactions. The Japanese Journal of Cognitive Psychology, 11–19 (2008)

A Scrutinized Analysis Method of the Human Error Potential due to the Introduction of New Digital Devices to Nuclear Power Plants

Lee and Yong Hee

I&C and Human Factors Division,
Korea Atomic Energy Research Institute (KAERI),
1045 Daeduk-Daero, Yoseong-Gu, Daejeon, 305-353, Korea
yhlee@kaeri.re.kr

Abstract. This paper describes a new method proposed for human error analysis (HEA) in case of the introduction of new digital devices to nuclear power plants (NPPs). Preventing human errors has been a main issue especially for the safety of NPPs. The hi-touch human interface must be proved to be safe before being introduced to NPPs. Although many good HEA methods are available, a scrutinized one is inevitable against to the new types of errors, for utilizing new digital devices and their human interfaces in NPPs. All possible interactions between the device and the user through the designed interfaces are investigated by the term of Interaction Segment (IS), and Error Segment (ES) is assessed by human factors criteria and their consequences to predict the human error potential (HEP). Results such as a list of ISs and ESs and their combinatorial sequences are provided to the human interface designers for qualifying the digital devices to NPPs.

Keywords: human error, human interface, digital device, nuclear power plant.

1   An Approach to Human Errors in Digital Human Interface

Human error has been notorious as a universal enemy which has potential to break down all barriers and protective features for system safety. Many researchers have investigated the task performance of human and its influence to overall level of functional reliability. They have performed the studies to predict and prevent the human error through probability and usability; however, inadequate decisions and/or unwanted behaviors are inevitable to human itself. It has been complicated to know the details mechanism of human errors previously as the high technology digital instruments have been developed and introduced. Thus, it was needed to predict the detailed error potential, and to prevent previously in design of, especially NPPs. ES and IS were defined according to exterior physical units and operation options of the digital devices. It could be possible to review all interactions through ES and IS for using digital devices.

This paper describes a new method proposed for human error analysis (HEA) in case of the introduction of new digital devices to nuclear power plants (NPPs).

C. Stephanidis (Ed.): Posters, Part I, HCII 2011, CCIS 173, pp. 308–311, 2011.
© Springer-Verlag Berlin Heidelberg 2011

Recently, the human interface has been drastically revolved by virtue of the hi-touch technology as well as the digital and computer technology. It is still strongly doubtful to find such an up-to-date interface in NPPs in near future. Every new design and new technologies must be proved to be safe before introducing to NPPs, and free from defects including all kinds of human errors.

The human error potential within the digital devices should be thoroughly investigated from the early phase of design to the integration and operational phase. Although many good HEA methods are available, a scrutinized one is inevitable against to the new types of errors, for utilizing new digital devices and their human interfaces in NPPs.

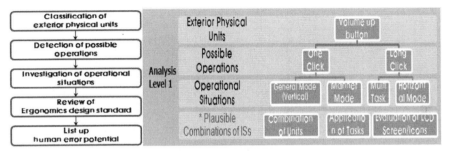

Fig. 1. Steps for HEA proposed

2   Interaction Segments (IS) and Error Segments (ES)

A digital device has various design factors of interface itself that might give very different impact to the user by not only the shape and color but also the operation methods, control states, and so on. Lee, et al. (2003) defined *Error Segment* as "the basic unit has the potential causing negative affect for use"[1]. In this study to find out the human error potential (HEP), two new terms such as *Interaction Segment (IS)* and *Error Segment (ES)* are introduced. All possible interactions between the device and the user through the designed interfaces are described in term of *Interaction Segments*. And *Error Segments* are assessed among the various combinations of ISs. They are enumerated into the combinatorial structures of all applicable tasks, nevertheless their frequencies might be extremely low.

The human error potentials of each *IS/ES* are respectively examined by human factors engineering criteria, and the plausible sequences of various combination of all ISs are assessed by their evolutionary paths to the ultimate consequences. Results such as a list of *Error Segments (ESs)* and their combinatorial sequences are provided to the human interface designers for qualifying the digital devices to NPPs.

3   Example Application and the Results

Three kinds of smart phones were analyzed and they are named type A, B, C. It has been using with the limited function in NPPs currently [2]. ES and IS were defined from instrument (device character, H/W and S/W design problem, and component breakdown), user (operation method, knowledge level, and user character), operation situation and so on. ES was classified by exterior physical units of the smart phone and IS was listed from user and operation situation. (LCD buttons are excluded just they are reviewed as an integrated icon in the applications.) They will be considered to a further research. Followings are results of example application of the proposed method to three different types of smart-phones for design review before NPP field applications. Table 1 shows a part of IS lists coded at capital alphabet. Figure 1 shows a comparative result about the total numbers of ISs. It is quite clear that type C smart phone has less exterior physical units and less ISs than the others.

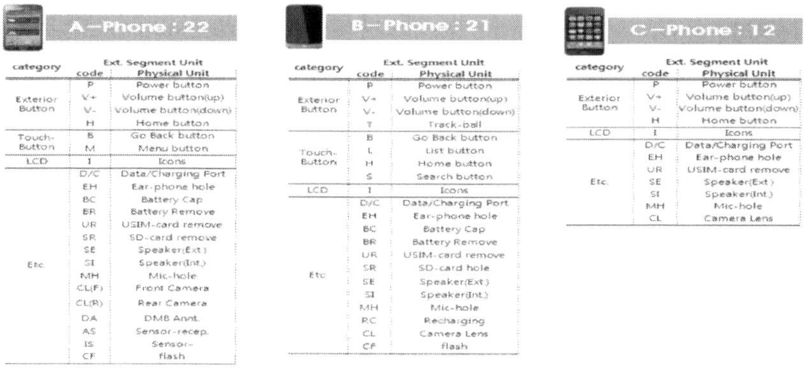

A–Phone : 22

category	code	Physical Unit
Exterior Button	P	Power button
	V+	Volume button(up)
	V-	Volume button(down)
	H	Home button
Touch-Button	B	Go Back button
	M	Menu button
LCD	I	Icons
Etc.	D/C	Data/Charging Port
	EH	Ear-phone hole
	BC	Battery Cap
	BR	Battery Remove
	UR	USIM-card remove
	SR	SD-card remove
	SE	Speaker(Ext.)
	SI	Speaker(Int.)
	MH	Mic-hole
	CL(F)	Front Camera
	CL(R)	Rear Camera
	DA	DMB Annt.
	AS	Sensor-recep.
	IS	Sensor-
	CF	flash

B–Phone : 21

category	code	Physical Unit
Exterior Button	P	Power button
	V+	Volume button(up)
	V-	Volume button(down)
	T	Track-ball
Touch-Button	B	Go Back button
	L	List button
	H	Home button
	S	Search button
LCD	I	Icons
Etc.	D/C	Data/Charging Port
	EH	Ear-phone hole
	BC	Battery Cap
	BR	Battery Remove
	UR	USIM-card remove
	SR	SD-card hole
	SE	Speaker(Ext.)
	SI	Speaker(Int.)
	MH	Mic-hole
	RC	Recharging
	CL	Camera Lens
	CF	flash

C–Phone : 12

category	code	Physical Unit
Exterior Button	P	Power button
	V+	Volume button(up)
	V-	Volume button(down)
	H	Home button
LCD	I	Icons
Etc.	D/C	Data/Charging Port
	EH	Ear-phone hole
	UR	USIM-card remove
	SE	Speaker(Ext.)
	SI	Speaker(Int.)
	MH	Mic-hole
	CL	Camera Lens

Fig. 2. The example of IS and ES for A and B type smart phone

Table 1. List of IS and ES (a part for smart phone)

IS Code.	Operation method	Test for ES by Operation situation				
		No option(Vertical)	Manner mode	Horizontal mode	Multi task	Lock
P	One Click	Screen on/off				
	Long Click	Pup-up window for option				
V +	One Click	Vol. up by stages	Manner mode cancel and vol. up by stages	Vol. up by stages (space compatibility) Oper. intended: down		None
	Long Click	Vol. up rapidly	Manner mode cancel and vol. up rapidly			None
V -	One Click	Vol. down by stages → manner mode	Vibration	Vol. down by stages (space compatibility) Oper. intended: up		None
	Long Click	Vol. down rapidly → manner mode	Vibration			None
T	Rotation	Move	Move	Move	Move	None
	Click	Selection	Selection	Selection	Selection	None

For an example, in case of HEP at 'V+' in ES and 'Horizontal mode' in IS, operators have different intention about Volume up button (V+) between no option and horizontal mode in IS. However they showed the same response. When V+ is in horizontal mode, it has performed to turn down the volume (V-). It caused confusion to operators by violating the space compatibility. If V+ is in horizontal mode, volume would be decreased by stage or rapidly. Because V+ is in the left of the device at horizontal mode, usually operators are likely to push the left button for decreasing the volume. The application includes a review by design criteria from the human factors engineering/ergonomics design standards such as functional availability, suitability of design, consistency, compatibility, effectiveness for use, and so on.(see Figure 2).

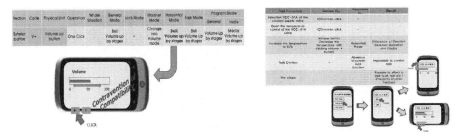

Fig. 3. Review on the interface by the human factors criteria

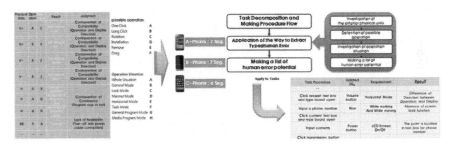

Fig. 4. Steps and results according to the applications to smart-phones

4   Conclusions and Discussions

A new HEA method summarized in figure3 can facilitate to specify HEP of a digital device based on the *Error Segment (ES)* and *Interaction Segment (IS)*. All possible interactions can be described in term of IS/ES, and HEP can be thoroughly investigated from the early phase of design by providing a list of IS/ESs to the human interface designers for qualifying the digital devices to NPPs. The results are to be verified through the experimental observation [3].

References

1. Lee, Y.H., Jang, T.I., Lim, H.K.: A modification of human error analysis technique for designing man-machine interface in nuclear power plants. Journal of the Ergonomics Society of Korea 22(1), 31–42 (2003)
2. Yun, J.H., Oh, Y.J., Lee, Y.H.: A development of the Extremely-Low Frequency Human Errors of Digital Devices. In: Proceeding of Conf. Ergonomics Society of Korea (2010)
3. Oh, Y.J., Lee, Y.H., Yun, J.H.: A Study on the Operator's Erroneous Responses to the New Human Interface of a Digital Device to be introduced to Nuclear Power Plants. In: Posters, Part I, HCII 2011. CCIS, vol. 173, pp. 342—345. Springer, Heidelberg (2011)

Understanding Users by Their D.I.S.C. Personality through Interactive Gaming

Qin En Looi[1], Swee Lan See[1], Chi Shien Tay[2], and Gin Kee Ng[2]

[1] Institute for Infocomm Research, A*STAR, Singapore 138632
[2] Catholic High School, Singapore 579767
{Qin En Looi,Swee Lan See,Chi Shien Tay,
Gin Kee Ng,stuqel}@i2r.a-star.edu.sg

Abstract. A key component of improving human-computer interaction is through the matching of users with their preferred computer interfaces and interaction styles. Understanding the users better would result in a customized gaming experience, leading to sustained user engagement. In this paper, we develop an alternative tool to aid in the measurement of the D.I.S.C. personality styles of users in the form of an interactive game. Through this game, we aim to predict the personality type of the gamer, from which invaluable insights about each type of gamer can be elicited.

Keywords: Alternative assessment tool, D.I.S.C. Personality Profiling, Interactive Gaming.

1 Introduction

With this growing need and pervasive use of information technologies, the study of Human-Computer Interaction (HCI) is undoubtedly becoming more and more important. Some studies have identified that the choice of computer interface and interaction style needs to match the users to result in good human computer interaction. Hence, it would be beneficial to understand users better and hence develop computer interfaces that could serve to improving human computer interactions.

We hypothesised that interactive social gaming could reveal the gamers' personality traits through the in-game decisions and activities. Hence, we decided to conduct further studies in this aspect of attempting to understand the users better through their D.I.S.C. personality traits.

In this paper, we would discuss about eliciting insights from user behaviours through the development an interactive game, followed by human behaviour assessment methods, which leads to the generic framework towards understanding users when developing an interactive game.

2 Personality Assessments

Personality is an important aspect as it shapes a human's mind and thoughts. Many personality assessment methods were developed and used by psychologist and

C. Stephanidis (Ed.): Posters, Part I, HCII 2011, CCIS 173, pp. 312–316, 2011.
© Springer-Verlag Berlin Heidelberg 2011

researchers. Basically, there are two major types of personality assessments, namely: *Projective tests* and *Objective tests.*

Projective tests assume that personality is primarily unconscious and assess an individual by how he or she responds to an ambiguous stimulus, like an ink blot. The idea is unconscious needs will come out in the person's response, e.g. an aggressive person may see images of destruction. On the other hand, objective tests assume personality is consciously accessible and measure it by self-report questionnaires.

Research on psychological assessment has generally found objective tests to be more valid and reliable than projective tests. Some of the notable objective tests include personality assessments such as the DISC personality profiling, the Myers-Briggs Type Indicator, Holland Codes, Minnesota Multiphasic Personality Inventory and many more.

Personality assessments can be scored using a dimensional (normative), a typological (ipsative) approach or both. Dimensional approaches, such as the Big 5, describe personality as a set of continuous dimensions on which individuals differ. On the other hand, typological approaches, such as the Myers-Briggs Type Indicator, describe opposing categories of functioning where individuals differ. Normative responses for each category can be graphed as bell curves (normal curves), implying that some aspects of personality are better than others. Ipsative test responses offer two equally "good" responses between which an individual must choose. Such responses (e.g., on the MBTI) would result in bi-modal graphs for each category, rather than bell curves. Personality tests, such as the Strength Deployment Inventory (r), which assesses motivation, or purpose, of behaviour, rather than the behaviour itself, combine a dimensional and typological approach. Three continuums of motivation are combined to yield 7 distinct types.

These personality assessments allow people to understand their way of thinking and how they react to certain situations. Through these personality assessments, researchers in the field of HCI are able to shape different programmes and ideas to suit different users of different personalities and hence, achieve the basic goal in the study of HCI. In addition, users who understand their personalities are able to understand their strengths and weaknesses as well, so that they are able to make better achievements in their career and life.

In this paper, we are attempting to improve understanding of people through the use of a personality assessment known as D.I.S.C personality profiling, which is similar to BIG FIVE, and at the same time through developing an interactive game. We use this personality assessment to extend the observation found in social gaming. D.I.S.C is a personality assessment developed based on the 1928 work of psychologist William Moulton Marston and the original behaviouralist Walter V. Clarke, et al. *D* represents Dominance (relating to control, power and assertiveness), *I* represents Influence (relating to social situations and communication), *S* represents Steadiness (relating to patience, persistence and thoughtfulness), and *C* represents Conscientiousness (relating to structure and organization).

3 Results and Discussion

The Preliminary Results were collected through the means of a quantitative questionnaire and the results are as shown in the figures below. 70% of the sample group have 'I' & 'S' personality types and almost all 'I' & 'S' personalities play computer games (Fig. 1), and form a potential gaming market, while 'D' & 'C' personalities are less engaged in computer games possibly due to their critical nature.

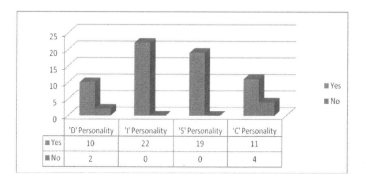

Fig. 1. Distribution of Personality Types in Gamers and Non-Gamers

Fig. 2 shows people of 'S' personality has the highest demand for a good quality game, for instance, games should meet standards such as having specific mentioned features in the games they play, even though this question asked them about their favorite game. Fig. 3 also shows that teenagers largely prefer multi-player games and interactive, role-playing games compared to less popular genres such as educational games In addition, from Table 1, we can further narrow down to people with 'D' and 'S' personalities being more demanding in their preference of their ideal game.

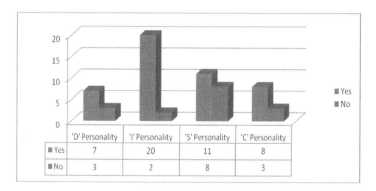

Fig. 2. Distribution of Personality Types and Favorite Game Expectations

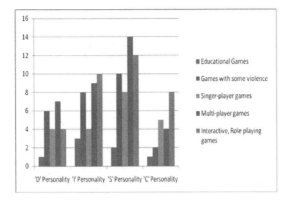

Fig. 3. Distribution of Personality Types and Favorite Game Expectations

Table 1. Personality Types and Ideal Game Characteristics

Personalities/ Characteristics	D	I	S	C
Good Graphics	✓	✓	✓	
3 Dimensional	✓		✓	✓
Good strategy	✓		✓	
Interactive		✓		
Able to Win	✓			
Realistic			✓	

From Table 2, we can see that certain features are only selected by certain D.I.S.C. personality types. For example, 'D' personalities prefer using console; 'I' personalities prefer playing speech-controlled games; 'S' personalities prefer playing first person shooter games while 'C' personalities showed no interest to these three features. This shows that people of each D.I.S.C. personality type do display distinct gamer behavior when playing games. Therefore, we are able to confirm with our hypothesis that gamers display their D.I.S.C. behavioral traits in the course of game play.

Table 2. Personality Types and Game Features Selections

Personalities/ Features	D	I	S	C
Gesture	✓	✓	✓	✓
Use of Keyboard		✓	✓	✓
3 Dimensional			✓	✓
Graphics			✓	
Real Life Simulation	✓		✓	
Speech Control		✓		
Console	✓			

Results from the Preliminary Questionnaire shows that the expectation level of a game varies with gamers of different D.I.S.C. personality types. 'D' and 'C' personality gamers, who dislike routine, and being more critical in nature, are generally found to be less engaged in online gaming. On the other hand, 'I' and 'S' personality gamers, who are generally interactive, and enjoy simple pleasures, are found to be more engaged in online games.

5 Conclusions

From this research, we found that users of 'S' personality style are better reviewers compared to users of other personality types. Game developers who would like to create better interaction interfaces should consult them for their inputs. However, as this is a preliminary study with small sample size, our future research would attempt to verify to confirm this finding.

In conclusion, from social gaming, we could understand the users better and can observe a user's personality. Through understanding users by their D.I.S.C. personality style, we could create better gaming interfaces to improving human computer interactions, thus enhancing user experience.

References

1. See, S.L., Tan, M., Looi, Q.E.: Towards better human robot interaction: Understand human computer interaction in social gaming using a video-enhanced diary method. In: Kim, J.-H., Ge, S.S., Vadakkepat, P., Jesse, N., Al Manum, A., Puthusserypady, K.S., Rückert, U., Sitte, J., Witkowski, U., Nakatsu, R., Braunl, T., Baltes, J., Anderson, J., Wong, C.-C., Verner, I., Ahlgren, D. (eds.) Progress in Robotics. CCIS, vol. 44, pp. 119–127. Springer, Heidelberg (2009)
2. Kim, J.-H., Ge, S.S., Vadakkepat, P.: Advances in Robotics. LNCS, vol. 5744. Springer, Heidelberg (2009)
3. Tan, M., Looi, Q.E., See, S.L.: Social Gaming: What Attracts the Most Attention? An Investigation Using an Improved Diary Method. In: Proceedings of the International Conference for Advances in Computer Entertainment Technology, p. 415 (2008)
4. Viswesvaran, C., Ones, D.S.: Meta-Analyses of Fakability Estimates: Implications for Personality Measurement. Educational and Psychological Measurement 59(2), 197–210 (1999)

Modeling Attention Allocation in a Complex Dual Task with and without Auditory Cues

Brian McClimens and Derek Brock

Naval Research Laboratory, 4555 Overlook Ave. S.W.,
Washington, DC 20375 USA
{brian.mcclimens,derek.brock}@nrl.navy.mil

Abstract. Navy watchstanding operations increasingly involve information-saturated environments in which operators must attend to more than one critical task display at a time [1]. In response, the Navy is pursuing a model-based understanding of human performance in multitask settings. Empirical studies with a complex dual task and related cognitive modeling work in the authors' lab suggest that auditory cueing is an effective strategy for mediating operators' attention [2,3,4]. Characterizing the effects of widely separated displays on performance and effort is an important ancillary concern, and a series of cognitive models developed with the EPIC cognitive architecture [5] is used for this purpose. These cognitive models verify a key finding from an empirical study; namely, time spent on the primary, relatively stateless, tracking task is regulated by state information retained from the secondary, radar task. These findings suggest that in multitask settings, operators use relatively simple state information about a task they are about to leave to gauge how long they can attend to other matters before they must return.

Keywords: Cognitive modeling, EPIC architecture, head-tracking, urgency, multitasking.

1 Introduction

Auditory display research at the Naval Research Laboratory (NRL) is motivated primarily by the U.S. Navy's need to improve efficiency in the Combat Information Center aboard ships, reducing required manpower. Research at NRL has shown that the use of auditory cueing can dramatically improve operator performance in information-saturated environments [2,3,4]. In order to better exploit the benefits of auditory cueing for the purpose of attention management, a good understanding of the underlying mechanisms driving attention switching in both cued and uncued settings is needed. This paper furthers the understanding of these mechanisms by presenting cognitive models of a method utilizing situational awareness to trigger attention switches in environments with and without external prompting, and evaluating these models using head-tracking data collected in a human subjects study.

C. Stephanidis (Ed.): Posters, Part I, HCII 2011, CCIS 173, pp. 317–321, 2011.

2 Background

The Dual Task. The dual task environment that provides the foundation for the models explored in this paper was developed at NRL in the early 1990s [6]. This dual task consists of a tracking task, in which subjects are asked to follow the movements of a target object on the primary display with a joystick, and a radar task, in which subjects make a series of rule-based classifications of objects that appear on a secondary screen.

The tracking task is a continuous task where performance is directly related to attention. Movement of the target is slow enough that subjects are capable of tracking well when attending to the task, but rapid enough that performance falls off abruptly when the subjects attend to the radar task.

The radar task is a more complex episodic task, requiring subjects to respond to individual classification events (sixty-five events over a thirteen minute scenario). Objects of three different types, referred to collectively as blips, appear near the top of the screen and travel towards the bottom of the screen over the course of about twenty seconds. Based on the speed and trajectory of these blips, subjects are asked to classify them as either hostile or neutral according to separate rules for each of the three blip types. Subjects are not permitted to enter their response until blips are approximately halfway down the screen at which point a blip will change color (and in some conditions an auditory alert will be presented), signifying that a response is needed. Blips may turn red, indicating that they are hostile; blue, indicating neutrality; or yellow, in which case subjects must rely on the rules alone to determine threat level.

In the Dual Task configuration addressed by this modeling effort, the two tasks were presented to subjects on different monitors separated by a ninety-degree arc. Two features of this setup are of critical importance. First, the separation angle is wide enough that subjects attending to one task do not have visual information from the other task available in their peripheral vision. Second, the cost for switching between tasks is significantly higher than it would be if the two tasks were on the same screen. Thus, rapid interleaving of the two tasks is not as feasible as in many other modeled multitasking environments.

EPIC. The EPIC cognitive architecture [5] has been used to build several models of this dual task in the past [3,7,8]. The models in this paper are an extension of previous modeling work at NRL, and again use the EPIC architecture. These models also make use of a custom-designed encoder for the hostility property of blips on the radar screen, and a timing mechanism that regulates the amount of time spent on the tracking task between attendances to the radar task.

Human Data. The design of this model relies on data collected in a human subjects study conducted at NRL [4]. Subjects wore a head-tracking device mounted on top of a set of headphones while performing the dual task in four conditions: one with no auditory cues to aid in their task, and three conditions that varied the type of sounds presented and the manner in which they were presented to subjects. This head tracking data allowed for analyses concerning the number of attention switches, response times to auditory cues, and the amount of time spent on any given instance of the tracking or radar tasks. A key finding from this study, shown in Figure 1, was the negative correlation between the time spent on the tracking task and the number of blips onscreen when subjects turned from the radar task to the tracking task. This correlation implies that subjects incorporate state information from the radar in their strategies for managing time spent on the tracking task.

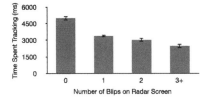

Fig. 1. Emprical data from [4]. The number of blips onscreen when a subject leaves the radar task to attend to the tracking task has a strong impact on the amount of time spent tracking before returning to the radar task. Error bars show the standard error of the mean (s.e.m.).

Upon completion of the four conditions, subjects were presented with a simpler version of the radar task. Blips were presented one at a time, and subjects were permitted to respond at any time; they did not wait for blips to become active. Each subject responded to 72 blips with auditory cues and 72 blips without auditory cues. This task provided a measure of classification and response times for situations in which no distractions were present.

3 Modeling

Base Model. All models were run under two conditions: one that made use of auditory cues to signify when a blip on the radar task became active, and one that used no auditory cues. Each of the models was run using four thirteen-minute scenario files that were used to drive the radar task in the human subjects study. A timing mechanism developed by Taatgen [9], and implemented in EPIC by Hornof [8] was used to determine the amount of time spent on the tracking task between episodes of executing the radar task. This timer adds a certain level of non-determinism to the model, so each condition-scenario pair was run ten times, and all recorded measures are averages of those model runs.

Two elements of note in the base model's strategy were influenced by information collected in the human subjects study. First, the classification of blips on the radar screen begins before they have become active. During the dual task, subjects spent less time on the radar screen after a blip had become active than it took them to classify a blip in the simpler single-blip task performed at the end of the experiment. This suggests that subjects began the classification process prior to a blip becoming active. Second, the model classifies blips in stages, with classification taking place over multiple attendances to the radar task. The duration of subjects' attendances to the radar task rarely exceeded 1500ms. Because blip classification and response were determined to take longer than this, it was concluded that subjects must classify blips over multiple attendances to the radar task. A custom encoder created in EPIC ensures that the model attends to blips for a 1000ms period, followed by a separate 565ms inspection period before the hostility of a blip is available to the model.

Modeling Urgency. When subjects looked away from the radar task to attend to the tracking task, the amount of time spent on tracking was inversely proportional to the number of blips on the radar screen. This is likely due to a sense of urgency that increased with the amount of activity on the radar task. We hypothesized that subjects used state information from the radar task to facilitate intelligently-timed attention switches, allowing subjects to spend more time on tracking when the radar task did not require attention, and to return to the radar task in a timely fashion when blips required a response. Such a strategy should improve performance in both tasks.

In order to test this hypothesis, our models were run in each of three modes. All models used the strategies described above in the Base Model section. The first model, referred to as mono-urgency, would spend approximately 2700ms on the tracking task each time it attended to it, regardless of the number of blips on the radar task. The dual-urgency model used two different durations on the tracking task: approximately 2450ms when there was a blip on the radar task, and 5915ms when there were no blips on the radar screen. A third, multi-urgency model made use of 5915ms, 2980ms, 2450ms, and 2000ms durations for tracking sessions beginning with zero, one, two, or at least three blips onscreen, respectively. All of these durations were based on data observed in the human subject study. In the sound condition, models used the same numbers to guide their tracking durations, except that if the model had already classified all blips on the radar task, it would wait for an auditory cue signifying that a blip had become active to return to the radar task.

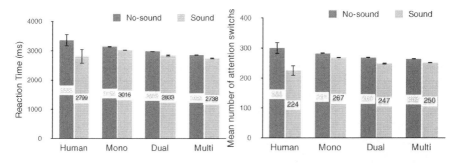

Fig. 2. Reaction times (left) and the number of attention switches (right) decreased as the model used more state information from the radar task. Note that error bars, which show the s.e.m., are present for the various models' measures. The variance is too small to see at this scale.

4   Results and Conclusion

Model performance was evaluated on reaction times in the radar task, the percentage of time spent on the tracking task and the number of attention switches between the two tasks. The models' reaction times in the radar task decreased as more information from the radar task was used to regulate time spent on the tracking task, as shown in Figure 2. In the no-sound condition, the models' mean reaction times were 3156ms,

2972ms and 2852ms for mono-, dual- and multi-urgency models respectively. In the sound condition, reaction times were 3016ms, 2833ms and 2738ms. The percentage of time spent on the tracking task remained relatively even, with mono-, dual- and multi-urgency models spending 64.9, 64.9, and 65.1 percent of their time on tracking in the no-sound condition, and 66.0, 66.3 and 66.0 percent of their time on tracking in the sound conditions. The number of attention switches decreased in the dual- and multi-urgency models, with 282, 273.2 and 282.4 attention switches in the no-sound condition and 284.4, 276.8 and 280.4 attention switches in the sound condition for mono-, dual- and multi-urgency models, respectively.

The human performance data suggests that subjects employ a strategy utilizing state information from the radar task to govern time spent on the tracking task, and data from the models suggests that this type of strategy can indeed be beneficial to the radar task without negatively affecting performance in the tracking task. However, the models fail to sufficiently capture the performance differences found in the sound and no-sound conditions, and further work must be done to ensure that a strategy utilizing state information from the radar task can be effectively applied in models that are more faithful to human performance in both of these conditions.

References

1. Hearn, J., Mills, J.H.: Finding the knowledge edge. CHIPS Magazine 13(3), 17–20 (2005)
2. Brock, D., Ballas, J.A., Stroup, J.L., McClimens, B.: The design of mixed-use, virtual auditory displays: Recent findings with a dual-task paradigm. In: Proceedings of the 10th International Conference on Auditory Display, Sydney, Australia (2004)
3. Brock, D., McClimens, B., Hornof, A., Halvorson, T.: Cognitive models of the effect of audio cueing on attentional shifts in a complex multimodal dual-display dual-task. In: 28th Annual Meeting of the Cognitive Science Society (2006)
4. Brock, D., McClimens, B., McCurry, M.: Virtual auditory cueing revisited. In: Proceedings of the 16th International Conference on Auditory Display, Washington, DC (2010)
5. Kieras, D., Meyer, D.: An overview of the EPIC architecture for cognition and performance with application to human-computer interaction. Human Computer Interaction 12, 391–438 (1997)
6. Ballas, J.A., Heitmeyer, C.L., Perez, M.A.: Evaluating two aspects of direct manipulation in advanced cockpits. In: Proceedings of ACM CHI 1992: Conference on Human Factors in Computing Systems, pp. 127–134 (1992)
7. Kieras, D.E., Ballas, J., Meyer, D.E.: Computational Models for the Effects of Localized Sound Cuing in a Complex Dual Task (EPIC Report No. 13). University of Michigan, Department of Electrical Engineering and Computer Science, Ann Arbor, Michigan (2001)
8. Hornof, A.J., Yunfeng, Z.: Task-Constrained Interleaving of Perceptual and Motor Processes in a Time-Critical Dual Task as Revealed Through Eye Tracking. In: Proceedings of ICCM 2010: The 10th International Conference on Cognitive Modeling (2010)
9. Taatgen, N.A., van Rijn, H., Anderson, J.R.: An integrated theory of prospective time interval estimation: The role of cognition, attention, and learning. Psychological Review 114(3), 577–598 (2007)

Relationship between Emotional State and Physiological and Psychological Measurements Using Various Types of Video Content during TV Viewing

Kiyomi Sakamoto[1], Shigeo Asahara[1], Kuniko Yamashita[2], and Akira Okada[2]

[1] Corporate R&D Strategy Office, Panasonic Corporation,
3-1-1 Yagumo-naka-machi, Moriguchi City, Osaka 570-8501, Japan
{sakamoto.kiyomi,asahara.shigeo}@jp.panasonic.com
[2] Department of Human life science, Osaka City University,
3-3-138 Sugimoto, Sumiyoshi-ku, Osaka, 558-8585 Japan n
{yamasita,okada}@ life.osaka-cu.ac.jp

Abstract. Using 42-inch plasma screens and showing four kinds of content, we experimentally evaluated the relationship between TV viewers' emotional state and selected physiological and psychological indices. Our results indicate that near-infrared spectroscopy (NIRS), representing nervous system activity, is a potentially useful index for evaluating emotional states that include "stressed—relaxed," "comfortable—uncomfortable," and "like—dislike." However, LF/HF and HR are affected by complex emotional states in each subject.

Keywords: Emotional states, physiological and psychological measurements, NIRS, Heart rate variability, TV viewing.

1 Introduction

Technological progress and changing lifestyles have led to significant changes in the everyday TV viewing environment. Bigger screens, and TV viewing styles that are becoming more diverse due to broadening content, such as video games and Web pages in addition to conventional TV programs, make it increasingly necessary to consider the effects of these changes on visual fatigue and health. Our previous study investigated visual fatigue with the aim of proposing optimum TV viewing conditions that correspond to the content being viewed and which do not cause eye strain [1]. However, measurements of users' emotional states in additional to visual fatigue are an essential element in designing and developing TVs to minimize visual fatigue while creating a sense of involvement and enjoyment. Current evaluation methods of viewers' emotional states depend chiefly on reports by subjects; however, these evaluations often show considerable variation between individuals. Thus, to be able to improve the accuracy and usefulness of these types of evaluations, it is necessary to measure emotional states objectively. In this study, the authors used both a physiological and a psychological approach. In our psychological evaluation, we

C. Stephanidis (Ed.): Posters, Part I, HCII 2011, CCIS 173, pp. 322–326, 2011.

employed questionnaires and interviews, and attempted to build an objective index of emotional state from two or more physiological indices.

2 Experiment

In the experiment, the participants engaged in TV viewing of four kinds of video content (a recorded concert, scenery, horror, and heartwarming material). Each participant watched all four 10-minute clips in one session, with a two-minute rest period before and after each clip. Physiological indices were monitored while the subjects performed the viewing test.

2.1 Methods

Subjects. Twelve adults aged from their 20s to 30s participated in this experiment.

Measurements. The following items were investigated.

1. Psychological state ("stressed—relaxed," "aroused—sleepy," "focused—distracted," "feeling of involvement—bored," "comfortable—uncomfortable," "like—dislike," "interest," "excitement," "fear," and "visual fatigue"), reported on a scale of 3 to –3, through questionnaires and interviews.
2. Near-infrared spectroscopy (NIRS): brain activity based on total hemoglobin or oxyhemoglobin, obtained by NIRS (NIRS detectors were placed on the left and right of the subject's forehead),
3. Heart rate (HR) and heart rate variability (level of sympathetic nerve activity: LF/HF (LF/HF is defined as the ratio of the low frequency band (LF: 0.04–0.15 Hz) to the high frequency band (HF: 0.15–0.5 Hz) [2] [3], calculated employing FFT analysis using the R-R interval based on heart rate variability obtained via an electrocardiogram),
4. blinking rate, and
5. β/α (Electroencephalogram: EEG; Cz reference).
6. Viewing distances: 165 cm (3H; H is the display height. H of a 42-inch screen is about 55 cm.).

Apparatus

1. The display device was a plasma TV (PDP) (Panasonic TH-42PX600; resolution: HD 1024 x 768, aspect ratio: 16:9, with a 42-inch screen.
2. The viewing distance was set at 3H (165 cm). Viewing distance was defined by screen-to-eye distance in terms of the height (H) of the screen. The display height of the 42-inch screen was set at 55 cm.
3. Test room conditions were maintained at constant levels: ambient temperature of 23 °C, relative humidity of 50%, and illumination of 150 lx. Humidity, which affects blinking rates, was strictly controlled. Illumination was set at 150 lx to simulate the average light level of a Japanese living room based on JIS standardization.

Procedure. Each trial included a 10-minute viewing test, with 2 minutes' rest time between tests. After each trial, the subject gave an assessment of their psychological state, on a scale of 3 to –3. Each item in the questionnaire included three parts: the first part for the early stage, the second for the intermediate stage, and the third for the last stage of the 10-minute viewing test. The order of type of content was different for each subject, chosen using a Latin square. Each trial consisted of two minutes' rest, followed by the ten-minute viewing test, and ended with another two minutes' rest. To prevent buildup of fatigue, a rest, lasting ten minutes, was scheduled between each trial. The measurement items were monitored during the tests.

2.2 Results and Discussions

Correlation among NIRS, HR, LF/HF of HR variability, blinking rate, β/α (EEG) and the subjects' evaluation of their psychological state: The results showed that brain activity, as measured by NIRS (total Hb), decreased in subjects who gave higher scores for "comfortable," with a significant correlation in nine of the twelve subjects; and for "like," and "relaxed," and there was a significant correlation in eight of the twelve subjects; but this was not the case for "feeling of involvement " (Table 1). Some subjects (S2, S4, S6, S7, S11, S12) gave higher scores for "uncomfortable," "dislike," "stressed," and "feeling of involvement," when viewing "horror." Other subjects (S1, S5, S8) gave higher scores for "comfortable," "like," and "feeling of involvement," when viewing "heartwarming material."

These results indicated that NIRS is a potentially useful index for evaluating emotional states that include "stressed—relaxed," "comfortable—uncomfortable," and "like—dislike." Heart rate (HR) rose with higher scores given by some subjects for "comfortable," and "like," but others showed the opposite pattern, with HR rising for high "uncomfortable" and "dislike" scores (Table 1). In six of the twelve subjects, LF/HF also rose, showing a significant correlation with higher scores for "comfortable," but showed the opposite pattern in two of twelve (Table 1). In six of the twelve subjects, LF/HF also rose, showing a significant correlation with higher scores for "relaxed," but in two of twelve, showed the opposite pattern (Table 1). These results indicate that LF/HF and HR are affected by complex emotional states in each subject.

In Figure 1, (a) and (b) show the relationship between the two psychological axes for horror content, and (c) and (d) in Figure 1 show those for heartwarming content. Figures plotted on the X-axis (score for stressed—relaxed) and the Y-axis (score for comfortable—uncomfortable) tended to follow the function ($Y = -X$). This relationship was independent of type of content, as seen in (a) and (c). On the other hand, figures plotted on the X-axis (score for stressed—relaxed) and Y-axis (score for feeling of involvement—bored) tended to follow the function ($Y = -X$) ((d): heartwarming material) or the function ($Y = X$) ((b): horror), and this relationship was dependent on type of content.

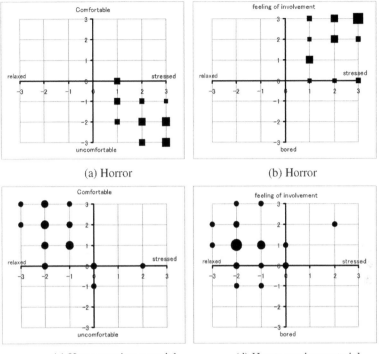

(a) Horror

(b) Horror

(c) Heartwarming material

(d) Heartwarming material

Fig. 1. (a) and (b) in Figure 1 show the relationship between the two psychological axes for horror content, and (c) and (d) in Figure 1 show those for heartwarming material content. The X-axis for (a)-(d) in Figure 1 indicates the subjects' scores for the "stressed—relaxed" psychological state. The Y-axis for (a) and (c) in Figure 1 indicates scores for ("comfortable—uncomfortable"). The Y-axis for (b) and (d) in Figure 1 indicates scores for "feeling of involvement—bored." The font size of the plot markers (●, ■, ◆ and ▲) on the graph grid indicates the number of points that were selected by subjects as their psychological scores. The total number of points was 36 (12 (the number of subjects) x 3 (each item in the questionnaire included in the three parts). The scale of font sizes is 1 to 7 points.

Table 1. Correlation between physiological and psychological states

	like –dislike			stressed– relaxed		
	NIRS	HR	LF/HF	NIRS	HR	LF/HF
S1~S8	N	NULL	P	P	NULL	NULL
S1	NULL	P	N	NULL	NULL	N
S2	N	N	P	P	P	N
S3	N	N	P	NULL	P	N
S4	P	N	NULL	P	N	P
S5	N	P	P	P	N	N
S6	N	N	NULL	P	P	NULL
S7	NULL	N	P	P	P	NULL
S8	N	NULL	P	P	NULL	N
S9	NULL	NULL	N	NULL	N	N
S10	N	N	N	N	N	N
S11	N	N	N	P	P	P
S12	N	NULL	N	P	NULL	NULL

326   K. Sakamoto et al.

Table 1. (*Continued*)

	comfortable–uncomfortable			feeling of involvement–bored		
	NIRS	HR	LF/HF	NIRS	HR	LF/HF
S1~S8	N	NULL	P	NULL	NULL	NULL
S1	NULL	P	P	N	P	N
S2	N	N	P	P	P	N
S3	N	N	P	NULL	P	P
S4	N	P	NULL	P	N	P
S5	N	P	P	N	N	NULL
S6	N	N	NULL	P	P	NULL
S7	N	N	P	P	P	NULL
S8	N	NULL	P	N	NULL	P
S9	NULL	NULL	NULL	P	N	N
S10	NULL	NULL	NULL	N	N	N
S11	N	N	N	P	P	P
S12	N	NULL	N	P	N	N

3 Conclusions

NIRS appears to be a potentially useful index of emotional states, including "stressed—relaxed," "comfortable—uncomfortable," and "like—dislike." However, LF/HF and HR are affected by complex emotional states in each subject, since there were significant negative correlations for some subjects and positive correlations for others between these indices.

Further investigations will be needed to gain a more precise picture of the relationship between emotional state and physiological and psychological measurements when viewing various types of content.

References

1. Sakamoto, K., Aoyama, S., Asahara, S., Yamashita, K., Okada, A.: Evaluation of the effect of viewing distance on visual fatigue in a home viewing environment. Journal of Human Ergology 39(1), 1–14 (2010)
2. Ishibashi, K., Kitamura, S., Kozaki, T., Yasukouchi, A.: Inhibition of Heart Rate Variability during Sleep in Humans By 6700 K Pre-sleep Light Exposure. Journal of Physiological Anthropology 26(1), 39–43 (2007)
3. Ishibashi, K., Ueda, S., Yasukouchi, A.: Effects of Mental Task on Heart Rate Variability during Graded Head-Up Tilt. Journal of Physiological Anthropology 18(6), 225–231 (1999)

Physiological Measurement Applied in Maritime Situations: A Newly Developed Method to Measure Workload on Board of Ships

Wendie Uitterhoeve[1], Marcella Croes-Schalken[2], and Dick Ten Hove[1]

[1] Maritime Research Institute Netherlands, P.O. Box 28,
6700 AA Wageningen, The Netherlands
[2] Maritiem Instituut De Ruyter, P.O. Box 364, 4380 AJ Vlissingen, The Netherlands
{w.m.uitterhoeve,d.t.hove}@marin.nl

Abstract. This article describes a method to measure the effects of workload and human performance on board of ships in navigation tasks. Physiological measurements and both objective and subjective observations were executed simultaneously. The added value in this design is the interpretation of physiological results together with the subjective and objective evaluation of experienced workload and performance. As all of the parameters separately are not indicated as absolute values to rule on workload, combining physiological information with subjective and objective observations leads to a more pronounced insight in workload. With this developed method entering a new terrain is possible, where scientific research of human performance is applied in nautical navigation.

Keywords: Workload measurements, human performance, navigation, manoeuvring simulator, physiological measurements.

1 Introduction

During all kinds of activities, there is a relation between task demand, the amount of effort someone has to put in and the performance. Most optimal is a combination of mediate task demand, minimum effort and maximum performance. By increasing effort an increase in demand can be balanced while performance stays optimal. But a too high demand leads to a decrease of performance. Avoiding such situations starts with measuring the actual workload and performance. Although such methods exist for aviation and automotive, they are not common in nautical settings [2], [3], [4].

2 Methodology

2.1 Basic Principles

The innovative aspect in the developed method to measure workload, effort and performance is the combination of several measurements. The physiological results are interpreted together with the subjective and objective evaluation of experienced

C. Stephanidis (Ed.): Posters, Part I, HCII 2011, CCIS 173, pp. 327–331, 2011.

workload and performance. As all of the parameters separately are not indicated as absolute values to rule on workload, combining physiological information with subjective and objective observations leads to a more pronounced insight in the relation between performance and workload.

2.2 Experiment Set-Up

In cooperation with Dutch pilots and Eagle Science, the developed method is tested during simulations on a full-mission manoeuvring bridge simulator and in real life on board of sea-going vessels. In this initial experiment the main task was to safely guide a car carrier underneath a bridge immediately after a quarter bend. Difficult in this scenario was the strong side wind, which made turning and lining-up just before the bridge a complex manoeuvre. During the so-called decision point the candidate had to decide whether to pass the bridge or not: if not lined-up correctly, the manoeuvre should be aborted and started again.

2.3 Detailed Description of Used Components

Reference Level. Indicating stressfull situations is difficult without recording a reference situation during relaxation. No exact number represents workload, only changes in several phenomenon give an indication of the level of workload. For that reason a zero load physiological measurement (in rest) expanded with an interview and anamnesis is essential.

Physiological Measurements. The human body responds in several ways to increasing effort. In this experiment three physiological aspects were measured using a portable multi-channel system carried by the candidates, namely the electrical activity of the heart muscle by an electrocardiogram (ECG), the respiration by measuring the expansion of the chest and abdomen and finally the electrical activity of facial muscles using electromyography (EMG). With these measurements information is collected about heart rate and heart rate variability, respiration rate and tidal volume, and the amount of muscle tension in the face.

Task Analysis. In order to get a feeling of the workload during the experiment, the amount of orders and/or operations was listed. This can be done by an observer or by analysing time traces of for example the steering actions or changes in the propulsion settings.

Performance Rating. In this experiment the main task, which was to safely guide a car carrier underneath a bridge, was rated in total by an expert using an assessment form. Hereby five key skills, specific for a piloting task, were defined and rated.

Effort Rating. Immediately after the simulation, the candidate has to fill in a Rating Scale of Mental Effort [1]. The candidate rates how much effort he had invested during the piloting task. This RSME ranges from 0 to 150, and is labeled from 'absolutely no effort' (score 3) to 'extreme effort' (score 114). Additionally the candidate is interviewed to get information about experienced effort during specific incidents, to be used as input for subsequent analysis.

Observations and Event Description. As stated before, no individual result is absolute in capturing the amount of experienced workload and human performance. Only a combination of several phenomenon, registered in one or more of the previous ratings and measurements, pointing in the same direction confirm a total view of the situation. In contrast with automotive and aviation, sailors have more freedom to move. A video registration of the operational pilot is not always sufficient. For that reason, additional observations by the researcher during the sailing are essential to get a total impression of the situation and to correctly interpret the outcome of the above mentioned variables.

3 Results

3.1 Applicability of Method

The experiment showed that it is possible to measure workload, experienced effort and performance. The interpretation of physiological results together with the subjective and objective evaluation of experienced workload and performance results in an overall picture of the situation. The answers from the interviews combined with the heart rate variability are a good estimate of the moment that the candidate experiences increased effort. In all the simulations the candidates identified the decision point as most strenuous, which was also visible in the HRV analysis. The performance during stressfull moments adds information about the ability to maintain the task. To find the cause of increased effort and/or decreased performance, information from the task analysis together with the findings of the observer can be used. Task analysis and subjective results were used to focus on the details of the physiological measurements.

3.2 Physiological Results

Two different ways of analysing the signals from the ECG give interesting results. The first is a spectral analysis, using three band-pass filters indicating not only the activity of the coherence between respiration and heart beat (MF 0.06-0.14 Hz), but also the activity of the autonomic nerve system, containing a sympatic part (active during stress, LF 0.02-0.06 Hz) and a parasympatic part (active during recovering, HF 0.14-0.45 Hz). Healthy people in rest show a larger value for the coherence parameter compared to people experiencing more stress, because their heart beat is more correlated to the respiration frequency. See also figure 1, shown below. Although in this figure the value for the amount of energy in the sympatic region seems the same, the absolute value during stress is much higher than during the relaxation moment. The amount of parasympatic energy is higher during the stress moment than in rest, which seems paradoxical. During the relaxation measurement there was no need to recover, while after the period with increased effort the parasympatic counterpart starts to recover the body. This leads to a larger absolute and relative contribution of the parasympaticus.

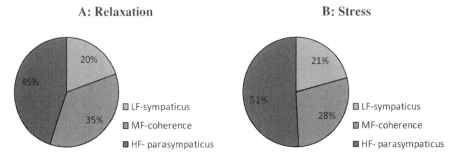

Fig. 1. Results from spectral analysis of heart beat. Presented is the amount of energy in three specific frequency areas. A: shows the values for a healthy person in rest, B: shows the values for the same person in a stress situation.

The second type of analysis is about heart rate variability (HRV). During relaxation large variation between two heart beats occurs, i.e. great HRV. The inter beat interval (IBI) becomes smaller and more constant in time if someone experiences increased effort. This is presented in figure 2 which shows the inter beat interval during a moment of relaxation and stress. Both the mean value and deviation of the inter beat intervals are larger in rest than during a moment of stress. In the stress situation, the cloud with inter beat intervals shifts to the lower left corner.

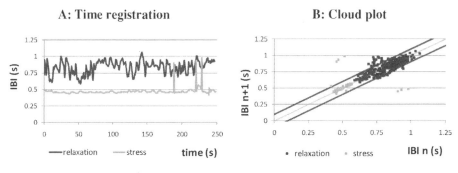

Fig. 2a. Time registration of inter beat intervals   **Fig. 2b.** Cloud plot of inter beat intervals

Both for the same person during relaxation and during the decision point (stress).

Although the usefulness of the heart beat measurement is very valuable, the results of the respiration and facial muscle measurement were insufficient to show any relation with performance and mental effort. A combination of technical problems during the measurement and results which were not clearly interpretable, made the respiration and facial muscle measurement subordinately.

3 Conclusions

The interpretation of physiological results together with subjective and objective observations gives a good evaluation of experienced workload and performance. The contribution of the physiological measurements, and especially the results from the heart, are an added value.

4 Future Applications

During a future experiment a more specific primary task, which time traces can be analysed afterwards, will be indicated. As an example deviation from a predefined track, speed or drift angle can be used as performance standard. The performance measurements can be expanded with rating a secondary tasks, using a so called peripheral detection task. The candidates reaction time by pressing a button when a light flashes, gives additional information about the relation between effort and performance. Also possible relations between task analysis, performance, RMSE score and physiological results will be examined.

With this developed method entering a new terrain is possible. A terrain where scientific research of human performance is applied in nautical navigation. Physiological measurements can substantiate employability of sailors, assessments and selections, but also contribute in developing new waterways or harbours.

Acknowledgments. Special thanks to the volunteers from the Dutch Pilot Association for their contribution in the experiment.

References

1. Zijlstra, F.R.H.: Efficiency in work behavior. A design approach for modern tools. PhD thesis, Delft University of Technology. Delft, The Netherlands (1993)
2. De Waard, D.: The Measurement of Drivers Mental Workload. PhD thesis, University of Groningen, Traffic Research Centre. Haren, The Netherlands (1996)
3. Veltman, J.A., Gaillard, A.W.K.: Pilot workload evaluated with subjective and physiological measures. In: Brookhuis, K.A., Welkert, J., De Waard, D. (eds.) Proceedings of the Europe Chapter of the Human Factors ans Ergonomics Society Annual Meeting in Soasterberg, Aging and Human Factor, November 1993, pp. 107–128. University of Groningen, Traffic Research Centre, Haren, The Netherlands (1996)
4. Grootjen, M., Neerincx, M.A., van Weert, J.C.M., Truong, K.P.: Measuring cognitive task load on a naval ship: Implications of a real world environment. In: Schmorrow, D.D., Reeves, L.M. (eds.) HCII 2007 and FAC 2007. LNCS (LNAI), vol. 4565, pp. 147–156. Springer, Heidelberg (2007)

Physiological Correlates of Emotional State

Andrea K. Webb, Meredith G. Cunha, S.R. Prakash, and John M. Irvine

Charles S. Draper Laboratory,
555 Technology Square, Cambridge, Massachusetts, USA
{awebb,mcunha,sprakash,jirvine}@draper.com

Abstract. This study examined the relationship between emotion and physiological measures of autonomic system response. Features of electrodermal, cardiac, respiratory, movement, and oculomotor response were measured from a population of normal subjects while they were presented standard acoustic and visual stimuli designed to evoke specific emotions. The subjects' assessments of their emotional response to the stimuli (self-report) were also recorded. We present results of a preliminary analysis of the statistical relationship between the stimulus category, the physiological features and self-report. We found significant differences across stimulus categories, as well as across self-reported emotions, suggesting that a combination of features could be used to classify the emotional content of a discrete stimulus. We also examine the dependence of physiological signals on the mode of stimulus presentations.

Keywords: Affect, emotion, psychophysiology.

1 Introduction

The emotional state has an important influence on an individual's cognitive and behavioral response to external events. As a result, there is increasing interest in the emotional component of social (Parkinson, 1996) and human-computer interactions (reviewed in (Brave & Nass, 2002)). An individual's emotional state, however, remains inaccessible to direct measurement and manipulation. A number of studies have examined the question of indirectly assessing the emotional state by measuring observable correlates of emotion (Cowie, et al., 2001): facial expressions (Fasel & Luettin, 2003; Pantic & Rothkrantz, 2000), gestures (Mitra & Acharya, 2007) and gait (Karg, Kuhnlenz, & Buss), speech and voice patterns (Murray & Arnott, 1993), self-reports of the subjects experiencing the emotion, and physiological signals. Of these measures, physiology is least amenable to being influenced by voluntary action on part of the subject, and is therefore a promising indicator of the "true" emotional state. However, the mechanisms relating emotion and its physiological correlates, particularly the autonomic nervous system are poorly understood, subject to a number of confounding non-emotional influences, and to large inter-individual variation. As a result, few human-computer interface systems incorporate physiological measurements to assess affective state.

C. Stephanidis (Ed.): Posters, Part I, HCII 2011, CCIS 173, pp. 332–336, 2011.
© Springer-Verlag Berlin Heidelberg 2011

In this study, we examine the relationship between physiological measurements and emotional state in a population of normal subjects presented standard affective stimuli. Prior work has found that there are differences in physiological responding when looking at pictures (Lang, Greenwald, Bradley, & Hamm, 1993) and for positive and negative emotions during directed facial action tasks (Ekman, Levenson, & Friesen, 1983; Levenson, Ekman, & Friesen, 1990). Prior work, however, typically has not looked at multiple stimulus modalities or included a broad array of physiological sensors. Our aim was to expand upon previous work by including a greater variety of physiological sensors and multiple emotion elicitation modalities.

2 Methods

32 participants (ages 19-55, 53% male, 47% female) were recruited from among employees of the laboratory. Informed consent was obtained, and the protocol approved by the New England Institutional Review Board.

Respiration and electrocardiogram (ECG) were collected with a Vivometrics Lifeshirt. Skin conductance (SC), finger pulse activity (FP), and gross body movement were collected with a Lafayette LX4000 polygraph. Pupil diameter and eye movement information were collected with a Tobii X50 eye tracker.

Emotionally evocative images and sounds were selected from the International Affective Picture System (Lang, et al., 1993) and International Affective Digital Sounds System (Bradley & Lang, 1999), respectively. Four stimuli for each emotion category and 4 neutral stimuli were selected, resulting in a total of 24 images and 24 sounds. E-Prime (Psychology Software Tools, Pittsburgh, PA) was used to control stimulus presentation. Each stimulus was presented for 6 seconds. Participants were then given 15 seconds to rate on a 7-point Likert scale (1=not at all, 7=a great amount) how much they felt of each of happiness, sadness, anger, fear, and disgust. For the mental imagery portion, participants were asked to remember for a 30-second period a specific personal event in which they felt the specified emotion. Participants then provided self-report ratings for how much they felt of each emotion.

CPSLAB (Scientific Assessment Technologies, Salt Lake City, UT) was used to remove artifacts from the signals, extract features, and perform within-subject standardization. Ten features were extracted for each stimulus: SC area to full recovery, SC level, respiration line length, activity line length extracted from the gross body movement, pupil diameter amplitude, FP level, FP rise time from the first low point, standard deviation of interbeat interval (IBI) derived from the ECG signal, and IBI area to full recovery. Averages were computed for each emotion, and within-subject z-scores were computed for each feature for each subject.

3 Results

The specificity of each response feature to the emotion category of the evoking stimulus was analyzed using discriminant function analysis, where the feature values were independent variables and the emotion category was the grouping variable. The results of this analysis are shown as a confusion matrix in Table 1 for images and

Table 2 for sounds, where the chance level is 20%. It can be seen from these tables that classification accuracy was above chance for each emotion for both images and sounds. Note that this is post-hoc analysis – cross-validation of these findings against and independent set of data is needed to improve our level of confidence in response classification.

We then examined the physiological responses to internally generated emotions (via the mental imagery task). The discriminant function analysis results for these data are shown in Table 3. We find that the correspondence between the emotional state and response is similar to that found for external stimuli, except when the intended internal emotion was *fear*.

We next examined how the subjects' self-report of their emotional state correlated with the emotion the external stimulus was intended to evoke. Figure 1 summarizes the findings across stimulus modalities. We see that on average, the emotion experienced most strongly by subjects corresponded to the emotion the stimulus was supposed to evoke.

4 Discussion

In this study, we wished to quantify indirect correlates of emotional state, particularly in autonomic physiological responses. The approach was to use established corpora of acoustic and visual stimuli purported to evoke specific emotions, and to examine relationships between stimuli and responses.

The results shown in Table 1 indicate that a linear combination of the set of physiological response features is significantly correlated with the stimulus category. The differences between the values for images and sounds suggest that auditory and visual stimuli result in slightly different physiological responses.

Table 1. Classification percentages for image (I) and sound (S) stimuli

	Disgust		Sadness		Fear		Anger		Happiness	
	I	S	I	S	I	S	I	S	I	S
Disgust	**58.6**	**50.0**	13.8	10.0	3.4	20.0	13.8	20.0	10.3	0.0
Sadness	6.9	6.7	**48.3**	**56.7**	10.3	13.3	24.1	10.0	10.3	13.3
Fear	3.4	10.0	20.7	20.0	**55.2**	**43.3**	6.9	6.7	13.8	20.0
Anger	24.1	13.3	6.9	3.3	17.2	10.0	**44.8**	**66.7**	6.9	6.7
Happiness	17.2	6.7	6.9	23.3	10.3	10.0	3.4	13.3	**62.1**	**46.7**

Table 2 shows that different emotional states evoked internally by mental imagery can also produce significantly different physiological responses. However, the differences between Tables 1 and 2 suggest that either the internal emotional states or the physiological responses produced by mental imagery may be different from those produced by corresponding external stimuli.

Finally, Figure 1 suggests that the stimuli in the corpora can evoke emotional responses with reasonable accuracy (as assessed by the subject). However, the evoked state is a mixture of different emotions. This dependence between the emotional categories could be used in optimizing the design of a classifier that uses physiological responses.

Table 2. Classification percentages for internal Mental Imagery

	Disgust	Sadness	Fear	Anger	Happiness
Disgust	**53.3**	10.0	6.7	13.3	16.7
Sadness	10.0	**53.3**	6.7	6.7	23.3
Fear	20.0	16.7	**16.7**	20.0	26.7
Anger	16.7	10.0	20.0	**50.0**	3.3
Happiness	0.0	20.0	20.0	13.3	**46.7**

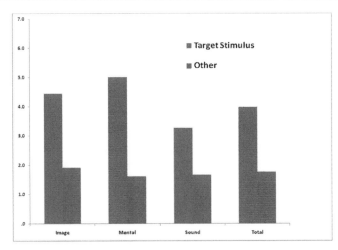

Fig. 1. Self-reported emotional responses to standard stimuli

Our measurements suggest that physiology offers a promising way to identify emotion, but the mappings from stimulus to emotional state and from emotion to physiology are subject to ambiguity. While our current results cannot resolve whether these ambiguities arise from systematic inter-subject differences or from large trial-to-trial variability within each subject, future studies will re-examine the data to develop subject-specific emotion inference methods, and study the test-retest reliability of these methods.

References

1. Bradley, M., Lang, P.J.: The International affective digitized sounds (IADS) stimuli, instruction manual and affective ratings: NIMH Center for the Study of Emotion and Attention (1999)
2. Brave, S., Nass, C.: Emotion in human-computer interaction. The human-computer interaction handbook: fundamentals, evolving technologies and emerging applications, 81–96 (2002)
3. Cowie, R., Douglas-Cowie, E., Tsapatsoulis, N., Votsis, G., Kollias, S., Fellenz, W., et al.: Emotion recognition in human-computer interaction. IEEE Signal Processing Magazine 18(1), 32–80 (2001)

4. Ekman, P., Levenson, R.W., Friesen, W.V.: Autonomic nervous system activity distinguishes among emotions. Science 221(4616), 1208 (1983)
5. Fasel, B., Luettin, J.: Automatic facial expression analysis: a survey. Pattern Recognition 36(1), 259–275 (2003)
6. Karg, M., Kuhnlenz, K., Buss, M.: Recognition of affect based on gait patterns. IEEE Transactions on Systems, Man, and Cybernetics, Part B: Cybernetics 40(4), 1050–1061
7. Lang, P.J., Greenwald, M.K., Bradley, M.M., Hamm, A.O.: Looking at pictures: Affective, facial, visceral, and behavioral reactions. Psychophysiology 30(3), 261–273 (1993)
8. Levenson, R.W., Ekman, P., Friesen, W.V.: Voluntary facial action generates emotion-specific autonomic nervous system activity. Psychophysiology 27(4), 363–384 (1990)
9. Mitra, S., Acharya, T.: Gesture recognition: A survey. IEEE Transactions on, Systems, Man, and Cybernetics, Part C: Applications and Reviews 37(3), 311–324 (2007)
10. Murray, I.R., Arnott, J.L.: Toward the simulation of emotion in synthetic speech: A review of the literature on human vocal emotion. Journal of the Acoustical Society of America (1993)
11. Pantic, M., Rothkrantz, L.J.M.: Automatic analysis of facial expressions: The state of the art. IEEE Transactions on, Pattern Analysis and Machine Intelligence 22(12), 1424–1445 (2000)
12. Parkinson, B.: Emotions are social. Br. J. Psychol. 87(Pt 4), 663–683 (1996)

A Study on the Operator's Erroneous Responses to the New Human Interface of a Digital Device to be Introduced to Nuclear Power Plants

Yeon Ju Oh, Yong Hee Lee, and Jong Hun Yun

I&C and Human Factors Division, Korea Atomic Energy Research Institute(KAERI),
Yuseong-Gu, Daejoen, 305-353, Korea
{ohyj,yhlee,jhyun}@kaeri.re.kr

Abstract. It is extremely difficult to investigate completely the defects in digital devices, and to prevent human errors in their interface during the design aspect of nuclear power plants (NPPs). Human interface errors have been investigated through usability studies and reliability analysis (HRA). Several methods and various programs are available for prevention of human errors. However, it is very limited to explain the detail mechanism of human errors by quantitative usability approaches. Therefore, we define Error Segment (ES) and Interaction Segment (IS) to predict a specific human error potential (HEP) in a digital device and its human interface. In this study predicted HEP is to be verified by experiments including data analysis of EEG, ECG and behavioral observations. Thus the HEP in the human interface of a digital device can be more carefully considered for preventing human errors in NPPs.

Keywords: human error, EEG, ECG, nuclear power plant, human interface.

1 Introduction

Human error means the potential to reduce the system efficiency, safety and performance. Researchers have tried to predict and prevent all human errors. However, it has been complicated to understand human error in past control room design that had been established by high technology digital instruments. This is due to the existing quantitative methods that include HRA and usability studies being problematic when considering marginal human errors by using new digital devices. Thus, it is necessary to predict the error potential specific to the device prior to the design. A new method is proposed to find out human error potential to digital device human interface [1]. The objective of this study is to verify the predicted erroneous responses by measuring physiological signal (EEG and ECG) and observing the human behaviors. By determining ISs according to the unit's physical exterior and operational options of the digital devices, and tested them as ESs.

Initially *Error Segment (ES) and Interaction Segment (IS)* are established and investigated by selecting two smart-phones (named A and B) [1, 2]. They have been used restrictively in NPPs. Type A has fewer physical exterior units and fewer segments than Type B. Table 1 shows a few ISs. We found a case of HEP at 'V+' in ES and 'Horizontal mode' in IS. Operators interpret the Volume increase button (V+)

C. Stephanidis (Ed.): Posters, Part I, HCII 2011, CCIS 173, pp. 337–341, 2011.
© Springer-Verlag Berlin Heidelberg 2011

differently according to a no option and a horizontal mode in IS. However they showed the same responses. When V+ is in the horizontal mode, it resulted in turning down the volume. It causes confusion to subjects by violating the interface design standard on space compatibility. If V+ of ES is in a horizontal mode, the volume decreases by stage or rapidly. Because V+ is on the left of the device in the horizontal mode, subjects are likely to push the left button for decreasing the volume [2].

Table 1. The example of HEP from IS and ES of A and B type smart phone

ES		IS				
Code	Operation method	Operation situation				
		No option(Vertical)	Manner mode	Horizontal mode	Multi task	Lock
P	One Click	Screen on/off				
	Long Click	Pup-up window for option				
V +	One Click	Volume up by stages	Manner mode cancel and volume up by stages	Volume up by stages (space compatibility violation	Volume up by stages	None
	Long Click	Volume up rapidly	Manner mode cancel and volume up rapidly	Operation intention: down	Volume up rapidly	None
V -	One Click	Volume down by stages → manner mode	Vibration	Volume down by stages (space compatibility violation)	Volume down by stages → manner mode	None
	Long Click	Volume down rapidly → manner mode	Vibration	Operation intention: up	Volume down rapidly → manner mode	None
T	Rotation	Move	Move	Move	Move	None
	Click	Selection	Selection	Selection	Selection	None

2 Experiments

We conduct an experimental verification to confirm the predicted HEP at 1.1. Two kinds of smart phones currently used by NPPs with some functions (logging system) are named type A and B. The Type A smart phone has fewer physical exterior units and fewer segments than those of type B. Five graduate students who were not familiar with the device (smart phone) procedures participated for monetary compensation on a voluntary basis. It was assumed that subjects were all on the same level of task procedure knowledge. The five subjects can be regarded as representative participants. Subjects were informed of the experiment method, and randomly complete each trial. After each trial was completed, ten minutes of rest was provided to the subjects. The task for this experiment is shown in (table 2). Task 2 was considered with the HEP.

The experiment includes three steps. The first one is a video recording and observation to determine the error rate and task performance during tasks. The second one is analyzing EEG/ECG by their frequency trends and patterns. These approaches are to find out the error potential and non-error section. There are several analysis methods to understand including law data graph trend, specific frequency pattern, brain activity, and statistical approach. After the experiments, all subjects evaluated their subjective workload by NASA-TLX. Figure 1 shows the experiment process.

EEGs and ECG were recorded in 8 channels by *POLYG-I of Laxtha*. It was measured by international 10-20 lead standard. Fp1, Fp2, F3, F4, P3, P4, O1, O2 leads were used with Ag/AgCl electrodes. The impedance was below 10☐ on all electrodes. Physiological signals were filtered by band pass filter, and sampled by 512Hz. The EEG components of the following four frequency bands are obtained delta (0.5~3.5Hz), theta (4~7Hz), alpha (8~12Hz), and beta (13~30Hz). We analyzed $\beta/(\alpha+\beta+\theta+\delta)$ by frequency band and also confirmed brain activity by mapping during performing tasks.

Table 2. Tasks designed for experiment

| Step | ES | IS | | Performance Item |
		Task 1	Task 2	
1	P			Power and screen on
2	M, I, T	One click	One click	Take a picture in the field
3	I, B	No option	Horizontal Mode	Send the message to MCR with short message
4	V			Turn down the volume during step 3

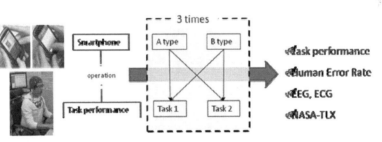

Fig. 1. The experiment procedure

3 Experimental Results

We tested the error rate, task performance (reaction time), EEG, ECG, NASA-TLX. Subjects were required to completely perform all preset task steps in the each task. The number of steps to complete the task was fixed. The total steps executed by a participant minus the steps preset would be the number of human errors. The number of error times was significantly more in task 2 than task 1 and significantly less in type A than type B. The average error rate is presented in table 3. Based on the results, there were significant differences between task 1 and 2 except the third repetition (*: $p\text{-}value<0.05$, **: $p\text{-}value<0.1$). The highest error rate was appeared in step 4. It was getting decreased after practicing about three times. The task performance of participants on different task types was analyzed as the reaction time. The reaction time between A and B type smart phone was significant ($p\text{-}value<0.05$). Also, the results showed that the average task performance (reaction) time was significantly different between task 1 and 2 (table 3). In the third repetition, there was no significant difference between tasks but the reaction time was the shortest. When a subject had an error in a specific part, the reaction time had sharply increased. One subject was confused and repeated the same procedure several times even though he was right because he didn't know whether it's right or not. One other subject performed the same task very quickly although he made errors. Thus, there was no correlation between reaction time and error.

Table 3. The results table for error rate and reaction times

Repeat	Analysis Items	Error Rate(%)				Reaction Time(s)			
		A type		B type		A type		B type	
		Task 1	Task 2	Task 1	Task 2	Task 1	Task 2	Task 1	Task 2
1	average	42	52	60	66	358.7	374.74	433.4	448.78
	S.D	10.95	4.47	7.07	8.94	41.45	54.13	50.11	52.34
	P-value	0.034*		0.007*		0.054*		0.077*	
2	average	22	30	36	42	279.98	311.76	359.8	374.32
	S.D	4.47	7.07	5.48	8.37	27.25	24.70	30.20	23.69
	P-value	0.099**		0.208		0.003*		0.01*	
3	average	10	14	22	24	147.82	230.26	252.6	273.18
	S.D	0	5.48	4.47	5.48	28.54	63.35	98.64	91.53
	P-value	0.374		0.178		0.696		0.225	

NASA-TLX results show that subjective workload of participants between task 1 and 2 were significantly different ($t=-2.807$, p-$value=0.038$). In task 2, all items had higher value than task 1. However, there was no significance difference between smart phone types. It shows that most participants had higher mental focus and concentrated efforts in performances than physical, temporal demand and frustration levels. (table 4).

Table 4. NASA-TLX

NASA-TLX		Mental	Physical	Temporal	Effort	Performance	Frustration
A type	Task 1	52.6	20.4	35	60	64	36
	Task 2	54	24	40	74	78	38
B type	Task 1	47.2	21	33	68.8	70	35.6
	Task 2	68	30	52	70	80	74

The heart rate in rest phase was continually recorded by ECG during and before the experiment. The heart rate difference was calculated in the rest status subtracted from average heart rate. The result shows that there was no significant difference between task1 and 2, and error and non-error section. Thus, heart rates by task types and error potential did not show any differences even though subjects felt some load subjectively.

Average beta activity of EEG data was showed as $\beta/(\alpha+\beta+\theta+\delta)$. The trends between task 1 and 2 look similar. The average beta band activity was increased from the front to the back of the brain. It was shown same results in type A and B, and there was significant difference between tasks (p-$value<0.05$). Figure 2 shows a comparison between error section and non-error section. Several statistical analyses were applied to the pattern of EEG graph, specific frequency band activity, and brain mapping. The error and non-error section could be separated by frequency band shown in figure 2. The error section has more frequency band than non-error one (p-$value<0.05$). However, the frequency data were mixed by noise; it is not easy to separate precisely.

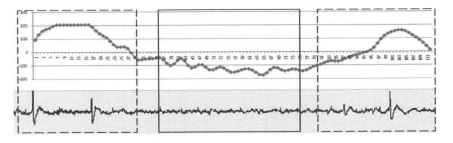

Fig. 2. The error and non-error section of a channel of EEG, the top graph is raw data from EEG according to recording time and the down graph shows two error section

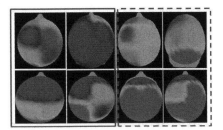

Fig. 3. The brain mapping between non-error and error section

Second, the section could be confirmed by brain mapping. The red area showed the brain activity was high. The high brain activity appeared when subjects concentrated on the task and became nervous because they had made an error.

4   Conclusions

Many alarms and user-friendly display features in digital devices were not enough to prevent human error in NPPs. The most urgent demand is to find out the detail mechanisms of human errors of digital device, and then consider them during the digital device interface design in NPPs. This study experimentally tried to verify the HEP predicted by ES and IS of a digital device by observation and measurement of EEG, ECG. We could discriminate the difference between error and non-error section, but it was not sensitive enough. A more detailed analysis technique is necessary to compare between the error section and non-error section. Since we are in a primary stage to find out the human error potential by experiments, further study is demanded to introduce the digital device without any human error in NPPs.

References

1. Hee, L.Y., Tong-il, J., Kyo, L.H.: A modification of human error analysis technique for designing man-machine interface in nuclear power plants. Journal of the Ergonomics Society of Korea 22(1), 31–42 (2003)
2. Hun, Y.J., Ju, O.Y., Hee, L.Y.: A development of the low extreme human error analysis method for using smart phone in NPPs. In: Proceeding of a Symposium for Recent Instrumentation and Control Techniques in Nuclear Power Plant (2010)

To Substitute Fast-Forward/Backward Keys for Numeric Keypad of TV Remote Controller

Horng-Yi Yu[1], Jui-Ping Ma[2], and T.K. Philip Hwang[3]

[1] Ph. D. Student, College of Design, National Taipei University of Technology, Taiwan
[2] Ph. D. Student, College of Design, National Taipei University of Technology, Taiwan
[3] Associate Professor, Dept. of Industrial Design,
National Taipei University of Technology, Taiwan
1, Sec. 3, Chung-hsiao E. Rd., Taipei,10608,Taiwan, R.O.C.
phwang@ntut.edu.tw

Abstract. This paper describes the problems of TV channel change using existing remote controller. French company Witbe (2008) have determined the average channel change takes 1.9 seconds by using the up/down button on a remote; 3.4 seconds if it's chosen directly by numeric keypad. Accordingly, the pilot study of this research revealed that the mental workload (frequency of visual focuses shifting between TV screen and remote controller) of using numeric keypad was higher than that of using up/down keys. A pair of dedicated keys were developed and located near up/down keys. The functions of dedicated keys were set as fast-forward 10 channels and fast-backward 10 channels respectively. An experiment was carried and the result indicates that mental workload of operating dedicated keys was significantly improved. The average vision focuses shifting frequency of operating numeric keypad and dedicated keys set were 2.5 times and 1.0 times respectively.

Keywords: fast-forward key, mental workload, remote controller.

1 Introduction

This paper describes the problems of TV channel change using existing remote controller, in which, up/down buttons provide users with channel browsing function, and, numeric keypad provides direct channel change. French company Witbe (2008)[1] have determined the average channel change takes 1.9 seconds by using the up/down button on a remote; 3.4 seconds if it's chosen directly by numeric keypad. Accordingly, the pilot study of this research revealed that the mental workload[2] (frequency of visual focuses shifting between TV screen and remote controller) of using numeric keypad was higher than that of using up/down keys.

---

[1] French company Witbe website, 2010.10.18, http://www.witbe.net/qoe/Presse/revue-de-presse.html
[2] During processing of information, attentional resources will be consumed. The extent of this consumption, the mental workload, will vary with the complexity of the processing task (quantity of information to be allocated attention, number of mental operations to be performed and processing structures involved) and with the time-margins available for completing the task.

C. Stephanidis (Ed.): Posters, Part I, HCII 2011, CCIS 173, pp. 342–345, 2011.
© Springer-Verlag Berlin Heidelberg 2011

1.1 Adjusting Visual Focus Provoked Mental Workload

A pair of dedicated keys were developed and located near up/down keys. The functions of dedicated keys were set as fast-forward 10 channels and fast-backward 10 channels respectively. The hypothesis is that the combined use of up/down keys and fast- forward/backward key would actually reduce mental workload of channel selection. Kazuteru et al. (2001)[3] performed remote controls operation tests with elderly subjects. The results of this subjective evaluation showed that subjects significantly prefer those controls without having to move visual focuses between TV screen and remote controller frequently within experiment task. In this case, shifting and adjusting visual focus provoked mental workload.

1.2 Pilot Study

In the pilot study, problems of using numeric keypad for channel switching were found, including error number operation and frequent shifting of vision focus between television screen and remote controller. The vision focuses movement of correspondents were recorded in the tasks of TV channel change using existing remote controller. Significant higher moving frequency of vision focus between TV screen and remote controller was found in direct channel change using numeric keypad, which indicated that much mental and perceptual demand was required.

2 Method

In order to improve the operation efficiency of channel switching, a pair of dedicated keys was utilized for fast channel switching. Two dedicated keys were set respectively near up/down keys (navigation key) and were design for the function of forward/backward 10 channels for every pushing down (as shown in Fig. 1).

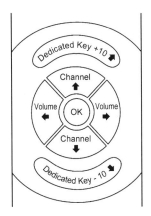

Fig. 1. A pair of dedicated keys were developed and located near up/down keys. The functions of dedicated keys were set as fast-forward 10 channels and fast-backward 10 channels respectively.

---

[3] Kazuteru et al.: Evaluation of usability of TV remote controls for elderly people in a GUI environment_full paper. 映像情報メディア学会誌, Vol.55, No.10, pp.1345-1352 (2001).

An experiment was carried out to verify the hypothesis by comparing the mental workload of operating dedicated keys set with mental workload of operating numeric keypad. 30 correspondents of 3 age groups were invited to complete 5 set of channel selection tasks individually. Moving frequency of vision focus between TV screen and remote controller was recorded, while response time and error rate were also recorded as reference.

2.1 Respondents

The experiment was carried out by testing respondents of 3 age groups: 10 to 20, 21 to 40 and 41 to 60 years old with equal number of males and females.

2.2 Procedures

The purpose of usability test is to to verify the hypothesis by comparing the mental workload of operating dedicated key set with that of operating numeric keypad. Respondents were tested through 2 steps:

1. Channel change tasks (reaction time and error rate) of operating numeric keypad of the existing TV remote control (SONY BRAVIA KDL-32V4000).
2. Channel change tasks (reaction time and error rate) of operating the dedicated keys of the designed TV remote controller (design outcome of this study).

2.3 Measures

The usability test employed SONY BRAVIA KDL-32V4000 TV and the sensor of infrared rays to simulate the situation of channel selection. The moving frequency of vision focus of correspondents will be recorded by the video camera. The response time and error rate were recorded followed by statistics comparison.

The processing seems to continuously provide output, whether or not the analyses are completed. Consequently, when the demands of a task exceed the available resources, mental overload will occur and task performance will deteriorate. When two (or more) tasks are time-shared, i.e. performed concurrently, attention will be divided between them, i.e., the tasks must share the resources that are available. If the total demand of the two tasks exceeds the available resources, the two tasks will interfere (Ross et al., 1996)[4].

Actions such as pointing at objects, changing their arrangement, turning them, occluding them, annotating and counting, may serve as epistemic actions that decrease the mental workload of a task by drawing upon resources that are external to the mind (Shaer, 2009)[5]. These mentioned factors were taken into consideration of tasks in this study.

---

[4] Ross T., et al.: HARDIE design guidelines handbook: human factors guidelines for information presentation by ATT systems. Luxembourg: Commission of the European Communities. (1996).

[5] Shaer, O.: Tangible User Interfaces: Past, Present, and Future Directions. Foundations and Trends® in Human–Computer Interaction, Vol. 3, No. 1–2 (2009).

3   Conclusion

The result indicates that mental workload of operating the designed TV remote controller was significantly improved. The average vision focuses shifting frequency of operating numeric keypad and dedicated keys set were 2.5 times and 1.0 times respectively. Among three age groups, older age group of 40-60 presented better improvement of mental effort (average 1.7 times decrease of vision focuses shifting frequency) by using dedicated keys set. Follows by younger age group of 10-20 and adult group of 20-40 (average 1.5 times and 1.2 times decrease of vision focuses shifting frequency respectively). (as shown in Table 1).

Table 1. The average vision focuses shifting frequency per user groups

Age groups	10 to 20		20 to 40		40 to 60	
operation keys	dedicated keys	numeric keypad	dedicated keys	numeric keypad	dedicated keys	numeric keypad
average frequency of vision focuses shifting	1.4	3.6	1.6	3.2	1.8	6.2

Presbyopia is the decreasing ability of the lens to focus with increasing age. people see the steady decline in amplitude of accommodation from the early forties, and generally by 45 years, most people begin to notice problems associated with this (Ross et al., 1996). Beyond the age of five years, the capacity to change the way the visual system works diminishes. When presbyopia sets in, symptom of difficult reading fine print, particularly in low light conditions (Pope, 2011), makes reading numeric keypad an unpleasant experience. Another symptom of momentarily blurred vision when transitioning between viewing distances (ibid.) also troublesome to older age group. These indications clearly illustrate why the 40 to 60 age groups performed better efficiency while less vision focuses shifting are required in the experiment task.

References

1. French company Witbe website (2010.10.18),
   http://www.witbe.net/qoe/Presse/revue-de-presse.html
2. Kazuteru, et al.: Evaluation of usability of TV remote controls for elderly people in a GUI environment_full paper. 映像情報メディア学会誌 55(10), 1345–1352 (2001)
3. Defence Standard 00-25: Human factors for designers of equipment. Part 7. Visual displays Issue 1, MoD (1986)
4. Ross, T., et al.: HARDIE design guidelines handbook: human factors guidelines for information presentation by ATT systems. Luxembourg: Commission of the European Communities (1996)
5. Shaer, O.: Tangible User Interfaces: Past, Present, and Future Directions. Foundations and Trends® in Human–Computer Interaction 3(1–2) (2009)
6. Patrick, B.G.: Why do we have to "get used to" presbyopic corrections? Eyewitness Fourth Quarter (2006)
7. Pope, W.K.: Common Eye Conditions And Treatment.,
   http://parkwoodvision.com (cited at March 26, 2011)

Part V
Inclusive Design and Accessibility

Digital Inclusion Index (DII) – Measuring ICT Supply and Usage to Support DI Implementation Planning Policies

Graziella Cardoso Bonadia, Nyvea Maria da Silva, and Cristiane Midori Ogushi

Fundação CPqD, Rod Campinas – Mogi-Mirim, km 118, 5 Fazenda Pau D'Alho, Campinas
{bonadia,nsilva,ogushi}@cpqd.com.br

Abstract. In a context where efforts are being made to increase access to computers and the internet, other barriers have become more visible: besides the physical and economic barriers, psychological, cognitive and linguistic barriers have gained relevance in the debate on digital inclusion, since they can also interfere in the intensity and quality of an individual's use of these technologies. The relevance of these aspects is quite evident in our Brazilian society, due to our social-economic structure, in great part formed by people of low income, with little or no literacy, and by people with disabilities. In spite of this, a large proportion of existing indicators represent primarily physical access to ICTs and the technological aspects of producing and spreading these technologies. An assessment of the scope of the data currently collected reveals that few indicators reflect psychological, cognitive and usability/accessibility barriers. With the objective of filling the existing gaps, we have proposed a new metric for gauging digital inclusion that will delineate its most diverse aspects and thus contribute to the elaboration of government policies that will effectively stimulate the development of an information society.

Keywords: digital inclusion, index, measuring, public policies.

1 Introduction

The conditioning factors for the complete assimilation of the benefits of Digital Inclusion (DI) transcend the existence of a computer or an Internet connection. In fact, it is of the utmost importance that indicators be adopted to reflect the characteristics of the diverse barriers to DI, particularly those that prevent total use of more complex information communication technology (ICT), such as the internet.

The objective of this paper is to propose an alternative way of measuring digital inclusion using a new index based on the concept of the different barriers to DI, as shown in Figure 1. We have used a layer model to clearly explict the different kinds of DI barriers that must be treated. The model was formulated based on Brazilian circumstances considering the social-economic, cultural and educational profiles.

C. Stephanidis (Ed.): Posters, Part I, HCII 2011, CCIS 173, pp. 349–353, 2011.
© Springer-Verlag Berlin Heidelberg 2011

Source: Holanda and Dall'Antonia (2006)

Fig. 1. Barriers to digital inclusion

Overcoming these barriers enables individuals to obtain the main benefits of the digital world, as represented in Figure 1 by the Information Society layer. This layer consists of total fruition and production of electronic content and services for educational, professional and entertainment purposes, as well as citizenship-related activities.

When considering all the physical, cognitive, psychological, social-economical and cultural DI barriers, the layer model can be useful in the formulation and assessment of policies and in the planning of actions to overcome these hurdles. Using indicators to reflect these barriers is an objective way of establishing goals and assessing the efficiency of proposed actions to achieve them. In a group, these indicators provide a synthesis of the country's current digital inclusion index.

The existence of gaps is what motivated the need to create a Digital Inclusion Index (DII) in the first place. To achieve this objective, indicators reflecting each layer of DI barriers were selected. Furthermore, aspects related to ICT supply and demand within each layer model were taken into consideration. These aspects can be determined by analyzing both individual/home accesses and collective/public accesses.

Broadband scope/coverage in the towns and cities and how important this service is to the development of each region must be observed in the Access layer. In the Accessibility and Usability layer, the issue of supply and demand can be determined based on the amount of access points with accessibility resources and the number of potential people to be qualified for ICT usage. The Intelligibility layer must be assessed considering also supply and demand, taking into consideration the number of qualified people using the services and the availability of electronic services with adequate language in each region. Finally, in the Information Society layer, a supply/demand analysis is important to portray the growth of internet usage and to determine the demand for different services. In short, assessing the supply will show ICT availability for the population regarding: coverage, scope, adequate services, terminals and equipment, and public access points. On the other hand, measuring demand will determine if the population is prepared and qualified to take full advantage of ICT services, assessing the level of interest they show in making use of these services.

These indicators were chosen to help formulate DI implementation policies, and to verify how efficiently and effectively these policies will achieve pre-established DI goals.

2 Existing Indexes and Their Adherence to the Digital Inclusion Layer Model

A survey was made of the indicators and indexes most commonly used to describe the diffusion and use of ICTs in society. Each one of the evaluated systems presents indicators that reflect, in different degrees, the barriers to DI illustrated in Figure 1.

In Table 1, there is a summary of the assessment of these metric systems according to the representativeness of each DI layer. This table demonstrates that access availability is the layer best represented by existing metric system indicators, followed by the fruition layer. The other barriers are poorly represented. The greatest gap can be observed in the Accessibility and Usability layer. This is explained by the difficulties encountered in gathering pertinent information. As for the intelligibility aspect, although indicators regarding educational level can be found, they become much scarcer when it comes to reflecting efforts at achieving digital literacy and adapting language for the general public.

Table 1. Overview of metric systems according to their representativeness of the DI layers (Legend: Y = yes; N = no; P = partially)

DI layers		GDI	INEXSK	ICTDI	Infostate	DAI	CAIBI	DOI	Eurostat	Core ICT ind.	NRI	SIBIS-DIDIX	BISER	Digital poverty	IDI
Information Society	Content Prod.	P	P	N	P	N	P	N	P	P	P	P	P	N	P
	Content Fruition	Y	P	P	P	P	P	P	Y	Y	P	Y	Y	Y	P
Intelligibility		N	P	N	P	P	P	N	P	P	P	Y	Y	N	P
Accessibility and Usability		N	N	N	N	N	N	N	N	N	N	P	P	P	N
Access Availability		P	P	P	P	P	P	Y	Y	Y	Y	Y	Y	P	Y

Does the metric system contemplate DI?

The diversity of indexes arises from the context and the objectives of their creation. For instance, while some systems focus on ICT diffusion among a country's population, others emphasize the dimensions of electronic commerce. However, none of them represent all DI aspects satisfactorily.

3 Digital Inclusion Index

To make up the DII calculation formula, besides the criteria of choosing indicators according to their representativeness of each DI layer, their collected values and the weight of each layer and each indicator were also used. To attribute weights to the layers of digital inclusion barriers and their respective indicators, the AHP (Analytic Hierarchy Process) methodology was used.

The following formula was used to calculate the digital inclusion index:

$$0 \leq \sum\nolimits_{j=1}^{4} b_j \sum\nolimits_{i=1}^{nj} p_{ij} Indicator_{ij} \leq 1 \qquad (1)$$

Where:

0 represents digital exclusion and 1 full digital inclusion

pij is the weight of indicator i of DI layer j

bj is the weight of the DI layer

Each layer and their respective indicators are presented next, together with the weights attributed by the AHP methodology. The current values of the indicators were also estimated in order to calculate the sub-indexes of each layer and the DII.

1. Access layer (Weight: 0.30): Proportion of the population covered by local broadband internet providers (Weight: 0.29; Current value: 0.78); Proportion of homes with broadband (Weight: 0.49; Current value: 0.10); Public access points (telecenters and LAN houses) for every 100 inhabitants without internet in the home (Weight: 0.22; Current value: 0.01). Calculation of Access Sub-Index: 0.28.
2. Accessibility and Usability layer (Weight: 0.20): Public access points with accessibility resources for every 100 inhabitants with disability or illiteracy (Weight: 0.19; Current value: 0.0); Proportion of internet users with disabilities over proportion of internet users without disabilities (Weight: 0.23; Current value: 0.0); Proportion of illiterate internet users over proportion of literate internet users (Weight: 0.38; Current value: 0.15); Proportion of general e-services with accessibility and usability (Weight: 0.19; Current value: 0.31). Calculation of accessibility and usability sub-index: 0.12.
3. Intelligibility layer (Weight: 0.14): Proportion of people with at least one internet skill (Weight: 0.40; Current value: 0.36); Proportion of functional literates (Weight: 0.20; Current value: 0.68); Proportion of general e-services with adequate language (Weight: 0.40; Current value: 0.55). Calculation of intelligibility sub-index: 0.50.
4. Information Society (Weight: 0.36): Proportion of individuals who used the internet in the last three months (Weight: 0.67; Current value: 0.34); Diversity of services (Weight: 0.33; Current value: 0.71). Calculation of the information society sub-index: 0.46.

Calculation of the Digital Inclusion Index (IID): 0.34.

To verify the behavior of the DI index in the face of future alterations that some of the indicators might undergo, a sensibility analysis was made of one indicator of each DI layer – always considering the indicator with the greatest weight.

Two effective indicators from the United Kingdom and two from Brazil were used as reference values for this analysis. Their values were doubled, while all the others maintained their respective values. The indicators chosen to receive doubled values were: Access: proportion of homes with broadband internet; Accessibility and Usability: proportion of illiterate internet users over proportion of literate internet users; Intelligibility: proportion of people with at least one internet skill and Information Society: proportion of individuals who used the internet in the last three months.

As mentioned previously, the DII is 0.34 and with the variation of the selected indicators, the following results were obtained:

When altering the indicator "Proportion of homes with broadband internet" from 0.10 to 0.63, in compliance with the United Kingdom indicator, the resulting DII is 0.42.

When doubling the indicator "Proportion of illiterate internet users over proportion of literate internet users" from 0.15 to 0.30, and doubling the indicator "Proportion of people with at least one internet skill" from 0.36 to 0.72, the resulting DII is 0.36.

However, when altering the indicator "Proportion of individuals who used the internet in the last three months" from 0.34 to 0.72, in compliance with the United Kingdom indicator, the resulting DII is 0.43.

4 Conclusion

Doubling the current value of indicators caused a less significant impact on the DII index than when using indicators with UK data. However, the "Proportion of homes with broadband internet" is an indicator that will very likely suffer alteration over time, since an investment in broadband internet is a priority for Brazil, as it is in other developing countries. Currently, according to United Nations data, although Brazil is the fifth largest cell phone and internet market in the world and the number of Brazilians connected to the web is high in absolute numbers, internet penetration in the country is still considered low. Based on projections that network data traffic will increase and that the world of internet is becoming increasingly dependent on high speed access networks, it is clear that there is a demand for this market and a real need for more investments on the part of the service providers. Another indicator that caused an expressive impact on the result when its value was altered was "Proportion of individuals who used the internet in the last three months." It is safe to assume that this alteration will occur sooner or later, since with the need for investment in infrastructure and the demand for broadband internet, the number of users and frequency of access should also increase.

References

1. Holanda, G.M., Dall'Antonia, J.C.: An Approach for e-inclusion: Bringing illiterates and disabled people into play. Journal of Technology Management & Innovation 1(3), 29–37 (2006)
2. ITU. Measuring the Information Society: The ICT Development Index. International Telecommunication Union, Geneva, Switzerland (2009)
3. UN-UNPAN. UN Global E-government Readiness Report 2008: From E-government to connected governance. New York: United Nations (2008)

Serious Game for Cognitive Testing of Elderly

Sangwoo Byun and Changhoon Park

Dept. of Game Engineering, Hoseo University,
165 Sechul-ri, Baebang-myun, Asan, Chungnam 336-795, Korea
karan99@imrlab.hoseo.edu, chpark@hoseo.edu

Abstract. South Korea now has one of the lowest birth-rates in the world and one of the most rapidly aging populations. In such an aging society, the most representative disease threatening the quality of old person's life is 'Alzheimer's disease'. In this paper, we will propose a screening test based on game technology. And, this game will be designed by applying Fitt's law and Hick's law to test cognitive function.

Keywords: Screening tool, Accessibility, Cognitive function, Alzheimer's disease, Fitt's law, Hick's law.

1 Introduction

South Korea now has one of the lowest birth-rates in the world and one of the most rapidly aging populations. At this pace, Korean society is expected to become a so-called "aged society" by 2018, only 13 years after its designation as an "aging society" in 2000. In an aging society, people aged 65 or older make up over 7 percent of the population, while in an aged society this number exceeds 14 percent. It took France 115 years and the U.S. 72 years to go from an aging society to an aged society; Japan took 24 years for this change. In such an aging society, the most representative disease threatening the quality of old person's life is 'Alzheimer's disease(AD)', and this Alzheimer's disease is social and ethical problem beyond medical problem and it's an important problem waiting solution to improve people's welfare.

As the prevalence of dementia increases, and novel and better interventions to delay the progression of dementia become available, the detection of early dementia, especially in the primary care setting, becomes important. But, most of the present dementia screening test tools have difficulty detecting early dementia and are not easy used in the primary care setting. To overcome this problem, [1] proposes a Computerized Dementia Screening Test (CDST) consisting of four test items which are all computerized as one program: the block test for spatial span, the memory impairment screen of Buschke, the judgment of the line orientation test and the Go No-go test. In this paper, we will propose a screening test based on game technology to provide the fun factor to improve the accessibility of the test for a long time.

2 Mild Cognitive Impairment (MCI)

Mild cognitive impairment (MCI) is a syndrome defined as cognitive decline greater than expected for an individual's age and education level but that does not interfere notably

C. Stephanidis (Ed.): Posters, Part I, HCII 2011, CCIS 173, pp. 354–357, 2011.
© Springer-Verlag Berlin Heidelberg 2011

with activities of daily life. MCI can thus be regarded as a risk state for dementia, and its identification could lead to secondary prevention by controlling risk factors such as systolic hypertension. Researchers have demonstrated the importance of identifying the declines in cognitive function indicative of imminent functional impairment. Therefore, investigators have been interested in the MCI prior to conversion to AD in recent era. Unfortunately, most of the present dementia screening test tools have difficulty detecting MCI and are not easy used in the primary care setting[2].

The diversity of the dementias and the diversity of the neuropsychological symptoms of dementia means that no single test is sufficient for the purpose of diagnosis or screening. Rather, a battery of neurocognitive tests is necessary. The commonality shared by all forms of dementia, however, indicates that an appropriate battery can comprise only a few well-chosen tests. This is important, because the major issue in dementia diagnosis is not necessarily to subtype the various forms of the condition, but rather to make the diagnosis as early as possible.

3   Screening for MCI

Computerized neurocognitive testing has been used in research since the days of the Commodore and the Apple 2e. The technology is well established in military and aerospace medicine, industrial medicine. Clinically, computerized tests are used routinely for attention deficit disorder (ADD) diagnosis and in sports medicine for concussion management. Computerized tests are reliable—in some respects more reliable than paper-and-pencil tests. They correlate well with conventional tests, are well-accepted by patients, and are capable of a high degree of accuracy. Some computerized tests generate results with millisecond accuracy, which is necessary for precise assessment of mild impairment in reaction times and information processing speed[3].

In this study, we propose a serious game for screening people with cognitive impairment. The fun factor of game can provide a way of monitoring human-computer interaction naturally. Monitoring data from occurring gameplay will be used to detect sustained changes in person's cognitive performance.

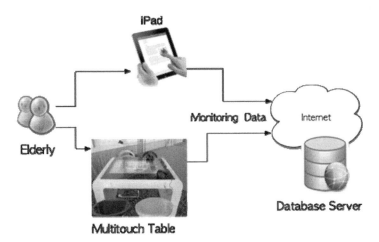

Fig. 1. Overview of system design

We present three mini-games for reaction time, short-term memory and discernment respectively. For inferring cognitive performance, these games are designed based on Fitt's law and Hick's law. Fit's law is a model of human movement in human-computer interaction and ergonomics which predicts that the time required to rapidly move to a target area is a function of the distance to and the size of the target. And Hick's law describes describes the time it takes for a person to make a decision as a result of the possible choices he or she has. By means of these two laws, we will control the difficulty of the game in order to test cognitive function.

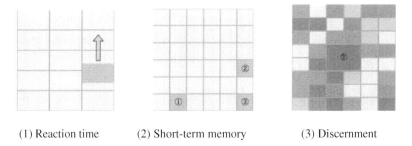

(1) Reaction time   (2) Short-term memory   (3) Discernment

Fig. 2. Three different tests for cognitive function

In the reaction game, the user should touch a colored block that is moving in one direction starting from the outline. The game for short-term memory changes the color of tiles randomly and disappear. Then, the user should touch these tiles in the same order. And, the game for discernment changes the color of the center. The user should touch the same colored tile. The difficulty of these game is controlled by means of not only time, speed, or number of changing tiles but also the size of tile. So, we can obtain user interaction data during gameplay naturally.

The goal of this research is to develop unobtrusive techniques of collecting long-term data that will allow us to detect sustained trends in cognitive performance. The inferences will be used to classify significant performance changes, and additionally, to adapt computer interfaces with tailored hints and assistance when needed.

4   Conclusion

In this study, we proposed a serious game for screening people with cognitive impairment. The fun factor of game can provide a way of monitoring human-computer interaction naturally. This game consisting of three test items: reaction time, short-term memory and discernment. Monitoring data from occurring gameplay will be used to detect sustained changes in person's cognitive performance.

References

1. Cho, B., Yang, J., Kim, S., Yang, D.W., Park, M., Chey, J.: The validity and reliability of a Computerized Dementia Screening Test developed in Korea. Journal of the Neurological Sciences 203, 109–114 (2002)
2. Gualtieri, C.T.: Dementia Screening Using Computerized Tests. Journal of Insurance Medicine 36(3), 213–227 (2004)
3. Fillit, H.M., Simon, E.S., Doniger, G.M., Cummings, J.L.: Practicality of a computerized system for cognitive assessment in the elderly. Alzheimer's & Dementia 4(1), 14–21 (2008)

Leisure Activities for the Elderly–The Influence of Visual Working Memory on Mahjong and Its Video Game Version

Chih-Lin Chang[1], Tai-Yen Hsu[2], Fang-Ling Lin[1,*],
Chuen-Der Huang[3], and I.-Ting Huang[2]

[1] General Education Center, Hsiuping Institute of Technology, Taichung City, Taiwan
[2] Physical Education, National Taichung University, Taichung City, Taiwan
[3] Dept. of Electrical Engineering, Hsiuping Institute of Technology, Taichung City, Taiwan
salamen@mail.hit.edu.tw

Abstract. Mahjong is not only a traditional game for recreation but an important leisure activity for elderly people in Chinese society. In this study, 8 elderly people of age 65 in average are selected as testees, their visual senses are sufficiently capable to continuously play mahjong for more than 1 hour. In addition, the testees all have more than one year of experience in playing mahjong. Also, a self-developed working memory inspection system is used to detect the influences of the working memory corrective ratio of version for elderly people under 350 Lux, the mahjong play duration as the variable. The study also may serve as a reference in designing environmental illumination and the duration for elderly people while playing mahjong.

Keywords: mahjong, working memory, entertainment, illumination.

1 Introduction

By the help of medical caring and economic conditions, the length of people life is going to increasing. According to the definition of WHO (World Health Organization, WHO), the society is called high-age society while the percentage of 65 aged people reaches 7%. In Taiwan, the population whose age is more than 65 years old has already reached 7.1% in 1993. Taiwan has become the so called high-age country already and becomes worse. All problems come accompany with the high-age problems such as health caring, service institutions, physiological problems, psychological problems and the social problems need a huge of cost. Therefore, how to deal with these high-age society problems has become an important task of country, not only in Taiwan but in many countries also.

Long living stands more leisure time, but it is not equal more healthy or happy living. Long living time might cause many negative consequences if the time is not spent on good things to approve the health of their own. To avoid the negative influences, everyone must aware of what kind of leisure is suitable for him. Ruled leisure activities, maintain a relaxed mood, keep good social life are the important

---

* Corresponding author.

C. Stephanidis (Ed.): Posters, Part I, HCII 2011, CCIS 173, pp. 358–362, 2011.

keys to active aging. A research showed that for the elder people they take 9 hours in sleep, 4 hours in daily living, and the rest 11 hours in leisure living[8][9]. Regular leisure activities are good for retired living or aged living. It is found that the activities of aged people can be classed into static and dynamic activities. The so called dynamics such as Tai-Chi-Chane, Yun-Chi dance, mountaineering, and invigorating walk. The so called statics such as chat, chess, Mahjong game are the favorites of aged people.

In addition to personal factor, the following factors all influence the vision ability[1] they are brightness (contrast), levels, and movement(the subject or the viewer moves). Also, when the subjects move with a fast speed, it will affect the vision[10] [11] [12]. When the subjects move speeds over 60 degrees per second the vision will deteriorate sharply[5]. After the optical stimulation to the retina of the eyes, there are three physical properties accompany with three kinds of psychological properties, there are hue (color), brightness and saturation. Color is decided by the length light, that is, different wavelengths of light will cause a different feeling. Amplitude of the light determines the luminosity of the light, the larger of amplitude the stronger of luminosity[3][4]. Purity of light determines the saturation of psychological properties. The so-called purity of light is by a stimulus light source containing different kinds of wavelength number, the less of type the better purity of light.

1.1   Goal of Research

To explore the effects of visual attention of the aged people engaged in leisure Mahjong 1 hour later.

2   Method

2.1   Object of Research

The Object of this study is the aged people whose age is over 65 years old. Eight aged peoples help the experiment to be testees. Some of them had taken mahjong as their leisure. The average age of them is 71.25(5.36) years old.

2.2   Process of Experiment

In the experiments, the test of vision including before and after play the game and the analysis data are based on the corrective rate.

The first step is to fill the table of each testee and told them about the steps and contents of experiments. The subjects was asked to familiar the soft of mahjong games[7]. They practiced then finished the attention test before formal played. After 60-minutes play period, the testees were asked to do the after-testing of attention. The state of attention of testees were analysis by using well done rate appeared on the soft of Vision Attention Soft.

2.3   Tools of Experiment

Self-developed tool called Visual attention system ver. 2.0 is used to do visual attention test[1]. Code figures series was black, font style was Arial, font size was 72, string length was 3 codes, appear on the screen with a white background on the 14-inch laptop screen. Target of stimulus was random string of numbers and was used to identify.

Table 1. Configuration parameters for working memory inspection

VDT pixels	Background color	Code color	Font size	Display duration	Code number	font	Inspection duration
1152×864	White	Black	72	0.5	3	Arial	10 Minutes

2.4 Data Analysis

Windows for SPSS12.0 statistical software package us used for statistical analysis, verification tests whether there are differences within the set to homogeneous, paired sample t test verification answer rate within the set is different, between factor (between factor) for the before and after the test's correct rate of significant level is Alpha = .05.

3 Results and Discussions

3.1 Results and Discussions

3.1.1 T-Test of Well Done for 1 Code, 2 Codes, 3 Codes

In the experiments all 3 codes appear is the standard, but in the experiments recorded 1, 2 and 3 code (all correct) number of questions answered correctly at the same time. The results show in 1, 2 and 3 codes well done before and after the test has not reached significant levels.

Table 2. T-test for 1 code, 2 codes, 3 codes

Variable	M	SD	df	t	P
1 code	.250	2.816	7	.251	.089
2 codes	-.125	2.997	7	-.118	.909
3 codes	-1.125	4.454	7	-.714	.498

$*p< .05$

3.1.2 The Age and Well Done 1, 2 and 3 Codes Single-Factor Analysis of Variance

Over 65 years of age and well done 1, 2 and 3 codes of single-factor analysis of variance found that age and well done 1 code ($*p<.05$), age and well done 2 codes ($*p<.01$), age and well done 3 codes ($*p<.001$) have reached significant levels. From the results that age is proportional to the character codes (1-3) number, and the more yards appeared, (3 codes), the more significant of test.

Tables 3. ANOVA for Ages within corrective codes

Variable		SS	df	MSS	F	p
1 code	Model	161.75	6	26.96	3.79	.036
	Error	64.00	9	7.111		
	Corrected total	225.75	15			
2 codes	Model	410.69	6	68.45	9.98	.002
	Error	61.75	9	6.86		
	Corrected total	472.44	15			
3 codes	Model	819.94	6	136.66	11.13	.001
	Error	110.50	9	12.28		
	Corrected total	930.44	15			

$*p< .05$

3.2   Conclusions

Regular leisure activities are positive influences for retired people and aged people. Those leisure activities of community for the aged people mainly are group activities such as Tai-Chi-Chane, YunChi dancing, and mountaineering are much enjoyed by aged persons of dynamic items. For statics, party chat, chess, mahjong games are the favorites especially mahjong. In Taiwan, there is more than 10% of population exceed 65 years old, July 2007. For such a huge group of aged people, proper leisure activities and the much safety activities has become the important topic to study.

Although this mahjong leisure activities study only in one hour and it will not affect the visual attention and the fatigue of the aged but the affection will increase while the play time is increasing[1][2]. It is known that the time spent in playing mahjong always exceed than one hour in fact. Therefore, to maintain good vision to pay attention to the environment and to avoid the dangerous is the most important thing.

Especially, several researches have told that working memory ability will decrease while the age increased [2]. In orient society, to study the optimal period that the aged people can play mahjong and still can keep their good vision abilities will be a worthy work in the future.

References

[1] Chang, C.L., Lin, F.T., Li, K.W., Jou, Y.T., Hsu, T.Y.: The Study of the Impact of IEEE International Conference on Networking, Sensing and Control, pp. 318–324 (2009)

[2] Chang, C.L., Li, K.W., Jou, Y.T.: The Influence of Gender and Age on the Visual Codes Working Memory and the Display Duration-a Case Study of Fencers, LNAI, 138-148 (2009)

[3] Classe, J.G., Semes, L.P., Daum, K.M., Nowakowski, R.L., Alexander, J., Wisniewski, J., Beisel, J.A., Mann, K., Rutstein, R., Smith, M., Bartolucci, A.: Association between visual reaction time and batting, fielding, and earned run averages among players of the Southern Baseball League. Journal of the American Optometric Association 68(1), 43–49 (1997)

[4]   Fujishiro, H., Mashimo, I., Ishigaki, H., Edeagawa, H., Endoh, F., Nakazato, K., Nakajima, H.: Visual Function of collegiate American Football Players in Japan. In: 13th Asian Games Scientific Congress (1998)

[5]   Hou, T.S., Chung, S.H.: Human Factors Engineering. Ding-Mao Publication Company, Taipei (2003)

[6]   Ishigaki, H., Miyao, M.: Implications for dynamic visual acuity with changes in age and sex. Perceptual and motor skills 78, 1049–1050 (1994)

[7]   Lin, F.L., Chang, C.L., Jou, Y.T., Pan, S.C., Hsu, T.Y., Huang, C.D.: Effect of the Involvement Degree of Playing Video Games on Brain waves for an hour. In: IEEE 17th International Conference on Industrial Engineering and Engineering Management, vol. 2, pp. 1043–1047 (2010)

[8]   Lin, Y.S.: The study of influence of video game violence on schoolchild attack behavior. unpublished master's thesis of Graduate Institute of Communications, Shih-Hsin University, Taipei (2001)

[9]   Lin, Y.J.: The study of videogame addiction tendency and its related factors. unpublished master's thesis of Graduate Institute of Psychology. Chung-Yuan Christian University, Taoyuan (2003)

[10] Marek, T., Noworol, C.: Bi-point flicker research and self0-ratings of mental and visual fatigue of VDT operators. In: Asfour, S.S. (ed.) Trends in Ergonomics/Human Factors IV, pp. 163–168. Elsevier, North-Holland (1987)

[11] Ridini, L.: Relationships between psychological function, test and selected sports skills of boys in junior high school. Research Quarterly 39, 674–683 (1968)

[12] Tsai, T.B.: The faculty train of sport vision for volleyball athletes. Science of Volleyball Coaching, 25-30 (2003)

An Empathic Approach in Assistive Technology to Provide Job Accommodations for Disabilities

Chien-Bang Chen

Department of Product and Interior Design
De Montfort University, UK
comous@hotmail.com

Abstract. When the psychologist Abraham Maslow first defined the five levels of human need in 1943, people started to realise how human needs should be fulfilled and many products have since been designed to fulfill these needs. Many researches have shown that the desire to achieve a higher level of need is no different between normal people and disabled people. However, social benefits only support a disabled person with their basic needs. To help them achieve a higher level of need, for them, finding a suitable job is the best way forward.An appropriately designed assistive technology (AT) allows the user to be more efficient at work, prevent them suffering occupational injury and enjoy a safe and comfortable work environment. It could be a good tool to help them reach their psychological needs, but designing an appropriate AT requires a designer with a high level of professional knowledge in AT, an understanding of the subject's abilities and being able to realise the task and environment that the subject needs to work in, all of which involve long term training. Additionally, the majority of designers are healthy people; it is very difficult for a healthy person to have the ability to understand the difficulties of a disabled subject, especially young designers. In this research, the researcher used a spinal injured lottery seller in Taiwan as the subject. The researcher observed and analysed his tasks and environment, collected professional suggestions from experts and, based on the user-centred design theory, compared the physical differences between the subject and healthy designers. Additionally, the results were applied to a design and an empathy tool was produced, when wearing it would allow the designers to empathise with the inconvenience of the physical conditions of the subject. The empathy tool was tested and evaluated by various product designers. The researcher designed a scenarios process and asked his participants to practice with it. The result showed that although the suit could not simulate the psychological conditions of the target user, it was, however, successful in mimicking the physical conditions of the subject and allowed the designers to realise the difficulties and problems of the subject through the simulation process. Thus, these experiences were transformed into design knowledge when designing assistive technology.

Keywords: Assistive technology, Empathic design, Disabilities.

C. Stephanidis (Ed.): Posters, Part I, HCII 2011, CCIS 173, pp. 363–367, 2011.
© Springer-Verlag Berlin Heidelberg 2011

1   Background

Job accommodation in eastern culture has a very long history. However, it was not officially managed by governments in the past and disabled people often found it hard to find a suitable job. On the one hand, according to traditional eastern thinking, no one is abandoned by God and every person should contribute to their society. This means that a person who has no "real job" will face strong pressure from their family and community, even if they have a disability. On the other hand, the help and support given by government and welfare services are often only enough for survival, meaning that disabled people need to earn a more sustainable income for their future life and family. Moreover, the ability to live independently is always the first thing that disabled people desire as earning money for themselves and their family enables them to gain people's respect and fulfill their higher psychological desires.

Sometimes, the process of helping a disabled person back to work requires the use of assistive technologies (AT) to support them within their work environment. However, many practical researches have found that most ATs are abandoned by their users after a very short period of usage.(Kintsch, A & dePaula, R, 2002) One of the main reasons is that the assistive technology bought is unsuitable. It has also happened that, in many job accommodation cases, users and their employer are often unsure which AT is suitable for the job. Consequently, when a wrong decision has been made, in some cases, it is just a waste of money. However, in more serious cases, it can often cause an occupational injury to the user.

An appropriate job accommodation design could avoid this problem. It would consider a user's physical character, work conditions, reasonable cost and work environment and would use professional knowledge and information to make an appropriate job accommodation assistive technology (JAAT) design. Moreover, an experienced job accommodation designer has more AT knowledge than the user himself and, with great vision and professional knowledge, he would know which kind of AT design would not damage the user's physical condition, even if it might make the user feel uncomfortable when they first try the AT.

However, it is not easy for an ordinary person to become an experienced designer and even experienced designers have difficulties in understanding some of their users' requirements and will sometimes make mistakes when designing the AT. Since there are so many varieties and types of disability in the world and every disabled person has different symptoms, working conditions and environment, designers find it hard to understand all situations. Therefore, in order to develop a suitable design rationale, the ability to understand the real needs of the disabled user is essential.

The empathic design model provides a process for designing commercial products and services. The model uses observation, simulation and role-playing techniques to help designers empathise with their users. It has been widely used during the design process of motor vehicles in many motor companies and it could also be employed in the process of designing AT for job accommodation.

When the empathic design model is employed to design a JAAT, the designer could use equipment to observe and record the environment but accurate simulation and role-playing techniques often require certain tools to help the designer to practice the real physical conditions and difficulties of the work environment. The precision of these tools could deeply affect the design results. Therefore, an appropriate tool design method plays a very important role in the process.

To make an appropriate tool design, the process has to consider the user's real physical condition and work environment and compare the differences between the disabled user and the health designer, whilst also collecting professional suggestions from the medical profession and the users' employer. Finally, the designer must use their product design knowledge to design and produce the design.

The goal of this research is to build an empathy tool which could help designer to understand the working difficulties of their disabled user; the result of the development process will be analyzed in order to build a design model of empathy tool design.

2   Research Methodology and Process

2.1   Subject Selection

To achieve the goal of research, the researcher selected a spinal injured lottery seller in Taiwan as his subject; since the lottery selling is a special permit job for vulnerable people in Taiwan. In addition, the lottery company does not provide them any equipment for their special needs. Therefore, an empathic design process to unfold their real need and help designer to build an appropriate AT for their job is essential.

The subject is a lottery card sales person with T12 spinal injured by an car accident in his ten years old, and he has moderate conversation difficulty because of his stone deaf. He has selling the lottery ticket for more than ten years at the outside of a night post office in Taichung city, Taiwan.

2.2   Literature Research

The existing literature review suggested that the job accommodation process should consider the physical and mental condition, abilities and preferences of the subject, the environment, employers, and the capability of the job; an appropriate match of these conditions could reduce the difficulties of the job accommodation.

Koskinen's research also indicated that "The key to empathic design is an understanding of how the user sees, experiences and feels some object, environment or service in the situation in which he or she uses the object" (Koskinen. I et. al, 2003). To make a successful empathic design is to allow the designer to step into users' world, and to wonder around in it   then to step back as a designer. Therefore, the empathy tool is the most essential equipment to help designers to do it.

2.3   Designer Research

In order to make the empathy tool correctly, the researcher analyzed the physical conditions of the subject as well as the ordinary designers. He observed and interviewed the subject and his care givers to collect the information of the subject. In addition, the Taiwanese Laborer Body Statistics Database (IOSH, 1996) is used to gather the mobility data of ordinary Taiwanese designers. By comparing the information from both sides, the researcher identified the differences of ability between the subject and ordinary designers.

The researcher also observed subject's work environment and his working process, and analyzed the tasks of the subject to find out the difficulties of the subject in his work. The results of task analysis indicated that the most difficult parts are installation of the work station, communication and un-install the work station. The identification of both his physical difference and task difficulties helped the researcher to develop the concepts of the empathy tool.

2.4 Design Rationales

Because the empathy tool is designed for general designers, the universal design principles were employed. Hence, the design rationales of the empathy tool design are:

- It should allow general designers to use.
- It should fit the sitting space of a standard wheel chair.
- It should limit the mobility of designer's lower limb.
- It should limit the designer's waist activity
- The construction of it should be able to afford the physical strength of ordinary health designer.
- It should not harm the users.

2.5 Empathy Tool Production

The empathy tool which the researcher designed and produced is separated into three parts to limit the mobility of waist, knees and ankles of designers; all of them are produced in the plastic workshop of the De Montfort University, Leicester, U.K. The main structure is built of PVC boards, and it used vacuum forming and cutting skills to construct; Nylon straps and click lock are also used to fix   designers' activities.

Without a proper scenario, the empathy tool may only let its users fool around in the subject's world. Therefore, the researcher also developed a role play SOP from the task analysis; it instructed the users what to experience step by step and gave a description of environment settings.

3   Evaluation

The empathy tool was tested and evaluated by product designers, assistive technology experts, and the subject. The results indicated that the empathy tool has enough strength to stand the muscle strength of designers, and designers did not feel uncomfortable in the empathy process; moreover, it successfully limited the activities in waist, knees and ankles of the participant designers.

4   Discussions

Regarding the views from the disabled subject, the subject appreciated the empathy tool design and believed it could simulate his situation for the designer users; the assistive technology experts suggested the researcher to shorten the waist part of the empathy tool as the subject is injured in T12, the mobility of spine should extend to the lower end of the chest; one of expert pointed out that the paralyzed lower limbs are without nerve feedback and muscle strength, which is different with the rigid constrain that the empathy tool made. However, the empathy tool designed to bend the lower limbs of the users in 90 degree angles, the users are very difficult to stand up without the help from others; they can only use their upper limbs to move body when they want to change positions, which is very similar with the experience of losing the muscle strength in lower limbs.

5 Conclusions

In conclusion, an empathy tool for simulating the spinal injured lottery seller subject has successfully made through this research; although it is very difficult to let a health designer to experience the paralyzed limbs of the subject, the empathy tool has let designers experience the difficulties of the subject without damage their body; the process of the empathy tool design has also be analyzed become a design model for further research of assistive technology in job accommodation.

References

1. Kintsch, A., de Paula, R.: A Framework for the Adoption of Assistive Technology. In: Paper presented at the SWAAAC 2002: Supporting Learning Through Assistive Technology, Winter Park, CO, USA (2002)
2. Leonard, D., Rayport, J.F.: Spark Innovation Through Emphatic Design, vol. 75(6), p. 102(12). Harvard Business Review (November-December 1997)
3. Galvin, J.C., Scherer, M.J.: Evaluating, Selecting, and Using Appropriate Assistive Technology, p. 233. An Aspen Publication, Maryland (1996)
4. Koskinen, I., Battarbee, K., Mattelmaki, T.: Introduction to user experience and empathic design. In: Empathic Design – User Experience in Product Design. IT Press, Finland (2003)
5. IOSH, Taiwanese Laborer Body Statistics Database. Institute of Occupational Safety & Health, Taiwan (1999)

A Study on Interface Design Guidelines of Web Maps for Elder Users

Chun-Wen Chen and Kevin Tseng

Department of Industrial Design, Chang Gung University
259 Wen-Hwa 1st Road, Kwei-Shan, 333 Tao-Yuan, Taiwan
junbun@mail.cgu.edu.tw, ktseng@pddlab.org

Abstract. The aim of this research is to find out the interface design guidelines of web maps from the viewpoint of elder people's acceptance. This stage of the research is a qualitative exploration to web map user experience to find out interface design issues and problems. Web map user experience of participants was explored with methods of observation and interview. Six elder participants were taught some basic operations to use Google Maps. From the result of data analysis, this study adopts natural mapping as a core concept of proposed design guideline. The interface design guidelines of web maps for elder users are proposed: (a) compatibility of map display and cognitive map, (b) mental model of interface operation, (c) learnability of interface platforms, and (d) physical dimension of map display and operation interface.

Keywords: web map, interface design, aging.

1 Introduction

The aim of this research is to investigate the interface design guidelines of web maps from the viewpoint of elder people's acceptance. Web map is a type of application service to support people for locating places and routes by spatial information with the form of maps via World Wide Web protocol on the Internet. For elder people, applications of information technology facilitate convenience in life, but obstacles in learning and accommodating also emerge. Because of the changing of elder people's psychological and physiological abilities, the design of information technology for elder people is similar to the design of home environment and life appliance; much more considerations are necessary beyond functionality.

Technologies can make life easier for elder people. Tacken [1] has found that elder users are satisfied with technologies. Rama [2] discussed that the problems elder users meet mostly are: (a) Complexity of user interface: a layered control panel with many functions may fail to provide information about the available functions, (b) Age: certain cognitive abilities including reasoning ability and working memory for spatial information change with increasing age, and (c) Technology generation: generations with different previous technology experiences could learn current products differently.

Aging changes the abilities of elder people in many dimensions. It makes declines of the physiological abilities, including vision, speech, hearing, and psychomotor

C. Stephanidis (Ed.): Posters, Part I, HCII 2011, CCIS 173, pp. 368–372, 2011.
© Springer-Verlag Berlin Heidelberg 2011

ability. It also makes declines of the psychological abilities, including attention, memory, and learning ability [3]. Hawthorn [4] has proposed interface design suggestions for elder users in such dimensions.

It is important to evaluate the proper size and position of interactive objects in interface for elder users. In addition to this, creating clear conceptual models to the new environment could be a more powerful solution for future interface design. The problem of elder users in future like us is not only decline of abilities, but a lack of previous experience and conceptual models. The transparency of conceptual models could help elder users' learning beyond ability limitation.

To consider the web map interface for efficiency, Fitts' law is a basic guideline to deal with time and distance factors. Fitts' law states the relationship between movement time, distance, and accuracy for people engaged in rapid aimed movements [5]. It's a model of human movement, predicting the time required to rapidly move from a starting position to a final target area, as a function of the distance to the target and the size of the target [6]. It can be applied both in the physical world and computer space. To consider web map interface for learnability, it is natural to arrange controls according to the directions of corresponding functions. Norman [7] has explained the principle of mapping. The principle is about the relationship between two things, such as the controls and the results in the world. If the mapping is natural, related to the desired outcome, and providing immediate feedback, it could be easier to learn and to remember.

2   Method

Participants. According to a research on policy of aging labor by Employment, Labour and Social Affairs Committee of OECD, the research defines elder people is above 55 [8]. The participants were recruited from elder volunteers of museums for their motivation of learning new technology. The participants' computer and/or the Internet experience were required. Six elder participants, including three male and three female, were recruited in this stage. Two were 55-60, one 60-65, and three above 65. The education of five participants was college or above.

Devices and Material. (1) Hardware: A desktop computer with 19 inch LCD monitor, 1280*1024 pixels, and a mouse. A smartphone (iPhone 3g) with 3.5 inch multi-touch screen, 320*480 pixels. A DV camera to record the behavior and protocol of the participants. (2) Software: Windows operation system with Chrome browser. Apple iPhone OS 4.2 with Maps app. Google Maps Traditional Chinese version. (3) Location of interview: Multi-function Classroom of Kuandu Museum of Fine Arts.

Procedure. The whole exploration for each participant would take about one hour. First, the investigator introduced the exploration observation and interview procedure. Second, tasks were given one by one for the participant to find the places on the map. During tasks, the participants were asked to talk about his or her behaviors, thoughts, and experience with the web map. Video and audio recordings were taken during the tasks and interview. Third, after all the tasks were completed, an interview was held to gain for a deeper understanding of each participant's inner experiences. The investigator would ask the participant some open-ended questions about the web map.

Data analysis. This study uses Glaser & Strauss' grounded theory as method of qualitative data analysis [9]. It utilizes a method of induction to analyze real phenomenon to conclude theoretic results. It is useful to explore a practical or interdisciplinary field, especially for the not well-defined concepts and relationship among concepts. In this study, the investigators tried to understand the user experience in web map use and to propose theoretic interpretation and guidelines.

3   Results and Discussion

3.1   Data Analysis

The result of data analysis consists of categories of problems as follows.

Some participants didn't understand the spatial structure of the neighborhood, for example, the related direction between geographic districts. Although the targets they searched were familiar places or paths, they cannot find targets quickly during browsing the map. They might try to read the labels one by one and recall some familiar place names near the targets. It is a searching method with lower efficiency.

Although with some experience, not all participants were familiar with user interface of computer operation system or web maps. For the interface operations such as clicking buttons or dragging objects/windows, they could not predict the computer's response properly and might feel frustrated. They may not have appropriate mental model for the interface operation. It was also found there was much difference between continuous and discrete interface. Continuous interface could help users explore and understand unfamiliar functions well.

Operating indirect physical interface, such as mouse and touch pad, was hard for participants with motor and cognitive difficulties. They had problems to operate mouse to locate the curser on proper positions. But with direct physical interface, such as a mobile phone with a multi-touch screen, participants had better learning experience and satisfaction. It is obvious that they did not have the problem of mental model. Only the interface device was changed to make the difference.

Poor ability to read labels and buttons was a problem for some participants who could not use web map well. They could not move their sight and attention fast. They must look at each object one by one. Detail and overview could not be examined in the same time. The trial-and-error period lasted longer. Smaller buttons were hard to click in the range of space that they covered. Errors might happen and result in unexpected events. It frustrated elder users to take following actions.

3.2   Proposed Design Guidelines and Discussion

From the result of protocol analysis, *mapping* is a core concept among all the factors. In the context of web map interface, including map display and controls, elder people perceive digital and physical environment and try to construct conceptual models to connect experience and phenomena. They check the feedback to confirm their actions, and mostly important their conceptual models. The appropriate and natural mapping is necessary between map display and cognitive map, between mental model and interface system image, between controls and display, and between senses and perception. This study adopts *natural mapping* as a core design guideline of web map interface for elder users to provide transparency of conceptual models.

Interface design guidelines of web maps for elder users are proposed: (a) compatibility of map display and cognitive map, (b) mental model for interface operation, (c) learnability of interface platforms, and (d) physical dimension of map display and operation interface.

Compatibility of Map Display and Cognitive Map. It is a complicated task to relate the map display to personal cognitive map. The problem is that they cannot recognize the spatial features and build the relationship between maps and their cognitive maps. For ones who understand the spatial structure of the neighborhood, they can recognize the positions of the targets from the shapes of features on the map, such as estuary or bend of rivers, without reading the labels. A layout to focus overview, such as a hierarchy structure in graphics, may help users browse a map with top-down methods to use their previous knowledge.

Mental Model for Interface Operation. Mental model is the model user relies on to predict system response. People construct mental model from observed phenomena. In the digital space, no natural characteristics help users understand the interface. Simulated shapes or materials, such as a digital image with physical button shading, may help give clues with meaning. The response of interface is another main phenomenon that can be observed. Continuous interface provides real-time visual feedback. It helps adjust the actions or directions and realize the principle of the interface. An appropriate mental model can be constructed. Discrete interface provides faster change without intermediate response. It is possible to get new image/layout faster, but the total efficiency and satisfaction is not necessarily high. Because the result can only be seen after action (clicking), it is not necessarily what the user needs. More efforts are necessary to adjust next step.

Learnability of Interface Platforms. New or unfamiliar interface platforms need time and efforts to learn. Indirect interfaces need more skills and learning time to coordinate the hand movement and cursor display. Although a smaller screen limits overview of information, the benefits of direct interfaces can overcome this issue. If touch screen of the same size is available, it should combine the benefits of direct operation and broader overview.

Physical Dimension of Map Display and Operation Interface. Because of the changing of elder people's physiological abilities, there are more limitations in reading text and controlling interface. It has been discussed much in literature. Larger size of map display and operation interface helps elder users to read labels and features and to click the correct positions. According Fitts' Law, larger target size and shorter distance can lower the movement time. It is more important for elder users.

4   Conclusion

Natural mapping is a core design guideline concluded in this study. The problems and issues analyzed in the observation and interview have the common concept of mapping. The suitable interface design guidelines of web map for elder users are proposed from the analysis. The guidelines consist of four parts: (a) compatibility of map display and cognitive map, (b) mental model for interface operation, (c) learnability of interface platforms, and (d) physical dimension of map display and operation interface. In next stage, further study will test the interface design guidelines from the viewpoint of elder people's acceptance.

Acknowledgments. This study was partly sponsored with a grant, NSC99-2410-H-182-031, from the National Science Council, Taiwan.

References

1. Tacken, M., Marcellini, F., Mollenkoph, H., Ruoppila, I., Szeman, Z.: Use and Acceptance of New Technology by Older People. In: Finding of the International MOBILATE Survey: 'Enhancing Mobility in Later Life'. Gerontechnology, vol. 3, pp. 126–137 (2005)
2. Rama, M.D., de Ridder, H., Bouma, H.: Technology Generation and Age in Using Layered User Interfaces. Gerontechnology 1, 25–40 (2001)
3. Hawthorn, D.: Psychophysical Aging and Human Computer Interface Design. In: Proceedings of Computer Human Interaction Conference, 1998 Australasian, pp. 281–291 (1998)
4. Hawthorn, D.: Possible Implications of Aging for Interface Designers. Interacting with Computers 12(5), 507–528 (2000)
5. European Commission: Section 7: Recommendations for the Best Use of Key GIS UI Functions. In: Guidelines for Best Practice in User Interface for GIS, ESPRIT/ESSI project no. 21580, pp. 69–84 (1998)
6. Fitts, P.M.: The Information Capacity of the Human Motor System in Controlling the Amplitude of Movement. J. Exp. Psych. 47, 381–391 (1954)
7. Norman, D.: The Psychology of Everyday Things. Basic Book, New York (1988)
8. Auer, P., Fortuny, M.: Ageing of the Labour Force in OECD Countries: Economic and Social Consequences. International Labour Office, Geneva (2002)
9. Glaser, B., Strauss, A.: The Discovery of Grounded Theory. Aldine, Chicago (1976)

Impact of Prior Knowledge and Computer Interface Organization in Information Searching Performances: A Study Comparing Younger and Older Web Users

Aline Chevalier[1], Paulette Rozencwajg[2], and Benjamin Desjours[2]

[1] Laboratoire CLLE-LTC (UMR 5263, CNRS, Université de Toulouse, EPHE),
Maison de la Recherche, 5 Allées Machado, 31058 Toulouse Cedex 9, France
[2] Laboratoire PSYADIC (EA 4431), Université Paris Ouest Nanterre, UFR SPSE (bât.C),
200 avenue de la République, 92001 Nanterre cedex, France
aline.chevalier@univ-tlse2.fr, paulette.rozencwajg@u-paris10.fr,
benjamin.desjours@gmail.com

Abstract. The present study addressed age-related differences in performance to find information by older and younger web users. More precisely, we determined the impact of prior domain knowledge (high level *vs* low level) of older and younger adults and the interface organization (taxonomical-HS *vs* tag-based organization-TBS) on information search performance. The main results showed that older users exhibited poorer information searching performance than the younger users only for Manga domain (for which the younger users had higher level of knowledge than the older ones). For the two domains, the TBS interface decreased age-related differences in performance. In contrast, the HS interface generated lower performances for the older adults in the two domains, especially faced to Manga domain in which older users had very lower performances than younger users.

Keywords: Information searching; aging; taxonomy organization *vs* tag-based organization; knowledge-domain.

1 Introduction

Since the 1990s, the number of websites has increased extensively, and older adults are shown to be one of the fastest growing demographic groups of web users that profit from the wide ranges of Internet services to search for information and communicate [9, 10]. However, various studies show that older people experience more difficulties than younger people in using such systems (for a recent review, see [11]). These difficulties may be exacerbated if the interface organization does not fit the users' cognitive specificities.

In a previous study, Pak and Price [5] instructed older and younger adults to search for travel information (domain for which older and younger adults had about the same knowledge) on two systems varied in their organization:

- A hierarchically organized system (HS), which maintained a one-to-one relationship between menu link and page.

C. Stephanidis (Ed.): Posters, Part I, HCII 2011, CCIS 173, pp. 373–377, 2011.
© Springer-Verlag Berlin Heidelberg 2011

- A tag-based system (TBS), with a many-to-one relationship between menu and page.

These authors observed that younger adults obtained better search performance than older adults. However, the TBS interface reduced age-related differences, as compared with a HS interface. The older adults could benefit from their higher vocabulary skills compared to younger adults in the TBS interface. Whereas the HS interface required more spatial abilities, therefore the younger adults, who had higher spatial abilities than older ones, could navigate it easier than the older adults. In their study, the young and old participants had the same level of knowledge in travel domain. So if older adults have more knowledge of a domain than younger adults, their performance in a TBS interface should be increased, and even greater than the younger adults.

Many studies focused on the role of prior knowledge on comprehension of hypertext systems (for reviews, see [1, 2]). In contrast, very few studies addressed the impact of prior domain-knowledge on the information searching activity as well as strategies carried out by individuals. These studies were carried out with young users, and frequently with students in various domains (e.g., [4, 6]).

To contribute to this topic, we carried out a new experiment in which we studied the role of prior domain knowledge on information searching performance of older and younger adults according to the interface navigated (HS *vs* TBS).

2 Method

2.1 Participants

20 younger adults (M=20.6 years, SD=1.7) and 20 older adults (M=73.43 years, SD=6.23) participated at this experiment. All participants were volunteers, in good health, and had normal or corrected-to-normal vision. The younger participants were students. The older participants were retired individuals. They lived in their own home, and did not need any assistance to perform daily activities. Older participants all scored over 27 (M=29.65, SD=0.67) on the Mini-Mental State Examination [3], which means that they had no cognitive impairment.

2.2 Materiel and Procedure

All the participants were instructed to search for information to answer 20 questions in a hierarchically organized system (HS), and a tag-based system (TBS) (10 questions per domain), providing information related to two domains:

- Manga domain for which younger participants had higher level of prior knowledge than the older participants (M_{young}=5.9, SD_{young}=1.2 *vs* M_{old}=3.6, SD_{old}=1.9; $t(34)$=3.941, $p<.0005$).
- Banking and insurance domain for which older participants had higher level of prior knowledge than the younger participants (M_{old}=5.9, SD_{old}=1.4 *vs* M_{young}=3.75, SD_{young}=1.5; $t(34)$=-3.671, $p<.001$).

In line with Pak and Price's study, for instance, in the HS interface of Manga, the page concerning "weekly preprint" could be located in four steps (four linked required to be clicked): (1) Manga marketplace, (1.1) Manga literacy marketplace, (1.1.1) Professional publications and (1.1.1.1) Weekly preprint. In contrast, in the TBS interface, the first three levels of links (1, 1.1, and 1.1.1) were displayed in alphabetical order. In the TBS, the participant could find correct answer from the previous three links and then open the fourth link (1.1.1.1); that corresponded to two steps. TBS explicitly allows information to have multiple keywords, resulting in an increased probability that a particular keyword generated by the participant is linked to the desired information.

2.3 Variables

A Latin square of three independent variables were designed: Age (young, old), interface organization (HD, TBS) and domain knowledge (Manga, Banking-Insurance).

We computed the two following measures of performances:

- A composite score of giving up and incorrect responses. Lower values indicated better performance.
- The task time (in sec.) needed to find the answer. As in the HS the participants required two steps more than the TBS interface, we computed a mean time to open a link, which we subtracted (for two links) from the initial task time.

3   Results

All results are presented in Table 1.

3.1   Composite Score of Giving Up and Incorrect Response

For the Manga domain, the ANOVA did show that older users exhibited poorer performance than the younger ($F(1,36)=17.612$, $p<.001$, $\eta_p^2=.33$). The interface had a significant effect ($F(1,36)=10.783$, $p<.005$, $\eta_p^2=.23$): the TBS interface generated better performance than the HS. The Age × Interface interaction had also a significant effect ($F(1,36)=11.975$, $p<.005$, $\eta_p^2=.25$). As expected, the younger participants had higher performance than the older participants when they dealt with the HS interface ($F(1,36)=29.317$, $p<.0001$) while no significant difference between the older and younger participants appeared for the TBS interface.

For the Banking-Insurance domain, the statistical analyses did not show any significant effect of the participants' age ($F(1,36)<1$, n.s.). On contrary, the interface had a significant effect ($F(1,36)=9.322$, $p<.005$, $\eta_p^2=.21$): the TBS interface generated better performance than the HS interface. The interaction between the age and interface was not significant ($F(1,36)=2.925$, $p>.05$).

3.2   Task Time

For the Manga domain, the age has a significant effect ($F(1,36)=37.242$, $p<.0001$, $\eta_p^2=.51$): the younger participants took less time than the older participants. The interface had also a significant effect ($F(1,36)=5.177$, $p<.05$, $\eta_p^2=.13$): the HS interface took longer than the TBS interface. The interaction between age and interface was not significant ($F(1,36)=2.717$, $p=.11$).

For the Banking-Insurance domain, the age had a significant effect ($F(1,36)=30.466$, $p<.0001$, $\eta_p^2=.46$): the younger needed shorter time than the older participants. The interface had no significant effect ($F(1,36)<1$, n.s.). The interaction between age and interface was not significant ($F(1,36)<1$, n.s.).

Table 1. Mean (SE) values for the number of composite score of performances, task time (in sec.) according to age group, the interface and the domain

Dependant variables		Manga		Banking-Insurance	
		TBS	HS	TBS	HS
Performance (composite score)	Younger participants	-0,35 (0,9)	-0.39 (0.61)	-0.39 (0.09)	-0.11 (0.2)
	Older Participants	-0.16 (1.18)	1.52 (1.56)	-0.48 (0.07)	0.36 (0.26)
Task time (in sec.)	Younger participants	35,33 (5,38)	40,35 (4,93)	33,65 (4,44)	29,95 (4,49)
	Older Participants	70,96 (7,64)	102,35 (12,01)	65,84 (6,27)	72,19 (10,13)

4   Conclusion

In conformance with prior works [9, 11], the results showed that the older adults took longer to find information than the younger adults regardless of the interface and the domain. More precisely, in the Banking-Insurance domain, although the younger participants took less time than the older participants regardless of the interface, these two age groups obtained close performance. Indeed, the older participants had better performance while they navigated the TBS interface than the HS interface, although they took approximately the same time in to two interfaces. The older adults may need high reflexive time before making decision when they had high level of prior domain-knowledge. This result corroborated Starns and Ratcliff's finding [7]: the younger adults attempt to balance speed and accuracy to obtain better performance, whereas older adults attempt to reduce errors by finding information more slowly.

The age-related differences in performance (composite score of giving up and uncorrected answer) was significant only for the Manga domain, especially in the HS interface, for which the older participants had lower level of knowledge than the younger participants.

For the two domains, the TBS interface decreased age-related differences in performance. In contrast, the HS interface generated lower performance for the older adults in the two domains, especially faced to Manga domain in which older users had very lower level of knowledge than younger users.

Based on these findings, two points are relevant to be considered for web designers:

- A tag-based interface supports older users in finding information. A tag-based organization should be used to facilitate the navigation, especially the older users' navigation.

- Although the prior knowledge level also has an important impact on information searching activity and allows decreasing age-related differences, the TBS facilitated the navigation of older participants.

References

1. Amadieu, F., Tricot, A., Mariné, C.: Comprendre des documents non-linéaires: Quelles ressources apportées par les connaissances antérieures? L'année Psychologique (in press)
2. Chen, S.Y., Macredie, R.: Web-based interaction: A review of three important human factors. International Journal of Information Management 30, 379–387 (2010)
3. Folstein, M., Folstein, S., McHugh, P.: Mini-mental state. A practical method for grading the cognitive state of patients for the clinician. Journal of Psychiatric Research 12, 189–198 (1975)
4. Hölscher, C., Strube, G.: Web search behavior of Internet experts and newbies. Computer Networks 33, 337–346 (2000)
5. Pak, R., Price, M.M.: Designing an information search interface for younger and older adults. Human Factors 50, 614–628 (2008)
6. Rezende, F., de Souza Barros, S.: Students' navigation patterns in the interaction with a mechanics hypermedia program. Computers & Education 50, 1370–1382 (2008)
7. Starns, J.J., Ratcliff, R.: The Effects of Aging on the Speed–Accuracy Compromise
8. Boundary Optimality in the Diffusion Model. Psychology and Aging 25, 377–390 (2010)
9. Stronge, A.J., Rogers, W.A., Fisk, A.D.: Web-based information search and retrieval: Effects of strategy use and age on search success. Human Factors 48, 434–446 (2006)
10. Sum, S., Mathews, R.M., Hughes, I., Campbell, A.: Internet Use and Loneliness in Older Adults. CyberPsychology & Behavior 11, 208–211 (2008)
11. Wagner, N., Hassanein, K., Head, M.: Computer use by older adults: A multidisciplinary review. Computers in Human Behavior 26, 870–882 (2010)

Sketching Haptic System Based on Point-Based Approach for Assisting People with Down Syndrome

Mario Covarrubias, Monica Bordegoni, and Umberto Cugini

Politecnico di Milano, Dipartimento di Meccanica Via G. La Masa, 1, 20146 Milano, Italy
{monica.bordegoni,umberto.cugini}@polimi.it,
mario.covarrubias@mail.polimi.it

Abstract. This paper describes the 2D sketching haptic system (2DSHS) designed for the assessment and training of sketching control movements. The system has been developed for people with Down syndrome, who can use the system for drawing simple and complex sketches. These users are able to feel virtual objects by using a haptic device, which acts as a virtual guide taking advantages of its force feedback capabilities; in fact, the haptic device is driven under the user's movements and assisted through the Magnetic Geometry Effect (MGE). The 2DSHS has been used as an input device for tracking the sketching movements made by a user according to the visual feedback received from a physical template without haptic assistance. Then, the 2DSHS has been used as an output device that provides force feedback capabilities through a point-based approach. Preliminary evaluation has been performed in order to validate the system. Two different tasks have been performed -sketching a template and hatching a surface- with the aim to obtain more information related to the accuracy of the device. The performance has been evaluated by comparing the analysis of the tracking results.

Keywords: Haptic technology, assisted sketching, unskilled people.

1 Introduction

A sketch is a rapidly executed freehand drawing that is not intended as a finished work. Sketching is one of the most complex human activities in which the hand movements are controlled by the central nervous system, which regulates the activity of the hand and arm muscles to act in synergy. The central nervous system receives dynamic feedback information from visual sensors and from other body sensors located on the skin, muscles and joints while regulating the motor output. In case of developmental disorders, such as Down Syndrome, motor control may be greatly affected [1]. People with Down Syndrome may demonstrate reduced sensory acuity, lengthened reaction time, hypotonia and altered postural responses to perturbation. One of the hypotheses suggests that the source of motor difficulties originates in deficit of the central representation of actions. As suggested by the literature [1, 2]

C. Stephanidis (Ed.): Posters, Part I, HCII 2011, CCIS 173, pp. 378–382, 2011.
© Springer-Verlag Berlin Heidelberg 2011

practice can have positive influence on the motor skill. Haptic guidance has a significant value in many applications, such as medical training [3], hand writing learning [4], and in applications requiring precise manipulations [5]. The guiding force can be either generated by a force-feedback device, such as a Phantom haptic device [6]. There are, however, only very few assisted applications for unskilled people in order to promoting them in a specific employment role. The aim of our study was to assess how the sketching control movements under haptic feedback are affected in people with Down Syndrome. We have designed the sketching haptic device for providing assistance movements while sketching through the haptic point-based approach.

2   The Concept

The sketching device concept has been developed through a series of virtual and physical prototypes to enable the evaluation of its potential for improving 2D operations (sketching and hatching). In order to enable the 2D operations by the user, several configurations have been analyzed. Figure 1 shows both, the CAD concept and the physical prototype.

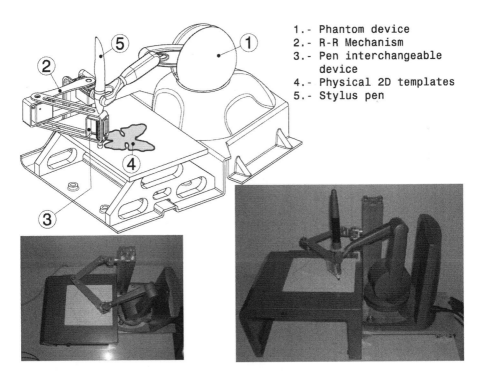

1.- Phantom device
2.- R-R Mechanism
3.- Pen interchangeable
      device
4.- Physical 2D templates
5.- Stylus pen

Fig. 1. CAD assembly concept and physical prototype of the sketching device

The Phantom device (1) is linked through the R-R mechanism (2) in order to provide 2 degrees of freedom. The pen interchangeable device (3) is used as a quick mechanism to change different pen's color; it is also possible to interchange the physical templates (4). The stylus (5) of the Phantom desktop is driven under the operator's movement and assisted by the Magnetic Geometry Effect (MGE). When this option is activated, a spring force tries to pull the sphere of the stylus (5) of the haptic device towards the surface of the virtual geometry that is used as a virtual guide. In fact, this effect is used in order to assist the user's hand.

3 Preliminary Test

We have carried out several preliminary tests in order to validate the sketching device while performing sketching and hatching tasks. The 2D operations accuracy has been measured using the Phantom device as input. The operations have been performed by tracking the stylus of the Phantom device through the DeviceLog command provided by the H3D API platform. The tracked sample rate is 25 Hz.

3.1 Sketching Operations

In this task, a 2D printed sketch has been provided with the same coordinate system of the 2D haptic sketch. First, we ask for a free sketching by using the device without the haptic support, and then the same sketch has been designed by enabling the 2D haptic sketch as a guide path.

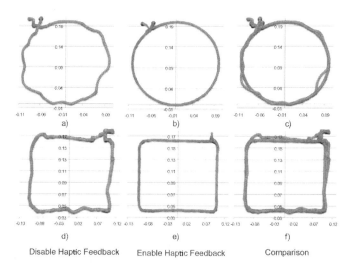

Fig. 2. Sketching geometry

Figure 2-a shows the resulting path tracked by the user's sketching operation in which the haptic feedback is off. Figure 2-b shows the same sketch operation with the haptic feedback enabled; we can observe a strong difference (Figure 2-c) in the accuracy of the operation. Similar task has been requested using a rectangle as can be seen from Figures 2-d, 2-e and 2-f. The most evident advantage provided by the 2D haptic sketches is the accuracy.

3.2 Hatching Operations

In the hatching task we request to fill the internal surface of the butterfly sketch as can be seen in Figure 3-a. Figure 3-b shows the hatching operation performed by the user without the haptic feedback, in fact, the 2D haptic sketch has been disable. Figure 3-c shows the hatching operation with the haptic feedback enable.

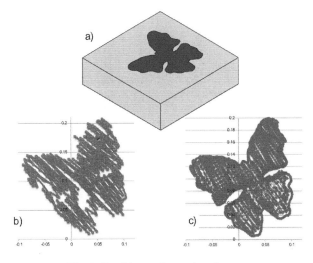

Fig. 3. Hatching an internal surface

Also in this operation, it is evident the advantage of using the 2D haptic sketches as a virtual guide for assisting the user's hand movement while hatching a region.

4 Conclusions and Future Work

The paper proposes a sketching system based on the point-based haptic approach. The main application of the haptic device is related to assisting people with Down Syndrome in the assessment and training of hand movements like sketching and hatching tasks. We explored user performance while using the haptic point-based approach. Results show that the effects of using the 2D haptic sketches increase the accuracy in the tasks operations. We are currently performing an evaluation with Down people in order to measure their improvements in 2D operations skills. In fact, this evaluation considers several parameters, which involve time, velocity, distance, and learning while the user is performing 2D operations with the sketching haptic device.

Acknowledgments. The authors would like to thank Emanuele Fedeli for his support in the preliminary evaluation of the sketching haptic device. Emanuele Fedeli provides specialized manual training for Down people at Laboratorio Artimedia (Calolziocorte, Italy).

References

1. Blank, R., Heizer, W., von Voss, H.: Externally guided control of static grip forces by visual feedback age and task effects in 3-6 year old children and in adults. Neuroscience Letters 271, 41–44 (1999)
2. Kurillo, G., Gregorič, M., Goljar, N., Bajd, T.: Grip force tracking system for assessment and rehabilitation of hand function. Technol. Health Care 13, 137–149 (2005)
3. Liu, A., Tendick, F., Cleary, K., Kaufmann, C.: A survey of surgical simulation: applications, technology, and education. Presence: Teleoper. Virtual Environ. 12, 599–614 (2003)
4. Teo, C., Burdet, E., Lim, H.: A robotic teacher of chinese handwriting. In: Proceedings of the 10th Symposium on Haptic Interfaces for Virtual Environment and Teleoperator Systems, HAPTICS 2002, IEEE Computer Society, Los Alamitos (2002)
5. Ahlström, D.: Modeling and improving selection in cascading pull-down menus using fitts' law, the steering law and force fields. In: Proceedings of the SIGCHI conference on Human factors in computing systems, CHI 2005, pp. 61–70. ACM, New York (2005)
6. PHANToM device, SenSable Technologies Inc., http://www.sensable.com (accessed February 16, 2011)

Helping Hands versus ERSP Vision: Comparing Object Recognition Technologies for the Visually Impaired

Marc A. Lawson[1], Ellen Yi-Luen Do[1], James R. Marston[2], and David A. Ross[2]

[1] College of Computing, Georgia Institute of Technology, Atlanta, GA 30332 USA
[2] Atlanta Vision Loss Center, 1670 Clairmont Road, Decatur, GA 30033 USA
{marc.lawson,ellendo}@gatech.edu
jim.marston@gmail.com, ross0128@bellsouth.net

Abstract. A major challenge for people with vision impairments ranging from severely low visual acuity to no light perception (NLP) is identifying or distinguishing the difference between objects of similar size and shape. For many of these individuals, locating and identifying specific objects can be an arduous task. This paper explores the design and evaluation of the "Helping Hand": A radio frequency identification (RFID) glove that audibly identifies tagged objects. In this paper we describe the design of a wearable RFID apparatus used for object identification. We evaluated the effectiveness of the glove by conducting a three-arm randomized controlled study. In our experiment, we compare a baseline (no assistive device), RFID (Helping Hand) and computer vision (ERSP Vision Software) in identifying common household objects. We also administered a questionnaire to obtain subjective data about the usability experience of the participants. Our experimental results show a reduction in the amount of time required to identify objects when using the Helping Hand glove versus the other two methods.

Keywords: object recognition, RFID, visual impairment, assistive technology, and computer vision.

1 Introduction

Over 314 million people worldwide are visually impaired, of whom 45 million are totally blind [1]. Presently, in the United States there are approximately 20 million people with visual impairments [2]. There are several different gradients of visual acuity – ranging from severely low visual acuity to no light perception (NLP). Many tests are developed to measure a person's level of vision. For example, Tumbling eye charts and the Snellen test measure an individual's visual acuity against the normal population curve. Performance scores are ranging from 20/10 to 20/200, where a score of 20/20 represents "normal vision" or what the average person can see at a distance of 20 feet. People with extremely low visual acuity have what is called a low vision evaluation. These evaluations are more comprehensive and measure a patient's ability to count fingers, observe motion or perceive light from varied distances [3].

C. Stephanidis (Ed.): Posters, Part I, HCII 2011, CCIS 173, pp. 383–388, 2011.
© Springer-Verlag Berlin Heidelberg 2011

A person with normal visual acuity can recognize complex images of objects varying in size, orientation and position within $1/10^{th}$ of a second [4]. Individuals with near total blindness, however, must rely on multiple senses like touch, taste and smell for object identification [5, 6], oftentimes making locating and identifying specific objects an arduous task. In using these other modalities a visually impaired person can sometimes spend a significant amount of their time trying to identify common everyday objects. The question is then, what tools can we offer to help reduce the time needed for such tasks?

Object recognition technology can be used to improve the visual perception process for the visually impaired by providing audible feedback describing objects. Our research evaluates the effectiveness of a wearable RFID design we have developed versus other established object identification methods.

2   Helping Hand System Overview

This section describes the components of the Helping Hand. The system is comprised of 3 different modules: a RFID Antenna, a Microcontroller board and a Secure Digital (SD) sound shield. Below we describe each module separately.

2.1 Main Board

The microcontroller board used in our prototype is the Arduino Duemilanove. The system software controlling the microcontroller was developed in Wiring and is programmed to recognize a number of passive transponder tags detected by an attached RFID antenna. When an incoming message ID is received it is validated and then associated with a wave file stored on an internal SD sound card. An audible wave file is then played as feedback. The board and battery are stored in a glove pocket positioned on the back of the wrist and lower forearm region. The mounting location for the components was selected for freedom of movement in the hand.

2.2 RFID Reader

The RFID reader module is a Parallax low frequency serial reader. It interfaces with our microcontroller board and sends serial data at a rate of 2400 bits per second. It can detect a HF passive tag within a distance of 2 – 3 inches from the antenna. In our design, the reading antenna is positioned on the back of the palm. This gives the antenna the best possible angle of detection and does not occlude the use of the hand.

2.3 Sound Shield

The sound shield provides audible feedback for our system. It connects to the main board and has a slot for a SD/MMC card. It plays 16 bit wave files stored on the SD card plugged into it. The audio files are preprogrammed and associated with transponder tags. When the reader identifies a tag, the associated sound identifying the object is played. The sound module possess a jack for headphones.

3 Methods and Results

To evaluate the effectiveness of our device versus other object recognition technologies, we conducted a within-subjects test design. Our goal was to capture performance variables for an objective comparison. In addition, we administered a questionnaire to obtain subjective data from each participant.

3.1 Subjects and Experimental Setup

In our study we tested 7 visually impaired participants consisting of 4 women and 3 men. We performed our participant testing at the Center for the Visually Impaired Georgia (CVIGA). Written informed consent was obtained from all subjects prior to testing. In addition, the participants provided information regarding their visual condition. Five of the participants were congenitally blind and had no light perception. The other two subjects, #4 and #7 were visually impaired due to the progressive diseases of Vogt-Koyanagi-Harada (VKH) syndrome & myopic degeneration respectively. These two subjects had been previously sighted. Subject #4 was totally blind and had light perception, while subject #7 was legally blind but could distinguish light, shape and color. The subjects were seated at a table throughout the entire experiment. Each participant was instructed on how to use both the Helping Hand and ERSP vision tools prior to being tested. Ten practice minutes were allotted for each tool. At the conclusion of the practice activity, a randomly selected object was placed in front of the subject on the table. Next, the participant was instructed on the identification method to be used and was asked to identify the object in front of them using that method. Each object identification method was tested 4 times. The objects were randomly selected to reduce any learned effects.

3.2 Objects

The objects in the study were arranged into four groups. Each group is consisted of common household items of similar size and shape. One group includes different flavors of soda packaged in identical bottles. The other groups of items were comprised of medication bottles, cereal boxes and non-toxic cleaning agents. The items in each group were similar; however the groups were of different categories. A subject could easily distinguish a box of cereal from a bottle of soda. Items were added to each group to randomize the number of possible objects and to reduce the possibility that participants can easily predict what the object is being tested.

3.3 Measures

We used two approaches to measure objective and subjective information in our testing. To obtain our objective data, a stopwatch was used to measure the amount of time required to correctly identify the objects. Object recognition times were recorded using 2 decimal point precision. For our subjective information we utilized a Likert survey which was verbally administered at the conclusion of each testing arm. The survey was comprised of four opinion questions scored on a seven-point scale from 1 (strongly disagree) to 7 (strongly agree). The questionnaire asked the participants to rank different aspects of the testing method based on the following four criteria: simplicity, practicality, predictability and preference.

3.4 Results

We measured the object recognition times for 7 visually impaired subjects using 3 different testing methods. The bar graph in figure 1 displays the percentage of improvement when using either Helping Hand or ERSP over the baseline (no device). In 6 of the 7 participants tested, the use of a technology, either with Helping Hand (RFID) or ERSP (computer vision), improved recognition times.

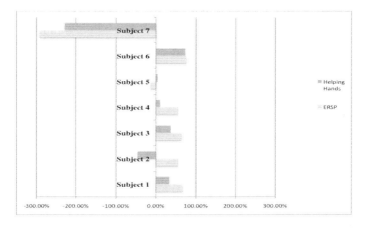

Fig. 1. Percentage of improvement for each participant using Helping Hand or ERSP over the baseline (no device)

For 5 participants, the Helping Hand prototype yielded the highest percentage of improvement. In one case (subject #7), the baseline (with no technology) was significantly faster than using either Helping Hand or the ERSP. Two factors could have contributed to this result. First, the data collected for subject #7 was averaged over 3 trials instead of 4. During one testing run, the camera used by the ERSP software malfunctioned resulting in an object recognition time delay of several minutes. This issue introduced a major outlier in our data set and was subsequently removed for others. An additional contributing factor could be the fact that even though subject #7 was legally blind, she was not totally blind. This subject's ability to perceive light, shape and form may have contributed to the significantly faster baseline times, as she could distinguish the objects without using any device.

Figure 2 shows the mean values for all the Likert survey scores. An analysis revealed the Helping Hand as the most simple to use (avg. 5.71, σ=1.25), practical (avg. 5.57, σ=1.13), predictable (avg. 6.00, σ=1.41) and preferred (avg. 4.57, σ=1.62) of all the tested methods. In comparison, the scores for the ERSP device are significantly lower than the baseline, particularly in simple to use (4.xx), practical (xx) and preferred (xxxx).

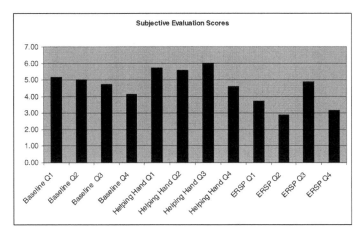

Fig. 2. Participants' subjective evaluation for ease of use scores in 7-point scale for Q1, simple to use, Q2, practical, Q3, predictable, and Q4 preferred

4   Discussion

To understand the effectiveness of our Helping Hand design, we evaluated our device against the baseline (no assistive device) and ERSP (computer vision). Our objective results revealed that the use of the Helping Hand produces faster object recognition times among the three methods studied. The results of our survey also showed positive participant opinion about the device. These are encouraging results. Meanwhile, the study revealed interesting results regarding partially sighted individuals using object recognition tools. Subject #7, a legally blind participant (who can distinguish light, shape and color) performed better when not using any assistive devices. This result leads to an interesting research question: Is there a low vision threshold for using object recognition devices?

In this study we show that the Helping Hand performs better when evaluated against a baseline and the ERSP method, but our participant pool was rather small. To conclude that the device truly outperforms others we would need to conduct study with a larger population or to include at least twenty participants. Finally, future evaluations should compare the Helping Hand with a non-wearable RFID technology, to determine if the wearable design is the reason for the better performance.

Acknowledgements. This material is based upon work supported by the Veterans Administration (VA), Atlanta Vision Loss Center (AVLC) and the Health Systems Institute (HIS) Seed Grant at Georgia Institute of Technology. Any opinions, findings, and conclusions or recommendations expressed in this material are those of the authors and do not necessarily reflect the views of the sponsoring organizations. We thank the Center for the Visually Impaired Georgia (CVIGA) for help in recruiting test subjects and providing a facility for us to run the comparative study.

References

1. Visual impairment and blindness. World Health Organization (May 2009),
   http://www.who.int/mediacentre/factsheets/fs282/en/
2. Vision loss United States Department of Veterans Affairs (May 2009),
   http://www.research.va.gov/resources/pubs/docs/
   Vision-Loss.pdf
3. Wendy Strouse Watt, O.D.: How Visual Acuity is measured (October 2003),
   http://www.mdsupport.org/library/acuity.html
   (accessed: 8/1/2010) (Online)
4. Bierdman, I.: Visual Object Recognition. MIT Press, An Invitation to Cognitive Science Cambridge (1995)
5. Lacey, Simon, Peters, A., Sathian, K.: Cross-Modal Object Recognition is Viewpoint-Independent. PMC 2(9) (2007)
6. Sensation and perception By E. Bruce Goldstein. p. 340 8th Edition Wadsworth

Examining the Current State of Group Support Accessibility: An Expanded Study

John G. Schoeberlein and Yuanqiong Wang

Towson University
7800 York Road
Towson, Maryland 21252-0001 USA
Jschoe4@students.towson.edu, ywangtu@gmail.com

Abstract. Group support applications are widely used in workplace to support group work. Unfortunately, persons who are blind often found it difficult to access group support applications, due to the highly graphical nature of the application; this hinders their ability to contribute to the group. As a result, persons who are blind often face problems in gaining and retaining employment. In order to expand on the knowledge gained from previous research, three additional focus group studies were conducted. The focus group studies show that accessibility and usability issues of group support applications are impeding persons who are blind from productive group work. The implications of the results from this research project are also discussed.

Keywords: Group support, accessibility, usability, blind.

1 Introduction

According to World Health Organization [5], about 314 million people are visually impaired worldwide, among them 45 million are blind. In today's global economy, many organizations utilize software applications, such as: email, document sharing, scheduling software, and conferencing systems for their collaborative work. Therefore, the ability to access these software applications becomes crucial for anyone to be able to perform well in the group environment. Unfortunately, current software applications are often not accessible to persons who are blind, because of the highly graphic nature of the interface. Thus, making it even harder for them to obtain and keep employment. With the unemployment rate for working age persons who are blind in the United States of 70% to 75% [4], the accessibility problems associated with group support applications become imperative.

As an early attempt on designing a more accessible group support application, a pilot focus group session and two field studies were conducted with five blind users who are the members of an access technology team in a Mid-Atlantic state, in the summer of 2010. The purpose of these studies was to investigate how persons who are blind work in groups, specifically the types of technologies they use, and their experience with software applications during group collaboration. It was discovered that the subjects did not use full-fledged groupware applications that support complete group processes. Instead, they utilized group support applications such as email, text

C. Stephanidis (Ed.): Posters, Part I, HCII 2011, CCIS 173, pp. 389–393, 2011.
© Springer-Verlag Berlin Heidelberg 2011

messaging, shared calendars, and track changes in documents, to support their group work. Various accessibility and usability issues were discussed during the sessions. For example, the subjects reported to have experienced problems, such as: reading the wrong message; not being notified of events; not being able to share the calendar in the monthly view; and, the contacts reading repeatedly when using Microsoft Outlook, the most frequently used email application by the subjects. Will users with less experience have similar results? Are there any different challenges less experienced users face?

In order to expand on prior knowledge and to understand how persons who are blind work in groups, the group support they require, and any accessibility and usability issues they encounter, three focus group studies were conducted during a Mid-Atlantic state convention of the National Federation of the Blind (NFB), in the fall of 2010. The following research questions were addressed:

- RQ1: How do persons who are blind work in groups?
- RQ2: What are the accessibility and usability challenges persons who are blind experience with software applications (specifically groupware or group support application)?
- RQ3: What kind of support do persons who are blind require so that they can perform group work?

2 Research Method and Procedure

Focus groups are group interviews that allow for the access of multiple points of view in a short time period (e.g. a single meeting) [1]. The size of the group can vary from 4 to 6 as a mini-group to than 10 as a full group [2]. The focus group studies allow the collection of data from multiple sources at a single meeting, the observation of the group dynamic as the group interacts, the gaining of agreement among several group members, and the validation of the group process and other data with the entire group. In order to gather feedback from people with different background, focus group is utilized. In this study, after preparing the meeting guide and questionnaires that collect background information about the subjects, each focus group session contained the following steps:

1. Conduct the focus group session, based on the meeting guide. The session is audio recorded. Researchers also take notes during the discussion.
2. Perform content analysis of the audio transcript and the researcher notes, to identify content categories;
3. Validate agreement of the coded content, using Cohen's Kappa; and,
4. Report findings.

3 Research Results

3.1 Demographics

Three sessions of small focus group studies were conducted with total of fourteen participants (nine females and five males, all blind, with no residual vision) during the NFB State Convention in a Mid-Atlantic state.

All of the participants utilized the computer daily and were adults with computer experience of at least 11 years. Tables 1, 2 and 3 show the distribution of age and their screen reader and computer experience.

Table 1. Age Distribution

Age	Number of Participants	Percentage
40-49	5	55.6%
50-59	2	22.2%
60 and over	2	22.2%

Table 2. Screen Reader Experience

Years of Experience	Number of Participants	Percentage
1-5 Years	1	11.1%
6-10 Years	0	0%
11-20 Years	3	33.3%
21-30 Years	5	55.6%

Table 3. Computer Experience

Years of Experience	Number of Participants	Percentage
11-20 Years	5	35.7%
21-30 Years	9	64.3%

3.2 Preliminary Results of Content Analysis

Content analysis was performed on the audio transcript and researchers' notes from the group discussion collected from the focus group study. Two research assistants performed as coders. Key points were grouped into categories. Cohen's Kappa was used as the indicator for integrator reliability [3] to make sure the consistency of the transcript coding. Total of 97 cases were identified with Cohen's Kappa at 0.94 indicating the acceptable agreement and reliability between the coders.

Six categories were determined as a result of this analysis:

- Groupware or group support software/features utilized;
- The tasks/steps necessary to complete a group project;
- Accessibility and usability issues;
- Group interaction techniques;
- Accessibility documentation and support; and,
- Accessibility design considerations.

While working in groups, participants reported that they use a screen reader to access software interface with software such as email and chat for communications and document sharing, and a note taking device for documenting meeting notes.

Outlook, Outlook Express, GroupWise, Google Calendar, chat tools such as Instant Messenger, Microsoft Office (Excel, Word, PowerPoint), SharePoint, and Word

Perfect were utilized to support group work. Outlook, Outlook Express, GroupWise, Instant Messenger and Google Calendar were used for their email, chat, task tracking, and group calendars features, while Microsoft Office, SharePoint and Word Perfect were utilized for document sharing and exchanging. All of these applications support group work, but are not considered full-fledged groupware. It appears that software features groups utilize the most include email, chat/text messaging, document sharing, task tracking, and sharing calendars.

The general project workflow discussed by the participants matched prior research during the pilot focus group study which includes identifying the purpose of the project, assigning a project leader, exchanging documents via *email*, followed by a *combination of face-to-face meetings, conference calls and additional email exchanges.*

Participants discussed some new accessibility and usability issues such as the difficulty to track changes, to follow a conversation in a chat session, to keep up with the software upgrades, and to use Windows ribbon menus. For example, track changes are garbled with so many inserts and deletes that it is difficult to comprehend the changes to a document. A participant commented, *"My track changes goes from the next comment to the next comment. It is hard to keep up with all of the information presented, and to determine the original and the change. Frequently, I just accept all of the changes. There is too much clutter with track changes."*

The inability to follow a conversation in a chat session was a concern for the participants. A participant commented, *"In a Chat Session – figuring out who said what, is an issue. You are no longer synchronous, when you have to look around the screen to figure out who said what. You are going to get behind the chat pretty fast. Even if you have access, chat is too difficult to keep up with the conversation."*

Since most of the participants make customizations to make applications work with screen readers, when new software upgrades are applied, the previous customizations or settings are lost. Most participants agreed with the comments made by one of the participants, *"I try to customize my interface but you loose your changes to the interface when upgrades occur When you get a new version of Office, for example. The new software comes out for sighted people, then the access technology people scramble to make the software function for persons who are blind."*

The ribbon menus added to new versions of Windows applications, were considered inaccessible and unusable -- *"The ribbons are not accessible – you have the up-and-down ribbons, and you are supposed to memorize the ribbons. It is not very usable. I cannot get to the other ribbons, like the spell checker for example. The prior design with the menus and the alt keys was a better approach for accessibility and usability."*

4   Conclusion

Multiple focus group sessions confirmed the results from previous study while also presented some new issues that were not discovered when we did the pilot study with more experienced users. Even though all the participants are elder adults with extensive experience utilizing computer and adaptive technologies while working in groups, they do encounter accessibility and usability issues while interacting with group support applications. Some common issues identified include the difficulty with track changes, following a conversation in a chat session, software upgrades, and Windows ribbon menus. The results from this study will serve as a guideline on what aspects of the applications need to be focused on when designing different group support applications/features. For example, when designing chat features for groups of more than two people, how to present the awareness in terms of what topic is discussed by which participant is extremely important; when designing document co-editing features, how to present changes or comments made by each co-worker clearly while not clutter the whole document.

References

1. Courage, C., Baxter, K.: Understanding Your Users. In: A Practical guide to user requirements. Methods, Tools and Techniques. Morgan Kaufmann Publishers, San Francisco (2005)
2. Greenbaum, T.L.: The handbook for focus group research, 2nd edn. Sage Publication, Thousand Oaks (1998)
3. Kurasaki, K.S.: Intercoder Reliability for Validating Conclusions Drawn from Open-Ended Interview Data. Field Methods 12(3), 179–184 (2000)
4. National Federation of the Blind. Assuring opportunities: A 21st century strategy to increase employment of blind Americans,
   http://www.icbv.net/National%20Issues/Opportunities.htm
5. World Health Organization,
   http://www.who.int/mediacentre/factsheets/fs282/en/

Verbalizing Images

Lisa Tang and Jim Carter

Dept. of Computer Science, University of Saskatchewan,
Saskatoon, Saskatchewan, Canada
lisa.tang@usask.ca, carter@cs.usask.ca

Abstract. Although a picture is worth a thousand words, how can you communicate its meaning and content in less than 250 words when that is all you have? Images are often used to convey information, supplement textual content, and/or add visual appeal to documents. The Usability Engineering Lab (USERLab) at the University of Saskatchewan developed an approach for generating informative alternative text for all types of images. This paper describes the approach and reports on the results of applying the approach by developers, content providers, usability and accessibility specialists, and the general public users.

Keywords: alternative text, images, description, captions.

1 Introduction

Textual content within a document often makes reference to images within the same document without explicitly explaining what is being communicated by the image. Alternative text helps people (both sighted and non-sighted) understand the image content by providing equivalent information to an image in a textual form. Alternative text can be beneficial in the following scenarios:

- when multi-tasking and interacting with the computer aurally (e.g. while driving)
- when using a device where the picture cannot easily be seen (e.g. on a smart phone in environments producing glare on the screen)
- when the person has a visual disability and relies on screen reader technologies
- when the person cannot comprehend the image.

While alternative text is beneficial to have, how should it be composed? There is a need for guidance concerning what to describe about an image. The purpose that an image serves and its context in the document can help determine what to describe. An image could encapsulate a vast amount of information. While it is desirable to keep as much information as possible, there may be too much for a person to process. Some of the information may also be irrelevant to the situation or context.

People need guidance on how to identify important information, how to rate the information, and how to transform the information into comprehensible prose. This paper proposes an approach for guiding people to create informative and descriptive alternative text for images and other graphical content. This work is being developed into ISO/IEC technical report 20071-11[b].

C. Stephanidis (Ed.): Posters, Part I, HCII 2011, CCIS 173, pp. 394–398, 2011.

2 Background

While there is much guidance on containers for providing alternative text [a], there is currently a lack of literature and research regarding the *composition* of alternative text, that is, what information to include and how to put the information together. We investigated the research areas of library science, image indexing, captioning, audio description, art description, and tactile representation for guidance.

Types of Information. It is important to know what information to convey to the user before beginning to write alternative text. The types of information that can be communicated through an image can be categorized into "What", "Who", "Where", "When", "Why", "How", and "How much".

Intended Versus Actual Information. An image chosen to convey certain information may be interpreted differently by a user, leading to miscommunication. It is important to ensure that the intended information is clearly communicated.

General Versus Specific. Information about an image can be generic or specific, yet accurately describes the image. For example, a general description could be "dog" and a specific description could be "poodle". While both uses the same number of words, the specific description is more descriptive. Vivid, succinct, and imaginative words provide the user with a better mental image within a limited time.

Importance Levels. Different pieces of information can have different levels of importance. It is important that the user receives essential information (that they want or need) as quickly as possible. Then if they so choose, they can request for additional, less significant, information. Considering time or space limitations, it is important to identify the essential information and present it first.

Purpose and Context. Depending on the purpose and context of an image, different pieces of information become important. The alternative text used in one instance might not be applicable in another. Therefore, a standard alternative text might not be appropriate to be used for any given image and a new version of alternative text may need to be generated with each use of the image.

3 Method for Identifying Information for Images

The creation of suitable alternative text should be based on a thorough understanding of the image, its components, and the document that contains it. This can be done by applying the following approach:

1. **Justification of the Image.** The purpose of each image is identified and described. This step will influence which image components and information are important for the user to know. This answers the question "Why?"
2. **Identification of the Image Components.** Image components are identified depending on the purpose of the image. Image components may be a person, place, object, or area of the image that the user should know about. This step is necessary to properly identify information about the image that may be of importance to the

user. Identifying image components is an iterative process. While identifying the image (or component) content, it may become necessary to separate that image (or component) into several image components, and so on.

3. **Identification of the Image (or Image Component) Content.** The content of an image and its components are described based on the purpose and context of the image, along with its importance. This involves answering the question "What?" Identifying content often involves expert knowledge in the field of the image. For example, an art historian would have expert knowledge on paintings from the 1800s and can interpret the painting. However, those without expert knowledge can also identify content based on what they see in the image without interpretation.

4. **Elaboration of the Content.** Elaboration focuses on identifying specific details that might be significant in understanding an image or component. This involves answering applicable questions relating to "What?", "Who?", "When?", "Where?", "How much?", and "How?" from a comprehensive set of questions that can elaborate on a wide range of images. Not all of the questions will apply to every image, so this step should focus on significant questions and information.

5. **Organization of Alternative Text Information.** Information obtained from steps 1 to 4 is organized to improve its readability and allocated to the short or long descriptions of an image or to the document textual content. This involves removing redundancies; considering the importance of each piece of information; ensuring flow with the rest of the document; and reorganizing the information for readability.

6. **Evaluation of Alt-Text.** The resulting alternative text should be evaluated by someone other than the person who created it to verify that it suitably describes the image within the context of the document within which it is contained. Ideally, this would involve actual user testing. However, it is important that this step not be omitted due to lack of available users or resources. Evaluation by a colleague or friend is better than no external evaluation at all.

4 Prototype Tool

To make the approach easier (and thus more likely) to use, we created an online prototype tool that guides individuals through the first four steps of the approach. The prototype tool lets the user add and delete image components, save responses to questions about each component, and review the information. The prototype tool provides an opportunity to further improve the guidance in ISO/IEC 20071-11.

The prototype tool presents the set of questions that the individual should consider about the image. While it is not required to provide a response to every question in the set, it is highly recommended that all the questions be considered. To ensure that a question is at least considered, the prototype tool forces the individual to provide a response, even if only "No / Not Applicable".

The set of questions can be answered from a depth-first or a breadth-first approach. To facilitate both approaches, there are options to expand or collapse each category of questions individually, as well as to expand or collapse all categories at once.

The individual can complete the approach and answer questions over several sessions. The prototype tool saves the information provided by the individual into a database for review between sessions and ensures that the information is accurate to the best of their knowledge.

5   Evaluations

We conducted two research studies: to evaluate the approach in a document format and to evaluate the prototype tool. Both studies were evaluated by four user groups: developers, accessibility specialists, content specialists, and general public Internet users. Each participant was given the approach (in the form of a document or prototype tool), five images to describe, and a feedback form.

5.1   Procedure Document Evaluation

After analyzing the descriptions based on quality and quantity, we found that most developers performed as well or better than the other user groups and generally identified a higher quality of information. The participants felt that the document was logical, but they were unclear as to how to apply the approach. This suggests that the focus needs to change from developing guidance to supporting its application.

Half of the time (51.2%), participants did not break the image down into components. This may be because the participants did not understanding the importance of components or they did not know how to identify components. There was an expressed need for examples in order to better understand how the approach should be applied. For the evaluation, the examples were deliberate removed from the document in order to see how the approach would be interpreted.

Half of the participants focused on the general questions (e.g., "What is in the image?") when describing the image and did not consider the detailed questions. Very few participants considered questions regarding relationships, location, or "When". Identifying image components would also help to identify more detailed information regarding the image.

The three-level scale for rating the importance of a piece of information raised many questions and concern. The participants were not clear as to when each rating should be used and felt that they did not have the necessary knowledge to make that judgment.

Despite the difficulties the participants experienced in applying the approach, many were capable of writing informative alternative text. To improve their experience, many participants recommended that a tool be created.

5.2   Prototype Tool Evaluation

The prototype tool was tested by the same individuals from the first study. Participants used the prototype tool to apply the approach on a different set of five images. The participants felt that the tool-based approach was easier to understand than the document. The comments and feedback were focused on the phrasing and presentation of the questions in order to improve the user experience.

Based on the web page format, the participants did not feel the same freedom to write long descriptions. The responses tended to be more concise and less descriptive. Also, because the prototype tool forced the participants to consider all general and specific questions about each image component, the approach took on average over an hour to complete for each image.

In the existing structure of questions, some questions (such as those related to actions) exist across multiple categories (such as "Who" and "Logical Relationships"). Reorganization of the questions may help identify applicable questions faster and decrease the amount of time spent on the approach. The questions can also be rephrased to extract detailed information quickly.

Several participants (23.5%) commented that there was too much content within a single web page. They were overwhelmed by the amount of information to process and the number of tasks to complete. They suggested that the image components be identified on a separate page and the set of questions be presented over several pages.

Ideally, the approach would be completed within five to fifteen minutes. With the additional improvements described above, a tool can help extract essential information in a timely manner while generating higher quality descriptions.

6 Future Work

Our procedure for creating alternative text for images has proven to be a feasible approach that can help in creating good alternative text. Some of the recommendations for the prototype tool were implemented and the prototype tool is now publically available [c]. Further research and development is currently underway in the following aspects:

- Evaluate the quality of the resulting alternative texts generated by the procedure.
- Identify information currently missing from the set of information types.
- Identify which information is of greater importance for certain types of images.
- Clarify the guidance on levels of importance.
- Enhance the prototype tool to filter non-applicable questions.
- Provide additional guidance on transforming the information into alternative text.

Acknowledgements. We would like to thank Microsoft Canada for their support.

References

[1] ISO/IEC WD 20071-11 Information technology — User interface component accessibility — Guidance on creating alternative text for images (2010)
[2] Usability Engineering Lab (USERLab). Alternative Text Prototype Tool (2010), http://userlab.usask.ca/AltTextTool
[3] W3C. Web Content Accessibility Guidelines (WCAG) 2.0 (2010), http://www.w3.org/TR/WCAG20/Overview.html

Experiencing Accessibility Issues and Options

Lisa Tang[1], David Fourney[2], and Jim Carter[1]

[1] Department of Computer Science, University of Saskatchewan,
Saskatoon, Saskatchewan, Canada
[2] Department of Mechanical and Industrial Engineering, Ryerson University,
Toronto, Ontario, Canada
lisa.tang@usask.ca, dfourney@ryerson.ca, cs@cs.usask.ca

Abstract. This paper introduces a comprehensive and well structured set of accessibility demonstration experiences (ADEs) that are accessible to a wide range of users. The ADEs are designed to help students as well as software and user interface designers understand the needs and expectations of users with disabilities. They cover a wide range of issues and options in accessible computing. The paper concludes with a discussion of lessons learned both about teaching using ADEs and making ADEs more truly accessible.

Keywords: Accessibility, demonstrations, experiences, web accessibility.

1 Introduction

The Usability Engineering Research Lab (USERLab) at the University of Saskatchewan has created a comprehensive set of Accessibility Demonstration Experiences (ADEs), which are interactive experiences designed to be delivered via the web to introduce people to various aspects of computer accessibility, including web accessibility.

ADEs are useful for:

- *Accessibility courses.* The set of ADEs can be used as hands-on tutorial exercises within a computer accessibility course.
- *Introducing accessibility for other courses.* Individual ADEs can be used within a general human-computer interaction course, an introduction to computing course to supplement a unit on accessibility, or an introduction to support professional development courses on accessible computing.
- *Providing accessibility experiences for the general public.* The set of ADEs are publically available at the USERLab website [4] so that anyone interested in computer accessibility can find and use them (without registration or purchase).

These exercises are specifically designed to help students as well as software and user interface designers understand the needs and expectations of users with disabilities. They provide experiences, rather than a complete set of answers, that are intended to motivate their users to want to explore the issues further on their own.

C. Stephanidis (Ed.): Posters, Part I, HCII 2011, CCIS 173, pp. 399–403, 2011.

There are two types of ADEs:

- *Accessibility Issues ADEs* focus on identifying and evaluating barriers to individual's abilities to access various forms of information technology. These issues tend to cross modalities.
- *Accessibility Options ADEs* focus on strategies and technologies for meeting the needs of users with specific partial or full disabilities, combinations of disabilities, or barriers due to the user's environment. These options focus on single modalities.

The original set of five ADEs developed in 2006 have expanded to the current twelve ADEs. The current set of Accessibility Issues ADEs explore: the impact of accessible design, how to test for accessibility, issues specific to learning disabilities, issues specific to cultural and linguistic adaptability, and secondary encodings. The current set of Accessibility Options ADEs explore: built-in accessibility settings and services available in modern operating systems, replacing and assisting vision, replacing hearing, and replacing and assisting touching.

Some of these ADEs are based on materials available via the web. The set of ADEs compile these sources together for a comprehensive set of material that represent the widest possible range of accessibility issues and options in a standard structure.

2   Methodology and Structure

The ADEs can be completed within one hour to fit the need to rapidly develop an understanding of the issues surrounding accessible computing beyond a theoretical understanding. The ADEs provide tutorial information as well as hands-on activities.

All of the ADEs share a basic structure of five major sections: an introduction to the topic, interactive activities, reflection, feedback, and references. Where an ADE tends to require a specific sensory ability, alternative versions (based on the same structure) have been developed, where possible.

Introduction to Topic. Each ADE starts with a multimedia presentation to motivate the students and to open their mind to the topic area. Where available, the multimedia presentations involve or come from an authoritative source. This also serves to introduce students to important individuals and organizations working in the field of accessibility. While most multimedia introductions are accessible, the job of increasing accessibility to all introductions is an ongoing development activity.

Interactive Activities. A set of interactive activities (IAs) are then used to engage students through first hand experiences with some representative aspects of the accessibility issue or option. There is no attempt to teach the students all they should know about the issue or option. Various techniques are used for creating interaction, including: simulations, using actual tools, and interactive dialogues.

Reflection Activities. Students are then asked to reflect on their experiences and to consider how they can apply them to the design of accessible computing. Specific questions about each IA focus on what was learned / experienced and how these experiences might be applied to improving design accessibility.

Feedback Activity. Students are also asked to evaluate their experience in terms of whether the ADE performed as expected. This allows us to update and improve the ADE to become even better experiences for future users.

Reference Activity. The last section of every ADE provides recommendations for further activities that students can do on their own. It contains a selected list of some sources that can provide further information relating to the topic area.

3 Accessibility Issue ADEs

Accessibility issue ADEs provide students with experiences and insights on barriers to the ability of individuals to access various forms of information technology.

Before and After Considering Accessibility. This ADE uses the area of website accessibility as a source of practical examples of technology access to provide students with an introduction to computer accessibility. Students explore the "Before and After Demonstration" provided by WAI [5] using both a graphic and a text-based browser. An alternate version is provided for where vision cannot be used.

Automatic Accessibility Evaluations. This ADE introduces students to evaluating computer accessibility. The ADE guides students in using readily available online web accessibility evaluation tools to evaluate a sample website and determine to what level the website adheres to the recommendations of the WCAG [6].

Cognitive issues. This ADE introduces students to cognitive disabilities by focusing on issues surrounding specific "learning disabilities". It helps students relate to these disabilities and draw some understanding of how software design decisions can impact people with these and similar disabilities by utilizing the "Misunderstood Minds" website [3] that simulates the classroom experiences of children with learning disabilities. An alternate version is provided for where vision cannot be used.

Cultural and linguistic issues. This ADE focuses on accessibility issues resulting from cultural and linguistic differences. Successful communication requires that users and systems share a context of use to be able to interpret the interactions of each other [1]. Colors, symbols, and poor translation are used as examples to illustrate the issues that arise from a lack of shared context. An alternate version is provided for where vision cannot be used.

Secondary encodings. This ADE explores secondary encoding, which results from the presentation style applied to the primary information. Secondary encoding often provides additional information to help the recipient to correctly interpret its intended meaning. During translation between media, secondary encodings are often ignored, leading to miscommunication. This ADE helps students experience the perspective of users who cannot detect secondary encoding affected by color, tone, and culture. Alternate versions are provided for where vision or hearing cannot be used.

4 Accessibility Options ADEs

Accessibility option ADEs provide students with insights related to strategies and technologies for meeting the needs of users with specific partial or full disabilities, combinations of disabilities, or barriers resulting from the user's environment to access various forms of information technology.

Operating system-based accessibility services. This ADE introduces students to specific accessibility features available on Windows: Magnifier, On-Screen Keyboard, and Narrator. This ADE provides a general introduction to accessibility options. An alternate version is provided for where vision cannot be used.

Replacing vision – Using a screen reader. This ADE goes into more depth than the operating system-based ADE to provide students with an introduction to using a screen reader to navigate a Web page that is not visible (constructed using white objects on a white background). The goal of the ADE is to experience some of the difficulties of navigating and using websites with a screen reader and to consider the impact of using speech as a primary output modality in navigation and reading tasks.

Assisting Vision – Using color shifting and shading. This ADE explores the needs of people who have a color vision deficiency (i.e., colorblind). It consists of a simulation of color blindness to help students experience the needs and expectations of a person who is colorblind, as well as the importance of contrast. It then introduces color shifting tools that can be used to help address these issues.

Assisting Vision – Using a magnifier. This ADE explores issues that people with low vision experience through simulations. It encourages students to consider magnification tools and how they can help those with low vision.

Replacing hearing – Using captioning. This ADE provides students with experience using captioning and visual cues. It encourages students to consider how well technology such as captioning can assist deaf and hard of hearing users as well as users for whom English is a second or other language.

Replacing touching – Using voice recognition. This ADE provides students with experience using a voice recognition system to navigate a user interface and complete tasks, where physical limitations preclude the use of touch-based inputs.

Assisting touching – Using single switch input. This ADE provides students with the experience of having severe physical limitations, where they are only able to communicate via a single switch input device. It makes use of an on-screen keyboard that is customizable to support individual software applications. This ADE is not just about entering text, it focuses on the whole input experience.

5 Lessons Learned

The ADEs have been used and evaluated by a diverse set of students, including one blind student, one hard of hearing student, and a number of students from cultures where English was not their first language. Developing the current set of ADEs has taught us a number of insights into providing accessibility demonstration experiences.

Depth vs. Breadth. While depth is needed to get to specific examples, getting students to this depth needs to be simplified so that they can get right into their IAs without needing a lot of background. Shortcuts to or automatic set-up of IAs allow students to get to the heart of an IA and complete it in a reasonable amount of time.

While breadth is needed to represent large issues (rather than to focus too much on details), the set of IAs need to be limited (to keep ADE length to a reasonable amount of time). It is important to achieve the maximum of breadth between each IA.

Openness to Additional Topics. The topics of the original five ADEs were largely selected to be significantly different from one another. Student projects to create additional ADEs have identified many possible ADEs and topics that could be added. While we believe that our current set of ADEs is comprehensive on a high level, we recognize that there is the potential for many additional ADEs to be added. Our latest efforts are focused on creating an ADE dealing with alternative text for images, based on USERLab research and an ongoing ISO/IEC development effort [2]. We invite submissions or suggestions that would further develop our set of ADEs.

Avoiding Platform Dependencies. When using specific forms of interactive technologies, specific instances of these technologies may be dependent on certain operating system and other technological platforms. While some ADEs were easier to develop using platform-dependent software, this limits the environments in which these ADEs can be used. We are creating alternate versions for the different main platforms where platform independent versions are not practical.

Making ADEs Accessible. Accessibility Issue ADEs tend to deal with multiple modalities. As such, they tend to combine modalities that may be accessible with those that may be inaccessible. The purpose of the ADEs can be fulfilled by having a sufficient variety of IAs so that each user can access multiple experiences. Some Accessibility Option ADEs, by their very nature, deal with issues related to a given set of abilities.

6   Conclusion

After iteration and student testing we have developed a comprehensive and well structured set of ADEs that are accessible to a wide range of users. These experiences cover a wide range of issues and options in accessible computing. In conducting this development, we have learned a number of valuable lessons, both about teaching accessible computing and in making our experiences more truly accessible.

References

1. Carter, J., Fourney, D.: Using a universal access reference model to identify further guidance that belongs in ISO 16071, vol. 3(1), pp. 17–29. Universal Access in the Information Society (2004)
2. ISO/IEC WD 20071-11 Information technology— User interface component accessibility — Guidance on creating alternative text for images (2010)
3. Kirk Documentary Group, Ltd., WGBH Boston. Misunderstood Minds (2002), http://www.pbs.org/misunderstoodminds
4. Usability Engineering Lab (USERLab) Accessibility Demonstration Experiences, ADEs (2006), http://userlab.usask.ca/ade
5. W3C Web Accessibility Initiative. Before and After Demonstration (2006), http://www.w3.org/WAI/EO/2005/Demo/Overview
6. W3C Web Content Accessibility Guidelines [WCAG] (2008), http://www.w3.org/TR/WCAG20/

Adopting User-Centered Design for the Translating of Barrier-Free Design Codes/Regulations

Tsai-Hsuan Tsai[1], Wen-Ko Chiou[1], Huey-Yann Liao[2], and Tai-Xian Tseng[1]

[1] Department of Industrial Design, Chang Gung University, Taoyuan, Taiwan
[2] Architecture and Building Research Institute, Ministry of the Interior, Taiwan
ttsai@mail.cgu.edu.tw

Abstract. Over the past few decades, barrier-free design codes/regulations have been integrated into many countries' national regulations. The existing guidelines, however, have been criticized for being too abstruse and professional for practical use by the general public. As a result, the aim of this research is to analyse the existing presentation of building codes and barrier-free design regulations, including the full variety of characteristics, behaviors and requirements, and identities of environments in order to translate the information within barrier-free design codes/regulations into suitable presentations that match the users' requirements and special needs. In addition, suggestions for the presentation of codes/regulations are provided in this study.

Keywords: barrier-free design codes/regulations, user-centered design, design for all.

1 Introduction

In order to provide accessible and safe environments that adequately address best practice concerns for people with disabilities, barrier-free design codes/regulations are proposed as guidelines for assisting designers and builders in complying with the construction requirements while avoiding errors and costly renovations [1]. Over the past few decades, these types of codes and guidelines have been integrated into many countries' national regulations [2]. The existing guidelines, however, have been criticized for being too abstruse and professional for practical use by the general public [3]. As a result, the aim of this research is to analyse the display of barrier-free design codes/regulations, including the extent to which they address users' needs and possess the characteristics for translating the information into a suitable presentation matching the users requirements as well as any special requirements. We consider the development, display, classification of disabilities, and characteristics of barrier-free environments as defined within the guidelines as attributes of this analysis.

2 Existing Presentation of Building Codes and Barrier-Free Design Regulation

2.1 Barrier-Free Design Codes/Regulations vs. Displays

In this research project, we present the development of barrier-free design codes/regulations step by step, beginning first with texts and lists, then progressing to

C. Stephanidis (Ed.): Posters, Part I, HCII 2011, CCIS 173, pp. 404–408, 2011.

descriptions with dimensional pictures, and finally including pictures of actual environments and situations. The display of existing design codes can be divided into four types, as follows:

Text: Text is the main format for communicating barrier-free design codes/regulations, including the types of barrier-free environments, dimensional data, the principles of accessible design, and the facilities inherent to barrier-free environments [1, 3-11].

Tables: The tables list the differences in design principles or facilities within the same projects and environments. For example, Table 221.2.1.1 in the '2010 ADA Standards for Accessible Design' is a formal type of table found in barrier-free design codes/regulations. It indicates the minimum number of required wheelchair spaces in assembly areas in relation to the total number of seats [5]. Table 3.8.2.1 of the Barrier-free Design Guide is similar [1].

Dimensional Pictures: For supporting the text description of barrier-free design codes/regulations, dimensional pictures present the visual forms of barrier-free design, environments and facilities. They also include the patterns of disabled users and anthropometry data, to explain how users will interact with the barrier-free facilities and the specific actions that will take place within the environment. For example, the picture of '2010 ADA Standards for Accessible Design' [5] is a formal dimensional picture with a display of the accessible range of a wheelchair user's arms. In creating the barrier-free facilities, designers must follow the guidelines of the height range.

Pictures of real environment: To support the text descriptions and explanations, some barrier-free design codes/regulations have implemented pictures of actual environments and scenarios, documenting users' activities. These are meant to ensure that readers will understand and apply the guidelines to real situations exactly, by comparing the pictures to the information contained in the text. According to the research, the use of such images will help developers to manage the fluidity of design [12]. Publications such as the Singapore "Universal Design Guide 2007" and the Taiwanese "Inclusive Design: Designing and Developing Accessible Environments" are existing codes that include pictures of scenarios within actual environments for supplying clearer introductions and explanations of barrier-free design [3, 8].

Enhancing descriptions with digital media: Utilizing pictures of dimensions and scenarios within the context of real environments is an existing trend in the presentation of existing barrier-free design codes/regulations. However, in addition to using scenario pictures, we can also utilize digital media to ensure that the translation of guidelines is more appropriate and specific to readers' needs and to an understanding for the general public. For instance, users can find scenario videos and animation addressing workplace safety and equipment operation in digital media formats on Institution of Occupational Safety and Health Web sites [13]. Similar presentations can be found on the official site of the Workplace Safety and Health Council [14].

2.2 Barrier-Free Design Codes/Regulations vs. User's Needs and Characteristics

Today, with a significant proportion of the population aging, the "World Population Aging 2009" report of the Department of Economic and Social Affairs at the United Nations states that "At the world level, the number of older persons is expected to exceed the number of children for the first time in 2045." This report also indicates that the percentage of elderly people will increase to 22 percent of the world population by the middle of this century [15]. Therefore, including elders as one of the user types in guidelines has been a trend in the recent years. As seen in publications such as the Singapore "Universal Design Guidelines 2007" and the United Kingdom's "The Building Regulation 2010", this principle has been implemented in many codes/regulations of barrier-free design [4, 8]. However, the existing codes/regulations are still questioned, because "often people with disabilities are presented as being members of a homogenous group having exclusively mobility impairments and, in conclusion, all their interests and requirements being the same [2]." Thus, the regulations must include the full variety of handicapped individuals who may interact with the environments in question, dividing the users' needs extensively and definitely [3].

As noted, the existing barrier-free design codes/regulations address many types of disabilities with detailed definitions. We can see that the elderly, people with impaired sight or hearing, and wheelchair users are the main categories of handicapped individuals. For translating the information contained in the barrier-free designs/regulations, the presentations must not only include the needs and characteristics of these users, but also must display the activities and behaviors of people with disabilities, so that the information in the guidelines will be applied suitably according to the exact requirements and actions of people with disabilities.

2.3 Barrier-Free Design Codes/Regulations vs. Spaces and Environments

For designing and planning spaces with friendly accessibility to disabled people, many countries have implemented barrier-free design codes/regulations into their national building guidelines [16]. In terms of spaces and environments, these guidelines tend to focus on the barrier-free design of new construction and the redesign of existing buildings. Some of these regulations also focus on the maintenance of historic architecture. Thus, for translating the barrier-free design codes/regulations into a form that can be understood by the general public, it is necessary for the presentation of guidelines to include the various forms of building design, and match the actual environments of readers as closely as possible.

3   Conclusion

For achieving the goal of matching users' actual needs and the concept of "Access-for-all", we have analyzed the existing "barrier-free design codes/regulations", including the full variety of characteristics, behaviors and requirements, and identities of environments in order to translate the information within barrier-free design codes/regulations into suitable presentations that match the users' requirements and special needs. According to the analysis of existing design codes/regulations, we suggest that these guidelines must include the following:

− To divide and consider the users' needs extensively and definitely, the presentation of codes must match the full variety of handicapped individuals' traits and behaviors, including for those of impaired hearing and sight, as well as those of wheelchair users. Additionally, for we are in an aging period, with the special needs and comprehensive disabilities of elders, the presentation of codes/regulations must take their needs into account.
− The design of content presentation must be based on the reality of the environment. Especially in terms of architecture and space, the translating must include the local building patterns, styles, and cultural characteristics, and strive to match the recognition of the general public, thereby making the application of design codes/regulations apt for the design of real environments.
− Adopting scenario design to simulate the real dwelling environments and facilities matching the design codes/regulations while also containing digital media for translating the guidelines to help the users of barrier-free environments and their families, friends and caregivers to obtain the required information and apply the regulations to real environments.

References

1. Alberta Municipal Affairs, Design for Independence and Dignity for Everyone, in T5J 4L4, Safety Codes Council, Editor, Barrier-Free Policy Administrator: Edmonton, Alberta, Canada (2008)
2. Vozikis, K.T.: I. Kontzinou The Understanding of Accessibility and Universal Design-Presented on Results from a Recent Survey with Future Design Professionals in Greece. In: Engineering Education. 2009: World Scientific and Engineering Academy and Society (WSEAS) Stevens Point, Wisconsin, USA ©2009
3. Liao, H.Y.: Inclusive Design: Designing and Developing Accessible Environments, Architecture and Building Research Institude, Editor, Architecture and Building Research Institude, Ministry of The Interior (2008)
4. The National Archives, The Building Regulations 2010, in 2214, Ministry of Justice, Editor, HM Government Publishing (2010)
5. Americans with Disabilities Act, ADA Standards for Accessible Design, U.S. Department of Justice, Editor, Americans with Disabilities Act (2010)
6. Architecture and Building Research Institude, Accessible Buildings and Facilities Designing Standards, Ministry of The Interior, Editor, Architecture and Building Research Institude (2008)
7. Building and Construction Authority, Code on Accessibility in the Built Environment 2007, Building and Construction Authority, Editor. Tower Block MND Complex (2007)
8. Building and Construction Authority, Universal Design Guide (commercial buildings), in Singapore 069110, Building and Construction Authority, Editor. Tower Block MND Complex. p. 11 (2007)
9. Hamiton Public Works, City of Hamiton, Barrier-Free Design Guidelines, in Version 1.1.Hamiton Public Works (2006)
10. National Blood Service, Approved Document M, Office of the Deputy Prime Minster, Editor. National Blood Service, London (2004)

11. Americans with Disabilities Act, Accessibility Guidelines for Buildings and Facilities, U.S. Architectural and Transportation Barriers Compliance Board (Access Board), Editor. Americans with Disabilities Act (ADA), Washington, D.C (2002)
12. Carroll, J.M.: Five reasons for scenario-based design. Interacting with computers 13(1), 43–60 (2000)
13. Institution of occupational safety & health. SuperBee Safe Safety and health promotion - Safety scaffold. Fall Prevention (2009),
    http://www.iosh.gov.tw/Media/Media.aspx?cnid=479#18
    (cited March 17, 2011)
14. WSHCouncil. Confined Space, Safety in Confined Spaces - Case Study and Lessons Learnt (English) Video Gallery (2011),
    https://www.wshc.sg/wps/portal/
    video?action=viewVideoDetail&videoID=VL2011010700059
    (cited March 17, 2011)
15. Economic and Social Affairs, World Population Ageing 2009, Economic and Social Affairs Population Division, Editor. United Nations, p. 8 (2009)
16. Vozikis, K.T., et al.: The Understanding of Accessibility and Universal Design- Presented on Results from a Recent Survey with Future Design Professionals in Greece. WSEAS (2009)

User Research for Senior Users

Kaori Ueda and Kazuhiko Yamazaki

Chiba Institute of Technology Graduate School
2-17-1 Tsudanuma, Narashino, Chiba, 275-0016, Japan
kaori0226@gmail.com

Abstract. The purpose of this research is to propose new user research method for senior users, and discover problems of user interface design, propose an idea for improvement using proposed method. Targeted user is senior user from middle 50s to late 60s, and targeted product is cellphone. The aim of proposed method is to find out more detailed problems and the intention of senior users to improve user interface design. Author conducted preparatory survey based on proposed method with the Diary method and the Ethnographical interview. The results were classified into the impact analysis table. From those result, "change main screen image" has problem the most. Author improves its user interface design based on the results.

Keywords: Cellphone, Senior users, User interface design, The Diary method, The Ethnographical interview, HCD, Cognitive science.

1   Introduction

In 2013, it is expected 1 of 4 people will become senior citizens in Japan. But most of products are complicated and difficult to use for senior citizens. Author believes it is not easy to find out actual senior citizen's life. This is the original point of this research.

2   Purpose of Research

The purpose of this research is to propose new user research method suited for senior user, and discover problems of user interface design, propose an idea for improvement using proposed method. The aim of proposed method is to find out more detailed problems of the product and the intention of senior users to improve user interface design, and find the causes of barriers against operations of the product.

3   Condition of This Research

Targeted user is senior user from middle 50s to late 60s, and targeted product is cellphone. Author asks senior users to use own their cellphone in survey. The condition of the examination targeted senior users is to lighten senior user's loads, and be easy to join in the survey like senior users live naturally. Considering this thing, the Diary method and the Ethnographical interview were chosen. Especially, the Ethnographical interview makes senior users to join our conversation actively because the survey take place in somewhere they can be relieved like their home.

C. Stephanidis (Ed.): Posters, Part I, HCII 2011, CCIS 173, pp. 409–413, 2011.
© Springer-Verlag Berlin Heidelberg 2011

4   Survey of the Diary Method and the Ethnographical Interview

Before the survey, author conducted 2 experiments to decide the contents and shape of the evaluation sheet of the diary method. The purpose of this experiment is to make new evaluation sheet to obtain good results from senior users. First, author used the evaluation sheet in the reference literature. But the results just indicated there were 2 answers; "Yes" and "No". Senior users hardly have complains and questions against their cellphone's functions. Second, author made the folding type evaluation sheet to fill in the screen layout and the operation. But it was difficult to fill in the content while operating cellphone, so that author could not find problems in this way. Finally, since these results, author made the evaluation sheet attached behind cellphone. It requests senior users to check what they did, evaluate usability evaluation scales against operated content by 5 step, and write down in the free blank if they noticed or felt something [Fig 1].

Fig. 1. The evaluation sheet (full scale) and the scene of the Diary method

Author conducted preparatory survey based on proposed method. 3 persons in 60s were chosen as examinee. Author explained the purpose of this preparatory survey, how to do each research, and tasks. Considering if examinees did not use their cellphone at all, 7 tasks were prepared: call, send a message, take 2 photos, attach a photo to message, change main screen image, search train route, and save the train route result. Author asked examinees to do the Diary method using improved evaluation sheet about a day, and the Ethnographical interview about an hour. In Ethnographical interview, author asked examinees to operate as same as they did in the diary method, and interviewed how they use their cellphone. And author filmed the situation as survey record. After survey, author asked examinees some questions about cellphone's operations and cellphone itself.

On the Diary method, the result was filled in the table each item: time, place, operation, useful, efficiency, satisfaction, and comment in the free blank[Fig.2]. The evaluated results by 5 steps were totaled up, and filled in the impact analysis table.

Diary method result   subject No.1   Sat. August 21st

No.	time	place	contents of operation	Effectivity	Efficiency	Satisfation	comments (anything I notice)
1	03:00	home	confirm the time	5	5	4	Is it always cosrrect with standard time?
2	03:20	home	other (music)	5	5	5	
3	03:30	home	mail arrangement	2	1	1	toublesome
4	04:00	home	web (searching train)	5	4	4	"from Ichikawa to Narita" it needs some annoucement which stn is better to go
5	14:30	home	call	5	5	5	call for gramma's house
6	17:00	home	mail	5	5	5	8 e-mails
7	17:30	home	mail	5	5	5	comfirmation of reception
8	18:00	home	camera	2	3	1	he tried to take a pic of newspaper by camera, but he doesn't know about graphic mode.
9	18:40	home	mail	5	5	5	comfirmation of reception
10	19:30	home	call	5	5	5	Call from his wife
11	21:30	home	mail	5	5	5	
12	21:40	home	mail	5	5	5	troublesome
13	21:50	home	other (movie play)	5	5	4	too short to film
14	23:00	home	other (movie shooting)	5	4	4	too old!!!
15	23:00	home	setting change	5	5	5	book in, delete staff date
16	24:30	home	other (miniSDcard)	5	5	4	substitution "why doesn't those digital tools have unification?"

Fig. 2. An example of the result of the Diary method

On the Ethnographical interview, the filmed data was filled in the table each item: speech, operation, screen content after the operation, and notices[Fig.3]. Some important points were picked up from the table, and filled in the impact analysis table below the operation name classified by results of the Diary method.

In the impact analysis table, items filled in "useful is low and middle" blank and "efficiency is low" blank treat as the most important problem. In this case, it refers to "change main screen image". From this result, author improves its user interface design based on speech of examinees and notice from the Ethnographical interview results. "I can do middle of operation, but I can not find the way to register" obtained from the Ethnographical interview results proved that "change main screen image" is necessary to improve the most [Fig.4].

Result of the Ethnographical Interview (Raw data)
Place:home / Operation:Searching train

Date : Tue, August 17th / Examinee : T.I / job : Housekeeper

No.	What examinee say	operation	contents after examinee operated	Notices
01	«You can jump to here, leave Ichi-kawaOhno station at 13:53 with Musashino-line..» "What is that?" «I think it is the place of train. It says you should ride on the train from middle to backward to change next train.» "I see, I should ride on here, backward." «And it says you ride on the train to Tsudanuma on Sonu-line, you can arrive at Tsudanuma at14:13. Now you finished searching, so I wanna ask you to save this screen.»	upper right	Submenu appeared on the screen	It is established about preview statement about examinee said about U turn mark. Examinees are gotten turned on by something red color.
02	"Is it right on favorite list? Save to Datefolder... Humm, let's just do it"... Where did I save it? just try to do it."	down→center	Choose Save to data folder, then appear the logo mark of EZweb	I feel examinees do tasks by guesswork. I asked to save as task, so I thought it is easier to connect to "save to screen memo", but the "screen memo" makes examinees confusion, examinees didn't choose correct answer.
03	"Hum?" <Answer is not date folder.> "See? Is it kind of pics, right?" So I should select clear button.	clear	Back to the result of searching	
04	<Move to submenu again, then...> "screens? favorite? memo? I have no idea. Which one?" <What are you thinking now?> "I have no idea where to register it. Let's try it." <Save to screen memo?> "screen memo... I think it's not favorite." <Do you think which word is adjusted to save?> What? What is the difference? Just... try to register to favorite?"	center	Choose the favorite list, move to the screen to edit URL and title	Do they have some realization like "save" means "date folder"? "MEMO" makes a kind of barrier to confuse examinees thinking process
05	"It seems okay, doesn't it?" Then if I press upper right button, does it register? <I think so.> "Okay I do that."	upper right	move to the list of folders	
06	"Register to favorite list, then press OK? NEW? OK? ..try to press OK."	center	Choose OK, "Finished to register" appeared on screen. move to the result of searching	
07	"Done, yes, oops! It is come out again! Then what happen? <You registered just now...> "So?" <Could you go back to idle screen?> "And then?"	power off 2 times	"Finish to connect with ezweb. Is it okay?" appeared as alarm. Choose 2 (finish), then move to idle screen	
08	"And I see here, how do we say it? Ezweb? sort of..."	EZweb	Top screen of ezweb	They remember it with place, not the sign name.
09	"I guess it's gonna be good. I'll try select second button on favorite list."	down→center	Move to the favorite list	
10	"Here it is Ichikawaohno station, Tsudanuma...	down→center	Choose the bottom item, then move the result of searching	
11	<It isn't same as before one.> "Really?" <is it not same screen you register just now?> "Not same? Oh, that's right" <I think this is the one you register yourself.> "I did myself when I was alone. So it isn't same." <Could you go back to preview page?>	clear	Top screen of ezweb	
12	<Could you do that from the favorite list?>	center	Move to the favorite list	
13	"Transfer... Here is also transfer. <I guess it is on bottom of this screen> "Is anything different?" Everything is same, isn't it?	down→center	Choose the bottom item, then move the result of searching	This examinee chose the bottom item with question. As I have same experience, only title doesn't appear anything what we register. It's so bother to reset tltime name just for it.
14	<Oops> "Hummm..." <It is something wrong...> "Oh! There is nothing!" <Give me a second> "Why? Why? Did I push anything wrong button? probabbly...	clear	Top screen of ezweb	Register to favorite list is just to register the site, not save the screen. But another examinee could register it. Does it depend on the site?

Fig. 3. An example of the result of the Ethnographical interview

5 level evaluation / scales	Effectivity — Did you want to do?	Efficiency — Did you do it smoothly?	Satisfaction — Do you have a complain?
Low (1,2)	Setting change (idle screen) · Those words on submenu are hard to understand, and it makes examinees confuse, they couldn't find clue for next step. · They wanted to reset time, but they had to reset from choosing images again. · They felt concern even though they set and the word "Finish the setting" appered on screen.	Setting change (idle screen) · Too many layers and flows for changing idle screen · They dont care about buttons bottom of the screen like "OK" or "Submenu" · Captions of the item appear bottom of screen, but sometime not.	Web · They wanna search easy way and shortcut in some wise. · Color of cousor should be vivid color, like blue or red. · They seem lack a sense of fulfillment after they got result of searching. Setting change(idle screen) · It's hard to see where is the cursor.
Middle (3)	Web · They have no idea which screen to start · They took time to enter some number. · They have no idea to check the parallel botton. · They tried to save the screen, but the screen wasn't saved. · They passed because the search botton isn't specialized.	Web · Letter size is only small on web screen even though their mobile phone has a function to change letter size bigger. · They didn't notice the cursor mark which button · They couldn't figure out where is the goal because they changed letter size bigger and they couldn't look down whole flow.	Camera
High (4,5)	Call E-mail Camera They could operate above 3 tasks to goal with no problem.	Call (address book) · They book in some good friends as mobile phone and homephone. E-mail : They use predictive transform before they enter whole words Camera : Timing of pres the button and shooting are not same	Call E-mail · One of examinee's friend told her "not to use pictograph anymore". Because those pictograph doesn't match every mobile phone. · Those pictographes with e-mail are rack up on date folder.

Fig. 4. Impact analysis table with 2 results

5   Future Agenda

Until now, some problems about operating cellphone were come out using 2 examination techniques. Author hereafter conduct another survey with considering about followings: contents of evaluation sheet, questioning technique on the Ethnographical interview, and analyzing for improving user interface design of screens which has some problems.

References

[1] The Cabinet Office, the Aged Society white paper, pp.2–6 (2010) (Japanese)
[2] The rate of cellular phone by household, Honkawa Date Tribune (2010),
    http://www2.ttcn.ne.jp/honkawa/6350.htm (Japanese)
[3] Hara, N., Shida, T., Naka, T., Nambu, M., Harada, E.T.: Characteristics of Cognitive Aging in Appliance Operation. Matsushita Technical Journal 51(4) (2005),
    http://panasonic.co.jp/ptj/v5104/index.html
[4] Nojima, H., Harada, E.T.: Shinyo Press (2004) (Japanese)
[5] Kurosu, M., Ito, M., Tokitsu, R.: Introduction to User-Centered Engineering -Think about usabiliry - specific approach to ISO13407, pp.132. Kyoritsu Press (1999) (Japanese)
[6] Imai, T., Takeo, H., Yoshimura, M., Sakata, A., Sakakibara, N., Sekine, C.: Improving the usability and learnability of a home electric appliance with a long-term usability study (2009)
[7] JIDA, Product Design -To all the people who are related to the product development-, pp.101, WORKS CORPORATION Inc. (2009) (Japanese)
[8] Tarumoto, T.: Usability Engineering -Practical Technique for user survey and usability evaluation, pp.4, 5, 183, 184, Ohmsha (2005) (Japanese)

Audio-Haptic Description in Movies

Lakshmie Narayan Viswanathan, Troy McDaniel, and Sethuraman Panchanathan

Center for Cognitive Ubiquitous Computing
School of Computing, Informatics, and Decision Systems Engineering
Arizona State University
Tempe, Arizona, USA
{lakshmie,troy.mcdaniel,panch}@asu.edu

Abstract. This paper proposes a methodology to enhance audio described movies (i.e., films augmented with additional narration to explain visual content to viewers who are blind or visually impaired) by providing positional information of on-screen actors through haptics. Using a vibrotactile belt, we map the location of a character across the screen to a relative location around the waist, and the relative distance of a character from the camera is mapped to a tactile rhythm. Character movement is subsequently conveyed through these two dimensions. All participants, including one visually impaired subject, felt the vibrations improved their visualization of the clips. This subject also felt that it was quite easy to combine the information received through audio and haptics, and that the vibrations were not obstructing the subject's attention to audio.

Keywords: Audio description, video description, described audio, descriptive video service, movies, tactons, tactile icons, vibrotactile belt, haptics, assistive technology.

1 Introduction

In literature, such as novels, an elaborate account of a scene, in terms of the location, ambience, and presence of characters, is presented prior or during the conversation of those characters in the scene. In movies, similar information is portrayed, but through the use of visual cues. For individuals who are blind or visually impaired, the visual content of a film is largely inaccessible, which makes its interpretation difficult without additional aids. To assist with visualization, an additional audio track of a narrator, who describes the scene and events, may be incorporated. These narrations are most commonly known as audio descriptions or descriptive video service (DVS). Audio descriptions are added to the audio track of a movie after it is completed to avoid overlap with the audio of the original movie, such as conversations, certain musical scores and sound effects. Given the limited duration available for audio descriptions, they are often stunted and abridged. A corpus based analysis by Salway [7] on 91 audio described movies suggests that the following character cues were the most commonly narrated: appearance, focus of attention, interpersonal interaction, relative location (with respect to other actors or objects), and expression.

An important visual cue that audio descriptions often fail to describe is the position of a character in terms of (1) his or her relative position on the screen; (2) relative

C. Stephanidis (Ed.): Posters, Part I, HCII 2011, CCIS 173, pp. 414–418, 2011.

distance from the camera; and (3) movements in front of the camera. Positional information is important for appreciating and interpreting a visual scene given the social interaction dynamics it can convey, as well as the structure of a scene in terms of where characters are located and how they are moving. To deliver this cue, we propose the use of a vibrotactile belt. Vibrotactile belts consist of vibration motors placed around the waist (in the form factor of a belt), and have been successfully used for applications where users require positional information such as navigation [8] and social interaction assistants [4]. Moreover, as natural interactions, both with our environment and those around us, are multimodal, extending film to incorporate a haptic communication channel may complement audio descriptions in that more visual cues may become accessible, potentially providing a richer viewing experience.

2   Background and Related Work

Peli et al. [5] conducted an experiment with people who had low vision, and found that when they were exposed to audio described videos, they answered more questions correctly compared to those who were not presented audio descriptions. Braun suggests in [1] that the success of the description lies in its ability to help individuals who are blind or visually impaired develop mental models, and in maintaining relevance and preserving coherence throughout the movie.

Research has explored the use of haptics during the production, post-production, and delivery of a movie. Woldecke et al. [8] used a vibrotactile belt to aid actors with their interactions with virtual objects during virtual studio productions. The lack of haptic cues as a delivery medium in movies has led researchers to provide tools to annotate movies with tactile or kinesthetic cues: Cha et al. [2] presented a framework for broadcasting movies augmented with haptics; by extending the MPEG-4 BIFS (Binary Format for Scene) format, they encoded tactile content as a grayscale video that was synchronized with audio-visual content. Rahman et al. [6] provided a mechanism for embedding and delivering vibrotactile feedback in traditional YouTube videos. The focus of these approaches is to provide users with haptic sensations that enhance the viewing experience; e.g., an intense vibration felt on the chest might simulate the feeling of a character being punched by another character on the screen; but contextual and social (non-verbal) cues are important as well.

Our contribution is with respect to tactile-visual sensory substitution of pertinent visual cues (this work focuses on positional information as a first step toward this goal) to aid individuals who are blind or visually impaired to better comprehend and appreciate films.

3   Proposed Methodology

To communicate positional information of characters in a movie, we propose the following visual-to-tactile mapping: the location of various characters across the screen will be mapped to a relative vibration location around the waist; their relative distance from the camera will be mapped to tactile rhythm; and their movements will be mapped to a combination of these two vibration dimensions, described next.

3.1   Vibration Location

A vibrotactile belt with six tactors, shown in Fig. 1, was used in this work. The tactors were equidistantly placed in a semi-circle on the subject's abdomen with the first and sixth tactor placed at the subject's left side (L3) and right side (R3), respectively. The third and fourth tactor were placed to the left (L1) and right (R1) of the navel. This arrangement of tactors around the waist was motivated by the work of Cholewiak et al. [3] in which belts of various tactor arrangements were explored to assess localization accuracy. When a tactor, L3 through R3, vibrates, it corresponds to a character's position across the screen, which is divided into six columns of equal width, also shown in Fig. 1.

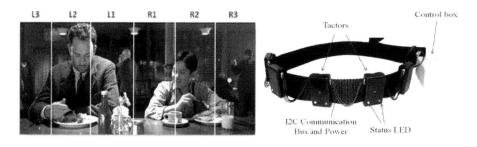

Fig. 1. (Left) Mapping of screen regions to tactors; (Right) Wireless, vibrotactile belt consisting of an elastic band, control box, and tactors (pancake motors operate at 150 Hz, and are fixed within custom plastic cases)

3.2   Tactile Rhythm

Three rhythms, inspired by the work of [4], were designed to correspond to the relative distance of an actor from the camera—see Fig. 2. The distances are categorized as near, middle, and far, with each rhythm having a length of one second. Rhythms are presented only once to inform a user of a character's distance with respect to their location across the screen. For a distance of near, a long, steady vibration provides an intense sensation, representing the intimacy of a character being close. At the opposite end of this spectrum, two short pulses represent the subtlety of a social interaction where a character is far away. For a distance between near and far, another rhythm was chosen that might fall in the middle of this spectrum: a long train of short pulses, creating a rough sensation.

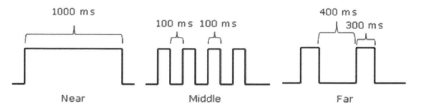

Fig. 2. The three rhythms used in this work for near, middle, and far distances. Through pilot testing, all three rhythms were verified as being distinct and intuitive.

4 Experiment

With the objective of taking the first step toward validating the idea of haptics for sensory substitution in movies, a pilot study with eight audio described movie clips, each of duration between one and three minutes, was performed with 14 participants, all from our lab, but neither involved in the project nor haptics research. Subjects were divided into two groups: the *control group* with four participants (3 males and 1 female; age group: 22-34; no visually impaired subjects), and the *haptic group* with 10 participants (8 males and 2 females; age group: 22-34; one visually impaired subject). A few subjects had used the vibrotactile belt once in the last 6 months, but not in the current configuration. The participants were allowed to listen to each clip once, with (haptic group) or without (control group) vibrotactile stimulation. They were not allowed to take notes. At the end of each clip, participants from both groups were asked to provide the number of actors in the clip; their location (L3, L2, L1, R1, R2 or R3); distance with respect to the camera; and movements during the course of the clip. To retain focus on the scenes, subjects of both groups were also asked to suggest the context (e.g., the ambience and subject of conversation) of each clip.

Subjects within the haptic group underwent a familiarization and testing phase, first with the vibrotactile cues (*part 1*), and then again on the clips with manually authored vibrations (*part 2*).

4.1 Results

The control group was not able to suggest the location of the actors present in the scene through the audio clips. Only one participant from this group was able to interpret the relative distance of actors from the camera in some clips based entirely on the loudness of their voice. This group was able to suggest the movement of characters, but failed to suggest how they moved in the scene. On the other hand, the haptic group was able to provide all the above information with high accuracy as shown in Table 1. This group also performed well in part 1 of the experiment as shown in Table 2.

Table 1. The accuracy achieved by the haptic group when considering (or not considering) correct association of vibrotactile cues to their respective actors

Part 2	*Association of actors to vibrations*			
	Not Considered		Considered	
	Mean	SD	Mean	SD
Localization	93.9%	6.49%	87.18%	10.92%
Distance	83.8%	12.29%	81.5%	12.7%
Movement	84.56%	7.85%	77.89%	12.94%

Table 2. Performance of the haptic group on the vibrotactile cues. A one-way Anova, for each parameter, suggested no significant differences indicating distinct, easily perceived cues.

Part 1	Accuracy		One-way Anova
	Mean	SD	
Localization (L1, L2, etc.)	97.5%	2.24%	[F(5,54)=3.5, p=0.6872]
Distance (Near, middle, far)	96.67%	3.14%	[F(2,27)=5.49, p=0.3252]

4.2 Discussion and Future Work

The haptic group sometimes associated vibrotactile cues to the wrong actors on screen as observed in Table 1. This seems to have been influenced by both the audio descriptions and in how the vibrotactile cues were authored. However, the haptic group, including the visually impaired subject, felt that the vibrations improved their visualization of these clips. This subject also felt it was quite easy to combine the information received through audio and haptics, and that the vibrations were not obstructing the subject's attention to audio. Based on these results, we are currently planning a more extensive study that will involve only visually impaired subjects.

References

1. Braun, S.: Audio description from a discourse perspective: a socially relevant framework for research and training. Linguistica Antverpiensia NS6, 357–369 (2007)
2. Cha, J., Seo, Y., Kim, Y., Ryu, J.: An authoring / editing framework for haptic broadcasting: passive haptic interactions using MPEG-4 BIFS. In: Proc. of World Haptics, pp. 274–279 (2007)
3. Cholewiak, R.W., Brill, J.C., Schwab, A.: Vibrotactile localization on the abdomen: effects of place and space. Perception & Psychophysics 66(6), 970–987 (2004)
4. McDaniel, T., Krishna, S., Colbry, D., Panchanathan, S.: Using tactile rhythm to convey interpersonal distances to individuals who are blind. In: Proc. of Ext. Abstracts CHI 2009 (2009)
5. Peli, E., Fine, E.M., Labianca, A.T.: Evaluating visual information provided by audio description. Journal of Visual Impairment & Blindness 90(5), 378–385 (1996)
6. Rahman, M., Alkhaldi, A., Cha, J., Saddik, A.: Adding haptic feature to YouTube. In: Proc. of ACM Multimedia, pp. 1643–1646 (2010)
7. Salway, A.: A corpus-based analysis of audio description. Media for All, Rodopi (2007)
8. Woldecke, B., Vierjahn, T., Flasko, M., Herder, J., Geiger, C.: Steering actors through a virtual set employing vibro-tactile feedback. In: TEI 2009, pp. 169–174 (2009)

Part VI

Social Interaction and On-Line Communities

Becoming Friends on Online Social Networking Services

Wonmi Ahn, Borum Kim, and Kwang-Hee Han

Department of Psychology
Yonsei Yniversity, Sinchon-dong,
Seodaemun-gu, Seoul, Korea
1meahn@gmail.com, borumkim27@naver.com, khan@yonsei.ac.kr

Abstract. The internet has become an effective tool in communication, and SNS (Social Networking Service), such as Facebook or Twitter, that allows anyone to disclose a variety of specific personal information. The purpose of the present study is to identify which profile factors provided SNS users (or viewers) with a positive first impression. Results from study 1, the three factors - basic information, profile picture and interests - were derived according to priority. In study 2, we established three major profile factors extracted from surveys that are crucial factors in SNS settings. We can assumed that more self-disclosure SNS users have the more socially attractive they will be by viewers.

Keywords: Social Networking Service, Profile, First Impressions.

1 Introduction

Interacting on the Internet is similar in some respects to interacting in a darkened room, in that one cannot see one's interaction partner, nor can one be seen. First impressions thus are formed based upon the information provided by the other person and perhaps also by the positive effect of our own acts of self-disclosure [1]. Online Social Networking Service (SNS) enables users to present themselves in a number of ways. Users can voluntarily display pictures in their albums, describe their personal interests, political views, favorite music/movies/books/quotes, and hobbies, and list their friends. A function of SNS is to help the users connect with those they already know and extend that connection to those they do not yet know [2]. If a person were to view an SNS profile before physically meeting, how might that affect the relationship? Which profile factors are important at the initial stages of a virtual friendship? Viewers may seek to the part of physical information such as photo or objective information such as age, gender, and major. And the ability to sustain and manage complex personal relationships requires elaborate cognitive strategies, and there is good reason to believe that the impressive cognitive abilities of *homo sapiens* evolved largely to accomplish this task [3]. Modern industrialized mass societies, where interacting with strangers is common. That's why we choose additional condition - information openness to public status. The purpose of the present study is to identify which profile factors provided SNS users (or viewers) with a positive first impression. Study 1 was designed to assess the three most influential three profile factors and Study 2 was designed to identify the effects of

C. Stephanidis (Ed.): Posters, Part I, HCII 2011, CCIS 173, pp. 421–425, 2011.
© Springer-Verlag Berlin Heidelberg 2011

these factors, extracted from study 1. This study aims to be an exploratory investigation of whether profile factors influence online relationships.

2   Study 1: Questionnaire

Under initiating friendship in cyberspace, what information is considered important as a SNS profile factor? We have subdivided six factors.

2.1   Method

Participants. Thirteen students participated in Study 1. (5 males and 8 females).

Measures. The questionnaire was designed to rate the presented options in order of priority from actual 6 factors - basic information, profile picture, relationship status, education & work, interests and contact information - based on Facebook, a popular means of SNS.

Procedure. The owner of the profile was called 'user' and those viewing the profiles were called 'viewer'. Participants acted as viewers and were asked to rank the profiles on preference and their reasoning for initiating a friendship with a stranger on a SNS.

2.2   Result

Results from study 1, the three factors - basic information, profile picture and interests - were derived according to priority (Fig. 1.).

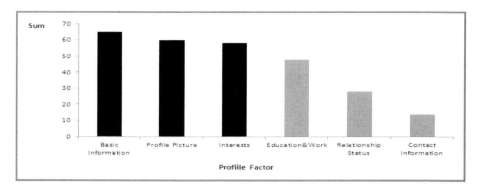

Fig. 1. Importance ranking on profile factors

The basic information was a cue for guessing the user's basic things and personality, and when we initiate friendship in online, an important factor for building personal trust is personal information.

"Just reading basic information, I can guess who user is like life environment, and it helps to avoid suspicious stranger"

Visual cues are important during early stage interaction and profile picture was only visual cue in SNS.

"First impression is very important to make friends, especially good feeling of picture gives more curiosity about user"

The factor of interests shows user's character. Having things in common creates a possibility for further intimacy. Besides, doing various social activities and interests is potential to have a good personality.

"User who have various interests maybe talk more fun".

3   Study 2: Experiment

An experiment was performed in study 2 under the result of study 1.

3.1   Method

Participants. Twenty seven participants (16 males and 11 females, mean age = 22) from Yonsei University took part in the experiment for class credit.

Measures. Twelve profile prototypes appeared randomly twice for each participant. Prototype is composited with basic information, profile picture and interests (study 1 main factor) formed from Facebook. Independent variable is openness to the public about user's information. A 2×2×2 within subjects design was conducted: 2(basic information conditions for public availability; private and public)×2(picture conditions for public availability: private and public)×2(cultural interesting conditions for public availability: private and public). The profile picture gender limited as a woman.

Procedure. Participants were given three questions about willingness to initiate to make friendship with on a 7-point Likert scale responses. Questions and profile prototypes are as follow (Fig. 2.).

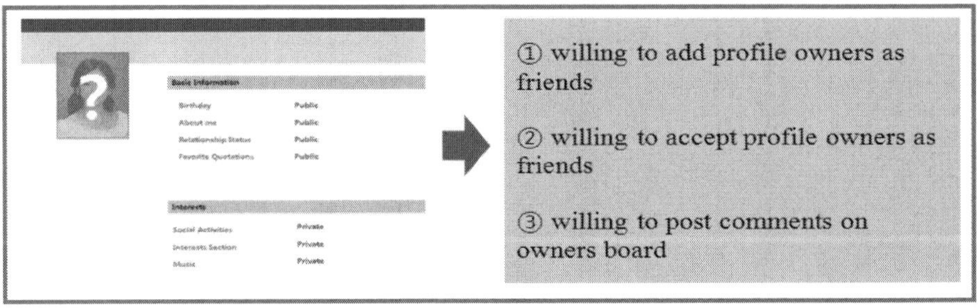

Fig. 2. Sample prepared profile prototype and question

3.2   Results

Willingness to become a friend (the average of 3 responses) was evaluated by repeated-measure ANOVAs and further analyzed by post hoc Bonferroni.

Profile information. The analysis indicated that profile information main effects were all significant. Under the 'to public' condition, viewers tend to initiate to make friends with user [Profile picture: $F(1, 26) = 30.330$, $p < .001$, $\eta_p^2 = .538$; Basic information: $F(1, 26) = 20.922$, $p < .001$, $\eta_p^2 = .446$;Interests : $F(1, 26) = 16.423$, $p < .001$, $\eta_p^2 = .387$] (Fig. 3).

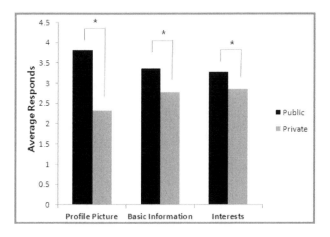

Fig. 3. Average responds each information status

Interaction between Profile picture and Basic information. The two-factor interaction of between profile picture and basic information was significant [$F(1,26) = 12.089$, $p < .05$, $\eta_p^2 = .317$]. When picture and basic information are presented at the same time, willingness to initiate friendship markedly increases.

4   Discussion

Having access to personal information is a fundamental requirement when initiating friendships. The empirical findings of this study suggest important implications for the understanding of how people decide to make friends in the virtual world. First, we posited the essential factors - basic information, profile picture and personal interests - would influence the willingness to initiate friendship with zero-history partners. There is support that visual can play a critical role during social interaction online and offline alike [4]. Seconds, we established three major profile factors extracted from surveys that are crucial factors in SNS settings.

Social interaction through SNS has become the primary use of a home computer [5]. We can assumed that more self-disclosure SNS users have the more socially attractive they will be by viewers.

Acknowledgments. This study was supported by Yonsei University and by the Brain Korea 21 project.

References

1. McKenna, K., Green, A., Gleason, M.: Relationship Formation on the Internet: What's the Big Attraction? Journal of Social Issues 58(1), 9–31 (2002)
2. Zhao, S., Grasmuck, S., Martin, J.: Identity construction on Facebook: Digital empowerment in anchored relationships. Computers in Human Behavior 24, 1816–1836 (2008)
3. Dunbar, R.I.M.: The social brain hypothesis and its relevance to social psychology. In: Forgas, J.P., Haselton, M.G., von Hippel, W. (eds.) Evolution and the social mind, Psychology Press, New York (2007)
4. Wang, S., Moon, S., Kwon, K., Ewans, C., Stefanone, M.: Face off: Implications of visual cues on initiating friendship on Facebook. Computers in Human Behavior (2009)
5. Amahai-Hamburger, Y., Vinitzky, G.: Social network use and personality. Computers in Human Behavior 26, 1289–1295 (2010)

On-line Communication as a Part of the "Symbolic Politics"

Evgeniy Ishmenev

Institute of Philosophy and Law, Russian Academy of Sciences,
Sophia Kovalevsky St., 16, 620137 Ekaterinburg, Russia
ishmenevev@mail.ru

Abstract. This paper analyzes the role of the "symbolic politics" in improving the design of on-line communication. Such explanations are beyond a classical paradigm as assuming the existence of various ways of supporting and an emotional involvement of users into the process of creating and consuming of political information. The concept presumes the analysis of rational forms that differ in their emotionality but can be united into symbols for creating the *certain image* of political world. The analysis of users' behavioral features enables to evaluate democracy condition at the moment. It is particularly essential for developing countries and countries with a transforming political system.

Keywords: symbolic politics, convergence media, political marketing, legitimacy, institute.

1 Introduction

At the early stage of the Internet development the potential of on-line communication was evaluated as an alternative type to off-line. Especially it took place in authoritarian and post-authoritarian countries looks like Russia with a big influence of the official institutes. The growth of usual Internet users is supposed to consider individual genres as well as forums, blogs, chats as some sort of a "new communication". This was evident in influence of the official mass media to be presented both ways. While lots of mass media had been presented off-line, it was not so much sources on-line.

The modern stage demonstrates that on-line communication can integrate different genres of off-line mass media. Increasing advertising incomes cause an interest in big media companies in transferring its resources on-line [1]. It enables research to define the Internet as a part of "convergence media". The development of on-line as some sort of multimedia communication when off-line media genres have possibilities to be united via modern technology is supposed to make correlation between created content and previous. Participation of professional journalists and official mass media representatives in on-line communication decreases the significance of individual communicative forms. As a sequence, most users, who consider the Internet to be as a sort of "alternative political tool" at first, need to change their attitude today.

C. Stephanidis (Ed.): Posters, Part I, HCII 2011, CCIS 173, pp. 426–430, 2011.
© Springer-Verlag Berlin Heidelberg 2011

Despite of the problems mentioned, the early period helped to recognize some specific Internet features. This is evident in discussion about a legal regulation of electronic mass media and blogosphere by Government and official institutes in Russia. Within the support of "Electronic Russia Programm" the item concerning "institutional and legal status" of on-line mass media has become an important part of "public discussion" to be argued by representatives of science, journalists and usual users. A lot of Russian users are interested in the fact how the electronic mass media would be registered: what sequence as well as preferences, opportunities and responsibility while creating "news" can be got as a result of the institutional regulation?

2   Theoretical Background

In recent time communication-study demonstrates an interest to the "symbolic politics" concept. In the middle of the 20th century, term was introduced by American and European scientists as a more positive definition of "propaganda" which had lots of negative connotation at the post-war period. Such authors as Murray Edelman and Ulrich Sarcinelli defined symbolic politics as a *mass communication* phenomenon. It suggested that mass communication for them was a "new instrument of propaganda" resisting the traditional political institutes and agents.

During the past two decades, the "symbolic politics" has received additional interpretation among researchers of post-authoritarian countries. The authors suppose that symbols can be defined as a main tool of political legitimacy for countries which haven't a long tradition of institutions' development [3]. The case-studies of Russia of 1990s demonstrate how lack of formal institutes has caused "mediatization" of politics [4]. In contrast to traditional rational features, such describing of institutional condition enables research to explain how mass communication becomes a part of "public discourse" and "public expressions". Such explanations are beyond a classical paradigm as assuming the existence of various ways of supporting and an emotional involvement of participants into the process of creating and consuming of political information.

Concentration on analysis of political symbols allows scientists to define "symbolic politics" as a source of political legitimacy [5]. The concept presumes the analysis of rational forms that differ in their emotionality but can be united into symbols for creating the *certain image* of political world. It supposes that political symbols can be not only an "instrument" of propaganda and manipulations for political leadership or the competing elites [6], but can be used for interpretive function, by which both political leaders and people try to grasp an understanding of the political universe.

Symbolic features of the Internet are becoming an important subject of scientific discussions in political science nowadays. In contrast to *commercial features*, symbolic and cognitive conditions enable research to explain on-line communication as some sort of *knowledge* about the political reality [7]. It is shared by both scientists who focused on the role of the Internet in formulating official political agenda and scientists who try to explain how usual users can articulate their private opinion concerning a current political process. Two points are directed to explanation of two problems:

- Where will the limits of participants' responsibility be?
- How new individual form of communication as well as blogging, twitter and forums will coexist with traditional mass media?

Besides, several aspects of symbolic politics are used in modern political marketing theory. Interest in politics by audience can be presented not only as the quantitative growth of on-line users but also as a sequence of individual choice by "consumers" [8]. Statistical measurement of different online genres, frames and discourses as well as advertising, politics, entertainment, feedback sites, social network and individual sites demonstrates how users' choice is reflected in political preferences. It is evidence in correlation between users' choice and electoral behavior in some European countries and USA in recent years [9]. Moreover, marketing effect takes place in analyzing of "convergence media" that allows keeping connection between specific of on-line discourse and off-line sociological data. The analysis of users' reaction to development and changes of a "new media" assumes use both qualitative and amount research.

The empirical base of research includes results of the largest Russian sociological canters: Fund of "Public Opinion" (FBO), VCIOM, Levada Center, Rambler, Gullop Media, Spy Log, Fund "Effective policy".

3   Case-Study: Symbolic Politics of the RuNet

3.1   Objectives

The development of the Russian Internet (RuNet) shows how participation of mass media and official institutes has transformed on-line symbolic politics. At this case, the important subject of the observation is evolution of an individual on-line genres and discourses at the RuNet-content in the last ten years. In addition to that, the behavioral of online participants is presented as the second subject of observation. Sociological data achieved in recent years helps to understand how transformations of the RuNet are reflecting in users' opinion and intentions.

Research aims in studying of correlation between RuNet-discourse and sociological data of the users' behavior. Approach is supposed to use both quantitative and amount methods where statistical data supplements the content-analysis. While the behavioral of on-line participants is an important part of a normative (institutional) approach, the analysis of users' reaction to development and changes requires qualitative and amount research that would explain the RuNet contemporary circumstances. Both subjects are presented as a part of "political legitimacy" problem in the post-Soviet countries. An attempt to show symbolic politics of the RuNet as a part of a normative model can be useful for understanding what place different symbols and discourse take in studying political legitimacy.

3.2   Results

The early period results help to understand some RuNet features. The majority of researchers concluded that quantity of users at the beginning of 2000s was much less than in another type of communication. It was the reason why most authors tried to define "potential" of the RuNet as a "new communication channel". A lot of researchers of this period made an attempt to opposite on-line and off-line communication – to define on-line communication as "alternative political tool" [10]. According to this point, some results revealed that users of the RuNet had their interest in political on-line information, but had close access limits.

Since 2005 the growth of users' quantity (total RuNet users included 28 million – almost 30% of population; constant users (daily using the Internet) included 11 million) allowed political actors to make use of the Internet as a tool in their activities. As sequence, most mass media (Kommersant, NTV, Nezavisimaya Gazeta) and official institutes have begun to open their representatives and "site-cut-aways" into RuNet. According to the 2005 and 2007 research, the on-line content looks like the content of off-line mass media at the early stage; especially in the case of political content [11]. While on-line content has become more thematically various, orientation of users to entertaining and commercial genres has keep the same traditional directions.

Despite of the innovation environment, the modern stage demonstrates how examination of on-line communication in the context of political legitimacy problem can be useful for explaining the RuNet evolution in recent 10-15 years. Consideration of the Internet connecting with the convergence media, where the Internet is defined not only as an "alternative political tool" but also as affiliation to off-line communication, allows finding out correlation between changes in the amount participants data and participants' behavior. It is presented in research of bloggers' attitude to their participation in on-line communication. According to the research of Levada Center, the "behavior model" of a Russian blogger is presented as a "tool for verifying his own environment" [11]. The participation user at this case is presented as attempt for identification [12].

References

1. Data of Association of communication agencies of Russia. Advertising size in means of its distribution (January-March 2007), http://www.akarussia.ru
2. Bjola, S.: The Impact of Symbolic Politics on Foreign Policy during the Democratization Process. In: Workshop on Southeastern and East-Central Europe, pp. 1–25. Harvard University (2000)
3. Zasursky, Y.: The System of Russian Mass-media. Aspekt-press, Moscow (2003)
4. O'Shaughnessy, N.: The symbolic state: a British experience. Journal of Public Affairs 3(4), 296–311 (2003)
5. Kauffman, S.: Symbolic Politics or Rational Choice. International Security 30(4), 45–86 (2006)
6. Lupia, A., McCubbins, M., Popkin, S.: Beyond Rationality: Reason and the Study of Politics, Cambridge (2000)
7. Scullion, R.: Investigation electoral choice through a 'consumer as choice-maker' lens. In: Lilleker, D., Jackson, N., Scullion, R. (eds.) The Marketing of political parties, pp. 185–206. M. U. Press, Manchester (2006)
8. Cornfield, M., Carson, J., Kalis, A., Simon, E.: Buzz, Blogs, and Beyond: the Internet and the national discourse in the fall of 2004. In: Negrine, R., Stanyer, J. (eds.) The Political Communication, Routledge, London, vol. 52, pp. 296–305 (2009)

9. Krasnoboka, N., Brants, K.: Old and New Media, Old and New Politics? On- and Off-line reporting in the 2002 Ukrainian Election Campaign. Routledge, London (2006)
10. Dubin, B.: Institutions, Networks, Rituals. Pro et Contra. 2-3, 24-35 (2008)
11. Fomicheva, I.: Sociology of Internet Mass-media. Moscow State University, Moscow (2005)
12. Fossato, F.: Is Runet the Last Adaptation Tool?. Russian Cyberspace, 1(1), http://www.russian-cyberspace.com/issue1/florian-fossato.html

A Displaying Method of Food Photos to Know Child's Dietary Life for Parents

Kenta Iwasaki, Kazuyoshi Murata, and Yu Shibuya

Kyoto Institute of Technology
Matsugaski, Sakyo-ku, Kyoto 606-8585 Japan
iwasaki@hit.is.kit.ac.jp

Abstract. There are many children who live far away from parents. The parents want to know their child's dietary life because it is important for his/her healthy life. However, there are no ways for parents to know their child' dietary life without troublesome in each other. We proposed the method which extracts the information related to child's meals automatically and displays it to know the child's dietary life easily for parents.

Keywords: displaying method, automatic extraction, dietary life.

1 Introduction

Most parents are taking care of their child who lives far away from them. In particularly, many parents want to know that their child's dietary life because it is important for his/her healthy life.

In general situation, parents know that their child's dietary life by calling or sending an email to him/her. However, it is often troublesome to take an opportunity to do so. FoodLog[1], which displays uploaded food images, might be helpful for the parents to know their child's dietary life if their child takes photos of food and uploads it whenever he/she eats. However, these actions should be troublesome for the child. In addition, the FoodLog is not enough to know the child's dietary life because parents can't know amounts of food which their child actually ate and how long he/she took to eat. Parents might know such thing by watching a recorded video but it needs much time to watch it.

This paper proposes a method to aid the parents to know their child's dietary life without troublesome actions.

2 Proposed Method

The proposed method consists of a meal information extraction method from the captured video and a method to show the information. In this paper, the meal information is defined as the information which parents want to know about their child's meals. Table 1 shows a list of meal information.

C. Stephanidis (Ed.): Posters, Part I, HCII 2011, CCIS 173, pp. 431–434, 2011.

Table 1. A list of meal information

Meal information	Reason why parents want to know
Food the child ate	If the child took balanced food, his/her dietary life might be good. If the child took unbalance food, his/her dietary life might not be good.
The amounts of food	If the child have proper amounts of food, his/her dietary life is good. If the child have too much or too little, his/her dietary life is not good.
Meal time: When did the child eat?	If the child ate at proper time of the day, his/her dietary life might be good. If the child ate too early or too late, his/her dietary life might not be good.
Meal time length: How long did it take for eating?	If it took proper time length, his/her dietary life might be good. If it took too long or short time, his/her dietary life might not be good.

2.1 Meal Information Extraction Method

The proposed method extracts the meal information, listed in Table 1, when the child has meal. In order to extract the information of food the child ate, we get the food images in each of the dishes when they are put on the dining table. These images show food in each dish before the child began to eat. Furthermore, in order to extract the information of the amounts of food which the child ate, we also get the food images in each of the dishes when it is taken away from the dining table. The parents are able to know the amounts of food which their child ate by comparing the food images between the beginning and ending of the meal. Here, the time when the first dish was put on the dining table is beginning of meals, and the time when the last dish was taken away from the dining table is ending of meals. We define intermediate between beginning and ending of the meal as meal time. As well as, we define the period from beginning of the meal to ending of the meal as meal time length.

In order to extract the time when the dishes are put on the dining table and the time when the dishes are taken away from the dining table, the method counts the number of dishes on the dining table and extracts the child's seating information. When the child puts dishes on the dining table and the standing child sit in front of the dining table, the number of dishes increases. On the other hand, when the child takes away dishes on the dining table and the sitting child stand to bring them, the number of dishes decreases.

2.2 Displaying the Meals Information

We propose the three methods of displaying the meals information for parents to know their child's dietary life easily.

(a) Displaying to know eaten food
Every stored food images are classified into several clusters with its similarity. We use color histograms as a basis for similar foods. Here, we use RGB color and HSV

color for color histograms. If the summation of distance of each color histogram value between foods is near, it is highly possible that the foods have similar appearance. We use Ward method[2] as clustering algorithm which classify with highly accuracy. By looking this displaying, the parents are able to know how many times their child ate each of appearances clusters. Therefore, the parents are able to know eaten food. Fig. 1 shows example of displaying to know eaten food.

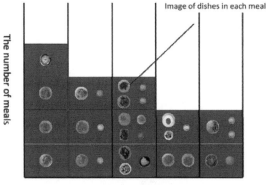

Fig. 1. Displaying to know eaten food

(b) Displaying to know the amounts of food

Every stored food images are classified into several clusters with its amounts of food. We use a total area of foods in each dish as a basis for amounts foods. While a total area don't show necessarily amounts, it is highly possible that the foods have large amounts if foods have large area and it is highly possible that the foods have small amounts if foods have small area. By looking this displaying, the parents are able to know how many times their child ate in each of the amounts clusters. Fig. 2 shows example of displaying to know the amounts of food.

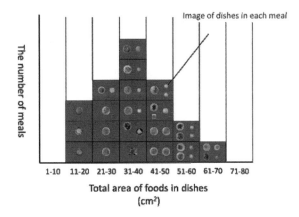

Fig. 2. Displaying to know the amounts of food

(c) Displaying to know meal time and meal time length

The displaying puts a point about each of meals. The place of each point depends on the meal time and meal time length. Furthermore, the displaying draws a square which indicates range of both meal time and meal time length averagely. Center of the square indicates average meal time and average meal time length. Width of the square indicates twice standard deviation of meal time. Height of the square indicates twice standard deviation of meal time length. By looking this displaying, the parents are able to know the meal time averagely and whether there are too early meals or too late meals. As well as, the parents are able to know meal time length averagely and whether there are too long meals or too short meals. Fig. 3 shows example of displaying to know meal time and meal time length.

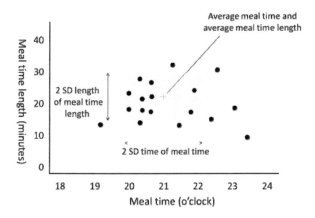

Fig. 3. Displaying to know meal time and meal time length

3   Conclusion

We proposed the method which extracts the meals information automatically and displays it to know the child's dietary life easily for parents who take care of him/her.

In future studies, we are planning to conduct a field study to evaluate proposed method. We are implementing the proposed method as a prototype system. A few families will be recruited and asked to use the prototype system.

References

1. Keigo, K., Toshihiko, Y., Kiyoharu, A.: Food Log by Analyzing Food Images. In: ACM Multimedia 2008 Demo Session, Vancouver, Canada, October 27-30, pp. 999–1000 (2008)
2. Joe, H.W.: Journal of the American Statistical Association 58(301), 236–244 (1963)

Memory Makers – The Experience of Camera Usage by Women

Yu-Lung Kao[1] and Ju-Joan Wong[2]

[1] Department and Graduated Institution of Industrial Design,
College of Management, Chang Gung University,
259 Wen-Hwa 1st Road, Kwei-Shan Tao-Yuan, Taiwan, 333, R.O.C.
[2] Department and Graduated Institution of Industrial Design, College of Design,
National Yunlin University of Science and Technology,
123 University Road, Section 3, Douliou, Yunlin, Taiwan, 64002, R.O.C.

Abstract. Abstract. This study focuses on gender perspective to explore the Taiwan married women's experience in using the camera. Unlike Western women who dominate the family photography for a long time, early family photography in Taiwan is mainly responsible by the male. Until the early '80s women had more shooting opportunities. In this study, through the interview to seven of Taiwan's middle-class women's camera usage, we focused on the impact of experience in photography for their lives. Preliminary study results indicated that: In addition to her husband's busy and rejection of photography etc. factors, women's self independent and outgoing nature make them more interested in photography. In addition, due to the computer knowledge they obtained through work and other interests, these women could be more initiatively to adopt digital photography, but they also reduced the chance to actually interact with people. According to the above, the study believes in the late industrialization countries, women are not always passive technology users, but are able to use technology to show themselves; and the future of technology in the development of photography should take a fresh look at women's ability to operate the technology, and to derive self-empowerment of each interacting process.

Keywords: Qualitative research, Camera, Feminist theories of technology, Married women, Family photography.

1 Introduction

In recent years' HCI study had started to pay attention to digital photography's impact to family life [1]. In particular, the current Anglo-American society's traditional families, originally women-led family's photography [2], but because children can use the computer better than parents resulted in the power of women in the family photography was affected. Related scholars provided design proposals for women as the main user [1].

If we put the issue in Taiwan's social connection into review, there are different historical process. Before 1970, the price of a camera is equivalent to the two-month

C. Stephanidis (Ed.): Posters, Part I, HCII 2011, CCIS 173, pp. 435–439, 2011.
© Springer-Verlag Berlin Heidelberg 2011

salary of a middle-class worker, and only until the retailers adopted monthly payment systems as a marketing strategy did family photography become popular in Taiwan. However, in the patriarchal society of Taiwan, the father represents the leader of the family, and possesses the power and control over resources. As a result, the purchase and usage decisions on camera, which was still considered a luxury product, were usually made by the father. Women had few opportunities in contacting photography. Therefore the study relatively discussed in the Western world the parents must face traditional film change to digital photography's adjustment and adaptation. Camera use in Taiwan also had the unequal women power relations of gender issues. As to the different East-West women position in the family photography, this study raised concerns about Taiwan unfair general situation of the family photo. Our purpose can be divided into two. First of all is to understand how women receive power to take the family photos, followed by discussion of the impact women face after the photography digitalized.

2   Literature Review

Hirsch [3], in a study on family photography, pointed out that photos are used to produce or reproduce an idealized and normal image of a family. But as the Anglo-American society, the family image is mainly held by women [2]. It was mainly due to at the early twentieth century, Kodak's invention and commercialized advertisement, allowed camera, originally the entertainment belonging to the rich, crossed beyond gender, age and economic constraints, and became a large number of popular product in Anglo-American society[4]. In the process it also shaped the image of women responsible for family photography [2]. However, the study of history of photography in Taiwan found that due to industrialization was later, not until the 80's camera became popular. Taiwan also did not experience the launch of the Kodak camera when promoting a dollar Brownie camera and the Kodak Girl advertising age, so the difference of camera commercialized and development of country's industrialization resulted in early stage Eastern and Western women's different experience on the use of the camera.

STS study for today's technology-neutral approach raised the question. It believed that the technology was affected by social impact and generated gender user's situation [5]. The initial design of digital camera was for male users, so women would have a problem in use [6]. In the study of human-computer interaction, there was more discussion of women's impact when facing digital photography [1].

Bardzell[7] pointed out that feminist study could help the application of human-computer interaction, and could develop a new design direction and to help in-depth understanding of the users. Wajcman [8] studied feminist theories of technology and from present developmental viewpoint, emphasized the development between gender and technology. This should be regarded as mutually shaping relationship. But now more technology discussed how to change the engendered issue, and had study less on development of how the gender itself change the technology[8]. So when women faced the digital photography technology's changes, and the camera engendered issues, we should return to women's own camera using experience as study focus. Henwood [9] argues that to change the gendered culture of technology, one should not merely focus on criticizing the characteristics of the gendered technology. One should understand women's subjective experiences and practices of technology and, based on this understanding, define or redefine technology.

3   Method

The study interviewed seven Taiwan's middle-class married women, ages 50 to 60 years old. They belonged to Taiwan's first experience of the camera popularity and are woman influenced by digital photography. The study will focus on qualitative study interviews. First of all use family photos to make married women had retrospective examination, then had in-depth interviews to investigate women's experience with the camera in order to understand how women described their contact with the camera, and the impact to their individual and family life.

4   Results

4.1   Novice Photographer

Since in the 70's photography in Taiwan was not popular, family photography opportunities were not common. The majority respondents said that their early age photography experience was mostly remained when shooting in the photo shop for family portrait. One of the respondents A described: "As a child I had very little chance to see the cameras. Mostly only in major festivals we have the opportunity to take photographs at photo shop, but we also rarely had a personal photo." Therefore, after they got married and when trained in taking family photo and album management capabilities, they could not refer to the past experience of their parents. They must learn and develop by self (Fig. 1). They were in the stage at the novice photographer.

Fig. 1. The album of Respondents f E

4.2   Promote Interpersonal Relations

Study found that: The purpose of women's first exposure to photography was hoping by photography to have the opportunity to interact with others. Regardless extroverted and introverted personality, women all mentioned: "Taking pictures help me make more friends." By interacting with photography, in addition to the communication during the shoot, or photo exchange after the photos produced will enhance the opportunity to actually interact with others.

4.3   Family Photographer

Women can obtain the power of family photography was mainly due to the interaction between the concept of husband and wife. Part of the respondents' husband was too busy. Husbands did not believe family photography as responsibility of women, but they just did not think family photography was important, so they would not have the conflict to fight for shooting photos with his wife. Secondly, from the interview we found the characteristics of the respondents were considerable confident in self. They showed lively and outgoing communication and were financially independent. In addition to photography, they took the initiative to pursue learning of other personal interests.

4.4   The Digital Impact

Computer skills' training of women was mainly from the work requirements in the workplace. In addition, individuals involved in computer learning by other means, to further enhance their ability to face digital photography. Respondents D who had involved in photography class said: "In order to let photographs look better, I especially learn the retouching software. In addition, because sharing of digital is way too convenient, there is no need to develop films and film exchange with others, which limits the actual experience of interacting with others.

5   Conclusion

While feminists have said the performance of family photos could limit the ability of individuals, and limit people in the family [10], but from the study it could be found, family photography for women is positive, because all these women in the history of life are a new group of using the camera. In the past it did not have a precedent to require them to do a record for the family, and therefore on the family album, they can have a lot of creativity and talents and show many different styles. In addition, family photography is not considered as housework, so after women who gain interested in photography, are not merely the family's photographer, in other areas they also show a different film form. Respondent D had a wonderful description and said: "The camera is not the housework equipment for women, but comparison it can release pressure, and is a relaxed self-leisure." On the other hand, although patriarchal ideology let men control the main source of family income and has more opportunity to the use of camera, also because of economic pressure they need to bear for the family, it limits their pursuit of personal life and interests. Although women are limited in domestic labor, also due to they assume less responsibility for economic pressure, they have more chance to pursue personal interest.

Wajcman [8] commented that the current emphasis on innovative technology mainly with the use of men as the main object, which often leaves women in vulnerable state. From the study we found that when women face the impact of digital photography, they can learn and adapt more initiatively, rather than adjust passively. Turkle [5] said: Although women and men have different ways in the use of new media, this does not prove that women inherently unable to control the technology. So the future development of photographic technology, in addition to positively view women's ability to adapt to technology, we should aim at universal design of avoiding continue to cause the emergence of vulnerable users.

In this study, we research from the perspective of Feminist theories of technology to explore how Taiwanese women shape the process of photographic technology. Since Taiwanese women's participation in the family photography is brief in history, it allows women to maintain positive and open concept to the family photography. Photographic technology for women is the media to show self-capacity. In addition, due to gender stereotypes so that both spouses have a limit of the power of family photography, but women's independent choice helps to change the status. In the future development of photographic technology, we should use universal design to avoid the disadvantaged users to be excluded by digital gap.

References

1. Durrant, A., Frohlich, D., Sellen, A., Lyons, E.: Home curation versus teenage photography: Photo displays in the family home. International Journal of Human-Computer Studies 67(12), 1005–1023 (2009)
2. Rose, G.: Family photographs and domestic spacings: a case study. Transactions of the Institute of British Geographers 28, 5–18 (2003)
3. Hirsch, M.: Family frames: photography, memory and post-narrative. Harvard University Press, Harvard (1997)
4. Olivier, M.: George Eastman's Modern Stone-Age Family: Snapshot Photography and the Brownie. Technology and Culture 48, 1–19 (2007)
5. Turkle, S.: Computational reticence: Why women fear theintimate machine. In: Kramarae, C. (ed.) Technology and Women's Voices, pp. 41–61 (1988)
6. Waner, F.: The Power of the Purse. Baker & Tayl,New York (2005)
7. Bardzell, S.: Feminist HCI: Taking stock and outlining an agenda for design. In: Proc. of CHI 2010: World Conference on Human Factors in Computing Systems, ACM, New York (2010)
8. Wajcman, J.: Feminist theories of technology. Cambridge Journal of Economics 34(1), 143–152 (2010)
9. Henwood, F., Green, E., Owen, J., Pain, D.: Establishing gender perspectives on information technology: Problems, issues and opportunities. In: Gendered by Design? Information Technology and Office Systems, pp. 31–49. Taylor and Francis, Abington (1993)
10. Kuhn, A.: Family secrets: acts of memory and imagination. Verso, London (1995)

Unique Motivation
for Using Global Social Network Site in Korea

Hyosun Kim[1] and Kwang-Hee Han[2]

[1] Graduate Program in Cognitive Science, Yonsei University, 134 Shinchon-dong,
Seodaemun-gu, Seoul, South Korea
[2] Department of Psychology, Yonsei University, 134 Shinchon-dong, Seodaemun-gu,
Seoul, South Korea
cogenghyosun@gmail.com

Abstract. This study is an attempt to connect the distinctive motivation of
Korean self-expression [1] with growth of the global social network sites
(SNSs) in Korea. To explore the motivation using global SNSs, we conducted
in-depth interview. The result of the interviews suggests that Korean expected
to look more attractive or charming when they have foreign online friends, thus
leading them to seek to make such foreign friends on Facebook, a widely used
SNS. In addition, a questionnaire was conducted to analyze the correlation
between the offline and online tendencies of Koreans to prefer foreign friends.
The results showed that the respondents perceived themselves as more
attractive if he (she) had a foreign friend offline and as more attractive if he
(she) was a person who had comments from foreign friends on Facebook. The
above results implicate that there are various motives for using global SNSs,
depending on the cultural backgrounds of the users.

Keywords: motivation, global Social Network Site, self-expression, foreign
friends, rich-get-rich theory.

1   Introduction

While global social network sites (SNSs) such as Facebook are growing in many
countries, many studies have shown that the motivation for using them can differ
according to different cultural backgrounds. According to data from an internet site
that compiles findings and statistics related to Facebook (www.socialbakers.com), the
penetration rate of Facebook has increased to 10.2 percent of the online population,
implying that nearly 4 million people use this SNS. Facebook have widespread appeal
in many parts of the world [2]. However, the growth of global SNSs does not indicate
a downward trend of local SNS use. Local SNSs grow with global SNSs together [3]
in that both show the importance of an online network. Regarding both local and
global SNSs, how different is the motivation for using them?

Many previous studies have investigated the motivation for using SNSs. Before the
growth of Facebook, studies were conducted within the framework of each country.
In Korea, Jung et al. [1] revealed six motivations for using Cyworld, which is the
representative local SNS in Korea, based on what was termed user-and-gratification

C. Stephanidis (Ed.): Posters, Part I, HCII 2011, CCIS 173, pp. 440–444, 2011.
© Springer-Verlag Berlin Heidelberg 2011

framework. Ahn and Han [4] explored the relationship between SNS use and personality. Recently, several researchers have explored the motivation for using a global SNS, and they have started to analyze the differences among cultures as it relates to the use of a global SNS [3, 5]. However, these cross-cultural studies are based on the results of research conducted from a western viewpoint. Hence, they may not be suitable by themselves to show the actual difference among cultures. If the results of studies of motivation for using local SNSs are applied to the study of global SNS, it would be helpful to reveal the true differences as regards other cultures.

Jung et al. [1] suggested six motivations for using the local SNS, Cyworld, in Korea: entertainment, self-expression, professional advancement, passing time, communication with family and friends, and trend-following. Among them, self-expression seemed to be a unique motivation in Korea. Given that self-expression is a distinctive motive in Korea, the aim of the current study was to connect the distinctive motivation of Korean, self-expression with the growth of the global SNSs in Korea. However, we did not insist on a hypothesis at the outset. Though in-depth interviews, we used a bottom-up approach to reveal the hidden motivations.

2   In-Depth Interviews

2.1   Method

We conducted in-depth interviews with three Koreans, two Britons and one German. In common, their countries have local (Korea-, UK- and Germany-based) SNSs, but all of them use Facebook more often than they use their local SNS. However, they have different cultures. The characteristic of Koreans can be revealed in the differences between how Koreans and Westerns reflect cultural differences through the answers to the interviews.

Participants. Interviewees were six undergraduate students at Yonsei University in Korea. Three foreign students came from the UK (2) and Germany (1) as exchange students for one year. Korean students participated in exchange for course credit. The foreign students received 30,000won(about €19) cash compensation.

Procedure and Measures. To explore the motivation using local and global SNSs, semi-structured interviews were conducted. They lasted 50~60 min. The interview questions were divided according to three main research topics: (1) Why did the participants start to use Facebook or a local SNSs? (2) Who were their friends on Facebook or the local SNS? (3) Why did the participants continue to use Facebook or the local SNS? The languages used in interviews were Korean and English.

2.2   Result

The results of interviews suggest that Korean students expected to look more attractive or charming when they have foreign online-friends (especially western friends). Therefore, they would like to meet foreign friends through Facebook. In contrast, western students did not care whether their friends were foreign or not. This result may have the two reasons: The first is the unique emotional state of Korean, as characterized by "being envy" [6]. Koreans feel envious of those whom they want to be. This emotion motivates Korean to approach a 'wannabe'. The second reason is related to the meaning of western culture in Korea. Western culture represents globalization in Korea. For example, many universities in Korea used English slogan to show their international abilities [7]. That is, becoming western means being good at English, being a very capable person, and being more attractive than others in Korea. A foreign person may be one whom a Korean wants to emulate. In addition, "being envy" and becoming western may be combined with the unique motivation of Korean, that being self-expression [1]. Korean would like to express their attractiveness and capability by showing that they have many foreign friends. In sum, Facebook offers the opportunity for them to express their attractiveness online by showing comments written by their foreign friends, thus realizing their 'wannabe' motivations online.

The results of interview were consistent with the rich-get-richer theory [8]. This theory seeks to explain the relationship between personality and social networking use. According to the rich-get-richer theory, personality is expressed online as it is in real life. For instance, a high extroverted person may have a large number of friends on Facebook [9]. The point of this theory is that the offline tendency can extend to the online tendency, which is in good agreement with the results of the interviews. Given that the point of the rich-get-richer theory can be applied to emotion or motivation as well as personality, the distinctive motivation for using a global SNS could begin from Koreans' eager offline traits. To clarify the relationship between offline and online propensities, a questionnaire was used.

3   Questionnaire

To examine whether Koreans' unique emotions and motivations expand to the online realm, a questionnaire was used to analyze the correlation between the offline and online tendencies.

3.1   Method

Participants. Forty-five participants (twenty five men and twenty women) responded in this questionnaire. The participants were undergraduate students at Yonsei University and participated in exchange for course credit.

Procedure and Measures. The participants completed an online survey. The questionnaire measure was organized in three parts. The first part assessed users' offline tendencies to prefer foreign friends. For example, one question was, "I will look more attractive when I have foreign friends." The second part measured the online propensity for comments written by foreign friends and perception of Facebook compared to local SNSs. For instance, two questions were, "A friend looks more attractive when I see a comment written by foreigners on friend's Facebook page" and "Facebook is more suitable for people my age than a local SNS." The last part concerned demographic information such as gender and the use of SNSs, such as the time spend using them. All questions were rated on a 7-point Likert scale.

3.2 Result

To examine whether Koreans' unique emotion and motivation also existed online, we analyzed the correlation between the preferences of comments written by foreign friends and SNS users eager make to foreign friends. The perceptions of Facebook compared a local SNS were added to the correlation analysis. The results are presented in Table 1. A user evaluated oneself as more attractive if he (she) had a foreign friend offline, and this was the same if a Facebook friend had comments from their foreign friends on their Facebook page. Concerning the relationship with the perception of Facebook, he (she) rated oneself as more attractive or more intelligent when using Facebook compared to a local SNS.

Table 1. Correlation between the preferences of foreigners' comments and eagerness to meet foreigners offline and the perception of Facebook and use of Facebook

	Attractiveness of friends with foreigners' comments	
	r	p
Use of Facebook		
The total number of friends	-.012	Not significant
The number of foreign friends	-.032	Not significant
Eagar to meet foreigners offline		
The person looks more attractive if they have foreign friends.	.615	$P < .001$
I would like to have foreign friends.	.396	$P < .01$
I look more attractive if I have foreign friends.	.706	$P < .001$
Perception of Facebook compared to a local SNS		
Facebook is more suitable for people my age than a local SNS.	.023	Not significant
A person using Facebook looks more intelligent than those using a local SNSs.	.545	$P < .001$
I look more attractive when using Facebook than when I use a local SNS.	.603	$P < .001$

4   Discussion

According to the result of the in-depth interviews, Korean users of a global SNS appear to consider that foreign online-friends make them look more attractive or charming. This is connected with the unique motivation of self-expression, as revealed by Jung et al. [1]. The motivation to express oneself as very capable or attractive is combined with the representation of western culture. Becoming western means becoming globalized, in the same manner as being good at English is regarded as the index of the possibility to succeed in Korea. In local SNSs, Korean had few opportunities to express this when using a global SNS. This result supports the rich-get-richer theory [8], which holds that the online propensity reflects the offline trend. To clarify the result of the in-depth interview and explain it as quantitative data, we used the questionnaire. The correlation result supported the result of the in-depth interview result. The more attractive he (she) evaluated oneself if he (she) has a foreign friend offline, the more attractive he (she) also evaluated a person who had the comments of foreign friends on Facebook.

This study shows that the motives for using local SNSs and global SNSs do not originate from a common motive. Although an approach that uses common factors to explain the differences among cultures is important in cross-culture studies, a method to reveal the distinctiveness of one particular culture is also meaningful. In addition, the results of this study suggest that there are various motives for using global SNSs depending on the different cultural backgrounds of users. Global SNSs have to consider local motivation for greater business success online.

Acknowledgments. This study has been supported by Yonsei university and Brain Korea 21.

References

1. Jung, T., Youn, H., McClung, S.: Motivations and self-presentation strategies on Korean-based "Cyworld" weblog format personal homepages. CyberPsychology and Behavior 10(1), 24–31 (2007)
2. Eldon, E.: ComScore, Quantcast, Compete, Nielsen show a strong December for Facebook traffic in the US (January 22, 2010).
   `http://www.insidefacebook.com/2010/01/22/`
   `comscore-quantcast-compete-show-a-strong-december-`
   `forfacebook-traffic-in-the-us/` (accessed 10.01.10)
3. Kim, Y., Sohn, D., Choi, S.M.: Cultural difference in motivations for using social network sites: A comparative study of American and Korean college students. Computers in Human Behavior 27, 365–372 (2011)
4. Ahn, W., Han, K.: Social Network use and personality. In: Proceeding of Korean Society of Design Science 2010, Wonju, South Korea (2010)
5. Vasaloua, A., Joinsona, A.N., Courvoisier, D.: Cultural differences,experience with social networks and then ature of "true commitment" in Facebook. International Journal of Human-Computer Studies 68, 719–728 (2010)
6. Cha, O.A.: Buroum: An Analysis of Benign Envy in Korea. Korean Journal of Social and Personality Psychology 23(2), 171–189 (2009)
7. Yang, C.Y.: Understanding the Linguistic Use of English Slogans in Korean University Homepages. Language and Linguistics 39, 91–111 (2007)
8. Kraut, R., Lundmark, V., Patterson, M., Kiesler, S., Mukopadhyay, T., Scherlis, W.: Internet paradox: A social technology that reduces social involvement and psychological well-being? American Psychologist 53, 1017–1031 (1998)
9. Amichai-Hamburger, Y., Vinitzky, G.: Social network use and personality. Computers in Human Behavior 26, 1289–1295 (2010)

Color Image Effect of Online Community on Age: Focusing on Self-expression

Jihyun Kim[1], Hyeryeong Kim[2], and Kwang-Hee Han[3]

[1] Graduate Program in Cognitive Science, Yonsei University,
134 Shinchon-dong, Seodaemun-gu, Seoul, South Korea
[2] MC Design Laboratory, LG Electronics,
221 yangjae-dong, Seocho-gu, Seoul, South Korea
[3] Department of Psychology, Yonsei University,
134 Shinchon-dong, Seodaemun-gu, Seoul, South Korea
jjyuny2@gmail.com, heheday@naver.com, khan@yonsei.ac.kr

Abstract. Online social network service prevents older adults from isolating. It can be the tool of self-expression in the social context as well as the mean of sharing information. Affiliated community itself can be a self-expressive symbol of the member sometimes. How the member feel the community can affect sense of belonging. This study investigated age difference on perceived self-expression depending on color image of online community webpage. The results indicated that two different age groups showed different perceived patterns to 'soft-hard' and 'warm-cool' image dimensions. This suggests that interface designers consider that color image of interfaces can provide different expression among different age groups.

Keywords: self-expression, color image, older adults, age, social network service, interface.

1   Introduction

As the average life expectancy is rising with the increased usage of advanced medical technology, the quality of life in late stage of development needs to be considered. As older adults experience economical and physical change, they gradually disengage from social relationship, which leads to social isolation. The opportunities of online communication through social network service, such as blogs or online communities, can improve subjective well-being of the elderly. The main purpose of using social network service is not only to share useful information with others and to maintain social network but also to express one's own idea, feeling or personality. The need for self-expression is strong in especially social context. As the group one belong to is one of self-expressive symbols, online community one belong to can be a self-expressive way. At this time, it is important to emotional aspects of interface in the services. Color is one of influential factors to make the first impression for interface [1]. If people felt that interfaces express themselves, their service use and preference could increase [2]. In the previous study, younger adults reported more self-expressive in the color combination of cool image than older adults and older adults perceived less

C. Stephanidis (Ed.): Posters, Part I, HCII 2011, CCIS 173, pp. 445–448, 2011.
© Springer-Verlag Berlin Heidelberg 2011

self-expressive in the color combination of hard image than younger group. However, that study excluded the context of usage.

The present study brought that to the context of interface, especially social network service such as online community and investigated that self-expressive color image of the interface among two different age groups, older adults and younger adults.

The color combinations applied in this study were tested in the previous study [2]. Those were extracted from Kobayashi's Color Image Scale(1990) [3]. The Image Scale represented perceived images of color combination according to two dimensions, "soft-hard" and "warm-cool". The present paper explored how the result of the previous study could apply to online community.

2   Methods

Prototype webpages were produced for this study. The webpages were colored by the color combinations that extracted and tested in the previous study [2]. That is, the community webpages represented specific images according to "soft-hard" or "warm-cool" color image dimensions. For example, a webpage has soft and warm image depending on specific color combination. This study investigated that older and younger adults groups perceived differently how much the communities express themselves when imagined to be a member of the online communities.

Participants. Twenty older adults were recruited through a welfare center in Korea (Mean age: 62.3 years, Men: 7, Women: 13). They were active computer users joined in computer community of the center. They were paid for 5000 won. 31 undergraduate students received course credit (Mean age: 21.5 years, Men: 19, Women: 12).

Materials. Webpage prototypes were the first pages of online community for computer users. The layout of the first page consisted of three areas; background, menu bar, and community information. Three colors of a color combination were randomly assigned to the three areas of the prototype to eliminate area effect of color image. Therefore, three different prototypes were produced for one color combination. Eight color combinations were used and total number of webpages was 24. Questionnaire sample for self-expression cited Carroll & Ahuvia(2006) [4]. The researchers regarded self-expression as both inner self and social self. When someone expresses himself, he considers not only self-image but also the way others see. The questionnaires were such as "this community mirrors the real me" and "this community has a positive impact on what others think of me.

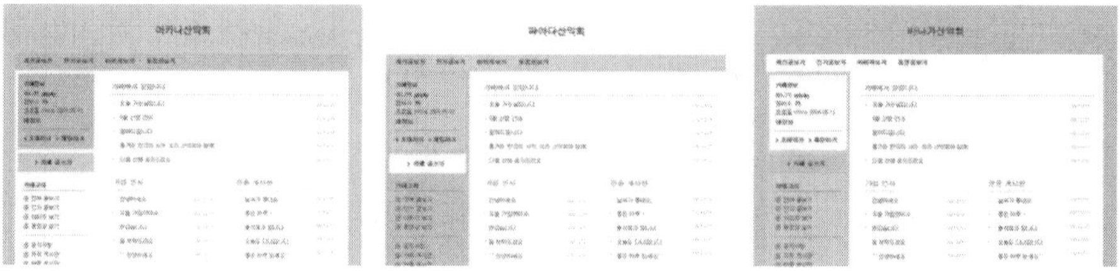

Fig. 1. Community webpage prototype; three pages for one color combination

Procedure. Participants conducted the survey through computers. They were asked to imagine that they were searching for a new community they wanted to join or browsing as an existing member of the community during survey. 24 community webpages were randomly presented one by one. Participants rated the webpages as the degree of self-expression on 7-point likert scale, clicking 1 through 7 buttons. The webpage prototypes and questionnaires were presented by Microsoft Visual basic 6.0. After the survey, they were debriefed.

3   Results and Discussion

Mixed ANOVA was conducted. The main effect results revealed that the community webpages of soft color image *(M* = 4.11, *SD* = .127) were perceived more self-expressive than those of hard color image (*M* = 3.70, *SD* = .144), *F* (1, 49) = 5.89, *p* < .05. However, no age difference was observed in "soft-hard" image dimension, *F* < 1. In addition, the result showed that the community webpages of cool color image *(M* = 3.77, *SD* = .111) were perceived more self-expressive than those of warm color image (*M* = 4.04, *SD* = .121), *F* (1, 49) = 8.04, *p* < .01. Interestingly, older group perceived self-expression not depending on "warm-cool" image of the online communities, but younger group perceived more self-expressive in the communities of cool color image(*M* = 3.85, *SD* = .151) than those of warm color image(*M* = 3.19, *SD* = .139), *F* (1, 49) = 16.02, *p* < .001.

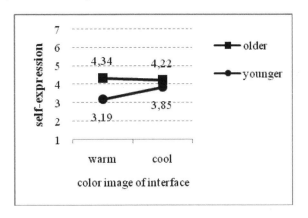

Fig. 2. Age difference on "warm-cool" color image

There was age difference of perceived self-expression from communities depending on "warm-cool" image dimension. This result was consistent with the previous study that younger group perceived more self-expressive in color combination of cool image than older group [2].

The present study suggests that interface designers take color images into consideration for the service or interface that needs for self-expression when service target age is different.

References

1. Cho, K.J., Sun, J.H., Han, K.H.: The Sensibility Effect of Color Combination and Layout in The Design of Web Site. Journal of Korean Society of Design Science, 56, 17(2), 209–220 (2004)
2. Kim, H.R., Kim, J.H., Han, K.: Color Image and Aging Effects on Perceived Self-expression. In: Conference of Korean Society for Emotion & Sensibility, Seoul, pp. 131–132 (2010)
3. Kobayashi, S.: Color Image Scale. Kodansha International Ltd., Tokyo (1990)
4. Carroll, B.A., Ahuvia, A.C.: Some Antecedents and Outcomes of Brand Love. Marketing Letters 17(2), 79–89 (2006)
5. Cailin, B.: Color Harmony for The Web. Rockport Publishers. Inc., Massachusetts (2001)
6. Kobayashi, S.: The Aim and Method of The Color Image Scale. Color Research & Application 6(2), 93–107 (1981)

Gender in the Digital Age: Women's Participation in Designing Social Software

Tânia Cristina Lima and Júlio Cesar dos Reis

Center for Information Technology Renato Archer (CTI) - Rodovia Dom Pedro I,
km 143,6, 13069-901, Campinas, SP, Brazil
{tania.lima,julio.reis}@cti.gov.br

Abstract. Women's participation in social network activities may be an essential condition for its maintenance. This article aims at presenting gender issues and their connection to information technology environment. In order to know what are the gender differences that should be considered in designing a Social Software, the process of creating a social network in the Web is discussed from a female perspective. Testimonies of various social actors and residents of a lower medium class peripheral neighborhood in the city of Campinas, Brazil, the Vila União, involved in the e-Cidadania project is analyzed making references to the paths chosen by the women during the design process, in the pursuit of technological knowledge required for this activity.

Keywords: Gender, Local Culture, Technological Environment, Inclusive Social Networks.

1 Introduction

At the beginning of civilization the human being was nomad and the individuals dedicated themselves to activities of gathering, hunting and fishing, having survival as the sole purpose. Along the time and experience they learned that an organized group functions efficiently, with the increasing importance of kinship and affinity links, family and clans. In order to keep their unity and to protect their identity, these groups created particular ways to express and communicate among individuals, thus establishing specific cultures. Eventually writing became used by most groups and nations in its many forms such as: books, magazines and newspapers, television, computer, satellite, and more recently by Internet and e-mails. Far from adopting a vision of technology as the engine of history, it is accepted that its use changes the type of relationship between people and alters the way of being in the world.

To understand how relationships configure group identity at the global level, it is important to consider the connection between social actors in this environment (World Wide Web) by setting its entry into the world and their cultural traits from this perspective. In these circumstances the main question considered is: how women receive the technology and how these technologies can contribute to empower the local culture?

C. Stephanidis (Ed.): Posters, Part I, HCII 2011, CCIS 173, pp. 449–453, 2011.

It is understood that the study of communication technologies, or rather its appropriation, considered from the gender point of view, is more appropriate and perhaps even more important when we want to elect the best features for a computer system.

Public policies are concerned with the inclusion of female in the digital world, so they try to support learning and communication practices that result in decreasing the digital divide. The e-Cidadania project [2] may be considered a good example of these practices, since its scope aims to achieve economic, political, and cultural changes.

Moreover, socio demographic data of women in Brazil show the rapid growth of female class and display their alternatives in search of visibility. It also shows that women still have a great lag of opportunities compared to men. Women living in large urban centers emerged as a significant contingent of people earning low income, few job prospects and low education [1].

This paper is organized as follows: the section 2 presents the female universe bringing updated data about the population social layer in the research context in Brazil. The section 3 is devoted to a theoretical discussion. The section 4 presents considerations about the feminine discourse; these are excerpts transcribed from interviews in order to enrich the debate on the subject. The section 5 finalizes the paper by also suggesting avenues for future work.

2   Gender and Life Quality

In the last 20 years the Brazilian society suffered demographic and socio-economic transformations that resulted in changes in the spheres of the family life, with prominence reduction of the size of families and the growth of the proportion of families whose responsible persons are women.

The *Vila União* neighborhood follows such change pattern, in which women's proportion responsible for homes is high. This fact is also reflected in the socio economic development of the families, both in cultural aspects, such as dissolution of marriage, until the lack of formal jobs. Among younger, there are those that look for a model of individual independence.

The women participants in the Inclusive Social Network (ISN) VilanaRede (built in the e-Cidadania context) represent the community's female population layer. Without opportunities in formal market jobs some of them stay home and exercise informal paid tasks. Concerning the way individuals deal with the technological environment, it is important to note that when faced with many features offered by the system, which were developed with and for the community, *VilanaRede's* women users choose preferably those that somehow would help them to develop their own business (*i.e.* they had a greater interest in certain features).

Given the geographical extent of the country and its population diversity, there is a sizable contingent that remains in the range of digital exclusion. There are different ways to measure the exclusion; for example, the access to information technologies may be measured from the approach of socio-economic development. In urban areas, in households belonging to D and E social layers, the Internet access reaches 1%, while households in the class A access reaches 93%. Another barrier to digital inclusion is the education; efforts must still be made to improve social and economic conditions that determine the level of education. Statistics on differences in education levels achieved by men and women indicate that there are more women included in lower levels. For example, the proportion of men with up to three years of study by the last Census in 2000 was 33.7%, while women were (37.6%).

Concerning the age structure it is important to note that the Brazilian population goes through a gradual process of aging, reducing the relative proportion of children and young people, due to falling fertility levels in recent decades. This change is also reflected in the average of the female population, which stood at 19.4 years in 1980 and reached 24.9 years in 2000.

3   Theoretical Reflections

The contemporary technologies that enable and enhance communication among people must mainly consider the culture of the group that it targets, among other factors. When this communication exists to support social networks, it is important to consider the cultural structure of the target group. The analysis of social interaction as the *locus* of cultural dynamics is studied by Edward Sapir [3]. Culture, resulting from interactions between different social actors, clarifies the modes of cultural construction on any scale of event.

Anthropology and social sciences in general understands the culture according to one of its first meanings: culture as an ideology - a process that produces specific features of culture, habits and behaviors by borrowing references from the dominant ideology. This ideological feature in culture formation relates to the maintenance of order and social integration. As an example, from the ideologically 'dominant' culture emerges the 'mass consumption culture' replacing the 'traditional culture'.

However, some authors like Williams [4] and Hall [5] recognize the authentic culture or traditional features as resulting from the combination of high culture elements, with those from the ordinary or popular culture. Both authors show that it is possible to verify the importance of culture and language in communication flow. Based on the Marxist concept of production and consumption the authors will explain the message transmission as a chain of communication that does not operate linearly. Understood as a complex structure of meanings, communication is not always received in a clear and transparent way. This means that there is not an overall logic that allows us to understand the meaning or the ideological meaning of the message implicit in the communication [5].

This can be verified in any technology environment that desires to be inclusive. We must consider population characteristics in the design and features of a computational system, such as: cultural capital and language, understanding interactions with computer and user's expectations with network. Writing about the electronic media, Hall and Williams, calling attention to the dual interpretation of the data related to its use, in which case the culture and language may be as much an obstacle as an opportunity to allow interactivity [6].

A technological artifact properly constructed to and with the community can bring about remarkable transformations of qualitative nature. It is a process that affects the lives of families and communities, while it requires the harmonious participation of all involved. However, the appropriation of technological innovation does not happen equally to men and women. That is why we address the effects of gender, involving specific benefits for women. For this reasons, it is not clear what the communication process brings to everyday life. We ask whether these innovations realized under the project would be fully used outside of that scenario.

This question can be answered with a positive increase on the relationship between human versus computer, leading to a more frequent use of the system and its features in a meaningful way. When looking at the practices of women from the construction and use of *VilanaRede* we can see this actually happening.

4 The Community and the Technological Use

In test scenarios of the new website *VilanaRede* users gradually gave evidence of good practice, demonstrating autonomy and self-assurance when making use of hardware tools (keyboard and mouse), and also software. Over time women began to post ideas and ads in the system in order to communicate. The ISN have become (it is now seen) as an alternative communication channel of long range to the community. The use of the network system increased the opportunities of work by increasing contacts.

The correct use of the PC is rewarded with recognition for the effort invested in learning to communicate through the machine. Women learn how to communicate and keep updated about many subjects: *"[...] everyone does it nowadays; you get outdated if you not run for it. PC is a working tool used a lot. (Vila União's residence number 4).*

Confidence, motivation and support are part of a group of taxonomies used to evaluate the system. According to Burnett [1] these are situations that should be taken into account when evaluating the design of the system.

The good practices related to gender are numerous: they are reported in the interviews and statements confirming the change of relation between the human versus the digital artifact, as the motivation for surfing in the Web, the autonomy for accessing that the good use of technology makes possible. They understand that every effort for learning is rewarded with improvement in quality of life that returns to them, to family and community.

From this community is observed that "being" in *VilanaRede* brought greater diversity to the community. It allowed access to information and make they felt satisfied with the dedicated effort. After applying their expertise in creating announcements in the ISN *VilanaRede*, using for that fully digital assets and artifacts such as cameras, photo, movies and chat, it is possible to see emerging a visible growth of their self-esteem, self-confidence and in their ability to use the resources offered by the system. They report that: *"[...] I have never imagined how was to construct a site"..."this knowledge has no price, there is no value. There is so many things that I didn't know and I learned." (Vila União's residence number 1).*

5 Final Considerations

This paper is an attempt to show that technology when associated to gender brings the capacity to emancipate people. The facility to access information is recognized as much important, as well as the capacity for interaction and collaboration between people that technology offers. There is no doubt that the contemporary technology gives to human the capacity to produce better and in more quantity. However, it does not point out what are the better choices in front of a variety of consumption and cultural options. That is the moment that makes difference to include the female population layer that habitat the huge urban centers.

Such significant contingent of people is capable to remake their traditional habits rooted in the local culture. They also are capable to understand the potential for communication brought by technology seeing the possibility to create and to express themselves. They realize accessing the digital world opportunities to overcome their social and economical situations, and also to improve their female condition mainly for recognizing the importance of self-esteem.

We pointed out that technology not distinguishes gender, in other hand just the gender appropriates it differently. In this sense, we are aware about the truths and myths created around the use of technology. However, a system that contemplates the differences regarding gender in design process of the computational system, must be useful to other kinds of users; *i.e.* although the reported experience has indicated to be efficient to women context, this just reinforce that potentially it can bring considerable impacts to their life (private and public). Further study can show the direction if this is enough to confirm new design methods that contemplate the female layer.

Acknowledgments. This work was funded by Microsoft Research - FAPESP Institute for IT Research (proc. n. 2007/54564-1). The authors also thank colleagues from IC/UNICAMP and from the *"Vila União"* Community.

References

1. Beckwith, L., Burnett, M.: Gender: An Important Factor in End-User Programming Environments? Visual Languages and Human Centric Computing. IEEE Symposium, 107–114, 30-30 (2004)
2. Baranauskas, M.C.C.: e-Cidadania: Systems and Methods for the Constitution of a Culture mediated by Information and Communication Technology. Research Proposal for the Microsoft Research-FAPESP Institute (2007)
3. Sapir, E.: Culture, Language and Personality. In: Mandelbaum, D. (ed). University of California Press (1949)
4. Williams, R.: Marxism and Literature. Oxford University Press, Oxford (1997)
5. Hall, S.: Da Diáspora – Identidades e Mediações Culturais. In: Horizonte, B. (ed.) UFMG Codificação/Decodificação, p.354 (2003)
6. MODELO DE REFERÊNCIA – Sistema Brasileiro de Televisão Digital Terrestre. FUNTTEL. Projeto Brasileiro de Televisão Digital. OS 40539. Texto em PDF (2006)

Study of Communication Aid Which Supports Conversation Held at Railway Station

Kaoru Nakazono[1], Mari Kakuta[2], and Yuji Nagashima[3]

[1] NTT Network Innovation Laboratories, Musashino-shi Tokyo 180, Japan
nakazono.kaoru@lab.ntt.co.jp
[2] International Christian University, Mitaka-shi Tokyo 181, Japan
[3] Kogakuin University, Hachioji-shi Tokyo 192, Japan

Abstract. We are developing a communication aid technique called VUTE (Visual Universal Talking Environment). VUTE aids people who have difficulty in spoken communication such as elderly hard of hearing people, Deaf people and foreigners. Its unique characteristic is that it does not rely on written language but uses motion pictograms. This paper presents the overview of VUTE 2010 that can be used at railway stations and the methodology for designing VUTE 2010. The results of the evaluation experiment of VUTE 2010 will also be discussed.

1 Introduction

We are developing a communication aid technique called VUTE (Visual Universal Talking Environment) that can be activated on a portable cellular device. VUTE can be used by elderly hard of hearing people, Deaf people and foreigners who have difficulty using spoken language.

We developed VUTE 2009, a system that aids people to make emergency calls when there is need for help or rescue in emergencies such as fire, sudden sickness, accidents, etc[1][2]. Following VUTE 2009 we developed VUTE 2010 a communication aid targeting traveler's communication in places such as railway stations.

This paper will report the methodologies for the development of VUTE 2010 such as collecting, classifying, grouping conversation sentences used during travel. Also the design of interface screen and motion pictograms will be explained. The results from our evaluation experiment will also be presented.

2 Design of VUTE 2010

2.1 Guideline for the Design of VUTE

There are 3 basic guidelines that we followed for the design of VUTE: (1) VUTE can be activated on a portable cellular device and this enables connection for database search and output of audio information, (2) VUTE can show motion pictograms, (3) Aspects of manga and expressions used by the Deaf were incorporated in the design of the pictograms. Commonly used pictograms are too

C. Stephanidis (Ed.): Posters, Part I, HCII 2011, CCIS 173, pp. 454–458, 2011.

simple and highly abstract. We believe that by using some aspects of manga the pictograms can be more expressive. Also by observing aspects of the expressions used by the Deaf, we believe that we can make the pictograms more universal and easy to understand.

2.2 Collection, Classification, Grouping of Traveler Conversations

We collected conversations used by foreign travelers in places such as stations and classified and grouped them to find out the general patterns in traveler conversations.

Collecting the traveler conversations
We restricted the collection of traveler conversations into conversation between 2 people, in which "the traveler" asks and "the respondent" answers. Simple greeting and complex conversations were omitted from our data. As a result, 266 conversation sentences remained.

Classification of the traveler conversations
We classified our traveler conversation data into 3 types focusing on "what the traveler basically wishes or hopes to gain from the communication"

1. **Sentences to question**: These sentences are for asking questions wanting to gain some information.
   Eg. *What time is the next express train? / Where is the toilet?*
2. **Sentences to express some desires**: These sentences express desires such as what you want to do and what you want to become.
   Eg. *I want to drink water. / I want to go on the train to _____ station.*
3. **Sentences to express trouble**: Sentences to express trouble, danger or something that is unpleasant for the speaker.
   Eg. *I forgot my bag. / There's a suspicious bag.*

If the message of the traveler is transmitted well, they can get some response and help from the respondent maybe using gestures or writing on paper.

Grouping of the traveler conversations
The 3 types of sentences to question, to express some desires, to express trouble were grouped as follows. These are based only on the usage at railway stations.

1. **To question**: Asking for something that the speaker do not understand
   (a) Where is _____ ? (Asking for the place)
   (b) What time is_____ ? (Asking for the time)
   (c) How much is_____ ? (Asking for the cost)
2. **To express some desires**: Want to do something
   (a) Want to buy _____ ? (eg. tickets)
   (b) Want_____ ? (eg. drinks and food)
   (c) Want to ride_____ ? (eg. train)
   (d) Want to go_____ ? (eg. place)

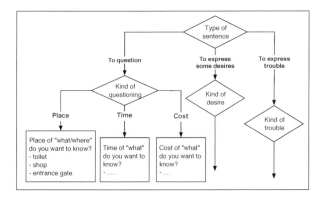

Fig. 1. Part of flowchart of VUTE 2010

3. **To express trouble**: Want to say that the speaker is in a troubled situation
   (a) Troubled situation concerning safety
   (b) Troubled situation concerning luggage/belongings
   (c) Troubled situation concerning the train
   (d) Troubled situation concerning health

For the above 11 groups of sentences, different words or phrases can be inputted into the blank, eg. For (1)-a "Where is _____ ?", words such as *toilet, shop, entrance gate* can be inputted.

Words or information that corresponds to these sentences were then designed into pictograms. By selecting pictograms appropriate for a specific sentence, the information that the speaker wants to transmit were gathered in detail. Part of the flowchart explaining this system is shown on Figure 1. We will call each stage on the flow chart, transaction. All conversations on VUTE 2010 will be formed in a 3 stage transaction.

The first transaction determines "The type of sentences that needs to be transmitted (Type 1, 2 or 3)". The second transaction is for deciding what kind of information needs to be transmitted (Kind (a), (b), (c) or (d)). The third transaction gains information in detail so that the final information can be formed (eg. If asking for the cost of the ticket, additional information such as the types of ticket i.e. express train or local train).

2.3   Design of Agent and Manga Pictograms

The sentences and the transactions described in section 2.2 were then converted into agent animation and pictograms. VUTE 2010 was designed so that each transaction was arranged in a different format so the user can know what stages they are at. If the system is used several times the user can understand how the final information and question is formed. The examples of the screen are shown on Figure 2. VUTE 2010 is a Web application using Flash.

(1)   (2)   (3)   (4)   (5)

Fig. 2. Screen capture of operating VUTE 2010

3   Evaluation Experiment

Seven Japanese subjects (2 male and 5 female, age 50 to 60) who do not daily use computers were asked to use VUTE 2010 to evaluate whether they can construct the information necessary using the system and to check whether there is any interface trouble.

3.1   Setting the Situation

Before the subjects used VUTE 2010, we had to explain to the subjects so that they can fully understand the situation they are in and what kind of information that they had to transmit. We made up 11 kinds of situations, where the user had to ask someone at the station for something. These situations were written in Japanese. Each situation was printed on one A4 paper and the subjects had to read and understand the contents.

The examples of the situations are (1) I am standing in front of the shop. I want a sandwich, (2) I am standing on the platform of the station. I want to go to the entrance gate, (3) I am standing on the platform of the station. I want to know where the locker is.

3.2   Method of the Experiment

We handed the situation papers to each subjects and asked them to read and fully understand the content. The subjects then used the mouse to select the pictograms of VUTE 2010 so that they can output the final sentence or information. The 11 types of situations were shown to each subject in an order that was set before the experiment and they had to use VUTE 2010 according to each situation. The subjects received no help or direction after the situation paper was shown. The time used by the subjects to complete the output for each situation was recorded.

3.3   Results

All subjects were able to reach the correct output sentence necessary for each situation although some had to repeat or redo the selection of the choices to

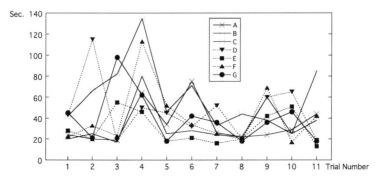

Fig. 3. Transition of accomplishment times for each subject

reach the correct answer. The average time was approximately 41 seconds and those between 15 – 25 seconds were the majority and only few were able to finish in less than 15 seconds.

Figure 3 shows the change in the accomplishment time for each subject. A to G indicates the 7 subjects. The numbers 1 to 11 in horizontal axis indicates the 11 different situations. The accomplishment time (seconds) are plotted along the vertical axis. From Figure 3, it can be found that many subjects had difficulty for situation 4 and situation 9. For these two situations the subjects had to scroll the page to select the pictograms and were complex compared to the other situations. For the other situations there were no big differences. We expected the accomplishment time to decrease as the subjects got used to the system but in this experiment there were no clear results concerning the decrease in time. We also found out from the accomplishment time that some specific pictograms were difficult to understand and we need to improve several parts of the system.

4   Conclusion

From the results of the evaluation experiment, it was found that many users can use this system and output the appropriate information without knowing how to use the system. We were also able to find out parts of VUTE 2010 that needs to be improved to further increase the understanding of the users. This research is granted by the Strategic Information and Communications R&D Promotion Programme (SCOPE) of Ministry of Internal Affairs and Communications, Japan.

References

[1] Nakazono, K., Kakuta, M., Nagashima, Y., Hosono, N.: Universal Communication Aid for Disabled People Using Motion Pictograms. In: Proceedings of HCI International, pp. 951–955 (2009)
[2] Nakazono, K., Kakuta, M., Nagashima, Y., Hosono, N.: Development of Universal Communication Aid for Emergency Using Motion Pictogram. In: Miesenberger, K., Klaus, J., Zagler, W., Karshmer, A. (eds.) ICCHP 2010. LNCS, vol. 6179, pp. 308–311. Springer, Heidelberg (2010)

Sociable Tabletop Companions at "Dinner Party"

Hye Yeon Nam and Ellen Yi-Luen Do

Georgia Institute of Technology
Atlanta, Georgia, 30332
{hnam,ellendo}@gatech.edu

Abstract. This paper describes the challenges and processes of developing a sociable interface and presents the implementation of one sociable interface, *Dinner Party*, in which a participant interacts with virtual creatures while dining alone. This paper explains how mundane objects can be sociable interfaces that interact with humans on a psychological level.

Keywords: Human-computer interaction, Sociable interfaces, Creative and expressive art experiences.

1 Introduction

In human-computer interaction, research pertaining to pervasive and ubiquitous computing [1] and tangible user interfaces [2] shows an increasing need for new interfaces that provide seamless integrations between the digital and physical worlds. Interface designers are currently exploring the possibility of these improvements in technology as tools, yet few designers approach them as sociable interfaces capable of perceiving human social behaviors and friendly communicating with people on cognitive levels.

This paper introduces a sociable interface called *Dinner Party*, which enables friendly interaction between a human and an everyday piece of furniture. While sitting by a dinner table, whenever a diner moves a cup, a fork, a spoon, or a pepper shaker, animated words describing imaginary creatures from *Jabberwocky* [3] appear on the surface of the table. These imaginary creatures move between the shadows of different eating utensils in a playful manner, forming a nice "Dinner Party" for the diner. This paper discusses the challenges in designing sociable interfaces and the processes of individuals' interpretation of objects as sociable interfaces that psychologically interact with them. This paper introduces *Dinner Party* as an implementation of a sociable interface.

2 Challenges in Designing Sociable Interface

Neurobiologists and psychologists alike have speculated that emotion is an adjusted, adaptive change in multiple physiological systems in response to the value of a stimulus from the environment. For several decades, developers have attempted to

C. Stephanidis (Ed.): Posters, Part I, HCII 2011, CCIS 173, pp. 459–463, 2011.
© Springer-Verlag Berlin Heidelberg 2011

create artificial intelligence that has emotions. Early AI researchers were optimistic about the future of AI producing intelligence equal to that of humans. In 1965, AI pioneer Herbert Simon stated "machines will be capable, within twenty years, of doing any work a man can do" [4]. However, AI does not yet match human level intelligence because machines are not able to think.

Searle [5] criticized early AI theories, calling them "strong AI," and said "no program by itself is sufficient for thinking." Instead of using the term "strong AI," he used the term "applied AI." Duffy [6] describes an artificial system as an illusion of intelligence according to the human interpretation of the actions of AI. For example, the ELIZA program [7], which was described by Joseph Weizenbaum in *Communications of the ACM* in January 1966, engages in friendly conversation with a user on the Internet. It chats with the user based on the user's typed input even though it does not understand either the contents or the contexts of the conversation. Even though Eliza is a simple chat system, people share personal experiences with the system, forming psychological attachments.

3   Psychological Notions

The projective intelligence in sociable interfaces is supported by the psychological notion of intentionality and perception.

3.1   Intentionality

A philosopher and psychologist in the 19th century, Franz Brentano introduced the concept of "intentionality" used in philosophy and cognitive science to explain why people believe that machines can think without any human level intelligence. He coined the term "intentional inexistence" [8] to explain mental phenomena. People have beliefs because certain objects trigger certain attitudes and behaviors (e.g., "The shower head is sad because it drops water.") The view is also supported by philosopher Daniel Dennett [9] in *Intentional Stance*. In his view, people apply three strategies to predict the behaviors of living organisms such as plants, animals, and humans, and even artifacts. Whereas some are based on the laws of physics, or "the physical stance" (e.g., "If you heat the water at more than 100 C., the water will boil."), others are determined by design, or "the design stance" (e.g., "The design of a door knob gives clues about how to open the door."). Sometimes neither the physical nor the design stance is accessible, so another stance, "the intentional stance," can be adopted. The intentional stance treats plants, animals, humans, and artifacts as rational agents with beliefs and desires in order to further predict how they are going to behave.

3.2   Imaginary, Symbolic, and Real Orders

The French psychoanalyst Jacques Lacan [10] showed the relationship between one's "self" and one's "separated self." Lacan divides human perception into three orders: the *imaginary*, the *symbolic*, and the *real*. In Figure 1, "a" in the lower left-hand corner designates one's self, or ego, and "a'" in the top right-hand corner is a projection and a reflection of one's identity, called the *imaginary* order. The *imaginary* order includes conscious, unconscious, perceived, or imagined identification in the outside world. They face each other in a symmetrical mirror. In this realm, one sees oneself as another person reflected in the mirror. Theories of narcissism are explained within the imaginary order. Later, in the early 1950s, Lacan introduced the *symbolic* order, in which one's identity is defined by outside contexts such as society, culture, language, or customs. Finally, Lacan explained the position of the *real* order, which is pure, and thus, only the final residues are left once all articulations are deleted.

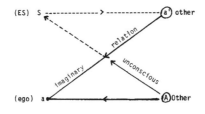

Fig. 1. Lacan's L-schema

Lacan explains how individuals perceive the world according to relationships between themselves and others and how they identify and negotiate boundaries. While perceiving, they consciously and unconsciously interpret the world as they are projecting themselves. When any objects in their surroundings display subtle cues so that a human can determine their functions, the human intuitively translates the complex behaviors of the objects into more familiar and understandable behaviors.

4   Dinner Party

4.1   Hardware/Software System

The *Dinner Party* interface consists of a computer, an IR-filtered camera, and a mirror, all inside of a table, and a plate, a cup, a peppershaker, a fork, and a spoon, all lying on top of the table. IR lighting on the ceiling focuses on the center of the table. An IR-filtered camera detects movement above the table surface, and the projector casts interactive letter animations onto the tabletop.

Fig. 2. Dinner Party setup

We developed *Dinner Party* using Openframeworks, an open source software framework based on the C++ programming language. Using a screenshot of the default image, we compared the default image pixels with the current image pixels on the table surface in real time. This computer vision system allows the computer to detect where the letter animations originate and move to.

4.2 Interaction

Dinner Party provides a space in which people meet and interact with the letter-shaped virtual creatures from Lewis Carroll's *Jabberwocky* [3]. When a participant sits down at the table and moves the utensils, the cup, and the shaker, the projector connected to the computer casts animated creatures hiding in the shadows of the objects. The table becomes an interactive platform between the participant and the imaginary creatures living in the shadows underneath the objects of *Dinner Party*. Creatures move from the shadow to other shadows while scattering or hiding in between objects (see Figure 3). Initially, the letters are entangled in a shape of large blobs. After a certain period of time, individual letters form sentences. Then they reveal themselves completely and display each sentence of the poem, *Jabberwocky*.

Fig. 3. Letter-shaped animation moves between shadows on the table surface

5   Conclusion

Dinner Party was exhibited at New York's Eyebeam Art Gallery in 2008 and showcased at the Siggraph Art Gallery in 2010 in Los Angeles. Hundreds of participants interacted with *Dinner Party*, and they commented that it was a "friendly" interface. Because the combinations of slow and fast movements of letter-shaped animations imitate the movements of living organisms, they trigger participants' imaginations, rendering the *Dinner Party* interface more life-like and sociable. This paper constructs two physiological notions to interpret meaning expressed in the interaction of visitors with Dinner Party. At first glance, the tabletop component of Dinner Party may not seem to serve any particular functional purpose other than as an ordinary table for food placement and dining activities. However, it transforms a mundane dining experience into a pleasant and friendly interaction with individuals when they project intentionality and perception. Although the objects, a table, a chair, and dining sets in *Dinner Party* are made of materials, people interpret their movements as those of an organism and perceive their interactions as psychological cues. In this manner, everyday gestures and objects become meaningful when a participant engages in friendly interaction with the Dinner Party tabletop.

References

1. Weiser, M.: The Computer of the 21st Century. Sci. Am. 265(3), 66–75 (1991)
2. Ishii, H., Ullmer, B.: Tangible Bits: Towards Seamless Interfaces between People, Bits and Atoms. In: Proceedings of CHI 1997, pp. 234–241. ACM, New York (1997)
3. Carroll, L.: Through the Looking- Glass and What Alice Found There. Electronic Text Center, University of Virginia Library (1871)
4. Crevier, D.: Ai: The Tumultuous History of the Search for Artificial Intelligence. Basic Books, New York (1994)
5. Searle, J.R.: Minds, brains and programs. Behav. Brain. Sci. 3(3), 417–459 (1980)
6. Duffy, B.R.: Anthropomorphism and the social robot. Robot. Auton. Syst. 42, 177–190 (2003)
7. Weizenbaum, J.: ELIZA—a computer program for the study of natural language communication between man and machine. Commun. ACM. 9(1), 36–45 (1966)
8. Brentano, F.: Psychology from an Empirical Standpoint. Routledge, London and New York (1995)
9. Dennett, D.C.: The Intentional Stance. The MIT Press, Cambridge (1989)
10. Lacan, J.: The Ego in Freud's Theory and in the Technique of Psychoanalysis, 1954-1955 (Book II). In: Tomaselli, S. (Trans.) The Seminar of Jacques Lacan, W.W. Norton & Co. (1991)

Quality of Community in Social Games

Kohei Otake[1], Tadakazu Fukutomi[2], and Tomofumi Uetake[1]

[1] Graduate School of Business Administration, Senshu University
[2] School of Network and Information, Senshu University
2-1-1 Higashimita Tama-ku Kawasaki 214-8580, Japan
uetake@isc.senshu-u.ac.jp

Abstract. With the widespread of Internet, 'Contents' on Internet are increasing. And, contents offered on Internet are transformed from a unique service into an undifferentiated service (Commodification of the Internet contents). And users' concerns may be changing from the value of contents to other in the near future. In social games, we think that the selection criteria will change from the value of contents to the value of the community. So, it is important for Social Game suppliers to offer the function to improve the quality of community. In this paper, we aim to examine how to improve the quality of community. We focus on Q&A sites that have services to improve the quality of community. We analyze the structure of the community and consider the factors to improve the quality of community.

Keywords: Social Games, Quality of Community, Commodification, Q&A service.

1 Commodification of the Internet Contents

Today, Free Service has infiltrated into our life, such as music, books, games, etc. These contents suppliers gather users and gain profit from advertising, freemium, and premium services [1]. In the present state of affairs, the quality of contents is an important factor to gather users. But contents may be transformed from a unique service into an undifferentiated service in the near future [2]. So, contents suppliers must think another way to gather users.

In this paper, we focus on Social Games which indicate the games offered by SNS sites. This type of game is now very popular. There are many SNS sites that provide these Social Games. So, it is important for SNS sites to offer unique services for users.

Social Games have following three special features.

— operating is simple
— playing time of the game once is short
— it is social

By the third feature, the quality of the members who are participating may become the major incentive for playing Social Games. In other words, we can say that 'Quality of Community' is important in Social Games.

C. Stephanidis (Ed.): Posters, Part I, HCII 2011, CCIS 173, pp. 464–468, 2011.
© Springer-Verlag Berlin Heidelberg 2011

2   Problems of Social Games

We think about the problems of Social Games by taking up a Japanese popular title "Bandit Nation". "Bandit Nation" is offered by Japanese major SNS sites such as "mixi" (http://mixi.jp/home.pl), "DeNA" (http://yahoo-mbga.jp/).

The aims of the "Bandit Nation" are becoming the leader of the banditry, and collecting treasures by stealing from other users. Moreover, the player can register other users as a companion. It comes to be able to exchange the item and the treasure when becoming a companion. Most users are playing a game in cooperation with friends. So, this game is fun when playing a lot of companions. Therefore, it is important for the SNS site to offer the function to increase the number of users who play together. The users who have the possibility of becoming companions are divided into following three types (see Fig.1).

A) Known users and playing the same game
B) Known users but not playing the same game
C) Unknown users but playing the same game

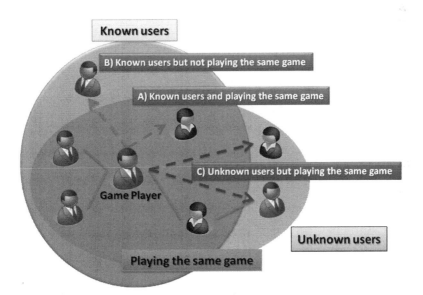

Fig. 1. The users who have the possibility of becoming companions

It is easy to contact with known users, but it is difficult to contact with unknown users. In this situation, there are three ways to contact with unknown users in "Bandit Nation".

1. Contact to the friends of known users
2. Use the search function that can be searched by the game level
3. Use the bulletin board of the gaming community

But, these ways are not enough to contact unknown users because there is little information about unknown users. Social game suppliers offer enough function to play with known users, but it is not enough to play with unknown users.

So, it is important to offer the functions to increase the number of unknown users easily who play together.

3   Communications with Unknown Users

We focused on the online question and answer (Q&A) service, because the Q&A service has functions that support communications with unknown users. The Q&A service is knowledge community service which purports the retrieval by person's power in internet. There are many types of questions that are from easy questions to difficult questions that require the exclusive knowledge.

Following sites are representative Q&A services in Japan.

— Hatena::Question   (http://q.hatena.ne.jp/)
— OKWave (http://okwave.jp/)
— Yahoo! Chiebukuro (http://chiebukuro.yahoo.co.jp/)

We focused on "Hatena::Question". We researched what the quality of community is and how to improve the quality of the service and defined elements to improve the quality of community as:

— Good manners
— High skill
— Active

Moreover, we found that three services are necessary to improve these elements (see Fig.2).

a) Disclosure of user information
b) Mutual evaluation by the user
c) Point system that can be used on other communities

In "Hatena::Question", all activities in the community such as member information, content of question, content of answer and evaluation to them are open to other users. "Disclosures of user information" take responsibility to their remarks. For example, it is assumed that a certain user did an irresponsible answer to the question. Information that the user answered keeps remaining afterwards, and is open to the public of other users. This negatively affects the "mutual evaluations by the user".

Moreover, the points are necessary to question on this site as the question fee (50 - 200 points, 1 point = 1 Japanese yen) in "Hatena::Question". Questioner must pay a fee whenever questioner opens one answer. So, they want to obtain profitable information as much as possible. The answerer can get points as a fee when the questioner opens the answer. And, the points can be exchanged for the points of other communities. This "point system that can be used on other communities" contributes to the improvement of the quality of community.

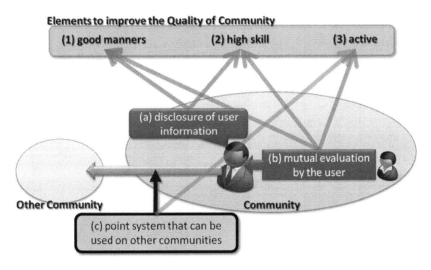

Fig. 2. Three services to improve 'Quality of Community'

4 Basic Ideas

Based on our analyses, we design functions to increase the number of unknown users easily who play together in the Social Games. These functions correspond to services (Disclosure of user information, Mutual evaluation by the user, Point system that can be used on other communities) that improve the quality of community. Basic ideas that achieve these functions are as follows.

a) Disclosure of user information

   To build this function, we focus on user profiles on SNS sites. Almost of the SNS sites offers user profiles. For example, a famous SNS site "Facebook (http://www.facebook.com)" offers detailed user profiles. By using these user profiles effectively, good manners may be feasible and users are easy to find the high skilled users.

b) Mutual evaluation by the user

   To build this function, we focus on the attribute information of the game (e.g. the level of the game, the number of friends, etc.). Moreover, we focus on the feedback ratings adopted on the auction sites. By using the information effectively, good manners may be feasible and users are easy to find the high skilled users and it becomes easy to activate the community.

c) Point system that can be used on other communities

   To build this function, we focus on the attribute information of the other games (e.g. the level of the game, the number of friends, the reputation, etc.). We quantify this information and standardize these values. By using this function, it becomes easy to activate the community.

Our system has a matching system and an extended BBS included above three functions. Our system image is shown in Fig.3. In our system, it is easy to contact unknown users by using our functions, because the user can easy to get the information about unknown users.

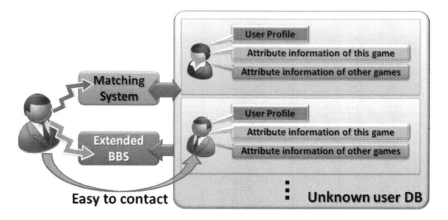

Fig. 3. System image

5   Conclusions and Future Work

In this paper, we focused on the Social Games. In Social Games, quality of community is especially important when the content is transformed from a unique one into an undifferentiated one. By analyzing Q&A sites, we defined elements to improve the quality of community as good manners, high skill, and active. And, we examined the system that enhances the value of the community in Social Games.

We believe that the improvement of the Quality of Community will become a valuable factor to corporations and contents suppliers in the near future. So, how to accept these systems ingenious in Social Games is our future work.

References

[1] Anderson, C.: Free: The Future of a Radical Price, Hyperion (2009)
[2] The annual On-line Game industry report in 2009 (2010)
[3] Junjiro, S., Noriyuki, Y.: Economics of free copy, Nihon keizai shinbun shuppan sha (2008) (in Japanese)
[4] Hirano, C.A., Hagiu, A.: Strategy of Platform, Toyo keizai shinpou sha (2010) (in Japanese)
[5] Kokuryou, J.: Strategy of Open architecture, Diamond sha (1999) (in Japanese)

Taiwanese Facebook Users' Motivation and the Access of Information Technology

Chun-Ming Tsai[1], Yu-Ting Huang[2], and Ji-Lung Hsieh[3]

[1] Department of Computer Science
[2] Graduate Program of E-Learning
Taipei Municipal University of Education,
No. 1, Ai-Kuo W. Road, Taipei 100, Taiwan
[3] Graduate Institute of Libary & Information Studies, National Taiwan Nomal University,
No. 162, He-Ping E. Road Section 1, Taipei 106, Taiwan
{cmtsai2009,yutingbelle,jirlong}@gmail.com

Abstract. With the increasing diversity in networked information communication technology (ICTs), the question arises whether users' social, entertainment and information needs are being met. Existing research on Internet information services and traditional portal or blog sites has not been extended to a more recent study of functional community websites such as Facebook. Therefore, this study was designed to administer a questionnaire survey in order to explore the motivation of Taiwan Facebook users of ICT's by analyzing their Facebook use. The study concluded that: (1) Facebook users were attracted to Facebook mainly by social motivations, though some were attracted by the Facebook game simulation of "Farmville", highly publicized in the media. A study of background variables further found that female users who had low education level and low age were more likely motivated by the gaming platform; male users who had low education level and a higher age were likely attracted by both a high degree of social interaction and high use of game-playing; (2) Facebook users were online more often, but for most there was no significant increase in the total number of hours online; (3) Facebook users who were motivated by both game play and social interaction do actually increase their online time using Facebook. The study indicated that Facebook facilitates increased use of information technology, and further recognizes that the gender of users accounts for significant differences in motivation. The findings of this study will lead to a better understanding of the motivation of Taiwan ICT users, specifically Taiwan Facebook users[1].

Keywords: Access of information technologies, motivation, social networking sites.

1   Introduction

As information communication technologies continue to develop rapidly, the public can access and disseminate information in increasingly diverse ways. Information

---

[1] This paper is supported by the National Science Council, R.O.C., under Grants NSC 99-2221-E-133-002-.

C. Stephanidis (Ed.): Posters, Part I, HCII 2011, CCIS 173, pp. 469–473, 2011.

services have changed from the single mode into multi-level applications such as Facebook, which provide access to information, business, communication, social and entertainment functions in the format of a new "community" website. Inspiration for this study stems from 2009, when a question was raised in Taiwan about the rise of the social gaming craze on Facebook. The motives and background variables of users who explore the community sites such as the Facebook social and gaming platform are studied to determine the impact of recent emerging information technology.

Accordingly, the purpose of this study is (1) to investigate the motivation of Taiwan Facebook users, and establish any correlation with the background variables, and (2) to determine whether Facebook users do actually increase the use of recent information technology. Finally, there is significant motivation to study the types of Facebook users, as the increased use of Facebook in Taiwan constitutes the largest reason for an increase in the number of hours of Internet access.

2   Research Methods

This study utilized a questionnaire survey method to collect research data from Taiwan Facebook users. The motivation of Facebook users is studied as the main variable, with subjects' personal background variables further investigated to explore the Taiwan Facebook user's online life, including the impact on their use of emerging information technologies to access Facebook. The area of Facebook user motivation is divided into social interaction, game-playing, game-playing with and without high social interaction, and those who did not favor either social interaction or game-playing. Background variables considered were users' gender, age and education level.

The questionnaire was designed to determine use of social and game-playing platforms. High reliability was indicated by Cronbach's Alpha scores for sociability (0.861) and game-playing (0.791). The questionnaire utilized a four-point Likert scale (strongly agree, agree, disagree, strongly disagree) for subjects' opinions on their own Facebook use. A subject scoring higher than 80% for both of the two types was classified in the high social / high game-playing; if the percentage gap was within 5%, the user was classified as not favoring either.

From October 2009 to October 2010, the study preparation stage *involved research* design and sampling. From October 2009 to May 2010, the first data was collected using a pre-test prototype questionnaire. A review of the literature was conducted, and research techniques for the study were further developed and modified. Beginning in June 2010, the researcher developed research tools including the formal questionnaire survey. The validity of the questionnaire was pre-tested in three phases in September, and in the process of pre-testing, some related findings were gained and taken into consideration for the purpose of revising the survey. Also, an experience researcher was invited to review the design of the questionnaire. His feedback was instrumental in the final survey design. Consequently, results were re-analyzed on a larger scale.

The references for specialized statistics on worldwide Facebook users were the checkfacebook.com website [1], and the Taiwan Institute for Information Industry 2009 study on social gamers, stratified by age [2]. The subjects of this study were Taiwan Facebook users, grouped into four categories: (1) High school students

(17 years of age and under), (2) College students (18 - 25 years of age), (3) Workers (26 - 34 years of age), and (4) Middle-aged users (35 years of age and over).

Herein, purposive sampling is adopted to obtain the samples. The formula (1) is used to estimate the number of samples required in order to obtain valid user data:

$$n = \frac{C^2 * P(1-P)}{E^2} \tag{1}$$

Note: n, the number of samples; C, the confidence level, P, the percentage, E, sampling error. The formula estimates that the study requires at least 384 samples. The study used 512 samples (496 valid samples). Their ages are given in Table 1.

Table 1. Ages of Surveyed Facebook Users

Age	Number of people	Percentage
8-17 years old	35	7.1%
18-25 years old	362	73%
26-34 years old	84	16.9%
More than 35 years old	15	3%

3 Experimental Results and Discussion

3.1 Background and Motivation of Facebook Users

Users' motivation for Facebook use and the background variables were analyzed using the chi-square independence test in order to determine the relationship between the variables. The existing data indicates that the primary motivation for Facebook users is to get the latest news (21%), both information and social aspects. Secondary social motivations include contacting friends (20.4%), finding people to contact (15%), and to become closer to friends (12%). Another group is solely motivated by the entertainment aspect of game-playing (6.6%).

In addition, from 2009 to 2010, the study results infer that the motivation for users of Facebook changed; in 2009, frequent Taiwan users of Facebook played games (67%) and took online psychological tests (8%) [3]; only about 20% of users utilized the social aspect of the site to make friends (9%), send messages (5%) and seek friends (5%). Studies also indicate that the motivation for early users of Facebook was an attraction to play online games, which attracted many new users. Interacting with friends was not the primary incentive to use the site. However, after 2010, the study found that the Facebook services which are most frequently accessed by users of the site have changed significantly. Currently, users are motivated to obtain information about friends (28%) and use the messaging bulletin board "wall" (21%). Gaming, originally a high percentage use in 2009, now has declined to only about 12%, indicating a transition from past high use of gaming to current social motivations of interacting with friends. The current study indicates that social interaction motivates the majority (70%) of users. Later users were not significantly motivated by the opportunity to play Facebook games.

With regard to users' backgrounds and the effect on their motivation, the chi-square test of independence was used. The effect of user gender is statistically significant ($x^2=0.013<0.05$). A higher proportion of females is motivated by game-playing (16.8% of women, 9% of men), whereas a higher proportion of males were highly motivated by both the game-playing and social interaction opportunities.

Age also plays a significant role in Facebook motivation, as lower age users, in particular the eight to seventeen years of age group, are easily attracted and motivated purely by the game-playing opportunities; older users, especially over the age of thirty-five, display characteristics of both high social interaction and high game-playing.

The study also indicates that users who have higher education display a significant social motivation; users with a low level of education, especially those in high school, are more likely to be motivated by the attractiveness of game-playing. High school students, more than the other age-groups, are motivated to use Facebook both for the game-playing platform and for the social networking capabilities.

3.2   Facebook Motivation and Its Impact on Information Technology Access

The study defined information technology access as the subjects' frequency and hours of use of online services. Participants were asked whether their use of Facebook had increased their information technology access. The results showed that about 62% of the subjects were online more often due to Facebook; the highest proportion of users (24%) reported being online with the highest frequency, five times weekly. About 61% of subjects do stay online longer specifically to use Facebook. Nearly 40% of the subjects are online three hours per week (about twenty-five minutes a day on average); however, only 22% report higher online use and more than three hours weekly. Overall, Facebook subjects are motivated to be online more often, but there is no significant increase in Internet time, displaying high-frequency/low-contact usage.

While this study determined that users spend an average of twenty-five minutes per day on Facebook, the Taiwan market research agency Insight Xplorer in a monthly survey of Taiwan Internet users found that users reportedly spend an average of 400 minutes monthly (about thirteen minutes a day) on the Internet social interaction site [4]. Both surveys clearly demonstrate that the community site Facebook occupies an important proportion of online time for Internet users in Taiwan.

ANOVA was used to analyze whether the motivation of Facebook users is correlated to information technology access (due to the increase in weekly Facebook online hours). The result of the F-test is significant ($P = .011 < 0.05$), which clearly demonstrates that the motivation for Facebook use had a substantial impact on the users' weekly time online. Table 2 presents a comparison to further understand in depth the users' different motivations for Facebook use. Results also show that users with high gaming and high social motivation significantly increase their Facebook online hours per week; this group has online use that is significantly higher than the group motivated by high sociability or the group that did not favor either of the subjects.

Table 3 indicates that the subject group which spent the most time on Facebook every week uses Facebook to interact with their friends, and also to utilize the social aspect of the game-playing platform. This group increased their weekly Internet access time by an average of 2.71 hours, or a range of about 21 to 43 minutes daily. However, most subjects showed no significant increase to the overall number of hours of Facebook use.

Table 2. Facebook users' motivation in relation to the increase in online hours per week

Facebook Motivation (I)	Facebook Motivation (J)	Mean Difference (I-J)	Significant (p)
High play / high social	Sociability	.834*	.017*
High play / high social	Do not favor either	.848*	.026*

Table 3. Facebook users' motivation in relation to the average increase in online hours a week because of Facebook. [Note: average of 1 (0 hours), average number of 2 (3 hours or less), average number of 3 (3 - 5 hours), average number of 4 (5 hours or more).]

Facebook Motivation	Average
High social and play	2.71
Social	2.02
Play	1.88
Does not favor either	1.87

4   Conclusions

The results of the study indicate that the emerging information communication technology is indeed having a significant impact on the Taiwan Internet users' Facebook online life. The subjects used Facebook more often, but there was no significant increase in the number of online hours. In 2009, social gaming was the motivation to join and use Facebook; currently, about 70% of users are motivated by interaction-based social networking. An analysis of background variables indicates that female users of low age and education level are likely to be motivated by the game-playing aspect, whereas male users aged thirty-five years and above, with low education (high school), are motivated to play games while also maintaining a high degree of social interaction. Those subjects who are motivated by both high social and high play spent the most time online.

References

1. Gonzales, N.: Facebook Marketing Statistic, Demographics, Taiwan (2011),
   http://www.checkfacebook.com/
2. Hsieh, T.C.: Analysis of Taiwan's online game players. Market Intelligence Center, Taipei (2009)
3. Pollster Technology Marketing Ltd. 67% of Taiwan's users favorite to play games (2009),
   http://www.cyberone.tw/ItemDetailPage/MainContent/
   05MediaContent.aspx?MMMediaType=pollster_Report&offset=192&MM
   ContentNoID=60311
4. InsightXplorer Marketing Ltd. Time users spend on social networking sites, 9 times for e-mail Web site (2010),
   http://www.insightxplorer.com/news/news_11_23_10.html

Connecting Generations: Preserving Memories with Thanatosensitive Technologies

Cyndi Wiley, Yun Wang, Ryan Musselman, and Beverly Krumm

Department of Art and Design, Iowa State University, Iowa, USA
{clwiley,yunwang,rmuss,blkrumm}@iastate.edu

Abstract. Hand-written letters have morphed over the past two decades from the physical realm of ink on paper to digital text displayed on a digital screen, making emails the most common digital format for letters. Old shoeboxes were used as storage spaces for hand-written letters and photographs, bound together with ribbons or rubber bands. The shoebox would then be tucked away somewhere in the house, only to see the light of day years later after a vigorous bout of house cleaning, on a special occasion or after one's death. Since email archives are not the physical artifact of a shoebox of letters and photographs, it is much more difficult to bequeath them to an heir after death. Our proposal is the development of an application named Shoebox that will connect family and friends through the bequeathing of Gmail archives, Picasa photos and YouTube videos.

Keywords: Interface design, User-centered design.

1 Introduction

"Death makes us do strange things; hold on in ways we would not otherwise," says Rev. Jennifer L. Hall, M.Div. our Subject Matter Expert (SME) for this project. "I have an email from my father, wishing me a happy birthday from June 2000. The message is short, just a few lines, hoping we can see each other soon and ending with the words 'love, Dad'. It is the last correspondence I have from him. He died the following April."

"Since that time, I have had many other email accounts with better spam filters and more up-to-date features, but I cannot bear to close the account that holds my father's final Happy Birthday message to me. I considered forwarding it to my most recent inbox, but it would not be the same. His name would not appear the way it does in that old discarded account. There is something important about seeing 'John Hall' in my inbox. It keeps me connected, somehow in touch with the man who was my father. Perhaps one day I'll be able to print the email, tuck it away in a file labeled 'Dad' and say goodbye to that account. Not yet, I still need to be reminded he was once alive and reached out to me."

The culture and conditions surrounding end-of-life traditions in the United States has remained primarily untouched by technology until very recently. There is a growing need for more technology to be designed related to the distribution of one's digital assets upon death, since what happens to these assets remains ambiguous in most cases.

C. Stephanidis (Ed.): Posters, Part I, HCII 2011, CCIS 173, pp. 474–478, 2011.

Thanatology [18] is the study of death among human beings. Designing thanatosensitive technologies is becoming an increasingly important topic for CHI, as our lives are becoming more involved digitally. Research on thanatosensitive technologies within the CHI domain has focused on memorializing the departed [1,8,9,14]. At CHI 2009, alt.chi, Massimi and Charise introduced the concept of thanatosensitivity [14]: to describe an approach that actively integrates the facts of mortality, dying, and death into HCI research and design. A technology heirloom, [8] targeting this definition, was introduced by Kirk & Banks at SIMTech '08, suggesting a way to pass down a physical object across multiple generations. With these works in mind, we have chosen to design a thanatosensitive technology for bequeathing email archives, photos and videos within the Google entities of Gmail, Picasa and YouTube.

1.1 Demographic Analysis

The population in the U.S., as well as around the world, is significantly aging [5]. The first of the Baby Boomer generation (those born between 1946 and 1964) will turn 65 in 2011 at the rate of 7,000 per day [11]. People at the age 65 and over are the fastest-growing group of people using social networking, followed by those ages 50 to 64, according to a Pew Research Center report [12]. Yet, this age group is considered under-represented in the field of human-computer interaction [5].

"Young adults continue to be the heaviest users of social media, but their growth pales in comparison with recent gains made by older users," explains Mary Madden, Senior Research Specialist and author of the report. "Email is still the primary way that older users maintain contact with friends, families and colleagues, but many older users now rely on social network platforms to help manage their daily communications." [12].

The Boomers have been trendsetting since they were born. As this is the largest and most diverse under-represented age group in the U.S. population, we have chosen to create our application to meet their needs while focusing on the user-centered design methodologies.

1.2 Problem Identification

Thinking of death and dying can present numerous emotions. Anticipatory grief is one emotion that can hinder the process of preparing for one's own death [10]. In March 2009, Carroll and Romano, the authors of *Your Digital Afterlife*, co-presented a "Core Conversation" at the South by Southwest (SXSW) Interactive Festival called "Who will Check My Email After I Die?" [4]. This is a critical question and there is not yet a best practice for dealing with deceased users' content [4]. To further complicate the situation, the law has been slow to keep up with the fast pace of technology [4].

Since email is the "master key" as Carroll and Romano phrase it [4], it is of utmost importance to name a digital executor(s) and keep an inventory of your digital assets. The most influential piece of your digital estate is your email account since it controls access to all other online accounts. Even with a digital executor, each email provider or ISP has a different set of terms and conditions to which you agree each time you set up an account. Some accounts, such as Gmail, have instructions for gaining access to a deceased user's account. Others, like Yahoo!, have a non-transferability clause that does not allow the account to be bequeathed to an heir. Herein is the most troubling problem. When a user dies and no one has been named as a digital executor or has access to the departed user's account, the account simply remains active for an undetermined amount of time. If a death certificate is produced, then the account will be deleted, not archived or transferred.

1.3 Design Concept

Email, as well as other digital media, is quickly replacing the physical artifact of the shoebox storage and retrieval system. Storing and retrieval now occur through virtual folders, files, tags and even the virtual trash or recycling bin.

Family and friends connect with one another on a daily basis through the exchange of emails and other online social media and networking sites. In 2009, almost 70% (or 215 million people) of all U.S. American adults sent or read emails [15]. This large number contributed to the 90 trillion emails sent worldwide in 2009 [16]. According to the 2011 Statistical Abstract, more than 1.7 million U.S. Americans aged 65 and over died in the year 2007 [17]. An estimated 375,000 active users [13], out of the 500 million [6], Facebook users will die this year. These data indicate that our target age group of users over the age of 65 uses email more than other social networking sites. Therefore, we envision the first part of our solution to be a 3rd party application for Google's Gmail, Picasa and YouTube accounts, for the account owner to tag each file with instructions on how the digital executor will bequeath data. The account owner will tag files based on following some rules for automation to make the process less tedious. We based the options of the Shoebox application within Gmail on a chart describing instructions of what an account owner should do in preparation with a digital executor for the bequeathing of digital data.

As the second part of the solution, we also propose an interface for the heir(s) to view the Gmail archives, Picasa photos and YouTube videos within a timeline-based environment. The timeline-based interface is designed for use on a touch screen mobile device (such as the Google Nexus, iPad, Galaxy Tab, or other smart device) that family and friends can view together to connect and share stories. Google TV would also be a viewing option for those to spend time together sharing. The application will also run on a desktop computer or laptop with an Internet connection. If the account owner chooses to provide Shoebox with a handwriting sample, the archived emails can be displayed in the owner's handwriting.

Since data is stored in Google's cloud, Shoebox will simply act as an archiving and viewing tool for the account owner until the time of death. Once the digital executor provides a death certificate, the Shoebox archive will be bequeathed to heirs.

Longevity and diversification are important to the designing of any thanatosensitive technology and Google is proving to be both financially and globally stable in the realm of cloud computing [7].

2   Existing Work

The Digital Beyond Web site, co-created by Carroll and Romano, lists 26 online services to manage your digital assets [3]. Some of the services are offered free for a basic account, but most charge a fee for premium services such as notifying a beneficiary after your death. Our hope is by integrating the Shoebox application within the existing Gmail, Picasa and YouTube interfaces, that your digital emails, photos and videos will be secure and accessible to your beneficiaries. In terms of socioeconomics, this application should be included free of charge to users with Gmail accounts.

3 Conclusion and Future Work

Ethnographic research needs to be compiled to determine specific user needs for this application and responses to such an application. Also, further research into the legalities of estate planning and the digital realm need to be analyzed. Possible limitations of the application are working within established user agreements when a user signs up for Gmail or adds the Shoebox to his or her account. Current user agreements may not be suitable and may need revision in order for the application to be added.

Privacy and security should be held at the utmost importance for this application and it is our intent that Gmail's existing standards would be applicable to the Shoebox.

Our current and future work includes (1) obtaining IRB approval to conduct user-centered evaluations of users age 65 and over, (2) developing other consistent and complementary visualization and interaction techniques for the Shoebox and (3) extending the Shoebox to integrate more complex digital file types and applications such as blogs (i.e. Blogger).

References

1. Banks, R.: Richard Banks: An introduction to technology heirlooms (2010),
   http://www.psfk.com/2010/04/
   richard-banks-an-introduction-to-technology-heirlooms.html
   (retrieved January 8, 2011)
2. Carroll, E.: Afterlife predictions for 2010. The Digital Beyond (2010),
   http://www.thedigitalbeyond.com/2010/01/
   digital-afterlife-predictions-for-2010/ (retrieved January 8, 2011)
3. Carrol, E.: The Digital Beyond (2011), http://www.thedigitalbeyond.com/,
   (retrieved January 8, 2011)
4. Carroll, E.R.J.: Your digital afterlife: When Facebook, Flickr and Twitter are your estate, what's your legacy? Berkeley, New Riders (2011)
5. Czaja, S., Lee, C.C.: Designing computer systems for older adults. In: Jacko, J., Sears, A. (eds.) The human-computer interaction handbook: Fundamentals, evolving technologies, and emerging applications, Lawrence Erlbaum Associates, New York (2001)
6. Facebook Statistics (2011),
   http://www.facebook.com/press/info.php?statistics
   (retrieved January 8, 2011)

7. Hitwise Top 20 Sites & Engines (2011),
   `http://www.hitwise.com/us/datacenter/main/`
   `dashboard-10133.html` (retrieved January 8, 2011)
8. Kirk, D., Banks, R.: On the design of technology heirlooms. In: SIMTech 2008, ACM, New York (2008)
9. Kirk, D., Izadi, S., et al.: Opening up the family archive. In: CSCW 2010, ACM, Savannah (2010), (retrieved January 8, 2011)
10. Kubler-Ross, E.: On death and dying: What the dying have to teach doctors, nurses, clergy and their own families. Macmillan Publishing, Co. Inc., New York (1969)
11. Love, J.: Approaching 65: A Survey of Boomers Turning 65 Years Old. Transitions. AARP (2010)
12. Madden, M.: Older adutls and social media. Pew Internet (2010),
    `http://pewinternet.org/Reports/2010/`
    `Older-Adults-and-Social-Media.aspx` (retrieved January 8, 2011)
13. Madrigal, A.: 375,000 Facebook users may die this year. What do we do with their stuff? The Atlantic (2011),
    `http://www.theatlantic.com/technology/archive/2011/01/`
    `375-000-facebook-users-may-die-this-year-what-do-we-do-with-`
    `their-stuff/68910/` (retrieved January 8, 2011)
14. Massimi, M., Charise, A.: Dying, death and mortality: Towards thanatosensitivity in HCI. In: CHI 2009 ~ alt.chi ~ Life, Love, Death, ACM, Boston (2009)
15. PewInternet.org, Online activities 2000-2009. Pew Internet (2011),
    `http://pewinternet.org/Static-Pages/Trend-Data/`
    `Online-Activities-20002009.aspx` (retrieved January 8, 2011)
16. Pingdom, Internet 2009, in numbers (2010),
    `http://royal.pingdom.com/2010/01/22/`
    `internet-2009-in-numbers/` (retrieved January 8, 2011)
17. U.S. Census Bureau (2011). Deaths by Age and Selected Causes: 2007. U.S. National Center for Health Statistics, National Vital Statistics Reports, Deaths: Final Data for 2007, vol. 58(19), U.S. Census Bureau (May 2010)
18. Walker, A.C.: Life span issues and end-of-life decision making. In: Balk, D. (ed.) Handbook of Thanatology: The essential body of knowledge for the study of death, dying and bereavement, Association for Death Education and Counseling, The Thanatology Association, Florence (2007)

Part VII
Work and Collaboration

Introducing CAPER, a Collaborative Platform for Open and Closed Information Acquisition, Processing and Linking

Carlo Aliprandi[1] and Andrea Marchetti[2]

[1] Synthema Srl
Via Malasoma 24
56121 Ospedaletto (Pisa) - Italy
[2] Institute of Informatics and Telematics (IIT) CNR
Via G. Moruzzi, 1
56123 Pisa - Italy
`carlo.aliprandi@synthema.it, andrea.marchetti@iit.cnr.it`

Abstract. We introduce the CAPER project (Collaborative information, Acquisition, Processing, Exploitation and Reporting), partially funded by the European Commission. The goal of CAPER is to create a common platform for the prevention of organized crime through sharing, exploitation and linking of Open and Closed information Sources. CAPER will support collaborative multilingual analysis of unstructured and audiovisual contents, based on Text Mining and Visual Analytics technologies. CAPER will allow Law Enforcement Agencies (LEAs) to share informational, investigative and experiential knowledge.

Keywords: Text Mining, Natural Language Processing, Semantics, Semantic Web Interlinking, Social Web.

1 Introduction

The revolution in information technology is making Open Sources more accessible, ubiquitous, and valuable. The specific term "open" refers to publicly available sources, as opposed to classified sources, usually referred to as Closed Sources.

The international Law Enforcement Communities have seen Open Sources grow increasingly in recent years. But up to 90% of electronic data is textual and most valuable information is often hidden and encoded in documents which are neither structured, nor classified. The process of accessing all these raw data, heterogeneous in terms of source and language, and transforming them into information is therefore strongly linked to automatic textual analysis and visualization with powerful Human Computer Interfaces.

Anyway, the availability of a huge amount of data in Internet and in all the Open Sources information channels has lead to the modern paradox of information overload. In fact, everyone experiences a mounting frustration in the attempt of finding the information of interest, wading through thousands of pieces of data.

C. Stephanidis (Ed.): Posters, Part I, HCII 2011, CCIS 173, pp. 481–485, 2011.

This paper introduces a collaborative content enabling system that provides deep semantic search and information access to large quantities of unstructured and multimedia data, offering information analysts a solution to information overload. CAPER provides a common platform for the prevention of organized crime through sharing, exploitation and linking of Open and Closed information Sources.

In Section 2 we present some state of the art of currently available systems; in Section 3 some distinguishing features of the CAPER System are presented. In Section 4 we describe conclusions and expected advantages.

2 State of the Art of Semantic Information Systems

Current-generation information retrieval (IR) systems excel with respect to scale and robustness. However, if it comes to deep analysis and precision, they lack power. Users are limited by keywords search, which is not sufficient if answers to complex problems are sought. This becomes more acute when knowledge and information are needed from different linguistic and cultural backgrounds, so that both problems and answers are necessarily more complex. Developments in the IR have mostly been restricted to improvements in link and click analysis or smart query expansion or profiling, rather than focused on a deeper analysis of text and building of smarter indexes. Traditionally, text and data mining systems can be seen as specialized systems that convert more complex information into a structured database, allowing people to find knowledge rather than information. For some domains, text mining applications are well-advanced, for example in the domains of medicine, military and intelligence, and aeronautics [1].

In addition to domain-specific miners, general technology has been developed to detect Named Entities [2], co-reference relations, geographical data [3], and time points [4].

The field of knowledge acquisition is growing rapidly with many enabling technologies being developed that eventually will approach Natural Language Understanding (NLU). Anyway, despite much progress in Natural Language Processing (NLP), the field is still a long way from language understanding.

The reason is that full semantic interpretation requires the identification of every individual conceptual component and the semantic roles it plays. In addition, understanding requires processing and knowledge that is not explicitly conveyed by linguistic elements. First, contextual understanding is needed to deal with the omissions. Ambiguities are a common aspect of human communication. Speakers are cooperative in filling gaps and correcting errors, but automatic systems are not. Second, lexical knowledge does not provide background or world knowledge, which is often required for non-trivial inferences. Any automatic system trying to understand a simple sentence will require - among others – accurate capabilities for Named Entity Recognition (NER), Deep Parsing, Word Sense Disambiguation (WSD) and Semantic Role Labeling (SRL) [6].

Current baseline information systems are either large-scale, robust but shallow (standard IR systems), or they are small-scale, deep but ad hoc (Semantic-Web ontology-based systems). Furthermore, these systems are maintained by experts in IR, ontologies or language-technology and not by the people in the field.

Finally, hardly any of the systems is multilingual, yet alone cross-lingual and definitely not cross-cultural.

The next table gives a comparison across different state-of-the-art information systems, where we compare ad-hoc Semantic web solutions, WordNet based information systems and tradition information retrieval with CAPER.

Table 1. Comparison of semantic information systems

Key features	Semantic web	Wordnet based	IR	CAPER
Large scale and multiple domains	NO	YES	YES	YES
Deep semantics	YES	NO	NO	YES
Automatic acquisition and Indexing	NO	YES/NO	YES	YES
Multi-lingual	NO	YES	YES	YES
Cross-lingual	NO	YES	NO	YES

3 The CAPER System

The CAPER project will create a common platform for the prevention of organized crime through sharing, exploitation and analysis of Open and Closed information sources. CAPER will support collaborative multilingual analysis of unstructured and audiovisual contents (video, audio, speech and images), based on Text Mining and Visual Analytics technologies. The integration of database technologies (ETL), application workflow and Semantic Modeling of processes will allow participating users, i.e. LEAs, to share informational, investigative and experiential knowledge. The CAPER platform will be built in close collaboration with the LEA users in order to understand their functional needs, how they can cooperate and share information, and within what legal and procedural framework they may acquire, process and exploit information from multiple sources.

The project is not focused on developing new technology, but on the fusion and real validation of existing state of the art to solve current bottlenecks faced by LEAs. So the design methodology will be based on an iterative development lifecycle, with several integration steps that will be carried out.

The 6 technology pillars of the CAPER platform, that currently is in a very initial stage of development, are:

- **Open and Closed Data Sources**: TV, Radio, and Information in closed legacy systems are the data sources to be mined and evaluated by CAPER, in addition to Open Internet data sources and Semantic Web data collections (Linked Data, for example, like Geonames, DBpedia or Yago).
- **Data Acquisition**: Depending on the information source type, different acquisition patterns will be applied to ensure acquired information is the richest possible and has a suitable format for analysis.

- **Information Analysis**: Each analysis module is geared towards a specific content type, i.e. Text, Image, Video, Audio and Speech or Biometric data. These modules interact with a 'Semantic mash-up' component, to interlink Semantic Web data.
- **Information and Reference Repositories**: source data and mined information will be stored in these repositories, separated by content type. Repositories will also store the reference images, text, keywords, biometric data etc. of interest to the LEAs.
- **Interoperability and Management Application**: This is the end users' workbench, the main Human Computer Interface. It will be built on a wiki platform. It will allow LEAs to collaborative create and configure their monitoring requests and analysis petitions. Through this HCI, Law Enforcement Officers will be able to create and configure their monitoring requests and analysis petitions. It will allow a structured collaboration between LEAs, who will also be able to configure their own internal closed information sources and control how and to whom the data is shared.
- **Visual Analytics (VA) and Data Mining (DM)**: VA and DM will provide the intelligence necessary to support the output of the system. They will allow LEAs to effectively mine processed data both from Closed and Open Sources, and to further relate it to Semantic Web sources when required.

The CAPER system will be designed from a linguistically neutral point of view. This design methodology will allow linguistic analysis and speech recognition components for any language to be added in the future. LEA users will provide reference images, keywords, biometric data, and define concepts to be used in information acquisition.

The design methodology will leverage standardization of data and interchange of tools: once a data format is accepted as a standard, tools can be adapted and shared with little effort. CAPER will also standardize the processing of language sensitive information by adopting KAF [7] (Knowledge Annotation Format), a multi-layered XML format for linguistic and semantic annotation of unstructured documents that has been proven to be suitable for the purpose of Information Processing.

CAPER aims at extending data representation standards to also cope with multimedia and structured data, particularly focusing on the analysis and exploitation of Social Web Content and Semantic Web Data. To collect and integrate these different kinds of online information sources, after a thorough analysis of social and semantic data from the point of view of the CAPER users, we will develop specific components for Named Entity and URI identification in the target Open Sources, exploiting results coming from [9]. Finally, we will develop specific components for interlinking Social Web Content, exploiting Tagpedia [9], a semantic resource for Tag Sense Disambiguation, by mining the structure of Wikipedia articles.

4   Conclusions

This paper has presented CAPER, a common platform for the prevention of organized crime through sharing, exploitation and linking of Open and Closed information Sources. After a brief survey of state of the art of similar systems, we have provided an overview of the system and its core features.

The CAPER design potential advantage is that, shifting the focus from a technology development model to a technology integration and standardization model, it will address the LEAs needs, structuring the development process around a cyclic process. The design methodology will take into account LEAs functional specifications but also the legal and procedural framework related to exploitation of information from multiple sources and from foreign countries and cultures.

Acknowledgments. This work is partially funded by the European Commission (CAPER project, 261712 FP7-SECURITY SEC-2010.1.2-1).

References

1. Grishman, R., Sundheim, B.: Message Understanding Conference - 6: A Brief History. In: Proceedings of the 16th International Conference on Computational Linguistics (COLING), Kopenhagen, vol. I, pp. 466–471 (1996)
2. Hearst, M.: Untangling Text Data Mining. In: ACL 1999, June 20-26, University of Maryland (1999)
3. Miller, H.J., Han, J.: Geographic Data Mining and Knowledge Discovery. CRC Press, Boca Raton (2001)
4. Wei, L., Keogh, E.: Semi-Supervised Time Series Classification. In: SIGKDD 2006 (2006)
5. Carreras, X., Màrquez, L.: Introduction to the CoNLL-2005 Shared Task: Semantic Role Labeling. In: CoNLL 2005, Ann Arbor, MI USA (2005)
6. Vossen, P., Agirre, E., Bond, F., Bosma, W., Fellbaum, C., Hicks, A., Hsieh, S., Isahara, H., Huang, C., Kanzaki, K., Marchetti, A., Rigau, G., Ronzano, F., Segers, R., Tesconi, M.: KYOTO: a Wiki for Establishing Semantic Interoperability for Knowledge Sharing across Languages and Cultures. In: Blanchard, E., Allard, D. (eds.) Handbook of Research on Culturally-Aware Information Technology: Perspectives and Models, Publ. IGI Global USA, pp. 265–294.
7. Bosma, W., Vossen, P., Soroa, A., Rigau, G., Tesconi, M., Marchetti, A., Aliprandi, C., Monachini, M.K.: a generic semantic annotation format. In: 5th International Conference on Generative Approaches to the Lexicon, Pisa (2009)
8. Aliprandi, C., Ronzano, F., Marchetti, A., Tesconi, M., Minutoli, S.: Extracting events from Wikipedia as RDF triples linked to widespread Semantic Web Datasets. In: Proceedings of HCI International 2011, 14th International Conference on Human-Computer Interaction, Florida, USA, July 9-14 (2011)
9. Ronzano, F., Marchetti, A., Tesconi, M., Minutoli, S.: Tagpedia: a Semantic Reference to Describe and Search for Web Resources. In: Social Web and Knowledge Management Workshop at the 17th World Wide Web Conference WWW 2008, Beijing (2008)

Secure Transmission of Medical Images by SSH Tunneling

Felipe Rodrigues Martinêz Basile and Flávio Cezar Amate

Research and Technology Center, Mogi das Cruzes University,
Mogi das Cruzes, Brazil
felipermbasile@hotmail.com

Abstract. Given the technological advances related to Telemedicine and eHealth together with the increase of cyber attacks in the internet. We can consider that studies are necessary to improve a secure transmission of medical images. A desktop application was developed for the transmission of medical images considering a secure environment using SSH protocol and cryptographic keys. In accordance to statistical analysis using test t there isn't significant difference $(p>0.05)$ when we compare the total time of transmission using SSH Tunneling with the total time of transmission using HTTP request, in the same way there isn't significant difference $(p>0.05)$ when we compare the average transmission rates using SSH Tunneling with the average transmission rates using HTTP request. Finally, we can affirm that a secure transmission of medical images using SSH tunneling is highly recommended because it can provide a secure way with a level of encryption on point to point transmission between client and server, observing national and international rules for telemedicine.

Keywords: SSH, HTTP, tunneling, telemedicine, secure, medical images.

1 Introduction

New technologies and the access to the Internet are making casual or malicious invasions of people without authorized access to information [1].

Between 1999 and 2009 there was an expansion of about 380% which can be estimated in approximately 1.7 billion of people connected on the World Wide Web [2].

The medicine has been using advances of information technology area to solve many problems. The Telemedicine as service is being used by physicians, hospitals and education institutions. This service is increasing mainly with the great number of computer networks with large bandwidth that allow experts to monitor long distance exams. Many studies in the literature show the use of these computer networks to transmit medical images [3],[4],[5],[6],[7].

The World Medical Association recognizes that there are many problems related to responsibilities and ethical standards in telemedicine services. This association defines as important questions: confidentially and security in the transmission of information in electronic format [8].

C. Stephanidis (Ed.): Posters, Part I, HCII 2011, CCIS 173, pp. 486–490, 2011.
© Springer-Verlag Berlin Heidelberg 2011

In face of this, there is the need of studies that may help the development of viable proposals to establish the transmission of medical images considering a secure environment and performances in telemedicine.

2 Materials and Methods

2.1 Web Application and Desktop Application

Desktop application and web application were developed for transmissions. The web application was created to allow the transmission of medical images using HTTP requests and the desktop application was used for the transmission of medical images using SSH tunneling. These applications allowed the comparison between transmissions of medical images using HTTP request and transmissions using SSH tunneling considering a secure environment.

The Shell Script language was used to create scripts to build the desktop application. In the code bellow there is a command line for the transmission of medical images using SSH protocol in version 2.

```
scp -2 <user name>@<ip number>:<location> <destination>

Example:

scp -2 felipe@200.246.78.4:/images/raw/*.raw /home/raw
```

In the above code we can observe the use of scp command to make a secure copy using the SSH protocol in version 2. Other parameters are necessary as: user name, ip number, location of images in the server and destination of images.

The SSH (Secure Shell) was used with RSA algorithm to encrypt medical images together with public and private keys. In Fig. 1 it is possible to observe the use of public and private keys and RSA algorithm in the process of information cryptography. In the first moment to encrypt a message sent and after to decrypt a message received.

Fig. 1. Transmission of medical Images using SSH Tunneling

2.2 Client and Server

The Server machine has the following characteristics: CPU AMD Athlon II X4 2.6 GHz; Memory 2GB; Hard Disc 40 GB; Operating System: Linux Ubuntu karmic Koala 9.1; Management System Database: MySQL 5.1; Web Server: Apache Tomcat 6.0.20.

The Client machine has the following characteristics: CPU AMD Athlon 64 bits 2.7 GHz, Memory 1GB; Hard Disc: 40 GB; Operating System: Linux Ubuntu karmic Koala 9.1; OpenJDK-6 jre.

2.3 Experiments

Subsequently we made experiments that simulate a data transmission between client and server tested with medical images. The original medical images were in pgm format. All 20 images (portable graymap) were converted and divided in two groups, 10 in raw format with total size of 17.408 KB and 10 in bmp format with total size of 17.408 KB, for a total of 34.816 KB of data transmitted. This way, we developed this test related to time and rate transmissions between HTTP requests and SSH tunneling. They were performed in three random stages.

3   Results

From the statistical analysis using t test the results showed that there is no significant difference (p>0.05) when comparing the total time with SSH Tunneling and HTTP request considering medical images in bmp and raw format (See Fig. 2).

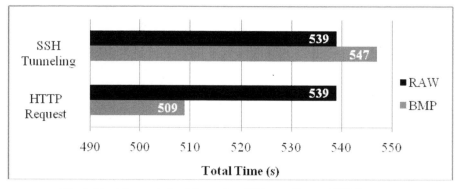

Fig. 2. Total Transmission Time using SSH tunneling and HTTP request

Likewise, there isn´t significant difference (p>0.05) when comparing the average transmission rates with SSH Tunneling and HTTP request considering medical images in bmp and raw format (See Fig. 3).

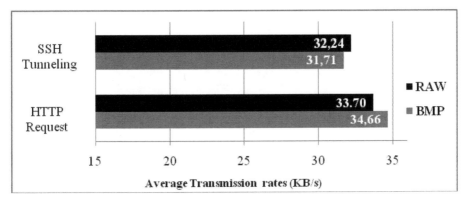

Fig. 3. Average transmission rates using SSH tunneling and HTTP request

4 Discussion

In summary, with tests it was possible to understand many aspects related to network and security. Many Losses of Connection were observed in HTTP requests, different from SSH tunneling. Several factors contribute to insecurity during a data transmission on Internet, among which we were able to identify some examples such as packet capture during the jump in traffic for a network and availability of files in web caches, which can provide storage of transmitted data. Despite the importance of VPN security [1], this feature is limited to the establishment of secure transmission between gateways, enabling the interception of data in the nodes that belong to the local network. Otherwise that doesn´t occur on point to point transmission tunneling, when it is possible to establish data encryption from client to server.

5 Conclusion

In brief this paper presents a new vision about the viability of secure transmission of medical images considering the average transmission rate and the total time of transmission by SSH tunneling compared to the transmission by HTTP request. The use of SSH Tunneling is highly recommendable because there isn't significant difference in the comparison of HTTP request and SSH Tunneling performances. Other important point is that the SSH can provide a secure way with a level of encryption on point to point between client and server avoiding problems in web caches and traffic between gateways.

References

1. Cao, F., Huang, H.K., Zhou, X.Q.: Medical Image security in a HIPAA mandated PACS environment. Computerized Medical Imaging and Graphics 27, 185–196 (2003)
2. Stein, S.: A cyberspace treaty - a United Nations convention or protocol on cyber security and cybercrime. In: Twelfth United Nations on Crime Prevention and Criminal Justice Salvador. United Nations, Brazil (2010)

3. Shimizu, S., Nakashima, N., Okamura, K., Tanaka, M.: One Hundred Case Studies of Asia-Pacific Telemedicine Using a Digital Video Transport System over a Research and Education Network. Telemedicine Journal and E-Health 15(1), 112–117 (2009)
4. Hahm, J.S., Lee, H.L., Kim, S.I.: A remote educational system in medicine using digital video. Hepato Gastroenterology 54(74), 373–376 (2007)
5. Liu, B.J., Zhou, Z., Gutierrez, M.A., et al.: International Internet2 connectivity and performance in medical imaging applications: Bridging the America to Asia. Journal of High Speed Networks 16(1), 5–20 (2007)
6. Fan, Y., Hwang, K., Gill, M., et al.: Some connectivity and security issues of NGI in medical imaging applications. Journal of High Speed Networks 9(1), 3–13 (2000)
7. Kiuchi, T., Takahashi, T.: High speed digital circuits for medical communication the MINCS-UH project. Methods of Information in Medicine 39, 353–355 (2000)
8. World Medical Association. Declaration of Tel Aviv: About responsibilities and ethical Standards the use of Telemedicine. In: 51st Annual General Assembly. Tel Aviv, Israel (1999)

Service Components for Unified Communication and Collaboration of an SOA-Based Converged Service Platform

Ki-Sook Chung and Young-Mee Shin

Service Convergence Research team,
Electronics and Telecommunications Research Institute
161 Gajeong-dong, Yuseong-gu, Daejeon, 305-350, Korea
{kschung,ymshin}@etri.re.kr

Abstract. Since there are lots of communication means and devices such as e-mail, short messaging, messengers, wired or wireless telephone and even social network services, we need some unified communication environment for the smarter work place. We introduce a converged service platform with open service components for the unified communication and collaboration in this paper. Using the converged service platform, the third party service providers can create applications easily by composing the open service components and execute their applications since the CSP covers the entire lifecycle of services. The CSP provides UCC (Unified Communication and Collaboration) components in the form of web services. The UCC components of the CSP cover basic communication functionalities as well as social collaboration functionalities and can be mashed up into various applications for the smart collaboration in a company.

Keywords: SOA, Service Component, Unified Communication.

1 Introduction

The SOA (Service Oriented Architecture) is one of the key mechanisms which enable service developers to create new applications rapidly using existent service component with high reusability. An SOA implementation can consist of a combination of technologies, products, APIs, supporting infrastructure extensions, and various other parts [7].

We introduce an SOA-based converged service platform that specifically supports the creation, execution, and management of service components and the core UCC (Unified communication and collaboration) components which are provided by the platform. These components have been designed to provide various communication functionalities including VoIP, short messaging, email, and chatting, and social functionalities such as micro-blogging, group discussion, and contents sharing among coworkers in a company.

More specifically, the UCC components can be categorized into user session management, third party call control, short messaging, e-mail, directory, presence,

C. Stephanidis (Ed.): Posters, Part I, HCII 2011, CCIS 173, pp. 491–495, 2011.
© Springer-Verlag Berlin Heidelberg 2011

direct messaging, bulletin board, and real-time group discussion services. These are implemented in the form of SOAP-based web services or restful web services and registered in the registry of the CSP and provide 54 operations related to UCC functionalities. As an implementation of SOA technology, these service components are opened to 3rd party service providers so that application developers can compose those components and make their applications rapidly.

2   Converged Service Platform

The core functional parts of the CSP are shown in the figure 1 and categorized into the following 3 main functional modules.

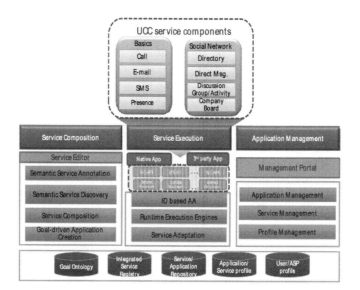

Fig. 1. Converged Service Platform Architecture

- Service Composition module. This module provides semantic service creation environment to application developers. We provide a graphic service editor tool which interworks with service registry. To enable goal-driven application, this module includes semantic service annotation and discovery functions using the goal ontology and service registry.
- Service Execution module. This module is responsible for running application logics and executing service components within the logic when requested. It also has identity-based authentication and authorization function to check the rights of requestors and the policies of each service component. This module has WAS (web application server) and ESB (enterprise service bus) as service execution facilities and interworks with other servers outside the CSP.

- Application management module. This module provides means for managing applications, service components, and users. This module consists of data repositories for user profile, service profile, application profile, and other management facilities for the maintenance of the platform. We provide management portal site where the third party service providers and platform operators can manage their applications and related data remotely. The portal allows the access to the resources according to the user level and authorizes users who try to manipulate their resources such as their applications and relevant data.[12]

3   UCC Service Components and Application Example

3.1   UCC Service Components

The main service components of the CSP are those for unified communication and collaboration. We have targeted the convergence of IT and telecommunication services according to the recent trends of the smart work.   Therefore, we implemented two categories of APIs: components for the basic communications and components for collaboration.

- Components for the basic communication. These components include email, short messaging, third party call including VoIP, as well as presence service. These are implemented as SOAP-based web service similar to ParlayX web services [1]. With these APIs, application developers who have no knowledge about network protocols can make applications using network capabilities.

Table 1. Service Components for Basic Communication

Communication Service Component	Functionalities	Type
Third Party Call Control	- make/end a Call - get Call Status	SOAP
Email	- send Mail	SOAP
SMS	- send Short Message - send Group Short Message	SOAP
Presence	- get/set User Presence - get Buddy List	SOAP

- Components for the collaboration. With the widespread population of smartphones, lots of people use SNS (Social Network Service) such as twitter [2] and facebook [3] as a means of communications. Due to these SNS, people can hear real-time news or small talks of others more rapidly and easily than before and new business models such as social commerce and social game are getting more attention.

Table 2. Service Components for Collaboration

Social Service Component	Functionalities	Type
Directory	- search/get a part profile - search/get a user profile - get Contact List - get/add/modify/delete Contact Information	Restful
Group Discussion	- get Group List/Group Information - get Activity List/Activity Information - get Activity Post List - add/delete/search Activity Post - get Activity Post Reply List - add/delete Activity Post Reply - get New Post Count of an Activity - get the Post Number of an Activity	Restful
Bulletin Board	- get Board List - get the Count of new Post on a Board - get/add/delete One's Favorite Post List - get/search Post List of a Board - get/add/delete Post of a Board - add new Post Reply to a Board - get Reply List of a Post - get the Count of Posts of a Board	Restful
Direct Message (DM)	- send/delete Direct Message - get DM List/DM information/new DM count	Restful

Using these functionalities, the company's employees can collaborate with each other and improve efficiency of their work inside and/or outside their company. The examples of the enterprise SNS are yammer [6], socialText [5], cubeTree [4] and etc.

3.2 Appication Eample – cocoTime Mobile App

We developed several applications by composing the UCC service components. Among them, we introduce a mobile application, "cocoTime", which is implemented for android smart phones.

The cocoTime application uses lots of UCC components and it has the following functions.

- Group discussion: People in a group, for example, project group, can write and read one's opinions in real-time so that they can collaborate.
- Company directory: Members of a company can search other member or teams and get information about them.

Acknowledgments. This research is supported by the IT R&D program of MKE/KEIT of South Korea. [KI002076, Development of Customer Oriented Convergent Service Common Platform Technology based on Network].

References

1. 3GPP TS 29.199 Open Service Access; ParlayX Web Services,
   http://www.3gpp.org
2. Twitter, http://www.twitter.com
3. Facebook, http://www.facebook.com
4. Cubetree, http://www.cubetree.com
5. SocialText, http://www.socialtext.com
6. Yammer, http://www.yammer.com
7. Erl, T.: SOA Principles of Service Design. Prentice Hall, Englewood Cliffs
8. Erl, T.: SOA Design Patterns. Prentice Hall, Englewood Cliffs
9. NEXOF, http://www.nexof-ra.eu/
10. SOA4ALL, http://www.soa4all.eu/
11. Lenk, A., et al.: What's Inside the Cloud? An Architectural Map of the Cloud Landscape. In: ICSE 2009 (2009)
12. Chung, K.-s., Kim, S.: A study on the application lifecycle management over SOA based application hosting platform. In: ICACT 2010 (2010)

Fine-Grained Adaptive User Interface for Personalization of a Word Processor: Principles and a Preliminary Study

Martin Dostál and Zdenek Eichler

Dept. Computer Science
Palacký University Olomouc, 17. Listopadu 12
77146 OLOMOUC, Czech Republic
{dostal,eichlerz}@inf.upol.cz

Abstract. We introduce novel fine-grained adaptive user interface for the OpenOffice.org Writer word processor. It provides a panel container with personalized user interface to an individual user. The personalization is provided on frequently or recently used user commands, user's preferred interaction styles and frequently used parameters to user commands. The next part of the paper describes a proof-of-concept usability study. We measured task completion times and error rates on the proposed adaptive interface, menus and toolbars on a word processing task.

Keywords: personalization, adaptive user interfaces, usability study.

1 Introduction

Today's users are faced with complexity of feature-rich applications, such as office suites, large information systems or integrated development environments. Such a complexity can result in worsening usability and frustration or dissatisfaction with the user interface. Reportedly [8], users usually use only a small fraction of the provided functionality. Moreover, it has been demonstrated [1] on usage of word processing applications that users are substantially different in used functionality and preferred interaction styles. These issues with complex user interfaces are addressed by user interface personalization. Systems for personalization of user interfaces tailor the interface to individual user's needs and habits. User interface personalization may be either user-driven (called *adaptable*) or system-driven (called *adaptive*) or *mixed initiative* (a combination of the previous two). Adaptive interfaces dynamically and automatically adjust the interface in order to conform user's needs and usage habits. Such systems implement a mechanism to understand the user and consequently provide a personalized user interface. Again, adaptable interfaces provide customization mechanisms which rely on the user to apply those mechanisms to do the adaptation. For instance, users can customize a menu or a toolbar structure or assign custom keystrokes. The advantage of user interface personalization is that the user is provided with a user interface that is customized to individual requirements. On the other side, personalization has also disadvantages; the user-driven adaptation is usually too complex for the "average user" [7,9]. Various studies [4,5,6,10] reported users' dissatisfaction with adaptive user interfaces when

C. Stephanidis (Ed.): Posters, Part I, HCII 2011, CCIS 173, pp. 496–500, 2011.
© Springer-Verlag Berlin Heidelberg 2011

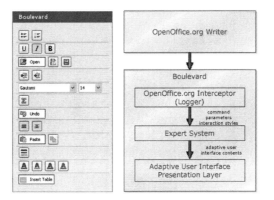

Fig. 1. Boulevard: screenshot (left), architecture (right)

usability design principles are violated. Also several comparative studies between adaptive, adaptable and static user interfaces [2,3,7] showed that users preferred a static or an adaptable user interface over the adaptive.

2 Boulevard: A Fine-Grained Adaptive User Interface

We introduce a fine-grained adaptive user interface for the OpenOffice.org Writer word processor. The system is called "Boulevard". We strive for fully adaptive, non-moving (or in any other way destructive for the user interface), easy-to-learn-and-use personalization. In contrast to many present adaptive systems, our system does not modify the static part of the user interface, but rather provides a panel container (see Fig. 1) that provides the personalized interface. The panel contents are adjusted to user's preferred commands (including user command parameters, e.g., used font sizes, colors or paragraph styles) and interaction styles. The personalization is driven by an embedded expert system which continuously evaluates the user activity in the word processor and constitutes the personalized user interface.

Boulevard organizes user commands in the panel container according to measured importance for the user. The importance of a user command is expressed by the so-called *rank*. It is a number between 0 and 1 and considers two factors of user command usage: *a recency* and *a frequency*. The frequency factor reflects a frequency of the user command usage. The recency factor reflects whether the command has been used recently in order to accelerate position of scarcely used commands to a more prominent position in the panel container. Conversely, whether such an accelerated user command is no longer one of recently used commands, it loses the accelerator and moves back to a less prominent position. The most prominent position is considered on the top, the least prominent at the bottom of the panel container. The rank of the user command x is computed according to the following formula:

$$rank(x) = w\frac{|x|}{|T|} + (1-w)\frac{\sum_{p_i \in P_x}(q - p_i + 1)}{\sum_{i=1}^{q} i} \tag{1}$$

In this formula, $|x|$ expresses the count of the user command x activations. T expresses the count of all commands activations. We maintain a queue of recently used commands, where each user command may appear in the queue of size q at multiple positions (the most recently used command's position is stored at position 1). We put a set P_x which contains the positions of occurrence of the user command x in the queue. $w \in < 0, 1 >$ represents the weight of long-time usage patterns (frequency), whereas $1 - w$ represent the weight of short-time usage patterns (recency).

Boulevard performs also a semantical grouping of user commands. Semantically similar user commands are organized at one particular row instead of appearance of several similar commands at separate rows. Fig. 1 (left) depicts a real example of Boulevard content. Most rows contains more than one user command due to mentioned semantical organization, e.g., first row contains bullets and numbering or second row which contains Bold, Italic and Underline. Boulevard also considers usage of interaction styles. The commands in the panel container are presented according to the most frequently used interaction styles. That is, whether a user invokes a particular command most frequently using a toolbar, the command is presented as a toolbar button. If a user invokes the command using a menu, the command is presented as a command button that mimics a menu item. If a user command is issued most frequently using a keystroke, then it is excluded from the panel container since the user is able to use the command without a visual representation.

3   Preliminary Usability Study

We conducted a preliminary study to verify the basic concepts behind the Boulevard. The study analyzed task times and error rates on selecting user commands using three different interaction styles: toolbar, menu and Boulevard. The study was participated by twelve users (nine males and three females) aged from 21 to 53 (M=28.75 years). Users had to select a particular user command in OpenOffice.org Writer according to instructions on a computer screen. The instructions depicted a command that should be selected and which interaction style should be used. Individual interaction styles were tested sequentially on somewhat different sets of user commands. User were shortly acquainted about the Boulevard immediately before the test. No training was possible.

3.1   Quantitative Measures

The task has been composed of three parts. In the first part, a user selected a sequence of sixty commands using a toolbar — fifteen particular commands, each four-times repeated in a random order (namely: Bold, Italic, Underline, FontHeight, CharFontName, RightPara, CenterPara, DefaultBullet, DefaultNumbering, IncrementIndent, FontColor, Undo, Copy, Paste, InsertTable). In the second part a user selected a sequence of sixty commands using a menu — twenty particular commands, each three times repeated in a random order(namely: SelectAll, Italic, Underline, FontHeight, CharFontName, View-Bounds, LeftPara, RightPara, SplitCell, DeleteRows, FontColor, Undo, Copy, Paste, InsertTable, DeleteColumns, TableBoundaries, Zoom, WordCountDialog, Ruler). Finally, the third part was devoted to selecting a sequence of seventy-eight user commands using Boulevard which were selected as union of commands from the toolbar part and the menu part, each was repeated three times in a random order. The data has been saved as a CSV file and analyzed statistically. Overall, users were able to select a desired user command at first attempt in 62.7 % of cases for toolbar, 53.3 % cases for menu and 66.4 % of cases for Boulevard. On the other side, users failed (i.e., were not able to select a demanded command during 30-seconds long period) in 67 cases for the menu part, 20 cases for the toolbar part and 11 cases for the Boulevard part of the experiment. Average task completion times were 5.29 sec. for toolbar (Mdn=4.29, Sd=3.93), 8.94 sec. for menu (Mdn=7.50, Sd=5.00) and 5.43 sec. for Boulevard (Mdn=4.17, Sd=4.27).

Repeated measures ANOVA showed a significant effect of interaction style on task completion time ($F(2, 22) = 63.76, p < .001$, partial $\eta^2 = 0.85$). Pairwise comparisons using t-test with a Bonferroni adjustment showed significant differences in task completion time between menu and toolbar $p < .001$ and between menu and boulevard $p < .001$. A significant effect of interaction style on average error rate has been found using repeated measures ANOVA ($F(2, 22) = 12.9, p < .001$, partial $\eta^2 = 0.54$). Pairwise comparisons using t-test with a Bonferroni adjustment showed significant differences in average error rate between menu and toolbar $p = .012$.

3.2   Qualitative Measures

The qualitative aspects were evaluated using a questionnaire. Users completed an online questionnaire immediately after finishing the benchmark test. A questionnaire evaluated a user satisfaction and reception of Boulevard which it is crucial for acceptance of adaptive interfaces by users.

The participants were asked to order the interaction styles (toolbar, menu and Boulevard) by perceived rapidness of individual interaction styles. Eight participants selected Boulevard, four participants selected toolbar, and no one indicated menu as the fastest interaction style to control the application. As second in order of interaction styles seven participants ranked toolbar, four ranked Boulevard and one menu. Eleven participants indicated menu, one toolbar and no one selected Boulevard as the slowest way to control the application. Participant also reported satisfaction with interaction styles. Six participants ranked Boulevard as the most satisfying interaction style and six ranked toolbar. Next in order, six participants voted for toolbar, six for Boulevard. Menu was marked as least satisfying by all twelve participants. In the next, participants were asked to evaluate the following statements on the five-point Likert scale. The questions were following:

– I do understand clearly the basic principles behind Boulevard (Mode=4,5, Mdn=4.5).
– Boulevard is intuitive and predictable (Mode=4, Mdn=4).
– Boulevard is interesting (Mode=4,5, Mdn=4.5).
– Overall, I like Boulevard (Mode=4,5, Mdn=4).
– I would use Boulevard (Mode=4,5, Mdn=4).

Such a positive responses from participants were somewhat surprising. It points to a promising acceptance by users. An interesting point there is that although Boulevard is not significantly slower or faster in task completion times in comparison to toolbar, users considered Boulevard as subjectively faster than toolbar. Also, the comparable error rates on Boulevard and toolbar shows that users were not significantly less accurate in selecting user commands using Boulevard. Note also, that participants were able to use Boulevard effectively despite no training was enabled.

4   Conclusion and Future Work

This paper introduced Boulevard — a fine grained adaptive user interface for OpenOffice.org Writer. The proof of concept study evaluated one of the possible designs of Boulevard and compared task times and error rates on Boulevard, menus and toolbars. Overall, the proof-of-concept study showed particularly promising results, the task times and error rates were found comparable to toolbar although Boulevard integrates both menu and toolbar and occupies significantly larger space than toolbars. Furthermore, the qualitative analysis showed promising reception of the Boulevard by users. However, this study is only a preliminary, proof-of-concept study which must be followed by various other studies concerned to particular designs of adaptation mechanisms.

References

1. Dostál, M.: On the differences in usage of word processing applications. In: Proceedings of the HCI International Conference, Springer, Heidelberg (2011)
2. Leah, F., Joanna, M.: A comparison of static, adaptive and adaptable menus. In: CHI 2004: Proceedings of the SIGCHI conference on Human factors in computing systems, pp. 89–96. ACM, New York (2004)
3. Gajos, K.Z., Czerwinski, M., Tan, D.S., Weld, D.S.: Exploring the design space for adaptive graphical user interfaces. In: AVI 2006: Proceedings of the working conference on Advanced visual interfaces, pp. 201–208. ACM, New York (2006)
4. Jameson, A.: Adaptive interfaces and agents, pp. 305–330 (2003)
5. Keeble, R., Macredie, R.D.: Assistant agents for the world wide web intelligent interface design challenges. Interacting with Computers 12(4), 357–381 (2000)
6. Kühme, T.: A user-centered approach to adaptive interfaces. In: IUI 1993: Proceedings of the 1st international conference on Intelligent user interfaces, pp. 243–245. ACM, New York (1993)
7. McGrenere, J., Baecker, R.M., Booth, K.S.: An evaluation of a multiple interface design solution for bloated software. In: CHI 2002: Proceedings of the SIGCHI conference on Human factors in computing systems, pp. 164–170. ACM, New York (2002)
8. McGrenere, J., Moore, G.: Are we all in the same "bloat"? In: Fels, S., Poulin, P. (eds.) Graphics Interface, pp. 187–196. Canadian Human-Computer Communications Society (2000)
9. Oppermann, R., Simm, H.: Adaptability: user-initiated individualization, pp. 14–66. L. Erlbaum Associates Inc., Hillsdale (1994)
10. Shneiderman, B.: Direct manipulation for comprehensible, predictable and controllable user interfaces. In: Proceedings of IUI 1997, 1997 International Conference on Intelligent User Interfaces, pp. 33–39. ACM Press, New York (1997)

Development of Learning Achievement Index for Project Human Resource Management

Yusuke Emori, Takuya Furusawa, and Tsutomu Konosu

Department of Project Management, Chiba Institute of Technology
2-17-1, Tsudanuma, Narashino-shi, Chiba, 275-0016, Japan
s0842031RN@it-chiba.ac.jp

Abstract. The problem of decline in the number of project managers and in their quality has been widely discussed. The proposed approach bases the learning goal evaluation index on the student group projects. The index uses item response theory that evaluates items regardless of the test used. Comparing the evaluation of the applied educational products with that of student retention from lecture tests and midterm and final exams resulted in nearly the same curves. The results showed that both evaluation methods test nearly the same characteristics. This study defined success as achievement of learning goal and compared the learning achievement goal with the assumed capability of the work group: approximately 32% of examinees in the 7th group work demonstrated an ability level below that required to achieve the learning goal. This study revealed that it is possible to predict whether a student will pass a lecture test before a periodic test.

Keywords: Education, Evaluation, Project Human Resource Management.

1 Introduction

In recent years, many corporations and organizations have discussed the problem of the decreasing number of project managers and the deterioration in their quality. However, it is difficult to train students in project management skills only by OJT (on-the-job training) because the time for delivery is short and the quality demanded is high. Thus, project management education at an earlier stage is needed in the university. In addition, it must be determined whether a student is able to acquire the required knowledge and techniques through education. However, evaluations of whether students have learned this knowledge are generally measured only by periodic testing on each lecture.

2 Current Method and Proposed Method

It is necessary to determine whether a learner is able to acquire knowledge through education. The drawbacks of such knowledge tests are that they require only memorization and lack practical application unitary knowledge. And become the knowledge for tests by the memories, and that it is lacking in practice power is felt

C. Stephanidis (Ed.): Posters, Part I, HCII 2011, CCIS 173, pp. 501–505, 2011.

uneasy about. In these circumstances, project management educational institutions consider it difficult to give the desired results. Therefore, we proposed focusing on GW performed in a lecture, with an evaluation of the accuracy of GW in attaining the goal of periodic testing. However, GW is a relative evaluation, while periodic tests are absolute evaluations. Because these evaluation methods are different, it is not possible to simply compare them. This study allowed an evaluation based on the same standards by applying item response theory (IRT).

3   Experiment

3.1   Overview

The curriculum is based on the Japanese Accreditation Board for Engineering Education (JABEE) standards in this department of project management, and students are evaluated using an absolute interpretation of a periodic test and a report. The student who scores 60% or higher on the test is considered to meet the JABEE educational standard. Thus, in this study, it is presumed that the ability (θ) for the correct answer probability (P) is 60%.

Objective. The objectives of this study are as follows: (a) develop the educational content and the GW to establish basic knowledge; (b) evaluate the individual and the GW in a lecture; and (c) develop an index for evaluating whether the learned knowledge meets the goal.

Method. The method of this research was (a) the basic knowledge required for a project manager was clarified, and the educational content and GW were developed; (b) the students were introduced to Project Management, and the examination data of the GW, a midterm exam, and a final exam were collected; and (c) the data obtained were analyzed using IRT, the item difficulty and ability were presumed, and the achievement index was developed.

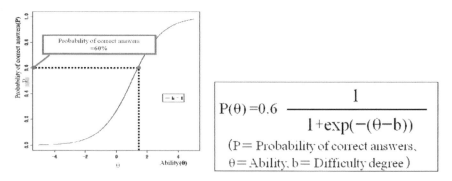

$$P(\theta)=0.6 \ \frac{1}{1+\exp(-(\theta-b))}$$

(P = Probability of correct answers, θ = Ability, b = Difficulty degree)

Fig. 1. Definition of the arrival target

Educational Contents. Material was developed based on the contents of PMBOK and PMP, and the knowledge of a de facto standard was taught low grade. The students were taught using these standards, and the examination data were collected.

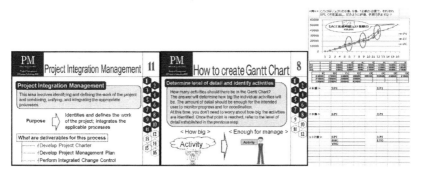

Fig. 2. Example of educational contents

3.2 Results

The obtained data were analyzed by applying the Rasch model, which showed a significant relationship (r = 0.94) between a midterm exam and the presumed ability. The final exam was also strongly correlated (r = 0.85) with the presumed ability. No matter what kind of test was used, the presumed ability had the same measure, and the correct answer probability could be presumed, provided the degree of the item difficulty was clear. Then, the test characteristic curve of a midterm and a final test was calculated from ability and item difficulty.

Ability to Estimate Participants. The two tests showed almost the same curves. It was proved that the two tests had almost the same characteristics. Moreover, the probability of achieving 60% of the correct answers was presumed from the curve: the midterm exam was presumed to be 0.500, and the final exam was presumed to be 0.400. A score of 0.450, which was the average, was defined as the ability to achieve the learning goal in this study.

Number of Candidates (Total:108)	Number of correct answers	Test score	θ	Model conformity
1	9	49	0.626	-1.166
2	11	53	1.563	-0.211
3	8	40	0.206	0.114
4	5	31	-1.071	0.671
5	11	58	1.563	-1.068
6	5	29	-1.071	-0.206
7	6	35	-0.626	-1.476
8	10	50	1.071	1.612
9	10	54	1.071	-0.313
10	10	60	1.071	-1.281

Fig. 3. Periodic Tests TCC (Measurement data)

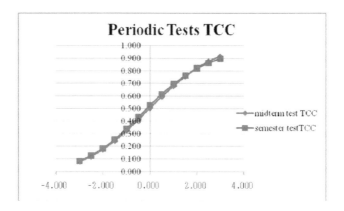

Fig. 4. Periodic Tests TCC

Learning Achievement Goal and Presumed Ability for GW. In addition, compared with the learning achievement goal and the ability presumed from the GW, about 32% of examinees in the 7th GW achieved less than the ability level of the learning goal.

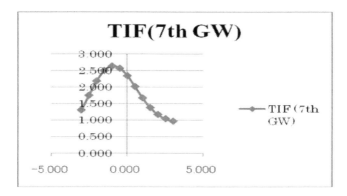

Fig. 5. 7th group work TIF

4   Conclusion

This achievement index using IRT can overlook temporary knowledge, which cannot be identified by the unitary evaluation of a standard test. In addition, it evaluates the use of GW at a suitable degree of difficulty; it was able to guidance to student before a periodic test. On the other hand, if the GW, model fit, and item information function are considered as the function of a periodic test, it can be expected that the student's learning of the material will improve continuously.

References

1. A Guide to The Project Management Body of Knowledge, 4th edn., Project Management Institute, Inc., pp. 3–413 (2008)
2. Baker, F.B.: The Basics of Item Response Theory, Heinemann (1985)

3. Milosevic, D.Z.: Project Management ToolBox: Tool and Techniques for the Practicing Project Manager, pp. 4–538. John Wiley & Sons, Inc., Chichester (2003)
4. Hambleton, R.K., Swaminathan, H.: Item Response Theory: Principles and Application. Kluwer-Nijhoff Publishing (1985)
5. Henning, G.: A Guide to language Testing: Development, Evaluation Research. Newbury House Publishers (1987)
6. Heldman, K., Mangano, V.: PMP Project Management Professional Exam Review Guide, pp. 2–314. Wiley Publishing, Inc. (2009)
7. Rasch, G.: Probabilistic Models for Some Intelligence and Attainment Test, Danish Institute for Educational Research (1960)
8. Waller, M.I.: A Procedure for Comparing Logistic Latent Trait Model. JEM 18, 119–125 (1981)

Design and Development of Information Display Systems for Monitoring Overboard

Tadasuke Furuya[1], Atsushi Suzuki[2],
Atsushi Shimamura[2], Takeshi Sakurada[2],
Yoichi Hagiwawa[2], and Takafumi Saito[2]

[1] Tokyo University of Marine Science and Technology,
2-1-6, Etchujima, Koto-ku, Tokyo, Japan
[2] Tokyo University of Agriculture and Technology,
2-24-16 Naka-cho, Koganei-shi, Tokyo, Japan
tfuruya@kaiyodai.ac.jp

Abstract. Recently, the number of incidents that suspicious person boards from a small boat to a boarding ship has increased. In case of a large ship, the number of crew is especially a few against the size of the ship. Under the circumstances, we need a method to easily grasp the state not only monitoring in the bridge but also inspecting inboard and taking a rest.

Keywords: monitoring, overboard.

1   Introduction

A navigator observes the movement of other ship by the naked eye and by using radar equipment's information when own ship is close to other one. Then, the navigator observes the movement of other ship by using the information of AIS (Automatic Identification System) when own ship is far from other one.

However, it is difficult to find a small ship which doesn't install AIS by using radar at nighttime. Especially, it is difficult to set the radar. When the sensitivity is strong, the wave influences the setting of radar. On the other hand, when the sensitivity is not strong, a small boat cannot be found. As a method for maritime surveillance, it has been proposed to use a night vision camera and a thermal infrared camera. By using them, guardians can almost find their objects in the bridge.

In this approach, there is a problem of oversight, because the location and the guardian which check the video are determined. Therefore, we propose an information display system that can watch how the patrol boats move. We just control about 10-inch touch screen PDAs, we can arbitrarily display thermal imaging camera images, infrared images and radar images as we want.

C. Stephanidis (Ed.): Posters, Part I, HCII 2011, CCIS 173, pp. 506–509, 2011.
© Springer-Verlag Berlin Heidelberg 2011

2   Our System Design

So that the ship shakes in its way, it is difficult to grasp the situation only by a real-time image. Moreover, the camera stabilizer cannot be put up to all cameras. The technique is needed for displaying the existence of the approaching objects, even if there is a shake of the ship. In such an environment, the accuracy of the automatic recognition is not high. The judgment by man is far better than the automatic recognition.

Then, we propose the technique for displaying the existence of the approaching objects. For example, we extract information from the time-line images taken with each camera, generate corrected image at a fixed time and present them. The image that collected this information is called "a gathering image [1][2]". The gathering image is generated by counting the amount of the change in a space of a fixed time and by gathering the large amount of the changes. Showing visualized data that compressed the time-line image data to be able to instantaneously judge makes it possible that a guardian's load reduction and the recognition time.

Image sequence to gathered time will depend on the distance between the object and frame rate. If the object is hidden from the camera's frame due to the large shaking vessel, a discrete track appears that the object is moving. However, because these waves have different movements, it should be readily apparent to monitor. Also, when capturing environment (e.g. at night) you need to select the appropriate equipment. Therefore, the image displayed is selected according to the situation.

The display image is divided into the following two.

– Night: The image that combines thermal imaging cameras and radar images.
– Rain: The image combines infrared images and radar images.

Using a combination images are gathered images. Gathered images are generated from captured images at a specific time interval. That one of a typical surveillance camera generated from the one hour, 10 minutes, and one minute's information. Real-time processing is so difficult. In this case, gathered time is set to a short interval time (e.g. 30 seconds).

In this paper, we report the status of fact, when we set the ship.

3   Experiments

We experimented with assuming suspicious person on board at night. The ship anchored 10 miles from land, are captured in a small boat near the radar. Figure 1 is a block diagram of the experimental environment. The radar images are the data from Automatic Radar Plotting Aids (ARPA). For safety reasons, ARPA can only be provided from the data. Camera control PC is networked. The mobile terminal connects to the control PC using wireless LAN.

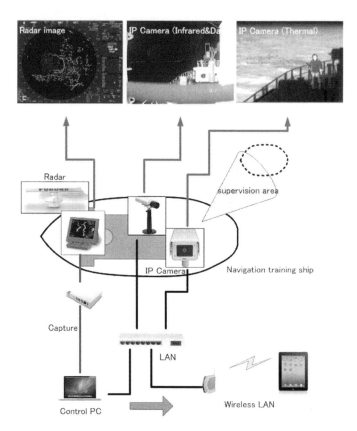

Fig. 1. The block diagram and layout of the system shows. ARPA has made use of the equipment used in practice. A navigation training ship for the experiment using a wired network, wireless network has been installed. ARPA display screen, Infrared & Daylight camera screen, Thermal camera image showing the top of the screen.

4   Result

We experimented with assuming suspicious person on board at night. The ship anchored 10 miles from land, are captured in a small boat near the radar. It put the case that a suspicious person on board the ship from the stern. In this experiment, IP cameras (thermal imaging, infrared imaging) were used. Radar image, thermal imaging, infrared images at night and the gathered images are shown in Fig.2. The two synthetic images (thermal and radar, infrared and radar) were compared. Small boat tracks extraction in radar images alone was difficult. The reason is that it is necessary only to produce images of the radar image to match the aggregate speed of the radar. However, it became possible to easily recognize images by combining the aggregate. The operation of small touch screen mobile device configuration change was difficult. Checking images of the ship is enough while it was moving.

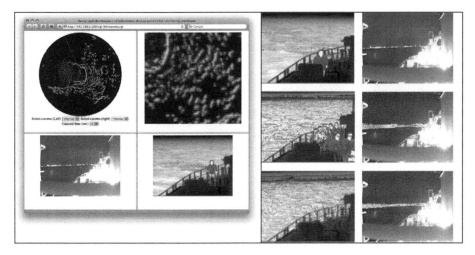

Fig. 2. Left: Display screen showing an Internet browser. ARPA Image (top left).Enlarge image the camera direction (top right). Infrared camera's live image (bottom left).Thermal camera's live image (bottom right). Right: Thermal camera image. The gathered image for 30 seconds. The gathered image for 30 seconds when there was no change. Infrared camera images. The gathered image for 30 seconds. The gathered image for 30 seconds when there was no change.

5   Conclusion

In this paper, we proposed a method to visualize the information in a variety of vessel operation (boarding of suspicious accident). Close object's presence shows in the gathered images that moving object's track can be easily understood. Gathered images of the proposed method are created with gatherers information on a certain time interval after extracting information from an image change in each camera.

This approach can also support the oversight accident. In this experiment, we could not due to the small number of surveillance cameras in one direction only. Next, we installed cameras on both sides, we will be observing the track of a small boat meandering.

References

1. Hirakawa, M., Uchida, K., Yoshitaka, A.: Content-Based Video Retrieval using Mosaic Images. In: Proceedings of 2002 International Symposium on Cyber Worlds: Theory and Practices, pp. 161–167 (2002)
2. Akutsu, W., Furuya, T., Miyamura, H.N., Saito, T.: Hierarchical Image Gathering Technique for Browsing Surveillance Camera Images. In: Smith, M.J., Salvendy, G. (eds.) HCII 2007. LNCS, vol. 4557, pp. 383–390. Springer, Heidelberg (2007)

Fault Diagnosis of Induction Motors Using Discrete Wavelet Transform and Artificial Neural Network

In-Soo Lee

School of Electronic & Electrical Engineering, Kyungpook National University, Sangju, Korea
insoolee@knu.ac.kr

Abstract. This paper proposes a fault diagnosis method for induction motors based on DWT (Discrete Wavelet Transform) and artificial NN. The proposed algorithm is based on ART2 NN (adaptive resonance theory 2 neural network) with uneven vigilance parameters. Proposed fault diagnosis method consists of data preprocessing part by frequency analysis of vibration signal, and fault classifier for fault isolation by ART2 NN. Especially, the data preprocessing part which converts the sampled signals into the frequency domain by DWT is very important to improve the performance of the fault diagnosis. In this paper both rotor and bearing faults of the induction motors are considered for diagnosis. The experiment results demonstrate the effectiveness of the proposed fault diagnosis method of induction motors.

Keywords: Fault diagnosis, induction motor, DWT, ART-2 NN.

1 Introduction

Induction motors are very important and virtually used in every industry. Fault diagnosis of induction motors is very important to ensure safe operation. The early detection of faults can help avoid major system breakdowns [1].

Methods for fault diagnosis of the system fall into two major groups [2]: 1) model free methods, 2) model based methods. The model based Fault diagnosis methods rely on the idea of analytic redundancy [3]. In practice, however, the mathematical model is not easy to obtain due to nonlinearities. Model free methods include limit checking, expert systems and neural network-based schemes. In recent years, neural network models have been studied extensively for the fault diagnosis [4-6]. It has been noted that neural network models consist of a suitable structure for representing the unknown nonlinear function generally. Therefore this model can be used as a powerful tool for handling nonlinear problems.

This paper proposes a fault diagnosis method for induction motors using DWT [7-8] and ART-2 NN with uneven vigilance parameters. Since ART2 NN [6] is an unsupervised NN the proposed fault classifier does not require the knowledge of all possible faults to isolate the faults occurred in the system. A DWT algorithm is also used to convert the sampled vibration signals to the frequency domain. We diagnosed rotor bar fault and bearing fault of the induction motors.

C. Stephanidis (Ed.): Posters, Part I, HCII 2011, CCIS 173, pp. 510–514, 2011.
© Springer-Verlag Berlin Heidelberg 2011

2   DWT and ART2 NN-Based Induction Motor Fault Diagnosis

2.1   Experiment Set-Up

Figure 1 shows the overall real-data acquisition system for fault experimentation of the induction motors, which consists of a NI cDAQ-9172 board for data acquisition, a vibration sensor, three induction motors, and the fault diagnosis algorithm.

(a) Rotor fault   (b) Bearing fault

Fig. 1. Real- data acquisition   **Fig. 2.** Fault of induction motors
system for fault experiments
of the induction motors.

We conducted fault experiments of induction motors for the following two fault types as shown in Figure 2: The rotor fault is simulated by artificially making a hole in the middle of the rotor bar as shown in Figure 2(a). The bearing fault is induced by injection of bits of iron in a bearing as shown in Figure 2(b).

2.2   Proposed Fault Diagnosis Method

A block diagram of the proposed diagnostic system configuration is shown in Figure 3. Proposed fault diagnosis method consists of data preprocessing part by DWT of vibration signal and fault classifier for fault isolation by ART2 NN. Vibration signal is digitized and recorded using NI cDAQ-9172 board. The fault diagnosis algorithm which is based on DWT and ART2 NN is implemented on a PC using MATLAB 7.1. The data preprocessing part is very important to improve the performance of the fault diagnosis. It converts the sampled vibration signals to the frequency domain by a DWT. The ART-2 NN with uneven vigilance parameters is also considered for fault isolation of the induction motors.

Fig. 3. Structure of the proposed fault diagnosis method

Feature extraction by DWT. The wavelet analysis is done similar to the STFT (short time fourier transform) analysis. The signal to be analyzed is multiplied with a wavelet function just as it is multiplied with a window function in STFT, and then the transform is computed for each segment generated. However, unlike STFT, in wavelet transform, the width of the wavelet function changes with each spectral component. The WT, at high frequencies, gives good time resolution and poor frequency resolution, while at low frequencies, the WT gives good frequency resolution and poor time resolution.

The CWT (continuous wavelet transform) is provide by below equation;

$$X_{WT}(\tau,s) = \frac{1}{\sqrt{|s|}} \cdot \int x(t)\psi^*(\frac{t-\tau}{s})dt \qquad (1)$$

where x(t) is the signal to be analyzed, $\psi(t)$ is the mother wavelet or the basis function. In the case of DWT, a time-scale representation of the digital signal is obtained using digital filtering techniques. The DWT is computed by successive low-pass and high-pass filtering of the discrete time domain signal as shown in Figure 4(a). This is called the Mallat algorithm. In the Figure 4(a), the signal is denoted by the sequence x[n]. The LPF is denoted by G_0 while the HPF is denoted by H_0. At each level, the HPF produces detail information, d[n], while the LPF associated with scaling function produces coarse approximations, a[n]. The reconstruction of the original signal from the wavelet coefficients is shown in Figure 4(b).

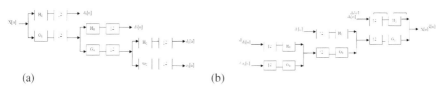

(a)   (b)

Fig. 4. Discrete wavelet transform

Fault isolation by ART2 NN with uneven vigilance parameters. In the proposed method, the ART2 NN with uneven vigilance parameters isolates the motor faults. Architecture of the ART2 NN is shown in Figure 5. The ART2 NN with uneven vigilance parameters [6] has the same architecture of the general ART2 NN [9]. But, in the proposed NN new vigilance test is used to classify the patterns. The distance between the input patterns and j-th output node is computed as follows:

$$d_j = \left\| W_j - X \right\|_\infty^E \quad \triangleq \quad \max_i \left| \frac{1}{\varepsilon_i}(w_{ij} - x_i) \right|, \quad j=1,2,\cdots,M \qquad (2)$$

where x_i is the input of the input node i, $i=1,2,\ldots, N$, N is the number of input nodes, w_{ij} is the weight from output node j to input node, M is the number of the output nodes. And $\|\bullet\|_\infty^E$ is the weighted infinite norm, $E = diag(\varepsilon_1^{-1},\varepsilon_2^{-1},\ldots,\varepsilon_N^{-1})$ is the diagonal weighted matrix, ε_i is the vigilance parameter for i-th input node. If the distance between the input patterns and the J-th output node is minimum, then the class J is selected winner node. Verification is done whether input pattern X really belongs to the winner class J by performing the vigilance test as follows:

$$\left\| W_J - X \right\|_\infty^E \quad < \quad 1 \qquad (3)$$

If the winner class J passes the vigilance test, adjust the weights of the class J by

$$W_j^{new} = \frac{X + W_j^{old}[class_j^{old}]}{[class_j^{old}]+1} \qquad (4)$$

where $[class_i]$ is the number of the patterns in the class i. On the other hand, if the class J fails the vigilance test, a new class is created with weight $W_{M+1} = X$.

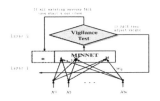

Fig. 5. Architecture of the ART2 NN

3 Experiment Results

Simulations are carried out to evaluate the performance of the proposed fault diagnosis method based on the ART2 NN and DWT using real data obtained from the induction motors. Three experiments have been done to produce three group(Healthy condition, Fault #1, Fault #2) sample data using induction motors and NI cDAQ-9172 board. The induction motor was operating at 1800 rpm and 0.1 ms sampling time was chosen. We chose 20 input nodes and vigilance parameters of the ART2 NN as $\varepsilon = 0.01*[1,1,1,1,1,1,1,1,1,1,1,1,1,1,1,1,1,1,1,1]$.

To verify the proposed method, two types of faults were introduced to the induction motor system at the 150-th sample number. The faults that were introduced into the fault diagnosis experiment are summarized as follows:

Fault #1 : Rotor fault,   Fault #2 : Bearing fault

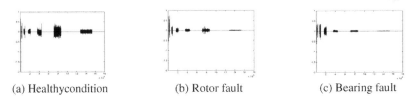

(a) Healthycondition   (b) Rotor fault   (c) Bearing fault

Fig. 6. Spectrum of the vibration signals by DWT

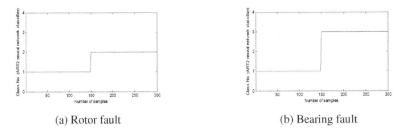

(a) Rotor fault   (b) Bearing fault

Fig. 7. Fault diagnosis results of the induction motor

The spectrum of the vibration signals by DWT for healthy motor, motor with rotor fault and motor with bearing fault are shown in Figure 6(a), (b) and (c), respectively. Fault isolation results for rotor fault and bearing fault by ART2 NN are shown in Figure 7(a) and (b), respectively. From the results, we can see that the proposed fault diagnosis system using DWT and ART2 NN successfully diagnoses the faults which were occurred in the induction motors.

4   Conclusions

This paper proposed a fault diagnosis method for induction motors based on DWT and ART-2 NN with uneven vigilance parameters. Since the ART2 NN is an unsupervised NN, the fault classifier does not require the knowledge of all possible faults to isolate the faults occurring in the system. A DWT algorithm was also used to convert the sampled vibration signals to the frequency domain. In this research we diagnosed rotor fault and bearing fault of the induction motors. From the simulation results using real data collected from induction motors, it is verified that the proposed method was successfully applied to diagnose the problem in the induction motors.

Acknowledgments. This Research was supported by Kyungpook National University Research Fund, 2010.

References

1. Ye, Z., Wu, B., Sadeghian, A.: Current signature analysis of induction motor mechanical faults by wavelet packet decomposition. IEEE Trans. Industrial Electronics. 50(6), 1217–1228 (2003)
2. Wagner, J., Shoureshi, R.: A failure isolation strategy for thermofluid system diagnostics. ASME J. Eng. for Industry 115, 459–465 (1993)
3. Isermann, R.: Process fault detection based on modeling and estimation methods-a survey. Automatica 20(4), 387–404 (1984)
4. Polycarpou, M.M., Vemuri, A.T.: Learning methodology for failure detection and accommodation. IEEE Contr. Syst. Mag., 16–24 (1995)
5. Srinivasan, A., Batur, C.: Hopfield/ART-1 neural network-based fault detection and isolation. IEEE Trans. Neural Networks 5(6), 890–899 (1994)
6. Lee, I.S., Shin, P.L., Jeon, G.J.: Multiple faults diagnosis of a linear system using ART2 neural networks. Journal of Control, Automation and System Engineering 3(3), 244–251 (1997)
7. Ionescu, R., Llobet, E.: Wavelet transform-based fast feature extraction from temperature modulated semiconductor gas sensors. Sensors and Actuators B 81, 289–295 (2002)
8. Huang, M.C.: Wave parameters and functions in wavelet analysis with filtering. Ocean Engineering 31, 813–831 (2004)
9. Kung, S.Y.: Digital Neural Networks. Prentice Hall, Englewood Cliffs (1993)

Study on Providing Multi-faceted Information on Technology Intelligence Service

Mikyoung Lee, Seungwoo Lee, Pyung Kim, Hanmin Jung, and Won-Kyung Sung

Korea Institute of Science and Technology Information (KISTI)
335 Gwahangno, Yuseong-gu, Daejeon, Korea 305-806
{jerryis,swlee,pyung,jhm,wksung}@kisti.re.kr

Abstract. In this study, we propose an information visualization method that provides multi-faceted information about technologies, research agents and research results on technology intelligence service supporting researchers to facilitate strategic planning and decisions. We consider selecting a suitable type among existing visualization types to increase the efficiency of information delivery and then customizing it for multi-faceted information. In this manner, we select an appropriate visualization type and then add meaningful information by using additional features such as color and size of node. As further work, we would like to develop an automatic explanation module for all visualizations in the technology intelligence service.

Keywords: Multi-faceted Information, Technology Intelligence Service, Information visualization.

1 Introduction

Due to the flood of information on the web, researchers require a system that enables them to analyze high volumes of data and subsequently valuable information that will be helpful to their research. We have developed a technology intelligence service that supports researchers in decision making and strategic planning by analyzing bibliographic information and implicit data in large-capacity academic literatures[1]. The technology intelligence service is a decision-making support system mainly composed of technologies, research agents (countries, institutions, and researchers), and research results (papers and patents). Information visualization displays high volumes of information on screens in the form of graphics, helping users to understand the information intuitively [2].

This paper describes an information visualization method that provides a large scale of information in an effective and intuitive manner, which is required to effectively express multi-faceted information on the technology intelligence service.

2 Types of Visualization for Multi-faceted Information

Types of visualization commonly used include tables, graphs, plots, maps, matrixes, and trees. A service developer selects a type of visualization that is suitable for the

C. Stephanidis (Ed.): Posters, Part I, HCII 2011, CCIS 173, pp. 515–518, 2011.

characteristic of data to effectively provide information to the user. As seen in the Table1, types of visualization can be divided by the characteristics of the data [3].

Table 1. Types of visualization divided by the number of dimension

One dimension	Two dimensions	Three dimension
Scatter plot	Table	Scatter plot
Line graph	Scatter plot	Heat map
Bar graph	Box plot	Rubber sheet
Tree	Matrix	Parallel coordinates
Basic chart	Bubble chart	

In general, most types of visualization tend to encompass difficulties in supplying comparison and analysis of multi-dimensional objects, because they are primarily designed to intuitively understand analysis of a single object and comparison between two objects. The reason for difficulties in displaying a multi-dimensional data lies in the 2D nature of the computer screen. Therefore, when 3D and higher data are represented on a 2D screen, some information is likely to be missed. Furthermore, users are more accustomed to 2D-visualization than 3D, and consequently have difficulties in understanding 3D data [3]. Multi-dimensional data can be represented in 3D by utilizing motions such as space or rotation, but due to restrictions on screen, the data is likely to be occluded by other points that might be in front of it. Accordingly, it is more effective to represent data in several 2D-data sets rather than in a single 3D-data set.

Hence, we exploit a method that combines several types of existing 2D visualization to represent multi-dimensional information of the technology intelligence service, rather than designing a new type of visualization. This is based on the idea that efficiency in information delivery can be maximized as the user is able to grasp the service intuitively.

3   Information Visualization on Technology Intelligence Service

In this chapter, we describes a method of visualizing multi-faceted information by citing a case of a Technology/Agent Map service that offers an analysis of correlations among technologies, research agents, and research results. The Technology/Agent Map service searches its related technologies and compares research results of the technologies by their technologies and also by their major researcher agents and also provides competitive/cooperative relations among research agents.

We adopted 'Bubble chart' that can show the multi-faceted relation among technologies, research agents and research results by three aspects such as a vertical axis, a horizontal axis and a node. That is, the X axis refers to research agents, the Y axis to technologies, and the node to research results. The amount of research results that a research agent achieved on a technology is represented with the size of the node. In addition, the user is allowed to change conditions so that he or she can get analyzed results from different points of views. More specifically, a select box and a sliding bar are placed on the X axis, Y axis, and node to change the technology relations (association relations, element relations), a granularity of research agents (researchers, institutes, and countries), and the type of research results (academic-centered, business-centered). However, it was difficult to represent competition and cooperation relations among agents researching a specific technology, and a paper/patent in research results on a screen. In order to resolve these difficulties, we considered adding explanatory notes on a node or representing the node as an image. However, in the case of a small node, this is likely to decrease discrimination of the node. Hence, we decided to display the information with color and chroma of a node.

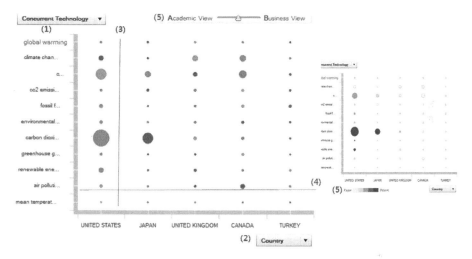

Fig. 1. Technology/Agent Map of Technology Intelligence Service shows as follows. (1) The technologies related to the searched technology, (2) Major agents researching the searched technology, (3) R&D results concentration of major research agents on each technology, (4) Competition/cooperation relations among research agents on each technology, (5) Research/business dependency of research agents on each technology.

Figure 1 shows a snapshot of the Technology/Agent Map when the 'global warming' technology is given as a target.

● The Y axis and the X axis display the target technology and its related technologies and leading countries researching those technologies, respectively. Research results can be compared among the research countries and also technologies.

● The level of concentration on research results can be compared by each node size of technologies and research agents. It is possible to understand which one among the technologies a specific research agent concentrates on. In the case of the US and Japan, they are found to concentrate on 'carbon dioxide' technology.

● The color of a node provides information on the competition/cooperation relations among research agents for each technology. Research agents whose nodes have the same color have cooperative relations while those otherwise have competitive relations. It is found that the US and Canada maintain cooperative relations in the 'air pollution' field.

- The chroma of a node is divided in five stages to provide the paper/patent ratio of research results, based on which research type of agents (academic- centered or business- centered) can be identified.

4   Conclusion

In this paper, we proposed an information visualization method where a technology intelligence service supporting researchers to make decisions can effectively provide massive amounts of multi-faceted information to a user. We selected a visualization type that suits the purposes and enables the user to understand the information intuitively and subsequently gave information by utilizing all functions of the visualization selected. This makes it possible to represent the visualization of multi-faceted such as technologies, research agents and research results. However, if a lot of information is delivered at once, intuition could be decreased, consequently making it difficult to provide clear information. When the information is represented with node colors in the "Bubble Chart" we chose, if there is no additional description on the color, a user could not be aware of the color information. In the future, we will additionally develop an automatic description module on the technology intelligence service to address this problem.

References

1. Lee, S., Lee, M., Jung, H., Kim, P., Kim, T., Seo, D., Sung, W.: Supporting Technical Decision-Making with InSciTe, The 9th ISWC, Semantic Web Challenge (2010)
2. Foss, C.: Tools for reading and browsing hypertext. Information Processing & Management 25(4), 407–418 (1989)
3. Fry, B.: Computational Information Design, Massachusetts Institute of Technology (2004)

Simulating Additional Area
on Tele-Board's Large Shared Display

Peter LoBue, Raja Gumienny, and Christoph Meinel

Hasso Plattner Institute, Prof.-Dr.-Helmert-Straße 2-3, 14482 Potsdam, Germany
peter.lobue@temple.edu,
{raja.gumienny,christoph.meinel}@hpi.uni-potsdam.de

Abstract. Digital whiteboard systems can simulate an infinite amount of surface area on a single display; however the hardware's limited size necessitates supplementary virtual tools to navigate the area. In what ways does this less convenient setup hinder established collaborative workflows? Participants in our pilot study were asked to synthesize data on either a traditional whiteboard setup with multiple touch displays or a single display that had to be navigated virtually. Results show that working under the restrictions of a single display required slightly more time, yet workflows could continue. Users accepted the visual restriction as a condition of working with a digital system. Team members were also impelled to work more closely together, which both helped and hurt collaboration.

Keywords: CSCW, whiteboards, simulated space, shared displays, creativity support tools, design thinking.

1 Introduction

Tele-Board is our digital whiteboard software system, designed to support collaborative creativity as ubiquitously as possible. It runs primarily on a single, large touch display, the most popular models of which currently only support a maximum resolution of 1280x960 pixels, yet it is meant for projects that take up a lot of space.

Our original approach to simulating more area was to make a virtual 3200x2400 pixel surface available and use the display as a window into this area. As more space was needed, users could pan the window in any direction to branch out their work. We assumed this behavior was appropriate for the fluid nature of creative processes. However, from observations during user testing, we noticed that when a window of area would fill up with sticky notes, drawings and other whiteboard artifacts, users would inevitably jump to an arbitrary blank location for a fresh slate. This corresponds to the physical action of fetching another whiteboard. To better support this convention we enabled users to manage multiple separate surfaces, or *panels*. (Users can more easily navigate through the history of an individual panel or share content with others on a per-panel basis.) Supplementary virtual tools are needed to navigate these panels while working. This raises the following questions, which we answer here by means of an experiment and analysis.

C. Stephanidis (Ed.): Posters, Part I, HCII 2011, CCIS 173, pp. 519–523, 2011.
© Springer-Verlag Berlin Heidelberg 2011

- Can team members continue their established workflows despite having visually restricted access to their information?
- To what degree do the restrictions frustrate users?
- How else might the extra tool set required to view all needed information influence team dynamics?

Display interaction research generally deals with extensions of traditional desktop features, such as enhancements to window management systems [5]. Research on creative tasks with large displays tends to focus on ideation exercises such as brainstorming [3] where only one shared display is needed. However, activities exist where people use segregated spaces in analog environments that could be replaced by digitally enhanced counterparts, for example organizing information and making sense of collected data. Recent research by Andrews et al. [1] explores how new meaning is added as users manage their content freely on a large display space. We are interested in whether the spatial relationships remain useful in the context of collaboration when access to this space is restricted by "coupled navigation" [6].

2 Experiment

Students of the HPI School of Design Thinking in Potsdam, Germany, volunteered in teams of one male and one female. The pairs were presented with 49 digital sticky notes. Each one contained a single fact or statement based on real interview results on the topic of trusting health information on the internet. The number of sticky notes along with their size was carefully selected so participants would be forced to use more space than the initial view provided, yet could easily manage within twice as much area. This forced teams to make a logistical decision on where to obtain it.

The participants were asked to *cluster* the sticky notes into meaningful groups, in order to deduce the most important insights. Every participant had practiced clustering before and knew what the result should look like, namely groups of two or more sticky notes, separated by whitespace or marker lines, each with a common theme. This provided a good balance between a mutually expected outcome and room for variability without needing to measure anything too abstract, such as levels of creativity. Also, clustering is an open activity done as a team. No personal space is required for individual work.

2.1 Conditions

In one out of two conditions, the *variable*, two panels were accessible on a single touch board, one showing the initial sticky notes and the other blank. To switch between them, users tapped a button on the bottom left of the display which contained a miniature snapshot of the other panel's content. Each panel had an available area of 1810x1358 pixels, or twice that of 1280x960, so at any given time only half of the panel's area was visible on the screen. Users could pan the space with a *move tool*, similar to the hand tool in Adobe Photoshop. A collapsible overview map showing the current screen's entire content was provided on the bottom right. See figure 1. We expected participants to decide early on how to obtain additional space, either by switching between panels or by spreading out on the first panel and ignoring the second. Either approach offered the same amount of area to work with.

In the other condition, the *control*, two touch board displays were set up next to each other, each with a resolution of 1280x960 pixels. One was filled with the sticky notes, and the other stood blank. Everything was visible, the user needed not think about navigating the area, and the extra tools to do so were removed. This is akin to traditional whiteboard setups.

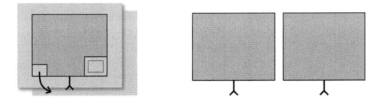

Fig. 1. Left: *Variable condition* with a button to switch between panels and an overview map for the current panel. Right: *Control condition* without navigational tools

3   Results and Discussion

Ten participating teams were randomly assigned to one of either condition. Four out of the five groups who tested the variable condition immediately opted to obtain additional space by switching between panels. They hardly used the move tool.

3.1   Content, Performance and Satisfaction

Between conditions, the groups' approach to clustering and themes for clusters did not differ appreciably. The average number of clusters in the variable conditions was 7.8, and in the control condition 6.8. No reason for this difference could be concluded.

Control groups needed an average of 32.8 minutes for task completion and variable groups 36.0 (10% more). Even so, as measured by a questionnaire on a 5-point Likert scale, as well as subjectively observed, the average levels of satisfaction with their results, amount of fun had and feeling of preparedness for the next step in the design thinking process did not differ substantially between the conditions.

3.2   Teamwork

In the variable condition, both participants physically stood closer together to work on the same touch board. Every time one participant wanted to see something not currently visible, before changing the view he or she naturally felt compelled to make sure the other's train of thought would not be broken. This resulted in much more verbal dialog between participants which kept them focused on the same action, like deciding whether a sticky note belonged in a certain cluster. Birnholtz et al. [4] achieved similar results by limiting input devices. The three individuals who recognized this phenomenon viewed it as advantageous. We see it as an opportunity to impel users to focus together on a given decision, ensuring the outcome is a product of true collaboration.

However, at times this setup excluded one of the team members. In the exceptional group from the variable condition that used the move tool instead of switching between panels, the male essentially completed the entire task by himself. As he moved the board and the sticky notes across it, he verbalized his actions as if to assuage his teammate's possible disagreement while she tried to keep up. During another group's experiment, the female twice lost focus and sat down for a few minutes, seemingly uninterested in her teammate's continuation of the task. (When this happens it is immediately obvious which person has receded. This could serve as useful information to an observer, for example in a teaching environment.)

In the control condition, no participants became this disengaged. Some pairs tacitly separated themselves into roles. For example, one person would *pick* (cut) the sticky notes that fit to an established theme, while the other would rapidly *drop* (paste) them on the other board and organize them into clusters. Here, content-based decisions were being made by one individual, while the other made presentation-based decisions. The roles would switch back and forth, often depending upon which board each person was closest to. At other times, the participants would work separately for several seconds or minutes and then reconvene and explain what they had just done.

3.3 Memory Retention

Only two individuals in the variable condition explicitly addressed the issue of not being able to see all their sticky notes at the same time. The female mentioned earlier, whose partner completed most of the task with the move tool, stated "at first it was difficult to assess the space, but then it was okay [with the overview map]." Another participant commented, "Normally you can turn your head to see whatever you need to. Here I had to make sure [my team member] was okay with moving the board."

Participants from the variable condition were able to recall an average of 4 clusters (by names and relative locations on the panel) after the task, while those from the control condition remembered 5.5 (38% more). Aside from the two quotes above, no effects of this difference in memory retention were palpable. This suggests that throughout the task, content left in the non-visible areas by the users did not need to be as prevalent in their memories to complete the overall task equally as well.

3.4 Ease of Use

The tool's perceived ease of use, as measured by various questions on a 5-point Likert scale, remained relatively constant between conditions. Users did not show frustration from having restricted visual access to their information. We infer that widespread acceptance of having restricted access to simulated space through a personal computer's monitor carries over to larger, shared displays.

Participants who used the move tool to achieve more space remarked that it was burdensome to change their stylus's function by means of virtual buttons on the display. Sharing the user's only input device between the marker and the move tool caused a lot of inconvenient switching back and forth. Newer touch display hardware that differentiates between finger and stylus input is becoming ever more available. We plan on mapping each of these mechanisms to the move and marker tools, respectively, as they are by far the most used functions on our whiteboard.

4   Conclusion

Replacing physical navigation with virtual navigation is generally believed to correlate with a slight decrease in performance [2]. However, our qualitative measures were intended to determine whether conventional workflows are severely interrupted in the context of whiteboards. We did not observe this to be the case. The relatively consistent level of satisfaction and experience across both conditions prompts us to further develop Tele-Board to take advantage of multiple larger, simulated spaces.

It remains to be studied precisely what effects the setup has on content and performance. More of such experiments are planned with more panels and methods to navigate them and tasks from different stages of creative processes. In the future, our team will focus more closely on how managing space can be utilized to enhance teamwork and ensure all users are contributing to the given collaboration.

Acknowledgments. This work was funded by the HPI-Stanford Design Thinking Research Program. We also thank the HPI D-School class of 2010, Lutz Gericke and Mia Konew.

References

1. Andrews, C., Endert, A., North, C.: Space to think: large high-resolution displays for sensemaking. In: CHI 2010 Proceedings, pp. 55–64. ACM, New York (2010)
2. Ball, R., North, C., Bowman, D.A.: Move to improve: promoting physical navigation to increase user performance with large displays. In: CHI 2007 Proceedings, pp. 191–200. ACM, New York (2007)
3. Bao, P., Gerber, E., Gergle, D., Hoffman, D.: Momentum: getting and staying on topic during a brainstorm. In: CHI 2010 Proceedings, pp. 1233–1236. ACM, New York (2010)
4. Birnholtz, J., Grossman, T., Mark, C., Balakrishnan, R.: An Exploratory Study of Input Configuration and Group Process in a Negotiation Task Using a Large Display. In: CHI 2007 Proceedings, pp. 91–100. ACM, New York (2007)
5. Czerwinski, M., Robertson, G., Meyers, B., Smith, G., Robbins, D., Tan, D.: Large display research overview. In: CHI 2006 Extended Abstracts, pp. 69–74. ACM, New York (2006)
6. Stewart, J., Bederson, B., Druin, A.: Single Display Groupware: A Model for Co-present Collaboration. In: CHI 1999 Proceedings, pp. 286–293. ACM, New York (1999)

Components Based Integrated Management Platform for Flexible Service Deployment in Plant Factory

Aekyung Moon·, Song Li, and Kyuhyung Kim

Embedded System Research Team, Electronics and Telecommunications Research Institute
161 Gajeong-dong, Yuseong-gu, Daejeon, 305-350, Korea
{akmoon,li.song,jaykim}@etri.re.kr

Abstract. The plant factory is a facility that aid growers to make the steady production of high-quality vegetables and ornamental plants all year round by artificially controlling the cultivation environment such as indoor temperature and humidity. There are various types of plant factory such as fully artificial light-type, sunlight-type and plastic house, etc. In this paper, we propose Intelligent Greenhouse Integrated Management Platform (IGIMP) that can support a variety of plant factory type with the flexible service deployment. To optimize the environment for crop growth automatically, it gathers environmental context information from various indoor sensors as well as outdoor sensors and provides appropriate control functions using the convergence of ubiquitous computing and agriculture technologies. Finally, we introduce implementation through small plant factory prototype a kind of fully artificial light-type greenhouse.

Keywords: Environment Control, Greenhouse, Plant Factory, Context, Ubiquitous Sensor.

1 Introduction

Recently severe weather conditions decreased agricultural productivity in South Korea and the extreme weather such as heavy rains, typhoons and droughts affects the open field agriculture. Consequently, these unusual weather phenomena cause that the volatility of food price is increasing rapidly. The requirement on the environmental control technology using the convergence of Ubiquitous Computing and Agriculture technologies derived to solve this problem. The plant factory is a facility that aids the steady production of high-quality vegetables all year round by artificially controlling the cultivation environment (e.g., light, temperature, humidity, carbon dioxide concentration, and culture solution), allowing growers to plan production. There are various types of plant factory such as fully artificial light-type, sunlight-type and plastic house, etc. In this paper, we propose IGIMP that can support to provide a variety of plant factory type with the flexible service deployment as well as artificially controlling the plant factory environment. For this purpose, we design component based six-layer architecture of the IGIMP. To optimize the environment for crop growth automatically, it gathers environmental context information from various

C. Stephanidis (Ed.): Posters, Part I, HCII 2011, CCIS 173, pp. 524–528, 2011.

indoor sensors as indoor parameters such as light strength, temperature, humidity, and CO_2 density. Moreover, it gathers from outdoor-sensors as outdoor-parameters such as outdoor temperature, sun light strength, wind speed and the amount of rainfall. Consequently, IGIMP provides appropriate control functions using current environment context gathered from the ubiquitous sensor network. And, we consider a component-based configuration for providing various types of plant factory with flexible service development and deployment. Plant factory management system has been studied for a long time. Recently, with the advancement of ubiquitous sensor network technologies, it has applied increasingly to greenhouse management.   As a result of recent study of Denmark IntelliGrow [1] and BipsArch [2] systems, and research results of University of Vaasa, Finland [3], Hungary's Sun SPOT system [4], and EY_THERMO project in Greece[5], the ubiquitous greenhouse management system[6] and so on.   However, most previous systems considered a specific greenhouse. Only exception is IntelliGrow and BipsArch.

The remainder of this paper is organized as follows. Section 2 proposes system architecture and scenarios. Section 3 describes case study. Finally, summary and concluding remarks are presented in section 4.

2   Intelligent Greenhouse Integrated Management Platform

The IGIMP is a platform for artificially controlling the plant factory environment and deploy service flexibly. The features of IGIMP are as following:

- **Artificially controlling the greenhouse environments**: To optimize the environment for crop growth automatically, it gathers environmental context information from various sensors indoor parameters such as light, temperature, humidity, and CO_2 density as well as outdoor temperature, sun light, wind and rain and provides appropriate control functions. Figure 1 shows the example of sensors and actuators for green house.

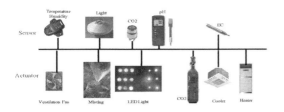

Fig. 1. Example of Sensors and Actuators in Greenhouse

- **Flexible Service Development and Deployment:** There are various types of greenhouses such as fully artificial light-type, sunlight-type and plastic house and so on that a variety of sensors and actuators for environmental monitoring and control. For this purpose, we provide the software component for sensors and actuators that are installed in the actual greenhouse.
- **Customize Service depend on Crop Stage (Growth Status)**: This will allow the operator to set up different growth conditions for the plants over a number of days or crop growth status. For example, paprika has vegetative and generative stages that it is important to control the balance of theses stages.

For this purpose, we design IGIMP, that divided into three major systems, IMS(Integrated Management System for greenhouse),GOS(Greenhouse Operation System and GC(Greenhouse Controller) as shown in Figure 2. IMS deploys software components for them that sensors and actuators are installed in each actual greenhouse.

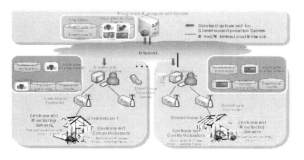

Fig. 2. System Architecture

GOS installs software components for sensors and actuators with software downloaded from IMS. The communication of IMS and GOS uses TCP/IP protocol. IMS have databases to store crop growth environment information for a variety of crops and database to store crop status information received from GOS.

Table 1. Six-layer Architecture of IGIMP

Layer	Function
GUI Layer	– Provides GUI with users according to user's roles. Users execute the service they need
Service Layer	– The application layer which contains all specific applications for the actual greenhouse operation For example, environment control service, environment monitoring service, etc.
Composer Layer	– Provides development environments for service deployment in user's greenhouse – Provide component creation/ composer IDE (Integrated Development Environment) – Creation of sensor/actuator/database component. Store component in component repository. Component discovery
Component Communication Layer	– Communication between components and execution of components – Component scheduling – Event registration and publishing
Component Management Layer	– Life-Cycle Management – Fault Management/ Recovery – Status Management of Sensor and Actuators
Basic Component Layer	– Database Component : Crop Growth DB, Crop Growth Environment DB, Environment Control DB, Greenhouse Profile DB, Environment Contextual Information DB – Sensor Component : Temperature, humidity, light, pH, EC, CO_2 density, leaf temperature components, etc – Actuator Component : Cooling, heating, artificial light, CO_2 dosing, water supply, irrigation, circulation fan, ventilation fan components, etc.

GC is consisted of embedded board with some control logics. GC gathers context information from various sensors installed in greenhouse environments. The communication of GC and sensors/actuators uses wireless protocols such as WiFi or Zigbee. And it delivers contextual information to green house operation system (GOS). The six-layer architecture of the IGIMP consists of GUI Layer, Composer Layer, Service Layer, CCL(Component Communication Layer), CML(Component

Management Layer), Basic component layer. Table 1 shows the functions of six-layer architecture.

3   Scenarios and Case Study

System provider or facilities installers can make new component for physical sensor/actuators using Component Creator IDE(Integrated Development Environment). And then they registers new component into Component Repository. Figure 3 shows operation process for component creation. (1) Sensor component creation step using SCC(Sensor Component Creator); (2) Actuator component creation step using ACC(Actuator Component Creator);(3) Database component creation step using DCC(Database Component Creator). Each new component is registered. Using Component Creator IDE, system provider or facilities installers can develop some logic for actual sensor/actuators.

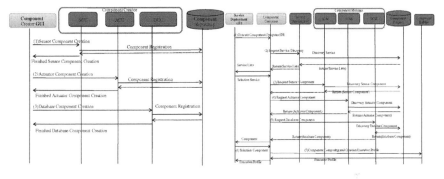

Fig. 3. Process of Component Creation (Left), Service Deployment (Right)

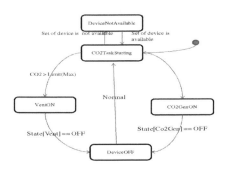

Fig. 4. Example of Component Scenario for CO_2 regulation

System provider installs applications for actual green house that consisted of component software for physical sensors and actuators. Figure 3 shows operation process for service deployment. (1) Service deployment step uses Component Composer IDE; (2) Discovery needed services for actual green house; (3) Discovery sensor components for actual green using SCM(Sensor Component Manager);(4) Discovery actuator components for actual green using ACM(Actuator Component Manager); (5) Discovery database components for actual green using DCM(Database Component Manager); (6) Select the needed components; (7) Create execution profile for deployment of physical green house.

To demonstrate the environment control and component-based system architecture, we designed two small plant factory prototype (2000(W) x 1900(D) x 2400(H) (mm). This is a kind of fully artificial light-type. Figure 4 shows the example of component scenario for CO_2 regulation. The proposed CO_2 regulation diagram uses limit value for CO_2. The diagram consists of five states: DeviceNotAvaiable, CO2TestStarting, VentON, CO2GenON, and DeviceOFF.

- CO2TaskStarting: This is the initial state. It branches to the VentON, CO2GenON, DeviceNotAvailable states depending on current CO_2 value or the sates of set of devices for regulation of CO_2.
- DeviceNotAvailable: This state indicates that the set of devices for regulation of CO_2 are not available. There are ventilation fan and CO_2 generators.
- VentON: This state means that the ventilation fan is turned on. If the CO_2 density is grower than Limit(Max), the ventilation fan is turned on.
- CO2GenON: This state means that the CO_2 generator is turned on. If the CO_2 density is grower than Limit(Min), the CO_2 generator is turned on.
- DeviceOFF: The set of related devices are turned off. Because device contention, it need to be checked the state of device before turn off.

4 Conclusions

In this paper, we introduce Intelligent Greenhouse Integrated Management Platform (IGIMP) that can support to provide a variety of plant factory type with the flexible service deployment. It can support a variety of greenhouses that is consisted of sensors and actuators. Therefore, it can easily upgrade an old greenhouse, and build a new greenhouse with low price. In the future, we implement sensor and actuators components for greenhouse of sunlight-type. Eventually, we expect that the proposed IGIMP will play an important role of greenhouse industry development by means of component-based architectures in various greenhouse types.

References

1. Aaslyng, J.M., Lund, J.B., Ehler, N., Rosenqvist, E.: IntelliGrow: a greenhouse component-based climate control system. Environmental Modeling & Software 18 (2003)
2. Aaslyng, J.M., Ehler, N., Jakobsen, L.: Climate Control Software Integration with a Greenhouse Environmental Control Computer. Environmental Modeling & Software 20 (2005)
3. Ahonen, T., Virrankoski, R., Elmusrati, M.: "Greenhouse Monitoring with Wireless Sensor Network. In: Proceeding of International Conference on Mechtronic and Embedded Systems and Applications (2008)
4. Kolokotsa, D., Saridakis, G., Dalamagkidis, K., Dolianitis, S., Kaliakatsos, I.: Development of an Intelligent Indoor Environment and Energy Management System for Greenhouses. Energy Conversion and Management 51 (2010)
5. Matijievics, I.: Advantages of Wireless Sensor Networks in Greenhouse Environment. In: Proc. of International Symposium on Intelligent Systems and Informatics (2009)
6. Xiao, J., Jiang, B., Jiang ming, K.: Design for Wireless Temperature and Humidity Monitoring System of the Intelligent Greenhouse. In: Proceeding of International Conference on Computer Engineering and Technology (2010)

Development of the Many Nodes Connected and Simple Operated HD Remote Lecture System by Automatic Control

Takeshi Sakurada[1], Yoichi Hagiwara[1], and Tadasuke Furuya[2]

[1] Information Media Center, Tokyo University of Agriculture and Technology,
2-24-16 Naka-cho, Koganei-shi, Tokyo, Japan
{take-s,hagi}@cc.tuat.ac.jp
[2] Faculty of Marine Technology, Tokyo University of Marine Science and Technology,
2-1-6 Ecchujima Koto-ku, Tokyo, Japan
tfuruya@kaiyodai.ac.jp

Abstract. We developed new HD remote lecture systems, which connected many universities in Japan. People can use this system easily, because people should only reserve the system through the web, then a system starts in ɖ eservetion time and sets the equipment automatically. Thus, this system can reduce a burden of a user. This system is a beginning in Japan, as for the remote lecture using a high-definition picture connected Japanese universities from the north to the south. We are expanding the system and total connection nodes number is over 36. We connect rooms nearby by this system and create some virtual big room. It is useful to connect not only the remote rooms but also neighborhood rooms together.

Keywords: Tele-conference, Remote Lecture, Automated system, High-Definition System.

1 Introduction

Before time, most Japanese universities have performed a remote lecture using Satellite communication system, which is called SCS (Space Collaboration System) [1][2] since around 1997. We also performed remote lectures, but we had many problems that trouble of machinery by deterioration, a satellite line linked down many times in SCS. In addition, a satellite connection fee was expensive, and a next system of SCS was necessary. Thus we must build a new system. It is necessary that the new system can be used same as using SCS. In addition, a system needs simple operations, stable running and multi-point bi-direct connection. In our plan, remote lectures will be held using new system and connecting 18 national universities in Japan (Obihiro University of Agriculture and Veterinary Medicine, Hirosaki University, Iwate University, Yamagata University, Ibaraki University, Utsunomiya University, Tokyo University of Agriculture and Technology, Gifu University, Shizuoka University, Tottori University, Shimane University, Yamaguchi University, Ehime University, Kagawa University, Kochi University, Saga University, Kagoshima University, University of

C. Stephanidis (Ed.): Posters, Part I, HCII 2011, CCIS 173, pp. 529–533, 2011.

Ryukyu). And new system is also required to hold parallel remote lectures connected several universities. In these lectures, documents, material or pictures are used for explaining. Thus the transmission of high quality video images is necessary.

2 Our System Design and Construction

2.1 New System Design and Choose Videoconference Devices

The following is necessary for a new system:

- Multi-directional communications that connected many sites at the same time
- Simple machinery operation
- Interoperability with the other videoconference systems
- Supported two screens with high-definition
- Provide high quality videos and sounds
- Many universities (more than 18 universities) can join same lecture.

To connect plural videoconference devices at the same time, MCU (Multipoint Control Unit) are necessary. Internal MCU of videoconference devices is only accepting 4-6 connections. We must connect over 20 nodes, we should use outside MCU device. We chose Polycom RMX2000-MPM+160 as MCU that could accept connection at 40 high-definition videoconference devices simultaneously.

Since many of Japanese universities are connected with SINET3 (The Science Information Network 3) [3], we use this network in this system.

A videoconference terminal, which was based on H.323 and SIP made by Polycom, Tandberg or Sony, has already introduced in many universities and companies. Because we think about interoperability with them and our constructing new system, we chose dedicated terminal type to our new system. In our new system, it is required to display high quality image of materials or documents at remote side, then we use a HD (High-Definition) system and this system has simultaneously two video image streams, a camera image and a PC (documents or material) image. Thus we use Polycom HDX-8006XLP, which supported two HD video streams, as base of our new videoconference system. HDX-8006XLP has interoperability with other HD and SD videoconference system made by other companies and has support 720p/60fps, 1080p/30fps video and stereo 22KHz sound.

2.2 Automation of Equipment Control

There are installed videoconference terminal only, equipment operations are difficult and system users are concerned. It is difficult to manage videoconference terminal because wireless remote commander of equipment has dozens of buttons. It is pushed the wireless remote commander of equipment carelessly, there are troubles that setting is changed, takes a sound mute and videoconferencing is finished.

We design the wireless touch panel and reservation system. And we do not let you use the wireless remote controllers attached to equipment. The reservation system eases operation of the devices by automation. On the other hand, we prepare wireless touch panel for operating a videoconference terminal, camera, and AV equipment (data projectors, large-sized monitors, a sound amplifier, matrix switcher, etc.) at the same time. Thus, we use a NI-3100 programmable system controller made by AMX corp. for local control. Reservation management system connects this controller by IP, performs to turn on and off automatically the remote monitor and operates the remote system from the distant place.

Fig. 1 shows installed equipment in each node. These are different in constitution by each node so that the facilities such as a video display unit or speakers are different by room size or the attendance number of people.

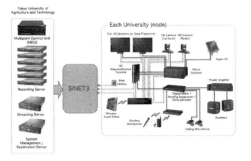

Fig. 1. System equipment

2.3 Reservation System Design and Construction

Fig. 2 shows a flow of using our constructed reservation management system. A user makes reservations by inputting the use date and time and connecting nodes into a reservation management system through the Web interface. The reservation management server starts up videoconference terminals and AV equipment by reserved connection plan before three minutes of the reservation time. It is about three minutes in time when equipment starts up. Then reservation management server makes a virtual meeting room in MCU and connects a videoconference terminal to MCU at reservation time. After one minute of the reservation end time, the reservation management system disconnects each node and shuts down AV equipment automatically. The system has few burdens of the user because it is automated.

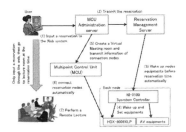

Fig. 2. How to use the system and system starts up automatically

2.4   Additional Design for Our New System

Some functions that became necessary came out at a stage of the construction.

People tend to exceed time when they concentrate on a meeting and a lecture. And it is difficult to extend reservation time from Web interface when holding a lecture or a meeting. Accordingly we design and construct extension function of reservation time. This function extends reservation time for 10 minutes when user selects the "Extend Meeting Time" on touch panel at one node. Therefore we set a notice announcement, "reservation end time comes soon", and system outputs the announcement from a speaker automatically before five minutes in reservation end time.

The connection of the videoconference is rarely breaking down by the state of the network. Fig. 3 shows reconnection function flow. If a user want to reconnect the system to virtual meeting room, touch the reservation time request button on the touch panel at a node. The touch panel connects reservation management server and search the reservation. If the node was to be connected by the reservation, a system displays reservation information on the touch panel and shows reconnect button. A user touch the reconnect button then the node is connected to the virtual meeting room.

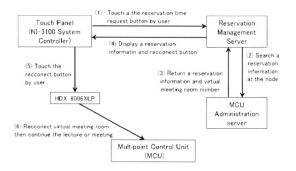

Fig. 3. Flow of reconnecting to remote conference

3   Using the System and Nodes Addition

The system that we made is already used [4]. Lectures and meetings were held 1115 times with this system for two year (from April, 2009 to January, 2011). In addition, it was used about 60 times for the briefing session of how to use the system and the test of the system. There are about 2 lectures and meetings per day. The extension function of reservation time was used 7 times. Many reservations seemed to have reserved time that was longer than the meeting plan. Reconnection function was used about 20 times. This function was used so that the network line to a node was unstable mainly when videoconference connection was down.

We thought that we used this system for the expansion of the room. In other words we connect rooms nearby by this system and create some virtual big room. And we add 13 nodes and total number of nodes is 36.

We sometimes connect four rooms of the neighborhood and hold lectures or conferences (Fig. 4). You can use the room without changing with a normally room because the system is automatically started. Therefore, it is useful to connect not only the remote rooms but also neighborhood rooms together.

Fig. 4. Flow of reconnecting to remote conference

4   Conclusion

We developed new HD remote lecture systems, which connected 18 Japanese national universities from north to south. This system is instead of SCS and many remote lectures are used our new system now. This system can reduce a burden of a user, because the user can use it with simple operation for reservation from Web, and a system starts automatically in reservation time and sets it. We designed an extension function of reservation time and a reconnection function, and we implemented these. These functions really understood that it was used. We are expanding the system and total connection nodes number is over 36. We connect rooms nearby by this system and create some virtual big room. It is useful to connect not only the remote rooms but also neighborhood rooms together. This system is a beginning in Japan, as for the remote lecture using a high-definition picture connected Japanese universities from the north to the south. In the future, this system makes advantage of usage with high quality videos and sounds, and it is expected to use widely.

Acknowledgments. We would like to thank Audio Visual Communications Ltd. for supporting construction this system. We want to thank 18 universities staff.

References

1. Kimio, K., Noritake, O.: Results of the Operation of Satellite Collaboration Network (SCS). IEIC Technical Report 106(1), 197–201 (2006), ISSN 0913-5685
2. National Institute of Multimedia Education Space Collaboration System, http://www.nime.ac.jp/SCS/
3. SINET3, http://www.sinet.ad.jp/
4. Sakurada, T., Hagiwara, Y., Furuya, T.: Construction of a Dual-HD Videoconference System For Remote Lectures Connecting 18 National Universities. In: 13th IASTED International Conference Internet and Multimedia Systems and Applications, pp. 124–130 (2009); ISBN 978-0-88986-804-5

Enhancing Flexibility of Production Systems by Self-optimization

Robert Schmitt[1,2], Carsten Wagels[1], Mario Isermann[2], and Marcel Mayer[3]

[1] Laboratory for Machine Tools and Production Engineering (WZL) of RWTH
Aachen University, Steinbachstr. 19, Aachen, Germany
[2] Fraunhofer Institute for Production Technology IPT,
Steinbachstr. 17, Aachen, Germany
[3] Institute of Industrial Engineering and Ergonomics of RWTH Aachen University,
Bergdriesch 27, Aachen, Germany
r.schmitt@wzl.rwth-aachen.de

Abstract. For establishing self-optimization in production technology, an extensive knowledge about the effects of process parameters on the product during the manufacturing processes is mandatory for the flexibility needed in complex production systems. In this regard, a controlling software that can autonomously detect this knowledge and use it for optimization is needed. Specific methods for the implementation of cognitive information processing are required. This paper focuses on the development of a self-optimizing controlling software architecture. In order to evaluate the optimization steps and simultaneously validate the rules used for it, an implementation for real production data of an automotive rear-axle-drive is described.

1 Introduction

Due to an increasing amount of competitive pressure, the manufacturing industry faces a difficult situation. New competitors, who typically generate their competitive advantage through lower labour costs, are steadily improving the technology of their production capabilities and create a massive cut-throat competition [1]. Companies are forced to innovate continuously to maintain their leadership in production technology. At the same time, production or labor costs must be decreased and productivity increased since changing consumers' behaviour demands that even innovative products have to be placed on the market at the lowest possible price. Additionally, differences between customers' requirements and the company's innovation targets complicate business [2].

Technologically demanding products are manufactured by adoption of modern production technology. The flexibility which is required for the ambitious technological processes needs a new kind of controlling mechanisms, which can only be reached by sophisticated optimizations.

C. Stephanidis (Ed.): Posters, Part I, HCII 2011, CCIS 173, pp. 534–538, 2011.

2   Cognition as Enabler for Self-optimization

2.1   Self-optimization

A self-optimizing factory is able to optimize the production processes concerning quality, costs and throughput time by repeating execution of the following actions [3]: 1) Continuous analysis of the as-is situation, 2) Identification of the objectives and 3) Adaptation of the system behavior in order to reach the objectives. Opposite to a classical regulation, a self-optimizing system is able to steadily redefine the various subobjectives and dynamically adapt the regulation process. Furthermore the ability of independent learning for target adaptation and variation of the regulation process, in this case the process chain, is required.

Self-optimization is connected to cognitive systems that gather information from their environment and convert it into actions which influence the environment. [4]

Such a cognitive system forms the core of a self-optimizing factory. [5] [6] The implementation of cognitive mechanisms on computer systems allows the analysis of big mounts of data and complex production processes with multi-layer dependencies.

In manufacturing, a cognitive, self-optimizing system modifies the production process by selectively changing tolerances in order to react to deviations of upstream process steps, which increases quality of the final product. In assembly, a cognitive system compensates dimension variations resulting from manufacturing by paring of individual parts and modifying actuating variables it.

During the inspection the data are collected and directly sent to upstream process steps and the cognitive system is able to detect correlations between production and product parameters of individual parts. In the following text, a cognitive software architecture will be suggested to be central element within the process chain.

2.2   Cognition

Processes that are executed by humans in their environment can be divided into three steps of information processing [7]:

Information input (Perception and interpretation): A physical stimulus is discovered or information is perceived through the various sense organs. This stimulus needs a certain threshold to be categorized as important. The interpretation follows the detection. The stimulus is compared to existing cognitive schemes.

Information processing (Decision): Having arrived at a receptor the stimulus is transformed into a cognitive representation and afterwards into a reaction. During their processing, the information is forwarded for task fulfilment. The decision is a conflict-solving process, which has to choose between several possible options.

Information output (Action): The information output process depends on the outer conditions and the constitution of the human being. It is important to exert influence on the environment. Human information output mostly takes places with the movement of body parts or speech. Both are controlled by the motion centers which are located in several brain regions.

3 Cognitive Software Architecture

In the project "Cognitive Tolerance Matching", a project of the Excellence Cluster "Integrative production technology for high-wage countries", a cognitive software architecture is being developed, with several layers and modules performing the actions of cognitive information processing (see Fig 1):

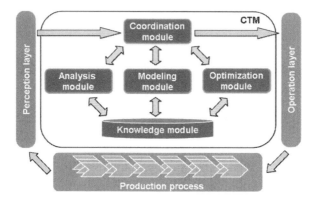

Fig. 1. Cognitive Software Architecture

The *Perception layer* acts as an interface for the production system. It collects sensor data and forwards it to the modules extracting information from it. The *Coordination module* is built as a C++-Framework and is responsible for the coordination and the internal communication of the different layers and modules. In the *Analysis module* a Pre-analysis of the considered data, accomplishment of correlation-analyses and data-reduction are implemented. The *Modeling module* includes a description of cause-and-effect chains of the production system to predict the result of single production steps focused in the optimization (3.1: ANN). The *Optimization module* is the Central part of the architecture. It autonomously generates optimization strategies and flexibly reacts to outer influences (3.1: Soar). The *knowledge module* contains relevant data as well as rules to derive decisions from it. The *operation layer* is responsible for the execution of the chosen optimization decisions and acts as interface to the production system's objects.

3.1 Cognitive Technologies

Cognitive perception of production data: As a first step data collection is a crucial factor. Given in the form of numerical values, the data can be analysed directly if production and analysis systems are connected. Data to be interpreted, e.g. the picture of contact patterns of gearbox components, need numerical values derive from it. One approach is image processing for the cognition of qualitative data.

Data mining operations performed by the analysis module: Data Mining tools and algorithms are used to detect structures within the production data and to derive optimization decision. They reduce model complexity by analysis of the influence of single parameters and hence help to focus on important data.

Optimization operations performed by Soar: In Soar, target-oriented problem solving takes place as a heuristic search in problem space. Operators are successively applied until the target situation is reached. The search in the problem space is implemented in a complex decision cycle. For knowledge representation, Soar offers two concepts: a short-term and a long-term memory.

In the first phase of information processing, productions of the long-term memory, which work on the working memory, become activated. New objects are generated, which in turn activate other productions and preferences, which are used in the second phase. Then, an operator is selected using the short-term memory. By successive application of operators, a target will be reached. In case of an impasse, problem space independent mechanisms like back-tracking are used. To avoid dead-ends, a chunking learning mechanism is activated each time a route out of a dead-end was found. Additionally, reinforcement learning remembers decisions by reward points. Soar is already used very successfully to simulate human behaviour [9], e.g. for robots and steering artificial enemies in flight simulators [10].

The modeling of the production system by ANN: Artificial Neural Networks are emergent systems with sub-symbolic information processing [11]. Artificial neurons emulate the processes of a biological nerve cell. Like them, artificial neurons possess input channels to detect signals as input values and one output channel to provide output values.

An ANN can be trained with sophisticated non-linear functions. The trained knowledge is represented in the weight structure of the neurons. In supervised learning, the network is trained with known input and corresponding output samples.

3.2 Interaction of Components

First, the model complexity is reduced by data mining algorithms to detect main influence parameters. Then, ANN emulate the behavior of the production system.

Soar generates decisions from existing rules and validates or extends them during their application. Soar learns from the effect of the particular application and transforms this knowledge into new rules. It varies those parameters, and ANN subsequently evaluate them. Hence Soar learns from the result by reinforcement learning to ensure an effective search in the space of possible production parameters.

The procedure is repeated until the results obtained by the neural network show conclusively that all product demands would be met in the actual production. Then this parameter set is used in the real production process and Soar will receive a success message. Otherwise, it learns from the miscalculations and corrects the rules used. If derivations occur, the network will be re-trained.

On the one hand, Soar considers fixed rules of known correlations in the production system, and on the other hand, reinforcement learning is used to obtain further process knowledge. Improvements can be achieved systematically and more quickly than by algorithms.

4 Current Applications

The appliance of the developed methods demands a use case which has been initiated in cooperation with RWTH Aachen University WZL, Fraunhofer IPT and BMW Group. For that purpose, a project to optimize the emitted acoustic of rear-axle-transmissions has been defined. The challenge lies in the holistic examination of the entire process chain, implying the production of the gear tooth system for power transmission and the complete assembly process of the differential. Focus is to analyze the interactions of the various tolerances and its impact on the rear-axle-drive's noise behaviour.

Acknowledgements. The authors would like to thank the German Research Foundation DFG for the kind support within the Cluster of Excellence "Integrative Production Technology for High-Wage Countries".

References

1. Tseng, M.: Industry Development Perspectives: Global Distribution of Work and Market. In: 2003 CIRP 53rd General Assembly, Montreal, Canada (2003)
2. Schmitt, R., Scharrenberg, C.: Planning, Control and Improvement of Cross-site Production Process Chains. In: Presented at the 2007 CIRP 40th National Seminar on Manufacturing Systems, Liverpool, GB (2007)
3. Schmitt, R., Beaujean, P.: Selbstoptimierende Produktionssysteme. ZWF - Zeitschrift für wirtschaftlichen Fabrikbetrieb 102(9), 520–524 (2007)
4. Strohner, H.: Kognitive Systeme. In: Eine Einführung in die Kognitionswissenschaft, Westdeutscher Verlag, Opladen (1995)
5. Zäh, M.F., et al.: The Cognitive Factory. In: ElMaraghy, H.A. (Hrsg.) Changeable and Reconfigurable Manufacturing Systems, Springer, Heidelberg (2008)
6. Zäh, M.F., et al.: Kognitive Produktionssysteme – auf dem Weg zur intelligenten Fabrik der Zukunft. ZWF-Zeitschrift für wirtschaftlichen Fabrikbetrieb 102(9), 525–530 (2007)
7. Schlick, C., Bruder, R., Luczak, H.: Arbeitswissenschaften. 3. Aufl. Springer, Berlin (2010)
8. Soar Technology, http://www.soartech.com (September 25, 2009)
9. Mayer, M., Odenthal, B., Faber, M., Kabuß, W., Kausch, B., Schlick, C.: Simulation of Human Cognition in Self-Optimizing Assembly Systems. In: Proceedings of 17th World Congress on Ergonomics IEA 2009, Beijing (2009)
10. Jones, R.M., Laird, J.E., Nielsen, P.E., Coulter, K.J., Kenny, P., Koss, F.V.: Automated Intelligent Pilots for Combat Flight Simulation. AI Magazine 20, 27–41 (1999)
11. Kratzer, K.: Neuronale Netze. Carl Hanser, München/Wien (1990)
12. Lehman, J., Rosenbloom, P.: A gental introducion to soar, an architecture for human cognition (2006)
13. Laird, J.E., Rosenbloom, P., Newell, A.: Chunking in soar: The anatomy of a general learning mechanism. Mach. Learn. 1(1), 11–46 (1986)
14. Sutton, R.S., Barto, A.G.: Reinforcement learning. Journal of Cognitive Neuroscience (1999)

Do They Use Different Set of Non-verbal Language in Turn-Taking in Distributed Conferences?

Hidekazu Tamaki, Suguru Higashino, Minoru Kobayashi, and Masayuki Ihara

NTT Cyber Solutions Laboratories, Nippon Telegraph and Telephone Corporation.
1-1Hikarinooka Yokosuka-Shi Kanagawa, Japan
{Hidekazu Tamaki,Minoru Kobayashi,Suguru Higashino,
Masayuki Ihara}@lab.ntt.co.jp

Abstract. Our aim is to create an environment where we can change a speaker smoothly. To avoid speech contention, we try to investigate what is the main reason of it. In this paper, we experimented to investigate what kind and how many non-verbal information appeared in distributed conferences. The result said that, non-verbal information such as nodding and back-channel feedback appeared decreasingly, even though they did conferences with video conference, no delay.

Keywords: Distributed conferences, Turn-taking, Non-verbal language.

1 Introduction

"Sorry, please go on!" This kind of phrase is often heard, when two or more attendees start to speak at the same time in Web conferences. Web conferencing is being widely adopted because people can save on installation and travel costs. However, Web conferencing systems provide somewhat limited video and voice quality than dedicated video conference systems[1]. The key reasons are that Web conferencing systems are established on best-effort networks, and that people participate via their desktop screens. Thus it is difficult for them to be aware of the other participants' movements and subtle face changes. Both deficiencies make it difficult to detect when others want to take the floor, and speech contention becomes frequent.

Our aim is to solve this problem and make an environment where they can turn-take smoothly. To solve this problem, we determine the cause of speech contentions in Web conferences. As you know, face-to-face communication avoids speech contention and realizes smooth turn-taking through the use of nonverbal information. We want to investigate what happens in Web conferences.

This paper presents an approach that we investigate what happens in Web conferences, experiment for first step of our approach, discussion of it and what we will plan to do next.

2 Approach

To solve the problem of the speech contention, we try to make an environment where they can turn-take smoothly. Therefore we have three things to do.

C. Stephanidis (Ed.): Posters, Part I, HCII 2011, CCIS 173, pp. 539–543, 2011.

1. To determine the cause of the speech contention
2. To make sure the key point to avoid the speech contention
3. To realize the environment that solve the problem of the speech contention.

To begin with, we tackled the first step of our approach, "To determine the cause of the speech contention". The process we planed to determine the cause of the speech contention is described following. We broke down the problem.

The biggest problem that two participants start to speak at the same time has two causes in our hypothesis. One is that a participant who is going to speak is not aware of that the other is also going to speak. And the other cause is that a participant who is going to speak is not aware of that the other starts speaking.

First we broke down the problem from the first cause above. Because if a participant was aware of that other is going to speak, she/he was able to avoid the speech contention. If our hypothesis was true, why participants were not aware of another was going to speak? As you know, face-to-face communication avoids speech contention through the use of nonverbal information [2]. We call some groups of motions common to people who wish to speak "pre-motions". In face-to-face communication, we know who seems to speak next from "pre-motions". In order to answer this question, we had to test that the reason of that participants could not be aware of who spoke next is that; they did not do "pre-motions" or they did the same "pre-motions" as in face-to-face communication but they did not carry.

3 Experiment

We conducted the experiment to investigate "pre-motions" appear or not in Web conferences. To analyze problem specify, four conditions were examined for the comparison; face-to-face, curtain, monitor and Web conference conditions.

3.1 Procedure

Four conditions described above were examined for the comparison; face-to-face condition, Curtain condition, Monitor condition and Web conferencing condition. All used the same discussion goal of brainstorming.

Each discussion lasted for 7 minutes for each condition and was active throughout this period. The order in which the conditions were used was set at random. A total of 56 men and women in their 20s to 50s participated in this experiment. They were split into 14 groups of 4 subjects. Before the experiment started, the subjects held a general conversation to develop some familiarity with each other.

Topics of the conferences were "generating ideas about the future of XXX". Where XXX was chosen from cars, houses, cell-phones, and TV; all discussions were intended to be quite informal, so that all subjects could make utterances easily.

3.2 Conditions

1. Face-to-face condition
   Four subjects sat around a table.

2. Curtain condition

Four subjects sat around a table. Curtains were set between each participant. They could not see each other.

3. Monitor condition

This condition was made by adding monitors and video cameras to curtain condition. They were set in front of each participant. Pictures of four participants were displayed on the divided area in the monitor.

4. Web conference condition

Four participants join the Web conference [3] by distributed room. Pictures of four participants were displayed on the divided area in the monitor.

The difference between the face-to-face condition and the monitor condition was that participants see each other directly or through the monitor. The difference between the face-to-face condition and the curtain condition was that there was visual information of other participants or not. And the difference between the monitor condition and the Web conference condition was that there was network delay or not.

For the face-to-face and curtain conditions, we used 1 camera per subject too to record each subject's bust image to observe their motions. The four pictures were displayed on a screen divided in quarters. Finally, we took videos of the screen. The voices were captured by a microphone hanging over the center of the table. For Web conference condition, we set a client machine and logged the proceedings by taking pictures of its screen, and also recording the voice streams. We analyzed the last 5 minutes of each discussion, because the subjects often did not immediately start discussing the intended topic.

3.3 Results

By checking the video of experiment, we counted "pre-motions" shown bellow that other researchers and we have already found when participants wish to speak.

1. Nodding
2. Back-channel feedback (using their voice to express a positive or negative attitude)
3. Laughing
4. Body motion (moving their body toward any side)
5. Hand motion (moving their hand to around their face)

Average number of each "pre-motion" in 5 minutes per group is shown bellow (figure 1, 2, 3, 4, 5).

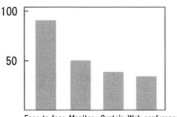

Fig. 1. Number of nodding

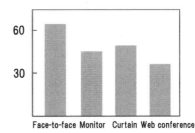

Fig. 2. Number of Back-channel feedback

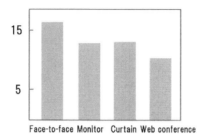

Fig. 3. Number of Laughing

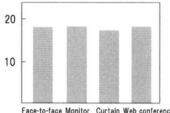

Fig. 4. Number of hand motions

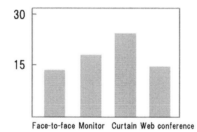

Fig. 5. Number of body motions

The result says that the largest number of nodding, back-channel feedback and laughing appeared in the face-to-face condition and the smallest number of that appeared in the Web conference condition. The difference between the numbers of these three "pre-motions" above in the face-to-face condition and in the monitor condition was much larger than that between the monitor condition and the Web conference condition. That shows that, people seem to do less nodding, back-channel feedback and laughing through monitor in communication, even though there is no network delay.

There were not large differences among the numbers of Hand motion and body motion in any conditions.

Nodding, back-channel feedback and laughing are used when they try to take a turn in face-to-face conferences. So we guess that, participants could not use these three "pre-motions" to take a turn through monitor in communication.

4 Conclusion

To realize the environment where participants can avoid the speech contention in remote communication, we are trying to determine the cause of it. The first step was to investigate whether they use "pre-motions" or not in Web conferences and why.

We conducted the experiment to compare the number of "pre-motions" that participants use in some different conditions. The result of it said that, people seem to use less nodding, back-channel feedback and laughing, which they use to take a turn in face-to-face communication, through monitor in communication.

Next step of our approach is that we test why they don't use "pre-motions" through monitor. We will make sure which is the reason; they cannot be aware of other participants' "pre-motions" or they have a feeling that their "pre-motions" do not carry other participants.

References

1. Sellen, A.J.: Remote Conversations: The Effects of Mediating Talk With Technology. Human-Computer Interaction 10, 401–444 (1995)
2. Vargas, M.F.: Louder than Words: an Introduction to Nonverbal Communication. Japan UNI Agency, Inc. (1987)
3. MeetingPlaza Information, http://www.meetingplaza.com/e/index.html

Floating 3D Video Conference

Kun-Lung Tseng, Wen-Chao Chen, Tung-Fa Liou, and Kang-Chou Lin

Electronics and Optoelectronics Research Laboratories,
Industrial Technology Research Institute, Hsinchu Taiwan
{KLTseng,Chaody,Alpha,gangchoulin}@itri.org.tw

Abstract. This paper proposes an improved algorithm based on Active Appearance Models (AAM) and applies on a real-time 3D video conference system with a novel 3D display device which can pop out an avatar out of the display in the air. The proposed algorithm utilizes an improved Adaboost algorithm [1] for face detection based on skin color information. Facial feature points are then tracked based on AAM [2] and we improved the algorithm to determine the rate of closing eyelid and the rotation angle of eyeballs. The novel 3D display device projects digital images on an actual human like object as an avatar and pops out a 3D image in the air via an optical module. With the proposed system, users can interactive intuitively with a popped 3D avatar. This system provides more realistic and representative visual effect for interaction in a video conference.

Keywords: Interaction, Floating, AAM.

1 Introduction

Human-Computer Interaction is a more important technique at this time. People hope to interact with computer via the movement of body instead of instructions. In order to detect user's movement accurately, we can utilize a sensor with special wavelength. When users attach the sensors, the system will get the movement of body by sensors and analysis it to execute the corresponding instructions. However, the attached sensors restrict the user. To avoid this, we will utilize a markerless tracking algorithm to detect the user movement and the user can interactive intuitively with system.

2 System Overview

In this chapter, we will introduce an improved algorithm based on Active Appearance Models (AAM) and Optic system. We will present the improved algorithm how to decrease the running time and detect eyes motion and the popped 3D image's features via the optic system.

2.1 Facial Expressions Tracking

Facial expression detection is an important part of Human-Computer Interaction. The system can use the result to detect the user's emotion and give him appropriate response. Active appearance models (AAM) fitting algorithm is a markerless facial

C. Stephanidis (Ed.): Posters, Part I, HCII 2011, CCIS 173, pp. 544–547, 2011.
© Springer-Verlag Berlin Heidelberg 2011

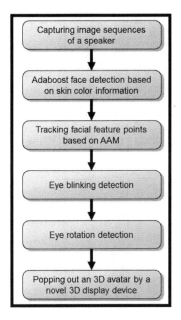

Fig. 1. The flowchart of the proposed system

tracking algorithm. Before tracking facial expressions, we have to select images with feature points and train database recording contour and color information of human faces. Utilizing the database information, system can fit the AAM to user's face and track user's facial expression by feature points. However, fitting an AAM to an image directly increases running time and error rate. The image includes not only human faces but also other things, but we only have to detect the area of human face. In order to detect the area of human face, the proposed system applies the Adaboost algorithm [1] for face detection. The detected result is often more than one candidate. Because we need to choose a candidate from the result and using this candidate to fit AAM, we will calculate the percentage of the pixel whose pixel value belongs to the range of human skin color. First, we change the image's color space from RGB to YCbCr so that we can remove the influence of ambient lighting. Second, we determine the region of human skin color in YCbCr color space. We will choose the highest candidate from the result to fit AAM. In this way, the running time and error rate are decreased substantially. However, the AAM algorithm can't track the rate of closing eyelid and the rotation angle of eyeballs. We propose a novel method based on AAM to detect eyeballs. We utilize the fitting result to get contours of eyes and calculate the gray level histogram. In order to remove the influence of ambient lighting, we set a special percent to detect eyeballs and accumulate the histogram from low to high. If the accumulative percent lower than the special percent, the value belongs to eyeball's color. In this way, we dynamic determine the threshold of eyeball's color and use the threshold to detect the rate of closing eyelid and the rotation angle of eyeballs. Utilizing information, user can do more interaction with the system (Fig.2-4).

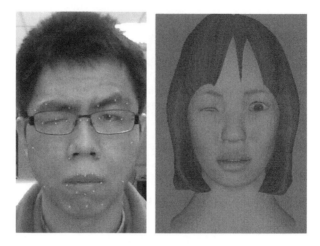

Fig. 2. Facial expression with eyelid tracking

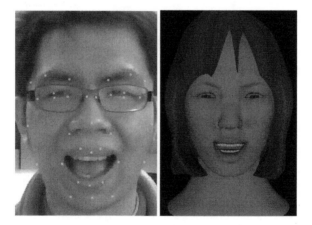

Fig. 3. Facial expression tracking result

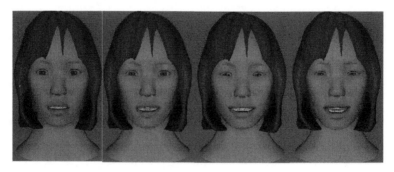

Fig. 4. Facial expression animation

2.2 Optic System

The novel 3D display device projects digital images on an actual human like object as an avatar and pops out a 3D image in the air via an optical module. Users can see the 3D image at 50 cm front of the system and interact with system. In this way, a vivid 3D object can be presented as a real image which is able to float in the air without causing crosstalk problems as traditional 3D display devices. (Fig.5)

Fig. 5. Floating 3D objects presentation

3 Conclusion

With the proposed system, users can see a 3D avatar in the air without any crosstalk problems in the air and interactive intuitively with a popped 3D avatar, which is animated with facial expressions and eye rotation and blinking. This system provides more realistic and representative visual effect for interaction in a video conference.

References

1. Ma, S., Du, T.: Improved Adaboost Face Detection. In: International Conference on Measuring Technology and Mechatronics Automation (ICMTMA), vol. 2, pp. 434–437 (2010)
2. Cootes, T.F., Edwards, G.J., Taylor, C.J.: Active appearance models. IEEE Transaction on Patent Analysis and Machine Intelligent (TPAMI) 23(6), 681–685 (2001)

Part VIII
Access to Information and Knowledge

User Interface Design for the Interactive Use of Online Spoken German Journalistic Texts for the International Public

Christina Alexandris

National and Kapodistrian University of Athens, Greece
calexandris@gs.uoa.gr

Abstract. A design of a user-interface for the interactive use of online spoken German journalistic texts is proposed to provide the in-context signalization of ambiguous or connotative linguistic and paralinguistic information to non-native speakers of the German language The online transcribed spoken journalistic texts are scanned by the proposed module and the User is presented with an output in the module's user-interface constituting the actual text with an in-context indication of all the instances of connotative linguistic and paralinguistic information, which are signalized according to error data obtained from European Union Projects and international MA courses for translators and journalists. The module is designed to be able to be compatible with most commercial transcription tools, some of which are available online.

Keywords: morphological processing, prosodic emphasis, paralinguistic elements.

1 User Requirements and Error Data

The present approach concerns a set of specifications for an annotation module and its user-interface for the interactive use of online spoken German journalistic texts. The proposed design targets to provide the in-context indication of ambiguous or connotative linguistic and paralinguistic information to non-native speakers of the German language, in particular, students, translators and journalists. The boundaries of possible differentiations in respect to the semantics of expressions become less evident in spoken journalistic texts, where they are highly context-dependent and determined by their usage in the language community.

For the successful implementation of the proposed module, a detailed approach to User Requirements is necessary [3], [8]. The target user-group usually has an above-average or even a fairly good fluency of a foreign language such as German or more than one foreign languages, but are either non-native speakers and/or often lack the necessary exposure to the culture related to the foreign language concerned, especially if the place of work/ correspondence changes frequently. Thus essential information in on-line texts presented either in a subtle form or in an indirect way ("explicitation", [4]), such as text-in-context relationships and socio-textual practices is often undetected. The international public is generally interested to be able to have an

C. Stephanidis (Ed.): Posters, Part I, HCII 2011, CCIS 173, pp. 551–555, 2011.
© Springer-Verlag Berlin Heidelberg 2011

insight in respect to a specific issue or event from a not always explicitly expressed insider's or an outsider's point of view or from an international perspective. Furthermore, the international public often has to make choices in respect to what types of online spoken/written journalistic texts to use for professional purposes and what types of online spoken/written journalistic texts to omit and/or discard. This decision-making process may be time-consuming, since the User is required to read or hear the text many times. Typical indicators of connotative features such as fixed expressions and idioms do not occur often enough in texts to signalize a point of view or attitude conveyed and many paralinguistic elements may be absent in some multimedia files, for instance in a cases where the speaker (for, example, a correspondent) is not visible. Furthermore, in languages such as Standard German, it is observed that speakers do not always demonstrate obvious changes in prosody when making subtle ironic statements, changes not easily detected by an international audience. Additionally, paralinguistic elements expressing speakers' or journalists' attitude may be misinterpreted or overlooked by an international audience, unless extreme emotions are expressed.

The proposed specifications and related annotation module is language-specific and its basic parameters are designed based on translational error-types retrieved from empirical data concerning the language pairs English, German and Greek. Most data involves mistranslations of spoken and written journalistic texts (data provided from graduate courses for professional translators), as well as failure to correctly interpret paralinguistic elements in online multimedia journalistic files by transcribers and professional journalists. The data was collected from graduate courses for journalists (M.A in Quality Journalism and Digital Technologies, Danube University at Krems, Athena- Research and Innovation Center in Information, Communication and Knowledge Technologies, Athens, Institution of Promotion of Journalism Ath.Vas. Botsi, Athens) and from data transcribed from spoken journalistic texts in European Union projects, especially the CIMWOS Project [9].

2   Combination with Transcription Tools and User Interface

The online transcribed spoken journalistic texts are scanned by the proposed morphologically-based module and the User is presented with an output in the module's user-interface constituting the actual text with an in-context indication of all the instances of (a) ambiguous or (b) connotative linguistic information and (c) language and culture-specific paralinguistic features, which are signalized in different categories, based on error data obtained from the above-mentioned sources [9]. These signalizations are the most commonly occurring types of such information observed in spoken German journalistic texts, namely (1) "Stress", (2) "Casual" and (3) "Non-neutral" and indicate elements stressed by the speaker (1), a casual tone (2) or connotative features (3) respectively. The module is designed to be able to be compatible with most commercial transcription tools, some of which are available online [10], [11] (Figure 1). Specifically, the module operates on keyword detection at morpheme-level or word-level based on interaction with a simple database which is, however, constructed on ontological principles, and may be visible and extended by the User. The database concerns a restricted set of word stems and suffixes as well as a defined set of verb stems that may be enriched. Incoming text may also be downloaded written journalistic texts from the internet such as blogs.

| www.visualsubsync.org | http://www.anvil-software.de/ |

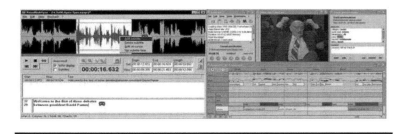

Fig. 1. Examples of commercial transcription tools available online

2.1 User Interaction and User Interface

The proposed module combines spoken words with paralinguistic elements, which are sometimes existent, such as in the case of prosodic emphasis, or sometimes they are non-existent or too subtle to be detected by non-native speakers. The combination of words with paralinguistic elements allows (a) a better understanding of the connotative elements in spoken texts and (b) may additionally also be used for research and development purposes in respect to mapping of spoken word and prosody and/or gesture. During the transcription written words belonging to the categories "STRESS", "CASUAL" and "NON-NEUTRAL" described in Section 3 are automatically highlighted. Sections with higher amplitude corresponding to prosodic emphasis are automatically selected and signalized, either from the automatically generated pitch contours provided by many available transcription systems or only as signalized peaks in amplitude in the simpler systems. The possibility of gestures, often occurring along with such words and prosodic emphasis, is retrieved in the respective temporal points in the wav file by the User.

User interaction may be described in three steps which correspond to three respective levels in the annotation module appended to the transcription tool employed by the User. In the first step, the User listens to the recorded speech and/or video and adds the respective text to the speech signal, a standard process for most transcription tools. When specific word types are written corresponding to possible connotative features, the proposed additional module highlights these word types in a respective color determined by the User (1). In the second step, the recorded speech and/or video can be replayed by the User. The points containing the previously highlighted words are compared to the speech signal and the respective tag, according to the amplitude of the speech signal, is produced namely "STRESS", "CASUAL" and "NON-NEUTRAL"(2). As an optional third step, the proposed annotation module allows the User to append additional comments, especially in respect to paralinguistic features not related to the speech signal such as facial expressions and gestures (3).

Table 1. Levels of proposed annotation module and transcription tool

AVAILABLE TRANSCRIPTION TOOL: Speech Signal and/or Video & Transcribed Text and annotation scheme /respective levels provided by tool
MODULE :
LEVEL 1: Automatic word spotting and highlighting & combination with speech signal and/or video in time
LEVEL 2: Mapping of highlighted words with speech signal and/or video in time & respective tag : "STRESS", "CASUAL", "NON-NEUTRAL"
LEVEL 3: (Optional) Template for additional comments by User (comparison with other paralinguistic elements)

3   Database: Combination of Word Categories with Paralinguistic Features

Words related to the tag "STRESS" for Spoken German are all word categories combined with prosodic stress, signalizing what the speaker considers important to underline and are detectable with a rise in amplitude in speech signal. The stressed words are of additional importance if they also coincide with the "NON-NEUTRAL" category described here. In less formal contexts, a casual and/or friendly or communicative attitude related to the tag "CASUAL" is signalized by specific sets of particles, adverbials and exclamations that are, however, not accompanied by prosodic stress. Typical examples are the expressions "doch", "eben", "gleich", "doch bitte" [1], [2]. In order to be classified as "CASUAL" elements, such words selected in text level should be accompanied by lack of prosodic emphasis, otherwise, they are marked as "STRESS" words.

The detection of specific sets of words is used in regard to the detection of "NON-NEUTRAL" elements. These words are often combined with paralinguistic elements. However, these features are not always present or not easily detectable by the international public. The detection of these words is based on the flouting of the Gricean Cooperativity Principle, especially in regard to the violation of the Maxims of Quality and Quantity [2], [6], [7]. Specifically, the strategy concerns morphological processing operating on (A) a word-stem basis [2] involving the detection of (1) adjectives and adverbials, containing semantic features related to (i) descriptive features (ii) mode (iii) malignant/benign action or (iv) emotional/ethical gravity, (2) verb-stems from verbs containing semantic features (including implied connotations in language use) related to (i) mode (ii) malignant/benign action or (iii) emotional/ethical gravity[2]. These verb stems are located low in an ontology, approachable with Selectional Restrictions [5] of the modifying type (and/or Wordnets). Morphological processing also operates on (B) a suffix basis involving the detection of (2) suffixes producing diminutives and (3) a predefined set of derivational suffixes resulting to a nominalization of verbs (derivational suffixes producing participles and actor thematic roles are excluded) or a verbalization or adjectivization of proper nouns. Thus, a specified and finite set of "marked" suffixes (such as, "-erei") is defined, as well as a defined group of "marked" verb-stems, such as "schuften" (partially equivalent to "to slave away"). Typical examples of the "NON-NEUTRAL" category occurring in the on-line spoken texts are the expressions "(ein) schoenes (Wahlversprechen)" ("that's some (ironic: great) pre-election promise) and "zurueckegerudert" (= to row back, used instead of the expression "to go back") (Speaker: Correspondent (Male), Spiegel Online, CDU/CSU-Wahlprogramm: Wer glaubt an Steuergeschenke? 29.06.2009).

4 Conclusions and Further Research

The present approach intends to capture the three most commonly occurring categories of lexical information related to paralinguistic information constituting connotative features in spoken German journalistic texts. For the international audience, the elements selected by the module can be "safer" pointers to the intentions and/or spirit of the speaker than most culture-specific paralinguistic elements related only to prosody and gesture. Further research in spoken German journalistic texts may provide more categories of connotative information not easily detectable to the international public. Implementation of the proposed annotation module to various user groups such as professionals and/or students will provide evaluation results for further development.

References

1. Alexandris, C.: Speech Acts and Prosodic Modeling in Service-Oriented Dialog Systems. In: Computer Science Research and Technology, Nova Science Publishers, Hauppauge (2010)
2. Alexandris, C.: English, German and the International "Semi-professional" Translator: A Morphological Approach to Implied Connotative Features. Journal of Language and Translation 11(2), 7–46 (2010)
3. Constantie, L.L., Lockwood, L.A.D.: Software for Use: A Practical Guide to the Models and Methods of Usage-Centered Design. Addison-Wesley, Reading (1996)
4. De Silva, R.: Explicitation in Media Translation: English Translation of Japanese Journalistic Texts. In: Proceedings of the 1st Portuguese Translation Conference, Caparica, Portugal (2006)
5. Gayral, F., Pernelle, N., Saint-Dizier, P.: On Verb Selectional Restrictions: Advantages and Limitations. In: Christodoulakis, D.N. (ed.) NLP 2000. LNCS (LNAI), vol. 1835, pp. 57–68. Springer, Heidelberg (2000)
6. Grice, H.P.: Studies in the Way of Words. Harvard University Press, Cambridge (1989)
7. Hatim, B.: Communication Across Cultures: Translation Theory and Contrastive Text Linguistics. University of Exeter Press, Exeter (1997)
8. Wiegers, K.E.: Software Requirements. Microsoft Press, Redmond (2005)
9. The CIMWOS Project, http://www.xanthi.ilsp.gr/cimwos/
10. Visualsubsync Subtitling tool, http://www.visualsubsync.org
11. Anvil Software transcription tool, http://www.anvil-software.de/

How the Shapes of School Emblems
for Colleges Convey Imagery

Mu-Chien Chou

Department of Digital Media Design, Chungyu Institute of Technology,
No.40, Yi 7th Rd., Xinyi District, Keelung City 201, Taiwan (R.O.C.)
chou.muchien@gmail.com

Abstract. School emblems express the spirit of the school, winning a sense of identification from teachers and students. We wonder if the imagery conveyed by school emblems is in agreement with how viewers feel. The following is a summary of our research results: (1) The horizontal axis in the imagery space is "fond - hateful"; the vertical axis is "concrete - abstract". School emblems are distributed in the space between the two axes. (2) The influences on imagery are simplified into four factors. The four factors, arranged in the order of importance, are "psychology", "shape", "times" and "strength". (3) In the design of school emblems, "circular", "club-shaped" and the like are more popular in Taiwan. In contrast, irregular forms are less welcomed and should be avoided when making emblems. (4) To give a sense of entirety, school emblems have to be closed figures. Circular and square emblems, in particular, have better completeness.

Keywords: shape of school emblem, convey imagery.

1 Introduction

A school emblem is a representation of its spirit. We wonder if viewers have a consistent feel about the imagery conveyed by school emblems, and what design elements and shapes can convey similar impressions. In consideration of this, we are conducting research on how the shapes of school emblems for colleges convey imagery, and expect to provide the results for reference in the field of emblem design.

This study has the following three purposes: (1) To search and collect school emblems for well-known colleges and make cluster analysis by card sorting; (2) to explore the connection of various school emblems with emotional vocabulary, and form cognition space for school emblem shapes by Multidimensional Scaling; and (3) to analyze the factor loadings of each pair of adjectives in each concept.

2 Literature Review

2.1 School Emblem Design

The term shape herein is similar to a German word, Gestaltung. It refers to a form with unified entirety. To give viewers comfortable sense of beauty, unity of

C. Stephanidis (Ed.): Posters, Part I, HCII 2011, CCIS 173, pp. 556–560, 2011.
© Springer-Verlag Berlin Heidelberg 2011

multiplicity is necessary [1]. For brand administration of a school, careful consideration should be given to such issue as how school emblem design clearly conveys the abstract managing philosophy with a concrete, visually distinguishable image, so that viewers can be deeply impressed.

2.2 Kansei Engineering and Method of Semantic Differential

Kansei engineering is a consumer-oriented technology created to develop and produce new products according to consumers' feelings and demand. Its definition goes as: "A technology transforming the public's feeling or imagery of a product into design elements [2]. Method of Semantic Differential (SD Method) was created by U.S. psychologist Osgood et al. This experimental method is to examine the testees' imagery for each sample product. The imagery is a form of synesthesia, a sensation felt when one of our sensory organs receives stimulation [3].

2.3 Multidimensional Scaling and Factor Analysis

Multidimensional Scaling (MDS) is a set of related statistical techniques often used in information visualization for exploring similarities or dissimilarities in data [4]. In some research, Factor Analysis is most often used to examine the validity of the data collected by questionnaire. This statistical method is using correlation coefficients to search for common factors of the questions in a questionnaire [5]. After card-classification of the school emblems and emotional vocabulary, the experiment was then conducted by questionnaire survey. The testees' cognition of the imagery conveyed by the school emblems was obtained by using MDS to analyze the factor scores.

3 Research Methods

In this study, we used cards to classify the samples and cluster analysis for statistical work. Next, questionnaire survey was carried out by using SD Method, and Factor Analysis Approach and Quantification Theory Type I were adopter to analyze the school emblem shapes. Twenty students from the graduate school of design cooperated in obtaining the samples of school emblems and emotional vocabulary. In the questionnaire phase, 40 high school students were selected and included in the survey, with SD Method used for evaluation. We got a response rate at 90% and 36 effective surveys. The testees sorted and sequenced 100 emblem cards and 100 pairs of opposing vocabulary on cards. They then selected the representative stimuli and their corresponding adjectives for cluster analysis. To build the imagery space for school emblem design, we used 20 shape designs for stimulus samples, and 7-point scale questionnaires with 20 pairs of adjectives on to conduct a survey for the students not design majors.

4 Result and Analysis

4.1 The Imagery Space in School Emblem Design

The imagery conveyed by school emblems for colleges needs to be elaborated by the relations between imagery space and vectors. The vectors of emotional vocabulary can be divided into several groups, and major two of them are as follows.

(a) Group 1: Six vectors like "unique-common", "outstanding-ordinary", "clever-clumsy", "fond-hateful", "noble-humble", and "pretty-ugly".
(b) Group 2: Five vectors like "concrete-abstract", "complete-split", "massy-linear", "organic-geometric", and "orderly-rebellious".

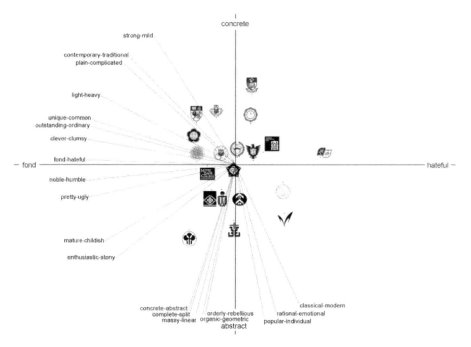

Fig. 1. The imagery space of school emblem design

From the imagery space of school emblem design, we can find that the two main axes are named after the pair of adjectives closest to the decided imagery in meaning. The horizontal axis is named "fond-hateful", and the vertical axis "concrete-abstract" (see Fig. 1.).

4.2 The Factor Analysis of School Emblem Design

The influences on imagery are simplified four major factors, whose eigenvalues are all greater than 1 and cumulative explained variance is 74.868%. The loadings of each variable are greater than 0.55. The four factors, arranged in the order of importance, are "psychology", "shape", "times" and "strength".

4.3   The Axial Investigation into School Emblem Design

We then picked four pairs of adjectives representative of each factor to further investigate into the imagery. They are "fond-hateful", "complete-split", "complicated-plain", and "mild-strong". Table 1 shows the sequence of projected stimuli on the vector of "fond-hateful". For the shapes of school emblems, we later found that the high school students not design majors have a preference for circular design, followed by club-shaped. In contrast, irregular forms are less welcomed.

Table 1. The sequence of projected stimuli on the vector of "fond-hateful"

Sequence	1	2	3	4	5	6	7	8	9	10
Stimuli										
Sequence	11	12	13	14	15	16	17	18	19	20
Stimuli										

For the vector of "complete-split", we found testees consider that closed figures give a sense of entirety. Circular and square emblems, in particular, have better completeness, although some of them are complex in design (see Table 2).

Table 2. The sequence of projected stimuli on the vector of "complete-split"

Sequence	1	2	3	4	5	6	7	8	9	10
Stimuli										
Sequence	11	12	13	14	15	16	17	18	19	20
Stimuli										

For the vector of "complicated-plain", testees all consider that an emblem containing too many design elements gives a sense of complexity. Combination of simple masses will give viewers a plain impression. From the result of Table 3, however, only opinions on the most complicated and the plainest designs are consistent; others are in disagreement.

Table 3. The sequence of projected stimuli on the vector of "complicated-plain"

Sequence	1	2	3	4	5	6	7	8	9	10
Stimuli										
Sequence	11	12	13	14	15	16	17	18	19	20
Stimuli										

The sequence of projected stimuli on the vector of "mild-strong" is shown in Table 4. From the sequencing result, we found testees consider that more complicated design gives milder impression; plainer design, on the contrary, gives a stronger feel.

Table 4. The sequence of projected stimuli on the vector of "mild-strong"

Sequence	1	2	3	4	5	6	7	8	9	10
Stimuli										
Sequence	11	12	13	14	15	16	17	18	19	20
Stimuli										

5   Conclusion

In the design of school emblems, "circular", "club-shaped" and the like are more popular in Taiwan. In contrast, irregular forms are less welcomed and should be avoided when making emblems. To give a sense of entirety, school emblems have to be closed figures. Circular and square emblems, in particular, have better completeness. In addition, the combination of too many design elements should be avoided in emblem design, as this will give a sense of complexity and separation. For a plain impression and strong feel, combination of simple masses is required.

References

1. Lewalski, Z.M.: Product Esthetics: An interpretation for designers. Design & Development Engineering Press, Carson City (1988)
2. Nagamachi, M.: Kansei Engineering: A new ergonomic consumer-oriented technology for product development. International Journal of Industrial Ergonomics 15(1), 3–11 (1995)
3. Osgood, C.E., Suci, C.J., Tannenbaum, P.H.: The measurement of meaning. University of Illinois Press, Urbana (1989)
4. Green, P.E., Frank, J.C., Scott, M.S.: Multidimensional Scaling: Concept and applications. Allyn & Bacon, Boston (1989)
5. Kline, P.: An easy guide to factor analysis. London, Routledge (1994)

Extensible CP-Based Autonomous Search

Broderick Crawford[1,2], Ricardo Soto[1], Carlos Castro[2], and Eric Monfroy[2,3]

[1] Pontificia Universidad Católica de Valparaíso, Chile
[2] Universidad Técnica Federico Santa María, Chile
[3] CNRS, LINA, Université de Nantes, France
{broderick.crawford,ricardo.soto}@ucv.cl,
{carlos.castro,eric.monfroy}@inf.utfsm.cl

Abstract. A main concern in Constraint Programming (CP) is to determine good variable and value order heuristics. However, this is known to be quite difficult as the effects on the solving process are rarely predictable. A novel solution to handle this concern is called Autonomous Search (AS), which is a special feature allowing an automatic reconfiguration of the solving process when a poor performance is detected. In this paper, we present a preliminary architecture for performing AS in CP. The idea is to perform an "on the fly" replacement of bad-performing heuristics by more promising ones. Another interesting feature of this architecture is its extensibility. It is possible to easily upgrade their components in order to improve the AS mechanism.

Keywords: Constraint Programming, Autonomous Search, Heuristic Search.

1 Introduction

Constraint Programming (CP) is known to be an efficient technology for modeling and solving constraint-based problems. It has emerged as a combination of ideas from different domains such as operation research, artificial intelligence, and programming languages. Currently, CP is largely used in diverse application areas, i.e., scheduling, configuration, diagnosis, engineering design, games, and bioinformatics. In CP, problems are formulated as Constraint Satisfaction Problems (CSP), which are defined by a triple $\mathcal{P} = \langle \mathcal{X}, \mathcal{D}, \mathcal{C} \rangle$, where $\mathcal{X}$ is an n-tuple of variables $\mathcal{X} = \langle x_1, x_2, \ldots, x_n \rangle$. $\mathcal{D}$ is a corresponding n-tuple of domains $\mathcal{D} = \langle D_1, D_2, \ldots, D_n \rangle$ such that $x_i \in D_i$, and D_i is a set of values, for $i = 1, \ldots, n$. $\mathcal{C}$ is an m-tuple of constraints $\mathcal{C} = \langle C_1, C_2, \ldots, C_m \rangle$, and a constraint C_j is defined as a subset of the Cartesian product of domains $D_{j_1} \times \cdots \times D_{j_{n_j}}$, for $j = 1, \ldots, m$. A solution to a CSP is an assignment $\{x_1 \rightarrow a_1, \ldots, x_n \rightarrow a_n\}$ such that $a_i \in D_i$ for $i = 1, \ldots, n$ and $(a_{j_1}, \ldots, a_{j_{n_j}}) \in C_j$, for $j = 1, \ldots, m$.

The common approach for solving CSPs is to employ a backtracking-like algorithm that interleaves two main phases: enumeration and propagation. In the enumeration phase, a value is assigned to a variable in order to check whether this instantiation is a feasible solution. The propagation attempts to prune the

C. Stephanidis (Ed.): Posters, Part I, HCII 2011, CCIS 173, pp. 561–565, 2011.

search space by filtering from domains the values that do not lead to any solution. The enumeration phase involves two important decisions: the order in which the variables and values are selected. This selection refers to the variable and value ordering heuristics, and jointly constitutes the enumeration strategy. It is well-known that those decisions are dramatically important in the performance of the solving process. However, to perform an a priori decision is hard, since the effects of the strategy are normally unpredictable.

Autonomous Search (AS) [2] is a special feature allowing systems to improve their performance by self-adaptation. This approach can smartly be applied to CP in order to reconfigure bad-performing processes produced by the use of an inappropriate heuristic. AS has been successfully applied in different solving and optimization techniques [3]. Among others, an interesting application is about parameter setting in evolutionary computing [5]. In this context, there exists a theoretical framework as well as different successful implementations. Unlike evolutionary computing, the AS-CP couple is more recent. A few works have reported promising results based on a similar theoretical framework [1], but little work has been done in developing extensible architectures for AS in CP.

The main advantage of AS in CP is to allow a self-adaptation of the search process when a poor performance is detected. The idea is to reconfigure the process by replacing bad-performing heuristics by more promising ones. In this paper, we present a preliminary architecture for implementing AS in CP. This new framework performs the replacement by measuring the quality of strategies through a choice function. The choice function determines the performance of a given strategy in a given amount of time. It is computed based upon a set of indicators and control parameters which are carefully adjusted by an optimizer. An important capability of this new framework is the possibility of easily update its components. This is useful for experimentation tasks. Developers are able to add new choice functions, new control parameter optimizers, and/or new ordering heuristics in order to test new AS approaches.

This paper is organized as follows. Section 2 presents the basic notions of CSP solving. The AS-CP architecture is described in Section 3, followed by the conclusion and future work.

2   CSP Solving

As previously mentioned, the basic idea for solving CSPs is to combine two main phases: enumeration and propagation. A general procedure for solving CSPs is depicted below.

```
load_CSP()
while NOT all_variables_fixed OR failure
   heuristic_variable_selection()
   heuristic_value_selection()
   propagate()
   if empty_domain_in_future_variable()
      shallow_backtrack()
   if empty_domain_in_current_variable()
      backtrack()
end_while
```

The goal is to iteratively generate partial solutions, backtracking when an inconsistency is detected, until a result is reached. The algorithm begins by loading the CSP model. Then, a while loop encloses a set of actions to be performed until fixing all the variables (i.e. assigning a consistent value) or a failure is detected (i.e. no solution is found). The first two enclosed actions correspond to the variable and value selection. The third action is responsible for the propagation phase. Finally, two conditions are included to perform backtracks. A shallow backtrack corresponds to try the next value available from the domain of the current variable, and the backtracking returns to the most recently instantiated variable that still has values to reach a solution.

3   Architecture

Our framework is supported by the architecture proposed in [4]. This architecture consists in 4 components: SOLVE, OBSERVATION, ANALYSIS and UPDATE. SOLVE runs a generic CSP solving algorithm. The enumeration strategies used are taken from the quality rank, which is controlled by the UPDATE component. OBSERVATION takes snapshots in order to store the relevant information of the resolution process. The ANALYSIS component studies those snapshots, evaluates the different strategies, and provides indicators to the UPDATE component. Some indicators used are for instance, number of variables fixed by propagation, number of shallow backtracks, number of backtracks as well as the current depth in the search tree. The UPDATE component makes decisions using the choice function. The choice function determines the performance of a given strategy in a given amount of time. It is calculated based on the indicators given by the ANALYSIS component and a set of control parameters computed by an optimizer.

Figure 1 depicts a general schema of the framework. The UPDATE component has been designed as a plug-in for the framework in order to easily be upgraded.

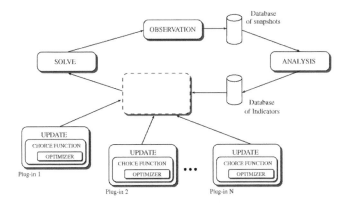

Fig. 1. Framework schema

Indeed, we have implemented a Java version of the UPDATE component which computes the choice function and optimizes its control parameters through a genetic algorithm. Another version of the UPDATE component, which is currently under implementation, uses a swarm optimizer.

3.1   The UPDATE Plug-In

In the current UPDATE component, we use a choice function [6] that ranks and chooses between different enumeration strategies at each step (a step is every time the solver is invoked to fix a variable by enumeration). For any enumeration strategy S_j, the choice function f in step n for S_j is defined by equation 1, where l is the number of indicators considered and α is the control parameter (it manages the relevance of the indicator within the choice function). Such control parameters are computed by the genetic algorithm, which attempt to find the values for which the backtracks are minimized.

$$f_n(S_j) = \sum_{i=1}^{l} \alpha_i f_{in}(S_j) \tag{1}$$

Additionally, to control the relevance of an indicator i for an strategy S_j in a period of time, we use a popular statistical technique for producing smoothed time series called exponential smoothing. The idea is to associate, for some indicators, greater importance to recent performance by exponentially decreasing weights to older observations. In this way, recent observations give relatively more weight that older ones. The exponential smoothing is applied to the computation of $f_{in}(S_j)$, which is defined by equations 2 and 3, where v_0 is the value of the indicator i for the strategy S_j in time 1, n is a given step of the process, β is the smoothing factor, and $0 < \beta < 1$.

$$f_{i1}(S_j) = v_0 \tag{2} \qquad f_{in}(S_j) = v_{n-1} + \beta_i f_{in-1}(S_j) \tag{3}$$

Let us note that the speed at which the older observations are smoothed (dampened) depends on β. When β is close to 0, dampening is quick and when it is close to 1, dampening is slow.

The general solving procedure including AS can be seen below.

```
load_CSP()
while NOT all_variables_fixed OR failure
   heuristic_variable_selection()
   heuristic_value_selection()
   propagate()
   if empty_domain_in_future_variable()
      shallow_backtrack()
   if empty_domain_in_current_variable()
      backtrack()
   calculate_indicators()
   calculate_choice_function()
   enum_strategy_selection()
end_while
```

Three new function calls have been included at the end: for calculating the indicators, the choice function, and for choosing promising strategies, that is, the ones with highest choice function. They are called after constraint propagation to compute the real effects of the strategy (some indicators may be impacted by the propagation).

4   Conclusion and Future Work

In this work, we have presented an extensible architecture for performing AS in CP. It allows the system self-adaptation by performing an automatic replacement of bad-performing heuristics. A main feature is perhaps the possibility of upgrading the UPDATE component. This allows users to modify or replace the choice function and/or the optimizer in order to perform new AS-CP experiments. The framework has been tested with different instances of several CP-benchmarks (send+more=money, N-queens, N-linear equations, self referential quiz, magic squares, sudoku, knight tour problem, etc) by using the already presented UPDATE component. A clear direction for future work is about adding new UPDATE components. This may involve to implement new optimizers as well as the study of new statistical methods for improving the choice function.

References

1. Crawford, B., Montecinos, M., Castro, C., Monfroy, E.: A hyperheuristic approach to select enumeration strategies in constraint programming. In: Proceedings of ACT 2009, pp. 265–267. IEEE Computer Society, Los Alamitos (2009)
2. Hamadi, Y., Monfroy, E., Saubion, F.: Special issue on autonomous search. Contraint Programming Letters 4 (2008)
3. Hamadi, Y., Monfroy, E., Saubion, F.: What is autonomous search? Technical Report MSR-TR-2008-80, Microsoft Research (2008)
4. Monfroy, E., Castro, C., Crawford, B.: Adaptive enumeration strategies and metabacktracks for constraint solving. In: Yakhno, T., Neuhold, E.J. (eds.) ADVIS 2006. LNCS, vol. 4243, pp. 354–363. Springer, Heidelberg (2006)
5. Robet, J., Lardeux, F., Saubion, F.: Autonomous control approach for local search. In: Stützle, T., Birattari, M., Hoos, H.H. (eds.) SLS 2009. LNCS, vol. 5752, pp. 130–134. Springer, Heidelberg (2009)
6. Soubeiga, E.: Development and Application of Hyperheuristics to Personnel Scheduling. PhD thesis, University of Nottingham School of Computer Science (2009)

A Hybrid Approach to User Activity Instrumentation in Software Applications

Martin Dostál and Zdenek Eichler

Dept. Computer Science
Palacký University Olomouc, 17. Listopadu 12
77146 OLOMOUC, Czech Republic
{dostal,eichlerz}@inf.upol.cz

Abstract. This paper introduces novel approach to logging user activity in software applications that provide accurate high-level information about issued commands, commands parameters and user interaction styles without a need for inferring user activity from logged user interfaces events as it is required on most loggers these days. We also demonstrate the proposed approach on a prototype implementation under the OpenOffice.org suite.

Keywords: usability instrumentation, understanding the user, user commands, user interface events.

1 Introduction

Automated capturing of user interaction is an integral and well established part of measuring usability. Although logging user interface events is one of the most commonly used techniques of instrumentation [1,4,6], it has serious limitations in situations where high-level, immediate and unambiguous information about user activity in an application is required since the recorded events must be further extensively processed in order to infer issued user commands from user interface events. Unfortunately, in some cases the user interface events do not provide enough information for correct inference of user commands. Linton [5] used a different technique to capture user activity which enables logging user activity at the level of user commands without processing user interface events. Unfortunately, his approach is unable to retrieve information about used interaction styles (e.g., whether a user command was initiated by a toolbar).

In this paper we introduce a hybrid approach to logging which advantageously combines the both mentioned techniques. Basically, our logging technique is based upon the user-command based logging which provides information about issued commands and their parameters (e.g., when InsertTable command is issued, the parameters contain information about a number of rows, columns and a table name). User command-based logging is surrounded by recording certain user interface events such as opening a menu or opening a window in order to infer information about used interaction style. The combination of the both logging techniques provide high-level, rich (user command and parameters used to issue the command) and accurate information about user activity including used interaction style. Next part of the paper introduces the OpenOffice.org

C. Stephanidis (Ed.): Posters, Part I, HCII 2011, CCIS 173, pp. 566–570, 2011.

Interceptor—a logging tool for the OpenOffice.org suite as a proof-of-concept implementation of the proposed hybrid approach. We also provide a description of the internal architecture and the background on the logging technique behind the Interceptor.

2   Techniques Used to Logging User Activity

In general, there are different approaches to capture user activity. This approach provides immediate and contextually rich information about user interaction with an application. Nevertheless, this way has serious limitations: it is time-consuming for the experimenter and thus not well suited for long term observations as well as for observing a broad group of users. Another, a more automated approach offers the screen recording systems which allow recording of the visual state of the screen and some low-level user events, such as mouse movements, clicks or key press events. The data is usually stored as a movie file. User activity can also be captured using loggers which automatically capture low-level or high-level user interface events or another type of appropriate events triggered by an application. The captured data is stored in a file called a *log*. This approach overcomes some disadvantages of human observation and screen recording systems; logging is usually light on system resources, the data can be further analyzed by corresponding software and logging can be used for short- as well as long-term analysis on a virtually arbitrary number of users.

2.1   Logging User Interface Events

Logging user interface events is based on recording low-level (e.g., keyboard input, cursor movement, mouse clicks or window resizing) and high-level (menu or toolbar selection) user interface events generated by running applications [3]. It represent the most widely used approach today. This approach is represented by MSTracker [6], AppMonitor [1] or RUI [4], for instance. User interface events-based logging provides very detailed, fine grained, low-level data which are useful for a certain kind of user studies such as determining optimal size and layout of user controls. On the other hand, for studies that focus on functionality of an application (e.g., which commands are used, how they are used, which parameter values are preferred) user interface events centered data is not well suited. Logged data must be further extensively processed in order to provide high-level, semantically rich information about user activity. We performed a simple experiment with RUI and AppMonitor loggers on logging a common user command for selecting the "Times New Roman" 14pt font in the font dialog in Microsoft Word 2003. RUI produced 1040 log entries, although due to the type of logged information it is not possible to extract information that the user performed a font change to "Times New Roman" 14pt. Using AppMonitor's default settings (that does not log low-level events) the same user command produced about 50 log entries. In our approach, such user activity would result in a single line of log file. Since MSTracker is not available for public use we could not perform the same experiment on this logger. Nevertheless, reportedly [6] a menu item selection would result in up to 150 lines in a log file. In addition, further log processing is an unwelcome property for applications which require an on-line, immediate and unambiguous response from the logging framework. This is the case of intelligent user interfaces which continuously track and evaluate user's activity in order to support the user.

2.2 User Command-Based Logging

User command-based logging has been used by Linton in the OWL [5] system to log user activity in Microsoft Word for Macintosh. In this approach, a logger directly captures issued user commands at the level of the underlying function call, not at the level of user interface events. The logging mechanism is thus entirely separated from the user interface elements. Unfortunately, it has one serious disadvantage; it is not possible to retrieve information about the interaction style (e.g., whether a user command was initiated by a toolbar button or a menu item) used to invoke the user command. For instance, if we invoke the "Open" command three times, firstly using a menu, secondly using a toolbar and thirdly using a keystroke, it will result in three identical log entries. User command-based logging has been used scarcely until today because there is no standard way to capture such information at the level of APIs provided by operating system.

2.3 A Hybrid Approach

We propose a hybrid approach to logging that advantageously combines the both mentioned approaches. Basically, our logging technique is based upon the user command-based logging. In order to enable logging of user commands including the information about used interaction style, we also process user interface events related to interaction styles such as opening a menu or opening a window. The information about the issued user command and logged user interface events is then processed using an interpreter that correctly assigns used interaction style to the corresponding user command. The interpretation of the data is non-trivial. We outline the interpretation algorithms used in the prototype implementation in Section 3.

2.4 Hybrid Approach Integration into Present Desktop Environments

Today's desktop environments strive for consistency and uniformity of applications not only in terms of user interfaces, but also to some extent to unify the internal architecture using various APIs or frameworks. For instance, modern desktop environments provide universal, system-wide APIs for managing user interface events, clipboard operations, undo/redo operations or accessibility (it provides the information about the contents of user interfaces for assistive technologies in order to meet specific needs of disabled people). Unfortunately, the problem with our hybrid approach is that the present environments do not provide such a standardized, system-wide API for logging user commands issued in applications. It makes the implementation of system-wide hybrid approach-based logger infeasible. However, such a simple "user command observing API" that would provide information on issued user commands and their parameters would be fairly easy for developers of desktop environments. In fact, it would be fairly similar to the implementation of an undo/redo framework which tracks issued commands and information on how to undo or redo changes caused by the command. The "user command observing API" would require information about the issued user command and parameters applied to the user command. For instance, when a user inserts a table named "Salary" which has two columns and four rows, the command would be "InsertTable" and parameters will be equal to: "TableName: Salary;Columns: 2;Rows: 4". The next

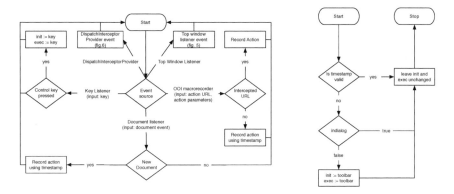

Fig. 1. The Logging Algorithm: The Main Part (left), Record action using timestamp (right)

section introduces the architecture behind the prototype implementation of the hybrid approach-based logger that operates under the OpenOffice.org suite. The "user command observing API" is there substituted by the built-in macro recording framework that provides the information about issued commands and their parameters.

3   Prototype Implementation under the OpenOffice.org Suite

This section describes the internal architecture, in particular the logging algorithm and some implementation issues of the Interceptor. The main algorithm is outlined on the left part of the Fig. 1. In fact, the depicted blocks of the logging algorithm is a way simplified. Most user commands imply that the logging algorithm must be performed repeatedly in order to assign used interaction style correctly. Note, the algorithm variables are not reinitialized at the start of each iteration of the logging algorithm.

   Most user commands and their parameters are logged by a custom macrorecorder which replaces the embedded one. Since we use the macrorecorder, Interceptor works under Writer and Calc only. However, some user commands are not macrorecordable. For those user commands we use a DispatchProviderInterceptor object (a part of the DispatchFramework) and a DocumentEventListener object (it listens for document-related events such as creating a new document).

   The main issue related to logging interaction style is that there is no straightforward way how to determine interaction style since user command calls are separated from the user interface events. Furthermore, a complication arises from the fact that the user command is logged after the originating user interface event. Nevertheless, the performed action must be associated with an originating interface event that was triggered by activation of the user command. We record events of a TopWindow - a general OpenOffice.org window object, represented by menus, pop-up menus and dialogs (not the system ones), and a keypress events (handled by a KeyListener). Also the Accessibility API is used in order to infer used interaction style. TopWindow events are used to inform about opening, closing or focus change of a TopWindow. We handle only certain kinds of a TopWindow, such as menus, pop-up menus and dialogs. A KeyListener is responsible for determining the keystroke interaction style.

The basic idea behind logging interaction styles is straightforward, see Fig. 1 (right): almost every user interface event initiate a setting of three variables: `timestamp` (current time in miliseconds), `init` and `exec` (interaction style used to initiate and execute user command, values depend on a particular user interface event). Therefore, when a user command is logged, the timestamp and current time values are compared. If the difference between the timestamp value and current time is less than 500 ms, then `init` and `exec` variables are proclaimed as valid and therefore, their values are used to identify the interaction style used to initiate and execute the user command. In other case, the variable values are considered as invalid and then in most cases we interpret such case as toolbar interaction style, since such a style neither do not cause opening or closing of any TopWindow, e.g., a menu or a dialog. The next important issue is related to handling dialogs, especially the non-modal ones. Between opening of non-modal dialog and executing user command from such a dialog the user can perform other user commands from other parts of application. That is why we handle an internal set of currently opened dialogs. This information is used when a dialog is used to execute a user command.

4   Summary

This paper introduced novel approach to logging user activity and a prototype implementation of the proposed approach. Since the architecture behind the logger has been outlined briefly we recommend a tech. report [2] that provides comprehensive implementation details. We believe that our logger could be useful to some other HCI researchers and practitioners and we provide the logger upon e-mail request for free use.

References

1. Alexander, J., Cockburn, A., Lobb, R.: Appmonitor: a tool for recording user actions in unmodified windows applications. Behavior Research Methods 40(2), 413–421 (2008), http://dx.doi.org/10.3758/BRM.40.2.413
2. Dostál, M., Eichler, Z.: The implementation of logging user activity in the openoffice.org interceptor. Tech. rep., Palacký University of Olomouc, Olomouc, Czech Republic (March 2010), http://dostal.inf.upol.cz/data/hci/ooi-techreport.pdf
3. Hilbert, D.M., Redmiles, D.F.: Extracting usability information from user interface events. ACM Comput. Surv. 32(4), 384–421 (2000)
4. Kukreja, Urmila, Stevenson, William, E., Ritter, Frank, E.: Rui: Recording user input from interfaces under windows and mac os x. Behavior Research Methods 38(4), 656–659 (2006)
5. Linton, F., Joy, D., Schaefer, H.P., Charron, A.: Owl: A recommender system for organization-wide learning. Educational Technology & Society 3(1) (2000)
6. Mcgrenere, J.: The Design and Evaluation of Multiple Interfaces: A Solution for Complex Software. Ph.D. thesis, University of Toronto (2002)

Web Resource Selection for Dialogue System Generating Natural Responses

Masashi Inoue[1,2], Takuya Matsuda[1], and Shoichi Yokoyama[1]

[1] Graduate School of Science and Engineering, Yamagata University, Yonezawa, Japan
[2] Collaborative Research Unit, National Institute of Informatics, Tokyo, Japan
mi@yz.yamagata-u.ac.jp

Abstract. Using Web information in example-based dialogue systems is considered to be a good way to increase the topical relevance of system responses. However, Web content is mostly written documents, not colloquial utterances. To alleviate the discrepancy in style between written and spoken language, we suggest that the corpus should be selected subsets of the Web, viz., online bulletin boards. The naturalness provided by casual utterances is especially important when the goal of a dialogue is chatting rather than formal question answering. By appropriately selecting the information source, our text-based dialogue system can generate friendly responses to users. These characteristics were evaluated with a questionnaire.

Keywords: Naturalness, Dialogue system, Web as corpus.

1 Introduction

In designing dialogue systems, two aspects must be considered. The first aspect is management of the dialogue's flow, and there have been statistical and rule-based studies on this [1]. The second aspect is refining the content of the textual responses. Chatting as entertainment is a functionality that we can expect from an advanced dialogue system that generates natural responses to user inputs. However, casual dialogue data are hard to collect. In this paper, we discuss our investigations into the utility of Web resources for this purpose. The style of Web text is an issue when using it as a corpus for a dialogue system. For example, although Wikipedia has plenty of well-organized entries, they are often too formal for the purpose of chatting. We overcame this problem in text style by utilizing an online bulletin forum as a corpus.

2 Colloquial Texts

We used the 2channel Internet bulletin board[1] as the source of natural colloquial utterances. This is considered to one of the biggest forums on the Web, and it was used in [2]. It has over a million posts per day, mostly in Japanese. Another smaller, but

---

[1] http://2ch.net

C. Stephanidis (Ed.): Posters, Part I, HCII 2011, CCIS 173, pp. 571–575, 2011.
© Springer-Verlag Berlin Heidelberg 2011

M. Inoue, T. Matsuda, and S. Yokoyama

still large Internet forum, is Slashdot. For example, 17,948 articles and about 3.8 million comments on it were analyzed in cross-media retrieval [3]. However, Slashdot mostly covers technical topics. 2channel contains many boards for users to discuss diverse topics ranging from "hacking" to "today's supper". The breadth of the topics in the target corpus may be disadvantageous when the system suggests quite minor topics that the majority of users have no interest in. To minimize such mismatches in interaction, we limited the topics to "trending" ones. Such topics are the most current ones on Internet forums, and it is likely that people will have something to say about them. There is a site that hosts trending topics[2]. Around 500 topics are posted every-day on this site. For each topic, 267 comments are posted on average[3]. The number is about ten times larger than the movie review site used in a previous study [4]. Of these 500 topics, we randomly selected five as candidates and presented them to users. Table 1 shows an example of the selected topic and comments associated with it.

Table 1. Example topic. Each topic has its original article and comments referring to it.

Topic
Cadburys says today's youngsters prefer lighter tastes - are they immature?

Article
According to a study by the candy maker Cadbury, the younger generation prefers lighter tastes. Cadburys says "The young people stick to simple seasonings … they are less interested in eating and having meals while they are playing games or using their mobile phones.

Comments
1 If you can appreciate lighter tastes, it means you have a sensitive tongue.   **2** Traditional seasoning is light.   …   **7** This is typical bad-mouthing of young people by the media.   **8** Bogus!   …

3 System Overview

The process of chatting is depicted in Table 2. Since the goal of this research was to investigate the utility of selective online resources, the base dialogue system was kept simple. It incorporated only those processes that were needed to generate minimally reasonable responses. Also, since we focused on the naturalness in single exchanges, we did not consider dialogue management. In step 1, topics with less than 100 comments were removed because the number of comments defines the pool of example utterances; fewer comments mean there is a smaller base of examples. About 51% of the topics contained more than 100 comments in our dataset. We found that the precision of keyword detection in step 5 was about 80%. In step 7, the scores of comments were calculated as the sum of frequencies of initial keywords and related terms in them.

---

[2] http://www.2nn.jp/
[3] accessed on 23rd Nov. 2009

Online bulletin boards were used to extract input-response patterns to generate utterances in the chat bot system [4]. In contrast, our system utilizes the original sentences to preserve its colloquialism and does not limit utterances to logical responses. We consider this aspect contributed to the naturalness both positively or negatively. In the future, we are going to analyze what constitutes naturalness.

Table 2. Illustrative flow of dialogue between a user and the system

	Internal Process	Visible Output and Input / [Internal Values]
1	The system shows a list of topics and the user selects a topic.	**System:** "Which topic do you want to talk about? *1: Cadburys says today's youngsters ...*" **User:** "1"
2	The system shows the details on the selected topic.	**System:** "The details on the topic are as follows: *According to a study by the candy maker Cadbury...*"
3	The user inputs a response freely.	**User:** "This is typical bad-mouthing of the young people by the media."
4	The system extracts nouns and noun phrases from user input through morphological analysis[4].	[*bad-mouthing, younger generation*]
5	It obtains keywords from the list by using the word scoring API[5].	[*younger generation*]
6	It obtains related words by searching the Web[6] and counting co-occurrences.	[*older, people*]
7	It ranks all comments based on the frequencies of the keyword and related words in them.	
8	It outputs highest ranked comment as its response.	**System:** "The older generation always wants to say something bad about younger people."
9	The user quits the interaction.	**User:** "Bye."

4 Evaluation

4.1 Experimental Setting

Although openings and closings in dialogues are considered to be important [5] to make dialogue systems more human-like, we focused on the naturalness of responses in the middle of the interactions under the assumption that such content was more influenced by the stored examples. That is, the goodness of interaction was measured by comparing the user input and system response texts (step 3 and 8 in Table 2). The results may change over time, since the system uses a Web API. Therefore, we did not let the participants use the system and instead showed them sample inputs and

---

[4] http://en.sourceforge.jp/projects/chasen-legacy/
[5] http://developer.yahoo.co.jp/webapi/jlp/keyphrase/v1/extract.html
[6] http://developer.yahoo.co.jp/webapi/search/

outputs in the form of a questionnaire. The sample inputs were randomly selected from example pools after eliminating meaningless sentences. Sample responses were generated by the system. This procedure also eliminates the influence of system speed and user interfaces.

The evaluation was conducted by asking volunteers to rate the utterances of our dialogue system. The participants were 30 undergraduate students majoring in computer science who were informed that the examples were taken from the output of dialogue systems. They were asked to rate the 10 sample responses made for each of the samples of input for the five topics in terms of naturalness and topical relevance. The scores ranged from one (not natural or not relevant) to five (very natural or very relevant). Naturalness did not necessarily correspond to the use of colloquial expressions because formal expressions might be construed as being more natural for some topics.

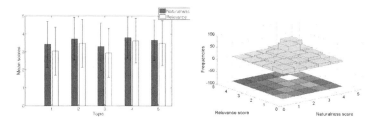

Fig. 1. Mean scores and standard deviations for five topics (left). Histograms for the first topics (right). The other four topics exhibit similar patterns.

4.2 Experimental Results

The average ratings awarded by the evaluators are plotted in the left graph of Figure 1. 300 scores were assigned to each topic. Although the scores for the same topic varied among evaluators and sample responses, as can be seen from the error bars, average naturalness scores exceed the borderline score 3.0 and the responses are categorized as natural. The right graph shows that there is a correlation between relevance and naturalness since the diagonal elements are most frequent. Kendall's τ coefficients for the five topics are 0.39, 0.55, 0.47, 0.64, and 0.57.

5 Discussion

Our experiment showed a positive result in term of naturalness. However, it should be noted that the naturalness scores might have been higher because young students participated in the experiment. The source collection contained a great deal of online jargon and dialects seen only in online communication. Such expressions may have been regarded as being friendly. In addition to the evaluators' demography, if the entire dialogue rather than a single message exchange were to be evaluated, the score would be lower. Furthermore, we need to figure out what influence different sources have. We are currently looking at Twitter as an alternative source.

6 Conclusions

We analyzed the effect of corpus selection on generating friendly responses by a chatting system. Our experiment suggested that the use of original expressions in an online forum as the system's output is a promising way of achieving naturalness. Besides our reliance on the intrinsic naturalness in a corpus, there are sentence modification approaches. For example, one can add disfluencies to system utterances [6], make sentences shorter [6], or add modalities [7]. We need to investigate the utility of a web corpus when such approaches are used to increase naturalness.

References

1. Xu, Y., Seneff, S.: Dialogue management based on entities and constraints. In: 11th Annual Meeting of the Special Interest Group in Discourse and Dialogue, pp. 87–90 (2010)
2. Ueno, M., Mori, N., Matsumoto, K.: Novel Chatterbot System Utilizing Web Information. Advances in Soft Computing 79, 605–612 (2010)
3. Potthast, M.: Measuring the Descriptiveness of Web Comments. In: 32nd International ACM SIGIR Conference on Research and Development in Information Retrieval, pp. 724–725 (2009)
4. Huang, J., Zhou, M., Yang, D.: Extracting Chatbot Knowledge from Online Discussion Forums. In: 20th International Joint Conference on Artificial Intelligence, pp. 423–428 (2007)
5. Cheepen, C., Monghan, J.: Designing for Naturalness in Automated Dialogues, ch. 11, pp. 127–142. Kluwer Academic Publishers, London (1999)
6. Marge, M., Miranda, M., Black, A.M., Rudnicky, A.I.: Towards Improving the Naturalness of Social Conversations with Dialogue Systems. In: 11th Annual Meeting of the Special Interest Group in Discourse and Dialogue, pp. 91–94 (2010)
7. Higuchi, S., Rzepka, R., Araki, K.: A Casual Conversation System Using Modality and Word Associations Retrieved from the Web. In: Conference on Empirical Methods in Natural Language Processing, pp. 382–390 (2008)

R&D Information System to Support
Knowledge Creation

Hyojeong Jin, Il Yeon Yeo, Youn-Gyou Kook, Byung-Hee Lee, and Jaesoo Kim

`{jin,ilyeon9,ykkook,bhlee,jaesoo}@kisti.re.kr`

Abstract. In this paper, we introduce a web-based national Research & Development (R&D) information system that is called 'Open R&D Knowledge Service'. It is based on the SECI model of knowledge creation theory for supporting knowledge creation process on a national basis. The R&D information system gathers and shares tacit and explicit R&D knowledge through three separate services – Open R&D encyclopedia service, Knowledge Q&A service and Precedent R&D Information service –utilizing crowdsourcing and accumulated government-funded R&D outcomes.

The system facilitates the conversion of individual tacit knowledge to national explicit knowledge and expands the existing national explicit knowledge.

Keywords: R&D Information system, Organizational knowledge, knowledge management, SECI model, Crowdsourcing.

1 Introduction

It becomes very significant for advancement of national science and technology to enhance the R&D knowledge creation since the knowledge is a core element in planning or performing R&D projects.

According to the SECI model proposed by Nonaka and Takeuchi which is one of the most widely accepted models for managing the knowledge, the knowledge is created through the spiraling knowledge processes of interactions between explicit and tacit knowledge. And the organizational knowledge creation is the process of making available and amplifying knowledge created by individuals as well as crystallizing and connecting the individual knowledge to an organization's knowledge system. In other words, ensuring what individuals come to know in their (work-) life benefits their colleagues and, eventually, the larger organization [1], [2].

In this paper, we consider systematic methods to support knowledge creation by applying SECI model and propose a web-based National R&D Information System that is called 'Open R&D Knowledge Service' to integrate and share R&D knowledge by utilizing crowdsourcing and accumulated national R&D outcomes database.

2 System Requirements Based on SECI Model

There are two types of knowledge, i.e., tacit and explicit knowledge. The tacit knowledge is normally gained from experience or intuition and difficult to state explicitly in

C. Stephanidis (Ed.): Posters, Part I, HCII 2011, CCIS 173, pp. 576–579, 2011.
© Springer-Verlag Berlin Heidelberg 2011

words, formulas or figures. On the other hand, the explicit knowledge is represented in a form of certain media and easily shared with others [1], [2], [3].

According to the SECI model, knowledge creation is a continuous process of dynamic interactions between the tacit and explicit knowledge. The four modes of knowledge conversion interact in the spiral of knowledge creation. The spiral becomes larger in scale as it moves up through organizational levels, and can trigger new spirals of knowledge creation [1], [2] (Fig.1).

- Socialization (tacit-to-tacit): where tacit knowledge is shared through shared experiences.
- Externalization (tacit-to-explicit): where tacit knowledge is articulated into explicit knowledge with the help of metaphors or analogies.
- Combination (explicit-to-explicit): where explicit knowledge is systemized and refined e.g. by utilizing information and communication technologies and existing databases.
- Internalization (explicit-to-tacit): where explicit knowledge is converted into tacit knowledge, e.g. by learning.

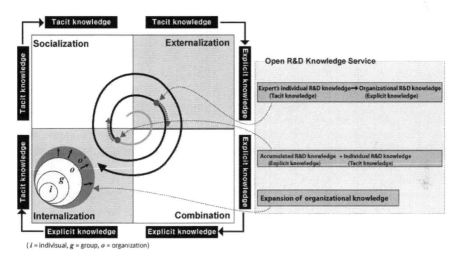

Fig. 1. SECI model & the proposed system's impact on the knowledge creation

By applying the SECI model, we suggest requirements of R&D Information System for R&D knowledge creation support, as follows.

- How to support the knowledge conversion process?
- How to support the expansion of the organizational knowledge scale?

To solve these requirements, the proposed system utilizes crowdsourcing based on open environment realized Web 2.0 and accumulated national R&D outcomes database.

In the open environment, users can draw up their tacit knowledge and easily interact with other users' knowledge or the existing organizational knowledge from database. Through this process, user's tacit knowledge is transformed into explicit knowledge, which expands existing organizational knowledge to new organizational knowledge. (Fig.1)

3 Providing Services in the System

The proposed R&D Information System that satisfies the two requirements provides three information services, 'R&D encyclopedia service', 'Knowledge Q&A service' and 'Precedent National R&D service', for sharing or concentrating R&D knowledge.

3.1 R&D Encyclopedia Service

R&D encyclopedia service aims to establish an encyclopedia in the field of R&D with the current and practical knowledge of the related experts. Experts who are selected from applications and recommendation from R&D management institute or government basically manage contents of R&D encyclopedia. R&D Encyclopedia experts engage in the whole contents life cycle, from an examination to deletion. Users can freely draw up their tacit knowledge (know-how, opinion, etc.), which are examined by experts before registration for reliability of contents.

This service also provides the link to concerned precedent National R&D outcomes. To search the concerned precedent National R&D outcomes in database, this service uses tagged metadata of contents.

By using this service, users' individual tacit knowledge can be transformed into organizational explicit knowledge and shared with other users, and the existing organizational explicit knowledge in database can be transformed into new organizational knowledge through interaction with users' tacit knowledge (the existing organizational explicit knowledge + the expert's tacit knowledge +users' tacit knowledge).

3.2 Knowledge Q&A Service

Knowledge Q&A service is question and answer service about R&D. There is no restriction or rule in this service, therefore users can freely ask any questions or draw up their tacit knowledge as answers.

This service enables to create new organizational knowledge (collective knowledge) with concentrating user's tacit knowledge.

3.3 Precedent R&D Information Service

Precedent R&D Information service provides R&D projects outcomes (e.g., reports) which are classified into success cases and failure cases.

Contents of this service are registered by user's voluntary registration and recommendation from R&D management institutes, hence accessibility to R&D cases can be improved, especially government-funded R&D projects.

This service enables to add user's tacit knowledge and shares through the discussion board of each R&D cases.

4 Conclusion

We introduced a national R&D information system that is capable of sharing R&D knowledge and interacting with tacit and explicit knowledge on national basis in this paper.

In this system, users can share their knowledge and create new knowledge based on national R&D knowledge of this system, and the related national institute can maximize the utilization of R&D Information and promote development of the national science and technology.

Acknowledgement. The introduced system is a part of NTIS (National Science & Technology Information Service), which is managed by NTIS Division of KISTI (Korea Institute of Science and Technology Information) and the Korea National Science and Technology Council.

References

[1] Nonaka, I., Takeuchi, H.: The Knowledge-Creating Company. Oxford University Press, Oxford (1995)
[2] Nonaka, I., von Krogh, G., Voelpel, S.: Organizational Knowledge Creation Theory: Evolutionary Paths and Future Advances. Organization Science 27(8), 1179–1208 (2006)
[3] Polanyi, M.: Tacit Dimension. Peter Smith Publisher Inc. (1983)
[4] Howe, J.: The Rise of Crowdsourcing. Wired 14(6), 1–10 (2006)
[5] Ahn, N.: A System Dynamics Model of Large R&D Program, Ph.D., MIT (1999)
[6] Blanning, R.W., David, K.: Organizations Intelligence, pp. 39–50. IEEE Computer Society Press, Los Alamitos (1995)
[7] Davenport, T., Jarvenpaa, S., Beers, M.: Improving knowledge work process. Sloan Management Review 37(4), 53–65 (1996)
[8] O'Leary, D.: Enterprise Knowledge Management. IEEE Computer 31(4), 54–61 (1998)

A New Method for Designing a Sitemap

Soheila Khodaparasti[1] and Marzieh Ahmadzadeh[2]

[1] Department of IT, e-Learning Faculty, Shiraz University, Iran
[2] Department of IT, Shiraz University of Technology, Shiraz, Iran
Soheila.khodaparasti@gmail.com, Ahmadzadeh@sutech.ac.ir

Abstract. Sitemap is a tool used by web designers to increase the accessibility of their site's information. The significance of sitemaps lies in providing their users with an overview of the contents of the website. In this article, a new method for designing a sitemap, which is based on different users need, is proposed. The customers of websites are usually at least one or two groups with specific information needs, needing to be provided with more help. In this proposed method, the requirements of these groups are first defined, and scenarios for moving through the site's pages are also recommended. These scenarios guide users to the right pages in a high level of quality (speed, ease of access and desirability of information). Each scenario leads to a page of website and may mark the other pages in its path. Using our designed sitemap, a proper understanding of the sitemap is expected.

Keywords: Sitemap, Website, Accessibility, Users' needs, Requirements, Scenario.

1 Introduction

The speed and quality of the users' accessibility to the required information in a website depends on two factors: web user skills and website structure. Frequent and experienced users can surf more quickly to access their required information than less experienced ones. An appropriate site architecture, including hyperlinks, information categorization, the logical and appropriate arrangement of hyperlinks, menus' options, and any other web guiding elements, can facilitate user's surfing and accessing to required information.

Although site navigation and menus can help users access their required information, it sometimes takes users considerable time to become acquainted with the site structure, and some useful information may not be noticed by users. Providing users with a quick overview of a site's sections can accelerate their accessibility to the required information. This facility is provided by sitemaps which are regarded indispensible by website designers.

Sitemaps, by offering an overview of web content, help users to be faster familiarized with a web structure and content. Sitemaps may take such diverse forms as alphabetical site indexes, categorized titles, and categorized titles along with subtitles. Sitemaps may be in the form of hyperlinks or plain texts. "Despite the prevalence of good sitemaps these days, users do not use them very much." [5] Based on the

C. Stephanidis (Ed.): Posters, Part I, HCII 2011, CCIS 173, pp. 580–583, 2011.
© Springer-Verlag Berlin Heidelberg 2011

research by Nielson Norman Group [5], the reason is the lack of knowledge of users about the presence of the sitemap. Therefore, it is necessary to notify the users somehow about the availability of sitemap. On the other hand, the inexperienced and unskilled users, even by using the sitemap, spend a considerable amount of time to find their needed information. The authors of this paper have encountered users who were not skilled enough to efficiently use the information provided in websites. Moreover, the provided regular sitemap has been of no help. This problem was even more serious when it came to visiting the crowded and complicated sitemaps such as large hospitals.

Usually for each website, there are a group of users who need more help and guidance. In this paper, we are seeking for a solution to improve the effectiveness of the sitemaps for this group of users, and we propose new version of sitemap that directs these users to their required information (or lead them to their desired web pages) by providing more guidance and supports.

2 Introducing the New Sitemap

In our introduced approach to design a sitemap, we identify the user groups who need more guidance and support. After determining the required information of this user groups, we identify the web-pages containing the corresponding information. Now, these identified pages are shown with special markings (bold, colored, reverse video, etc). The idea is to present the main respective pages with a certain color and the other associated pages with alternative colors. Consequently, the resultant sitemap proposes some distinctively colored pages to these users.

Our objective is to enable this group of users to quickly have access to these webpages after entering the website without much effort. Therefore, it is necessary that the users see a notice at the same time they enter the site, and they should be able to declare their purpose of visiting the site by selecting the available choices. Based upon their selection a customized sitemap should be presented.

Indeed, this notice should not impose any restriction for other users. Therefore, infrequent users are one click away from their required information and frequent users do not need to do any extra work.

3 Designing the New Sitemap

For implementation of the new sitemap, we first need to identify user groups based on their needs. This helps us to create a user profile. The profiles are obtained through analysis of requirements, interviews, polls and studies. Using these profiles, the information requirements of users are identified and then, they are categorized and prioritized. Based on the acquired results from profiles, the required website pages of users are also identified, categorized and prioritized. The marking of these pages in the sitemap leads into improvement in the usefulness of the new sitemap as compared to the conventional ones because following specifying the information requirement in the initial notice page, these users observe a sitemap that has specified the pages with distinctive colors and commensurate with their information needs.

In this sitemap the user can select more suitable pages or the ones with higher priority (bolder) ,these selections are considered as the first suggestions of the website, and if they are willing after visiting them, they can choose other colored pages (the pages containing related information) by returning to the sitemap. In this new sitemap, we focus on the routes that users should traverse to obtain their required information. For reaching to the required information of a certain user, one or several routes might be defined. These routes include the hyperlinks by successive selection of which the users can reach their destination (required information). We call the most suitable route for reaching a page containing the needed information "**user's circulation scenario**". This scenario is a route which is selected by the sitemap designers as the optimal route among all the existing routes and is used in designing the sitemap.

Each scenario is a sequence of hyperlinks. These hyperlinks may be located in separate pages of the website. In this case, the user proceeds towards their needed information after visiting successive pages corresponding to each hyperlink. In addition, these hyperlinks might be as part of a menu and in this case, the users can see the hyperlinks existing under each menu by selecting any of them, and they can proceed toward the respective information by selecting the next hyperlink. Therefore, every scenario leads into a final page of the website and; it can mark other relevant pages for users' application on its way. In comparison with conventional sitemaps, these scenarios guide users to the right pages in a higher level of quality (speed, ease of access and desirability of information). Thus, the defined scenarios for a specific user group indicate a set of pages and optimized ways for reaching the pages in the sitemap for a certain group of users. This marking can be done with specific colors. The destination page is specified with a certain color and the other related pages are specified with different relevant colors.

In this way, the new sitemap is like the same ordinary sitemap but due to markings of some pages based on the proposed scenarios of the site designer; it might provide the users with more information as compared to regular sitemaps. It helps the users to find the required pages in the shortest possible time and also to attain a suitable insight about the spatial situation of these pages.

We believe that comprehending the situation of the site is a crucial factor for users' familiarity with the structure of the site. They identify graphically their own situation and the situation of pages related to their information needs. The users see the pages suggested to them in the new sitemap. In addition to familiarity with the situation of each of the website pages, the users can decide to visit or not to visit those pages. The user can see the related pages recommended to them by the site (specified with other colors). These observations altogether result in a better and faster understanding about the site and help the user to obtain their required information more rapidly. As all the users do not need commonly used sitemaps, all of them do not require this new sitemap too. The proposed sitemap is recommended for aiding certain groups of users.

Practically, implementation of the new sitemap is not mandatory and reasonable for all groups of users because all the website users (including skilled users) do not need such supports (services). According to Nielson Norman Group [5], the sitemaps:

- *"They do not hurt people who do not use them.*
- *They do help a few people.*
- *They incur very little cost."*

These statements are also true concerning the new sitemaps, of course their cost is higher than commonly used sitemaps but instead, they provide more help to certain groups of users. We recommend that for some websites (such as hospitals website), the site's user groups shall be identified and an exclusive sitemap shall be designed for one or several groups of users, particularly when some groups are likely to be lost in the website regarding the extensive sections and information. The authors has not test the idea practically however users and stakeholders showed great interest to support the idea.

Therefore the future work will be to provide such a system, run an experiment to elicit detailed user requirements and to evaluate the effectiveness and efficiency of this proposed approach.

4 Conclusion

In this paper, a new method for designing a sitemap is proposed. The idea is to select a group of users who need more support. Then their requirements in terms of finding the relevant information are gathered and a proper scenario is defined. The defined scenarios for a specific user group mark a set of web pages as well as the paths to those pages. Referring to this sitemap, users can have a proper understanding of their location on the website, and they can also see the location of the web pages.

With this suggested method, we help first time users to recognize proper paths easily as efficient as frequent users. This approach will be useful for websites that their users have pre-identified needs. A user will be presented with a sitemap that is relevant to his/her choice of requested information. Frequent and advanced users will have no need to use such a sitemap.

References

1. Buede, D.: The Engineering Design of Systems: Models and Methods. John Wiley & Sons, Inc., Hoboken (2009)
2. Yip, A.: The Effects of Different Types of Site Maps on User's Performance in an Information-Searching Task. In: 13th International World Wide Web Conference on Alternate Track Papers & Posters, pp. 368–369. ACM, New York (2004)
3. Maguire, M., Bevan, N.: User Requirements Analysis: A Review of Supporting Methods. In: 17th IFIP World Computer Congress, pp. 133–148. Kluwer Academic Publishers, Montreal (2002)
4. Bernard, M.L., Chaparro, B.S.: Searching Within Websites: A Comparison of Three Types of Sitemap Menu Structures. In: IEA 2000/HFES 2000 Congress, pp. 441–444. HFES, Santa Monica (2000)
5. Tedesco, D., Schade, A., Pernice, K., Nielsen, J.: Site Map Usability. Technical Report, Nielsen Norman Group (2008)

On-line Handwritten Signature Verification Using Hidden Semi-Markov Model

Daw-Tung Lin and Yu-Chia Liao

Department of Computer Science and Information Engineering,
National Taipei University,
151, University Rd., San-Shia, New Taipei City, 237 Taiwan

Abstract. Handwritten signature has been extensively adopted as biometric for identity verification in daily life, as it is the most widely accepted personal authentication method. Automatic signature recognition technologies can definitely facilitate the verification process. Many research attempts and advances have occurred in this field, automatic signature verification still is a challenging and important issue. This work presents a novel and robust on-line signature verification approach using Hidden Semi-Markov Model (HSMM). The proposed system comprises three stages. First, dynamic features are extracted according to the local statistical information of velocity, acceleration, azimuth, altitude, and pressure. Next, the extracted features are normalized into unified observation length. To improve the verification accuracy, features with slight variation are clustered into the same class using K-means classification algorithm. Furthermore, the Forward-Backward algorithm is utilized to accelerate the computation of HSMM parameters. Finally, the system builds a unique HSMM for each identity and estimates the signature baseline in corresponding to the features. To assess the recognition performance of the proposed algorithm, experiments were conducted using SVC2004 signature database. Analytical results reveal that the proposed method is very promising.

Keywords: On-line handwritten signature verification, dynamic features, Hidden Semi-Markov Model, Forward-Backward algorithm.

1 Introduction

Handwritten signature biometrics is commonly adopted for person identity verification and authentication in daily life, such as authority of financial transaction and document approval, etc.. Automat recognition technologies can definitely facilitate the verification process. Many research attempts and advances have occurred in this field, automatic signature verification still is a challenging and important issue. Srihari *et al.* have done a comprehensive survey to online and offline handwritten signature recognition and applications [1]. Lai and Chen considered the virtual stroke feature and made a fusion of real and virtual stroke to develop Chinese signature verification systems [2]. Bovino *et al.* developed a multi-expert method which matches the position, velocity and

C. Stephanidis (Ed.): Posters, Part I, HCII 2011, CCIS 173, pp. 584–589, 2011.

acceleration of each stroke with weighting to verify handwritten signatures [3]. Martens *et al.* employed Dynamic Time Warping (DTW) for signature verification and improved the efficiency of DTW by modifyied feature extraction procedure [4]. Quan *et al.* developed an online signature verification system by fusing the HMM and Artificial Neural Network (ANN) [5]. Rigoll *et al.* utilized HMM and combined several features to classify the signature [6]. Fierrez *et al.* also made extensive discussions about feature extraction and model issue on the verification system using HMM [7]. This work presents a novel and robust on-line signature verification approach using Hidden Semi-Markov Model (HSMM).

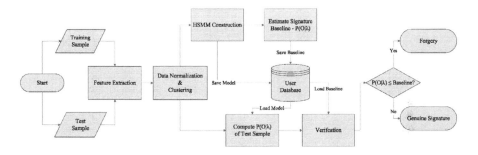

Fig. 1. System flowchart

2   Proposed System Architecture

The proposed system comprises three stages. Figure 1 depicts the flowchart of the proposed system and is described in detail as follows.

2.1   Feature Extraction

Generally, signature is captured from tablet device, on-line information such as velocity, acceleration and pressure is available. In this work, we employ various features for signature verification including velocity, acceleration, pressure, pen tilt orientation, and total signature time.

2.2   Data Normalization and Outlier Clustering

Due to slight variation of signature duration, the data captured from tablet device needs to be normalized to the same observation length or unit for further process. We divide the time sequence data into same number of frames for each signature. Then, the feature of each frame is represented by the average of all data in a single frame. Besides, although each signature has been unified to the same observation length, there are still too many outlier variations that the features could be. Thus, we adopt K-means algorithm to cluster the feature outliers for each signature. By clustering the feature value to limited classes and giving each class an index, signature feature representation can be simplified with limited types.

2.3   HSMM Construction and Verification

In this work, each signature was converted into a index sequence with the observation length T: $(I_1, I_2, ..., I_T)$. We employed the advanced version of HMM, Hidden Semi-Markov Model (HSMM), to perform signature verification [8]. Typically, signature is written starting from the first stroke. Therefore, we set $\pi_1 = 1$, while the other states are not activated, i.e. $\pi_2 = \pi_3 = \cdots = \pi_N = 0$, where π_i denote the probability of initial state i. Based on the specific signature strokes sequence of each person, the characteristics can be transferred and feeded into the HSMM. The state transition in HSMM is based on the variable duration of each state. In this work, we simplify and set each state with a constant duration, i.e. $d_1 = d_2 = d_3 = \cdots = d_N = 1$, so that the state number N is equal to the observation length T. Then, the HSMM state transition probability a_{ij} between state i and state j is determined by the time shift: $a_{ij} = 1$, if $j = i+1$; otherwise $a_{ij} = 0$. Suppose there are Q training sample sequences, the observation sequence $O^{(q)}$ for the q-th training sample is expressed as: $O^{(q)} = [I_1^{(q)}, I_2^{(q)}, ..., I_t^{(q)}, ..., I_T^{(q)}]$, where $I_t^{(q)}$ means the feature cluster index of the t-th observation point. Define $W(I_t^{(q)})$ as the weight of feature cluster index of each observation point and set $W(I_t^{(q)}) = 1$, if $I_t^{(q)} = k$; otherwise $W(I_t^{(q)}) = 0$. The probability of the feature cluster index k under state j is computed by accumulating the number of times that index k occurred under this state: $b_j(k) = \frac{\sum_{q=1}^{Q} \sum_{r=0}^{R-1} W(I_{1+r}^{(q)})}{Q \times R}$, where R is the number of observation points of state j. Since we assume each state with the constant duration $d = 1$, we set $R = 1$.

After establishing the initial HMM λ, we can compute the signature probability in model λ, i.e. finding $P(O|\lambda)$ to determine the verification result. Intuitively, $P(O|\lambda)$ can be obtained by the brute-force method, however it is time consuming. Instead, we employ Forward-Backward algorithm [9]. The forward variable is defined as $\alpha_t(i) = P(I_1, I_2, \cdots, I_t, S_t = i \mid \lambda)$, i.e, the probability of partial observation sequence, $I_1, I_2, \cdots, I_t$, (until time t and state i), given the model λ. Then we can solve the forward variable $\alpha_t(i)$ inductively as follows.

$$\text{Initialization:} \quad \alpha_1(i) = \pi_i b_i(I_1). \tag{1}$$

$$\text{Induction:} \quad \alpha_{t+1}(j) = [\sum_{i=1}^{N} \alpha_t(i) a_{ij}] b_j(I_{t+1}). \tag{2}$$

$$\text{Termination: } P(O|\lambda) = P(I_1, I_2, ..., I_T \mid \lambda) = \sum_{i=1}^{N} P(I_1, I_2, ..., I_T, S_T = i \mid \lambda) = \sum_{i=1}^{N} \alpha_T(i) \tag{3}$$

Equation (1) initializes the forward probabilities as the joint probability of state i and the initial cluster index I_1. Equation (2) shows the heart of forward process, which computes the probability that state j can be reached at time $t + 1$ from N possible states with observed index sequence $I_1 I_2 I_3 \cdots I_t$. Notice that we used the concept of HSMM as the main design to deal with the index sequence of signature, so there is only one state i at time t can reach state j at time

$t+1$. Next, Eq. (3) shows $P(O|\lambda)$ can be obtained by summing terminal forward variables $\alpha_T(i)$. The backward procedure is similar to the forward procedure by computing the backward variable $\beta_t(i)$ reversely in time. Finally, by fusing two procedures, the proper $P(O|\lambda)$ can be computed as follow :

$$
\begin{aligned}
P(O|\lambda) &= P(I_1, I_2, ..., I_t, ..., I_T \mid \lambda) \\
&= \sum_{i=1}^{N} P(I_1, I_2, ..., I_t, S_t = i \mid \lambda) P(I_{t+1}, ..., I_T \mid S_t = i, \lambda) \\
&= \sum_{i=1}^{N} \alpha_t(i) \beta_t(i)
\end{aligned}
\tag{4}
$$

Moreover, we can further compute $P_k(O|\lambda)$ for various types of feature (X types) and associate it with proper weights as: $P_{overall}(O|\lambda) = \sum_{k=1}^{X} P_k(O|\lambda) W_k$ Therefore, when several genuine signatures has been trained with user's HMM λ, and find an appropriate $P_{overall}(O|\lambda)$ as the baseline of user's signature, then a test sample can be verified by comparing the $P_{overall}(O|\lambda)$. The higher the $P_{overall}(O|\lambda)$ is, the more likely the signature is true.

3   Experimental Results

To assess the performance of the proposed system, experiments were conducted using 40 data sets consisting 1600 signatures of SVC2004 database with 20 genuine signatures and 20 skill forgeries in each set [10]. Five-fold cross validation was performed. To attain an ensemble accuracy, fifty complete five-fold cross-validations were performed on each database. The observation length T was set to 60, and the number of feature clusters is six. The complexity is reduced to $P(O|\lambda)$. Table 1 shows the experimental results of using single feature as the base of verification, and Table 2 shows the results when we associate multiple features with different weights.

Table 1. Experimental results using single feature

		Velocity	Acceleration	Azimuth	Altitude	Pressure
Training	EER mean	7.38%	9.25%	10.03%	15.45%	9.95%
Set	EER SD	4.75%	4.8%	6.78%	8.23%	8.33%
Test	EER mean	18.83%	23.88%	18.15%	26.8%	19.03%
Set	EER SD	11.66%	12.35%	12.33%	14.09%	14.14%

Table 2. Experimental results with multiple features

Feature	Weights							
Velocity	0.75	0.6	0.5	0.7	0.6	0.5	0.5	0.2
Acceleration	0	0	0	0	0	0	0.05	0.2
Azimuth	0.25	0.4	0.5	0.2	0.3	0.3	0.3	0.2
Altitude	0	0	0	0	0	0	0.05	0.2
Pressure	0	0	0	0.1	0.1	0.2	0.1	0.2
EER mean	15.93%	16%	16.03%	16.3%	16.28%	16.35%	17.7%	17.93%
EER SD	10.99%	11.09%	11.07%	11.44%	11.39%	11.52%	9.43%	9.48%

4   Conclusion

This work presents a novel and robust on-line signature verification approach using Hidden Semi-Markov Model (HSMM). The proposed system comprises three stages. First, dynamic features are extracted according to the local statistical information of velocity, acceleration, azimuth, altitude, and pressure. Next, the extracted features are normalized into unified observation length. To improve the verification accuracy, features with slight variation are clustered into the same class using K-means classification algorithm. Furthermore, the Forward-Backward algorithm is utilized to accelerate the computation of HSMM model. Finally, the system builds a unique HSMM for each identity and estimates the signature baseline in corresponding to the features. Analytical results reveal that the proposed method is very promising. This system is expected to further improve the performance and reliability by incorporating additional features such as virtual strokes.

References

1. Plamondon, R., Srihari, S.N.: Online and off-line handwriting recognition: a comprehensive survey. IEEE Transactions on Pattern Analysis and Machine Intelligence 22(1), 63–84 (2002)
2. Chen, J.H.: Chinese Signature Verification Using Combination of Real-Stroke and Virtual-Stroke Information. Master's thesis, National Central University (2005)
3. Bovino, L., Impedovo, S., Pirlo, G., Sarcinella, L.: Multi-expert verification of handwritten signatures. Document Analysis and Recognition 2, 932 (2003)
4. Martens, R., Claesen, L.: On-line signature verification by dynamic time-warping. In: Proceedings of the 13th International Conference on Pattern Recognition, vol. 3, pp. 38–42 (2002)
5. Quan, Z.H., Liu, K.H.: Online Signature Verification based on the Hybrid HMM/ANN model. IJCSNS 7(3), 313 (2007)
6. Rigoll, G., Kosmala, A.: A systematic comparison between on-line and off-line methods for signature verification with hidden Markov models. In: Fourteenth International Conference on Pattern Recognition, vol. 2, pp. 1755–1757 (2002)

7. Fierrez, J., Ortega-Garcia, J., Ramos, D., Gonzalez-Rodriguez, J.: HMM-based on-line signature verification: Feature extraction and signature modeling. Pattern Recognition Letters 28(16), 2325–2334 (2007)
8. Yu, S.Z.: Hidden semi-Markov models. Artificial Intelligence 174(2), 215–243 (2010)
9. Rabiner, L.R.: A tutorial on hidden Markov models and selected applications in speech recognition. Proceedings of the IEEE 77(2), 257–286 (1989)
10. Yeung, D.Y., Chang, H., Xiong, Y., George, S., Kashi, R., Matsumoto, T., Rigoll, G.: SVC2004: First international signature verification competition. Biometric Authentication, 1–30 (2004)

Accessing Previously Shared Interaction States through Natural Language

Arthi Murugesan[1], Derek Brock[2], Wende K. Frost[2], and Dennis Perzanowski[2]

[1] NRC/NRL Postdoctoral Fellow
[2] Naval Research Laboratory, 4555 Overlook Ave. S.W.,
Washington, DC 20375 USA
{Arthi.Murugesan.ctr,Derek.Brock,Wende.Frost,
Dennis.Perzanowski}@nrl.navy.mil

Abstract. An important ambition of human-computer interaction research is to develop interfaces that employ natural language in ways that meet users' expectations. Drawing on elements of Clark's account of language use, this idealized form of human-computer interaction can be viewed as a coordination problem involving agents who work together to convey and thus coordinate their interaction goals. In the modeling work presented here, a sequence of interrelated modules developed in the Polyscheme cognitive architecture is used to implement several stages of reasoning the user of a simple video application would expect an addressee—ultimately, the application—to work through, were the interaction goal to locate a scene they had previously viewed together.

Keywords: natural language; coordination problem; common ground; salience; solvability; cognitive modeling; Polyscheme.

1 Introduction

An important ambition of human-computer interaction research is to develop interfaces that employ natural language in ways that meet users' expectations. Drawing on elements of Clark's [1] account of language use, this idealized form of human-computer interaction can be viewed as a particular type of coordination problem [2] involving agents who work together to convey and thus coordinate their interaction goals. People rely on a procedural convention for doing this that can be summarized as follows: in posing a coordination problem for an addressee to solve, one is expected to set things up so that the effort needed to work out the intended solution is minimized. "Setting things up" entails the use of a system of straight-forward practices that includes 1) making the focus of the coordination problem explicit or salient and 2) posing a problem one expects the addressee can solve.

In the modeling work presented here, a sequence of interrelated modules are developed with the Polyscheme cognitive architecture [3]. These modules simulate the stages of reasoning a user of a simple video application [4] might expect a real person standing in for the application to execute, if the goal were to find a frame or scene in the video they had both seen at an earlier time. The user's verbal description of the

C. Stephanidis (Ed.): Posters, Part I, HCII 2011, CCIS 173, pp. 590–594, 2011.
© Springer-Verlag Berlin Heidelberg 2011

scene is treated as a coordination problem that the application must try to solve. Accordingly, each word and the higher-order semantics of the description—its conceptual references to objects, places, and events—are matched against a body of domain-specific lexical and schematic representations held by the application. Barring any failures at this level, the product of the preceding stages is then used to infer which scene, among those the user has previously inspected, is the one the user intends for the application to find.

2   Coordinating the Expression and Interpretation of Intentions

Natural language can be viewed as a collaborative means for expressing and interpreting intensions [5] through a body of widely shared conventions [2]. Clark [1] characterizes the challenge of conveying an intention from one agent to another—for example, from a speaker to an addressee—as a coordination problem that participants must work together to solve. To get to the intended solution, or a solution that will do, individuals routinely proceed in a conventional collaborative way. In particular, they rely on certain heuristic presumptions regarding a set of actions they expect to carry out together, which includes posing and grasping the problem and working out and acting on the result. Instantiations of three of these presumptions are modeled in this work from the point of view of the addressee. They are: 1) *common ground*—it is expected that the speaker has taken into account knowledge believed to be shared with the addressee as a basis for the words and actions that are used to convey the intention; 2) *salience*—the words and actions the speaker uses are expected to make identification of the intention and its implications prominent or obvious on the basis of common ground; and 3) *solvability*—the speaker is expected to have an intended result in mind and to have framed the expression of the intention so the addressee can readily "solve" or work out what the intended result must be and act on it.

3   Application Setup and Tools Used

The three heuristics cited above are implemented to work with a simple application that is loosely based on an experimental test bed known as InterTrack [4] used in the authors' lab for research on advanced traffic monitoring and user-interaction techniques. In this variant of InterTrack, a scene of interest is "shared" with the application by clicking somewhere in a video frame, which is then referred to as a "card." Automated identification of objects and events in shared scenes has not been implemented, so what the application "knows" about a specific scene is currently coded by hand. Once a shared card has been created, the user can then access it at a later time with a written sentence.

Computational implementation of natural language interactions is a complex undertaking that requires both cognitive modeling and linguistic tools. The Polyscheme cognitive architecture [3] is used in the present effort because of its role as the substrate for recent modeling work in sentence comprehension [6] and intention-based reasoning [7], which are both needed to model linguistic communication as a collaborative activity. Head-driven phrase structure grammar (HPSG) [8] is also used in the modeling work because of its lexical integration of syntax and semantic constraints and the computational advantages of its framework.

4 Modeling Expectations in Language Use

The models described in this section are conceived as a set of interrelated modules. Reasoning about the user's sentence input is performed at different levels in stages that roughly correspond to the heuristics outlined above. Although the presumption of common ground is addressed in grossly simplified terms, the salience and solvability heuristics are applied, respectively, to the utterance level of the user's sentence and, in two stages, to its linguistic and practical implications.

4.1 Common Ground

Because of the complexity in modeling common ground, we proceed on two simplifying assumptions, leaving certain issues for future investigation. First, the application interacts with only one user, and second, we only model the listener's interpretation, and do not address issues concerning a speaker's generation of language. In this simplified model, knowledge is limited to a subset of actions and objects in a vehicular traffic domain. HPSG feature structures of words are encoded in Polyscheme (Fig. 1).

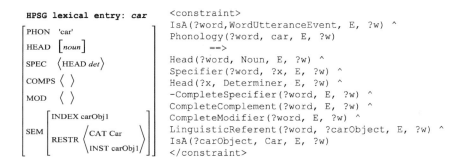

Fig. 1. The HPSG feature structure of the word "car" is shown on the left. On the right is its Polyscheme constraint in XML. Propositions on the right of the arrow ==> (consequents) are inferred from propositions on the left (antecedents). Note, "?" used as prefix denotes a variable.

4.2 Salience

Clark's principle of salience [1] suggests, roughly, that the ideal solution to a coordination problem is one that is most prominent between the agents with respect to their common ground. Thus, for example, when the user enters "…the red car…," it is expected that these words are intended to make objects tied to this phrase more prominent than other objects in the knowledge and experiences the user shares with the addressee. This effect is achieved with a reasoning "specialist" in Polyscheme.

4.3 Solvability

Stage 1—Natural language understanding. Although an addressee's syntactic, semantic, and pragmatic processing may overlap in real-world collaborations, these levels are currently staged in separate models. Basic syntax and semantics are thus handled first, producing a set of "atoms" such as those shown in Fig. 2.

```
IsA(car1, Car)                                 SpeakerOfUtterance(mePerson1)
Color(car1, red)                               IsA(displayEvent239,
IsA(car2, Car)                                 DisplayEvent)
Color(car2, black)                             Agent(displayEvent239,
IsA(passingEvent280, PassingEvent)             personListener242)
Agent(passingEvent280, car1)                   Beneficiary(displayEvent239,
Theme(passingEvent280, car2)                   mePerson2)
IsA(personListener242, Person)                 Theme(displayEvent239,
ListenerOfUtterance(personListener242)         passingEvent280)
IsA(mePerson1, Person)                         Mode(displayEvent239,Directive)
```

Fig. 2. Semantic output (simplified) after parsing "Show me the red car passing the black car"

This output is then processed by a second model in this stage that applies Polyscheme "constraints" representing common sense and domain knowledge to achieve a higher-level understanding of the user's sentence. The example in Fig. 3 shows how this model reasons about the higher-level implications of the atoms in Fig. 2.

```
DOMAIN KNOWLEDGE          COMMONSENSE KNOWLEDGE       INFERRED OUTPUT
<constraint>              <constraint>                Direction(car1,dir1)
IsA(?p,PassingEvent,      IsA(?u,Person,E,?w)         Direction(car2,dir1)
E,?w)  ^                  ^ListenerOfUtterance(       InMotion(car1)
Agent(?p,?pOb,E,?w)       ?u,E,?w)                    InMotion(car2)
   (.9)>                  ==>                         IsA(user1OfIntertrack,
InMotion(?pOb,?t,?w)      LiteralReferenceOfMeta-     Person)
</constraint>            phor(?u,                     SpeakerOfUtterance(
                         IntertrackApplica-           user1OfIntertrack)
                         tion,E,?w)                   LiteralReferenceOfMeta-
                         </constraint>                phor(listener242,
                                                      IntertrackApplication)
```

Fig. 3. Examples of domain and commonsense knowledge constraints: (left) the agent of a passing event is in motion with a probability of 0.9; (middle) the application is the addressee (listener). The atoms on the right are inferred based on the semantics from Fig. 2.

Stage 2—Task recognition. When one agent's intentions must be grasped and acted upon by another, addressees presume the speaker has a practical task outcome in mind they can recognize and help achieve. Hence, in this stage, the model marks a recognized directive or a question as an expected task (Fig. 4 left), and, barring any problems, executes the appropriate application command (Fig. 4 right).

```
<constraint>
Mode(?entity, Directive, E, ?w) ^
Agent(?entity, ?entsAgent, E, ?w)
^ LiteralReferenceOfMetaphor(
?entsAgent,IntertrackApplication,
E, ?w)
  ==>
ExpectedTask(?entity, E, ?w)
</constraint>
```

```
<constraint>
ExpectedTask(?entity, E, ?w) ^
IsA(?entity, DisplayEvent, E, ?w)^
Ability(IntertrackApplication,
DisplayEvent, E, ?w) ^
Theme(?entity,  sceneToBeDisplayed,
E, ?w)
  ==>
Perform-
Task(MatchCardWithAnswerWorld,
?sceneToBeDisplayed, E, R)
</constraint>
```

Fig. 4. Example of task identification (left) and application processing capability (right)

5   Conclusions and Future Directions

Modeling coordinated activity between agents has the potential to offer more flexibility to users than other types of interfaces, e.g., menu-driven systems. The models outlined here focus on an addressee's heuristic expectations of a speaker's use of common ground, salience, and solvability in the coordination of meaning and understanding. Related heuristics that remain to be modeled are those of sufficiency and immediacy [1]. An advantage of modeling these stages of an addressee's processing is the ability to identify the precise nature of the problem when coordination failures requiring repairs arise. In future work, models of repair will be pursued by allowing the user to correct or clarify various types of misunderstandings such as the use of unfamiliar words or the inability to perform a particular task, etc.

References

1. Clark, H.H.: Using Language. Cambridge University Press, Cambridge (1996)
2. Lewis, D.K.: Convention. Harvard University Press, Cambridge, MA (1969)
3. Cassimatis, N.L.: A Cognitive Substrate for Achieving Human-Level Intelligence. AI Magazine 27(2), 45–56 (2006)
4. Pless, R., Jacobs, N., Dixon, M., Hartley, R., Baker, P., Brock, D., Cassimatis, N., Perzanowski, D.: Persistence and Tracking: Putting Vehicles and Trajectories in Context. In: 38th IEEE Applied Imagery Pattern Recognition Workshop, Washington, DC (2009)
5. Allen, J., Perrault, R.: Analyzing Intentions in Utterances. Artificial Intelligence 15(3), 143–178 (1980)
6. Murugesan, A., Cassimatis, N.L.: A Model of Syntactic Parsing Based on Domain-General Cognitive Mechanisms. In: Proceedings of the 28th Annual Conference of Cognitive Science Society, Vancouver, pp. 1850–1855 (2006)
7. Bello, P., Cassimatis, N.L.: Understanding Other Minds: A Cognitive Modeling Approach. In: Proceedings of the 7th International Conference on Cognitive Modeling, Trieste (2006)
8. Sag, I.A., Wasow, T., Bender, E.: Syntactic Theory: A Formal Introduction, 2nd edn. University of Chicago Press, Chicago (2003)

Japanese Sentence Input Method
Using Acceleration Sensor

Masaki Sugimoto[1], Kazufumi Nakai[1], Nobuo Ezaki[1], and Kimiyasu Kiyota[2]

[1] Toba National College of Maritime Technology 1-1 Ikegami-cho,
Toba-shi, Mie, 517-8501 Japan
[2] Kumamoto College of Technology 2659-2 Suya, Koushi-shi, Kumamoto, 861-1102 Japan
{sugimoto,nakai-k,ezaki}@ezaki-lab.com,
kkiyota@kumamoto-nct.ac.jp

Abstract. Digital pens are used for character input method without training. Some lecture support systems were developed by using pen input, because of collecting remarks of student in a real time. We proposed a lecture support system by using Wiimote for character input method. Because Wiimote has 3D acceleration sensor, a student writes a character in the air, and our system can recognize a written character. After that the recognized character is displayed on an electronic blackboard. We are using two recognition algorithms by only real-stroke. And we adopt the error correction method by using a tree search algorithm that uses word dictionary. The Japanese characters used in this paper are Hiragana (71 characters), Katakana (71 characters), Kanji (1006 characters taught elementary schools in Japanese) and numerals. The recognition accuracy was 78.9%. Also, the recognition accuracy of phrase was 91.7% by bi-gram model. We confirmed the required performance for utilization.

Keywords: Character Recognition, Wiimote, Gesture Recognition, N-gram Model.

1 Introduction

Digital pens are used for character input method without training. Some lecture support systems were developed by using pen input, because of collecting remarks of student in a real time. We proposed a lecture support system by using Wiimote for character input method. Because Wiimote has 3D acceleration sensor, a student writes a character in the air, and our system can recognize a written character. After that the recognized character is displayed on an electronic blackboard. The advantage of our system is simple equipment investment.to aggregate student's opinion, other systems need input device such as a pair of pen-tablet and personal computer for each student, but out system enable it with Wiimote only.

We are using two recognition algorithms by only real-stroke. However, it was difficult to distinguish similar characters to use these methods that are the recognition algorithm for the one character order. Therefore we adapt the error correction method by using a tree search algorithm that uses word dictionary.

C. Stephanidis (Ed.): Posters, Part I, HCII 2011, CCIS 173, pp. 595–599, 2011.
© Springer-Verlag Berlin Heidelberg 2011

2   Input Method of Japanese Sentence by Using Wiimote

The way of writing a letter is: users push the "B" button, and release it whenever they finish writing one stroke. And, users push the "A" button when they finish writing one letter.

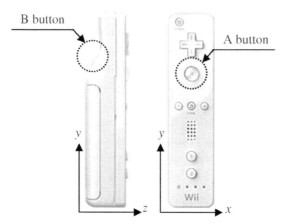

Fig. 1. Wiimote and axes

3   Improvement of Character Recognition Method

3.1   Reconstruction of Written Character Shape

We adopted bi-axial accelerations (x-z plane) gotten from tri-axial acceleration sensor of Wii remote. This method is described below. As a preparation, we integrate acceleration got from acceleration sensor of Wii remote, and calculate velocity. Then, we integrate it again, and calculate trajectory of Wiimote. But, gravity acceleration is always included in z-axis. We have to rid gravity acceleration for us to calculate trajectory. When analyzing frequencies of acceleration, we realized that the frequency of gravity acceleration appeared as DC component. So, we removed gravity acceleration by using high-pass filter. Figure 2 shows reconstructed characters of Japanese.

Fig. 2. Reconstructed shapes

3.2 Character Recognition Method

Written characters are recognized by using trajectory gotten from preparation. Two kinds of character recognition algorithm; namely, the TRRS (Time Ratio of Real Stroke) method and the LSDS (Line Segment Directions in a Stroke) method [1] have been proposed for this system. TRRS method is based on the time ratio of real strokes (trait). A feature parameter set is expressed as a set of codes that correspond to each line's input time ratio. We defined codes from 0 to 7. Here, let R_i and F_i denote the direction in the ith stroke on a template and give an evaluation value as follows;

$$P_i = \begin{cases} 2, if\ F_i = R_i \\ 1, if\ F_i = R_i \pm 1 \\ 0, Others \end{cases} \tag{1}$$

The corresponding sum of the P_i

$$T_{TRRS} = \frac{\sum_{i=1}^{N} P_i}{2N} \tag{2}$$

is calculated.

We checked that real stroke is relatively-stable feature quantity. We can't give an accuracy value from an imaginary stroke (an imaginary stroke means an imaginary line between a pen-up point of the stroke and a pen-down point of the following stroke). LSDS method is that a stroke is divided into several line segments by the same segment length. A feature parameter set is expressed as a set of eight direction codes that correspond to each line segment. Here, let $R_{i,j}$ and $F_{i,j}$ denote the direction of the jth line segment in the ith stroke on a template and give an evaluation value as follows;

$$Q_{i,j} = \begin{cases} 2, if\ F_{i,j} = R_{i,j} \\ 1, if\ F_{i,j} = R_{i,j} \pm 1 \\ 0, Others \end{cases} \tag{3}$$

The corresponding sum of the $Q_{i,j}$,

$$T_{LSDS} = \frac{\sum_{i=1}^{N} \sum_{j=1}^{n} Q_{i,j}}{2nN} \tag{4}$$

is calculated where n means a segment number on a certain stroke. The combination of the two methods is desirable to recognize all type of Japanese character written by using Wii remote. This method is named the Fusion method in this paper. The sum of the T_{TRRS} and T_{LSDS} is used as recognition in the Fusion method. Adding weight ratios (W_{TRRS} and W_{LSDS}) of the T_{TRRS} and T_{LSDS} are 50:50 in the case of the character having more than three strokes and 0:100 in the case of one stroke character in the following formula.

$$T_F = W_{TRRS} \cdot T_{TRRS} + W_{LSDS} \cdot T_{LSDS} \tag{5}$$

3.3 Error Correction Method

It was difficult to distinguish similar characters to use the Fusion method for one-character order. Therefore we adapt the error correction method by using n-gram model. The candidate character sequences are produced from each characters transition probability and the character pattern similarity.

Then the system outputs the 1st candidate phrases using Viterbi algorithm. In the normal algorithm, to calculate all combinations of characters takes time for extract the 2nd and 3rd candidate phrases. Thus, we adapt simplification algorithm for the reduction of the processing time in our system. It is re-calculated to replace only one character from the 1st candidate phrase. In almost all cases, only one character of a character sequence has mistaken from a correct phrase. Therefor our proposed simplification algorithm is effective from a viewpoint of the both of processing time and a recognition improvement.

4 Performance of Recognition Accuracy

We tested the performance of the proposed improvement recognition algorithm. The Japanese characters used in this paper are Hiragana (71 characters), Katakana (71 characters), Kanji (1006 characters taught elementary schools in Japanese) and numerals. The recognition accuracy was 78.9% in the 1st candidate by using the Fusion method (Table 1).

The recognition accuracy of the 1st candidate phrase was 91.7% by bi-gram model (Table 2).

Table 1. Performance of recognition (One-character order)

Candidate	TRRS	LSDS	Fusion
1st	54.5%	68.3%	78.9%

Table 2. Error correction method performance of recognition (Phrase order)

Method	Tester A	Tester B	Tester C	Average
Fusion only	78.1%	74.3%	81.0%	77.8%
Fusion with Error correction	92.3%	92.9%	90.0%	91.7%

5 Conclusion

We proposed Japanese sentence input method using Wiimote as acceleration sensor. We are using two recognition algorithms by only real-stroke. One of recognition algorithm is LSDS method. However, this method doesn't adapt if a stroke length is short. Therefore, the other recognition algorithm is TRRS method that it uses the ratio at the input time of each stroke.

However, it was difficult to distinguish similar characters to use these methods that are the recognition algorithm for the one character order. Therefore we adapt the error correction method by using a tree search algorithm that uses word dictionary.

The recognition accuracy was 78.9%. Also, the recognition accuracy of phrase was 91.7% by bi-gram model. We confirmed the required performance for utilization.

Reference

1. Ezaki, N., Kiyota, K., Kamei, T., Takizawa, H., Yamamoto, S.: An Improvement in the Character Recognition Accuracy in the On-line Japanese Input System for Blind Persons. Japanese Society for Medical and Biological Engineering 40(4) (2002)

Where to Put the Search Concepts in the Search Result Page?

K.T. Tong and Robert W.P. Luk

Department of Computing,
The Hong Kong Polytechnic University
csrluk@comp.polyu.edu.hk

Abstract. This paper looks at where to put the search concepts in the search re-sult pages by asking over 40 subjects. Four (layout) designs are used where the search concepts are placed differently, and subjects are asked to rank them. Re-sults show that there is preference to place the search concepts near the snippets.

1   Introduction

Search results are typically organized into a rank list of found items (e.g., Google). The use of rank list is supported by the probability ranking principle [1]. Recently, search concepts are proposed to organize search results by grouping the found items that relate to the particular concepts. By clicking these concepts, a smaller rank list of found items relating to a particular concept is shown. Using concepts in this way is found to be effective by Ko et al. [2]. These concepts may be search categories or Wikipedia entries. While such concepts are useful to organize search results, it is not known where to put them in the search result page.

There are search engines that add search concepts on the left hand side of the rank list (e.g., Vivisimo) or on the right hand side of the rank list (e.g., those in Web of Science). Fig. 1 shows an example search result page and its related, placed items (e.g., recommendations and sponsored links). It is not known where users prefer to put these search concepts in this congested result page even though they are placed on the left. Putting concepts on the right hand side has the disadvantage that it blocks the typical (Google's) area to display sponsored links.

We carried out an experiment that asks over 40 subjects about their preferences to put the concepts in the search result page. Apart from the sides of the ranked list, we also presented alternative places to put the concepts. We investigated the learning effect due to carrying out part of the questionnaire. The results show that there is a clear preference to put search concepts near the snippets, and the subjects prefer only about five concepts to be displayed in a row.

The rest of the paper is organized as follows. Section 2 reports the research meth-odology and the related demographics. Section 3 discusses the questionnaire results about the four designs of the search result pages where the search concepts are placed differently. Finally, Section 4 concludes.

C. Stephanidis (Ed.): Posters, Part I, HCII 2011, CCIS 173, pp. 600–604, 2011.
© Springer-Verlag Berlin Heidelberg 2011

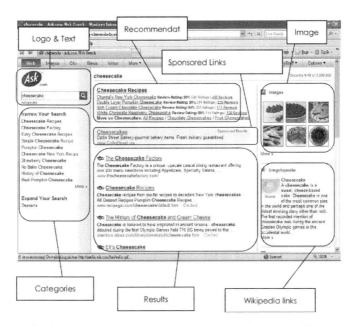

Fig. 1. An example search result page and its related, placed items

2 Research Methodology and Demographics

We administered the questionnaire to 60 subjects. The subjects were asked about the designs of the search result pages, and Fig. 2 shows some example questions in the questionnaire. Each design placed the search concepts differently or used different interface devices to see if this affected the ranking of the designs by the users. There were four different designs altogether.

The questionnaire was divided into two parts. In the first part, each subject was asked one design after the other without knowing how many designs there are and without knowing what were the subsequent designs. In the second part, the subjects knew that they had seen all the designs, and they were asked about the design one after the other again. The questionnaire was divided into two parts in order to see if there were any learning effects on ranking the designs.

Amongst the 60 subjects, 53% of them are male and the remaining are female. Note that 46% of them are under 24 years old, 23% are between 25 and 49 years old, and 21% are over 49 years old. In terms of frequency of search per week, 18% of them make less than 10 searches per week. 50% of them make between 10 and 20 searches per week, and the remaining 32% of them make more than 20 searches per week. Google is always used by 58% of the subjects.

Questions 11-13 related to the snippet

11. Have you read the snippet before clicking the link?
    A. Always
    B. Sometimes
    C. Rarely
    D. Never
12. Could the snippet provide sufficient and suitable information to you
    to choose the website?
    A. Always
    B. Sometimes
    C. Rarely
    D. Never
13. What do you prefer to show in the snippet?
    A. Sentences
    B. Keywords related to the webpage
    C. Empty

Fig. 2. Example questions in the questionnaire

3   Results and Analysis of the Questionnaires on the Designs

This section reports one by one the results of the questionnaire on the four designs.

3.1   Design A

Fig. 3(a) shows design A which groups the ranked items into different search concepts. Each group is displayed horizontally and the ranked items of each group are indented to show that they belong to the group, the search concept of which is shown immediately above.

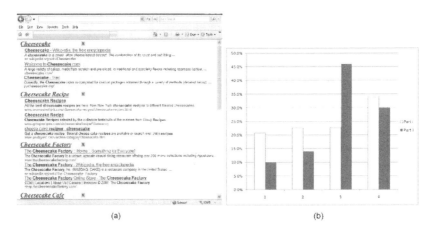

(a)   (b)

Fig. 3. Design A (a) Layout and (b) Ranking Results

Fig. 3(b) shows the ranking results of the questionnaire for part I and part II. Results for Part I show that the ranking is more evenly distributed than the results for Part II, which show that the majority of the subjects rank the design to be between three and four. Therefore, knowing all the designs facilitates the subjects to agree more sharply on which rank to select.

3.2 Design B

Fig. 4(a) shows design B layout which shows the search concepts below the snippet. Each search concept has a check box to invite the subjects to click it if the search concept is relevant. A "modify" button is included which modifies the query by adding the clicked search concepts to the original query when the button is clicked.

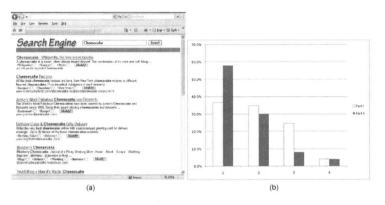

(a)   (b)

Fig. 4. Design B (a) Layout and (b) Ranking Results

Fig. 4(b) shows the ranking results for Part I and II. Part II shows that the majority of the subjects appear to know more clearly that the ranking of this design is between one or two.

3.3 Design C

Fig. 5(a) shows design C layout which is almost the same as B apart from the check boxes being replaced by crosses and apart from removing the "modify" button.

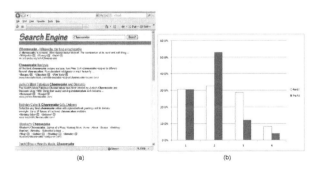

(a)   (b)

Fig. 5. Design C (a) Layout and (b) Ranking Results

Fig. 5(b) shows the ranking results for Part I and II. For Part I, the results are evenly distributed between rank one and three. For Part II, the majority of the subjects voted rank two and one for this design. This shows that the minor interface device change has an impact on the ranking of the design.

3.4 Design D

Fig. 6(a) shows design D layout which places the search concepts on the right, blocking the sponsored links.

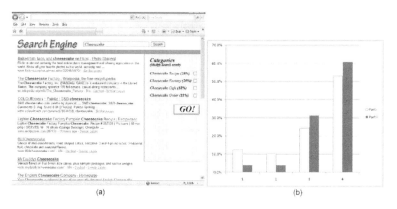

(a)   (b)

Fig. 6. Design D (a) Layout and (b) Ranking Results

Fig. 6(b) shows the ranking results for Part I and II, which do not differ much. Intuitively, the subjects seem to know this is not a preferred design and they rank it between three and four.

4 Conclusion

This paper shows that the preferred location to place the search concepts is near the snippet. Search concepts placed on the right hand side are not preferred. Empty check boxes are preferred over boxes with crosses.

References

1. Robertson, S.E.: The probability ranking principle in IR. Journal of Documentation 33(4), 294–304 (1977)
2. Ko, P.Y., Luk, R.W.P., Ho, K.S., Chung, F.L., Lee, D.L.: Are concepts useful for organizing search results? In: 22nd British HCI Group Annual Conference on HCI 2008, pp. 153–154 (2008)

Kansei Modeling on Visual Impression from Small Datasets

Shunsuke Uesaka, Kazuki Yasukawa, and Toshikazu Kato

Chuo University, 1-13-27 Kasuga, Bunkyo-ku, Tokyo 112-8551, Japan
{s_uesaka,k_yasukawa,kato}@indsys.chuo-u.ac.jp

Abstract. Large datasets are generally required for machine learning. In order to improve the efficiency of the system, our team proposes a new Kansei modeling method, which requires users to collect only a small dataset. Using our method, the small datasets can search and collect large datasets classified in detail. As a result, our method creates the well-tuned Kansei model only from small datasets without the trouble of collecting many datasets.

Keywords: Kansei Modeling, Machine Learning, Image Retrieval System.

1 Introduction and Problems

Impressions and feelings evoked by an image vary depending on who is looking at it. In the image search by keywords, the same result is presented to any users and it is difficult to retrieve an image suitable for each user's impression. Our team has been researching the Kansei modeling, a computational modeling of visual impression process, for scenery photos to retrieve an image suitable for each user [1].

In the earlier study for the Kansei model, our team analyzed the relation between information given in the photo and users' evaluation based on the visual impression using discriminant analysis [1]. However, this previous methods had the following problems, placing a large burden to the users.

(A) Detailed classification of datasets: Users train the system by providing classified datasets with impression words. However, because impression is something subjective for the users, dispersions of image features of the impression data tend to become larger. This results in lower modeling accuracy. Therefore, training datasets for modeling requires detailed classification in order to avoid this problem.

(B) Preparation of large datasets: Generally, when data prepared is small for machine learning, modeling accuracy gets lower. Therefore, users must prepare large datasets for machine learning.

For the reasons stated above, we propose a new Kansei model method, which requires only small dataset classified roughly. The problems can be solved by detailed classification and a searching system that automatically collects similar datasets based on image features of training data provided by the user. This method will greatly decrease the users' load.

C. Stephanidis (Ed.): Posters, Part I, HCII 2011, CCIS 173, pp. 605–609, 2011.

2   Solution

2.1   Detailed Classification of Datasets

To solve the problem identified in Chapter 1 (A), we propose a method of subdividing datasets by K-means. This method is effective for machine learning because subdividing datasets decreases dispersion of data sets and increases the modeling accuracy.

For K-means, the number of clusters needs to be specified. For our research, the number of clusters was set so that correlation ratio is maximized. The correlation ratio η is defined by the following expression.

$$\eta = 1 - \frac{\mid S_w \mid}{\mid S_T \mid}$$

S_W means within-groups sum of squares and products matrix. S_T means total sum of squares and products matrix.

2.2   Preparation of Large Datasets

To solve the problem described in Chapter 1 (B), we propose a method of automatically searching large impression image datasets, which share common characteristics with the small data provided. As a result, large datasets can be prepared just by small datasets given, and machine learning can create a model with high accuracy.

When users subjectively judge the degree of similarity of images, the users do not equally evaluate each characteristic in the image or weigh values that users stress [2]. Therefore, the similar images need to be searched by taking into account users' different attention degrees to various image features.

We assumed that we can measure the extent of users' consistency in selection criteria by assessing dispersion in the distribution of users' values on image characteristics. We also assumed that as the distribution is more dispersed, the users' selection criteria become inconsistent or that the users do not focus on particular values. Conversely, as the dispersion narrows, the users' selection criteria become consistent, or the users focus on the certain values.

The images below show search results obtained by estimating characteristics that users focus on from a few sample images.

(a) Search key   (b) Search results

Fig. 1. Example of searching images by estimating characteristics that users stress from a few sample images

3 Experiment to Evaluate Search System

This experiment verified the accuracy of our image search system, which estimates image characteristics that users focus on in accordance with detailed classification of datasets.

In the experiment, we used a database comprised of approximately 1,725 landscape images taken by a professional photographer. Impression words were assigned to each landscape image. Each impression word had the following number of images as shown in Table 1.

Table 1. Number of images for each impression words in experiment

Impression words	Number of images
Fresh	436
Natural	437
Modern · Classic	430
Elegant	422

First, the search system randomly selected 10, 20, and 30 traning image data for each impression word above from all the experimental images. Then, in order to verify the accuracy of the search system, we examined the top 200 search results based on the training data and calculated the conformity level between pre-assigned impression words and results' impression words. The experiments were repeated 20 times. The average value of the conformity level is shown in Fig.2.

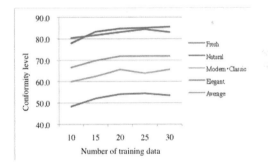

Fig. 2. Relation between the number of data sets and conformity level

The conformity level went up when the number of data sets increased (Fig.2). Also, the results of 'Fresh' and 'Natural' kept high accuracy because the resulting colors and textures were similar for each of those two impression words; data sets of 'Fresh' had images of sky and ocean, and 'Natural' had images of forest and mountain. Therefore, our system could easily search suitable images that share the same characteristics as the training data.

Conversely, the results of 'Modern · Classic' and 'Elegant' had low accuracy. Training datasets of 'Modern · Classic' and 'Elegant' all had similar images such as buildings and night scene. Accordingly, the resulting colors and textures among those impression words were similar without clear difference. Because our system could not evaluate impression well for those impression words lowering the conformity level, we must reconsider the amount of characteristics to input so that the system can evaluate images correctly.

4   Experiment to Evaluate Kansei Modeling

We create Kansei model with SVM (Support Vector Machine) to evaluate user's Kansei quantitatively. This experiment verified the accuracy of our Kansei modeling using image data searched by our system. We created four types of Kansei model by using 200 datasets for each. The datasets were three combinations of 10, 20, 30 training datasets and complementary search results in the previous experiment (Chapter 4) and 200 datasets selected randomly without using our search system. The conformity level for each model is shown in Table 2.

Table 2. Relation between number of search results and the conformity level

Training Data	10	20	30	200
Search Result	190	180	170	0
Fresh	89.6%	85.2%	83.1%	91.0%
Natural	86.0%	90.8%	84.8%	95.0%
Classic·Modern	62.1%	65.6%	66.0%	72.5%
Elegant	51.7%	49.0%	49.4%	63.5%
Average	72.3%	72.7%	70.8%	80.5%

According to Table 2, our proposed system can create Kansei model by a small dataset at the same or a little lower level of the model obtained from 200 training data sets. However, the accuracy of model for 'Classic·Modern' and 'Elegant' obtained from search results was especially lower than the model from 200 training datasets. This low accuracy occurred because the images came from the search result in the previous experiment, which could not find adequately suitable image for impression words of 'Classic·Modern' and 'Elegant' (Chapter4).

Acknowledgements. We extend our gratitude to all the people at Amana Holdings Inc. and Amana Images Inc. for their important advice and data sets; to Dr. Masahiro Tada at ATR Intelligent Robotics and Communication Laboratories for his advice on statistical analysis and learning algorithms; and to all the people at the Human Media Lab, Faculty of Science and Engineering, Chuo University, and at the Sensitivity Robotics Research Center for their discussions on research and their cooperation.

This experiment was supported partly by a Grant-in-Aid for Scientific Research and Fundamental Research (S) from the Japan Society for Promotion of Science, and a joint research Grant from the Institute of Science and Engineering, Chuo University.

References

1. Tada, M., Kato, S.: Analysis and study of visual impressions using SVM and the application to automatic image classification. Technical Report of The Institute of Electronics, Information and communication Engineers 104(573) (20050114), 45–50 (2004)
2. Tada, M., Kato, S.: Analysis of characteristics of similar visual impressions and modeling of visual sensitivity. Thesis Report of The Institute of Electronics, Information and communication Engineers D-II J87-D-II(10), 1983–1995 (2004)
3. Chichiiwa, H.: Viewing colors by mind? Color psychology design., Fukumura Shuppan Inc.
4. Shigematsu, R., Kato, T.: Learning Efficiency with Automatic Classification of Teaching Data – Using Global Graphic Features and Structured Graphic Features. In: The 11th Proc. of Japan Society of Kansei Engineering,
5. Nanbu, F., Hachimura, K.: Image search system which automatically configure similar judgment criteria, Symposium on Human Science and Computer (2002)

A Movie Recommendation Mechanism Based on User Ratings in the Mobile Peer-to-Peer Environment

Chian Wang[*] and Dai-Yang Lin

Department of Information Management,
National Changhua University of Education,
Changhua, Taiwan
cwang@cc.ncue.edu.tw

Abstract. In this paper, a movie recommendation mechanism in the mobile peer-to-peer environment is proposed. Our idea is that users can now easily exchange information with their mobile devices. Thus, if they can have ratings of the movies that they watched, then the ratings can be used to recommendation some movies that they have not watched. When two users approach, the mechanism can determine if they have similar interests in movies by exchanging the ratings. Then, the mechanism can generate a movie recommendation list by estimating a user's ratings of the movies that he has not watched.

Keywords: recommendation systems, mobile environment, peer-to-peer applications.

1 Introduction

Due to the progress of information technologies, mobile devices become quite common in our daily lives. By using mobile devices, we can connect to the Internet with less constraint. With this trend, many new types of applications are developed. Among these applications, the peer-to-peer (P2P) architecture is a promising technology that can help users to get information more effectively and efficiently. The major characteristic of the P2P architecture is that no centralized server is required. In stead, each peer acquires resources from other peers while providing resources to other peers. In this way, the centralized server's work load will not be a service bottleneck, especially in large-scale applications. Because as more peers join the system, more resources are shared and available to other peers. However, the problem of information explosion becomes essential as P2P applications become more and more popular and widely accepted. From a user's perspective, it's harder and time-consuming to get really useful and needed information. In this paper, we will develop a movie recommendation mechanism for the mobile P2P environment. Our idea is that users can now join a P2P application structure more easily with mobile devices. Currently, most users use movie titles as keywords to search for the desired resources. If a user is not sure about the exact title or he just wants to watch a specific genre of movies,

---

[*] Corresponding author.

C. Stephanidis (Ed.): Posters, Part I, HCII 2011, CCIS 173, pp. 610–614, 2011.

e.g., comedies starring John Travolta, it's not easy to find the desired movies. Worse yet, he may have to filter the search results manually to get what he really wants. Based on these situations, a mechanism that can help users to get the desired movies more easily and efficiently is preferred. In this paper, we will describe the development of an active recommendation mechanism that can help users to handle the huge amount of resources more efficiently and effectively.

With the proposed mechanism, a user rates each movie he watched to represent his evaluation and interest about the movie. When two users approach, the mechanism exchanges the rating information stored on each user's mobile device to determine if they have similar interests. When a user's interest is determined or matched, the mechanism generates a recommendation list containing movie information, e.g., title, genre, director, stars, plot, etc. After developing the recommendation mechanism, we will also have some system evaluations. Our analysis is based on the acceptance rates and the satisfaction degrees of the recommendation results.

2 Data Exchange

Using our recommendation mechanism, there is a data table on each user's mobile device. The table is used to store the user's preference and the ratings of the movies that he watched. There are two parts of the rating data, as illustrated in Table 1.

Table 1. The rating data table

f1	f2	f3	f5	tg1	tg2	tg3	tg4	tg5
8	7	2	4	4	2	8	3	9

In Table 1, f_i means the user's rating of movie i and tg_i represents his preference of movie genre i. The ratings are from 1 (the lowest) to 10 (the highest). When two users approach, the ratings stored in their tables are exchanged in order to generate movie recommendations. There are three ways of exchange.

(1) Unlimited exchange. Whenever two users get into a specific range, all the items in their data tables are exchanged. This is the simplest way of exchange. However, some items may be duplicate if they watched the same movies before. Moreover, as a user meets more other users, the amount of data increases rapidly.

(2) Limited exchange. In order to prevent the problem of flooding, each rating can be associated with a time-to-exchange (TTE) value. When a rating is exchanged, its TTE is decreased by one. When the TTE becomes 0, the rating can not be exchanged anymore.

(3) Exchange with similarity. In this paper, we adopt Pearson correlation to measure the similarity of user interests. If two users' interests are similar, then their rating data can be exchanged. By considering user interests, the recommendation results can be more accurate and acceptable.

Using the proposed mechanism, the similarity of two users' interests $W_{A,B}$ is determined as follows.

$$W_{A,B} = \frac{\Sigma (r_{Ai} - \overline{r_A})(r_{Bi} - \overline{r_B})}{\sqrt{\Sigma (r_{Ai} - \overline{r_A})^2 \Sigma (r_{Bi} - \overline{r_B})^2}}$$

where r_{Ai} is user A's rating of movie i,
r_{Bi} is user B's rating of movie i,
r_A is the average of A's ratings, and
r_B is the average of B's ratings.

$W_{A,B}$ is between 1 and -1. If $W_{A,B}$ is closer to 1 (-1), it means that A and B's interests are quite similar (different). If $W_{A,B}$ is larger than a specific threshold, *TH*, then A and B's rating data can be exchanged. Otherwise, their rating data are not exchanged in order to prevent the problem of flooding.

For example, Tables 2(a) and 2(b) show the rating data of A and B, respectively.

Table 2. The rating data of users A and B

f1	f2	f3	f6	tg1	tg2	tg3	tg4	tg5
8	7	1	4	4	2	9	1	9

(a)

f1	f2	f3	f5	f6	tg1	tg2	tg3	tg4	tg5
7	9	3	9	2	3	2	7	3	8

(b)

Then, their $W_{A,B}$ is 0.8322. If *TH* is set to 0.6, then A and B can exchange their rating data.

3   Recommendation Generation

There are several basis when generating the recommendation list, including user A's ratings of movie genre and watched movies and other users' ratings of movie genre and watched movies. Based on these parameters, the recommendation mechanism can generate a movie list to each user that he has not watched but may be interested in. The mechanism adopts a neighborhood-based algorithm to estimate the rating of a movie that the user has not watched. The estimation is measured as follows.

$$P_{a,i} = \overline{r_a} + \frac{\Sigma_{u=1}^{n}(r_{u,i} - \overline{r_u}) \cdot w_{a,u}}{\Sigma_{u=1}^{n} w_{a,u}}$$

where $P_{a,i}$ is A's estimated rating of movie i,
r_a is the average of user A's ratings,
r_u is the average of other users' ratings,
$r_{u,i}$ is other users' ratings of movie i, and
$w_{a,u}$ is the similarity of A and other users.

Table 3 illustrates how the recommendation decisions are made.

Table 3. The data table of user A after exchanging with users E and F. (Null means that the movie was not watched).

	f_1	f_2	f_3	f_5	f_6	f_7	tg_1	tg_2	tg_3	tg_4	tg_5
User$_A$	8	7	1	Null	4	Null	4	2	9	1	9
User$_E$	9	Null	7	6	Null	2	4	3	6	3	10
User$_F$	7	4	Null	8	4	3	3	3	7	2	8

To make movie recommendations to user A, the mechanism has to estimate A's ratings of movies 5 and 7. First, the mechanism calculates r_A, the average of A's ratings, as follows.

$$\overline{r_A} = \frac{8 + 7 + 1 + 4 + 4 + 2 + 9 + 1 + 9}{9}$$

$$= 5$$

Then, the similarities of A and E, and A and F can be calculated, too.

$$W_{A,E} = \frac{\sum (r_{Ai} - \overline{r_A})(r_{Ei} - \overline{r_E})}{\sqrt{\sum (r_{Ai} - \overline{r_A})^2 \sum (r_{Ei} - \overline{r_E})^2}}$$

$$= 0.5863$$

$$W_{A,F} = \frac{\sum (r_{Ai} - \overline{r_A})(r_{Fi} - \overline{r_F})}{\sqrt{\sum (r_{Ai} - \overline{r_A})^2 \sum (r_{Fi} - \overline{r_F})^2}}$$

$$= 0.6921$$

So, A's estimated ratings of movies 5 and 7 are

$$P_{a,5} = 5 + \frac{(6 - 6) * 0.5863 + (8 - 4.9) * 0.6921}{0.5863 + 0.6921}$$

$$= 6.6775$$

$$P_{a,7} = 5 + \frac{(2 - 6) * 0.5863 + (3 - 4.9) * 0.6921}{0.5863 + 0.6921}$$

$$= 2.1369$$

Finally, the mechanism recommends movie 5 to A because of the higher estimated rating.

4 Conclusion

Currently, we are developing the corresponding application system and having a real-world system evaluation. Our evaluation is based on several criteria.

(1) Mean Absolute Error (MAE)

$$\bar{a} = \frac{\sum_{i=1}^{N}|P_i - R_i|}{N},$$

where P_i is the estimated rating of movie i,
R_i is the real rating of movie i, and
N is the number of movies.

The purpose of MAE is to evaluate the difference between the real and the estimated ratings. If MAE is smaller, it means that the mechanism can generate more satisfactory recommendations.

(2) Precision.

$$P = 1 - \frac{\sum_{i=1}^{N}|P_i - r_i| / MAX(|R_{max} - r_i|, |R_{min} - r_i|)}{N},$$

where P_i is the estimated rating of movie i,
r_i is the real rating of movie i,
N is the number of movies,
R_{max} is the maximum possible rating, which is set to 10, and
R_{min} is the minimum possible rating, which is set to 1.

The purpose of precision evaluation is to measure the correctness of the estimations. Precision is between 0 and 1. When precision is closer to 1, the estimation is more satisfactory. Otherwise, the estimation is less correct.

Author Index